Ed "Strangler" Lewis

Facts within a Myth

Ed "Strangler" Lewis

Ed "Strangler" Lewis

Facts within a Myth

Steve Yohe

Foreword by
John Pelan

Editing & Design by
Gavin L. O'Keefe

An IHC Project

RAMBLE HOUSE
2015

First American hardcover edition

This edition © 2015 Ramble House

Ramble House
10329 Sheephead Drive
Vancleave MS 39565
USA

'The Ring Record of Ed "Strangler" Lewis'
Researched & Compiled by:
J Michael Kenyon, Don Luce, Mark Hewett,
Steve Yohe, Dan Anderson, Fred Hornby, Richard Haynes,
Libnan Ayoub, Steve Johnson and Scott Teal.

ISBN 13: 978-1-60543-856-6

CONTENTS

Acknowledgments

I want to thank the major researchers who's work is the backbone of this project. J Michael Kenyon is the major collector of Strangler Lewis information and he guide me during the year I worked on this project. I always consider Ed Lewis to be his baby and I never would have taken the task, if he hadn't given me the permission. I've lived off the research of Don Luce for years and he's helped me in every project I've ever worked on. Also want to say thanks to Mark Hewitt who's specialty is the time period I enjoy the most. Dan Anderson was a huge help in writing the early history of Bob Friedrich's career in Wisconsin. Other names I should mention are Koji Miyamoto (Lou Thesz's unofficial son and historian), Tim Hornbaker, Steve Johnson, Greg Oliver, Kit Bauman, Jack Cavanaugh (author of the great boxing book, *Tunney*), John Williams, Haruo Yamaguchi, Dave Meltzer, Fred Hornby, Dan Westbrook, Scott Teal, Libnan Ayoub, Alex Meyer (Stecher historian), Frankie Cain, Norman Kietzer (Photos), Ken (Viewer) Sandler (photos), Mark Nulty (of Wrestling Classics.com), Ed Lock, Steve Phersons (whoever you are) and my wife Maria Yohe. Also should mention the staff of the Amateur Athletic Foundation's Paul Ziffren Sports Library, mainly Mike Salmon and Shannon Boyd. The design of the book was done by Gavin L. O'Keefe, and the book is as much his as anyone's. Most of all I want to thank John Pelan, who encouraged me into turning this project into a book and then edited it so that it's readable. He had the faith and obsession to spend time and money on a project that has no chance of ever making a profit. He and I, and all the names above, are dedicated to seeing that pro wrestling has a written history, something thought impossible fifteen years ago.

A Tale of Two Champions

John Pelan

SINCE YOU'RE HOLDING this book in your hands, this indicates a couple of things. First (unless you're admiring someone else's copy, not having purchased your own yet), you've shelled out a not-inconsiderable-amount of money in order to possess this particular tome, as this is a volume made available through what we call "modular printing," "print-to-order," or "print-on-demand" — which are lofty sounding terms that simply mean that the book can be produced on an as-needed basis, saving the publisher the tremendous costs of printing several hundreds or thousands of copies all at once and then having to warehouse said copies until they sell. The disadvantage of this approach is that you won't see colorful displays of this book at your local bookstore; you'll have to have heard about it from someone and then sought out a copy. Secondly, one can surmise that you have a pretty strong interest in professional wrestling of a by-gone era, and at the very least a nodding familiarity with Ed "Strangler" Lewis, the subject of this book; or possibly familiarity with Steve Yohe, the author of this tome; or, as may well be the case, you're acquainted with both the subject and the author — in which case this foreword is going to be of very little use to you, as you already know the information I'm about to pass on.

Since its very inception, professional wrestling has been a hotbed of hyperbole and exaggeration — by its very definition it features larger-than-life morality plays enacted by larger-than-life individuals. This leads to adjectives like "extraordinary," "super-human," "iconic," and "immortal" getting thrown around quite a bit. In some rare instances, they are actually merited. When we look at "Strangler" Lewis' career and the popularity and notoriety that came along with it, the adjective of "extraordinary" is certainly called for. Anything less than that would be a denial of fact. "Extraordinary" is also a term that should be applied to the author of this book.

Why "extraordinary"? Simple — wrestling history is a strange chimera-like beast, quite unlike anything else. I myself am quite active as a researcher in a couple of other areas — major league baseball and genre fiction (specifically mystery, fantasy, horror, and science fiction) — and the differences are astonishing. In the two fields wherein I have somewhat of a bit of expertise, research is actually quite easy. Baseball is a game of statistics: since its earliest times there have been records kept, not always as detailed as one might wish, but records nonetheless. There's an entire organization (The Society for American Baseball Research or S.A.B.R.) dedicated to compiling the most detailed data imaginable. Genre fiction is a bit more difficult, but publishers kept pretty detailed records of what they paid and to whom for which item. Professional wrestling is a horse of a different color indeed. To characterize wrestling promotors in general as "lying liars who lie," while unkind, is woefully accurate. Attendance figures and box office receipts given to the newspapers and the I.R.S. can practically be guaranteed to bear little resemblance to each other. Worse than that, there's a trickle-down effect to the performers where "protecting the business" leads to all manner of distortions, ranging from one's age to ethnic heritage to earnings to marital status, and pretty much any fact that might be altered to suit the occasion.

The amount of truly great wrestling historians can be tallied on one's fingers. It's an incredibly difficult and for the most part thankless endeavor, and the amount of time that one has to spend sifting through various sources of information — many of which are questionable, at best — is daunting to most. What in any other sport is a simple matter of looking at the record book, in professional wrestling research often necessitates *creating* the record book out of whole cloth. Steve Yohe is one of the individuals that has done this and done it very well indeed.

This book is the result of a passion for the sport that takes place inside the squared circle. It takes a champion caliber researcher to put a book like this together. Steve Yohe merits that distinction: he has not only raised the bar for others that follow — he's redefined what a historical book on our favorite sport *should* be. There are indeed two champions here: the subject of the book, and its author.

Ed Strangler Lewis

Ed "Strangler" Lewis: Facts within a Myth

Birth, Family and Nekoosa

ROBERT HERMAN JULIUS FRIEDRICH, who later took the famous alias of Ed "Strangler" Lewis, was born on June 30, 1890 in the Wisconsin town of Sheboygan Falls.[1] Lewis, during his lifetime, always claim that he weighed 12 pounds at birth.

His parents were Jacob Friedrich (b. December 28, 1858) and Mary (Molly or Molla Guildenzopf, or perhaps Amelia Gueldenzopf) Friedrich (b. March 22, 1866). Jacob was born in Deinheim Hessen, Germany and came to the United States when he was 23 years old to make central Wisconsin his home. He had worked as a farmer, woodcutter, and butcher but, by the time of Robert's birth, he was working in the finishing room of the Nekoosa-Edwards Paper Company. On February 1, 1912, at age 53, Jacob took a job on the Nekoosa police force and stayed employed for 28 years. He weighed 200 pounds and had a reputation as a strong man, but it seems that Robert resembled his Mother Molly more than his dad. Molly weighed almost as much as Jacob and was well-proportioned. At church picnics, she would enter and win the young woman's races. She was a hard worker and the backbone of the family.[2] The two had married on September 26, 1888, in the town of Port Edwards.

Robert, who went by the name Bob, was the third of five children: Fredrich (b. Oct. 1887), Minnie (b. July 1889), Hattie (b. Jan. 1893) and Mary/Emily (b. Oct, 1994). It seems that the family left Sheboygan Falls—possibly to Nekoosa, Wisconsin—but returned in 1894. In 1895, they returned to Nekoosa, where Bob spent most of his childhood. The actual home may have been four miles north-east of Nekoosa in the small town of Port Edwards.

Nekoosa was a village of about 1,000 people, but it had a large paper mill where the father had found work. It was in Nekoosa that Bob attended public school. He grew big and active, doing all the things young boys do. As time passed, he started coming home with his clothes torn and dirty. This was a problem because it was costing money that the family had very little of to waste. One day, Jacob was walking by the schoolyard and found his son wrestling just about every boy in the school. His patience had worn thin by this time, so he grabbed Bob and beat him in front of all his classmates. Bob was so embarrassed that he refused to return to the public school, so he was sent to a German Lutheran school. He later was confirmed in that faith.

Bob played basketball, track and wrestled, but his favorite sport was baseball, and during the summers he played on the town's team. One Saturday they played a game in Pittsfield, Wisconsin. They won the game but were short on money for the trip home (that's the story, but I think Pittsfield is only 19 miles from Nekoosa and it seems like a plan that needed time to execute.). In the area was a local wrestler named George Brown, who had trained with the great Fred Beell. The baseball manager arranged for young Friedrich to wrestle Brown at the local opera house, with admission being 50 cents.

Bob claimed to know only one hold—the bear hug—but Brown fainted, giving Friedrich his first pro win. The gate was $60 and Bob's cut was $15.

Around that time, Lewis claimed that the local barber, a Carson Burke, gave him a book on human physiology, and his studying of the human body would later give him an advantage in the wrestling ring. (He was the Gorilla Monsoon of his time.) Burke also gave Bob the Spaulding guide to wrestling. He used this knowledge to twist the bodies of every boy in the neighborhood. This brought a line of complaining parents to the door of the Friedrich home, so Robert was once again in trouble.

At around 11 years old, Bob got a job as a water boy for a construction gang working on widening the road from the power plant to the paper mill. Near where the men rested was a narrow bridge or log going over a large stream or river. The men would get exercise by throwing each other off the bridge into the water. Their fun was ruined when the water boy started throwing all the grown ups into the pond. The boy's reputation grew with the locals and many times farmers would stop their work to watch him throw large men around. When he wasn't wrestling the crew, Bob played watchdog, looking out for the boss, as the crew napped the afternoons away under shade trees.

When not toiling for the construction crew, Bob worked in a store for a Mrs. Gutheil, making deliveries and lifting heavy loads on to farm wagons. Stories were told of Bob picking up 280 pound barrels of salt and carrying three bags of flour at a time. This Mrs. Gutheil had two or three other young girls working in the store, so Bob took to exercising in the back yard near a window in the hope of impressing them.

During this period, stories have Bob being trained by his Nekoosa neighbor, Fred Bentz. He may have also made contact with famed Wisconsin wrestler Fred Beell.

Every Saturday, Bob would work out with a 220-pound farmer named Albert Coon. Friedrich pinned Coon over and over, but the big guy never stopped coming back for more. Then came a lucky day when Albert got a pin over Bob. After that, Coon stopped training, and wouldn't wrestle his friend. After Lewis became a great star, he would beg his pal for a rematch but Coon refused—happy with his one victory over a champion wrestler.

Wrestling was the sport of farmland America. Roads were hard to run on, gyms were rare, and baseball took too many people, but farmers could always find someone to wrestle. A whole cultural ritual surrounded shoot "catch as catch can" wrestling in the mid-west and other areas of the country. Sundays were usually days off and local picnics were places for young men to gather and prove themselves. Bob was always a star at these events.

A major challenger to Friedrich was an older and larger boy named Art Crowns. They were friends, but a great rivalry formed between the two. A professor at a local school set up an official style match between the two, which Bob won after a throw which almost caused Art to bite off his tongue. A few days later, Bob had to fight Art's brother, George. Bob won that encounter, too. The two Crown boys grew up to become attorneys in Wisconsin.

Besides wrestling, Bob's next interest was young girls, and he dated a Sioux woman named Maude Brooks for a period of time. It seems she also taught Bob a few holds.

Bob was good natured and likeable, with his reputation as a local champion growing by the week. In the winter, another such champion, Fred Abel of Madison, Wisconsin, challenged Robert. The match was set up at the local opera house. The hospitable Bob met Abel at the train station and introduced him to the locals. This helped the gate. Bob won the match, but most thought the match looked like a "friendly" affair.[3]

A few months later, another wrestler named "Lindsey," from Neelsville, challenged Bob. Lindsey had a cauliflower ear and wasn't nearly as friendly as the first wrestler. Lewis claimed the match was a two-hour draw that had Lindsey riding him the whole time, rubbing his face into the mat. My feelings are that Lindsey was a pro working under an alias, trying to take advantage of the local gamblers. The people in Nekoosa formed the opinion that Bob had "worked" a least one of the two matches and felt betrayed.

His friends' reaction hurt and offended Friedrich, so he decided to leave Nekoosa. Bob's Uncle Emil was a superintendent at a paper mill in Rhinelander, Wisconsin, and offered Robert a job, and it was accepted.

Rhinelander

Bob's job at the Rhinelander Paper Mill was working with a machine that spit out 100-pound paper bundles. He had to pick up two of them a minute and stack them from the floor to a height of 15 feet. He worked at this labor for 12 hours a day for over two years. At first he was an assistant to a George Fisher, but George broke down from the work, and Bob continued by himself. Lewis claimed this monotonous work was the hardest time of his life. During his later life as a pro wrestler, in a tough match that stressed his endurance, he'd think of his Rhinelander Mill job and say to himself: "If that didn't break me—nothing will!" You can see how a job like this would turn young Lewis into a super strong athletic with the physique of a Hercules. It wasn't the static lifting of weights in a gym; it was the lifting of awkward objects up and down, over and over, for hours and hours, that would created the strength and stamina need in a great wrestler.

One of the social centers in Rhinelander was a roller skating rink. It was known as an acceptable place for young boys and girls to meet. In the back of it Bob once battled the local bully in what Lewis claimed was an hour-and-a-half long fist-fight in 30-degree weather. It was stopped after Friedrich had knocked the other boy down 25 times. Ed claimed he was happy about the stoppage because he was tired from all the punching.

Bob was apparently also playing basketball in the area, and one report had him playing ball for Antigo at a basketball tournament in the town of Portage. He also was with an encampment of the Rhinelander company of the state militia around July 1908.

While in Rhinelander, Bob dated and fell in love with a girl named Mabel. He described her as fair of skin, blue of eyes, a Madonna with black hair who was sweet, genteel, kind and amorous. He went with her for two years and the only reason they didn't get married was because they were only 17 years old. When Bob left Rhinelander, he left Mabel. 20 years later, while wrestling in Fort Worth, he received a letter from a District Attorney. Mabel had became a drug addict, due to a bad marriage, and both husband and wife were in jail. Lewis bailed her out and told her to return home to Rhinelander. Of course, she didn't. She showed up at a wrestling card in St. Louis a year later looking worse. Lewis gave her more money and never saw her again.

You'll read that Ed Lewis was a playboy. Always playing the field, having a good time. To me, he didn't seem to be that type. He appears to be more of a good-natured type, always falling in love while thinking about and getting married. My definition of a true playboy doesn't have the word marriage in it.

Minneapolis

Stanislaus Zbyszko

Friedrich's reputation as a wrestler was building and he needed to move on to another level in his career. He traveled to Minneapolis around the year 1909. Minneapolis was the closest metropolis to Rhinelander and a major wrestling center. He got a job in the drug store of an Oscar Zirker, working as a clerk. He lived in an apartment located at 11th and Hannepin. His room-mate was a cook and the rent was $5 a week.

Henry Ordemann, one of the best wrestlers in America, worked out with Bob. He trained in a gym owned by three boxing brothers. At the Cook's gym, he met a Billy Potts, who acted as his manager, but was never paid.

Potts was able to book Friedrich into a handicap match versus the great Stanislaus Zbyszko on February 10, 1910, at the Dewey Theater in Mineapolis. Zbyszko was in the middle of a huge national push, coming off wins over Frank Gotch (handicap match Buffalo, Nov. 25, 1909), Fred Beell (Buffalo, Jan. 1, 1910), Tom Jenkins (Cleveland, Jan. 7, 1910), and Charles Cutler, (Jan. 11, 1910) to set up a super return match with the undisputed world champion, Frank Gotch. He was probably the second best wrestler in the world.

After a burlesque show, Zbyszko had agreed to pin three men in 30 minutes. The three were Joe Carr, Carl Mattson, and Robert Friedrich (spelled Frederick). Mattson was pinned in 2½ minutes. Carr (a very tough middle weight) lasted six minutes, and Bob was pinned in 12½ minutes. After the match, Stan made a speech, saying that Friedrich was the strongest man of his age he had ever wrestled. This match was Lewis' introduction to big time pro wrestling.[4]

During this period, Friedrich was having hard times. Food could even be a problem. His room-mate cook worked at a lunchroom and Bob would hang out with a starved look on his face. Bob had too much pride to say anything, but after a while the staff would slip him something and the cook would bring home a sandwich for his friend. I wonder if this helped lead Lewis to one of his major vices: food.

Bob then got a job on the shipping room of the Jenn-Semple Hill warehouse, lifting things like stoves and kegs of nails. In Rhinelander, he had brought three or four suits of clothes, and with the money from a new job, he was turning into a clothes hog. He seemed to have very good taste, but he had very little restraint when spending money.[5]

North Dakota

He was then offered $2,500 to play on a pro minor league baseball team at Beach, North Dakota. He continued to wrestle, beating a good heavyweight named J. Power in the town.[6]

This fellow wrestler Power liked Bob, and help him set up a match with a pro named Jack James, who was coming off a hard battle with Henry Ordemann in Minneapolis. Bob knew a lot of important rich men in Beach and they were hot to bet on Friedrich. With strangers in town looking for Friedrich money, Bob told his friends that he didn't think he could beat James. He was right and his objectivity saved some people money. Bob later felt that Power was setting him and his friends up the whole time.

Ed Lewis in 1912

After the baseball season, Bob got a job working for a friendly jeweler. For four months he froze, running a general store that stood alone on the prairie trail, 25 miles north of Glenn Ellen.

After that, a beautiful Indian girl got Bob a cowboy job on her father's ranch near Terry, Montana. He always wanted to be a cowboy, but the actual experience wasn't as romantic as expected and this led him to take the trip back home to Nekoosa.

Back in Wisconsin

The local Elks Club of Grand Rapids, WI, knowing Friedrich's reputation and hearing he was home, offered him a match with Fred Beell of Marshfield. Fred Beell was one of the greatest pound for pound wrestlers in history and the last man to ever beat Frank Gotch.[7]

The match took place in Grand Rapids, WI, on January 3, 1911. The young Friedrich couldn't do anything with Beell, who played with him. After seven and a half minutes, Beell choked him out using what was called a reverse headlock. The second fall saw Beell pin Bob in twenty-two minutes. Friedrich was glad when it was over. Beell gave a speech saying that Bob would one day be champion. Bob received $25 plus a neck with no muscular control for two weeks.[8]

Fred Beell

Bob then barnstormed the area with matches through out Wisconsin. During this period he beat Walter Miller, Dave Sharkey and his trainer Albert Abel. He was positively involved with the pro wrestling business and his days of only thinking about "shooting" would seem over. To be a "pro" meant knowing how to "work."

On September 4, 1911, Friedrich traveled to Chicago for a few days to watch the great Frank Gotch defend his title verses the first true world champion, George Hackenschmidt. The match itself was a disappointment, but it drew over 20,000 fans and $87,000 to Comiskey Park. As with most of Gotch's matches he blew off his challenger in a stinker of a match, and the fans went home so unhappy that Chicago would remain dead to pro wrestling for a number of years.

Frank Gotch vs George Hackenschmidt. Gotch is going for his toehold.

Frank Gotch and Jess Willard, Giant Boxing Champ

Gotch, a discovery of Farmer Burns, had been the dominant wrestler of the early 20th century. In bringing the world's title to America, he became one of the country's first sport stars. Only the heavyweight boxing champion was bigger, but by 1911 he was rich enough to be thinking about retirement. Promoters knew their futures were dependent on the creation of a new star and champion. A problem was that every time they develop someone, Frank would come out of retirement to beat him. Gotch was great for Gotch, but he was beginning to kill the business.[9]

McGregor, Iowa

On the northeast corner of Iowa was a small city located on the Mississippi River across from Wisconsin. This town, McGregor, was connected via riverboat with Lansing, Iowa, 30 miles north of it. Joe Zimmerman, a wrestling manager and hotel owner, offered Bob work and matches in McGregor. After a match in the town, a DeForest Wolfe offered Bob a job cleaning chickens during the day and operating a movie projector in a small movie house at night. While living in McGregor, Bob was making $4 a day and feeling pretty good about himself.

Friedrich started thinking of ways to make even more money. On April 15, 1912, the world was shocked by the sinking of the ocean liner R.M.S. *Titanic* off the coast of Newfoundland, and it wasn't long before people were attempting to make money off the public interest in the disaster. On May 14, 1912, a film called 'Saved From The Titanic' premiered, 29 days after the event. A Dorothy Gibson, who was one of the lucky few rescued after the sinking, wrote and starred in the movie. The movie was filmed in less than a week and was 10 minutes long. This was 1912 and movies were still a new art form.

Friedrich and DeForest Wolfe, after a trip to buy a copy of the movie and a new projector, remodeled an old store in Lansing into a theater (named The Princess Theater). Within two weeks of the idea, they were showing 'Saved From The Titanic' to packed crowds. Most movie tickets cost 10 cents in 1912; Bob and Wolfe were charging 25 cents to see the smash hit.

One problem the two hadn't thought about was the Dunlevey family, who controlled and pioneered the movie business in Lansing. The Dunleveys went to the town newspaper and revealed that the *Titanic* movie being shown by their rival was not from the actual sinking, but a re-enactment with actors playing parts. In 1912, this blew the minds of the mid-west public, and Bob's theater was soon out of the business.

In Lewis' unpublished and unfinished biography, written around 1947, Lewis compared his movie experience to pro wrestling. He said that, just as the people of 1947 had trouble believing the 'Saved From The Titanic' story, while the 1912 public believed the film was reality—so would people in 50 years find it hard to believe that wrestling fans once thought that they were watching a "bona fide athletic contest," when they were actually being entertained by a carefully prepared theatrical spectacle.

Friedrich was unable to renew this license to run the theater because of the exposé by the Dunleveys, who not only ran the movie business in Lansing but also the mayor's office, the postmaster and the newspaper.

Bob lost his temper and in a rage tore up the newspaper office and pushed a lot of people around. Bob was convicted of disturbing the peace and fined $50. It seems the Dunleveys weren't very popular, because the incident made Bob a local celebrity and his fine was paid by Dunlevey's opposition, and he may have even got his license renewed.

There was another girl in Lansing, a banker's daughter named Meta. Bob got along with the mother, but the father wasn't interested in seeing his daughter married to a wrestler.

In Iowa, we have a record of Bob meeting Helmuth Preuss, Ed Prior, Jack Little, Joe Carr and a man named Avery. The spelling of Bob's name, as early as the Zbyszko match in 1910, is Bob Frederick. So it seems to have been his first ring name.

A New Name and Lexington, Kentucky

Late in 1912, Bill Barton, promoter and manager of Bill Demetral, came through Lansing. He was impressed with Friedrich and invited Bob to come to Kentucky for a series of matches. Friedrich agreed, but when the time arrived, Barton sent his letter with details of Friedrich's bookings to Lansing, Michigan instead of Iowa.

Without Bob knowing it, Barton booked Bob Frederick to meet William Demetral in Louisville on January 10, 1913. As the match approached, Barton realized his new star wasn't coming, so he looked for a substitute.[10] He found the veteran wrestler Bob Managoff willing, but Bob Frederick had been billed for a week. Managoff was always willing to change his name or nationality for a payday. So Barton used Managoff, under the name Bob Frederick, and it was he who did the job for Demetral.

With in a week, the real Bob Frederick (Friedrich) showed up in Louisville. With another Frederick (Managoff) in town, Barton created a new name for Bob. He became Ed "Strangler" Lewis, a take-off of the name of the famous wrestling champion of the 19th century, Evan "Strangler" Lewis. There was no intent of honoring an old champion, they just liked the sound of it.

On January 24, 1913, Ed "Strangler" Lewis had his first match in Louisville, or anywhere else, beating none other than Bob Frederick. He would use that name, given to him by Bill Barton, for the rest of his life.[11]

Kentucky was one of wrestling's hottest areas in 1913. Based mainly in Louisville and Lexington, it had a good promoter who booked regular cards using major talent from Chicago. Lewis liked Lexington

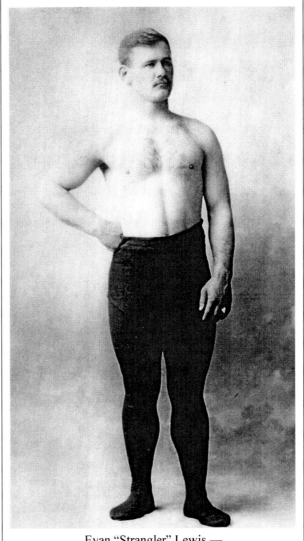

Evan "Strangler" Lewis —
the wrestler Ed Lewis stole his name from.

and would homestead the area for over two years. For much of his career he would be billed as being from Kentucky.

Lexington was one of the richest cities of the South. During the Civil War, it had been occupied mainly by the Union and wasn't destroyed like much of the South. It still had the feel and culture of the pre-war South, and it was the center of the horse racing industry. It was occupied by a large sporting crowd, coupled with a very sophisticated and unique social life. Lewis' personality seemed to take on much of the characteristics of the southern gentleman as he grew as a person and a wrestler in the city.

Dr. Ben. F. Roller

Lexington was promoted by Jerry M. Walls (or Wallus) and he managed Lewis for the next few years (with a verbal contract). During 1913, Lewis had wrestling programs with William Demetral and Dr. Ben F. Roller. Both men were world class wrestlers. Demetral was called the Greek champion and Light Heavyweight world champion. Roller was a main eventer on a national level, a true hooker, with good skills as a performer, but, like a true pro wrestler, willing to exchange wins and losses for a good payday. In his losses, he liked to use the same finish, always getting injured in the deciding fall. Through it all he still maintained the reputation of being one of the sport's best wrestlers. Lewis' association with Roller in 1913 gave Lewis the status of a true main eventer, and he was seen by most fans as a true contender for the world title.

During the summer of 1913 (July & August), Lewis worked in a Wisconsin (some reports say Oregon) lumber mill, chopping wood to improve his strength and condition.

On September 18, 1913, Lewis won a version of the American title from Dr. Ben F. Roller when the Doctor injured his ribs and couldn't continue. Lewis wrestled Demetral on September 29 in a match so violent that it was stopped by police, and both wrestlers were charged with disorderly conduct. That resulted in Mayor J. E. Cassidy banning pro wrestling in Lexington, but he was overruled by the local board of commissioners. Lewis lost his claim to the so-called American title on October 21, 1913, when he was hurt from a fall into a orchestra pit during the rematch with William Demetral.[12]

On April 1, 1913, Frank Gotch had his last major title defense, defeating the great European champion George Lurich in two straight easy falls. He once again announced his retirement and Gotch said he wasn't interested in wrestling again unless he was offered a major match with someone who could draw major money. No one at the time realized it, but Gotch's health was failing.

Frank Gotch working out with Charles Cutler in Chicago

Chicago in 1913

In November 1913, Lewis was brought into Chicago and given a major push by promoters Ed White and Joe Coffey. It was Ed's audition for a major national push.

On November 3, 1913, Lewis debuted at the Chicago Globe Theater on the first card of the wrestling season. He was matched in the main event with Paul Martinson, a semi-star, but someone willing to "job." In the semi-final was Charles Cutler, who was the biggest name wrestler working out of Chicago and an off and on claimant of Frank Gotch's old American title. Lewis was billed as a college boy from Lexington, who was teaching at the University of Kentucky and being described as the new Gotch.

Ed Lewis in 1913

Much of a pro wrestler's persona depends on the finishing hold they use. With Ed "Strangler" Lewis, he promoted himself around his one single hold more than just about any wrestler in history. His first finishing hold in Lexington was the strangle hold, due to his name, but that couldn't be used long term because it was illegal in most places. He, or the people around him, must have realized this in 1913, and Lewis started using a hold called a "neck yoke." This hold was a type of reverse nelson bordering on being a strangle hold but legal under wrestling rules. Lewis would take the hold like a front face lock and force his opponent's chin into his own chest; this cut off much of his air supply. The weakened wrestler was then flipped to the mat as Lewis skillfully applied a leg scissors and arm bar on the way down. The stunned wrestler would then be an easy pin. It seemed to be a move that required some technique, but Ed weighed only 205 pounds and was known then for his quickness and ability to move. In Chicago, the promoters claimed the young "Strangler" was "famous" for the move.

Lewis demonstrating on future manager Billy Sandow
the finishing hold used in Chicago in 1913.

Ed defeated Martinson in impressive style[13] and remained unbeaten throughout the month, setting up a major match with Charles Cutler on November 26. The promoters were trying their best to promote the Cutler/Lewis match, even having the two wrestlers stage a mock fight in a downtown restaurant on November 17, a move that backfired when the press treated the event as a made-up publicity stunt.[14]

On the 26th, in a match described in the pro-Lewis press as Ed's first big test, the Strangler was defeated by Cutler. Cutler took the first fall in 1:01:30 with a cross body lock. Ed came back to win the 2nd fall with his "neck yoke" in 11:45. The last fall ended suddenly when Lewis submitted in a Cutler head scissors at 29:00. The attendance in burned-out Chicago was around 1,000.[15]

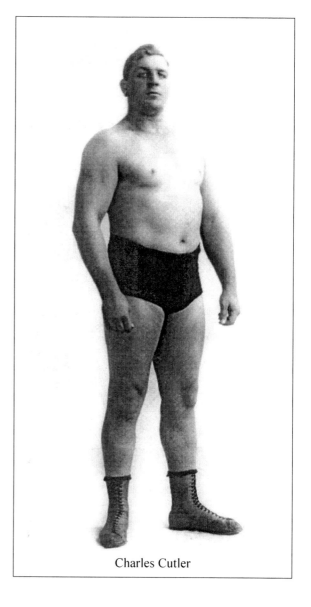

Charles Cutler

Later Chicago promoters would push Cutler as world champion, but I don't think it was an attempt to turn him into a major star. I think they viewed him as a "trail horse" and were just using him as a champion to lose to the next true star, and that star wasn't going to be Strangler Lewis.

The Lewis push continued. Two days after the Cutler match, Ed got a huge write up in the Sunday *Chicago Tribune* with photos of young Ed using the feared "neck yoke." He gave his history and talked about his education, with most of the story made up.[16] I call this lying, but nicer people use the term "ballyhoo."

Lewis' next major match in Chicago was against Gus "Americus" Schoenlein, on December 29, 1913. Americus was a major national star, especially huge in Baltimore, and had wrestled every major wrestler in the sport. Americus defeated Lewis in straight falls, pinning Ed twice after he was thrown by a "under crotch hold" in 5:10 and 50:00. The second fall saw Ed land on his head with a thud. Lewis was carried to the dressing room, unable to walk.[17]

This pretty much ended the first great Lewis push in Chicago. The Cutler match was a hard struggle but Americus had shown superior weight (25 pounds) strength and the victory was without any excuses by Lewis. The critics claimed that Lewis was quick and strong but lacked weight at 205 pounds (without any fat to be seen) plus experience versus the top wrestlers. The next wrestler to get pushed in Chicago was Wladek Zbyszko, the younger brother of Stanislaus Zbyszko.

1914 and Billy Sandow

Lewis went home to Lexington, but returned to Chicago for another major match versus Fred Beell on February 2, 1914. Lewis tricked Beell with a "side roll" to win the 1st fall in 9:37, Beell made Lewis submit to a headlock in the 2nd and he pinned Lewis in 10:35 after a toe hold in the last fall. So Lewis lost again and he didn't return to Chicago for the rest of 1914.[18]

Before 1918, most of the power in pro wrestling was in the hands of managers. To be a major star in the sport, you needed a strong manager. Managers didn't just manage bookings and money, they provided training for their performers and probably booked the actual matches. The manager with the biggest star, who could draw the most money, would control who won or lost.

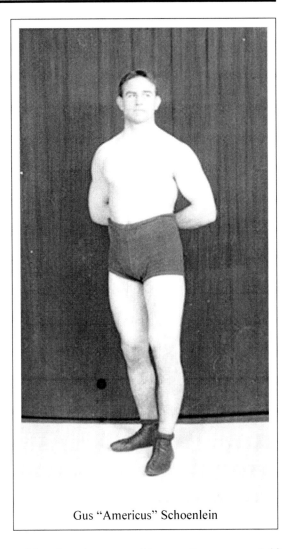

Gus "Americus" Schoenlein

Farmer Burns

Most of the time that meant his wrestler won, and, if another manager didn't like the situation, he didn't have to take the big money match. Sometimes the dominate manager would pull a switch if there was more money to be made losing. Even Gotch did big money losses to Jenkins and Beell. The manager also made bets and made sure his grappler got his cut from gamblers. A good manager might have meant more to a wrestler than great wrestling ability.

By 1900, Farmer Burns was the biggest manager in wrestling, and he controlled most of the major wrestlers and ran barnstorming through out most of American. In 1914 he was in decline and losing control, with his champion Frank Gotch wanting out of the business. Most felt Gotch had one more big match in him, but it would have to be against someone worth his time, who could give him that last big payday.

Farmer Burns training boxing champion James J. Jeffries
before the famous fight with Jack Johnson

In Lexington, Lewis was managed by Jerry Walls, a carnie who became involved with wrestling as a promoter and showman. He worked with Lewis for two years without a written contract. Ed didn't seem to respect him very much. After he got Lewis through the door of stardom, he didn't seem smart enough to get him any further.

On January 28, 1914, Lewis was once again matched up with Dr. Ben Roller in Lexington. Roller won the first fall with a crotch lift and slam for the pin in 41 minutes, and Lewis won the second using the "neck yoke" in 21 minutes. The match was filled with a lot of out-of-the-ring fighting and after one such occasion Roller slammed Lewis to get the pin, but it seemed to be a mistake by referee Wallace Yeager because Ed's shoulders were clearly off the mat. The fans were upset over that, and the fact that *Police Gazette* rules state that the two wrestlers on the ropes needed to return to the center of the ring before grappling restarted. So Roller's win over Lewis was a cheap one and another match would be needed down the road.[19] This was a pattern most Lewis matches would follow.

During his stay in the South, Roller was being managed by Billy Sandow. Sandow was a fine lighter weight wrestler, who worked as a trainer and ran a gym in Chicago. His true last name was Baumann, and he had two brothers, Julius and Maxwell, involved in the wrestling game as promoters. In 1914, he was trying to make a name for himself as a manager. Roller loved to talk, so he didn't need Sandow out front, but it would seem that Sandow was working with Lewis and helping the young wrestler get over via his series of matches with the Doctor. We know Sandow was connected with Lewis in Chicago because, in photos of Lewis published in the *Chicago Tribune* on November 30, 1913, Ed is shown working out with Sandow.

On February 4, 1914, a Lexington storyline created for the newspapers was that Billy Sandow was bringing in a well known "unknown" to meet homeboy Lewis. The "unknown" was later revealed to be Marin Plestina, the last great heavyweight developed by the Farmer Burns camp.

Marin Plestina

On February 5, Lewis was taking on all comers at the Lexington Ada Meade theater. The deal was that a challenger would get $1 for each minute he lasted versus the Strangler. Lewis wrestled Sandow that night and pinned him in 10 minutes. Billy made $10, or so it seemed.[20]

Lewis and Plestina met on February 10, 1914, at the Lexington Opera House. The match ended up being a two hour draw, so a return match was set up for February 18, with the strangle hold being legal. Referee Heywood Allen, a promoter in Louisville, disqualified Lewis in 43 minutes for rough work, including wrestling off the mat and refusing to break. Plestina then pinned Ed after a slam in five minutes. Even in losing two straight falls, Lewis had a way of not losing clean. Sandow was present at both matches.[21]

With Frank Gotch claiming to be retired, the best wrestler in the world was most likely Stanislaus Zbyszko, who was attempting to claim his own world title. Zbyszko met Lewis on March 23, 1914, in front of the largest crowd in Lexington wrestling history. The match was a handicap match in which Zbyszko had to pin Ed twice in an hour. This type of a match was considered an exhibition, with no title or record in danger, but these were done constantly in the early days of pro wrestling. I believe they were done mainly for gambling, which generated more money than gates or attendance. It was also a way to build to rematches and advance wrestlers. Most of the major stars of the time had lost such matches, including Frank Gotch losing one to Zbyszko (Buffalo, November 25, 1909) before their famous match in Chicago on June 1, 1910.

The pro-Lewis crowd cheered their boy on, as Lewis broke hold after hold put on him by Zbyszko. In fact, it seemed like Ed was being tied into knots by Stan, and was only breaking them with sheer strength. At the forty-one minute mark, Stan put on a toe hold Ed couldn't get out of, and Lewis gave up. For the last 19 minutes, Lewis ran around and even off the non-roped mat to avoided contact with Zbyszko and, as the crowd cheered, time ran out. Referee Heywood Allen announced Lewis the winner.[22]

Zbyszko was blind with rage because Lewis played with him by leaving the ring and refusing to wrestle as an honorable wrestler would have, and may of the fans also hated Lewis' tactics—but referee Allen stated that there was nothing he could do if Lewis followed his order to return to the ring. If Lewis had refused to return, he would have given the match to Zbyszko. Allen then said Zbyszko could have requested a roped off ring, but didn't—so it was his own fault.

This Zbyszko match, with Lewis refusing to lock up with the champion, wouldn't be the only time he'd use the tactic to frustrate a superior wrestler. In fact, it would become the style he'd become famous for.

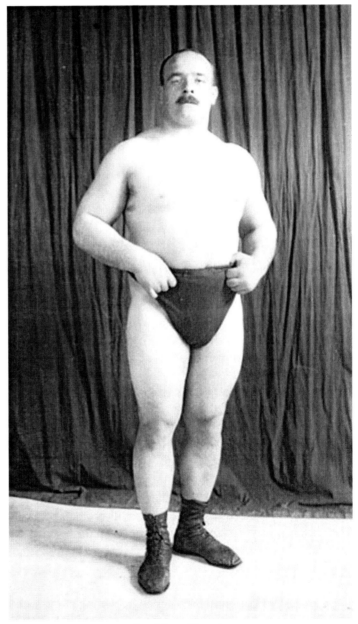

Stanislaus Zbyszko

Wladek Zbyszko

Wladek Zbyszko followed his brother Stanislaus to America in 1913. He claimed to have won the European title in a Paris, France tournament in 1911, and, unlike most European performers, was well schooled in catch-as-can style (Catch Style) of wrestling. He was a big man and probably had one of the best bodies in wrestling. Highly skilled as a wrestler, he was also an elegant gentleman with social graces when out of the ring. In the ring, his size, strength, and skill were coupled with a sadistic will to hurt opponents. And he didn't like to lose.

Lewis claimed he hated Wladek from the first moment he watched the wrestler in a dressing room attempting to sing opera. In later life Lewis would have little good to say about Wladek, but it was his series of matches with Zbyszko, and Joe Stecher, that created his legend and reputation.

In 1914, Wladek was getting the push that Ed wanted. The giant had beaten Tom Jenkins and Roller, with the promoters looking to feud him with Alex Aberg, the Greco-Roman style world champion in New York City. Lewis had been in Chicago with Wladek, and made a point of challenging him, even going so far as to distributing printed petitions for a match. The night of Lewis' Chicago loss to Beell, Wladek attempted, before the match, to attack Ed in the ring. Detroit promoters induced Wladek to meet Ed in their city, so the first Zbyszko/Lewis match was booked for April 4, 1914, at the Armory. This was only two weeks after Ed match with Stan Zbyszko, and on that night Lewis bet the older brother a suit of clothes that he would win.

Wladek came to the arena with the assurance of Ed's manager, Jerry Walls, that the match was going to be a "work" and he assumed that he was "going over." Lewis never seemed to co-operate in first matches, and, once in the ring, Wladek found he had been fooled. Lewis blocked Zbyszko's every move and the foreign wrestler couldn't do anything with him. Frustrated, Wladek then began to foul Lewis by eye gouging, finger twisting and elbowing. Lewis complained to the referee but nothing was done. Lewis then hit Wladek with three hard punches to the face. With a riot about to take place, a flock of police jumped into the ring and the match was stopped after 20 minutes. It was ruled a no contest.[23]

A rematch took place on April 23, 1914, in Buffalo, NY. Lewis battled Wladek as an equal in the first fall, but after an hour Zbyszko got rough. After two terrific slams, the second on his head, the Strangler was pinned. Lewis was almost knocked out and couldn't return for the second fall. Wladek Zbyszko was declared the winner.[24]

Following a loss to Charley Cutler in Lexington on April 27, the record shows Lewis to be inactive for a period of time. I believe Lewis was sick with a stomach problem. Ed claimed his hatred for Wladek caused the condition, and he returned to Lansing, Iowa for rest and training.[25]

In July, Lewis began wrestling in the Virginia area. During that month he defeated Hjalmar Lundin, Yussiff Hussane, and John Perilli in Richmond. Dr. Ben F. Roller was also in the area, being managed by Billy Sandow. The Doctor was once again claiming the American title. Lewis (being managed by Jimmy Ross) and the Roller/Sandow group seemed to be getting along well and they staged a title switch between the two performers.

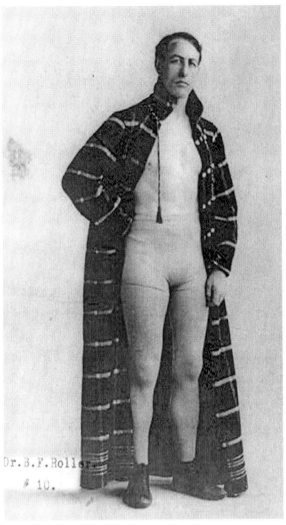

Dr.B.F.Roll[er]
10.

Dr. Ben. F. Roller

On September 3, 1914, Lewis defeated Roller for the American title in Richmond, only to drop it back to Roller three weeks later on September 29, 1914. Lewis' victory seemed to have been clean, but the Ed loss came via a disqualification. Lewis won the first fall in a little over an hour, but dropped the second via disqualification, after his second wrestler Gus Costello bumped against the Doctor. Roller then beat him in the third fall.

After Roller left the area, Lewis took friend Billy Sandow on as his permanent manager.

Billy Sandow was a wrestler, trainer, and manager with strong family ties in wrestling. His real name was Baumann, and he worked closely with his three brothers. Jules was the oldest, who promoted areas in upstate New York. Max operated out of Savannah and played the part of John Pesek's manager for a time. Another brother, not really involved much in pro wrestling, was named Alexander. Working out of Chicago, Sandow and Lewis had known each other for some time. Sandow had managed Ben Roller, Yussuf Hussein and Marvin Plestina in matches with Ed, and the two appear training together in Chicago photographs. Sandow, and just about everyone in wrestling, saw the promise in Lewis, and the union between wrestler and manager was formed by the end of 1914. This handshake agreement would last for almost 20 years.

Billy Sandow was the "big time" manager that Ed Lewis's career need. Sandow was ruthless in his promotion of his young wrestler. Sandow had acquired wrestling smarts and contacts from years of being around the business, so knew the value of "ballyhoo" (a wrestling term, which is a nice way of saying "lies used in self promoting"). Sandow, hard working and energetic, would do anything or say anything to get Ed Lewis over. Under no condition would Billy never admit he was wrong about anything.

He seemed to be honest in his dealing with Lewis and other wrestling insiders. His word seemed to have credibility, and he was always willing to make deals. This made him seem to be easy to work with, but he always knew how to get what he wanted.

There were many weasel type managers in wrestling, but when you compare Billy Sandow with the other major dignified managers in the late teens—Earl Caddock's Gene Melady, Joe Stecher's Tony Stecher, and Wladek Zbyszko's Jack Curley—Sandow comes off as the major heel.

Sandow was also a top-level trainer, who claimed to use a system called "Kinetic Stress" to get the best out of Lewis. The Kinetic Stress system of conditioning seemed to be the stressing of muscle groups by the use of pulleys, levers and straps. I don't know how much of this system applies to the training of pro wrestlers nor how much of the theory was created for public relations and the press, but Lewis did seem to improve under Sandow. Ed's weight was always credited in his defeats, but, under Sandow, Lewis went from 195 pounds in 1913 to 215 in 1915. After Sandow, Lewis's size became one of his strong points and he was able to keep his quickness and balance.

Under Sandow, Lewis's finishing hold was changed from the "neck yoke" to the "head lock." In the early years of pro wrestling, the brutal element of the sport was played down and sportsmanship played an important role. The main object was to pin your opponent, not make him submit. All the famous finishing holds of the era were used to pin wrestlers, and injuring someone was considered unsporting. Gotch's toe hold, Stecher's body scissors, and Caddock's head scissors were pinning moves. Lewis's headlock was used for the same purpose. Ed would weaken his man with the headlock, which was said to cut flow of blood to the brain, and then hip lock the wrestler to the mat with a violent slam with the giant Lewis handing on top, ready to pin his opponent. Most of the time he would have to use a series of headlock before pinning his man. This was the basic hold he used during his career, but it may have sometimes been used as a submission after about 1922, as styles changed. This form of a standing headlock take down would seem to have been a "show" move for worked situations. In a contest, a wrestler would not want to put someone in a position to get behind him while standing. (Today, how many standing headlocks have you seen used in the UFC?) It's used today, in every pro wrestling match, as a take down, and no one thinks much about it. Its days as a spectacular finisher are now long gone.

Sandow created a gimmick training aid, called a headlock machine. Built by one of the lesser known Baumann brothers, Alexander, it was a wooden head, cut in half,

Ed Lewis using the headlock machine

with a railroad spring attached in the middle. The story is that by forcing the two half's together Lewis developed the strength need to apply the headlock. It was mainly a P.R. tool, used to get copy in the press.[26] Sandow later developed a similar machine to publicize Everett Marshall's full nelson hold.

The famous wooden dummy machine devised by Sandow for Lewis to squeeze in training after the "Strangler" had kicked over his sparring play-house by treating the boys too roughly. The wire springs are reminiscent of those attached to locomotives.

The New Champion Finds A Contender

In April 1912, Dodge City, Nebraska's Joe Stecher began his wrestling career with a win over friend Earl Caddock. By 1914, he was the talk of the wrestling world and the man insiders felt would replace Frank Gotch as the next wrestling superstar. Stecher was a farm boy and a wrestling machine, who was beating Nebraska's best wrestlers in shoots, in straight falls and in short time. He took pleasure in beating the best students of Farmer Burns, so Burns sent his best, Marin Plestina, to Lincoln, Nebraska to take care of him. On March 25, 1914, Stecher wrestled rings around Plestina, winning in two straight quick falls. Plestina ended up not even being a good test for Stecher.[27] Burns then sent Ad Santel, under the name Otto Carpenter, to Fremount, Nebraska on January 5, 1915 to show up the young Stecher. Santel was also destroyed in two straight falls. In 1915 Stecher seemed like the safest bet in wrestling, and the Nebraska farmers saw no way they could lose money by putting it on Joe to win.

Joe and Tony Stecher working out for reporters

On February 20, 1915, Charles Cutler and his manager William Rochells went into the downtown offices of the *Chicago Tribune* and claimed the world title. They justified this by saying Frank Gotch was retired and Cutler was undefeated in two years as the American title holder. Cutler posted a bond with the *Tribune* reporter and challenged all contenders to meet him.[28] A short time later a major match was signed for him to meet Joe Stecher in Omaha on July 5, 1915.

On May 10, 1915, Charley Cutler defended his claim versus Ed "Strangler" Lewis in Lexington. After an hour and fifteen minutes, with neither wrestler gaining a fall, Lewis complained that Cutler was using a strangle hold. He then blew his cool over the injustice and knocked Cutler down with two punches. The match was then awarded to Cutler on a foul. The newspaper reported that the two continued the fight in the dressing room, but was stopped by officials.[29] So it looked like Lewis had another blood feud like the one with Wladek Zbyszko, but the next report we have is Ed going to Chicago to help train champ Cutler for the Joe Stecher match.[30]

On July 5, 1915, Lewis was ringside in Omaha to watch Joe Stecher take Charles Cutler's world title claim. The new champion won his two straight falls in 18:04 and 10:00 using his leg scissor. In the betting, the farmers of Nebraska won thousands from the Chicago fans who came by trainloads to see the match. Lewis and Earl Caddock trained Cutler, and Ed, in his unpublished biography, claimed the two of them lost $2,800 betting on Charley. It's a hard story to believe since the two of them must have known it was a "work."

The crowd was listed as 15,000, which, at the time, was one of the biggest non-Gotch attendance marks in wrestling history.[31] After the defeat, Cutler went to Stecher to say: "Joe, you are a champion if there ever was a champion born."

Stecher in the Navy during WWI

Stecher as world champion, with his famous belt

Ringside watching the match sat the old champion, Frank Gotch. That night Stecher would receive his first public offer for a showdown with Gotch. Chicago promoter offered the Stechers $25,000 for the match. No deal was made.

Lewis's old friend Bill Barton was promoting wrestling in Evansville, Indiana, and was able to book a championship match, to a finish, for Ed versus the new champion on October 21, 1915. Stecher had been busy defending his title and to Joe, who had never seen Lewis perform, Ed was just another contender standing in line. Lewis, however, hadn't had a match since May and had been in training, first with Cutler and then in his own camp with Sandow. He had watched the match in Omaha and knew Stecher's every move.

Although he knew all the fundamental holds, Ed Lewis was not a great technical wrestler, moving in and out of holds, like Caddock, Pesek, Gotch or even Londos. His strong point as a wrestler was strength, size, balance, coordination, intelligence, and stamina. The stamina didn't seem to come from training so much as from an ability to relax in the ring. He was a defense wrestler, who took pride in not letting his opposition get behind him in a position of control. Whenever he was faced with a shoot situation, he would revert to this defense style, which never seemed to beat anyone, but did frustrate opponents and fans. It didn't bother Ed to have long boring matches, just so long as he didn't get pinned.

Lewis vs Stecher

The first Stecher/Lewis match took place in Evansville on October 20, 1915. At the pre-match press conference, Stecher was the farm boy, timid around the press, but still showing the pose of a champion. This contrasted with the well-dressed and street wise Lewis, who was always willing to talk with the press or anyone else. Lewis looked heavier and stronger but once in the ring this illusion evaporated.

For two hours, Lewis ran and refused to lock up with Stecher. Having scouted Stecher, he claimed Joe only had three or four take downs and every time he saw Stecher's "tell" he just moved away. Lewis was able to block Stecher's every move, but he did nothing on offense. Stecher had no fear of Lewis and four times he dove in for a take down and Ed was able to get behind him on the mat. Each time, Lewis gave up his position and got back up on his feet. He was afraid that on the ground Stecher would reverse him and apply the scissors. Tony Stecher, Joe's trainer, complained to the referee that it was the contender's job to attempt to defeat a champion and that Lewis should wrestle, but Lewis would not change his strategy. The boring match upset the spectators and boo's filled the hall.

At the two hour mark, the upset Stecher rushed Lewis and Ed had nowhere to go but over the ropes to the floor. In the fall, Ed hit his head on a chair. He laid on the floor and Billy Sandow told the referee that he was injured and couldn't continue. The ringside physician, Dr. Phil Warter, ruled that he was not injured and could still wrestle. Lewis refused. The referee, Bert Sisson, then gave the first fall to Stecher and announced that he would give the champion the match if Lewis refused to return after a 15 minute rest period.

In the dressing room, between falls, two other doctors examined Lewis and said there was no reason he couldn't wrestle. When he didn't return to the ring, Stecher was awarded the second fall and the match. Reports printed the next day said that everyone present felt that there "was no doubt of the outcome. Sooner or later, Stecher would have gotten his deadly hold on him."

Back in the arena, hell broke out. The mayor of Evansville, who's last name was Bosse, got in to the ring and gave a speech. He complained that "the match was not on the square." He had the Chief of Police hold up the receipts and promised to give most of it to charity. The police claimed they had received telegraphs and phone messages before the match saying "Stop fake wrestling match tonight."

Lewis was taken to the hospital and the next morning a report was issued saying he had a minor groin injury. Mayor Bosse allowed promoter William F. Barton expense money, but Lewis and Stecher were never paid (they were going to split up $400). I don't think they cared—they both probably made far more from the gamblers. With Stecher being unbeatable, the major betting was on how long his opponents would last. It was very convenient for Lewis, to take his dive out of the ring, right after the two hour mark of the match.[32]

You would think this embarrassing match would have killed The Strangler's career, but once back in the big cities of Chicago and New York, Sandow and Lewis told reporters stories of a great match in which Lewis out-manoeuvered and out-thought the great Stecher for two hours. In time, the two even changed the result, with most believing the match was a draw or no contest. Sandow believed that if you told a lie and it got printed enough, it became truth. Sandow may have been right, because by the time Lewis got to New York City in November 1915, he was considered a major star and a top challenger to Stecher's title.

Sandow was ruthless in his promotion of Ed "Strangler" Lewis and he did a brilliant job in creating the myth that lives today. Billy Sandow's style was quite similar to the job boxing manager Jack Kearns did for young Jack Dempsey. I think the difference between the two is that Sandow remained friends with Lewis and seemed honest with money, or at least up to the standards of pro wrestling. Telling lies was just part of Sandow's job and he did it well. Kearns alienated everyone, including Dempsey.

1916 and The New York Tournament

By 1915 the history of American Greco (or Graeco)-Roman pro wrestling (GR)[33] was on its last page. It had been popular at the end on the 19th century due to great GR champions like William Muldoom, but most Americans preferred the Catch-as-Catch-Can style and GR was rarely used or talked about after Frank Gotch destroyed George Hackenschmidt in 1908 and 1911. GR wrestling is a sport of strength and endurance in which huge powerful giants (sometimes more fat than big) lock up in a wrestling contest in which no holds are allowed below the waist. It's much different than the Catch style, so most of the champion GR performers from Europe were used to job to American stars. It is a limited form of wrestling that would have contestants locked in strength holds for long periods of time, but it didn't have the moment or variety of holds of the Catch style.

But in 1915, a New York City Opera promoter named Samuel Rachmann, took advantage of a migration of European wrestlers trying to escape from the wars on the continent, and the large emigrant population of New York City, to promote two major GR tournaments in the city during 1915.[34]

The first, and lesser known, took place in May and June. The final match took place on June 25, 1915 between the GR world champion Alexander Aberg and Wladek Zbyszko. The title match was ruled a draw after three hours and forty minutes of brutal wrestling. Aberg seemed to get the better of the contest, as Wladek fell into a "semi-conscious" state for three days following the match. A rematch for the GR title took place on October 25, 1915 in Madison Square Garden, with Aberg defeating Wladek in one hour and four minutes. These matches with Aberg were losses, but they were putting Wladek over in the city making Lewis's old friend a big star.

From November 8, 1915 to January 29, 1916, Rachmann ran his second and most famous GR International tournament at the Manhattan Opera House.[35] It is famous today for the creation of the first masked man and for Strangler Lewis's domination, but the original goal was to put over Alex Aberg and then Wladek Zbyszko. Because of the beginning of wars in Europe that would lead to WWII, Rachmann was able to put some of the major wrestlers in the world on salary for as low as $50 a week. Some of the stars used were Ben Roller, Charles Cutler, George Lurich, Dimitrius Tofalos, Yusif Hussane, Renato Gardini, Ivan Linow and, of course, The Masked Marvel. Lou Daro (The Great Daro) and Frank Leavitt (later Man Mountain Dean) also made short appearances. Alex Aberg was the GR champion and considered unbeatable. He was never beaten in the tournament but he was booked as a GR idealist who refused to perform in the Catch style.[36]

They wrestled six nights a week with two matinees on weekends. Most matches were 20 minutes but if a challenge was made wrestlers could and did wrestle what were called finish matches. But, regardless of their name, they had to end by the city's one o'clock curfew. The early matches were all GR, but once the promotion started to tank, they allowed the catch style to be used. This tournament pretty much ended the use of GR in American pro wrestling.

The tournament began on November 8, but Lewis didn't show up until November 22. Since it was an International Tournament, Lewis was billed as being from Germany. Ed was as International as the House of Pancakes, but many Americans were being billed as foreigners, so the German speaking Lewis fit the billing. He was pushed from the beginning and won five straight matches before wrestling a 20 minute draw with Wladek Zbyszko on November 30. A large number of these matches, because of the short time limit, ended up as draws, and Lewis then entered a long period of them. His overall record during his stay in the tournament was 21 wins, one loss and 15 draws. At one point he wrestled six draws in a row. During the tournament he had four draws with Wladek (who had at least 13 draws in the tournament).[37] This type of booking was normal in GR tournaments in Europe.

Lewis went to a 20 minute draw with Aberg on December 4, which led to another Aberg draw on December 9 which lasted 1:04:00 before being stopped by the curfew. It was said to be an action-filled match and Ed did well wrestling in the GR style against the champion. The match barely got any mention in the press because that night marked the debut of The Masked Marvel.[38]

A young Wladek Zbyszko

Alex Aberg

The idea for masked wrestlers seems to have originated with a opera promoter named Mark A. Luescher. Using the hero of a novel *That Frenchman* by Archibald Clavering Gunter, he dressed an opera diva named La Belle Dazle up in a red mask and toured the country to sell-out crowds. Luascher suggested a masked mystery gimmick to Ben Atwood, press agent for the opera house wrestling shows. Atwood went to Jack Curley, who was managing Yusif Hussane in the tournament but not promoting, and Charlie Cutler, and two came up with a wrestler to play the part with a mask for him to hide his identity.[39] Up until his debut into Rachmann's tournament, the fans were losing interest in the show, but with the masked man headlining they started seeing box office drawers fill with money. The masked man was really Mort Henderson, a Rochester performer, who had been picked by Cutler and Curley while wrestling in Pennsylvania. Once outfitted with a proper mask, the unknown became a major wrestler over night. His only true major victory was a win over George Lurich but he wrestled many long draws with the best like: Wladek Zbyszko (Dec. 17, 2:13:00, Dec. 30, 1:56:00 and Jan. 5 1:58:00), Aberg (Dec. 17, 2:21:00), and

George Lurich

Lurich (Jan. 12, 1:27:00). The Masked Marvel got good reviews in the press as a performer and everyone seemed willing to make him look good. He was not the first masked wrestler, but he was the first to be promoted to the top level for any length of time. Did the gimmick expose the business? Yes, but no one seemed to care with good money being made off him.

The mystery didn't last long. On December 16, the *Brooklyn Daily Eagle* printed that The Masked Marvel was Mort Henderson. I believe the reporter got the information from Mort's manager, Ed Pollard, who then denied the charge. The angle continued like nothing happened.

Lewis became the first man to defeat The Masked Marvel on December 20, when the Strangler tricked the Marvel using a headlock followed by a wristlock and pin in 11:50. The ending happened so fast that it took the crowd a minute to realize the Marvel had been pinned. After the crowd regained its breath, it gave Lewis an ovation that he never forgot. The paper claimed he cried in the ring. The match had been an even affair, so a finish match was held on December 22, which ended up in a draw in 1:59:00. A third match between the two took place on January 3, and it also was a draw but lasted two hours and thirdly one minutes.[40]

Lewis had his big GR showdown with Alex Aberg on December 29, 1916. Lewis started fast but after 20 minutes he found Aberg gaining in strength. Aberg put Lewis into a double nelson and after Ed broke the hold, he seemed groggy. After 50 minutes Lewis was slammed by Aberg and pinned by an inside arm lock. Lewis had to be helped out of the ring and later claimed Aberg wasn't human and "the strongest wrestler before the public in 1915."[41]

On January 15, 1916, Ed Lewis defeated Dr. Ben Roller under catch rules. The next day manager Billy Sandow was interviewed in the newspaper saying that Ed Lewis was the catch style world champion due to the victory. He also claimed the first Stecher match was a draw and only stopped after The Strangler had held Stecher in a bridge for twenty-three minutes and Joe broke his finger to break free. This appeared around the same time that Jack Curley announced that the true world champion Joe Stecher would defend his title verses Wladek Zbyszko on January 27 in Madison Square Garden.

On January 17, Lewis scored one of his biggest wins at the Opera house in pinning Wladek Zbyszko in 1:21:07 under catch rules. The win and his continuing title claim put Sandow back on the sports page, claiming Lewis should replace Wladek against Stecher. Sandow and Lewis would claim, through the following years, that they won the catch section of the tournament. No one knows for sure, but in no place is there a mention of a "catch-as-catch-can" tournament in any newspaper. Ed Lewis could say he was the star during his two months stay at the Opera House and the strongest catch wrestler, but there is no straight-out mention of a catch tournament. There was only a GR tournament champion and that was Alex Aberg.

Lewis and Sandow then left the tournament before it completed. Rachmann wanted to take Lewis on a American tour meeting Aberg, but Sandow wanted more that the $200 a week he was getting in New York City. Lewis then started working on the East Coast, probably for Jack Curley, with an agreement to wrestle Stecher again in Omaha around July 4.

On Jan. 24, 1916, Alex Aberg defeated Wladek Zbyszko to win the GR tournament title. As was the habit of most major cards in pro wrestling's early period, the match was terrible and an insult to the fans who paid to be present. At 25:52 Zbyszko was thrown from the ring crashing him into the back of the stage. Wladek struck the floor and then rolled over on a table, laying still. When he was attended to, he claimed an injury, saying he couldn't continue. The fans yelled "quitter" and "fake." They shouted down any announcement and it looked like a riot was about to take place. A doctor came into the ring and said that Wladek could continue, but

Zbyszko refused. Zbyszko then announced that he was injured but would continue if the spectators desired him to do so. The crowd, being unsympathetic to Wladek's plight, made it plain they wanted him to wrestle, so Wladek walked off the stage and did not return. 50 minutes later referee George Bothner declared Aberg the winner.

Jack Curley had been a force in boxing for most of the 1900's, but he also had experience as a wrestling promoter in Chicago and the North West; and had managed Hackenschmidt, Roller and Yussif Hussane. Curley was the boxing promoter who found America's white hope, having staged famous Jack Johnson/Jess Willard fight in Havana, Cuba on April 5, 1915. Jack Curley was about as big and powerful a promoter as you could find in the world, but his position in boxing was challenged by a new man named Tex Rickard. Curley, not willing to offer the big guarantees, nor take the chances of Rickard, left boxing to concentrate on controlling the world of pro wrestling.[42]

Jack Curley (big guy with hat, in middle of group, listed as #5) at the camp of Jim Flynn, before Curley promoted match with Jack Johnson.

In January of 1915, he booked the champion Joe Stecher into Madison Square Garden at the same time Rachmann was still running his Opera House tournament. At first, Curley had Stecher set up to defend versus Wladek Zbyszko, but three day before card Wladek made a fool of himself in the January 25 match with Aberg and became unusable. So Curley contacted The Masked Marvel and Strangler Lewis to take Zbyszko's place in the title match. Rachmann didn't see anything in the idea for him, so he took Curley to court claiming both wrestlers were under contracts. It turned out that Henderson was being paid $100 a week and Lewis was getting $200, "engaged to take part in the wrestling performances, just as actors are engaged to perform" in stage plays.[43] Curley was friends with Rachmann and the two came to terms by the next day, so Jack made the announcement that Stecher would be meeting The Masked Marvel that night.

The statements in court blew the cover of Rachmann's tournament and confirmed The Masked Marvel's identity as Mort Henderson. Most of the air left in the Opera House Tournament then fled for a cleaner environment.[44]

On the day of the match, Sandow was in the newspapers again complaining that Stecher shouldn't be billed as Catch world champion because that title belonged to Lewis. But the new champion Stecher seemed to be getting most of the fan's attention and very few thought much of Sandow's comments.

On January 27, 1916, Stecher's first showing in New York City was a great success. Joe beat The Marvel in straight falls, 9:50 and 5:51, with his scissors hold. In outclassing one of the major stars of the Opera tournament, the paper claimed he "gave competitive sports a tremendous boost by his sportsmanlike actions" and that "Not since Frank Gotch showed here has there been such a wrestler" in the city. Stecher was a hit in front of one of the largest crowds in New York City in years. High society had turned out and approved of the sport. So Jack Curley had found a home in New York City and he remained the dominate wrestling promoter in town until 1937.[45]

The last card of Sam Rachmann's tournament took place on January 29, 1916. Alex Aberg received a $5,000 purse for winning first place in the GR tournament. No prize for catch wrestling was mentioned. The main event had The Masked Marvel losing to Sula Hevonpaa. There were challenges printed about Aberg wanting a match with Joe Stecher, but the match never seemed to have taken place. Hachmann had plans on a GR tournament to tour the country but it also never happened. For the most part, Greco-Roman wrestling in America just seemed to die.[46]

In late 1915, reports were that Gotch was coming out of retirement for the Stecher match. In January 1916 Frank traveled to Los Angeles on a family vacation but the real reason was to train. He later signed a contract to wrestle Ad Santel in San Francisco on February 22, but dropped out due to a lack of conditioning. This led to him being sued by the promoter.

On February 24, Gene Melady, arguably the most powerful wrestling promoter in American, said he had options on both Stecher and Gotch for a match at the Omaha Fair Grounds on Labor Day. He planed to erect an arena big enough to draw a $150,000 gate. It all would depended on Gotch's feelings after training a few weeks. Other reports of the match, taking place in Chicago and Sioux City, follow.

In March, Gotch had two matches. In one he beat William Demetral at the Los Angeles Athletic Club (March 10, 1916) and in the other he won a handicap match over Herman Strech, Jack White and Sam Clapham in San Diego (March 12, 1916). On both nights he looked terrible.

On April 4, Gotch returned to his home, Humboldt, Iowa, and announced he had signed to appear with the Sells-Floto Circus, starting on April 15. He said he would be paid $1,100 a week or $1,350 if he signed to meet Stecher. By May 1, Gotch had stomach problems and couldn't eat. Weighting only 185 pounds, he canceled his contract with the circus. Saying the condition started in California, he went back home to Humbolt but returned to the circus on May 24, noting that he needed the money. On June 14, Harry Tammen, owner of the Sells-Floto Circus, claimed Gotch has signed to meet Stecher in Chicago. On July 18, 1916, Frank Gotch broke the fibula bone in his left leg wrestling an exhibition match with Bob Managoff. Everyone involved then realized that a Stecher/Gotch super match would never happen.

Stecher had spent much of 1916 wrestling minor opponents and spinning his wheels waiting on Gotch. At some point he realized he needed a new rival to make big money off of. All signs pointed to Strangler Lewis to be the first to play the part.

Lewis and Sandow had continued to claim the world title, even after Alex Aberg got a temporary injunction from a judge telling them to stop. Aberg sited his win over Lewis as proof.

Four Hours and Fifty One Minutes of Boredom

In June, a Stecher/Lewis July 4, 1916 rematch was signed for Omaha. The match was contracted "to a finish" and set up in an outdoor stadium to meet the demands of fans from all over the mid-west. Starting at 4:00 in the afternoon, it drew 18,000 fans and lasted 4 hours, 51 minutes and thirty three seconds of total boredom.

Once again Lewis stayed on the defense for the entire match. Stecher couldn't take him down or even get a hold on him. Basically, nothing happened for five hours. Stecher was more wary in this match, always the aggressor, but he never took any chances that would allow Lewis to get behind him or hook him. Several times Joe got in the down position in the middle of the ring, and let Lewis get on top, but on the call for action by the referee Ed Smith, Lewis just stood back up in the defense position. At 8:00, darkness set in, and the promoter, Gene Melady, proposed that the match be stopped and resumed in the morning. This would have allowed them to wrestle all day. Stecher agreed but Sandow and Lewis said the contract read that it was "to a finish" and not to be stopped. As darkness fell, automobiles with their headlights on were brought in to surround the ring and light the area. So it continued, with Lewis doing nothing but backing away. The fans, for the last half hour, threw seat cushions in an attempt to hit the wrestlers and jar them into action. When a finish was called at 4:51:33, the police, jumping into the ring, were hit by six of the cushions. Promoter Melady, who was more of a sportsman that a wrestling promoter, wanted to continue the match the next day, but, by the next day, no one else cared. A committee of sports writers decided the match was over and it was called a draw.[47]

The result was a scandal that came close to killing pro wrestling in Omaha. The purse of both Lewis and Stecher, $5,022, was held up until July 7, when Sandow started to file a suit over the money. Both were blamed for the terrible match but the hate fell on Lewis because Joe was the homeboy and the aggressor. In Omaha and most of the mid-west, Lewis was never forgiven and he was always forced to play heel—a role he seemed born to play.

It wasn't just a bad match—the people of Nebraska lost thousands of dollars betting on Stecher. Before and after the match, no one felt Lewis had a chance of beating or pinning Stecher, so the real bet was on the length of the match. Joe won all his matches in short time and straight falls, so the farmer types thought it was a safe bet to put their money on "Stecher under 60 minute" or even under 30 minutes. As the match continued, they kept raising their bets with each half hour. A small fortune was made by the Lewis beaters and big city gamblers all over the country. Lewis was willing to stall and ruin the contest because the money was in the gambling, not winning a match or a title. Stecher, himself, was probably in on it and made money. The word "mark" was a gambling term long before it was used by the wrestling world—so figure that out.[48]

In the days following the event, Stecher attempted to pacify the fans by making a promise that he would not wrestle Lewis again unless the match was in Omaha. He seemed to intend to keep his word, because the next year he refused a Lewis match in San Francisco, using this promise as a reason.

Once Lewis was out of reach of anyone who had actually seen the match, Sandow told stories of a brutal five hour match that had Stecher so worn out that he couldn't have lasted another ten minutes. Billy claimed that Stecher spent the night, after the match, in a hospital with a pulse of 134, while Lewis went out dancing. He said that the car lights were used after darkness, because the match was getting better as it went on and the fans didn't want to miss any of the action. He also claimed the cries of "fake!" were because the Nebraskan fans couldn't believe someone could last with their champion. So a scandalous and embarrassing movement was turned into a Lewis triumph just by the used of lies.[49]

Earl Caddock

From 1915 to 1921, four wrestlers dominated pro wrestling. Three of them, Lewis, Stecher and Wladek Zbyszko, we have already been introduced to. The fourth was Earl Caddock. From 1909 to 1914, working out of Anita, Iowa, Caddock was the best amateur middleweight and light-heavy weight wrestler in the country. After winning both the AAU light heavyweight and AAU heavyweight titles in San Francisco on April 17, 1915, Caddock turned Pro in May 1915. Like Stecher, he ran off a line of victories over some of the best wrestlers in the sport, beating Jesse Westergaard, Charles Challander, Clarence Eklund, Bob Managoff, Mort Henderson, and John Freberg. On December 1, 1915, Caddock out classed Marin Plestina in two straight falls at Atlantic, Iowa. Gene Malady was present at the match and signed Caddock to a contract. As one of the most influential sportsmen in America, he would manager Caddock to the top of the profession. Caddock was probably the best true wrestler, pound for pound, of his, and maybe all, time. Called "The Man of a Thousand Holds" he never weighed more than 190 pounds but had wins over the giants. He was a great worker who never had a bad match.

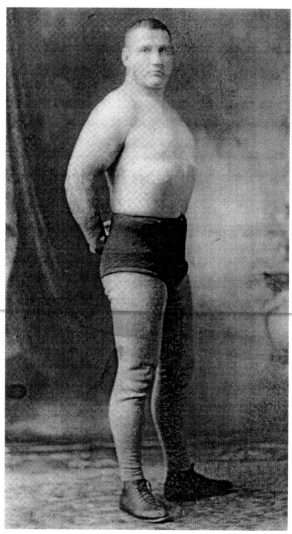

John Olin

In May and June of 1916, Caddock was training with the Sells-Floto Circus working with the Farmer Burns group, but left on June 7. It was on July 18 that Gotch broke his left leg ending any thought of a super match with Stecher. With out the ex-champ, the Stechers looked to Caddock to be the next major contender on his schedule.[50]

In late 1916, Lewis was working out of Savannah, Georgia, a town promoted by Billy Sandow's brother, Max Baumann. Late in the year Sandow signed Ed for two matches in San Francisco, California. On the way Lewis wrestled and defeated the Irish wrestler Pat Connolly at Billings Montana on November 30. Lewis injured his ankle in the match and he was in a great deal of pain on the train ride to San Francisco. He was treated by a female doctor named Ada Scott Morton, whose office was in San Jose. She treated Ed on the train and at her hospital in San Francisco. Ed's ankle improved, as did his love life, when a romance followed.[51] At the time, the lady Doctor was married to a Dr. Andrew W. Morton of San Jose. They divorced around February 1917.

On December 11, 1916, Stecher ran into some trouble of his own that ended his period of invincibility. At Springfield, he was matched with an Olympic silver medal winner in John Olin. Olin was a Finn who seemed lost in America. On taking the match, he was only interested in his purse, and seemed pleased to be picked to do a job with the great Joe Stecher. It didn't seem like an important match and Tony Stecher, the champion's manager, didn't attend the match.[52] Olin's manager for that one night was another wrestler, Hjalmar Lundin. Olin agreed to put on a show with the champion, but wanted some respect. Lundin went to talk about the match in Stecher's dressing room but couldn't find Tony. He decided to play with Olin's head, who didn't understand much English, so on return told him that Stecher planned to beat him in one minute. This upset the Finn, so the match turned into a shoot. Two hours into the match, Olin wanted to quit, but Lundin told him that there were armed Finn gamblers in the crowd, who had bet $1,000 on him, and they were going to shoot him if he quit. At four hours and 40 minute, the two wrestlers were "rough housing" outside the ring, and Stecher just quit and left for the dressing room. He had an injured right shoulder, and without Tony Stecher to protect or control him, he just walked off. Olin was announced as the winner but he didn't claim the title (he seemed more interested in getting a larger purse) and Stecher did not pronounce him as new champion. So Joe remained the world champion in the eyes of the public, although some were confused. It wasn't until 1917 that promoters got a hold of Olin to create a title line, which we call the "Olin line."[53]

San Francisco, under the promotion of Frank Schuler, was a major wrestling town in 1917. The major star in town was Ad Santel who was a rival to Clarence Eklund, Jim Londos, and Earl Caddock for the title of the best light heavyweight in America. Lewis wrestled Santel at the San Francisco Civic Auditorium on December 12, 1916 in a match with a two hour time limit. Lewis pinned Santel in 1:42:04 using his headlock after Ad made the mistake of stopping to pull up his tights. Lewis jumped on him and gave him a flying cross buttock (hip-lock) to the matt. Santel tried to break out using a bridge but Ed wouldn't let go and a pin was ruled. I don't know when Lewis first used his headlock and made it the focus of his attack, but this is the first report that I can be sure the hold was in effect. The report also referred to the hold as the "famous headlock."

Santel fought like a tiger for the last 17 minutes but was unable to win a fall before the two hour time limit ran out. So Ed won the match by the "won only fall" (WOF) rule. It was a very good match and (a statement we'll see in many Lewis matches versus smaller wrestlers) a moral victory for Santel because he was out weighed by 42 pounds. It drew 7,500 and a gate of around $10,000, which was very good at the time.[54]

1917 and The Olin World Title

Lewis had a rematch with Santel on January 2, 1917, that ended up a 2:30:01 draw. Stecher was to meet the winner and he picked Santel wanting the Lewis rematch in Omaha.[55] On February 22, Stecher destroyed Santel in two straight falls. The match drew 12,000 fans and $12,643.

Stecher spent two weeks at the end of January at Excelsior Springs, Nebraska receiving treatment on his right shoulder. Doctors recommended that he take three months off but he returned to the ring on February 7. There were also rumors of a nervous breakdown.

Between Stecher and Lewis, I feel that Stecher was the superior wrestler, but the one area that Lewis dominated was his durability—which gave him the ability to take punishment night after night in championship contests. Stecher's body would break down and he needed time off to recover, while Lewis's powerful body seemed able to absorb punishment and keep going.

Stecher continued to follow Lewis around the West Coast, and both wrestled matches in Los Angeles. They were billed as the two greatest wrestlers in the world. While training at the Los Angeles Athletic Club, Stecher complained of a knee injury, a result of the match with Santel.

In early 1917, Lewis appeared in an early Douglas Fairbanks movie, either as a stunt man or an extra. The name of the five reel film was 'Reaching The Moon.' I would think Lewis knew Bull Montana, Fairbanks' trainer and friend, or met Fairbanks at the Los Angeles Athletic Club. Lewis may have been involved in a short fight scene in the film. The movie was released on November 17, 1917.[56]

In February and March, Lewis wrestled in Canton, Ohio, Norfolk, Virginia, and Houston, Texas beating some of his old favorites, Charley Cutler, Ben Roller, Paul Martinson, and Ivan Linow, in two straight falls.

The tired Stecher, injured, sick, and newly-married, lost his title for real on April 4, 1917 in Omaha to his old friend and undefeated rival Earl Caddock. Stecher forced the action in the first fall, because Caddock was on the defense for an hour, so his local fans could win their bets on him lasting 60 minutes. Earl then came out of his shell, but the champion won the fall in one hour and 22 minutes with a scissors and body lock. In the 2nd fall, Caddock went after Joe. At the 55 minute mark, he seemed to pin Stecher using a head scissor and a

English arm bar, but the move was not allowed by the referee, who claimed he had ordered a break and a return to the center of the mat. The match continued for another 40 minutes until Caddock took the fall with a full nelson and pin. The crowd went nuts seeing Stecher pinned for the first time in his career. When the break between falls ended, Stecher didn't return to the ring. After notice was served to seconds (Joe Hetmanek) to produce Joe or else—else happened, and Caddock was given the third fall and world championship.[57]

There are a lot of reasons given for Stecher's refusal to return. He might have been injured, or sick, or just too worn out. Joe would claim he wasn't ever told to return by his manager, and such a double-cross was possible because the Stechers had attempted to dump manager Joe Hetmanek for the Gotch camp in December 1916. I think it was a worked ending that was 1917's version of a screw finish. Stecher needed time off and just dumped the title to trusted friend Earl Caddock.[58]

Stecher wrestled two minor matches in April, then didn't wrestle until September. On September 3, 1917, he beat Marin Plestina in Omaha. On Sept. 12, the Stecher's contract with Joe Hetmanek ended, and Tony Stecher took over as Joe manager.

Earl Caddock in 1916

John Olin

By 1917, promoters had convinced John Olin to claim the world title, so on May 2, 1917 he defended this title verse Strangler Lewis in Chicago. The match was refereed by Frank Gotch, and Lewis won his first true world championship when Olin injured his shoulder and couldn't continue after two hours and 37 minutes. Olin admitted defeat but complained that referee Gotch was coaching Lewis at times during the match. After the match, Gotch praised Lewis saying he was the best wrestler in the world.[59]

The Olin Title line was forgotten by our time and got little recognition in 1917, but some may have thought of it as the true "in the ring" world title, so it has to be considered a big moment in Lewis's career.

Gotch is of very little help to historians of 2015, with his quotes and titles bequeathed to various wrestlers over his later years. In June 1917, his health worsened and in October he was admitted to a Chicago hospital. On December 16, 1917, Frank Gotch died from Uremic (ureic) poisoning (usually meaning kidney failure) around noon at his home in Humbolt, Iowa. The proud champion weighed 115 pounds and had lost much of his mental faculties by the time of his death. He was a rich man, owning two farms, an auto dealership and land in the Dakotas, Seattle, and Canada. He was also a bank director and president of a local street railway and an electric light company. His funeral was held on December 19 in front of 2,000 people, with his eulogy given by the governor of Iowa. There would be no more Frank Gotch comebacks. Pro wrestling would have to survive without him.

On May 11, Olin lost to Wladek Zbyszko in Louisville when he was again unable to continue due to an injury.

After Joe Stecher's destruction of hometown favorite Ad Santel in February 1917, San Francisco wrestling fell back into hard times. Promoter Frank Schuler gave up his position as promoter to allow a mark named Charley Newman, whose real job was owner of the largest saloon on Market Street, to take control.

Back in New York, Jack Curley had a young man named Jack Kearns working odd jobs for him. Kearns, later become famous as the manager of Jack Dempsey, but in 1917 he was hated by everyone in New York City. Early that year, Curley got rid of Kearns by sending him to San Francisco to manage a wrestler named Tony (Anton) Irsa. Ad Santel's reputation had been damaged by the beating given to him by Stecher and he was having trouble with his promoter Schuler. Santel at a local gym offered to work out with Irsa. His need to get back on the good side of Schuler motivated a double-cross on Kearns. Santel shot and destroyed Irsa in front of the local sports writers.

With his wrestler ruined, Kearns was left in Oakland with nothing to do. So he found a down on his luck boxer named Jack Dempsey and started managing him around April 1917.

Kearn becomes buddies with Charley "what me worry" Newman[60] and talked him into bankrolling a Lewis/Zbyszko title match in San Francisco. Using his contacts with Curley, Kearn got Newman to give $3,000 guarantees to both Wladek and Lewis, plus expenses.

Lewis and Sandow arrived in town for a week of training before the June 6, 1917 match. Wladek and his manager Jack Curley did the same. Around that time, Kearn disappeared, leaving Newman alone to think about the large guarantees. He soon realized that these just guaranteed he was going to lose a lot of money. With Curley, Sandow, Lewis, and Kearn all in one city working over a mark like Newman, you can understand the mess going on. Newman wanted to cancel the card, but the group of wrestling pros managed to get him to the arena that night, mainly because he had already given them expense money.

At 9:00 they counted $836 in the box office. Newman freaked and twice the match was cancelled. Newman refused to pay, saying Kearn should pick up half of the bill. Kearn told everyone that Newman was handling the financial end of the affair. At 9:30, fans were starting to riot in the arena and the police were brought in. At some point, Curley agreed to a compromise of $1,400 for Wladek and Sandow agreed to $2,000 for Lewis.[61]

At 10:58, Lewis and Wladek entered the ring. It ended at 1:45 AM. The two and a half

Frank Gotch

hour time limit ran out with Zbyszko winning the only fall on a fluke. Lewis had Wladek in a hold with Zbyszko holding the ropes as Ed pulled. The referee told Wladek to let go—so he did, and both performers fell into the ring, with Wladek on top. This was ruled a flying fall for Zbyszko. Lewis was the aggressor and looked to be the better man, but he lost. No title was ever mentioned in the San Francisco newspaper, but later, in Boston, it was made plain that Lewis lost his Olin Line world title in the mess.[62]

Ed Lewis on the mat

The newspaper pronounced wrestling dead in the city, and Newman said he would never promote again after losing at least $2,100. Then, two days later, old promoter Frank Schuler stepped forward, saying the city was still alive and he was again taking over the promotion. San Francisco wrestling was back in the hands of professionals. Curley was mad at Kearns over the incident, so Kearn was never involved with the wrestling game again. He was stuck with the managing of Jack Dempsey.

Ed Lewis was happy because he got to spend three weeks courting Dr. Ada Scott Morton in San Jose. On June 21, Lewis gave a deposition in a court case involving Ada and her ex-husband Dr. Andrew W. Morton. Andrew was seeking to recover $70,000 worth of property (an orange grove) deeded to his former wife in a divorce settlement in February 1917. He was claiming fraud and misrepresentation, possibly as a result of her relationship with a certain wrestler.[63] Lewis produced affidavits that proved he was on the East Coast and not in the West on the date charged.[64]

Lewis got a rematch with Wladek on a big July 4 card at Braves Field in Boston. Wladek won the first fall in 57:45 by reversing a crotch hold into a body roll and pin. Zbyszko injured his right elbow and a knee during the 2nd fall and when he was thrown out the ring. Lewis then pinned him with a half-nelson in 24:44. Zbyszko had to be carried to the dressing room for the rest period and everyone was surprised at his gameness in returning for the 3rd falls, but he was no match for Lewis. The match was stopped in 45 seconds. This match was billed for the Olin world title and Ed regained it. The crowd was said to have been one of the largest in Boston sports history.[65]

Wladek got his title rematch on September 3, 1917, wrestling a draw with Lewis at Birmingham, Alabama.

World War I

On April 6, 1917, President Woodrow Wilson ended his policies of isolationism and the U.S congress declared war on Germany. The government quickly passed the Selective Service Act, which required all males between the ages of 21 and 30 to register for military service. This affected most of the major wrestlers in 1917, including Lewis and Stecher, but none more so than the new champion Earl Caddock.

The world champion Caddock was a true patriot, who did everything he could to join up. In May 1917, he joined a civilian training camp, similar to basic training, to prepare himself for enlistment. On August 4, Caddock appeared before a military draft examination board at Atlantic, Iowa. Three physicians determined that he was unfit for military service due to an infection caused by previous tonsil surgery. He also needed dental work.

The Army had given him an out, but Caddock didn't want it. He was twenty-nine years old, the World Wrestling Champion, one of the most famous athletes in the country who was at his peak as far as making money—but Earl Caddock wanted to fight Germans.

September saw him in Rochester, MN at the famed Mayo Clinic receiving treatment and further surgery on his tonsils under care by Doctors Charles and William Mayo. On October 5, the U.S. Army accepted him. On December 26, 1917, Caddock entered the U.S. Army and was stationed at Camp Dodge, Iowa.[66]

All of this, of course, caused a major problem for wrestling promoters. Caddock wasn't just playing soldier for public relations, he had every intention of leaving the country and taking an active part in the fighting, which was killing and mutilating much of the young men of Europe. It was apparent to everyone involved with pro wrestling that the title had to be taken off of him before he left for war.

Both Lewis and Stecher felt the public pressure to join the war, but both, unlike Caddock, took their time and didn't join the effort until July 1918. Wladek Zbyszko was drafted in 1917. He attempted to get an exemption because of a sister and mother in Austria, but it was refused. He even appealed his case to President Wilson, only to fail. On October 25, 1917, Wladek became a member of the National Army, Maine contingent, 303rd Heavy Artillery located at Ayers, Mass. But he was soon discharged because his cauliflower ears were affecting his hearing.

In late October, Lewis and Sandow accepted a date to wrestle Wladek Zbyszko in Houston, Texas for promoter Frankie Edwards. Promoter Edwards had a grand idea to bring big time pro wrestling to Houston and had made his bookings through Joe Coffey of Chicago. He paid transportation money of $200 to Lewis/Sandow, Zbyszko//Curley, and big time referee Ed W. Smith (Sports Editor of the *Chicago American*

Newspaper). Lewis got to Houston early, but the two days before the match date November 1, 1917, Charley Cutler walked into Edwards' office, telling him he was a replacement for Zbyszko. Wladek couldn't get a furlough from his heavy artillery unit and wasn't coming.

Edwards' pre-sale of tickets made him think he was going to break all attendance records in Houston, but once he made the announcement, fans began asking for refunds on their $5 tickets and then buying a $1 general admission. By the night, he still had a $1,000 gate in the house but Billy Sandow and Lewis had been promised $1,000 each for the match, and they refused to wrestle for anything less. The 2,000 fans stayed in their seats until 10:00, when they realized something was really wrong and in groups of three's they headed for the door or, worst yet, the long refund line.

Edwards left the arena for his hotel room but someone filed a report with the police and he was picked up by detectives. At the police station, he stated that he planned to reimburse everyone, but he had advanced expenses for the two wrestlers, a referee and had paid $250 rent on the building. He also had paid $252.68 to the war tax and would have to ask for the money back from the United States District Attorney. Edwards was quoted: "I've had hard luck with my matches. I have never made a penny in Houston and I have brought the best wrestlers in the world here. Can any wrestler, or any wrestling patron, point out a single instance where he lost money through one of my matches?" He again promised to refund everyone's ticket prices.

Charley Cutler was interview back at the arena, standing in the doorway of his dressing room, watching the crowd rush for the door. "A raw deal for Edwards" he said scornfully. "What does Lewis think he is, a prima donna? I guess he thinks he doesn't owe something to the promoter who takes all the risks to put on the bout. If it weren't for the promoter where would the delicate little wrestler be? You don't see me laying down do you? I am dressed ready for the match. I was ready to go on tonight on any terms that would help. The usual guarantee to a substitute wrestler is 25% gross, but if Lewis is so dead set on taking the lion's share, why didn't he take me on at winner take all?"

Billy Sandow claimed he could not afford to have Lewis go on without his guarantee. "Any week I can't make $1,200 with Lewis is a poor week. When Edwards said he didn't have $1,000 in the house, we simply refused to go on. What is a guarantee worth anyway?"[67]

Jim Londos

Jim Londos's pro wrestling career began in Oakland, California in February 1914. He actually was from Greece and migrated to San Francisco around 1910. No one knows how to spell his real name but it was similar in sound to Christopher Theophelus.[68] After a few matches mainly in Oakland and San Francisco, he left main stream pro wrestling and joined a vaudeville show as part of a acrobat act. By the end of 1915, he had an act of his own, in which he stared billed as a weightlifter, wrestler and classic poser. Londos was intelligent and so industrious that he probably had his life planned from the time he arrived in America. He was a fantastic athlete, who trained as a wrestler, gymnast, bodybuilder and weight lifter. In 1916 he returned to wrestling and worked out of Sioux Falls, North Dakota. He was pushed from his first match, billed as the world light heavyweight title holder. One of the most handsome men in the world with a perfect body, he was a huge draw. He was an excellent worker and a hooker. His only drawback was his small size. Early in his career he weighed in around 190 pounds and never in a career, that lasted over 40 years, weighed much more than 200. In July 1917, Londos moved his home to Canton, Ohio, where he hoped to take advantage of a large Greek population.

On October 8, 1917, Lewis was in Canton to watch Londos defeat Ed Schultz. He must have seen the potential in the young Londos and there seemed to be a plan to match the two. Billy Sandow booked Lewis to wrestle Alan Eustace (a famous shooter and Kansas farmer) in Canton on October 29. On the day of the match, Sandow cancelled because Lewis had a major match in Houston on November 1 (see above), and couldn't take a chance on a long match with Eustace. Londos replaced Ed and wrestled Eustace to a draw that almost lasted three hours. On October 19, the two wrestled again with Londos getting a match with Lewis by beating Eustace two out of three falls.

The first ever match between Strangler Lewis and Jim Londos took place in Canton on November 29, 1917. In defending his Olin world title, Lewis won the match but looked like a loser. Londos out wrestled him for almost two hours. During the match, Ed was able to get less than a half dozen holds on Londos and the Greek had counters to all his moves. Lewis was only able to break holds by pure strength and use of his 35 pound weight advantage. At one point Londos stopped the match to allow Ed to tie his shoe. At the one hour and 57 minute mark, Londos also bent to tie his shoe lace but Lewis, unlike baby face Jimmy, jumped on him like a tiger and flipped him to the mat using his headlock. Ed really cranked on the hold as the Greek was pinned. Londos's neck was injured and he was unable to return for the second fall. Most of the fans present felt that Londos was the better man, and there was a huge demand for a rematch. So Lewis beat Londos, but in allowing the young performer to save face, the Greek remain someone to promote and make money with in the future.[69]

Caddock was scheduled to enter the Army on December 26 and no one knew if he'd be able to continue wrestling or even how much time he had left in the States. In December 1917, Jack Curley promoted another major tournament in New York City at the Lexington Theatre (December 3 to 22). Curley's power was increasing, and I think this was an attempt to influence the national storyline and resolve the title problem. He probably overestimated his influence at the time.[70] The tournament was in the Catch style and the winner was to be billed as world champion in the state of New York. Wladek (managed by Curley) and Lewis were both entered with other names being Ben Roller, Youssif Hussane, John Freberg, Tom Draak, and even Frank Leavitt (who in 1934 took on new life as Man Mountain Dean). Earl Caddock was to make his debut in the city during the tournament, arriving in the middle of the month.

On December 14, 1917, Caddock had his first match in New York, thrilling the biggest crowd of the tournament, beating Dr Ben Roller with a head scissors and crotch hold in 40:59.[71] On the next night (December 15, the day before Frank Gotch's death), he beat John Freberg. Caddock then left the tournament and was inducted into the Army base at Fort Dodge on December 26. I believe Curley had planned on Caddock jobbing the title to the winner of the tournament, probably Wladek Zbyszko (who was managed by Curley and rid of any draft problems).

Caddock's manager was Gene Melady, who was a rich sportsman that promoted most of the major cards in the mid-west and probably the most powerful man in the sport after the fall of Farmer Burns and Gotch. I think he saw Curley as competition, and didn't like the deal that was offered, so he refused to have Caddock drop the title. He probably knew that the Army would allow Earl to continue wrestling while in camp waiting for orders to leave for Europe, and had ideas of promoting title matches of his own in the next year.

On the undercard or co-main event of Caddock / Freberg, Lewis and Zbysko worked one of their draws. This set up a major finish match the next night.

On December 17, in front of a sold-out 3,000, Lewis defeated Zbyszko in 1:21:33. At first Ed's headlock had little effect but, with each one, Wladek weakened. The finish saw Zbyszko wave to give up, but in those times the object of defeat was being pinned and submissions were rare, so the referee, George Bothner, didn't stop the match. Wladek's manager Jack Curley stepped on the mat and the match was stopped. It was the equal of a boxing manager throwing in a towel, but it may have been considered a DQ, but the newspaper called it a submission loss. The report claimed that the match ranked with the best ever held in the city.[72]

Gene Melady

Both suffered no more losses and met in the tournament final on December 22, 1917. After a long one fall match, Billy Sandow started an argument with a wrestler in Wladek's corner, claiming the man was coaching his wrestler illegally. Lewis turned his head to watch the argument, and Zbyszko leaped in to pin Lewis with a scissors and a body hold. Time was 1:47:37 and it was a sellout with many turned away. Lewis wrestled under a handicap as his headlock was not allowed. Lewis showed superiority and would have been given a decision if he hadn't gotten himself pinned.[73]

Wladek Zbyszko was presented a belt by the state of New York and claimed the world title. It would be the only title belt ever awarded a wrestler by the New York State Commission. Nothing was said about Lewis's Olin world title and it seemed to not have been at stake. Whatever, as he always did, Lewis continued to claim the world title.

1918 and The Age of Jack Curley

Lewis stopped off in Canton on January 1, 1918 to give the young Jim Londos his rematch. This time they went to a two and half hour draw. Londos out wrestled Lewis for the first two hours, but in the last 30 minutes Lewis' 40 pound weight advantage wore the Greek down. In the last ten minutes Lewis applied his headlock five times but Londos manage to hold on until the time limit ran out. Referee Jerry Walls ruled the match a draw, but most fans thought Ed would have won in a finish match. Still, lasting two and a half hours and getting a draw with one of the top four men in the world made Londos a major player.[74]

On January 4, 1918, Lewis was back in Savannah wrestling Wladek Zbyszko in a match under GR rules. Both were claiming a world title. The match was a 1:15:00 draw with Lewis working well in the GR style, but fans preferred Catch wrestling and the promoters stated that they would stick with the American style from that point on. Lewis may have injured a rib during the match, but was back wrestling in 20 days.

In January 1918, Earl Caddock, the person just about everyone recognized as the true world champion, was stationed at Fort Dodge teaching bayonet fighting to other troops and coaching sports teams. A deal was made with the Army and Caddock was given passes while his unit was in training, so he was able to continue his wrestling career. In late January, a promotional battle took place between Curley, Oscar Thorson (the major promoter of Des Moines) and Gene Melady of Omaha, over the site of a title unification match between Caddock and Wladek Zbyszko. Des Moines won the match and the date was set for February 8.

In the press, Sandow did his best to discredit Caddock. This lead to Melady saying a match with Lewis would be considered after he finished with Wladek. The quote: "The refusal to meet the Strangler is not based on any belief that he is not a good wrestler, but simply on the fact that so many of his contests have proved unsatisfactory. Lewis and his manager have succeeded in killing the game nearly everywhere they have appeared, because Lewis whenever he meets a man of ability has shown a penchant for playing on the defensive alone. His most notable offense was in Omaha when he wrestled Joe Stecher five hours without once trying to take the offensive."[75] Melady stated that he was willing to have Caddock sign for a Lewis match, if Sandow would put up a forfeit or bond that insured that the Strangler would wrestle instead of stall.

On February 8, 1918, either before or after the Caddock / Wladek match, Jack Curley called a meeting between the major wrestling promoters, such as Gene Melady, Oscar Thorson, Carl Marfigi and Otto Floto, and major newspaper man such as Ed Smith, Sec Taylor, and Sandy Griswold. Curley proposed rule changes such as time limits, decisions, and one fall matches. It was Curley's idea to make wrestling like boxing with pins being like KO's and decisions accepted as true victories. Curley walked away from the meeting with his rule changes—some of which lasted over time (note New York City's reliance on one-fall matches), while the less popular were hidden or thrown away. Never the less, Curley and NYC had shown newfound power over the sport.[76]

It seems the rules were focused on Lewis with time limits and decisions were put in effect so a wrestler couldn't stall through a match with the hope of an opponent blowing up after hours of standing around. This would give the fans insurance that they were going to see both men work to the best of their ability.

As for the unification match, Caddock won a two and half hour decision over Wladek. Caddock won the first fall in one hour and twenty minute with his head scissors and wrist lock. Zbyszko outweighed the champion by 45 pounds and when Earl had a body scissor applied, Wladek stood up with Caddock on his back. He then fell backward and Caddock landed on his back and head to be pinned in thirty one minutes. To the fans it seemed like a fluke, but it was only the second fall ever lost by Caddock. In the third fall Caddock out-wrestled Wladek, but the Pole's strength stopped any pinning attempt. Referee Ed Smith gave the decision to Caddock. Many Zbyszko fans thought Curley's insistence on a time limit cost Wladek the title because Caddock seemed injured in the third fall. The match drew 7,000 with 4,000 of them from out of town.[77]

Around March of 1918, Curley traveled to the mid-west and signed agreements with Joe Stecher and Ed Lewis. Most of the major matches were being held in the small cites of Iowa, Kentucky & Nebraska who drew large crowds from the countryside for holidays such as Fourth of July or The Kentucky Derby. The agreement by Curley, Sandow, and the Stechers formed a "Trust" that would take wrestling out of the small towns to the large cites of the East, such as New York City, controlled by Curley. Curley also had a large stable of talent that he would book out to emerging promoter along the East Coast and into the South. I don't know if Gene Melady agreed to the pact and that may have had something to do with the inability of Earl Caddock, guided by Melady, to drop the World Title back to Joe Stecher before being sent to Europe and WWI.[78]

Wladek Zbyszko

Joe Stecher had returned to wrestling slowly in the last four months of 1917. He appeared for Curley on January 29, 1918, beating Yussik Hussane on the first of four cards booked into Madison Square Garden between January 29 and April 26. All four cards were sellout for Curley.

On March 1, 1918, on the second card, Stecher wrestled Wladek Zbyszko to a two hour draw. The referee George Bothner ruled that the match was a draw but most reports felt Stecher should have been the winner. Sandow and Lewis were making noise in the newspapers, saying that Caddock and Stecher were refusing to meet him.[79] That did seem like the storyline, but the next two cards had Ed in the main event verses Wladek and Stecher. He must have signed up with Jack. Perhaps the alliance took place on March 9, when Sandow was in the New York office of Curley signing for another Zbyszko match.[80]

Lewis' headlock was becoming an issue. Many insiders claimed the move should be banned because Lewis would slide his arm down on the windpipe and turn the hold into a strangle. Lewis and some officials, such as George Bothner, claimed he was just blocking blood flow to the brain. All of the talk was turning Lewis's headlock into the most famous hold in sports. In the 1917 tournament loss to

Wladek, Lewis agreed to not using the hold, but in the New York rematch it would be legal.

On March 19, 1918, Lewis met Wladek Zbyszko in a "packed" Madison Square Garden, in a match called the fastest and wildest in the history of New York City wrestling. There was bad blood between the two from the bell. Zbyszko kept head-butting Lewis and Ed caught the Pole a dozen times in the headlock. Walter's eyes looked ready to pop in Lewis' vise-like grip but he wriggled his way free each time. At 38:28, Zbyszko hit The Strangler with another head butt and Lewis fell helpless out of the ring. The referee Billy Roche awarded the decision to Lewis on a foul. A riot followed with the sold out crowd trying to get at Wladek. One spectator hit Zbyszko over the head with a cane that inflicted a bad cut. For the win, Lewis was given his rematch with Joe Stecher.[81]

Following this match, Lewis developed an "infectious disease." I believe Dr. Ada Scott Morton, now his long-time girl friend, had been traveling with him, possibly being passed off as his wife.[82] She took Ed back to San Francisco, where she had him seen by a specialist. The report doesn't say what kind of a disease he had, but it was a threat to his career. Lewis was know for having the eye disease Trachoma, but 1918 seem too early for him to have been infected. He was also known for various skin problems such as carbuncles. By the end of April, he returned fit enough for his match with Stecher.

Lewis got his third match with Joe Stecher in Madison Square Garden on April 26. Reports called it a great match, with the grapplers punishing each other with deadly holds that were cleverly broken just as they seemed on the verge of defeat. Stecher was quicker and more aggressive, but found his scissors countered by Lewis' great strength. Stecher countered Ed's headlock and it was never an issue. After two hours, the match was called a draw by referee Billy Roche. The arena was sold out and it was said to be the best match of the season.

Some of the fans and reporters in Nebraska were upset that Stecher had broken his promise to not wrestle Lewis outside of the state, but they also realize that New York City was too big for a small city, like Omaha, to compete with.

On May 8 in Chicago, Wladek Zbyszko got another shot at Earl Caddock's world title. Once again he lost a two hour decision. Caddock's perfect physical condition and a superior wrestling knowledge proved too much for the Pole, but fans were beginning to talk about Caddock's inability to pin the large (at least 47 pounds with Wladek) contenders. Wladek, like his older brother, had a way of lying face down with no one able to turn them or put a major hold on them. (Stan Zbyszko used this trick versus the Great Gama in Europe during the 1930's). Most thought the match was boring and the new unsatisfying decision rule was disliked by fans.

Two days later, Lewis won a decision over Wladek in Louisville. Zbyszko won the first fall in 1:34:00 with a double hammerlock and Lewis took the second in 35:00 with the headlock. Ed was the aggressor throughout and was awarded the decision after two and a half hours. Wladek would also lose a decision to Stecher in Omaha on June 12.

On May 14, Sandow traveled to Des Moines to arrange a match with Caddock. He argued that Lewis had been drafted into the Army and if the two were ever to meet, now was the time. Lewis was still claiming the Olin world title and was willing to accept any terms asked to get the match. Agreements were made for June 21, 1918 in Des Moines.

Caddock wrestled rings around Lewis although he was once again unable to pin a contender. But the champion was so far ahead on points that referee Ed Smith quit keeping score after two hours of the 150 minute match. Only once was Ed able to secure his headlock and it was broken with ease. Every other hold Lewis applied was broken at Caddock's will and half the time the champion would reverse the move to end up behind the challenger. Lewis took no chances and stayed on defense except for about 15 minutes of the entire two and half hour match. Four times it seemed the champion was about to take a fall but Ed's superior weight helped him break away. Whenever the two were on the mat, Caddock was always behind. The match was a Caddock show from start to finish. Caddock claimed he was the undisputed heavyweight wrestling champion. Gate was $22,000.

The drafted Strangler entered the Army on July 27, 1918 and was stationed at Camp Grant at Rockville, Illinois. He was promoted from private to sergeant before he was given a uniform, serving as an instructor in physical education and athletics. He spent his off time entertaining by wrestling at the YMCA building and at hospitals. Billy Sandow was also in the service, he claimed he gave instructions in hand to hand fighting at

Ed Lewis in army uniform at the end of WWI

five different training camps. Sandow then attended officer's training school at Camp Gordon. He was then sent to Camp Hancock and was waiting for his commission when the armistice was signed.[83]

Joe Stecher joined the Navy on July 30 and was stationed at the Great Lakes Training Center in Chicago. Tony Stecher was turned down because he was the father of two twins. A third brother, Louis, had graduated from Annapolis and was an officer serving in British waters. At one point, Lewis's Camp Grant was to meet Stecher's camp in wrestling and there was talk of the two meeting, but nothing came of it.

On August 4, 1918, Earl Caddock's Eighty-Eighth division left for the East Coast, with orders to sail overseas with in the following week (August 7). He was off to the war, taking the undisputed world wrestling title with him.

By August 20, Caddock was stationed at Hericourt, France. The Eighty-Eighth was stationed safely far behind the lines, but Caddock felt a need to see action. Occasionally, in the evenings, he would ride a motorcycle to visit the front and spend a few hours in the trenches. It was during one of these clandestine visits that a green cross shell exploded near him and some of the poisonous phosgene gas reached him before he could adjust his gas mask. Caddock was not seriously injured but was sick for a few weeks.[84]

Around September 14, the Eighty-Eighth relieved the Twenty-Ninth Division at Belfort on the lines opposite to Mullhaus and Germany. It was a quiet front with shelling being the main danger. On October 4, 1918, a ceasefire was called between Allied forces and Germany.

November saw Caddock sent to officer training school, which he hated. He was treated badly, and it rained all the time. The food and his health were poor and he spent $500 of his own money on food. The conditions for the troops in France were a nightmare. Over 112,432 men died in their short stay, fifty percent of that number from disease.

The Eighty-Eighth had orders to attack Germany on November 12, but on November 11 the Armistice was signed at Compiegne, France, and the war was over. Around November 28, the Eighty-Eighth left Belfort.

Lewis defeated Bob Managoff on November 29, 1918. In December, Lewis was discharged for the Army and beat old friend Dr. Ben Roller at Montreal. He then went home for the holiday. One report said he was recovering from an injury suffered in the Army.

Stecher was discharged from the navy on December 19, 1918, he had been in training during his service and claimed to have gained 20 pounds of muscle.

Ed Lewis and Billy Sandow during WWI

1919 and the Battle For The Title

In January of 1919, Lewis went to Chicago for a few matches and to train for his comeback. In February he wrestled in Boston and Norfolk (beating John Olin on the 12th).

Jack Curley then got busy booking his three available stars to a series of matches. Over the next year, Curley would book the three in a number of match, exchanging wins and loses, which were designed to keep all of them strong and give meaning to every match.

Lewis signed to meet Stecher in Chicago on March 3, 1919. He completed his training for the match in Chicago.

Before he met Lewis, Stecher was matched with Wladek Zbyszko on February 25 at Sioux City. The two had wrestled a draw on November 26 in Madison Square Garden for the United War Campaign, that was so bad that fans were throwing fruit at the wrestlers. The result at Sioux City was worst. The match was billed for the World's Wrestling Championship and the PR promised the match would not end in a draw. So, the match ended in a two hour draw. At one point, Zbyszko laid flat on his stomach and Stecher was unable to turn him as Wladek winked at ringsiders. Fans were yelling "fake!" by the hour mark. The end saw the fans rioting and chasing Stecher, Wladek and Jack Curley back to the dressing room where they could be protected by an army of police. They were later escorted from the arena under police protection. The next day, Zbyszko was awarded a decision, but no one in Sioux City cared. They wanted wrestling matches with over 175 pound performers banned in the city.[85]

Curley's ideas of making pro wrestling like boxing with decisions ended that day. The fans had spoken and they wanted clean finishes with winners and losers. The decision rule remained on the books, but it was rarely used. Jack Curley and pro wrestling had learned a lesson.

The conditions for the March 3 Stecher / Lewis match called for a two out of three fall match, but if no falls were recorded in a hour and a half the match would became a one fall affair. The public also was promised a winner or the admission price would be returned.

The match that took place was faster and more entertaining than anticipated by the 7,000 fans (close to a sellout) that paid $16,000 to see the match. The contest was mostly stand up for the first 30 minutes, with Lewis back on the defense. Stecher then applied a grapevine and took Ed to the mat. Ed got to his feet but two minutes later was taken down again. At 47 minutes, Stecher turned a grapevine into a double wristlock and got behind Lewis, but Ed regained his feet with the two pulling on each other standing until the hour mark. They stayed standing for most of the next 30 minute but Lewis was more willing to mix than in past matches. At one point Ed was taken down again but managed to get behind Stecher—but nothing happened. They were on the mat as the timekeeper announced the hour and a half mark. Lewis broke a Stecher half nelson and bobbed to his feet. The match then speeded up with Lewis at times taking the offense. At two hours, Stecher went for the scissor but Ed got his arm between Joe's legs and broke the hold. What followed was the highlight of Lewis' career. Lewis backheeled Joe and as the two fell backward, Ed put Joe into a flying headlock. Stecher struck the mat with a loud thump. Lewis twisted the

James J. Corbett, Jack Curley & George Carpentier

headlock and put his legs around Joe moving for the pin. Stecher attempted to squirm and bridge out but he was locked in, and Lewis had his shoulders on the mat. The referee counted him pinned.[86]

This was the first clean loss in Stecher's career and one of Lewis's biggest victories. The win put him on the same level as Stecher and proved he could beat anyone in the sport.

The result also shows Jack Curley's booking power, and it showed a promoter taking control of storylines from the egos of wrestlers and managers. It was a good match and booked for the benefit of everyone. Stecher's willingness to put over Lewis just gave him an opponent he could make big money with for the rest of his career.[87]

In January Earl Caddock had been admitted to a hospital with what was called influenza. His health was failing him and he had lost weight. He had been in officer school, but on graduation he refused his commission and was order home. His orders were cancelled on January 20, and he was sent back to France to train the Second Army Athletic Team for competition in the A.E.F. championships.

On February 21, word reach the States that Caddock was going to retire from pro wrestling and take up farming when he did return from Europe. On March 3, Jack Curley claimed the world title for Wladek Zbyszko, who was coming off a win over Stecher and would soon defeat Lewis. On April 1, Caddock's manager Gene Melady denied the reports of any retirement and said Earl planed to defend his title on his return, but by then Zbyszko was being billed as champion.

March 7 saw Wladek and Lewis wrestle a two and a half draw in Norfolk, VA, with the title on the line.

Three days later on March 10, Zbyszko cheapened Lewis' win over Stecher by defending his title against Joe and beating him in a 2 / 3 falls match. Stecher won the first fall in 22:25 with a scissor and armhold

Lewis and his first wife

pin. Wladek won the second fall in 2:14:25 with a reverse body hold and then pinned Stecher in 14:03 to win the third fall.[88]

On March 21, Lewis was booked in another title match with Zbyszko in Madison Square Garden, NYC. Once again, the promoter announced that the gate would be returned to the fans if there wasn't a clean finish, and the Garden was jammed with the biggest crowd since the beginning of the war. The claim was that 5,000 people were turned away.

Lewis was the aggressor throughout and was the favorite with the crowd until a groggy Wladek picked up Ed and threw him to the mat so violently that the Strangler laid in a heap, exhausted and defeated. Zbyszko pinned him with a simple body hold in 1:34:36.[89] With this win, Zbyszko took away Lewis's Olin world title, which Sandow had always claimed for Ed. Everyone thought it was a great match.

Lewis then beat old rivals from his Lexington days, Gus "Americus" Schoenlein (Norfolk, March 26) and Dr. Ben Roller (Harrisburg, April 1),[90] the only difference being that the wins were routine and in two straight falls.

After beating John Olin on April 4, 1919 in Kansas City,[91] Lewis announced his engagement to Dr. Ada Scott Morton. He said the wedding would take place following a rematch with Zbyszko on April 28 in Chicago.

The windy city saw Lewis lose another match to Olin line champion Wladek Zbyszko, only this time it was reported that Zbyszko had out-classed The Strangler with superior strength and conditioning, pinning Lewis with a body scissors in 2:14:09. The match was held under AWA rules which meant that the match was 2 / 3 falls but reverted to a one fall match if no pin took place in the first two hours. Zbyszko out worked Lewis from the bell and there was no fluke or luck to the win.[92]

May 1 saw negotiations start for a late May rematch, in Omaha, with Joe Stecher. Lewis pulled out of the match when promoter Gene Melady demanded that Lewis and Stecher both post a $1,500 bond which would be forfeited if the match didn't go to a finish, two falls out of three. The people of Omaha still remembered the July 4, 1916 disaster and want some insurance that Lewis would be willing to wrestle this time. Billy Sandow blocked the arrangements, after the Stechers agreed. The plan seemed to be to have the match take place on the anniversary of the mess, July 4.[93]

Lewis had his own plans. On May 8, 1919 he married long time girlfriend, Dr. Ada Scott Morton, at Mercer, Pennsylvania. The event took place the same day as the divorce from Dr. Andrew W. Morton became official. The new Mrs. Friedrich was a well know surgeon with practices in San Francisco and San Jose. She had studied under the famous Mayo brothers and took graduate studies at the Royal College of Physicians and Surgeons at London, England. She still attended clinics annually in the East, England and France. She owned a large estate a few miles from San Jose and land in Southern California. By the time of the marriage she had already built a large gym on the property for Lewis. It had weights, a ring and a swimming pool, all enclosed by glass. She seemed to enjoy the idea that she was Lewis' trainer, and there was an electric piano next to the ring because she believe training should be done with music. Billy Sandow didn't seem to like her much. Stories are that Billy later put a clause in Ed's contract forbidding any more marriages. Both Ed and Ada were dedicated to their professions and both continued working.

Joe Stecher re-won his world title on May 9, beating Wladek Zbyszko in one hour and forty-eight minute using his famous body scissors at Louisville. The match took place the day before the forty-fifth running of the Kentucky Derby, with 50,000 sports fans in town. He took whatever claim Wladek had including the Olin line world title.[94]

The real world champion, Earl Caddock, sailed into New York Harbor on May 23. His wife was sick and he used the situation to persuade the army to allow his return. The Army had plans for him; one idea was to have him serve in President Wilson's personal guard, but he refused everything. The pre-war patriot had been turned into a post-war cynic. He told reporters that he would only fight again if the U.S. was invaded and never again on any other nation's territory. It was a view held by many soldiers. He was discharged by the U.S. Army on June 1, 1919. He traveled to Walnut, Iowa to see his wife and new born child. He then claimed his old title and began training to defend it.

The story believed by most wrestling writers is that Caddock's post-war performances were poor because he was weakened from being gassed in France. This may be true, but he had many great matches during this period—some over two hours, performed at a fast pace. After his return from the war he talked about his health, but didn't single out the gassing incident. He talked a lot about poor food and he did suffer from influenza in January 1919. Influenza was a major disease during the war, and had killed over 50,000 soldiers. Also, it has been claimed that Caddock suffered from tuberculosis as a child. Tuberculosis is a very serous problem, which would have been hard to treat before 1900. Today doctors use months of antibiotic treatment in isolation to subdue it, but antibiotics didn't exist until World War II. Caddock probably had some other type of respiratory illness, possibility asthma. Either way, these were illnesses that would not go away, and perhaps the gassing or unhealthy conditions of a war zone caused a relapse. From press clipping, there is no indication of any deterioration in his work rate. Storylines in some matches were that he wore down, but that was believable plotting considering just about everyone out-weighed him by 30 to 40 pounds. These matches were works, not shoots, and Caddock had many major victories and great matches after World War I. In fact, his good reputation as a wrestler and worker came from this period. Caddock himself is on record saying he didn't feel like himself for almost a year after his return from France.[95]

Lewis was signed for a Chicago match with Wladek Zbyszko on May 19. During May, Lewis worked in the training camp of Jack Dempsey. Dempsey was readying himself for his title winning victory over Jess Willard on July 4. Boxers in the early part of the 20th century usually had a wrestler in camp to help train. Dempsey and Lewis develop a friendship. Dempsey himself was a good wrestler and remained a part of the wrestling business long after his boxing career was over. His manager was the same Jack Kearns that promoted the Lewis / Wladek match in San Francisco back on June 5, 1917.

The May 19, 1919 Lewis / Zbyszko match was one of their best. Wladek won the first fall in 1:36:52 with his reverse body lock. The Pole looked the master during the fall, and Lewis looked spent. With defeat staring him in the face, Lewis crawled through the ropes for the second fall with a determination that could not be denied. A series of headlocks led to a Wladek defeat in 48:35. Lewis went after the giant Pole in a vicious third fall, and with the use of another headlock pinned Wladek in 12:56. Lewis claimed the world title because of the night's win and the win over Stecher in Chicago. The match drew 6,000 fans and $9,000.[96]

On June 11, 1919, Lewis returned to Omaha for the first time since the now-famous five hour draw with Stecher, to again wrestle the young star Jim Londos. Lewis took the first fall in 1:34:45 using the headlock. Londos hurt his neck, but returned to finish the match. Londos carried the fall, getting several dangerous holds and nearly pinning Lewis twice, but finally succumbed to another headlock in 17:30. Londos, out-weighed by 40 pounds, gave Lewis one of his hardest matches and didn't lose any fan support. Lewis returned to San Jose to train for his next big match.[97]

It was not by chance that the same promoter booked the same two wrestlers in the same city, on the same day in July. Pro wrestling and everyone connected with it was looking for vindication of the July 4, 1916 mess. Stecher had promised the people of Omaha another match with Ed "Strangler" Lewis, and on July 4, 1919 the promise was fulfilled. The famous 1916 match would, at last, have a finish. Gene Melady signed Lewis and Stecher on June 21, and to insure the fans a battle from start to finish, it was made a "winner takes all" match. Pro wrestling had gone through a lot in the three years, and like All Japan Wrestling in 1989, it learned that fans need clean finishes.[98]

The match took place at the Omaha Auditorium, which was equipped with new larger seats and a cooling system to insure the comfort of the fans. The arena attendance was a sold out 5,000 fans as their hero Joe Stecher, who had never actually pinned the Strangler, entered the ring. There was three men in the ring claiming the world title: Lewis and Stecher, plus the true world champion, referee Earl Caddock.

Lewis tried repeatedly to get his headlock around Stecher, but was unable to get a pin. Twice Caddock was forced to break the hold after Lewis dropped down into a strangle. Several times Stecher just broke the hold. The post war Stecher had developed new upper body strength and he showed improvement in the use of arm holds. Several times he had Ed in dangerous positions from which he was barely able to wiggle free. At no time did the Strangler threaten Stecher. Three times Stecher had Lewis almost pinned, but the sweaty wrestler was able to slip away. At one hour and 47 minutes, Joe caught Lewis in the body scissor with a wrist lock to get the pin and first fall. The second fall was also won by Joe using the same hold in 14 minutes. So Stecher got his hand raise by Caddock and took revenge for July 4, 1916 by winning two straight falls over The Strangler.[99]

Putting over Stecher took a lot of heat off Lewis in the Midwest, but in their eye he would always remain the villain.

Lewis seemed to spend the rest of July into October in San Jose with his new wife. On August 19, he lost a handicap match to Jim Londos in San Francisco. He agreed to pin both Dante Petroff and Londos in two hours, but only pinned Petroff in 1:15:32. Londos lasted the rest of the time limit, so it was considered a exhibition loss for Ed. So once again we find Lewis going out of his way to put over Londos.[100]

In September, Lewis was at his wife's ranch or orchard near Santa Ana, California, when an intruder pulled a gun on him. Lewis took the gun away and then spanked the man before sending him on his way.[101] In October he was training at the gym in San Jose with Dick Daviscourt for another match with Stecher in New York City.[102] Ed was doing double duty because around this time Dr. Ada became pregnant.

On October 10, 1919, the Cincinnati Reds defeated the Chicago White Sox to win the 1919 World Series. The "worked" series would lead to a national scandal with a number of players banned from the Major Leagues. Authorities clamped down on anti-gambling laws in most large cities. The major promoters realized that pro wrestling, a worked sport, was vulnerable to prosecution and would have to survive by being entertainment and clean itself of the idea of using gambling to make a buck.

Leading up to November of 1919, Jack Curley announced that he was going to promote a series of matches, with no time limits, to decide once and for all the true world champion. The three major title claimants—Ed Lewis, Joe Stecher, and Wladek Zbyszko—would meet in a double elimination tournament, with the winner getting an undisputed title match with Earl Caddock in Madison Square Garden. The first match would be between Joe Stecher and Ed "Strangler" Lewis on November 3 in the Garden.

The sold out Garden cheered the wrestlers as they entered the ring. Both wrestlers had gained strength during the war, and Lewis had put on some weight. Lewis forced the action at the start and threw Stecher around the ring roughly, but Joe was too agile to get an effective grip on him. Lewis repeatedly floored Stecher, but the farm boy bounced up as soon as he hit the carpet. At the 20 minute mark, Stecher got Lewis in a head scissor and almost got a count but Lewis wriggled free. Lewis took a lot of punishment from a Stecher toe hold, but his great strength didn't let him down as he kicked out and almost threw Stecher out of the ring. Twice Ed applied his headlock and the second brought Joe to the mat with the crowd yelling for a pin, but the champion twisted free. At the hour mark both wrestlers began to tire. Stecher tried some Jiu-Jitsu throws, but Lewis refused to be caught unaware. Lewis took the offence and twice applied the headlock with his arm clutched around his opponent's head like a steel band. But the hold was broken, and Stecher raped his legs around his opponent like a grapevine. The two crashed to the mat, with Lewis slowly turned on his back. He bridged to fight off the eventual but Stecher clinched both of his wrists as his knees rode the Strangler's shoulders to the mat with the weight of his own body. The Joe Stecher win lasted 1:31:25.[103]

Joe Carroll Marsh was the last of the Farmer Burns group that once ruled pro wrestling. His real name seemed to be George M. Marsh (also know as Joe Carroll or Ole Marsh). Marsh was one of the men who claimed to be the manager of Frank Gotch. In 1909 he was promoting wrestling in Seattle and engaged in a wrestling war with Jack Curley. In 1909, he was indicted by authorities as being part of the Mabray Gang. This gang was a nation wide group of swindlers that scammed people by fixing horse races, boxing and even wrestling matches. Marsh pleaded guilty and served a year in Leavenworth Prison. Many of his problems he blamed on Curley, who had moved on to New York City and bigger things. In 1919, he was managing Marin Plestina, the last of Farmer Burns' good heavyweight wrestlers. Plestina was big and could wrestle, but nothing on his record makes him seem like a superstar hooker. He lost major matches to Stecher (3-25-14) and Caddock (12-1-15), early in their careers when a true shoot was possible, and later he proved nothing in matches with John Pesek and Jim Londos. He did have an early win over Lewis, but it seemed to everyone like a worked match.

Joe Carroll Marsh

In 1919, Marsh was making a lot of noise in the press, claiming that there was a wrestling trust composed of Curley, Sandow, Melady and the Stechers controlling the sport, and all were refusing to meet Plestina, who swore he never work a dishonest match. He exposed the worked nature of the sport under Curley and gave away future results and storylines. Marsh was friends with Bert Collyer, who published a racing publication called *Collyer's Eye*, so Marsh had a forum for his exposé. Marsh also flooded the major newspapers with letters exposing the sport while claiming Plestina could defeat all the title claimants in one night. At one point, Marsh revealed that Curley was going to run a tournament and the final would be Caddock verses Stecher, with Stecher winning. None of his talk had much of an effect in 1919, but it embarrassed Curley and the other promoters. These reports were in the newspapers as Lewis prepared for his second tournament match, this time with Wladek Zbyszko in Boston on November 27.

Wladek, after losing his title claim, seemed to be on the down side. Besides losses to Stecher and Lewis, he was upset by John Pesek on June 14, 1919 at Gordon,

NE. Pesek, who would rival Caddock as the best pound for pound hooker in history, beat Zbyszko with a wrist lock in 2:03:15. Going into the Boston match, Lewis seemed to be a big favorite.

The 6,500 fans crammed into Boston's Mechanics Building witnessed a different result. Lewis was the aggressor throughout the match, but after four attempts to put on the headlock, Zbyszko threw him and put him into a body hold with a head chancery to pin Ed in 38 minutes. The loss was Lewis' second in the tournament, and he was eliminated.

Stecher won his return match with Caddock by pinning Zbyszko with a head scissors and wrist lock in 2:24:16 in Madison Square Garden on Dec. 8. Before meeting Caddock he also beat title claimants in John Olin (12-15-19 in Springfield) and John Pesek (1-16-20 at Omaha).

1920 with Joe Stecher as Champion

After the Wladek loss, Lewis headed back to San Jose after first wrestling a few matches in the Chicago area. He was in San Jose for the holidays, then wrestled his way through Kansas and Missouri and had a few matches in Utica and Boston. He was present at the Caddock/Stecher title unification match on January 30, 1920.

Many of pro wrestling's greatest events, such as the Gotch/Hackenschmidt matches, the first two Stecher/Lewis match, and you might even say the first Stecher/Caddock match, ended up as scandalous disappointments, but this match between wrestling's best lived up to its full potential. It drew a sold out 10,000 and had a $75,000 gate, with the city's best sitting in seats going at $22 a spot. It was promoted as an upper class affair.

Caddock was the aggressor for the first hour, but the physical and emotional strain seemed to wear him down during the one fall finish match and he ended up in Stecher's body scissors, being pinned after two hours and five minutes. It was considered a classic match in which both men showed all their speed and skill. Stecher and Caddock were paid $30,000 for the motion picture rights and forty minutes of the match remains on tape today. Even in today's age of moonsaults and chairshots, the work holds up and many even consider the match a shoot. After the pin, Stecher lifted Caddock to his feet and Earl's handshake followed. The two limped to the dressing room, but neither man would be forgotten by the New York fans. They would return to wrestle again, but never against each other.[104]

Stanislaus Zbyszko

With the win, Joe Stecher became the first undisputed world champion since Frank Gotch. His purse was $25,000 plus his cut of the movie money. A report in the *Fremont Evening Tribune* of February 3 claimed that Stecher was part of a syndicate of five sports gamblers, and that group had covered all Caddock bets in Dodge before the title match. Stecher's share in the syndicate pool was 20% of the gross amount "and then a share of what was left."[105]

In January 1920 came a report that Stanislaus Zbyszko was returning to American. Back in 1914 he was probably the best wrestler in America, and the only defeat on his record that fans would know of was a June 2, 1910 loss to Frank Gotch in Chicago. He returned home in 1914, and was held under house arrest in Europe through 1919. In the process he had lost his fortune and was hungry to wrestle any of the top wrestlers.

Jack Curley recruited Jim Londos about the same time and the Greek left Canton in January for the big time: New York City. Curley not only stole Canton promoter Mike McKinney's biggest star, but also stole the match he had been promoting for months.[106] On January 5, 1920 Jim Londos defeated William Demetral for the Greek wrestling title at the 71st Regt. Armory in Manhattan. After the match, fans and old timers claimed that it was without doubt one of the most grueling bouts they had ever witnessed. Londos won with a double-arm scissors after 1 hour 49 minutes and 20 seconds of vicious wrestling. The win gave Londos a title match with Stecher.[107]

Both Lewis and Londos were working in Norfolk, Virginia. Heel manager Billy Sandow was making claims that Lewis could throw the small star three times in two hours, and Londos took him up on the challenge.[108] The match took place on February 4, 1920 at Norfolk Club. Lewis needed to pin Londos three times in two hours to win the handicap match. Londos, out-weighed by 45 pounds, was never in trouble and the contest went the full two hours without a fall. In fact, Lewis was out-wrestled and at one point even called a time out to save himself from being submitted. The house was full and the match was the best seen that year.[109]

A lot in the years that follow is made of the rivalry between Ed Lewis and Jim Londos, but it is very clear that up until 1926, the established star Lewis was doing everything he could, next to a clean job, to put Londos over. It's also very clear that Lewis was very good at playing the subtle heel—and most of the time, he wasn't too subtle.

Lewis then traveled to Kansas City where he defeated Wladek Zbyszko on February 16.

Londos got his title match with Joe Stecher at the 71st Regiment Armory on February 20, 1920. It was printed that Jimmy gave Stecher the hardest battle of his career, but he was still pinned in 2 hours 13 minutes and 34 seconds with a wrist lock. The arena was sold out with no standing room, so the police had to lock the doors to keep thousands outside. The only thing between Jimmy and a championship victory was weight.[110]

Ten days later, March 2, 1920, Jack Curley, realizing he needed a bigger building, booked Londos to meet Strangler Lewis in Madison Square Garden, which attracted a capacity crowd with every nook and cranny filled. The police were ready this time and there was no disorder outside in the streets. The Lewis/Londos match was a stubbornly contested affair, in which brute strength was the ruling factor. The grapplers went at each other in violent rushes which caused them to tumble into the press roll frequently. Londos was agile, extremely clever on the defense, successful in his attack and several times had Lewis on the verge of defeat. In the end, however, the Strangler's crushing arm power and headlocks forced Londos to submit. At the two-hour mark Lewis appeared to be tiring and Londos looked fresh. Three times Londos broke out of Lewis' headlock. In the first, Lewis held the hold for some time as the Greek twisted into position, the powerful Londos rising erect with Lewis clinging to his head. The Strangler was then just shaken off. Londos duplicated the feat more than once while the crowd yelled loudly. The efforts, however, sapped Londos' strength and when, at the 2 hours 2 minutes mark, Lewis again secured his hold, the Greek was forced to submit. Lewis got the win while Londos got the adoration of the crowd.[111]

Less than two weeks later, on March 15, 1920, Curley booked Lewis in a match that would have to be considered one of the highlights of his career. Ed was to wrestle Caddock, the ex-champion and number one contender for Stecher's crown. Lewis was number two on the list, and Curley billed the contest as an elimination match for a title match. Caddock had only one known loss, to Stecher, on his record, and very few could say they had ever pinned the Iowan for a fall. As champion Caddock had beaten Lewis via decision and was a huge favorite in New York City. Pound for pound, the 185 pound Caddock was considered the finest technical wrestler in the world. With his war record and wrestling style, there was no more popular babyface in the sport.

On March 15, 1920, the two major contenders squared off in front of another sold out Madison Square Garden of 11,000. The crowd had picked Caddock to win and cheered the war veteran's every move. Until the finish, Caddock had justified the crowd's support by out pointing Lewis in every way. Although lighter and smaller, he had displayed a speed and aggressiveness that more than countered The Strangler's weight. The first indication that Earl was weakening came after 1 hour and 33 minutes, when Ed threw the Iowan to the mat heavily and almost pinned him with a face lock and leg hold. Caddock broke free after a tortuous struggle. Lewis then resumed the attack with the suddenness and quickness of a lightning flash. A head lock and hip throw slammed Caddock to the mat and Lewis slowly turned the ex-champ over on his shoulders for a three count by referee George Bothner. Time was 1:35:45.[112]

In the ring, Caddock was examined by a doctor, and it was announced that his collar bone was broken. Earl would later tell reporters that it was Ed's face lock that injured him, but every fan in the building believed it was Lewis's headlock that did the damage. Lewis's victory was unpopular, but he had won his chance to meet Stecher. Ed was on a big win streak in 1920, beating Londos, Wladek and then Caddock, and many reporters and insiders felt that The Strangler would soon take Stecher's title.

Curley booked the event into the Seventy-first Armory on April 16, 1920. The days of Lewis and Stecher wrestling five hours without touching each other were long gone. The two now knew and trusted each other and the fact that both had the same boss in Jack Curley smooth out any bumps in the relationship. Stecher had returned from his training during WWI a bigger, stronger wrestler in perfect condition, who no longer based his style solely on the scissors. In 1920, his style was well-rounded and he seemed the master of every hold. Lewis, on the other hand, had grown in size and weight with his feared headlock becoming more and more the tool he used to bring excitement to his matches. In fact the headlock was taking on a life of its own— sometimes overshadowing Lewis himself. Lewis was a gentleman outside the ring, well-liked by everyone. He wrestled clean but his headlock was taking on heel dimensions all of its own with fans and sports writers. It was seen as a brutal hold that caused injury. Some of the old hardcore fans thought it was too brutal for the scientific sport of wrestling, that used to be a contest of pinning a foe, not hurting them. The injury to Caddock had lifted the Lewis headlock, over Gotch's toe hold, as the most famous hold in pro wrestling history.[113]

The most remembered Stecher/Lewis matches are either the 5 hour draw in Omaha in 1913 or the Lewis title wins, but my favorite match between the two is the April 16, 1920 match. Stecher had been considered the champion wrestler for some time and was coming off of two major wins over Lewis. In Jack Curley's booking style, he didn't like long-term world champions and his ability to get results from performers came from the fact it was his booking style was to keep everyone strong. Of the big four wrestlers of 1915 to 1921, Lewis was the only one not to have been promoted by Curley as undisputed world champion. It seemed like his turn had come. I think that the smarts of April 1920 saw Lewis beating Stecher for the title, and some money was probably bet that way. It seemed like the smart move by booker Curley, but it wasn't. Jack was smarter than they thought.

The 71st Regiment Armory was Curley's choice as the site. It held 3,000 less than the Garden and it didn't have the prestige that was associated with Madison Square Garden, but its rent was lower and it had a better location in the city. Curley also didn't have to deal with his rival Tex Rickard, who managed the Garden and had drove Curley out of the sport of boxing. You will find that the gates pre-1929 and the Depression were larger that later, because Curley and others could charge as much as $20 for a ringside seat. There may have been less fans in the arena, but there were more dollars. I have no gate or attendance for the April 1920 match, but they made good money.

The bout turned out to be a terrific match of grueling endurance and skill that lasted three hours, four minutes and fifteen minutes. There was action throughout the match. The early portion saw Lewis get in close to the champion to take him down to the mat in a body lock. At one point he put on the headlock but Joe broke the hold. Lewis used the lock many times during his matches and wrestlers were able to break it or get lose, but it was used to wear down his foes and it only needed to work once for victory. Both hit the mat in the early going, with both scrambling to get out of harm's way. At one point both fell thought the ropes to the floor. Both the headlock and the scissors were worked during the match. For three hours there was nothing to choose between the two. Every known submission hold was used and broken. At that point, Stecher seemed to weaken and four times he was almost pinned by headlocks. On Lewis' fifth try, the champion made a spectacular comeback, with amazing strength he lifted Lewis off his feet while still in the headlock. He then threw the huge hulk of the challenger to the mat with Lewis landing on his head. (Sounded like Stecher knew Thesz's side suplex.). He then raped his legs around Ed and, using an arm bar, pinned Lewis flat for the pin. The crowd stormed the ring to congratulate Stecher on defending his title.[114]

All we have today is a newspaper report, but it seems like a spectacular wrestling match that should be remembered as one of wrestling's greatest contests. At that point, Lewis's record versus Stecher was one win, two draws and four major loses. Lewis would do better in the future.

On May 20, 1920, the James J. Walker Bill was signed into law by the New York Governor Al Smith. The bill legalized boxing in the state and set up a three man commission to control boxing and wrestling in the state. The Commission, which still exists today, ruled that anyone connected with ring sports had to be licensed by the state.

The mid-west was still sore over Lewis' New York win over Earl Caddock, and a lot of talk was being made in a build up to another match. Billy Sandow claimed that Caddock was afraid of Lewis' headlock and would never have the nerve to get back into the ring with Ed. Gene Melady, manager of Caddock, claimed that Earl had Lewis pinned at the 30 minute mark of the New York match, but the referee was distracted by Sandow and no count was made. He also called the headlock a strangle and complained about the match being only one fall. Caddock refused another New York match and there was no way Lewis would wrestle in Omaha. One of the major promoters, Oscar Thorson of Des Moines, Iowa, traveled to Boston in May and was able to sign the match. The date would be June 8 in Des Moines and it would be a two out of three fall match to a finish.

That night saw the Des Moines Coliseum filled with 6,500 Iowans looking for revenge over Lewis. Caddock reversed a headlock into his favorite hold, the head scissors, to win the first fall in 43:30. Lewis came back to win the second fall with the headlock in 27:00. Lewis had a 40 pound advantage over Caddock but he was almost as fast, and the match was judged by the reporter as exciting and spectacular as any ever held in the city. Caddock turned defeat into victory in the third fall with a toe hold and wrist lock that pinned The Strangler's shoulders to the canvas in 7:00. Caddock's fine condition had won over Lewis' vicious headlock and the crowd departed shouting praise for their ex-champ.[115]

This is a quote from the June 10, 1920 *Des Moines Register* by reporter Sec Taylor: "… from the 6,000 or more persons who saw it one hears thousands of words of praise… with the occasional word of criticism from those who steadfastly believe that all of the mat contests of the present day are cooked up for the fans. The charge that the wrestlers whispered to each other, that the result was prearranged and similar talk is always heard after the big matches, but the fact remains that even those who make these accusations are always among the spectators and apparently fear they will miss something good if they stay away. Even the few who are skeptical admit that Tuesday night's match was the best they ever saw and that it was worth the price of admission. It was full of hard wrestling, clever, and fast work by both contestants, exciting moments when the issue was in doubt and spectacular and thrilling moves on the part of both men."

In July Lewis returned to San Jose to be present at the birth of his daughter. Ada and Ed decide to name the poor girl Bobada, a conglomeration or combination of the first names of both father and mother.[116]

In July Joe Stecher, working out with the minor league Stecher Club of Dodge, Nebraska, injured his left arm. The baseball injury took him to Excelsior Springs, Missouri, for treatment.

On October 27, Lewis traveled to Montreal, Canada, to defeat Wladek Zbyszko. Ed's old rival was losing his national push and this was his third defeat to Lewis in 1920. This didn't stop Jack Curley from booking the two back into the 71st Armory on November 23 in another contender's match, with the winner getting a title shot. Lewis once again pinned Wladek Zbyszko with the use of the headlock in 1:25:45 in front of 10,000 fans. Wladek claimed that Lewis had

Wladek Zbyszko

changed his headlock and that the move had become even more deadly. This would be the last match between the two foes until 1931.[117]

A rematch between Stecher and Lewis was set for the 71st Regiment Armory on December 13, 1920. On December 5, both Lewis and the champion began training in New York City. Lewis did his roadwork in Central Park while both wrestlers trained at George Bothner's gymnasium up until the day of the match. It's interesting that Boxing champion Jack Dempsey was also in Central Park, doing his running for a December 14 title match at the Garden with Bill Brennan.

The eighth Stecher/Lewis match filled the Armory with almost 9,000 people. The building was so overflowing, with people standing on the main floor and in the gallery, that the Fire Department ordered the doors closed and late-comers, even with tickets, were turned away. Once the match started, there was little to choose between the two wrestlers—they tugged, pulled, pushed, and mauled each other for over an hour without either being able to apply a finishing hold. Lewis tried arm bars, half-nelsons, toe holds and slams in the early going to wear Stecher down so he could work him into the headlock, but the Nebraskan invariably slipped the hold without any loss of strength. Time and again Stecher tried to clutch Lewis in his powerful legs, but Ed was too strong to be held for any great period of time. After one hour and thirty-five minutes, Stecher seemed to be the stronger of the two, but the last seven minutes saw Lewis break lose with speed and agility to take control of the match. Reports claim that those seven minutes were wrestling's most dramatic. Lewis locked on a headlock and threw Joe to the canvas. For 54 seconds Stecher squirmed, twisted, jumped and sought by every means to extricate himself—before breaking free. The champion had hardly regained his feet and was tottering and swaying with the dizziness that resulted from the use of the Strangler's finishing hold, when Lewis jumped on him like a lion playing with a sick deer. Another vice-like grip saw Joe fighting for another 35 second before pulling himself free. He rose to his feet like a boxer who had taken a 9 count. Lewis, with a lust for victory and the title, leaped in again with the left arm looping eagerly for the hold which would finish his prey. A third headlock threw Stecher to the mat with the crowd standing knowing the end was

Studio portrait of a young Ed Lewis

near. But the effort was taking its effect on Lewis, too, and Joe broke free in only 7 seconds. With both nearly exhausted, Lewis rushed in for a forth headlock, but Stecher countered and threw Ed to the floor. Like a flash, Stecher was on him as the crowd let out a deafening yell. Tony Stecher and Billy Sandow screamed encouragement to the men that couldn't possibility be heard thought the noise and the excitement of the moment.

Stecher slipped on his famous scissors and applied so much pressure that the sweat oozed from both men. The veins of Stecher's upper extremities stood out as though his head was going to explode, but Lewis wouldn't give up or allow himself to be turned for a pin. For two minutes Joe applied the killing pressure in a last attempt to retain his honor, but Lewis fought savagely to release himself. Finally, Stecher's strength slowly gave way and Lewis, with one tremendous lunge, pulled himself free.

Stecher could barely stand as the exhausted Lewis dove at him for a fifth headlock. It looked like the end, and the crowd, sensing the result, changed its yells to shouts of encouragement for the toiling Lewis. Ed held the hold for 30 seconds but Stecher somehow pulled free. But back on his feet he staggered drunkenly about the ring until Lewis leaped in with another hold, which was also broken. The hold robbed the champion of the little he had left, so Lewis lurched forward and clamped on the seventh and last headlock. The hiplock throw followed with Stecher crashing on the mat. Lewis pinned Stecher with the little strength he had left. The graceful champion had finally been defeated.

Lewis let go of the grip after he felt the victorious slap on the back. Amid a din which threatened to lift the roof off the Armory, Lewis staggered weakly against the ropes. Billy Sandow jumped into the ring to hold him upright and he was placed on a stool. The handlers of Stecher ran to the fallen man and assisted him to another stool facing Lewis. For some time, the handlers worked to revive the two men who had battled for 1:41:56. Stecher needed the most attention but he was the first to his feet. He swayed drunkenly toward his corner, as if to leave the ring, but stopped. Then, as if in an afterthought, staggered on weary legs back across the ring to where Lewis was sitting and clasped the Strangler's hand. Many times over the preceding years Ed had believed he was world champion and said so—and now everyone believed it.[118]

The Strangler's First Title Reign

Soon after Lewis left New York for home by train, but it seems appropriate that he would have been present the next night at Madison Square Garden to watch friend Jack Dempsey defend his Heavyweight boxing title verses Bill Brennan. It was a bad night for Dempsey. Brennan gave him a very tough fight and the battle was even until Jack finish Brennan with body punches in the twelfth round. The worst part of the night was the booing Dempsey received from the New York fight fans for being a "slacker" during WWI. Ed must have been glad he hadn't make the same mistake. Ed did seem impressed with Dempsey's purse for the night, and it made Lewis and Billy Sandow wonder if some of that boxing money could be within their reach. Gene Tunney was also present that night, and he was impressed with the way Dempsey missed right hands, leaving himself wide open for a counter.

Joe Stecher returned to Nebraska. On December 23 he was admitted to Omaha's Fenger-Danish Hospital with neuritis in his left arm. While there he also had some bad teeth removed by dentists. His first match as ex-champ was on March 7, 1921 in Omaha, beating John Olin in straight falls.

Lewis's train arrived in San Francisco on December 21, and he was met by Ada Scott and five-month-old daughter Bobada. The couple claimed, even with Ed being on the East Coast for two months, that the baby still recognized her father.

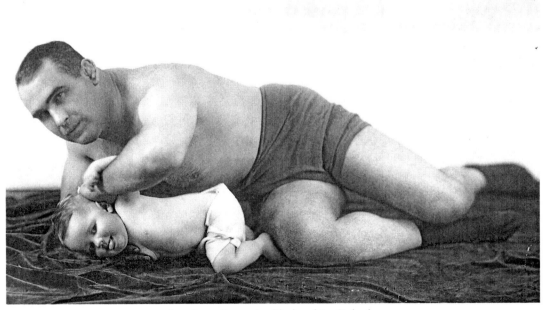

Lewis on the mat with daughter Bobada.

The most important revelation, in a newspaper report, was the complaint Lewis made about his eyes. He called his train ride the longest of his career because he couldn't read and had to wear dark glasses. His vision was so bad that a friend had to read aloud to him. This was the first account we have of Lewis' life-long battle with Trachoma. He claims he got the aliment before training started for Stecher, then it went away, but returned by match time.

Trachoma is an eye infection that comes from contact with the bacterium *Chlamydia trachomatis*. It was highly contagious and came from direct contact with eye, nose, or throat secretions from affected individuals, or from infected objects such as towels or wrestling mats. Multiple episodes of the infection could and did lead to blindness. Scarring in the eyelid lead to a distortion of the vision, with buckling of the lid so that the lashes rubbed on the cornea of the eye. The creation of antibiotic in the late 1940's ended the treat in major countries, and today it exists only in the poorest parts of the world. Sanitation standards also helped put a stop to the problem and today it would be considered just "pink eye."

In 1920 there was an epidemic of Trachoma in New York City and it plagued everyone in the wrestling world. There is a story in *The Unfinished Lewis Biography* claiming that the wrestler Chris Jordan brought the disease to wrestling after a tour of India. I don't know if that is true, but it was in the America way before 1920, and by 1913 emigrants going through Ellis Island were being tested for it and President Woodrow Wilson had designated funds for the eradication of the disease.

The year 1920 saw just about every major and minor wrestler in New York City, including Jim Londos, Earl Caddock, Dick Daviscourt, William Demetral, Johnny Meyers, and Wladek Zbyszko, become infected.[119] Everyone found a cure except Ed "Strangler" Lewis. This seems strange, because he was married to one of the country's best and richest doctors The disease would stay with him for the rest of his life, and there is no way to tell how many people Lewis himself infected. In his biography, he said that if anything in his life failed to make sense or needed more explaining, the answer probably had to do with the curse of Trachoma.

Lewis' first title defense was in Boston for promoter Lou Daro on January 6, 1921, against Renato Gardini. Gardini was a good performer in the 1920's and a major draw in towns with a large Italian population. Lewis won with the headlock, which set off a small riot in the crowd of 6,000. The headlock's fame continue to grow when Lewis beat Dick Daviscourt in Rochester on January 21. The report in newspapers was that Daviscourt suffered dislocated vertebrae from the hold.

Lewis' first show for Jack Curley was on January 24 versus Earl Caddock in the 71st Armory. Caddock, the big favorite with the New York wrestling crowd, was considered the top contender due to his clean win over The Strangler in Des Moines. At the weigh in, Lewis registered 228 to Caddock's 188, a difference of 40 pounds. The match drew a crowd of almost 8,000. As the match progressed the crowd showed in unmistakable terms just where its sentiments rested. Every Lewis attempt at a hold was booed, and every Caddock move sent the crowd into ecstasies. In every movement the Iowan reflected the easy grace that went with perfect physical condition. He was fast on his feet, agile as a jungle cat, worked quickly and variably with his hands and feet and carried crushing power in his well-developed arms. The former champ had a variety of holds and a comprehensive knowledge of every trick in the wrestling art. Lewis was lumbering and relied almost solely on his headlock. Fifteen times Caddock broke the hold or just evaded it. But after one hour and a half, Lewis got to Caddock and the Iowan began to tier. In the last four minutes of the match, Lewis hit five headlocks. The last one gave Lewis the victory, but Caddock lay still and inert on the mat, conquered in a manner which left not the slightest room for doubt as to the punishing effect of the hold.

It looked to everyone that the favorite Caddock was truly injured as he laid unconscious in the center of the mat. The crowd then went into a frenzy of excitement, with a major riot about to take place. With Caddock looking like a dead man, the gathering transformed into a spectacle which had seldom been seen in New York wrestling. The crowd was thrown into a fury and rushed the ring, trampling chairs, railings and high priced society members in ringside box seats. Officers guarded the inside of the ring, as Caddock's handlers, lead by manager Gene Melady, rushed to work on the limp Caddock, as Lewis stool over watching. The crowd cried "kill the murderer." After two minutes, it seemed his senses were restored and he was placed on a stool. After a further rest, he rose to his feet and shook Lewis' hand. That seemed to calm some in the crowd, but when Lewis left the ring he had to have guards surround him as they forced their way through the crowd to the dressing room. After being away from the East Coast for two months, Lewis, the new world champion, probably thought he would be treated better than Jack Dempsey, but it seems the two were in the same boat.[120]

On January 27, Lewis beat a Gustav Sulzo in Kansas City and left him unconscious after a headlock. Another fan riot followed. The days of popular champions, like Stecher and Caddock, seemed over.

Joe Stecher kept his title belt after losing the championship. So Lewis needed a belt of his own. In January 1921, Strangler Lewis was awarded a $10,000 championship belt by the Central Athletic Club of Kansas City. Storyline says it was set with 39 diamonds and plated in gold. Historians have called this belt the "Lewis Belt."

On January 30, 1921, Jack Curley announced that the feared headlock would be banned in any match promoted by him in New York City. Curley was the booker who had help promote Lewis' headlock, but he must have been under great pressure from the new Commission and by the classily high-paying fans who had been stomped on by the mob. He couldn't afford another riot, and he was attempting to put all the heat on Lewis, Billy Sandow and the hold. Lewis, being powerful but less skilled than the lighter stars, was someone that fans resented more than hated, but I think they never had any love for Sandow. So what they had at the time was the first true heel world champion. Curley, like Frankenstein, had created a monster, and it was a new enough concept that he didn't know what to do with it.[121]

The first reaction from Lewis' camp was negative, but they soon realized they needed Curley. After a few days Lewis announced that he had consented to no longer using the headlock.

On January 31, Lewis returned to Lou Daro's Boston Mechanics Hall and again beat Renato Gardini, this time with the headlock banned. Ada Scott was ringside.

On February 3, 1921, Jack Curley mailed telegrams to the top 50 promoters in American, asking them to meet in Kansas City around March 20 to discuss the making up of new rules and the banning of dangerous holds like the headlock. This could have been pure public relation to take heat off himself, and I don't know if the meeting ever took place. The state legislature in Albany was working on a bill to bar, not only the headlock, but also other dangerous holds like the Strangle, toe hold and the body scissors.[122]

It seemed that the next super match was going to be with Stanislaus Zbyszko, who on March 14, 1921 beat ex-champ Joe Stecher at the 71st Armory. After suffering from Stecher's scissor, Zbyszko body slammed Joe and got the pin with a crotch hold in 2:16:10. Attendance was 7,000.

On March 15, Lewis purchased an airplane (a Laird Sparrow) so he and Sandow took flying lessons. This was 1921, and airplanes were far from safe—but the two can take credit as the first wrestling insiders to fly from card to card, at least while Ed was world champion. I don't believe that Ed or Billy ever really learn to fly the plane themselves, but they hired a pilot to get them from city to city in one piece. Lewis loved to fly—Sandow hated it.[123]

Lewis sits in the rear of his Laird Swallow, with his manager Billy Sandow in front.

John Pesek was in the process of becoming the next big star. He was the best wrestler to come out of the shoot world of Nebraska after Stecher. He had wins over Wladek Zbyszko and Londos, and was in the process of his first major East Coast push. Pesek wasn't much bigger than Caddock and, through history, fans have argued over who was the best wrestler pound for pound. Pesek, unlike Caddock and Stecher, wasn't just a hooker. He was what was called a "ripper," which meant in wrestling terms that he liked to hurt people. It was Curley and Sandow's idea to use him as a policeman for Lewis. On the under card of a February 28 Stan Zbyszko main event in New York, Pesek wrestled a new legitimate wrestler from Finland named Aromas Lateen, who was talking about making trouble for Lewis. Peek almost broke his arm and the Lateen problem was solved. This coming during the uproar over "rough wrestling" probably didn't help Curley.[124]

Curley did sign Lewis to wrestle John Peek on April 4, 1921 at the 71st Armory with the headlock banned and the title on the line. Lewis seemed upset with Pesek and said he would retire if beaten by him. Lewis weighed 232 to Pesek's 195. Lewis had slowly been gaining weight over the last year and it didn't help that he keep getting booked with true wrestlers, small but always in top condition, like Caddock, Londos, Pesek and Stecher. There were some reports that described Ed as a "whale" or "corpulent", but he still wasn't the fat Lewis that he'd become in the late 1920's.

The bout was full of action from the start, but it soon became apparent that the loss of the headlock cramped the champion's style. As in all these match, Pesek wrestled rings around him. Within two minutes, Pesek had a near pin using a double wrist lock. Lewis seemed to need his headlock while Pesek had every hold in the book to used. When Lewis did get Pesek in a dangerous position, Pesek would twist out doing a head stand landing on his feet. At one point Lewis forgot and put on a headlock, that was followed by a cry from everyone in the house, and the hold was broken by referee George Bothner. But as he usually did, Lewis made his comeback—Ed got a good wrist lock on that lasted two minutes—but just when it looked like Pesek would be turned for a pin, he twisted out of the hold. But Pesek's right arm was dead. Lewis clamped on the hold again and Pesek had lost the strength to resist any longer. Lewis switched to a bar and hammer lock for the pin in 1:34:32. So the good news was that Ed proved he could beat a major 195 pound wrestler without the headlock, but the bad news was that the 71st Armory attendance was a poor 4,000.[125]

On April 12, 1921, Lewis and Earl Caddock were signed for a rematch at Des Moines Coliseum, which had added new seats, for promoter Oscar Thorson. It was said that the match up drew the largest indoor crowd in history, outside of New York City. In the match, the headlock was legal. Lewis had one of his best matches, beating the small Caddock in two straight falls. The first fall lasted 1:34:00 and the second 7:38, both won with Lewis' headlock. The victory didn't stop the "boo's" or the insulting reporters who called him fat. After the victory, a fan threw a rock at Lewis but for the most part the crowd seemed stunned by Caddock's defeat. They lingered for a short time afterward before filing slowly out of the Coliseum.[126]

The next day, April 13, Lewis and Sandow flew to Chicago to wrestle Jim Londos. It was called a spectacular match, with both using every known hold in wrestling. Six headlocks finished Londos, who was out-weighed by 35 pounds, in 1:52:00. On the undercard, Stanislaus Zbyszko defeated John Pesek with a crotch and half nelson in 1:22:00.[127]

The Chicago 2nd Regiment Armory was sold out.

Stanislaus Zbyszko

Jack Curley announced that he had booked Strangler Lewis to defend his title versus Stanislaus Zbyszko at the 22nd Regiment Armory on May 6, 1921. Zbyszko was old. He was born in Poland on April 1, 1880 (some say his birth date was 1878). But, by 1921, he was between 40 and 43 years old and looked the part (some New York papers claimed 42). After the retirement of Frank Gotch, he was considered the best wrestler and biggest star in the sport. But in 1915, he left the country and got tied up with wars in Russia and Europe and didn't return to America until 1920. His younger brother was Wladek Zbyszko. He was a small 5 foot 8 inches but powerful, with a 22 inches neck and 55 inch chest. His major attributes were great strength and endurance. Stan was smart and sophisticated, but he wasn't a technical wrestler. The same could be said about most former Greco-roman style performers. He was a good friend of Jack Curley, who managed his brother, and when Sandow and Lewis found out Curley's intentions, it didn't sit well. At one point leading up to the match, a report was out that Lewis planned to retire after the match, although the report was later called a misunderstanding.

Stanislaus Zbyszko

Stan weighed 226 for the match to Lewis' 235. Zbyszko had lost 50 pounds since his return to wrestling, and he had taken on the look of a shaved head. Some felt the new bald style was to be used as a defense against the Lewis headlock.

10,000 fans were present the night of May 6. The match was fast and spectacular, with Lewis the aggressor. Being more agile, quicker and more resourceful than Stan, he pushed him all over the ring, with Zbyszko willing to stay on the defense until a mistake was made. Ed seemed to be trying to tire out his old rival, but it didn't work. Stan's sweaty bald head and 22-inch neck seemed the perfect match for The Strangler's headlock. Lewis jumped to apply the feared hold after 20 minutes, but Zbyszko hunched his shoulders and Lewis missed his target. Ed flew through the air and landed fat on his back. Stanislaus lurched forward and quickly encircled the stunned Lewis in a neck hold, which pinned the Strangler's shoulders to the mat and gave the world title to the Pole. Time was 23 minutes and 17 seconds.[128]

The fans rushed the ring, this time to cheer for the new champion.

So Ed Lewis' first title reign ended after 4 months and 24 days. I've always felt that the poor crowd for the Pesek match was the factor for Curley taking the title off Lewis, but in writing this it just seems that Curley was fed up with all the pressure he'd gotten from officials, politicians and arena management, from having a heel world champion after years of respectable champions like George Hackenschmidt, Frank Gotch, Joe Stecher and Earl Caddock. Perhaps it was just a result of Curley's booking style, liking to switch title holders and keeping everyone in his company strong. Curley saw Stan Zbyszko as a sophisticated cultured man who the public would support. He was wrong. But in looking at Lewis' first short title reign, you'd have to say he failed as a major champion.

At some point in 1921, Jack Curley lost or gave up his control over Pro wrestling. Up to this moment, I've never really figured out why. The thought has been that he had some sort of trouble with the new Athletic

Stanislaus Zbyszko and Ed Lewis, May 6, 1921

Commission and couldn't get a license from the New York License committee. I don't know if that's true anymore, and can't find that in print. I think now that Curley was fed up with pro wrestling and saw bad times ahead. From interviews it's clear that he felt that the wrestling business went in cycles or waves. The good times were always followed by the bad. He brings this theory up in a few interviews, and always says that 1922 to 1926 was his down period. 1915 to 1921 had been great for wrestling and Curley, so it was time for things to change. Curley wasn't just a wrestling promoter—he started with pro boxing and invested in other areas like tennis and Broadway shows. I think it was Curley's plan to sit out a few years until pro wrestling became a money-making proposition again.

There also was a problem with the use of the National Guard armories in New York. Up until late 1921, wrestling and boxing bouts in New York armories were under the supervision of the State National Guard, and, under the Walker Law, the commission had no authority over these matches. So Jack Curley was able to run cards in the 71st Armory without a license from the commission, but at some point in the year the Adjutant General's office investigated promoter's use of all of its buildings as wrestling and boxing arenas. Resulting rule changes gave the commission more jurisdiction. A ruling was made that armory promoters would, thereafter, need to be licensed. Curley had no license because he didn't need one up to that time. On December 30, 1921, the commission announced that Curley had applied for a license to promote in the 71st Regiment Armory, but nothing more was written. It does explain why Curley stopped using Madison Square Garden in early 1921.[129]

Curley was very close to light-heavyweight boxer George Carpentier, having promoted a major bout between him and Battling Levinsky on October 12, 1920. Carpentier's win in that match set him up for a heavyweight title match with Jack Dempsey. Curley attempted to promote the title match, but was outbid by his rival boxing promoter, Tex Rickard. Rickard knew very little about actual boxing, but was a bold investor who was willing to take chances. To get the Dempsey/Carpentier match and house the bout, Rickard was willing to build an arena in Jersey City at the cost of half a million 1921 dollars. The fight ended up as boxing's first million dollar gate, drawing 80,000 fans and $1,789,238. It is a fact that Curley added Carpentier's manager, Marcel Deschamps, in negotiations with Rickard and everything else right up to the fight date on July 2, 1921. There was much more money in boxing than pro wrestling, and I believe everyone, including Curley and Sandow/Lewis, were banging their heads on the wall to think of a way to get a cut of it. It's very possible that Curley spent much of his time with Carpenter in 1921 and let the wrestling business fall apart.[130] Curley or his people did promote wrestling in Boston and New Jersey during this time.

Carpentier was too small and no one ever thought he had a chance against Dempsey. He was box-office and that's all. So Curley hid George from the press by locking out visitors from the training champ. At the fight, Rickard made Dempsey agree to carry Carpentier for four rounds to insure enough fight footage to show in movie theaters. So Jack won by KO in the 4th round. It was "worked" as well as any wrestling match.

George Carpentier (middle) & Jack Curley (far right)

Joe Stecher was still wrestling and, on May 26, he put over the new champion Stan Zbyszko in Kansas City. Joe then traveled to San Francisco to beat Ad Santel on September 28 (or 27).

San Francisco promoter Frank Schuler was then able to book ex-champ Stecher with home town ex-champ Strangler Lewis on October 10, 1921. It was a two-out-of-three fall match with a two-hour time limit. The match went the full time limit and Joe Stecher won a referee's decision. The match was another good one and close, but it was Stecher's condition which won the match for him, and there was no question it was the right decision. Dr. Ada Scott Friedrich ringside even shook her head in confirmation. Lewis' condition was off and the sick ex-champ coughed through most of the match, so Stecher had another victory over Lewis. It was no surprise at the time, but in the years to come it would be a rare happening.

This match had Jack Curley's booking written all over it. He was keeping his men strong and paying Joe back for the two jobs to Zbyszko. Over the next years we see that Sandow wanted nothing to do with Stecher, and it had to have been Curley that got the two in the ring that night. I think it's right after this match that Curley loses control over the sport.

Billy Sandow and Lewis broke away to form their own company. Somehow they talked champion Stan Zbyszko into joining up with them. The company also included Sandow's brothers Maxwell and Jules Baumann.

Tex Rickard Becomes a Wrestling Promoter

Madison Square Garden, managed by boxing promoter Tex Rickard, wanted pro wrestling back into the building, so Rickard decided to bring in his own group of wrestlers made up of those available and not under contract. One he picked was Marin Plestina, whose manager Joe Carroll Marsh had for over two years been hounding Curley's wrestlers for matches. The two would show up before major matches in places like Boston and Des Moines and get stories printed saying Curley's men were fakes and Plestina could beat guys like Caddock, Stecher and Lewis in one night. Marsh also sent letters to sports editors all over the nation exposing storylines before they happened. He also was hated by Sandow and Lewis.

Tex Rickard, boxing promoter

For Rickard's first card in the Garden on November 14, 1921, he booked Marin Plestina to meet John Pesek, who had employment as a "policeman" in the Curley promotion but was now part of the Sandow group. The storyline was that Zbyszko would meet the winner. It was the "trustbuster" Plestina's chance to show that he was a true contender and that his claims were true. Most fans felt they were going to see one of the rare "shoots" in pro wrestling. Present ringside was Lewis, Sandow, Tom Jenkins, Ernest Roeber, and Dr.

John Pesek

Roller The commission ruled that all the holds used in the past in the city would be legal as long as they were used for pin falls and not to punish. It was also billed as a two-out-of-three fall match.

Billy Sandow had made his orders clear to Pesek: he wasn't looking for a pin, he wanted Plestina hurt and humiliated.

Pesek went to work as soon as the match started. His favorite trick was gouging. Pesek would dig his thumb into Plestina's right eye over and over. The referee cautioned him within the first five minutes, but Pesek had his orders and he wasn't going to stop. The only hold attempted by Pesek was a reverse headlock, but Plastina broke it without difficulty. When he wasn't gouging, Pesek was head butting. At 11:19 he was disqualified for the first fall by the referee. Despite warnings by the referee and the commission, Pesek continued to eye gouge, strangle, head-butt and punch the "trustbuster." At one point they went to the mat with the Tigerman on top, but the large Plestina just stood up and shook him off like he was nothing. At 24:02, Pesek was disqualified for the second fall. With the fans looking like they were going to riot over the lack of a contest, the commission ruled that they would go one more fall to a finish. This was like a tonic to Pesek, who became even more daring in his fouls, while Plestina didn't say a word. With the butting and gouging continuing and the crowd rushing around the ring like a riot was coming, the referee disqualified Pesek for a third time at 7:05. It was a disgusting spectacle, with Plestina left bleeding from the nose, mouth, and cuts on various places on his face. Both his eyes were closed from all the gouging. He was taken to and treated at the Manhattan Eye and Ear Hospital.

Plestina was declared the winner due to fouls and John Pesek's money was held up, with the commission banning him for "life" from participating in bouts under the New York Commission's jurisdiction. Pesek did wrestle a few times in New York in the following years, but he was never a major draw on the East Coast again. Sandow and his followers would twist the story over the years to make fans believe that Pesek took Plestina apart in a shoot, but nothing near that happened. At the time, it was called the most unsatisfactory match in the cities history, and it ended up a repugnant mess.

Pesek's manager, Larney Lichtenstein, and Joe Marsh had their licenses suspended pending an investigation. Lichtenstein claimed he knew nothing and quit as Pesek's manager. Max Baumann, Sandow's brother, paid him $22,000 for the Tigerman's contract.

Plestina reputation was exposed in the match and he was never taken seriously by fans again.

The New York Athletic Commission was become stranger by the week. It first banned all punishing holds, but by November 14, 1921, was allowing all the old holds as long as they were used to pin foes and not used to injure or force submissions. It then made all main events two-out-of-three falls, but if no falls were recorded in two hours, the match would become one falls. If the one fall lasted another hour without a pin, the referee could then give a decision. But the worst ruling was the return to the old way of determining bouts, called rolling falls or flying falls. Under this system, a wrestler was pinned as soon as his shoulders touch the mat. So they eliminated the three count, and both shoulders didn't have to be on the mat at the same time. A man could just roll through on his back and be considered pinned. (Wish I could explain this better, but I don't really understand it myself.) What the commission did was return pro wrestling back to the rules of Greco-Roman wrestling of pre-1900. The result was giving the fans of New York City pro wrestling one more thing to hate.

Tex Rickard then booked a rematch between Lewis and Zbyszko at Madison Square Garden for November 28, 1921 under the new rules. To add to the excitement of the new rules, Rickard donated a $5,000 diamond studded belt to be presented to the winner. This was something he did with his boxing champions, and the belts were all called "Rickard belts." During Lewis' first reign, he used his "Lewis belt" and it had been passed on to Zbyszko the night of the title loss. So the winner of the rematch would have two belts. The two belts did not look alike. With a heavy rain outside, the Zbyszko/Lewis rematch drew only 7,000 to the Garden.

The Tex Rickard Belt

Lewis won the first fall in 17:31 with a headlock and pin to a thunderous ovation from the crowd. Lewis forced the advantage in the second fall, but Stan was declared the winner when he seemed to have forced Ed's shoulders to the mat while the challenger was striving to free himself from a neck and crotch hold. The crowd booed the referee's call on the rolling fall and a riot was only held down by the five-minute intermission between falls. The third fall saw Lewis throw Zbyszko with a bodyhold, and as the pair went down with the strangler on top, Ed attempted to apply his headlock. Being unsuccessful, he shifted and sought to grab Zbyszko's wrist, but the Pole turned suddenly, forcing Lewis clear of the mat by sheer strength as he wriggled upward, Zbyszko crashed his rival down and then clutched Lewis in a double armlock for the decisive fall (14:56). Some reports say it was also a rolling fall. Zbyszko was then presented with the new championship belt (Rickard Belt) and the Lewis Belt, to the applause of the crowd.[131]

Lewis spent early December wrestling in Kansas before returning home to San Jose to spend the holiday with his family. Ada Scott held a big party on Christmas Eve for the poor and needy of the city. An elaborate tree was erected in Ed's home gymnasium, and it was rumored that Lewis played Santa Claus, giving candy, toys, and other presents to children, many of which had been donated by the city. The home was located on Alum Rock Avenue.[132]

On January 6, Lewis defeated Dick Daviscourt in one of their many matches in Wichita, and then traveled to Havana, Cuba for a match. Sandow turned down a Boston rematch with Stan Zbyszko (January 19), thinking Lewis would have a better chance wrestling him in Wichita or Kansas City where he wouldn't have to deal with strange rules like rolling falls.

On January 22, 1922, Lewis was in New York City training for a Febuary 6 Renato Gardini match in the Garden when he awoke to read newspaper headlines saying that Tex Rickard had been arrested on charges of having sexually abused a number (later set at seven) of young girls ranging in age from eleven to fifteen. Over the next few months stories were published from the testimony of a grand jury investigation and later from a trial. It was claimed that Rickard, who was married and living on Madison Avenue, picked up the young

Madison Square Garden, 1922

girls at a swimming pool at Madison Square Garden and had sex, or tried to rape them, at his suite in the Garden Tower. Madison Square Garden was known for its risqué nude statue of the god Diana overlooking the city and for rumors of wild parties in its rooftop cabaret.

The trial took place in March of 1922, and there were other little pieces of drama in the days leading up to the event. One of the girls, being questioned by the police, was kidnapped on January 27 by a former boxer named Nathan Pond. On a tip, the police found her on a farm two weeks later. Pond was alleged to have offered the girl, Nellie Gasko, a bribe not to testify against Rickard after she had already signed papers saying that Tex had attacked her on three occasions. Other people claimed to have been bribed and some others just disappeared. Stories were published about Rickard's early life as a gambling casino and brothel owner in the wild west. One story had Tex seducing a young girl and then being whipped by the girl's mother, who then committed suicide. (I don't know if the deceased was the girl or the mother.)

At the trial, the girls all turned out to be older than first reported, the 11 year old became 15, and most had been arrested for theft, robbery, forging checks, begging and a variety of other offenses. Rickard's lawyer produced an impressive list of character witnesses to vouch for Tex, even Kermit Roosevelt, the son of former president Theodore Roosevelt. All claimed his reputation was impeccable. Rickard testified that on the day

of one of the major rapes, he was at the November 12 Dartmouth-Pennsylvania football game with witnesses. Tex explained that why he couldn't remember who won or what the color of the team's uniforms were was because he didn't like football and it was the first game he had ever gone to.

On March 27, 1922, it took the jury an hour and a half to return a not guilty verdict. Regardless of the verdict, Rickard's reputation was tarnished, and claims were made that he was through as a sports promoter. However, after a few months Rickard returned to his position of promoting boxing at the Garden. But the year 1922 was a bad and busy one for Rickard, and the result had Billy Sandow and Jack Dempsey running free.[133]

On February 6, Lewis defeated Renato Gardino on the under card of a Stan Zbyszko defense against the popular Earl Caddock in Madison Square Garden. The card was said to have drawn 12,000 fans, but everyone left the arena upset after Caddock lost both of his falls by rolling falls. In both Caddock's shoulders touched the mat for the "slightest fraction" of time and Caddock's winning fall, the second, was conventional and there was no doubt over its legitimacy. Once again a big card had been ruined by the rules of the Commission.[134]

Tex Rickard

Renato Gardini with a title belt,
in Chicago in 1916

Lewis' Second Title Reign and the
Obsession With Jack Dempsey

Around February 13, newspapers all over the country ran the story of Jack Dempsey challenging wrestling champion Stanislaus Zbyszko to a mixed match. Dempsey was quoted: "I'll knock out Zbyszko and a half dozen other champion wrestlers in the same night." Following the Carpentier match, which drew over 80,000 and the first million-dollar gate with a total of $1,789,238, Dempsey had hardly been busy, shooting minor movies in Hollywood and touring with vaudeville shows. Lewis and Dempsey were friends and Billy Sandow knew Jack's manager "Doc" Jack Kearns from San Francisco. Tex Rickard and Kearns felt that a lot of title defenses for Dempsey would hurt his box office, so Dempsey was just playing around in Hollywood looking for something to do. Sandow looked at the math and figured that a good boxing gate was more that Lewis could make in years of wrestling. A "worked" mixed match between champions would be an easy way for both sides to make some good money without taking any risks. But the champion was Stanislaus Zbyszko, and if Sandow and Lewis were to get their full cut of the boxing money, a change would have to be made.

On February 21, Wladek Zbyszko defeated Joe Stecher in Madison Square Garden using a rolling fall. The bogus pin once again upset the now small and apathetic crowd. On the under card, Lewis defeated Cliff Binckley also using a rolling fall. For Wladek, he was awarded the American title for the win, but after that night I can find no further mention of the new title. In fact, you would not find Lewis, Stecher, or Wladek together on the same card for a long time.[135] It also was the last wrestling card in Madison Square Garden until March 1928. Tex Rickard did attempt to promote a huge Garden wrestling show in December 1923, but his request for a license was turned down by the New York license committee, who claimed there were only enough wrestlers and good matches in New York City for one major promoter, and that promoter was Jack Curley.[136] So Tex Rickard left the wrestling business and died at age 59 on January 5, 1929 in a Miami hospital from an infection following surgery on a gangrenous appendix.

Jack Dempsey

Lewis and Sandow waiting for start of match, March 3, 1922

On March 3, 1922, Ed "Strangler" Lewis regained his undisputed world title, beating Stanislaus Zbyszko in a two out of three fall match in Wichita, Kansas, under traditional rules that didn't include "rolling falls." Zbyszko won the first fall in 41:20 with a body scissors and arm lock. Zbyszko was said to be overconfident in the second fall, he worked on Lewis' arm and was attempting another winglock, but Ed swung around to push or "punch" the champion in the face. Zbyszko fell across the ring and landed on his back. The Strangler jumped on him to apply the headlock and pin in 18 minutes. Stan's manager claimed a foul but it wasn't allowed by the referee Paul Sickner. Stan was dazed and was an easy victim to Lewis' headlock during the three minute third fall. Stan's manager Jack Herman cried foul, but Lewis left that night the champ. In winning the match, Lewis was awarded two belts. One was his original belt (the Lewis belt) and the belt Zbyszko won on November 28, 1921 in Madison Square Garden (the Zbyszko belt or Rickard belt).

The match was attended by a crowd of 4,925, and the gate was below $17,000. Stan was paid $7,000 for the loss and Ed made $5,000, so promoter Tom Law didn't do so well. Bad weather and muddy roads were a factor.[137] The true reason for staging the match in Wichita is unknown, but gambling was still a factor in that area and it may have been a good place for an upset title win.

Rumors are that this was the first wrestling match ever recorded by network radio. I believe that, because 1922 was a big year in the development of network radio and for the expansion of the medium in America. (The first boxing match on radio was the Dempsey/Carpentier match on July 2, 1921.) This had the same effect on pro sports that TV would have on wrestling in 1948. Radio didn't seem to help the popularity of pro wrestling in 1922, but it did create a major star in "Strangler Lewis," whose name recognition would rank with the other made stars of the Twenties like Babe Ruth, Dempsey, Bill Tilden, Bobby Jones, Jim Thorpe, and many others that are still legendary today. By 1924, names like Stecher, Wladek Zbyszko, and even Frank Gotch seem minor when compared with the popularity of Strangler Lewis' name that had been created by the use of radio.

Jack Dempsey

Trying to not waste too much time, March 16 saw Billy Sandow announcing that new champion Strangler Lewis had posted a $5,000 bond with the sports editor of the *Nashville Banner* as a challenge to boxing champion Jack Dempsey. Sandow claimed that Ed would beat the boxing champion in less than 20 minutes or forfeit the $5,000. In New York City Jack Kearns stated that Dempsey was willing to meet Lewis in a mixed match or in a wrestling match.

Lewis as champion took on a busy schedule. Wrestling five nights a week during March, he traveled thought the South, Kansas, Iowa and Missouri. He was hampered by a bad case of carbuncles that cause him to miss two minor shows, but he recovered well enough to defeat Yousiff Mahmout on March 27 in Wichita.[138]

On March 13, 1922, Lewis made his first appearance in St. Louis beating Jack Jurka, a wrestler billed as being Australian. St. Louis hadn't yet achieved its reputation as the center of American wrestling, but Lewis was brought back on March 29, 1922 for a big match with the town's favorite wrestler, Ed's old protégé, Jim Londos.

Jim Londos

The match drew the largest crowd in St. Louis history, estimated at 5,000. Lewis won the first fall in 1:17:10 with the headlock. Londos surprised everyone in the building by winning the second fall in 14:45 with his Japanese armlock coupled with a wrist lock. The headlock finished Londos in the third fall in 22:40. It was an interesting match all the way, with Lewis the aggressor, but he could not trick the Greek. Londos on more than one occasion brought the crowd to its feet by getting his armlock on the champion. Londos was faster and a more of a clever grappler, but he couldn't overcome Ed's 40 pound weight advantage. Londos winning a fall, over the most famous wrestler in the world, could only have helped his career.[139]

After WWI, Billy Sandow lived in Cherryvale, Kansas, in Montgomery County, near Kansas City. He became friends with his grocer, a man named Sam Avey. Sandow brought Avey into pro wrestling, where he was used as a referee. In 1922, Sandow set up Avey as the promoter in Tulsa, Oklahoma. During that year, Lewis wrestled at least four times in Tulsa and over the years it became one of Lewis' strongest city. Late in Ed's life, he even lived in Oklahoma. Avey developed Tulsa into a major wrestling town and became a rich man owning a pro hockey team and a radio station. He also played a major part in the development of the careers of wrestling stars Leroy McGuirk and Dick Hutton.[140]

Lewis remained active thought the rest of 1922 up until July 4. Some of his big matches were:

- On April 13, he defeated Earl Caddock in Wichita, winning two out of the three falls.

- On April 19, Lewis beat Dick Daviscourt in Boston in two straight falls using the headlock (1st fall 1:13:31, the 2nd fall 14:10).

- On April 25, Stanislaus Zbyszko got his first rematch against Lewis in Kansas City. He lost two out of three fall to the champion.

- On June 7, Ed returned to Boston and again beat Earl Caddock two out of three falls. Lewis took the first in 22:02 with a headlock, Caddock won the second with his head scissors and wristlock in 7:08, and the champ won the third with the headlock in 10:33. Lewis' policeman John Pesek defeated Dick Daviscourt on the under card.[141]

- The tour stopped on July 4 in Wichita, where Lewis beat Alan Eustace. The other wrestlers he met and defeated (most more than once) during the year were Jatrinda Gobar, George Hill, Cliff Binckley, John Freberg, John Grandovich, Farmer George Bailey, and Jack Sampson.

Toots Mondt Enters

Lewis and Sandow then spent a working vacation at Colorado Springs training for a European tour that never took place, or was very short. More that one historian thinks it's possible that Lewis was being trained at the Springs by Joe "Toots" Mondt, who was coaching wrestling 33 miles away at the Colorado Agriculture College (later renamed Colorado State University). Mondt was a feared shooter and a willing performer who had some very good wrestling ideas. It's very likely that a friendship was formed between Toots, Ed, and Sandow, so agreements were made for him to join the group later in the year as talent and as a trainer for Lewis. I don't know how Mrs. Ada Scott Friedrich felt about this vacation, but my guess is that Billy Sandow wasn't happy with the training Ed was getting in San Jose. Lewis was putting on weight and Billy, who took pride in being a trainer, never liked the added pounds and nagged his wrestler to lose weight.

The group was in Colorado on July 20, 1922, but Lewis wrestled at Madison, Wisconsin on August 21. There was a lot of time off in this period, and I wonder why Ed went back home to Wisconsin.[142] Perhaps just to visit the family and visit his summer ranch, but the events of the next year makes me think he was unhappy and seeing lawyers. He then went home to San Jose and defeated Renato Gardini in San Francisco on September 26.

Lewis and Sandow then went back to work. On October 10, 1922, Ed defeated Goho Gobar

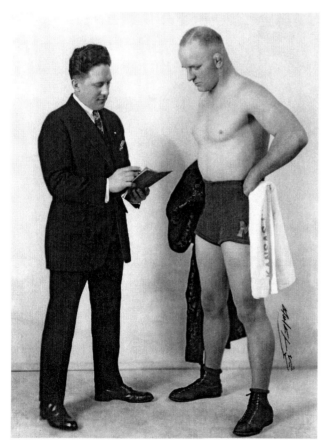

Billy Sandow and Toots Mondt

at Eaton, Colorado on a card promoted by Toots Mondt's brother, Ralph Mondt. Many historians, mainly me, think that Toots Mondt joined the Lewis/Sandow group at this time. He became a trainer for Lewis and also acted as one of Ed's policemen, protecting the champion from trustbuster type wrestlers or anyone undercutting the credibility of the world title. He was also pushed as a contender and major star, and the skilled Mondt had no trouble getting over with the fans. Toots, himself, thought he was a better wrestler than Lewis.[143]

Lewis started up full time in November, wrestling threw Missouri, Iowa, and Columbus, beating Jatrinda Gobar, Demetrius Tofalos, Anton Borsa, and Cliff Binckley. On November 10, Lewis defeated Toots Mondt in Boston with promoter George Touhey as referee. To get Toots over he was booked to win the first fall, pinning Ed in 30:15. Lewis then came back to beat Mondt in the next two falls (32:15 and 2:05).

At one point in late 1922, Mondt beat Lewis in a handicap match at Kirksville, Kansas. Lewis had agreed to pin two men in 75 minutes, with Mondt the second wrestler in. Ed beat the first wrestler but failed to do anything with Toots for the last 42 minutes. Reports say that Lewis quit the match with five minutes left because boils on his neck and arm were annoying him.[144] Within a few weeks, Sandow had turned Mondt into a major star.

Lewis defended the title against George Kotsonaros in Boston on November 17.

On November 26, Lewis while wrestling in Nashville, released a statement to the national press saying that he was willing to wager $25,000 that he could defeat Jack Dempsey in a mixed match.

On December 14, he defeated ex-champ Stanislaus Zbyszko in St. Louis. Zbyszko won the first fall in 41:15 with the use of the flying mare, but dislocated his right shoulder in the second fall. Lewis won the second fall with the headlock (24:25) but used several types of arm and wrist locks to win the third in 14:50. The gate was $16,400 and Lewis' purse was $7,500.[145] By this victory, Lewis, after three wins in three contests with the belt at stake, won permanent possession of the Rickard Belt.

On December 25, Lewis returned to his home on Alum Rock Avenue in San Jose to eat Christmas dinner with Dr. Ada Scott. Lewis was suffering from an infected arm, which he injured in a December 8 match in Kansas City verse Wallace Duguid. As soon as the Christmas festivities were over, Lewis was admitted into a local hospital where Dr. Ada performed an operation. I wonder if she was lancing one of Ed's many boils from which he suffered throughout his career. Ada must have been some doctor because it was revealed in the report that she had also amputated her 75 year old father's leg, removed her brother's appendix, and had operated on fifteen other blood relatives.

December 28 saw the recovered Lewis beat Jack Turner (Joe Zigmund) in San Francisco. The attendance was said to be "fair, though by no means large."[146]

Boxing champion Jack Dempsey had spent most of 1922 making minor films in Hollywood, appearing on vaudeville shows, and touring England, France and Germany. When Dempsey and Doc Kearns returned to New York City on May 19, they were ready for a title defense, but found Tex Rickard tied up in his scandal. With their big money promoter tied up, they may have returned to the idea of fooling around with the wrestler, Strangler Lewis. These strange matches were not new to Dempsey, who had done exhibition fights against both Douglas Fairbanks and Al Jolson, for a lot less money.

The storyline at this time was that Dr. Ada was training Lewis at the home gym for the match with Jack Dempsey. He did make a short trip to Los Angeles to visit with Dempsey and arrange for a wrestling match in Hollywood. On

Ed Lewis fighting Wayne Munn

December 30, Lewis announced to the press that arrangements had been completed for a mixed match with the boxing champion to be held at Wichita. In Los Angeles, Dempsey said that nothing had been signed but he was ready for the match. Tom Law, wrestling promoter in Wichita, claimed to know nothing about the match or the purse of $300,000, but on January 7 stated the bout was on and the rules were agreed on. No date was even revealed and the match never happened.

In the early part of 1923 Dempsey and manager Doc Kearns accepted an offer of $300,000 to defend his title verses Tommy Gibbons on July 4, by Shelby, Montana a small oil town, desperate to make a name for itself. I don't know if the offer was serious or just a PR stunt, but it backfired—as Kearns had them sign a contract before they could think twice. The fight has been called "The Sack of Shelby" in boxing books. Tommy Gibbons had been a good fighter but was considered washed up by 1923. He ended up giving Dempsey a hard fight and lasting 15 rounds, making the champion look bad in his first title defense in two years. Some of the banks of Shelby ended up being bankrupted at a result, but Doc Kearns didn't care, as he had made $272,000.

When that fight was over, Tex Rickard was back at work in Madison Square Garden and offered Dempsey and Kearns $500,000 to fight Luis Angel Firpo, the "Wild Bull of the Pampas." So Dempsey didn't need a Lewis match and Rickard probably knew it was a bad idea. Over the years, as they both grew older, Dempsey and Lewis would continue their talk of a match, but it never happened, and Sandow never got his big payday.

1923

In 1923, Los Angeles was just into a few years of Hollywood movie making and was becoming a hip place to live. Frank Gotch had spent a little time, late in his career, in Los Angeles but the town had a very limited history as far as pro wrestling was concerned. Lewis defended the title in Los Angeles at the Hollywood American Legion Stadium on January 10, 1923 against Demetrius Tofalos. Tofalos was a famous Greek wrestler/strongman, who probably was the manager of Jimmy Londos at the time. Londos was on the undercard beating an Angelo Taramaschi. The card drew 7,000 and became the largest crowd ever see a wrestling match in Los Angeles.[147]

Nat Pendleton was a major amateur wrestler who had made a national name for himself by winning the Silver medal at the 1920 Olympics, and he was being developed as a pro wrestler by Jack Curley. Curley was laying low in New York City but he was engaged in a Boston wrestling war between promoter George E. Tuohey and wrestler Paul Bowser. It was a funny kind of war that had cross promotional cards at one point. A lot of noise was going on about a match between Nat Pendleton and Bowser. At one point, on November 21, 1922, Pendleton's manager, Stuart Robson, made a claim that Nat could beat Bowser, George Calza (a big star in Boston) and Ed Lewis in one night. Billy Sandow probably didn't care about any of the names but Lewis, but he couldn't have been too happy with Curley's new star throwing Ed's name around. Paul Bowser became the major Boston promoter by 1923, and after a lot of talk he got Nat Pendleton to come to Boston to wrestle an "unknown" on January 25, 1923. Pendleton wanted to meet Bowser, but the "unknown" turn out to be none other than Lewis' policeman, John Pesek. The "shoot" handicap match needed Pesek to take two falls in 75 minutes to win, but Pesek made short work of the Olympic medallist by breaking his ankle (actually a torn ligament) in the first fall and winning the second fall in a total time (both falls) of 41 minutes. Pendleton never made it as a major pro wrestling star, but did become a big time supporting actor in Hollywood films. Paul Bowser went on to become a Lewis/Sandow ally and one of the major promoters in the history of the sport.[148]

Lewis returned to Missouri and met Toots Mondt on a Gabe Kaufman card in Kansas City on January 23. The match was two out three falls with a two hour time limit. During the two hours Mondt showed he had a defense against the head lock and broke the hold at least 15 times. Every time Lewis hooked Toots head, he was crotched by the challenger and slammed. Mondt carried the match to Lewis but Ed beat him with a toe hold to win the first fall in 1:25:15. For the rest of the match, the two went after each other like a pair of bulldogs in a pit fight. They rolled, tumbled, kicked, and broke holds with lightning rapidity. When the time limit expired, Lewis was ruled the winner by taking the only fall, but Lewis looked tired at the end while Mondt looked fresh. Most of those present fell that Mondt would win in a finish match. The attendance was around 8,000. The idea was for Lewis to meet John Pesek next in the city, but Mondt's showing made promoter change his plans.[149]

Toots Mondt in his prime

So the rematch took place on February 15 with Lewis winning two out three falls from Mondt in a finish match. Mondt won the first fall in almost two hours but the strenuous wrestling wore him out, and he was only a toy in the hands of Lewis while losing the next two falls. The Kansas City attendance was more than 10,000. (This is the first time that I have a report of Lewis reaching the 10,000 mark during his second title run.) It should be noted that the only two arenas capable of holding that amount of people were Madison Square Garden and Kansas City's Convention Hall. Kansas City was an old cow town and a major connecting point for all the mid-west rail lines. It wasn't hard for fans all through the connecting states to use the trains to come to Kansa City for a major match. It was a major wrestling city during this period going back to Frank Gotch's title reign. Gotch claimed that, for him, only Chicago was a better city.

Jim Londos had become a sensation in St. Louis and a title rematch with Ed Lewis was booked for the St. Louis Coliseum for the night of February 20, 1923. Both Lewis and Londos had spent much of the preceding week in town training at the National Athletic Association gym. Both men were bigger. Londos claimed he had gained eight pounds of muscle and was much more confident. Lewis weight in at 235 pounds.[150]

Lewis won the first fall in 1:46:34 after using ten headlocks to ware down and pin Londos. In most of Ed's matches his opponents would play dead and a quick finishing fall would follow, but Londos wasn't a normal opponent. The second fall saw Londos surprise Lewis by reverse an attempt at a headock into a jiu-jitsu wrist and then armbar. With painful and punishing twists, Londos forced the 35 pound heavier Strangler's shoulders to the mat. The pin came at 13:15. After headlocks failed him, Lewis captured the third fall with a hammerlock in 19:10.[151] The card seemed to have been a sellout, but no numbers were released.

In 1923, Lewis returned to Chicago. On March 6, Lewis defended the title against Alan Eustace at the Chicago Coliseum on a Joe Coffey promotion which drew 6,500 in his first appearance in the city during his second reign as undisputed world champion. On the same night, a John Krone promotion drew 2,100 using George Calza in the main event and long time locals like Charley Cutler, Bill Demetral, and Bob Managoff on the undercard.[152]

On March 7, Lewis returned to St. Louis to get an easy win over Dan Koloff.[153] April 3 saw Ed back in Chicago in front of 7,000 beating Renato Gardini. On April 15, he defeated and injured Wallace Duguid at

Nashville. The report had Duguid suffering through nineteen headlock and a hospital stay after sustaining a concussion with a neck strain. He had been unconscious for 30 minutes after the match was stopped.[154]

On April 12 John Pesek defeated ex-champ Stanislaus Zbyszko in Kansas City. As a result, Pesek won himself a title match with Lewis on May 2.[155] Lewis trained in Kansas City leading up to the match, while Pesek worked out on his Ravenna, Nebraska farm. The match was billed as a "shoot" match and some may have been thinking "title change" because it was known that Lewis was planning on touring Europe in mid-June.

The promoter Gabe Kaufman and Billy Sandow went out of their way to discourage betting on the match. No odds were posted by bookmakers, who as a rule quoted odds on any sport and one report said: "The wrestling game has so many knocks and so often has the finger of suspicion pointed at it, that bookmakers will not quote odds or make bets on wrestling matches."[156] I think wrestling promoters had abandoned the gambling world and, as a "worked sport," worried about the law exposing what little legitimacy it had left.

The May 2, 1923 match in Kansas City ended with Lewis destroying Pesek in two straight falls. Lewis, trained down to 218 pounds, had the skills of a ring general, and took no chances. He evaded Pesek's wristlock and out roughed Pesek while matching the Nebraskan's speed. Lewis won both falls with the toehold, the first in one hour and two minutes, and the second in two minutes and 30 seconds.[157]

Lewis using a headlock in workout.

The crowd was estimated at 15,000. They filled Convention Hall with every seat occupied and hundreds standing. It seemed to be the largest crowd in Kansas City history, but everyone didn't come out of the match in better shape. John Pesek's reputation was destroyed by his showing. Quote from the *Kansas City Star*: "John Pesek fooled the folks around here. A lot of them, anyway. They thought he was a great wrestler, but his showing against Lewis was a thing of sorrow to those who liked the Nebraskan. He had been called the 'Tiger Man.' For Lewis he was a tame tiger. Pitted against other wrestlers Pesek had been a real demon at wrestling with strength, skill, and fury. Matched against the champion he presented a sorry plight... He may be able to go elsewhere and stage a 'come back,' but it will have to be in Boston or some other favored city. It will not be Kansas City."[158] So in one night, Sandow/Lewis took one of their best contenders and a match capable of drawing 15,000 and destroyed any chance of it making money again.

On May 22, Lewis again beat Stan Zbyszko. This time it was a one fall 1:39:00 victory in Minneapolis.[159] Lewis then return to Nekoosa and stayed for some time with his parents.

On June 21, 1923, the Associated Press issued an announcement stating that wrestling champion Strangler Lewis had obtained a divorce from his wife at Stevens Point, Wisconsin. The degree was signed by Judge Byron B. Parks of the circuit court of Wisconsin and the divorce charge was "cruelty." Lewis then left for the East Coast.

Dr. Ada Scott Morton Friedrich learned of her divorce from reporters. She stated that she didn't believe "Bobby" was gone for good—but he was. On July 2 the divorce was listed in *Time Magazine*.[160] A few years later, on February 22, 1926, Dr. Ada Scott Morton announced she had married a Wells Clark, wealthy real estate operator working out of San Francisco and Washington D.C. They met and were married on the East Coast.[161] No one has any knowledge of what happened to Lewis' daughter Bobada, although she does seems to make an appearance in Tulsa later in Lewis' life.

Before air conditioned arenas, pro wrestling was seasonal, and usually the time off took place during the Summer and the baseball season. In mid-June, Lewis and Sandow took a tour of Europe. It was mainly a vacation for both, but Lewis did wrestle in six minor matches. He seemed to have started in England and then moved on to France. In Paris on July 27, his trip to Germany was delayed 24 hours when his laundry failed to show up at his hotel. There were no shirt collars in Paris over a size 17 and none of the others fit Ed's neck. He left for Berlin the next day. The two then traveled through Italy, Belgium, Holland, and Switzerland. It appears that they returned to American around September 1, 1923.[162]

Toots Mondt, who had spent the summer hunting and fishing in the Ozarks near Springfield, Missouri, met up with them and they settled into a training camp. Lewis had put on more weight drinking beer and having a good time in Germany, so he needed a lot of training.

At various times in October, Lewis announced an engagement to a member of the Russian nobility, a Princess Maria Traivaska (or Trawaski). She claimed to have fled Russia during the Bolshevik uprising and was living at Wiesbaden, Germany when she met Ed. The report was that the two would be married around Christmas and the honeymoon would be in Europe. Another report said the site would be Chicago. Nothing comes from this and I don't think the wedding took place. I've read reports that said the relationship was broken up by Billy Sandow. After a couple of months, Lewis never mentioned the Princess again. Whenever I read about the Princess Traivaska/Strangler Lewis romance, I think of Henry Fonda and Barbara Stanwyck in the 1941 Preston Sturges movie "The Lady Eve."[163]

Around November 16, Lewis returned to San Jose to effect a property settlement with the divorced Ada Scott and he took most of the month off.

Ada wasn't the only trouble Ed would have at the end of 1923. Joe Stecher had taken off most of 1922 and 1923 in an attempt to start up a baseball career,[164] but he had come to his senses, and was becoming more active and aggressive as a wrestler, seeming to want his title back. He had become a featured main eventer for the new St. Louis promoter, Tom Packs, and headlined Packs' first three cards in late 1923.

Joe Stecher working out with Tony Stecher

On December 7, Lewis returned to Kansas City to win another big rematch with Stanislaus Zbyszko. Ed and Sandow then traveled to St. Louis for a title defense against Josef Gurkeweicz on December 13.

Lewis was out-wrestled by the young Pole, Gurkeweicz, like he was in most matches, but still won two straight falls. The story of the night was Joe and Tony Stecher's appearance at ringside. Before the match would start, Billy Sandow refused to wrestle if the Stechers were allowed to enter the ring to challenge the champion. This resulted in an argument, resolved by having Joe enter his public challenge to Lewis during the break between falls, when Ed and Sandow were in the dressing room. The conflict with the Stechers resulted in Lewis and Billy being booed the whole match. After the Lewis' win, Sandow said that he would be glad to meet Stecher, if Joe, the ex-world champion, would first prove himself by beating Stan Zbyszko, Toots Mondt and then John Pesek. Tony Stecher then offered $15,000 for a title match, but he had been given his answer.[165]

Joe Stecher and the Policemen

I've often wondered why Lewis and Sandow needed the use of policemen. Gotch had used one or two policemen, but why did the great shooter, Strangler Lewis, use a whole stable of them in Zbyszko, Toots, and Pesek? You would think Ed could handle his own problems, but then you remember Joe Stecher was still around. Ed may have had an idea that he was better, but he wasn't sure, and it was far from a sure thing with everyone else. Stecher had no doubt that he could beat Lewis—he always had—and was coming off a decision win over Lewis in his hometown of San Francisco on October 1, 1921.

Telling someone to meet your policemen is the standard line a weak or non-wrestler type champion does when he's challenged by someone he knows he can't beat. It was a tool used by wrestlers like Munn, Sonnenberg or O'Mahoney later on in wrestling history. The idea is to direct the challenger to a stronger shooter, so the guy will disappear—and it usually works. But this was Joe Stecher, and he wouldn't back off. Following the statement by Sandow, Stecher challenged all three policemen. He then had trouble getting them in the ring, so he guaranteed Zbyszko $10,000 to meet him in St. Louis. That was a lot of money, so Stan agreed and the match was booked for January 22.

On December 15, 1923, Stecher traveled to Kansas City to repeats his $15,000 challenge to Lewis and to say he was ready to meet anyone to get to the champion. It seems odd, but in the cities like Kansas City and St. Louis, which were two of the strongest cities for the Lewis/Sandow group during his second reign, Stecher was portrayed as the face by the reporters and fans, while Lewis played heel.[166]

Also on December 15, Lewis beat Taro Miyake at Wichita in a wrestling world title verses a Jiu-Jitsu world title. Lewis was named the new Jiu-Jitsu world champion after the victory.[167] Then everyone forgot about it.

On December 28, Lewis was also in Wichita winning a match over Dick Daviscourt. The challenger won the first fall using Lewis' headlock in 1:06:00. Lewis came back to win the next two falls in four minutes and then one minute. After the match, Lewis was arrested by police on charges of assault and battery on a William Goodman. It seems that after the first fall loss, by his own headlock, he was booed by just about everyone. On the way to the dressing room between falls, someone hooted in Ed's face, and he punched Goodman. Later at the police station, Goodman said he wasn't the guy and that Ed had punched the wrong person. Ed said he was sorry for picking the wrong fan to batter, and everything was fine with the police. Charges were dropped.[168]

In late December, Toots Mondt was in the Kansas City newspaper saying that he should get the title match with Lewis, not Stecher, and he was willing to beat the former champion to prove his point. This resulted in Lewis signing to wrestle him in Kansas City on January 10.[169]

On December 31, 1923, the *New York Herald* printed a story that said, of all the pro sports, wrestling attracted the least attention in 1923. It said the sport was dead in New York and this condition was the same through out the country with little activity of major importance. It said Strangler Lewis was a champion that defended his title only infrequently because of the death of suitable opposition and lukewarm interest. It said fans were waiting for a match to renew their enthusiasm.[170] This report goes against everything that was printed about the period in the book *Falls Guys: The Barnums of Bounce* in 1937, which portrayed the time as a golden age run by a "Gold Dust Trio" (Sandow, Mondt and Lewis).

Toots Mondt had always given Lewis a hard time in title matches in Kansas City, but on January 10, 1924 it was different. Ed won the first fall in 1:44:02 and the second in 28:30, both with the use of a toe hold.

So Toots lost two straight falls. The result probably had something to do with Toots' coming matches with Stecher.

On January 18, in Wichita, Joe Stecher and Toots Mondt wrestled a handicap match in which no fall was recorded in 90 minutes. Stecher had agreed to pin Mondt twice before the time limit ran out, so Mondt was ruled the winner. Handicap matches were considered exhibitions, so the result wasn't looked upon like a real loss by fans. They were just a way to build up to a bigger match and give credibility to lesser wrestlers, without a star actually getting beat. Kansas City promoter Gabe Kaufman was present and said the match was great, so he signed a rematch for a February 11 match with no time limit. Stecher being in with Lewis' policeman made "smarts" think it was going to be a "shoot," with the winner getting a title match with Lewis.[171]

On January 25, Stecher wrestled a draw with Dick Daviscourt in Rochester, NY. This was a card promoted by Jules Baumann, brother of Billy Sandow, and Ed Lewis sat ringside for the match. This would make it seem like Lewis was helping in the promotion of a match with Stecher.

Ralph and Toots Mondt with family

On January 27 Stecher met Stan Zbyszko in St. Louis. As was the condition of the match, Zbyszko was presented his purse of $10,000 before the match. The attendance was 6,500 and the gate was $11,000. The wrestlers cut was $6,600, so Stecher ended up giving Zbyszko $3,400 for the match and a chance to wrestle Lewis, if he won.[172]

After losing the first fall to Stan in 22:55, Stecher took the next two using the scissor in 13:40 and 35:15. Lewis later agreed to wrestle Stecher but he wanted $30,000 to step into the ring. That was way too much money and match didn't happen.[173]

The Stecher/Mondt match took place in Kansas City on February 11. The report in the following day's newspaper was slim. All we know is that Mondt, after winning the first fall, punch Stecher with a closed fist and lost the match on a disqualification. Bare knuckled fights were against the law under state rules and the reporter thought that Mondt would be banned in Kansas City (though he wasn't).[174]

If you believe in "shoots," it should be noted that the guy who gets disqualified for punching is always the guy who thinks he's losing and has to save face. Jenkins punched Gotch in a "shoot" when he was losing and Ray Steele would later bale out in a Lewis shoot by punching Ed. If Toots was kicking Stecher's ass, why would Mondt blow the victory by fouling out and getting himself banned? It doesn't add up.

If you do believe there was heat between Mondt and Stecher, it sure seems like Stecher was not afraid of Lewis or his army of policemen. He wrestled Zbyszko and then Mondt twice, and was stepping into traps left and right. Joe also was pushing for a John Pesek match as part of the storyline in St. Louis.

Lewis defended the title in St. Louis on February 5, beating Renato Gardini in two straight falls. Gardini had earned his shot by beating Jim Londos. The crowd was called "fair."

On February 13, Ed Lewis returned to New York City to beat Pat McGill in front of 3,000 in 1:15:36. The card was at the 71st Armory and was called a wrestling revival. No mention was made of Jack Curley or who the promoter was, but McGill was a Paul Bowser wrestler. On the undercard, Wayne Munn defeated Big Beth in 7:10. Munn was a former collage football player, who had great size with good proportions and muscular development. He had already failed as a pro boxer, but Billy Sandow was in the process of pushing him like he was Hulk Hogan.[175]

Lewis was spending more time in Boston working for promoter Paul Bowser. On February 14 Ed beat Greek wrestler George Kotsonaros in the city. This was the third match of the year in Boston and the fans were very upset over Billy Sandow's coaching of Lewis, so Bowser ruled that the manager could no longer stay ringside during the match.

Stecher traveled to Tulsa to lose a handicap match to Cliff Binckley on February 14, winning only one fall after promising two with in two hours. He then returned to Kansas City and wrestled an exhibition at an athletic show. The report said that Joe would return the next month for a match. The next day, both Tony and Joe Stecher had a conference with promoter Gabe Kaufman. The topic was "the match." Kaufman also talked with Billy Sandow the same day.

Nothing mentioning Stecher or the "match" follows. Lewis wrestles Taro Miyake on March 3 in Kansas City, with both Wayne Munn and Mondt on the undercard.

Reports said that the finish to the Stecher/Mondt match was unfortunate and Toots was sorry and regretted it deeply. They also promised that a foul in an early fall wouldn't end a match in the future. The offended wrestler would be given a rest and then have to continue. It's funny how this set up the finish of the Lewis/Munn title change the next year.

Stecher never got his title match with Ed Lewis in 1924, and he may have tried out with the Philadelphia Nationals baseball and went south for spring training for a period of time, before realizing the money in pro wrestling was too good to pass up. Or maybe he just got cut.

I think the whole storyline was a work and that both sides were willing to do a match in March 1914 in Kansas City. I don't know if Billy Sandow realized that Stecher had been promise the title and expected Lewis to job it back, at least for a short period. Lewis had blown off all his major contenders and liked the idea of a big money match with Stecher, but Sandow would never let Lewis drop the title because there was no way to get it back, if Joe didn't keep his word.

I think Sandow got the idea to push Wayne Munn in the middle of the Stecher storyline and decided to go in that direction. Munn would be under his control, something he couldn't count on with Stecher. The title was the power and he felt safer with a football player.

The Stecher/Mondt bout, of February 11, seemed to be a worked first fall, followed by a potato to the ex-champ. It was kind of a wake-up call, and Sandow's way of telling Tony and Joe the deal was off.[176]

Another Marriage as Ed thins his Contenders

Lewis wrestled Stanislaus Zbyszko again on February 26, this time in Chicago. Lewis won the first fall using the headlock in 24:29 while Stan took the second with a short arm scissors in 7:30. In the third, Stan kept tying the champion up with arm locks until Ed reached up and punched Zbyszko. The Pole fell backward

Lewis with his second wife, Miss Bessie McNear

and his head hit the mat with a thud. Lewis then jumped on him for the pin. Referee wrestler Pat McGill ruled that Stan wasn't punched but "heeled," and Lewis was declared the winner. The fans then went nuts over the verdict, and both Lewis and referee McGill had to be escorted to the dressing room by police. Fans were so upset by Lewis that the city commission rules that Lewis couldn't wrestle in Chicago until Zbyszko got a rematch. Promoter Joe Coffey and Ed White were happy to provide one.[177]

The rematch drew 12,000 fans and a gate of $23,000 on March 25 at Chicago's Dexter Park Pavilion. Zbyszko used a wing lock secured in a standing position, and took Lewis down to pin him with a reverse body lock in 32:05. Lewis came back with a vengeance in the second, and after injuring Stan, pinned him using a toe hold in 8:40. With Stan injured, Lewis used a double toe hold to win the match in 9:15. After years without doing a job, Stan Zbyszko then had seven straight loses to Lewis and other losses to Stecher, Mondt, Pesek and Hans Steinke.[178]

After Ada Scott Morton and Princess Maria Traivaska, Billy Sandow claimed that he had a rule written into Lewis' contract, which the two always claimed was unwritten, that Ed could not get married again. So on March 27, 1924, Sandow was locked in his hotel room while The Strangler married his second wife, Miss Bessie McNear of Kansas City. The photos I've seen of Bessie show a nice looking girl who seemed the type to like "fun." Sandow was upset and claimed "it was the first time Ed ever double-crossed him", but he got over it. It all was probably just storyline anyway.[179]

Londos' size stayed the same but in 1924 his push kept getting bigger and bigger in St. Louis. On April 1, he got another title match with Lewis. Ed won the first fall with his third headlock in 1:02:00. Londos came back to take the second fall with a stepover toe hold in 22:35. The Strangler then took the deciding fall, after escaping another painful toe hold, by knocking Londos out with a "knee thrust." Jimmy was unconscious for fifteen minutes and had a "tumor" the size of a walnut below his left ear. The match took place in front of one of the largest crowds of the season.[180]

Philadelphia got its first title match under its state commission on April 8, 1924, when the Stan Zbyszko coached Renato Gardini wrestled Lewis to a two hour draw. They split two falls and Gardini worked Ed over during the last 24 minutes but the bell saved the champion. At one point Lewis broke a hold by going to the ropes, and then refused to come to ring center to wrestle for a half minute. The pro Gardini crowd went crazy throwing junk and even a knife into the ring. A hard piece of glass shattered in the ring, and the match was held up until the junk was removed from the ring. After the match, it took two men to carry the champion out of the ring. It sold out the Philadelphia Adelphia and set the gate record for the city. Promoter Aurelio Fabiani had been in Philadelphia for six months and had been using fellow countryman Gardini to bring Italian fans to the arena. If there was a Philadelphia Hall of Fame today, Renato Gardini would have to be in it.[181]

It seems strange, considering how many times they wrestled from 1914 to 1920, that once Lewis took control of the title he never wrestled Wladek Zbyszko. In 1924, it seemed Wladek was going to get his shot when he was matched with the Paul Bowser wrestler Stanley Stasiak in Boston on March 13, with the winner to meet Lewis for the world title. But Wladek never got his match, because Stasiak beat him.

I don't know a great deal about Stanley Stasiak, but I envision him as a big brawler with a boxer background. Bowser was giving him a huge push in 1924. Stasiak wrestled in other areas of the country, but I don't consider him a national star. That being said, he went over huge in Boston. On April 13, Lewis agreed to meet Stasiak after Bowser offered a larger bid or purse over a bunch of major promoters in a fake auction. The match took place on May 8. Some of the promoters mentioned in the auction were S. E. Avory (St. Joseph), George "Farmer" Bailey (Battleboro, VT), Charley Donnell (Norwood), Joe Turner (Washington DC), Jack McGrath (Worcester), Ed White (Chicago), Tom Law (Wichita), and even Jack Curley. Farmer Bailey, was said to be ready to offer $10,000. The "big" surprise was that Paul Bowser won by giving Lewis and Sandow a $12,000 payday.

Lewis wrestled Mike Romano four times in Chicago during 1924 and all the matches drew well and were major battles in the city. Romano wasn't what I'd call a major star—more of a mid-card worker who did some main events—and these 1924 title matches with Lewis seemed to be the high point of his career.

A first match took place on January 15 and Lewis won, but they worked some type of gimmick finish, so the rematch drew 10,000 on April 30 at the Chicago Coliseum. Mike Romano used the headlock and the match was billed as a battle of finishing holds. After being punished by Romano's headlocks, Lewis won the first fall in 41:20 with a vicious toe hold. Romano limped around but Lewis had to be carried to the dressing room during the rest period between falls. Romano threw Lewis around the ring in the second fall using Ed's headlock and pinned him in 12:50. Before Lewis, championship wrestlers did not go to the ropes to break holds. It was considered unsportsmanlike behavior and you could get disqualified doing it. The old rule used to be that, after a rope break, the two wrestlers had to return to the center of the ring before restarting the match. In the third fall, Lewis was still suffering from the punishment given in the first two falls and he started hanging on to the ropes. Romano, with victory in sight, grabbed Lewis around the waist and tugged hard. Ed let go and Romano fell backward landing on his back with Lewis on top. It was ruled a pin fall win for Lewis. An uproar followed and the crowd rioted, howling and breaking up chairs. The police had to be called to disperse the rioters.[182]

This finish has been used a million times since 1924 and maybe it had been done before, but Sandow/Lewis were getting more and more creative in keeping defeated rivals strong. Toots Mondt, who didn't travel with Lewis, may have played a part in creating ideas, but other than him taking credit we have no proof.

On May 1, Lewis, Billy Sandow and his new wife arrived in Boston to set up a training camp with Joe Alvarez at the Tyler Street Gym for the May 8 match with Stanley Stasiak. Lewis' now famous $10,000 belt was displayed in the window of a local jeweler to build interest in the card. On May 3, Lewis and sparring partner George "Farmer" Bailey got into bare-knuckle brawl during a work out. Bailey was fired and I wonder if the argument had anything to do with the Farmer being connected to Jack Curley.

Stanley was giving public work-outs at Combination Park at Medford. Some of the work-outs were drawing crowds of 2,000.

On May 5, Lewis traveled to Rochester to defeat Toots Mondt when he won the only fall before the time limit ran out. The Jules Baumann card drew 3,000.

The Lewis/Stasiak match took place at Boston Arena on May 8, 1924 and drew 9,000 fans—a city record. Stasiak won the first fall in 49 minute using a body scissors and wristlock. In the second fall, Lewis resorted to chock-holds and also landed a punch to the jaw. Stasiak retaliated by head-butting and kicking Lewis. The ring exploded in pandemonium as the referee, seconds, managers, police and even ushers rushed into the ring to break them up. Referee Sam Avery of St. Joseph disqualified Stasiak. The crowd went nuts and booed the decision, as they were doing at all of Lewis' matches. A rematch would be needed.

Lewis returned to Philadelphia on May 21 to defeat Renato Gardini when the Italian was unable to continue. The match drew 6,500.

A third match in Chicago with Stanislaus Zbyszko took place on May 28 at the Coliseum. Lewis won the first fall with the head lock in 24:05. In the second fall, Stan head-butted Ed, knocking him down. Then he picked him up and slammed him and got the pin in 12:55. The Strangler took the third in 9:50. The champion out-wrestled Stan and beat him decisively. Chicago and Stanislaus was running out of steam, with the newspaper calling him "poor old Stan." The attendance was down to 5,600 and the gate was $9,500. It was at least Lewis' eighth straight win over Zbyszko and he seemed to have proved his point.[183]

Lewis beat Jim Londos in St. Louis again on June 12. Jimmy won the first fall and lost the last two with the head lock and Ed's extra 30 pounds being the difference. The gate was $14,410. The crowd was hostile, but Lewis seemed unmindful of the taunts and boos. Londos was game and had The Strangler in trouble many times but some thought the champion was holding back.[184]

Lewis and Sandow then returned to the East Coast for a Toots Mondt rematch for Billy's brother Jules Baumann in Rochester. On June 26, while training at Conesus Lake, Lewis and Sandow had the first of a series of car accidents when their auto skidded on a wet road and landed in a ditch. The damage was minor and no one was hurt. Sandow seemed to be driving. On June 28, the champ defended the title in Rochester beating Mondt. (One wonders if Toots was also in the car.)

A rematch with Lewis was set up by having Stanley Stasiak beat poor old Stan Zbyszko in Boston on June 12. Lewis defeated Stasiak in Boston on July 1, 1924, winning the last two falls of the title defense. The victory was booed by those in attendance and Ed was attacked by several fans as he left the ring.[185]

After beating Mike Romano in a Chicago rematch on July 11 in two straight falls, the Sandow troop of wrestlers left for new territory, the west coast and Los Angeles.

Lewis in Los Angeles — 1924

Lou Daro was a side-show strong man and pro wrestler who went under the name The Great Daro. By 1921 he had turned promoter and was running cards in Boston for Jack Curley. He came out second best in a wrestling war with Boston's George Tuohey and, in 1923, set out for himself to develop Los Angeles into a wrestling empire. By 1923, Daro was running weekly cards in Long Beach, California using Jim Londos, Ray Steele, and Bull Montana. He had lease problems and by 1924 was concentrating on working in Los Angeles.

For an Arena, Daro used the Philharmonic Auditorium, an impressive building at 5th and Olive Street. It was a nine-story Gothic building built in 1906, that at one time was the largest concrete building in America. A lot of it was office building, but the arena section held 5,500 for wrestling. It was the home of classical music in Los Angeles and, beginning in 1920 was used for concerts by the Philharmonic Orchestra. At times it was used as a movie theater and in 1915 the world premiere of D. W. Griffith's film 'The Birth Of A Nation' was held there. It was an occasion remembered for the long line of Ku Klux Klan members riding horses in the streets of downtown Los Angeles. It overlooked Pershing Square and was across the street from the Biltmore Hotel, built in 1923, which had become the major hotel in town, where presidents and foreign royalty stayed, and where the first Academy awards were held. After the Music Center was built in 1964, the Philharmonic Auditorium lost its purpose and was torn down. Today it is an expensive parking lot that I pass on the way to do wrestling research at the downtown library.

Before Daro, the pro wrestling activity could only be found at the Los Angeles Athletic Club. It was a gym and social club for prominent rich men and threw the early year had infrequent wrestling and boxing cards. The gym had a wrestling section and many famous pro wrestlers coach there. Dan McLeod held the position in 1912 and Walter Miller, Middle-Weight champ, worked at the club for years. Late in his career, Lewis would work there as a coach and greeter. Many famous pro wrestlers have worked out there including Frank Gotch, Joe Stecher, and Antonio Inoki. Gus Sonnenberg was once mugged on a street a block away. The Athletic Club played a major role in bring sports to the city and for years owned The Olympic Auditorium, leasing it to the local wrestling promoters like Lou Daro, Cal Eatons, and Mike LeBell, for very little rent. The gym is still a great looking building located south of Pershing Square.

Stan Zbyszko was the first of Sandow's wrestlers to reach the West Coast, working in both San Francisco and Los Angeles. On July 9, 1914, Lou Daro ran a show at The Philharmonic with Zbyszko beating Yussif Hussane, drawing a crowd of 3,500. Daro then drew a "large" crowd on July 23 for Toots Mondt winning a handicap match over Zbyszko.[186]

Lewis was in the area and on July 29 drew the largest crowd in San Francisco since Stecher/Santel, for a win over Stanislaus. The report was kind of a comical review but it said that Lewis had travel across the country by car.[187]

Hollywood was in its prime, with great weather and parties every night. To the rest of the world, Los Angeles seemed like the great place to live in 1924. Newspapers and movie theaters across the country were filled with photos of beaches and beautiful people. Everyone wanted to move there and the population was growing by the day. Ed Lewis and Billy Sandow loved the place, but it needed a money making wrestling promotion.

Ed Lewis working out with University
of Southern California coach Howard Jones

The storyline was that Ed was training for an August 13 title defense against his major rival Toots Mondt, but on August 11, he, Mrs. Lewis and his brother-in-law C. B. Glenn were having a good time in Tijuana, Mexico. On the drive back, Lewis crashed into a car driven by a Mrs. Daisy Haynes. Daisy was very upset and forced Lewis out of his car so he could inspect the mess he had made out of her auto. Words went back and forth, some of which were insulting to Daisy. These remarks were resented by Charles Haynes, her son, so Lewis punched him out. Then Ed punched another son, Leo Haynes, and the last guy in Daisy's car Charles Fatherios. Daisy got roughed up too, because her clothes were torn and she later showed black and blue marks on her arm. Lewis and his party drove away, but later in the day the highway patrol pulled him over for speeding. Ed refused to get out of the car when ordered, so "back up" was called. With two more state traffic officers present, Lewis was arrested and charged by the San Diego Justice Court with four separate charges of battery and one of disturbing the peace. Lewis pleaded not guilty and was released on $500 bail.[188]

But Lewis made it to the Philharmonic on August 13, defeating Toots Mondt by winning the only fall in a two hour match. Mondt looked fit, while Ed seemed fat and had a bad eye. Except when Lewis came alive to win the fall at the 90 minute mark with a head lock, the match was dominated by Toots. Reporter Braven Dyer of the *Times* claimed both grapplers had shed gallons of sweat. "Had the perspiration lost by both giants been tanked and shipped to the orange belt, region ranches wouldn't have to worry about irrigation water for the next six months." The arena was sold out with 5,500 in the building and over 2,500 fans turned away. Daro was very happy but he was thinking that Los Angeles needed a bigger arena.[189]

Daro drew another sellout (5,500) on August 27, with Lewis defending (again) against Stanislaus Zbyszko. Lewis won the first fall after a series of headlocks in 21 minutes. Stan took the second with a toe hold in 14 minutes. In the third, both wrestlers fell to the mat but Ed was on top. The referee, ruled a pin (4 minutes) and Lewis was the winner. Zbyszko went crazy, claiming there was no pin, and the crowd was in a rage. The police had to be called to restore order. Everyone loved the show and claimed it was the best in the history of the city. The newspapers all praised Daro.[190]

On September 2, Lewis beat Pat McGill in San Francisco. The headlock knocked McGill out at the end of the first fall and the challenger had to spend the night in the hospital. After the match, Lewis was served a warrant charging him with speeding through the town of San Juan.[191]

On September 3, 1924, a report came from Boston that a newspaper man named Arthur Duffey had reported that Ed "Strangler" Lewis would soon retire from active wrestling due to eye trouble. It was claimed that due to his eye infections (trachoma), he had been near blind for most of 1924.

Everyone in Los Angeles thought Stan Zbyszko deserved a rematch with the champion and Lou Daro gave it to them on September 4. The match was to a finish and fans were told to bring there own food because the Philharmonic refused to allow Daro to set up a hot dog stand in the lobby. A condition set forth in the contract stated that the match had to take place in a roped ring, and not just on an unenclosed platform. That rule makes me think that September 4, 1924 was the first time a normal roped wrestling ring was used in Los Angeles. Zbyszko won the first fall with a flying mare in 24:01, but Lewis proved the Pole's master winning the next two falls in 39:45 and 4:17 with the headlock. It was an easy win for the champion. Once again Daro sold out and it was called the greatest crowd in Los Angeles wrestling history—but it was also written that Daro cried over the several thousand paying customers turned away.[192]

On September 25, Daro promoted a Lewis/Mondt rematch at the Philharmonic. It was another great show that sold out at 5,500. The two hour time limit ran out with both men having won a fall, so the match was called a draw.[193]

A rematch was booked for October 13, 1924. Daro was fed up with good customers being turned away, so he rented the Washington Ball Park to house the event. The storyline was that Lewis was wanted back East and didn't like the idea of a finish match, so Daro had to offer him a purse of $17,500 to wrestle. Mondt got $2,500 or 15% of the gate.

A lot of smart fans were hearing the reports and thinking that Strangler Lewis' time as champion was coming to a close. Some of them felt Toots Mondt had been picked to replace Ed. He was five years younger and Lewis was getting fatter by the week. So an outdoor show in Los Angeles would be a good place for the title change.

Lewis was shown in the newspaper with his biggest fan and mascot: Billy Sandow, Jr., the four-year-old son of his manager, who had been present with Mrs. Sandow at all of the Lewis matches in America and Europe. A photo of Lewis and the kid was shown in the newspaper. I never heard anything about Junior again.[194]

On October 13, 10,000 fans filed into the Washington Ball Park and paid $31,000 to watch a brutal battle. Mondt won the first fall in 34:09 with his jack knife scissors. Photos of the finishing move make it look like a rolling short arm scissors that end with cradling his foe for a pin. Lewis had to be carried from the ring by two seconds during the 10 minute rest period, but he came back fighting. The second fall was brutal, and at one point the two exchanged punches in the middle of the ring. Lewis overcame a lot of punishment to reverse the jack knife scissors and made Mondt submit after a Lewis' toe hold (41:51). Mondt returned injured and Lewis finished him with another toe hold in 4:19. The next day reporters agreed that the superior wrestler was Strangler Lewis.[195]

As late as the 1970's, promoters have always believed and stated that there was only 10,000 real wrestling fans in Los Angeles. They may not have known it, but that belief may go back to October 13, 1924 and this record crowd. It may also explain why Los Angeles built Lou Daro, in 1925, an Olympic Auditorium that held 10,400.

With all the major contenders beaten and used up, the Sandow company headed back to Chicago. Lewis had two matches in Chicago in late October 1924 and then seems to take the month of November off. On December 1, it was announced that Lewis was going to tour Europe, starting on December 16 and lasting for six months. On December 18, the story was changed to Ed sailing on January 16, 1925. Sandow claimed that Lewis was going to make $30,000 a week meeting all comers.

On December 11, Lewis defeated Hassalin O. Giles in two straight falls in Kansas City. The only thing that makes this match note worthy were the rules. There were none and there was no referee in the ring. Lewis won both falls with the strangle hold. The attendance, for what seemed like a death match, was estimated at 10,000.[196]

December 16 saw Lewis finish off Mike Romano in Chicago. Ed won two out three falls on a card that drew 11,000.[197]

After two weak years, business had pick up for the Sandow group in 1924. They had drawn very well in Kansas City and Chicago, with other cities like St. Louis, Boston, Los Angeles, and Philadelphia taking form as major wrestling promotions. But the center of the wrestling world, New York City, was dead. Sandow's champion, Ed Lewis, had become a famous sports celebrity due to radio, improved sports sections in the newspapers and the public's new obsession with professional sports—but Ed was 34-years-old, fat, and losing his desire to train. His eyes were so bad that he was almost blind at times, and his performances were growing worse as a result. He was the first truly heel world champion, and some of that was because of planning, but the plan may have been needed because he really wasn't liked by fans. As an actual person, he got along great with the press and other insiders—and he dressed and looked like a true champion—but Lewis really wasn't popular in any of the major cities. He had no home base. Boo's and riots followed every match.

Wayne Munn and The Big Blunder of 1925

By the end of 1924, everyone of Lewis' major contenders had been blown off. Old Stan Zbyszko had been beaten at least 11 straight times in publicized matches, in every major city. Toots Mondt, Dick Daviscourt, Renato Gardini, and Mike Romano had been beaten to death and were then being used to put over lesser wrestlers who couldn't draw. Jim Londos, although beaten, had gain in popularity but he had ideas of his own and Sandow didn't have complete control over him. Earl Caddock retired in July 1932. John Pesek wasn't trusted, didn't like to do jobs, and had been destroyed in his strongest town by Lewis. Sandow was afraid of Joe Stecher, who had been lied to and promised his title back, and Wladek Zbyszko, had been forgotten by just about everyone. There was no new super star to draw a huge house against—unless Sandow created one. Sandow, Lewis and Max and Jules Baumann got together, and the idea they came up with was Wayne Munn.[198]

Wayne Munn was born at Colby, Kansas in 1899. Later his family moved to Fairbury, Nebraska and he played on the football team at The University of Nebraska from 1916 to 1918. He was the first of four athlete brothers and a star lineman on a team that defeated Notre Dame 7 to 0 in a famous 1917 game. He majored in medicine but left the school to join the Army during WWI. Like most athletes during the war, he never left stateside and instead toured as a star on a all-star football team, out of Camp Pike, that beat every other southern army camp. He attended officers training camp and was discharged as a Lieutenant. After the war, he worked as a teacher, preacher, and even took a turn on the vaudeville stage. But by 1923 he was selling cars in a dealership in Omaha, which led him to Sioux City and a job in the oil business. Being 6'6" and over 315 pounds, he attempted to start a career as a pro boxer. By November 16, 1923, Munn had lost 55 pounds

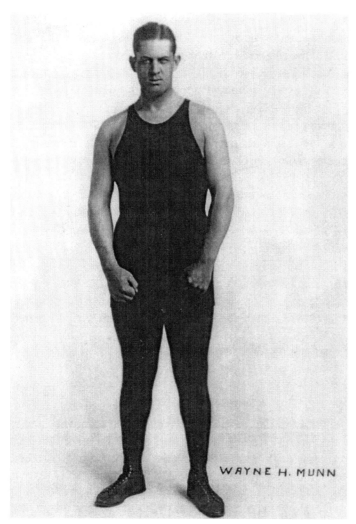

WAYNE H. MUNN

Wayne Munn

in training but was knocked out by Jack Clifford in the second round in Sioux City. Clifford's record was 3-22 at the time. On December 8, 1923, he fought a Charley Paulson (0-0) in Sioux City and was put away in the 4th round.[199] Wayne had helped put two brothers, Wade and Monte, through college and both became prosperous lawyers. Monte became a member of the Nebraska State Legislature. A third brother, Glenn, was doing well as a athlete at the university while Wayne was champion and would follow his brother into pro wrestling.[200]

Billy Sandow thought he would do better in a "worked" sport and spent most of 1924 having him trained as a pro wrestler. He was huge, good looking for the 1920's and powerful, but a terrible wrestler. The only real hold he could be taught was his finisher, the body slam. He could pick 'em up and slam them—but that was about all. Hulk Hogan, as a worker, would look like Volk Han next to him, but there are a lot of similarities between the two stars. He seemed to be a nice guy and a good person, so Sandow wouldn't have to worry about a wrestling ego.

By the end of 1924, Billy Sandow and promoter Gabe Kaufman had managed to get him over in Kansas City. He had been given wins over Toots Mondt and Wallace Duguid, showing little wrestling ability but a lot of power. A match was booked between the champion Ed Lewis and the giant Munn for January 8, 1925 at the Kansas City Convention Hall.[201]

The 15,000 fans present cheered Wayne Munn from the moment he entered the ring and all Lewis could get, after many bouts in Kansas City, were boos. Lewis' weight was announced as 235 pounds and Munn weighed 260 pounds of muscle. The two spared around for most of the first fall. Ed attempted to use the headlock, but the giant just shook him off. At the 21 minute mark, Munn picked Lewis up in the crotch hold and slammed Ed through the mat, and pinned him. The feared Strangler just writhed and groaned in agony. His 10-minute rest period between falls ended up being 20 minutes. Two minutes into the second fall Munn picked Lewis up again and threw him high over the top rope, crashing on to the apron and then falling on to the floor. Billy Sandow jumped into the ring yelling "foul", and for a period of time it seemed like he and Munn were going to have a fight of their own. The crowd rushed the ring, thinking Munn would lose the match on a foul, but a riot was averted when referee Walter Bates ruled Munn had lost the second fall on the foul, but Lewis had to return in fifteen minutes ready to wrestle or lose the match and title. Lewis was carried to the dressing-room at the back of the hall, as fans booed and threw paper balls at his limp form.

This ruling goes back to the Stecher/Mondt match of February 11, 1924, where the promoter changed the Kansas City rules and stated that a foul in a early fall would only lose that fall and not the complete match.

The fans sat with watches in hand waiting for the champion's return. 20 minutes passed with no Lewis and at one point a doctor was called. When Lewis returned, his back was bandaged and he had to be helped into the ring. Billy Sandow stated that Lewis was wrestling the rest of the match under protest and that the decision would be contested.

At the bell, the two wrestlers met at the center of the ring. Lewis tried for a headlock but was once again manhandled by Munn and slammed. Lewis didn't move as he was pinned at 50 seconds of the third fall.

The crowd cheered and rushed the ring as the referee Bates raised Munn's arm as new world champion. The fans jumped into the ring, passed the police, as they praised the new hero.[202]

Lewis laid forgotten by everyone in the building, just as his past foes had been forgotten after being crushed by his headlocks. For a while he watched as the fans paraded around Munn. He later was taken from the ring to boos and a ambulance drove him to St. Lukes hospital to which Ed was admitted, but by morning his injuries had still not been determined. Rumor were put out that he would have to be put into a full body cast—which was a joke. In the days that followed it was claimed he had an injured back, but no fracture was seen on any x-ray. The doctor's statement was that "his condition is very favorable to a speedy recovery."

Billy Sandow continued to protest the match and refused to give Wayne Munn Lewis' two championship belts. One was the Lewis belt, that was awarded to him in 1921 by Central Athletic Club of Kansas City, and the other was the Zbyszko belt that had been awarded to Stanislaus by Tex Rickard in New York City. Sandow's and Lewis' argument was that the Munn foul in the second fall should have given

Wayne Munn

them the match, thus they were still the rightful title holder. Sandow cancelled all engagements including the European tour. Sandow promised to take his case to court. Lewis stayed in the hospital for a short period and was back in the gym by mid-month.

On January 14, Munn announced he had signed a $2,500 a week contract to join the vaudeville tour that would last from February 1 to mid-April. If the plan with Munn was anything like Paul Bowser's push of Danno O'Mahoney in 1925, Sandow and Toots Mondt was working out Munn every day, trying to develop him into a performer that fit the standards of a normal pro wrestling worker. The local vaudeville tour was probably a way to not expose him in the ring until he was ready. His "worked" manager, Gabe Kaufman, said he might be able to wrestle a few minor matches during that time, but nothing with Lewis was planned.

To keep the storyline in the press, Sandow had both sides treating to take each other to court to stop the other wrestler from claiming the title. In late January, Munn filed a petition to stop Lewis and Sandow from claiming the championship. So, in effect, Billy was suing himself.

There was a lot of print about how Wayne Munn's victory had broken up the trust that had dominated pro wrestling since 1915, with Stecher, Lewis, Caddock and the Zbyszko brothers taking turns with the title, but another article was printed in the *Wichita Eagle* on January 11 that blew everyone's cover. It stated that Billy Sandow owned Wayne Munn's contract and was the actual manager of the football player. The reporter also claimed that the newspaper received a letter from a wrestling insider in Kansas City in the week before the Lewis/Munn match, stating that Lewis was going to drop the title to Munn. He also claimed that Wichita fans had lost interest in pro wrestling.[203]

On January 21, Wayne Munn was presented to the House of Representatives at Lincoln, Nebraska, by his brother Monte Munn, who was an elected member. Monte gave a speech and Wayne was congratulated for his victory over Lewis by the house. The brother stated there was nothing "shady" about the title win. Each member was given tickets to see Munn's vaudeville appearance that night at a local theater.[204]

A storyline was created where Munn signed to make a title defense against Stanislaus Zbyszko in Chicago on February 3, but Sandow stopped the match by claiming he had filed an injunction suit. So Wayne Munn's first match as champion was moved to Kansas City and the date was set for February 11.

Lewis took the February 3 booking at the Chicago Coliseum and agreed to meet anyone the promoter selected, who turned out to be Joe "Toots" Mondt. Lewis beat Mondt in two out of three falls while claiming the world title. On the undercard, Wayne Munn gave an exhibition of the holds (or hold) he used to defeat Lewis in Kansas City. This was probably his vaudeville act. The card drew 9,000 for a gate of around $21,000.[205]

Munn made it to Kansas City for the February 11 match with the ex-champ Stanislaus Zbyszko. Munn easily beat Stan in straight falls. Stan looked short, old, and fat and was no match for the giant champion. Munn was never in trouble. Zbyszko was pushed and thrown all over the ring. Wayne body slammed Stan with a crash to win the first fall in 16:40 and then repeated the result in 12:45. Munn grew well with 12,000 in the Convention hall. Munn dropped the vaudeville job about this time and started accepting wrestling dates.

Joe Stecher and Jack Curley were becoming more active in 1925.[206] Stecher was working full time being booked in St. Louis, Wichita, Memphis and New York. On February 19, he presented a written repudiation of an Omaha interview to the New York Athletic Commission. In the interview Stecher was quoted admitting he had engaged in fixed matches. He denied he had authorized the interview and suggested some enemy was responsible. He appeared in front of the commission that Friday when an investigation was conducted. Nothing resulted from it.[207]

Tony and Joe attempted to force a John Pesek match in Wichita during the first two months of the year. Pesek was the only one of Lewis' policemen he hadn't beaten and Joe seemed obsessed with wrestling him. He offered a side bet of $10,000 to Pesek and the Tiger seemed willing, but his manager Max Baumann never seemed to be in town the same day as Tony Stecher. A $20,000 bet was also offered to Toots Mondt, with nothing happening other than talk. Most of it merely used in an effort to quiet Stecher, whose demands for a title match were getting more and more embarrassing to the Lewis group.[208] Earlier in the year, Stecher had defeated another Sandow wrestler in Dick Daviscourt twice. One of them in St. Louis on February 5 saw Daviscourt disqualified for foul tactics in the third fall. Daviscourt came out of it with a swollen eye. On March 6, 1925, Stecher won two out of three falls from Ad Santel in Wichita.[209]

Jim Londos was also showing up in New York on Jack Curley cards. One wonders if Londos had jumped ship from Sandow group at this time, perhaps because he wasn't considered for the Wayne Munn part in the storyline.

From the beginning, Billy Sandow's plan was for the Munn/Lewis rematch to take place on the Decoration Day holiday, May 30, at an outdoor stadium in Michigan City, Indiana. His plan would build to a super match that would be the first $100,000 gate in pro wrestling history. One wonders if that would have been the site and date for the Lewis/Dempsey match, if things had worked out.

Lewis and Munn both worked main events in Chicago during February and March. Both were billed as world champion. Lewis beat Joe Zickman twice and Tom Draak. Munn beat Mike Romano on February 18 drawing 7,500, and on March 31 he beat his trainer Toots Mondt in front of 8,000 fans with a gate of $22,000. Mondt got his shot at the title by beating Stanislaus Zbyszko on March 3. Munn also beat Pat McGill in Rochester and Wallace Duguid in Cleveland.

A boxing promoter, named John Curley, was running wrestling cards in Philadelphia against Aurelio Fabiani. This John Curley, not Jack Curley, was aligned with Sandow and he booked a rematch between Munn and Stan Zbyszko for April 15, 1925 at the Philadelphia Arena. Actually, the choice of Stan Zbyszko as the challenger was made by the Pennsylvania State Athletic Commission, not the promoter.

Wayne Munn went through the motions of training in Philadelphia during the week leading up to the match. On the night before, Munn, Manager Gabe Kaufman and promoter John Curley attended the season opener of the Philadelphia baseball team, as a guest of Connie Mack.

That same night, April 14, Joe Stecher was wrestling former Harvard coach Frank Judson at the Philadelphia Adelphia for promoter Aurelio Fabiani. Stecher won the match. The reporter claimed the bout was "free of play acting which damages so many matches and had no exaggerated groans or writhing, either facial or otherwise." It was a clean test of strength and was as "clean as a tooth of a hound."[210] Stecher was still playing the part of a legitimate champion wrestler and hadn't adapted to the new style of Billy Sandow.

Stanislaus Zbyszko was in Philadelphia that night too. His birthday on April 1 had probably made him wonder how much longer he would last as a wrestler. Before 1922 he had gone years without doing a job, but by 1925 he had gone from being champion to top contender to setting up lesser wrestlers. He had dropped 11 straight major matches, all over America, to Lewis and then did jobs for Pesek, Mondt, Steinke, Londos and now the footballer Wayne Munn. A lot of wrestling purists hated Sandow's new gimmick and hated the turning of the sport into a circus, with brawling and men flying out of the ring. They believed the fans would tire of the style and the sport would die. From his statements late in life, I believe Stanislaus Zbyszko felt the same. Stan was an intelligent man, and he knew putting over a "performer" would mean the end of his career. Billy Sandow had no more use for him and he would be looking for work soon. He claimed in the paper that he no longer had a manager, and I'm sure that he talked to Jack Curley, Aurelio Fabiani and Tony Stecher in the days leading up to the match. Curley had always been a friend, who had managed his brother and helped bring him to America. He also probably talked to Wladek, whose feud with Lewis had build the Strangler into a star but had never got any big money title matches once Sandow controlled the belt.[211] This continued even after Wladek went to work for Sandow ally Paul Bowser. All Billy Sandow had to rely on was Zbyszko's character and professionalism—and it was a mistake. Stan must have had a lot to think about as time ran down before the match.

On April 15, 1925, the Philadelphia Arena was filled with a "standing room only" crowd of 8,000, said to be the city's indoor sports record. The under card saw John Pesek pin Frank Bruno five times in a handicap match that lasted less than 30 minutes. Stanislaus enter the ring with a boxer named Lew "Kid" Palmer as his only second. Wayne Munn entered with his manager Gabe Kaufman. The match itself wasn't much. In the 13 minutes, the two were not on the mat for more than a half dozen times. Zbyszko showed complete mastery, and all Munn could do was hope Stan would fall into his body slam. The first fall lasted 8:11, and, with Zbyszko showing lightning movement belying his seeming corpulence, he ducked under Munn's reach and got back control. He then lifted the 6'6" giant up and slammed him on to the mat. With Munn stunned, Stan applied a forearm hold and a hatch lock to lower the champion on to his back for the three count.

Munn and Kaufman jumped from the ring and rushed to the dressing room. Zbyszko refused to leave the ring during the rest period. He put on his robe and sat in his corner looking out across the ring. Kid Palmer stayed on the floor watching his back. A number of alleged representatives of Munn came to the ring to talk, but Zbyszko just shook his head and they left. Then Max Baumann, brother of Billy Sandow and manager of John Pesek, came to the ring and got so close to Stan that he could whisper in his ear. No one knows what Max said to Stan but one rumor is that he threatened to sent Pesek out to replace Munn for the second falls.

Whatever he said it was answered by a negative nod of Zbyszko head, as he stared out across the ring waiting for Munn's return.

Wayne Munn had the guts to return but he didn't have the skill to do any better. The fall lasted 4:53 with almost the same winning move. Munn once again reached out only to have Stan duck under his arms to get back control. Munn flew through the air, landing on his back. A Zbyszko's forearm hold was converted into a hammerlock and the champion's shoulders were forced down for a count of three. Stanislaus Zbyszko was once again champion and on top of the wrestling world.

Stan was surrounded by admirers and led to his corner, where he posed for photographers. Kid Palmer led a line of police into the ring and Zbyszko was escorted by cordon of police to his dressing room. They guarded him like a king whose assassination had been planned, until he changed and then was led out of the arena to a taxicab and a ride to his hotel. Kid Palmer stayed with Stan in his room guarding his door, but the new champion couldn't sleep. At 2:00, he got up to walk the streets by himself until morning came.[212]

Wayne Munn walked from the ring and back stage then into his star's dressing room. Rumors were spread that he fainted once inside. Manager Kaufman claimed he was sick and had a temperature of a 104. The commission doctor said he didn't have a temperature before the match, but was suffering from tonsillitis.

The next day Zbyszko was met in his hotel by representatives of every major promoter in wrestling. Floyd Fitzsimmons, promoter of the Michigan City card, offered $30,00 to Zbyszko to replace Munn against Lewis. Max Baumann went on record offering Stan $10,000 for a match with John Pesek. It would seem that Zbyszko also received offers from Aurelio Fabiani, Tom Pack, Jack Curley, and Tony Stecher working as a group.

The Zbyszko brothers, Stanislaus and Wladek, with Wladek's wife.

Wayne Munn's defense was that he had been sick from tonsillitis and anyone could have beaten him that night. He claimed he wanted a rematch. On April 28, Munn, billed in the Kansas City report as ex-champ, went through an operation to remove his tonsils.

Sandow's and Lewis' reaction was that Munn was never a champion to begin with. So Zbyszko's win meant nothing.

On April 18, 1925, Fabiani met with Stan Zbyszko and Jack Curley in New York City. He returned claiming that everyone had agreed that Stan would defend his title verses Joe Stecher at a Philadelphia outdoor ball park in June. Stanislaus had agreed to a purse of $50,000.[213] Later the location was moved to St. Louis and the date was set for Decoration Day, May 30—the same day as the Lewis/Munn rematch at Michigan City.

Lewis's rematch with Munn became official on April 23, when both signed contracts and posted $5,000 appearance bonds. The purse was said to be 60% of the gate and Lewis would receive 60% of that. Lewis' $10,000 Rickard belt would be at awarded to the winner.[214] Lewis was billed as champion and it was then billed as a Lewis title defense, even though some fans still considered it a title unification match.

After the mess in Philadelphia, Munn claimed he was sick and cancelled all matches. The next night, April 16, in Boston, Lewis subbed for him and defeated Alex Lunden. Ed then beat Tom Draak in Philadelphia (May 1) for Dick Curley, before a return to Boston and another win over Lunden on May 7. He was billed as champion while doing as much P.R. for the May 30 match as possible. After that both Lewis and Munn went into training, first in Chicago and then Michigan City.

Stan Zbyszko was an active champion, wrestling mostly in the North East, but he didn't sell many tickets. His return to Philadelphia with a win over local star Renato Gardini drew only 4,500 on April 23, and a match in Boston, for promoters Alex Maclean (Jack Curley's man in the city, who was going up against the Paul Bowser promotion), drew the "smallest house ever for a world champion in the city" on May 1 versus Oreste Vadalfi.

The Zbyszko group filled an injunction against Ed Lewis in an attempt to stop him from calling himself world champion, but on May 26 the application was turned down by Judge Hugo Friend, a former University of Chicago athlete.[215]

Floyd Fitzsimmons had for a long time been losing money promoting sports at the Blue Sky Arena in Michigan City, Indiana, located 60 miles from downtown Chicago on the other side of Lake Michigan. So he was looking for a huge payday with the Lewis/Munn rematch. He didn't get a $100,000 house, but he seemed happy to make some money for a change. The match drew between 13,000 and 14,000, and took in $64,000. It was claimed that 4,000 no shows ended up marooned on the congested highways leading from Chicago to the Arena. Billy Sandow got his 50% from both Lewis and Munn, so he made money, but no one made the fortune that had been planned on at the beginning of the year.

The May 30, 1925 match took place under a bright sun and blistering heat. Wayne Munn entered first, sporting a cut over his left eye after training for weeks with Toots Mondt. The champion Lewis, looking in good shape, followed and there was a long conference with referee Walter Bates, the same man who officiated the first match. Most of the first 15 minutes was all stand up. Three times Lewis attempted to clamp on the headlock but the huge Munn was able to shake him off with out any problems. Munn took Lewis down at one point but was unable to hold him and Ed broke lose. Ed kept away from Munn's crotch hold by going down on one knee or hanging on to the ropes. At times, Lewis seemed to be having trouble seeing and later claimed to have sore eyes from getting resin in them during a match in Boston. It may have been a result of Trachoma. At 24:55, Munn broke a minute long headlock and slammed Lewis to the mat for a pin and the first fall.

At the end of the rest period, manager Kaufmann announced that Munn wouldn't continue unless Lewis's championship belt was placed in the hands of promoter Fitzsimmons. Half a dozen police brought the $10,000 belt ringside and the match continued.

Munn was full of himself and he raced across the ring to get at Lewis. He chased Ed down and for 20 minute the two tugged and mauled each other in the center of the ring. Munn faded and by the end of the fall (32:12) he had been the victim of 20 headlocks and a huge slam before he was pinned by Lewis. Munn laid still in the ring for a minute before he was helped by his seconds to the dressing room.

Munn still look beat when he returned for the last fall. Lewis dragged him all over the ring and after 7 more headlocks and seven minutes, he was pinned. Lewis was announced as champion and the belt was placed around his waist.

On the same day in St. Louis, Joe Stecher regained the world title taking two straight falls from Stanislaus Zbyszko. The match, held on the St. Louis University Athletic Field, drew 13,500 and a gate of $43,315.

A motion picture company also paid $15,000 to film the event. For losing the title, Zbyszko was paid $50,000. Stecher himself paid $10,000 to Stan and wrestled the match for free. To most of the wrestling world, the true world champion was then Joe Stecher.[216]

The Wayne Munn gimmick turn out to be a disaster for the Sandow group, and it might be considered the greatest blunder in the history of the pro wrestling. In losing control of the world title, at least in the eyes of most of the country, Sandow lost most of his power. Zbyszko, Londos, Gardini, Pesek, Daviscourt, and others all jumped to the Stecher side, which was strengthened by the creation of new territories, arenas, and talent. Pro wrestling became big time under Stecher and really took off after the elevation of Jim Londos. Ed Lewis would come back, but other than for a couple of short periods, he would never be the central figure in the sport again. Billy Sandow was a very smart wrestling insider and would carry on being a power, but he never would regain the control he had from 1922 to 1925. Ed Lewis' great period has to be his first and second title reign from the end of 1920 to the beginning of 1925. It was the period when he became a national star, due to radio, improved sport pages, and the public awareness of pro sports. From a box office stand point, 1922 and 1923 didn't seem like much (it probably could be described as poor) but it picked up in 1924.

So what would have been the result of the Lewis/Munn rematch, if Zbyszko had done the job in Philadelphia? No one knows anything for sure, but for years I felt Lewis, with his bad eyes, was looking for a vacation and would wait a year or so before regaining the title. But now I agree with others, like historian John Williams. Lewis would have beaten Munn, pretty much as he did, and then tried to forget the football player had ever been champion in their storylines. (Look up Antonio Inoki and the WWF Title for an example or Ed Carpentier and the NWA title in 1957.)

I also have to believe that it bugged the hell out of Toots Mondt that he was never considered by Sandow to be the champion.

What was left for the Sandow group was Chicago, Kansas City, Boston, Tulsa, Texas, and the towns run by the Baumann brothers. All the rest of the major promotions or territories were backed the Stechers, and as wrestling grew in the late 1920's, so did the Stechers' side in the war. When Lewis did appear in major cities, like Los Angeles, it was for the minor outlaw groups, not the major promoters.

In 1925, the Sandow/Lewis group was never more creative with their lies used to discredit Stecher's title claims. In early June, Sandow house referee Walter Bates, who was the official of both Munn matches, came out in an attempt to over turn his decision in the first match and ruled, because he had changed his mind five months after the event, that Lewis had actually won the match on a foul and was still champion. Tom Law, promoter of Wichita, countered this Sandow move by having the referee of the March 3, 1922 Lewis title win over Stan Zbyszko, Paul Sickner, claim that he also made a mistake, and Ed was actually disqualified for punching Stan, so Zbyszko was the champion when he lost to Stecher.[217] The small part of the population who happened to be smart and paying attention thought it was all very funny.

The Lewis people tried other tricks. During early 1926, Boston promoter Paul Bowser began promoting wrestler Joe Malcewicz as the uncrowned world champion. He created a story that Malcewicz had wrestled champion Earl Caddock in December 1919, before the famed Earl Caddock title loss to Joe Stecher in Madison Square Garden, and been given a decision win at Utica, NY. They claimed the champion's loss was hushed up by Jack Curley, and Malcewicz was too stupid to make any title claims until 1926.[218] This untrue story remained with Malcewicz for the rest of his career. The facts are that the match didn't happen in 1919, but on January 14, 1921, long after Caddock had dropped the title. Stecher also defeated Malcewicz in a title match on February 11, 1920 at Utica.

Over the years, Lewis also changed the finish of the first Munn match, leaving out the part about being pinned in the third fall. His description had him being unable to continue after being thrown out of the ring. He also avoided the fact he was pinned in the first fall. That is the version that ended up in the book *Fall Guys* in 1938 (with the Malcewicz title win story), and has been repeated over the years.

There isn't a lot of important Lewis matches in the rest of 1925. He seemed to be only wrestling a few matches a month and only the rematches with Wayne Munn had any importance. He wrestled Wayne Munn at least three times. The first one was in Tulsa on October 8 and Lewis won two out of three falls. On November 16, he beat Munn in Houston and on December 9, 1925, Lewis took two out of three falls from Munn in Denver.

Two weeks later, Wayne Munn returned to pro boxing for a match with Andre Anderson (15-22-3). Anderson knocked out Munn in the first round. Munn's comments following the so-called fight were:

"I guess I wasn't cut out for boxing. I'll stick to wrestling." Anderson's quote was: "I'm through throwing fights and laying down whenever they want me to!" Three months later Anderson was shot dead by a gangster. According to police it was because Andre refused to job for Munn. Wayne told the press that he would spend money and find the killer but Munn's ruse never came up with a name.[219]

Munn wrestled Ed Lewis at least ten times in nine different cities, each time drawing less. On May 11, 1928, Munn lost at Worcester to the next great football star to try pro wrestling, Gus Sonnenberg. That's about all I know about Wayne Munn's wrestling career. After leaving sports, he got back into the oil business. In 1930, he moved to San Antonio, Texas, to be near relatives and became sick. He refereed a few matches and spoke before schools and clubs, but his condition gradually failed. He died from Bright's disease on January 9, 1931 at the Fort Sam Houston Army Hospital at age 35.[220]

The Stecher Reign of 1925 and 1926

After beating Zbyszko, Stecher defended his title in Wichita against local favorite Dick Daviscourt (June 5). Then he travel to Los Angeles to get away from the Midwest heat and work one match. On June 10, 1925, Stecher defended the title against Dan Koloff, who was a powerful looking Russian wrestler and thought of as a very good worker, but was never pushed out of the contender level for some unknown reason. The match took place at the Exposition Park's One Hundred and Sixtieth Regiment Armory. Joe won the match.

The promoter was Lou Daro, who told Stecher of the city's plans to build a 10,000 seat arena near downtown Los Angeles. In 1925, in a time when only two cities (New York City and Kansas City) had indoor arenas with seating of over 10,000, it would be billed as the largest sports palace in America. The city was growing faster than any place in America and he promised Joe that his payoffs would grow with it. Tony and Joe both loved the beach and the movie stars, so they made plans to return for the opening of The Olympic Auditorium.

Stecher was in Lewis' town, Chicago, to defend the title against Frank Judson on June 26 at the Coliseum. He drew 6,000 and $8,500, which may have been a near sell out at the time. Lewis and Sandow seemed to be living in Kansas City with a lot of time being spent in Chicago and Tulsa. Both wrestlers were billed as champion in Chicago and the battle between the two made more news than in any other city. The windy city was Lewis' home but Stecher wasn't afraid to visit.

Stecher wrestled a rematch with Stan Zbyszko in Wichita (July 1) and then traveled through the South, into Ohio and finished up in Minneapolis.

The Stechers returned to Los Angeles on July 19. They both brought their families and moved into new houses in Long Beach, a large resort town south of the main city known for its beaches and large amusement park. At the time it was like living next to Disneyland.

Stecher signed to appear as the first main event on a wrestling card at the new Olympic Auditorium, which opened with a boxing card on August 5, 1925. The build-up consisted of Stecher training with boxing champ Jack Dempsey at the Manhattan gym (July 28) and an appearance at the Hollywood Athletic Club (August 8), which had a membership of every major movie star in town.

On August 10, 1925, Stecher opened the new Olympic Auditorium by drawing 8,800 in defeating Renato Gardini. The newspapers claimed that the building was the largest in the country with a capacity of 15,000, but that was a lie. The real

Photo by "Dick" Whittington

The Olympic Auditorium in the early years

capacity was around 10,000 in those years, with 12,000 possible, with standing room only. This means people sitting in the aisles. The 8,800 was an indoor California state record.[221]

On the undercard was Los Angeles's favorite wrestler, Jim Londos and ex-champ, Stan Zbyszko. The fans loved the great looking and hard working Londos and the Stechers wouldn't hold him back, like Billy Sandow. Londos wasn't a promoter, but he had a whole line up of Greek promoters behind him, a stable of wrestling friends (Ray Steele, Gardini, and Daviscourt) on his team, and he was popular in every city he appeared in. The only thing not in his favor was size. Londos and the Stechers got alone well and matches were booked to advance both of them. On the first Olympic card, Londos beat Jim Browning in 55:26.

A report in the Tulsa newspaper on August 28, 1925, said that Lewis and Sandow had invested in an oil well located at Quincy, Kansas. The report just said they were drilling for oil—it didn't say they found any.

At the new Olympic, Stecher defended the title against Goho Gobar (August 24), and ex-champ Stan Zbyszko (September 28). On November 9, Stecher won the only fall before the two-hour limit expired against Jim Londos, giving him another win at the Olympic. The champion then defended in San Francisco, Chicago, Columbus and Cleveland. He returned to Los Angeles on December 14 for a two-hour draw with Londos.

The only city where Lewis could hold his own with Stecher was Chicago, but on January 11, 1926, Lewis drew a crowd of 1,200, beating Wayne Munn in Denver.

January 25 saw Stecher beating Frank Judson in Chicago in front of 2,000. Four days later, on January 29, Lewis beat Stanley Stasiak drawing 7,000.

Curley brought the champion, Joe Stecher, back into New York City on February 1 and drew a sellout 10,000 using 57 year old European legend Ivan Poddubny as a challenger. Stecher then defeated Jim Londos in St. Louis on February 10, drawing a sellout 12,000 and $38,000 with thousands turned away.[222] In Philadelphia he beat George Calza, whom I believe is one of the most underrated wrestlers in history.

Sandow was able to get photos of Lewis posing with 12 year old Frank Gotch Jr. in newspapers all over the nation on February 20. The Strangler claimed that Gotch senior had taught him many things early in his career, and he was going to pass the knowledge on to Junior. Lewis promised to take Junior "in tow" and make a wrestling champion out of him, just like his Dad. It was brilliant PR by Sandow but, 20 years later, Junior was working as a financial analyst in Houston. I also found it funny that the report called Lewis the ex-champion.[223]

Lewis and Stecher went against each other in Chicago on March 1, 1926. Stecher was to wrestle George Calza at the Coliseum, but Calza no-showed and Renato Gardini was used as a replacement. Fans were used to seeing Gardini job in title matches, so the card drew only 1,500. Lewis defeated Stanley Stasiak at Dexter Park Pavilion with his title on the line and drew 9,000 and $18,000. So Lewis won the night. It should be noted that Stecher was in the Coliseum, while Lewis' match was at the Chicago stock yard.

Paul Bowser was in Chicago that night looking for one of the two champions to wrestle Joe Malcewicz in Boston. He returned home with an agreement with the Stechers that Joe would wrestle in Boston on March 11, 1926 against a unknown wrestler for a purse of $12,500. Tony Stecher was led to believe the promoted "unknown" would be Jake Brissler and

Paul Bowser standing between wrestlers
George Clark (left) and Nick Lutze (right)

he could bring his own referee. Bowser weird style of promoting cards made the Boston fans think Joe Malcewicz would be in the main event.[224]

Joe Malcewicz

Stecher also wanted his purse paid before the match. On the day of the match, Bowser told Stecher he couldn't pay him the $12,500 but offered him a percentage of the house. Since the guy he was wrestling wasn't major, Joe agreed, but wanted his money before the match started. Bowser agreed, and the deal was made that Tony would be given a check before the start of the match. The Stechers must have suspected a dirty trick before even going to the arena.

Jack Brissler was the first in the ring followed by Joe and Tony Stecher. Then the Stecher/Jack Curley referee, Lou Grace, was not allowed into the ring and he was replaced with a Bowser referee, Leon Burbank. A group of men formed around Brissler, and he was hustled out of the ring. Joe Malcewicz, who had been sitting ringside in street clothes, jumped into the ring, undressed, and was declared by the ring announcer to be the "Unknown." Faced with the obvious double-cross, the Stechers jumped from the ring and returned to the dressing room as the announcer proclaimed Malcewicz "the new heavyweight champion of the world by forfeit."[225]

As Malcewicz wrestled sub Ned McGuire, the Stechers held a press conference in the dressing room explaining their side of the mess. They stated they were willing to meet Malcewicz at any time for a side bet of $10,000 and stated that the worry was the Bowser referee Burbank. The press reported the mess for what it was—a failed double-cross—and the wrestling public, used to double crosses after the Zbyszko/Munn match, never paid much attention to it. Malcewicz did claim the title in Boston, and used the match as PR over the rest of his career, but no one thought Stecher was afraid of him. Stecher was banned by the New York Athletic Commission (March 26) for a short period of time while the champion was on the West Coast, but that was lifted when Joe returned to the East to wrestle Jim Londos in May 1926.[226]

On March 6, 1926, a news release said that Billy Sandow had purchased the contract of Joe "Toots" Mondt, which had three years to run, from Ralph Mondt (Toots' promoter brother). You might wonder what that was about, if books like *Fall Guys* were right that Toots was a partner with Sandow and Lewis. I think Sandow, and most of the wrestling world in 1926, used verbal contracts and that Toots was just "talent." Most of Sandow's major wrestlers had jumped to the Curley/Stecher group, and maybe Sandow was worried about Mondt, so he wanted the contract on paper.[227]

For the first ten months of his title reign, Stecher had refused to wrestle Lewis. He claimed it was "pay back" because Lewis had refused to wrestle him while champion. It was something that champions did and would always do when faced with a trust buster type shooter. Joe Stecher wasn't a great thinker and all he really wanted to do was wrestle. He wasn't afraid of Strangler Lewis or John Pesek. Over the first ten months, their had been many offers by promoters from both sides for another Stecher/Lewis match. Chicago promoter Paddy Harmon offered $50,000 (June 3, 1925), St. Louis' Tom Pack offered $50,000 (June 29, 1925), Denver's Ralph Mondt offered $30,00 (January 8, 1926) and there were many more offers that didn't make the newspapers. After the mess with Malcewicz in Boston, Joe changed his tactics. He began to accept the challenges of Lewis and Pesek and it was Lewis and Sandow who backed down. Pesek, of course, was out of a job and game for anything.

On March 26, 1926, all the major promoters of the Stecher group met in Omaha for a conference. Present there were Jack Curley of New York, Tom Pack of St. Louis, Lou Daro of Los Angeles, Joe Coffey of Chicago, Tom Law of Wichita, Gene Melady of Omaha, and Aurello Fablani of Philadelphia, plus officials from Memphis and Atlanta. The meeting lasted into April. It would seem that the group discussed the movement of talent between territories and created a formula for the touring of the champion between cities. I believe this was a power play by the promoters to control national storylines and the world champion. They wanted the choice of champions to be in the hands of all the promoters and not controlled by individual managers like Tony Stecher, Billy Sandow or a Farmer Burns.

I believe that Tony Stecher gave in, at least in part, to their demands. The system would be less work for him, he'd have all the promotional problems taken care of, and contenders would be over with the fans before he ever got to a town. All he and his champion would have to worry about would be transportation to the next city.[228]

We know about this conference because a storyline in St. Louis came out of it. Joe Stecher told the members that he wanted a match with John Pesek and would stop wrestling on April 7 and begin intensive training at Hot Springs, Arkansas. The storyline, in St. Louis, was that all the promotions were bidding on the Stecher/Pesek match and that Tom Pack of St. Louis won. On April 16, both Pesek and Stecher signed for a St. Louis match on April 29.

On April 1, Lewis got himself into another auto-accident. This one resulted in a fist fight with a 52 year old Charles Wheeler in front of an apartment house at 430 Surf Street in Chicago. The brawl took place in a snow drift and was broken up by the police. They found Wheeler in a choke hold and Lewis bleeding from his lip. The two appeared together in front of Municipal Judge Padden. After both men shook hands and said they were sorry, the charges were dropped. Wheeler was quoted as saying: "If I had known who that big gorilla was, I wouldn't have tried it."

Lewis then beat Munn in Boston on April 5 and return to Chicago (April 19) to pin Rafalle Grenna in front of another good crown of 8,000 for promoter Paddy Harmon. Shortly after (May 11), a new Boxing and Wrestling Commission in Chicago banned all wrestling and amateur boxing shows until they could issue licenses to promoters. On June 19, a report had the commission drawing up new rules to govern wrestling. Perhaps this resulted in neither Lewis or Stecher appearing in Chicago for the rest of 1926.

On April 29, 1926, Ed Lewis was ringside at the St. Louis Coliseum to watch Stecher defend the title against John Pesek. Pesek won the first fall in three hours and fifteen seconds with a double wrist lock. Stecher returned to take the second fall with a double wing lock in 33 minute and 56 seconds. When the third fall had reach 40 minutes and 35 seconds, Stecher picked Pesek up for a slam, but John wiggled around forcing the worn out champion to drop him. Pesek fell through the ropes and landed on his head, to be counted out of the ring. Pesek had a concussion and was taken to a local hospital. Stecher was held under technical arrest by the police until it was revealed that Pesek injury wasn't serious. The decision by the referee was that the fall on to the floor wasn't the fault of the champion, so the winner was Stecher.[229]

Jim Londos continued to be Stecher's top contender and on June 10 the two drew 15,000 people to the first event at the new Philadelphia Municipal Stadium. Stecher defeated Londos in 1:50:26. Londos, who had trained for the match with Jack Dempsey, had an unusual ability to gain popularity with each loss, and was becoming one of sport's biggest draws.[230] The Stechers then returned to Los Angeles to draw more than 10,000 at the sold out Olympic Auditorium on June 16, again beating Ivan Poddubny.[231]

Bowser continued his push of Joe Malcewicz in Boston and on July 1, 1926 staged a super match between two title claimants, Strangler Lewis and Malcewicz, at the outdoor Braves Field. The match drew over 10,000 fans and ended up a draw. The two split falls in a contest that lasted three hours, twenty-two minutes and thirdly seconds. To me it was the highlight of Lewis' year.

A month later (August 2), Lewis met Malcewicz in Tulsa in front of a crowd of 8,000. The Strangler was billed as the champion but the promoter, Sam Avey, billed Malcewicz as having a title claim on the East Coast. Paul Bowser was present and billed as Malcewicz's manager. In a first fall, lasting one hour and twenty-three minutes, Malcewicz broke Lewis' headlock 30 times, but Ed looked like a sure winner—until the challenger caught Ed coming in and hit the Strangler with a side suplex (reverse flying mare) and got a pin.

After a 25 minute rest period, the two resumed with Lewis once again attempting to wear down Malcewicz with headlocks. After a third headlock, Malcewicz, dazed by the sleeper effect of the hold, threw Lewis out of the ring. Under the rules agreed upon before the match, referee Ted Tonneman disqualified Malcewicz. Sandow claimed Lewis had injured his side and refused to let the champion return to the ring, so Lewis won because of the foul without a third fall. This made the crowd unhappy, and while booing Lewis they lingered around ringside for 20 minutes yelling for a third fall, until the police broke them up.

1926 promotional photo of Ed Lewis

Los Angeles and the 1926 Forfeit

In August 1926, Billy Sandow and Ed Lewis took the wrestling war and their company to Los Angeles to battle the Stechers and Lou Daro face to face. It was another mistake.

On July 14 Stecher defeated local favorite Nick Lutze at The Olympic. A week later John Pesek defeated Lutze in the same ring. Lou Daro then announced that he had signed a Stecher/Pesek match for August 24.

Vernon is a small city located on the Eastern border of Los Angeles. It's an industrial city and the home of railroad lines and truck yards. The most famous business in the city is Farmer John, maker of the Dodger Dog. City taxes don't exist, and manufacturers are free to run their companies as they seem fit. No one really lives in Vernon; the 2000 census counted 91 people, all leasing buildings owned by the city. Vernon has its own power plant and charges every business in town for their power. Today it's claimed that the city has a surplus of 100 million dollars. In the big city of the angels, the sale of alcohol was illegal and the sport of boxing was controlled by a ton of rules. In 1907 an entrepreneur Jack Doyle opened what was called the "longest bar in the world" in Vernon. It had 37 bartenders. Next door Doyle opened the small Vernon Avenue Boxing Arena in 1908 and claims are that 20 championship matches took place in the small building. I believe the arena held around 4,000 fans.[232]

On August 3, 1926 a promoter names John De Palma held his first card at the Vernon Arena. The main event had local Los Angeles Athletic Club coach, Walter Miller, meeting Joe Parelli, but the under card was filled with Billy Sandow wrestlers like Bill Demetral[233] and Toots Mondt. My guess is that Toots Mondt was the booker.

While Stecher was in training for the Pesek match at the Olympic, Lewis and Sandow showed up in town ballyhooing a match with Stecher. The two posted a $5,000 check with the State Athletic Commission for a match with Stecher and went so far as to offer to "meet Stecher in some telephone booth" to "settle this matter once and for all."

John Pesek

Now, throughout history, the normal move for a wrestling champion is to tell a "trustbuster" type challenger like Lewis to get a reputation by beating a "policeman." Joe Stecher didn't do that. The champion signed a contract with Lou Daro to meet Ed Lewis at any time and posted his own $5,000 check with the commission. This move called Lewis' bluff.[234]

Capt. Seth Strelinger, chairman of the California State Athletic Commission, then stated that he had decided to act as matchmaker and ordered both parties to meet in his office. He promised a Stecher/Lewis match or someone would lose $5,000. On August 23, Lou Daro, with Tony Stecher, and Vernon promoter John De Palma, with Billy Sandow, met in Strelinger's office. After an argument, Strelinger gave Daro the match and De Palma received a payment from The Olympic to allow Lewis to wrestle at the larger arena where more fans could see the match and more taxes would be paid to the state. Strelinger and Daro wanted to stage the match two weeks after the big Stecher/Pesek match and Stecher agreed. Sandow refused, and claimed he needed over a month to get Lewis in condition and wouldn't be ready until after September 28. All this came after Lewis had been claiming in town for a month that he would wrestle Stecher "any place, any time." A date for the super showdown was set for October 6, 1926, at the Olympic.[235]

John Pesek, like most of Sandow's other wrestlers, had left the camp of Sandow and couldn't, at the time, be considered Lewis' policeman—but he still was very independent and posed a major problem for any champion. Pound for pound, he is considered by many historians as a contender for the title of "best shooter in wrestling history." Most champions would avoid meeting him in a title match, because he had money of his own and was very capable of a double-cross. Stecher knew Pesek and felt size made him the better wrestler, but the two were also friends and had trained together in Dodge many times. Pesek was not a stranger to Joe.[236]

On August 25, Stecher and Pesek wrestled to a two-hour draw. Now the result was predicted in local newspapers, so that would make the match seem like a "work." But the match was described as an uninteresting match with lots of boring stand up and Stecher spending a lot of time on the defensive. The reports were also pretty bare, without much detail. This makes me wonder if Pesek was playing around and the match was a "shoot." I checked most of the local newspapers and the only clues I saw was one report that the referee seemed to refuse to count a fall on Stecher when Pesek had him in a jam at the hour and a half mark. Perhaps the two wrestlers, who were both considered the best shooters in the sport, had some agreement to do a "contest," or I'm just seeing something that wasn't there. Either way, we will never know. This match is the least remembered of the three Stecher/Pesek matches of 1926, and mostly overlooked considering the events that follow.[237]

Lewis defeated old friend Mike Romano in Vernon on August 31. Romano was bleeding from the nose and mouth, so the ringside doctor stopped the match before the second fall could start. On the under card, Wayne Munn beat Howard Cantonwine and Toots Mondt beat Bill Demetral.[238]

On September 14, Lewis defeated Wayne Munn in Vernon two straight falls. Toots Mondt beat Mike Romano in the semi-main event.[239]

On September 25, it was announced that the October 6 Stecher showdown with Lewis was off because the Strangler had broke a bone in his left elbow training with Toots Mondt at their Garden Grove gym. The commission doctor stated that Lewis would not be able to perform for six weeks.[240]

More bad news followed when Lewis's illusions of a mixed match with Jack Dempsey were crushed when Dempsey lost every round of a ten round title fight with Gene Tunney in Philadelphia on September 23, 1926. The rules in Pennsylvania only allow 10 round fights, but it was a good thing for Dempsey because it looked like Tunney would have KO'ed him if the bout had lasted any longer.

Daro claimed all the seats in the Olympic were sold out and a major opponent was needed to fill the hole left by Lewis' no show. Billy Sandow offered Toots Mondt, but Daro went with a rematch using John Pesek against Stecher. This time the match would be to a finish.[241]

The October 6, 1926 Stecher/Pesek match ended up as one of the most controversial matches in wrestling history. The sold out Olympic fans saw Stecher win the first fall in 41 minutes and 10 seconds with a double-arm bar pin. Pesek evened the count with a head scissors and wrist lock in 21 minute and 45 seconds. The first fall was said to be unexciting grappling, while the second fall was a wild exhibition of the wrestling science. At some point—most think the last fall but from the report it may have been earlier—Pesek double-crossed the champion. Pesek is said to have torn into Stecher and at one point the referee broke a finishing hold for no good reason. Then, with the crowd in a frenzy, Pesek had Stecher submit after what looked like a wrist lock. At first the crowd thought the referee had ruled Pesek the winner, some even stated that Pesek's arm was raised, but then the referee, Tommy Travers, ruled Pesek's hold an illegal arm strangle and disqualified Pesek. The crowd hissed and booed the decision as they threw objects into the ring in protest. Claims by the Pesek's relatives have Stecher crying in the ring but Dodge historians claim it was Pesek crying.[242]

A hearing was conduced two days later with all sides present with the referee. Apparently no two people could agree on what actually happened. It was alleged, by some, that Pesek had thrown Stecher with all sorts of holds, ranging from "figure fours" to hammerlock cradles and crotch, wristlocks, strangle holds and just plain muscle wrenching. Nothing came out of the hearing, and referee Tommy Travers' decision was upheld. Legend says that Joe Stecher gave the winner's share of the purse to Pesek.

It may be that John Pesek still had a contract with Max Baumann, but John had split from the Sandow group by the end of 1926 after an argument with Toots Mondt in a Kansas City gym during the training for the first Wayne Munn match. There was a gym (shoot) match between the two and Pesek won. Sandow was upset and a talk with Max Baumann resulted in John quitting the company. In 1926, Pesek's affairs were being handled by a cousin named Joe Dus, but Tom Pack was also helping the "Tiger Man." Some claim that Pesek's double-cross of Stecher was a plot by Billy Sandow—that Sandow or Max Baumann had paid off Pesek or still had some type of control over the ex-policeman. I don't know, but it seems to fit Pesek's ego and I feel he was on his own. I respect John Pesek as a true hooker, but as a "pro wrestler" his conduct against Stecher and Marin Plestina was a disgrace.

The Pesek double-cross was also a major blotch on Stecher's career. Up until that night, his history and record made him seem like the best wrestler in the sport and he believed it. The Pesek affair seemed to hurt him personally and professionally, and change his opinion of himself. He became just another pro wrestler working matches, and these feelings might have been a major factor in his retirement a year later.

Billy Sandow had actually left Los Angeles on September 30, having to travel east because of the death of his father-in-law. On October 8, 1926, Lewis went into the commission office and told Capt. Strelinger that the Stecher match was off and he wanted to go home. He said he hated Los Angeles so much that he was willing to forfeit the $5,000.[243]

In early November, there were reports coming out of Chicago that a businessman had offered $100,000 for a title showdown between Stecher and Lewis. The next day, November 6, Chicago promoter John "Doc" Krone offered a $75,000 purse for the match.

Lou Daro had scheduled the Stecher/Lewis match for December 1 at the Olympic but on November 22 Billy Sandow sent word to the California commission that he refused to have Strangler Lewis wrestle Stecher in Los Angeles, and wanted the $5,000 transferred to another state. Daro then replaced Lewis with Jim Londos, and the two stars wrestled to a two hour draw in front of another sold out Olympic. On December 2, the Stechers and Lou Daro were awarded Lewis' $5,000 appearance bond. Both sides received $2,500 of Billy Sandow's money.[244]

After Sandow and Lewis left town, there are no more wrestling cards in Vernon, and promoter John De Palma disappears. In early July 1927, a fire burned the Vernon Arena (or Coliseum) to the ground.

At some time during 1926, Sandow published eight handbooks on conditioning, self-defense, and how to wrestle. It was similar to the Farmer Burns and Frank Gotch books written while he was champion. The books were filled with photos of Lewis, Mondt and Sandow demonstrating holds and training exercises. They were called *The Sandow-Lewis Library* and can be bought today through Paladin Press.[245]

Stecher went out on tour wrestling through the South and Wichita, into Philadelphia and New York City, before hitting St. Louis. The East had reopened its doors to pro wrestling and it had a new hunger for entertainment, with new arenas being built for the sporting public. New stars were created and styles changed to fit a public who didn't see pro wrestling as a true sport but something to have fun with and be entertained by. There was a need for wrestler/performers, and the idea of only true shooters being the stars went out the window. The number of cards in each city and the number of matches on each card increased. More wrestlers were needed, but the number of actual shooters remained at a stable number, so over time the number of performers began to dominate the true wrestler types. For the most part, the championship matches were still presented in a serious way, but the undercards were filled with brawling and wrestlers flying out of the ring into the audience. The promoters gained more control and they wanted the power to say who would be champion in their own small company. The days of Gotch, Stecher, and Lewis controlling wrestling were coming to an end.

The idea in 1927 was that the promoters would work together to make agreements and promote a national storyline that would benefit everyone, but as the sport progressed into the 1930's it found that satisfying the needs and ideas of the many groups wasn't that easy. Wrestling wars were created that made the Stecher/Lewis troubles in the 1920's look small time.

A strange event took place on December 19, 1926. Strangler Lewis defeated Mike Romano in Philadelphia. Now, there is nothing strange about Ed beating Romano—he beat him all the time. The weird part is the promoter being Ray Fabiani and Jim Londos wrestling on the undercard. A major member of the Stecher promotion booking Lewis might show that the ice between both groups was melting.[246]

Lewis then was in Boston on January 13 to wrestle a two-and-a-half hour draw with Pat McGill for promoter Paul Bowser.

On January 21, 1927, a report pops up saying that after Toots Mondt lost to Joe Malcewicz in Tulsa, he and Billy Sandow had a heated argument in the dressing-room. Some believe that the two broke off their business partnership at that point. I don't know. It may have just been a worked storyline, after all the reports of Toots training with Lewis in 1926.

Stecher defeated Nick Lutze in Philadelphia on January 7, 1927. On the under card, a new major star named Ray Steele (Pete Sauer) defeated Jim Londos by decision. In the following years, Steele would become Londos' greatest opponent, wrestling each other in every major city in the country. Both were working for Stecher at the time and on January 18 Stecher got a win over Steele at Atlanta. Steele, who was billed under his real name Pete Sauer in the South and Los Angeles, was a major hooker and a fine performer. Fans seemed to love him win or lose and he was a major draw across the country.

On January 23, Billy Sandow and Lewis with the Stechers present met with Aurelio Fabiani in New York City. They talk about a title match in Philadelphia. No news came from the meeting.[247]

Champions worked a much tougher schedule after 1927. Gotch, Stecher, and Lewis used to train in large cities for a least a week before major matches, but under new agreements and with every territory

Ray Steele

wanting a title match, the champion might be on the road for 4 to 6 matches a week. The title matches became shorter but there were more of them. For the first 3 ½ months of 1927, Stecher was working all over the country and didn't get a rest until mid-April.

Other than his trips to Boston, Lewis' travels consisted of mainly mid-west trips. He wasn't making much money and he was forced to read all the newspaper stories about him running out of the Stecher match in Los Angeles. On February 28, Lewis beat Romano in Chicago. It was the eight match between the two in the Windy City. He and Sandow realized they needed a new plan.

Stecher defended the title against Renato Gardini at New York City on March 7 in front of 10,000 for Jack Curley.[248] Stecher then wrestled for Tom Pack in St. Louis (March 15) beating another new star in Paul Jones.

Pack then traveled to Philadelphia to meet with the Stechers. The topic was Ed Lewis. Pack wanted to promote the super match with Lewis. Tony Stecher knew that he also needed the big money match, but didn't think, after what happened with Pesek, that it was wise for the champion to wrestle someone outside their trust or company. I think they agreed that Joe would be willing to work with Lewis if he would dump the idea of the Sandow group and cross the line. Of course, the story was released to the public in a different form. Pack's storyline was that Lewis hadn't wrestled a major wrestler in over two years and needed to meet one of the contenders, but, if he did that, Stecher would wrestle him.

Pack then traveled to Kansas City and ate dinner with Billy Sandow in his home (around March 20). Pack explained the plan to Billy. The idea was for Lewis to come over and at least work with the Stecher side. The first step would be a major match with John Pesek in St. Louis on April 4. Sandow knew he hadn't made major money during the war with the Stechers and they could make a ton of it if they just worked with the new promoters and quit playing games. So Sandow, Lewis and Bowser agreed to Pack's plan. Others like Fabiani, Daro, and Law were in on the deal, but I don't know if Jack Curley was happy with the idea.[249]

The Lewis/Pesek match was announced in the press, and on March 24 Lewis and Sandow visited Pack in St. Louis to scout locations for a training site. The plan had Lewis training at the National Gym during the week leading up to the April 4 match.

After the October 6 attempted double-cross on Stecher, Pesek didn't wrestle for the rest of the year. Pesek was friends with Joe Stecher, and I don't think Joe held any resentment against his fellow Nebraskan. I think Joe felt the champion should be the best wrestler and it was his own fault in letting Pesek get the best of him. Sometimes you make a friend out of a bully by beating them, but then I'm probably goofy as hell. As for everyone else but Tom Pack, Pesek had killed his career and didn't wrestle again for the rest of 1926.

Tom Pack was helping manage Pesek, who was still a major star in St. Louis. The only performer bigger in the city was Jim Londos. So Pack booked Pesek against Londos on January 25, 1927.

Jimmy was also kind of damaged goods at the time. In Memphis, on January 14, he was taken into police custody, and booked for larceny.[250] A Mike Casseras of Jackson, Mississippi, charged he was ripped off of $12,000 after betting on the outcome of a fake Londos wrestling match in 1925. Ripping off amateur gamblers was how pro wrestlers made their living in the early part of the century and Londos would have been playing the game too. But by 1925 most wrestling promoters realized they were looking for major trouble if they encouraged fans to bet on a "worked" sport and they had moved away from their gambling past. These charges against Londos were published across the nation and would be brought up by his enemies for the rest of his career, but when the charges were thrown out of circuit court on March 3, 1927 very little was written. In most people's eyes, you had to be really dumb to bet major money on a pro wrestling match in 1925. We know Londos never went to trial, but one of wrestling's major stars being arrested ended, for sure, any involvement the sport had with gambling. The same cannot be said of boxing, baseball, basketball, and about every other sport in America.

It would seem, at least to most smart fans, that Londos was going over the Pesek that everyone in the wrestling world was mad at, but that didn't happen. The match ended up being a four-hour classic. The 185 pound Pesek lost 13 pounds and the 200 pound Londos lost 10—and the match. Pesek won the first fall with a head scissors and arm lock in one hour and twenty-seven minutes. Londos won the second fall in one hour and forty-two minutes after five rolling headlocks. Pesek then won the third fall in 49 minutes and 10 seconds. The 10,000 fans called the match "great", and reports claimed there was no rest holds! The semi-final between Rudy Dusek and Paul Jones lasted 1:10:30. They loved that match too.[251]

The result cost Londos a match with Stecher and seemed hard to explain at the time but Tom Pack had plans for Pesek. He wanted Pesek over in St. Louis before a match with Lewis.

On February 25, 1927, a story in *Collar's Eye* and reprinted in the *Lincoln Ne Star*, stated that John Pesek was back in the Stecher trust. It claimed that the promoters held $21,000 of his money and that he could only get it back if he return and behaved himself. The money seems to have been impounded after the October 6 match. As punishment he would be asked to do a number of "jobs." On March 16, Pesek lost two straight falls by disqualification to Jack Sherry at Columbus.

Lewis' first match in St. Louis in almost three years did take place on April 7, 1927. It was a finish match and Tom Pack started the contest before the semi-final of Paul Jones and Joe Zigmund (Mayor of Brainard, Nebraska) at 9:00, so that fans might get some sleep in case of another wrestling marathon. The pre-match publicity was filled with all the normal Lewis' lies. He had only been a pro 12 years, misspelled his real name, talked about his college degree, the five-hour draw with Stecher was a brutal match, he lost to Munn by a foul, the record with Stecher was even, and he had only met Pesek one other time, but he was billed correctly as the ex-champion.[252] Pesek weighed 188 pounds to Lewis' 230, a difference of 42 pounds. There were 9,000 fans in the St. Louis Coliseum, but the paid attendance was 8,672.

The Strangler won the first fall in 1:03:19 after four headlocks. Pesek fought a tough battle but Ed's size overpowered him. Pesek came back in a glorious fashion, pinning Lewis using a flying mare off an arm lock in 29:05. Looking fit and as fast as ever, Lewis pinned Pesek in the third fall with a combination head scissors and a arm bar in 7:51.[253]

Tom Pack then visited the Stechers who were vacationing at Hot Springs, Arkansas, around April 13. Pack offered Joe a large purse, said to be $75,000 (I don't believe that number) for a title match with Lewis in St. Louis. Reports are that Tony and Joe were willing to "play ball" and this time they weren't talking about baseball.[254]

Following the Lewis match, John Pesek's career took a downward turn. On June 9, he has given a St. Louis rematch with Jim Londos and got beat. He then returned to Los Angeles to wrestle a draw with Jimmy (July 20). On August 3, he had a contenders match with Paul Jones, and, if he had won, he would have gotten a rematch with world champ Joe Stecher—but he lost. Pesek then went to Philadelphia for loses to George Calza (October 12) and Nick Lutze (November 18).

On April 11, 1927, Lewis' old friend Wladek Zbyszko finally got a shot at the world title, something Ed would never give him, losing to Stecher in New York City. Stecher also beat Wladek in Atlanta on May 26. Twice during the year Stecher defended the title in front of 10,000 fans in Philadelphia (August 2 & October 28).

On June 2 there is another report, this time out of Boston, that Toots Mondt was breaking off his relationship with Sandow and Lewis. Regardless of the rumors, Toots continued to wrestle and lose to Lewis in title matches and was still one of Ed's trainers.

Old friend Bill Demetral had been giving Billy Sandow trouble in Chicago. Demetral had obtained a $5,000 loan from Sandow, with his home as collateral. Demetral reported to the *Chicago Tribune* sports editor that the money and the fear of foreclosure was a tool used by Sandow and his trust to make sure Demetral wouldn't beat Lewis during a title match. The newspaper published that story and others exposing the workings of pro wrestling in the city. This may have been a reason why Lewis stopped working in Chicago in late 1926. The governor of Illinois ordered an investigation and threatened to ban wrestling in the state. A Legislature committee, investigated the charges, caused the cancellation of a big outdoor June 16 card at Wrigley Field, Chicago, where Ed Lewis was booked to wrestle Joe Malcewicz. Sandow spent a lot of money in an effort to stop the probe but on July 1, 1927, he, Lewis and Demetral appeared before the committee and testified under oath. It's claimed that Lewis saved the day by claiming he wasn't afraid of any wrestler and was willing to wrestle Bill Demetral then or at any other time to prove there was no way the Greek could beat him. Demetral declined the challenge and the investigation ended.[255]

On September 27, 1927, Jack Dempsey lost his rematch for his heavyweight boxing title to Gene Tunney in Chicago. This was the fight with the most famous round in boxing history. Dempsey had been out classed for six rounds by Tunney, but in the seventh he caught him with a right hand and followed up with a series of hard punches as the champ fell near the ropes. Dempsey didn't go to a neutral corner and referee Dave Barry refused to count until Jake moved away. Tunney got a "long count" and made it back to his feet. Dempsey had two minutes left in the round to finish the hurt champion, but was out-boxed for the rest of the round and for the next two rounds. By the end of the tenth round, Dempsey was out on his feet and Tunney won an easy decision. Once again Tunney had proved himself to be Dempsey's master, but over the years all the public would remember was the seventh round and the "long count."

There are many similarities between Ed Lewis and Jack Dempsey: both were creations of manipulative managers, both were hated by the public as champions, but became hugely popular after their careers ended, perhaps because they represented a type of credibility their sports had

Ed "Strangler" Lewis

lost. Dempsey fought only one major fighter as champion—Willard was an oaf, Brennan was sick, Carpentier was small, Gibbons was old, and Firpo was unskilled. He ran from men like Harry Wills and Harry Greb. The only top level fighter he met was Gene Tunney, and he lost at least 18 out of 20 rounds. Tunney's problems were that he was an intellectual who lived with the upper class and read books, he didn't care what the public thought of him, and didn't believe in the idea that a champion fought until beaten. Because he was only allowed to fight Dempsey in 10 round fights, he was also the first heavyweight boxing champion to win his title by decision. Tunney was not the type of fighter the American public and reporters wanted. As time passed, Dempsey remained in the public eye and he was remembered as a great champion. But Dempsey had his Tunney, as Lewis had his Stecher. Worse for Lewis, he also had a Londos.[256]

Knowing the friendship between Lewis and Dempsey, it's very possible that Ed was at the Chicago fight that night. Everyone else in the world was.

On November 8, Lewis defeated Paul Jones in St. Louis in two straight falls. During that month Billy Sandow posted another $5,000 bond with the Athletic Commission for a title match with Joe Stecher. On the 28th, the Stecher brothers visited with Tom Pack in St. Louis.

The February 20, 1928 Stecher/Lewis Match

On December 21, 1927, contracts were signed with Tom Pack, by both Lewis and Stecher, for a world title match in St. Louis to be held February 20, 1928.

The match was billed as a "shoot" from day one. In January 1928 Lewis had 4 matches beating Wayne Munn twice, Rudy Dusek, and Toots Mondt. He then went into strict training. Working with Mondt, Marin Plestina, and Pat McGill, he ran in the morning and wrestled all afternoon. After working at a training champ in Kansas City, he moved to the St. Louis University gym on February 14. He seemed to be in perfect condition on arrival. His weight was officially 224 but reports were that he at times it had gone as low as 217 pounds. Photos taken before the match back up all the claims.[257]

Stecher had been training for the match since December 14 in Dodge and moved to the St. Louis Knights of Columbus gym in the week leading up to the match.[258] He had been through a hard active two years and eight months as champion, traveling back and forth the country defending the title against such wrestlers as Jim Londos, John Pesek, Ray Steele, Wladek Zbyszko, Dick Daviscourt, Jim Browning, Paul Jones, George Calza, Rudy Dusek, Nick Lutze, Charles Hanson, Renato Gardini, Yussif Hussane, and many others. He had backed down from no one and had accepted every challenge. But in 1927, something had changed in Stecher. Around his hometown of Dodge he became more withdrawn and did less socializing with the people in the town. Rumors were being spread that he was worn-out and talking about retirement. Up until the Los Angeles match with John Pesek, he had believed he was the true champion able to actually beat everyone. Perhaps the double-cross took away Joe's idea that there was sport in pro wrestling. He began to see it as just entertainment and a fantasy for others. By 1928 Joe didn't want to play the game anymore. He had left wrestling at least twice before and 1928 seemed like a good year to say good-bye forever.

The February 20, 1928 match drew more than 7,500 people, including the acting Mayor of St. Louis, two State Senators, the Circuit Judge, the City Registrar, twenty city officials of Evansville, Ind., more than fifty newsmen, two wirer services, and most of the major wrestling promoters in the nation, including Jack Curley, Julius Siegel, Paul Bowser, Ed White, and Ray Fabiana. (I think Lou Daro called in sick, having lost a street fight to one of his wrestlers, Mohanned Hassen, in January.) Special trains arrived from such cites as Hannibal, MO, Kansas City and Chicago, and the price for a ringside seat was $25. The gate ended up at $65,000. Offers for a national radio broadcast were turned down by the promoter Tom Pack, and overtures from film companies were refused because the high powered lamps would produce too much heat for the wrestlers and the fans. On the night the arena was actually very cold, with overcoats being used by just about everyone.

$25 ticket to the February 20, 1928, Stecher / Lewis match

The rules were set for a two out of three fall match with no time limit. A foul would end a fall but not cost the guilty wrestler the complete match. A rule was made that stated that when the wrestlers were separated on the ropes, they would return to the middle of the ring in a standing position before continuing the match.

The under card had Jim Londos and Toots Mondt winning matches. Lewis was the first to enter the ring with Billy Sandow, Pat McGill and Marin Plestina. Stecher followed accompanied by Tony Stecher and Nick Lutze. Lewis weighed 227 and Stecher was 225. Stecher was announced as the World Champion. Lewis was the challenger, announced as the "headlock king."

The first fall saw both men wrestling defensively, with Lewis slightly the aggressor. Most of the fall saw the wrestlers standing, but Lewis did take Stecher down a few times, but no real holds were applied. Unlike in past matches, Ed was more willing to mix, with Stecher waiting for Lewis to make a mistake. Neither wrestler received much punishment. Things seemed to speed up at the two hour mark and the end came unexpectedly. At two hours, sixteen minutes and 32 seconds, Lewis took Stecher down and rolled him into an arm lock and body block for the pin. Tony Stecher protested the fall, claiming Joe was given a fast count by referee Harry Sharpe.

Back in the dressing room, Stecher was given a "pep" talk by friends Jim Londos and John Pesek (who were sitting together). They told him to stop playing the defensive game and take it to The Strangler.

Lewis returned back stage to the warm congratulation of his followers. Ed threw out his chest and mumbled, "Billy, it's easy."

Again Lewis was the first to enter the ring at 47 minutes passed midnight, followed by Stecher who was given an ovation by his fans. At the bell, the two circled, then Lewis dove for a bear hug type takedown, the same move that had worked to win the first fall, but Stecher stepped nimbly away, whirring around to land on top of Ed. Stecher put Lewis in the same type arm lock that had cost him the first fall. Stecher was then awarded the second fall in 56 seconds.

After another rest period, the third fall started at 13 minutes past one in the morning. Lewis continued to attack using body locks in an attempt to take Stecher back to the mat. Stecher was able to block his first few moves, but the two got entangled and fell to the canvas. Lewis got an arm lock and got on top of Stecher's shoulders. Knowing he was in big trouble, Stecher rolled, bridged, and wiggled in a desperate attempt to throw off the heavier Lewis, but Ed couldn't be kicked off. Stecher got to the northern edge of the ring and his left leg hit the lower rope. He then moved several more inches, and his right leg became twisted around the second rope, so far over that his foot was over the front row of seats. It was a test of strength, with Lewis having the vice-like grip as Joe fought to stop his shoulders from being forced to the mat. From Stecher's corner, front row, box seats, and the balcony came the chorus: "Ropes, ropes, ropes." With the crowd in a frenzy, referee Sharpe laid beside the two wrestlers as the champion, with no leverage to kick out, was forced down by the weight and strength of Lewis. With both shoulders firmly pressed on the canvas, he patted Lewis on the back and gave the signal that made him the undisputed world champion.

Billy Sandow jumped into the ring and led Lewis to his corner. Stecher, dazed, got to his feet and moved to the center of the ring, expecting to continue. He appeared amazed to see Lewis and Sandow celebrating the victory. Hundreds of fans rushed up to the ring yelling at the ref, while pointing to the ropes. The referee, Harry Sharpe, gave his decision to the announcer and Lewis was pronounced as the new champion. The time of the third fall was 12 minutes and 50 seconds.[259]

The next day, the result of the match was reported in every newspaper in America. Reports in out-of-town, pro-Lewis papers claimed there was no controversy over the result,[260] but in St. Louis the paper was filled for days of stories of Tony Stecher complaining about Joe being pinned with his feet in the ropes. Joe, himself, had very little to say. His statement was: "I have no alibis and am willing to take the result as a sportsman should. It was just the breaks of the game that it turned out as it did. But I still believe I can throw Lewis."[261]

Lewis stated that there wasn't any room for doubt in anyone's mind who was the better man. "Some people thought I'd either hop on a bicycle or get rough. I didn't do either, and did all the aggressive work. Stecher is game, I'll say that for him. He took a lot of punishment. But I don't think he is good enough to ever beat me." When asked if he would be willing to defend against Stecher in a rematch, he said: "Why should I? I think he showed that he is not to be rated with the top contenders." Lewis also made the point that he didn't win a title, he defended one.[262]

Joe Stecher retired a short time later to run his concerns in Dodge which included farms, a local movie house and a grain business. At the time, he seemed to have all the money he would even need. He was wrong.

Regardless of the screw finish, it has to be said that Joe Stecher's shadow no longer clouded the career of Strangler Lewis. Stecher's record versus Lewis at the time was five wins, three loses and two draws, but Lewis won the two title changes, and that's all the public would be allowed to remember. Unless you consider this 1928 match, in which he was billed as the challenger, a Lewis title defense—Strangler Lewis never defended a world title against Joe Stecher.

Now that the storyline has been covered, lets get to the politics. Why did the Stecher side allow Strangler Lewis to regain his title? When Sandow and Lewis agreed to join Tom Packs in March 1927, I don't believe he did so with the promise of getting the title, but Sandow may have been able to read the situation and anticipated that the promoters would look to Ed. The public had been promised a Lewis/Stecher match for at least six years, and it was too much of a build-up to let get away. With everyone agreeing that the match had to take place, the next problem was the finish. That also worked out, in that Stecher was tired out, had run through most of the major contenders, and was more than willing to retire. Unlike what you would think after three years or more of war, Joe liked Lewis and respected him as a wrestler. The name "Strangler Lewis" was bigger than his own and there would be no loss of "face" in losing to him. Especially if you threw in a screw finish—like having Joe's feet tied up in the ropes. The money would be good too.

Sandow, of course, wanted Lewis back on top, but Ed was almost 38 years old, not always in condition, and his eye

Lewis putting the traditional head lock on Babe Ruth

problem was an on-and-off thing. For most of us today, we are used to seeing photos of the rotund Lewis, and the idea of a fat Lewis fits in with our images of the wild 1920's and other fat personalities like Babe Ruth and Al Capone. The promoters and fans of that time were far less willing to accept that image of an out-of-shape champion wrestler. The promoters and Billy Sandow were always pushing Ed to lose weight. I think Lewis' weight loss before this match wasn't because of a possibility of a shoot but because the promoters wanted Lewis to look like a champion. By the date of the match, he only weighed three pounds more than Stecher. So Lewis was given his title back. It was billed as his third title reign but if you include the two Olin title wins: five.

With this said, I don't believe the promoters were thinking of keeping Lewis champion. Lewis and Stecher had dominated pro wrestling's storyline since 1915, and it was time to give the fans new stars to watch and spend money on. I think promoters wanted the big national star Strangler Lewis on top, so they could make a new star out of the guy who knocked him off.

Who were these promoters that made Lewis champion? Tom Packs, Tony Stecher, and Billy Sandow for sure. Fabiani seemed in on it. Paul Bowser was always close to Sandow, maybe even the true third member of the trio. We do know that Jack Curley, who sat in the front row during the title change, was against it. The day after the match (February 21), an Associated Press story stated that the New York Commission would not recognize Lewis as world champion until he met and defeated contender Hans Steinke. Steinke was a 275 mass of muscle that Curley had brought to New York from Germany. No one knew how good he was, and that meant Billy Sandow would be afraid of him and Lewis would stay away. This fact, played up in the newspapers, would give Curley, Fabiani, and the states of New York and Pennsylvania reason to create a title line of their own.

Hans Steinke

The 1929 Title Reign

Following the February 20 title change, it didn't take Lewis long to get back in action. On February 29, he defeated Joe Malcewicz in Kansas City for promoter Gabe Kaufmann. Reports claim that Lewis was planning to tour Europe in the summer and that someone in Hollywood had offered the champion $200,000 to star in a movie.[263]

On March 6, he defeated Paul Jones at Atlanta and then attempted to defend the title in Chicago March 12. The big city was still being plagued by a "mark" commission. Lewis was to wrestle Alex Garkawienko, but the Chicago Commission was split about allowing the card to take place. One of the commissioners claimed that Garkawienko wasn't a European champion from Russia, was managed by Billy Sandow, and not a fit opponent for a world champion. The match was allowed to take place after Lewis agreed to post a $5,000 bond to meet the winner of a Chicago tournament to decide a true undisputed champion. The "mark" Illinois Commission would continue to disrupt Chicago for years, and do harm to one of the best pro wrestling markets in the country.

From day one of his new title reign, Lewis had the reputation of a champion who was guarded and wouldn't meet worthy contenders. The truth is that he was just wrestling Paul Bowser wrestlers, like Malcewicz, Garkawienko, Joe Komar, George Mcleod, Stan Stasiak, Lutze, and Howard Cantonwine.

On March 17, 1928, Tom Packs announced that he and Philadelphia promoter Fabiani would bar Ed Lewis from wrestling in their promotions unless Ed agreed to meet "legitimate title contenders." Lewis did not defend this title in St. Louis for the rest of 1928. It seems to me that there was a power struggle between promoters and Paul Bowser won the prize. The storyline in St. Louis was that Packs wanted Lewis to wrestle Jim Londos and Lewis refused. It's possible, but no sure thing, that Packs wanted Lewis to drop the title to his star Londos, but Sandow and Bowser had other ideas. This is the first sign of the rivalry between Lewis and wrestling next huge super star Londos.

Lewis believed, and justifiability so, that he "made" Londos. He didn't do jobs for Jimmy but he did put him over in many matches in Canton and St. Louis. The larger Lewis, in size and "push," had lost exhibition matches to Londos and given him falls. Lewis and Sandow felt they had made a lot of money for Londos and expected some loyalty, but after Munn's loss to Zbyszko, Londos jumped to the Stecher side, taking a bunch of other wrestlers with him. Lewis had developed a strong hatred for Londos and he was willing to do anything that would make him look bad.

On March 30, Lewis beat Toots Mondt at Houston. This was the last time Ed would defend this title against his old trainer and friend.

Lou Daro still had a use for Lewis and his title so he became part of the Sandow/Bowser alliance. Daro had a major territory in Los Angeles and a good arena with low rent, so throughout the 1920's and 30's he was able to use whatever talent or promoters he wanted. Daro was willing to work with anyone who could make him money. For the next few years, Los Angeles would be one of Lewis' strongest city. On May 2, 1928 Lewis returned to LA and defeated Nick Lutze at the Olympic Auditorium in front of almost 9,000 fans. The match lasted 1:29:35.[264] Lutze was very popular and a rematch to a finish took place on June 13 at The Olympic. Lewis won two out of three falls and drew a sellout 10,000 with a gate of $16,000.[265]

The Olympic's biggest draw early in the year was Jim Londos, but he disappeared from the city as soon as Lewis began making appearances.

On June 25, Lewis defeated Malcewicz in Houston and drew a record crowd. At the time, the National Democratic Convention was in town. The party ended up nominating Al Smith, who went on to lose to the Republican Herbert Hoover. So Smith, Malcewicz, and the country all ended up as losers.[266]

On May 28 and on July 9, Lewis defeated Marin Plestina in Minneapolis.[267] There was a story told in the book *Fall Guys* by Marcus Griffin. The story says that Toots Mondt ran into the trust buster Plestina at the Hotel Pfeister in Milwaukee around June 1926. The two went to Mondt's room for a drink. Mondt made Marin an offer to leave his manager Joe Marsh and join the Lewis group. He told Plestina he could go with him to Lewis summer home in Nekoosa, Wisconsin. Marian would then wrestle Lewis in a gym shoot, and if Plestina could win that match, Ed would drop the world title to him with in two months. If he lost the shoot, Marin would then "play ball," work matches and still make good money. Plestina had gotten a lot of publicity from manager Marsh, but very little cash. He was getting old and he had a family to support, so Plestina agreed.

In stories told by Mondt and Lewis, it was always Billy Sandow who had no faith in the Strangler and wouldn't let him take on "trust buster" types in contests. It was their way of telling fans that Lewis was game and not to blame for avoiding major contenders over the years. So this story is important to Lewis supporters.

Marsh got Plestina to Nekoosa, and Lewis liked the idea, but Sandow hated it. So they wrestled and Strangler Lewis beat Plestina two falls in less than thirty minutes. Griffin then claimed that Lewis defeated Plestina in "almost every big city in America."

I would love to believe that story and the idea of Ed beating Plestina in a "shoot" match, but there are problems. From results we find that Plestina had left Joe Marsh and was working for the Jack Curley group by April 1925 in Boston (against Bowser). The time line of the match, taking place in June 1926, seems realistic because Plestina was one of Lewis's known trainers before the Munn matches and the title win over Stecher. But the first match in an arena took place in May and then July in 1928. The record only has Ed defending the title verses Plestina three times. Why did they wait so long to wrestle? By the time they got in the ring, everyone was getting old. Was Sandow afraid of a guy working for him? Pesek, and even Dick Shikat, worked for him, and Ed avoided them too.[268]

I think Plestina needed a good job and joined up with Sandow, first as a trainer and later agreed to be talent for a few more bucks. As for Lewis being able to beat him in a shoot, I believe it. Nothing makes me think Plestina was a top level shooter.

Another wrestler would begin a career in 1928 that would become an important figure in Ed Lewis' career. Gus Sonnenberg was born on March 6, 1889, on a farm in Green Garden, Michigan.[269] After attending a country school, he moved to Marquette, Wisconsin in 1912 to live with his older sister while attending high school. He was known for his line play on the football team at Marquette High School. Sonnenberg played right guard and later was moved to tackle. He also was a kicker. In 1916 the Marquette football team went undefeated, took the U.P. championship and out scored the opposition 211 points to 7. After graduating, Gus then passed up scholarships to major colleges to go to Dartmouth. The university didn't offer athletic scholarships, so Gus worked small jobs to support himself while playing football. Possible because of WWI, he left Dartmouth to teach and play ball back in Marquette. He returned to Dartmouth in 1920 to play on a good team and he was good enough to make the all-American team at tackle. In the 1920 Dartmouth-Pen game he kicked an important 80 yard punt and was considered a major football star. He was smart, well spoken and

known as a lover of good poetry. He then left Dartmouth for the University of Detroit. He graduated in 1922 with a Law Degree. He then worked for an automotive company but would take time off to play pro football. Pro football was small time in the 1920's and Sonnenberg didn't make much money, even while being a star. From 1922 to 1928, he played with The Green Bay Packers, Columbus, The Ohio Tigers, The Detroit Panthers, and The Providence Steam Rollers. In Providence, he played alongside of John Spellman, who was also a pro wrestler. One night a bunch of the player went to the match to watch Spellman perform. Gus thought the sport was a joke and he claimed he could do better than anyone on the card. So on a bet, Sonnenberg was taken to a gym and trained as a pro wrestler. To the surprise of everyone, Gus was better than everyone.[270]

Gus Sonnenberg had his first match in January 1928, and followed that by winning 28 straight matches. He was a natural with the persona of a true star. It wasn't long before he came to the attention of Boston promoter Paul Bowser, who saw his potential and pushed him to the top level.

Unlike Wayne Munn, Sonnenberg was a good worker who had a feel for pro wrestling. He was small at 5' 7" and 200 pounds, but was explosive and powerful. His

Gus Sonnenberg

style was to work everything around a move called The Flying Tackle. He would fly across wrestling rings, like he did on football fields, to drive his head into the chest and stomachs of his opponents. He was quick on his feet and could deliver a series of tackles before the other wrestler could recover from the first. The true finisher was a tackle where he grabbed his opponents two legs and combined the football move with a double leg take down. The other wrestler would crash to the mat, hitting the back of his head on the canvas. When he missed the move, he would fly out of the ring into the crowd or to bump on to the arena floor. In a way, Sonnenberg was the first wrestler in 3D. A fan or news reporter at ringside had to keep their head up because at anytime Gus could end up in his lap.

Sonnenberg revolutionized pro wrestling. From the beginning of time, the major stars were defensive wrestlers like Gotch, Londos and even Stecher. With Sonnenberg, his offense was his defense. He was aggressive and never let up. There was action from the first minute to the last, and the fans loved the style. Gus's matches were short and sweet. His style was a result of the fact that he wasn't a "wrestler." He was an athlete and a "worker." Any mid-level true wrestler could have beaten him in a contest. But Gus was very tough and physical and the style could be called "stiff", but the idea was to put on a good show and entertain.

Within a few short months, wrestlers all over the country was using the flying tackle. Gus Sonnenberg probably influenced the sport as much as any wrestler in history. A lot of hardcore insiders and fans hated the style and called him "Gus the Goat," but the crowds he drew overcame any criticism.

On May 11, 1928, Sonnenberg defeated Wayne Munn at Worcester to set up a title match with Lewis. Bowser signed champion Lewis and Sonnenberg with the biggest guarantee in New England history. The story was that Lewis was promised $15,000 and Gus would get $7,500. The date was June 29, 1928, and the place was Boston Arena.

Bowser did a great job of promoting the match, filling the newspapers with stories of Sonnenberg and the storyline of a young wrestler meeting the feared Strangler. The advance sale of tickets was huge. The only true fear was the idea that the young performer, with only 40 matches and five months of training in his career, might choke and mess up the match. Lewis and Joe Malcewicz took a fast train from Houston and arrived in Boston the day before the match.

The match sold out the Boston Arena with 12,000 filling the building. It was only the third time in its history that the Arena had been sold out. The "standing room only" crowd sat in their seats, stood rows deep along the back fringes of the seats, and even hung from the bare girders that hung from the roof. It was a Sonnenberg crowd from the moment the bulky, square-rigged little figure poked his head out and walked to ring. Lewis followed him to the ring. Announcements were made and group photos taken, then the bell rang and the match started.

The first five minutes was slow, with both wrestlers feeling each other out, but Sonnenberg took Lewis down to the mat with an arm lock. It was soon broken, but from then on there was action every minute, with Gus always making the war and Ed always warding him off with a speed remarkable for a 230 pounder. Twice Lewis attempted the headlock and twice Sonnenberg hurled him across the ring to the delight of the partisan crowd. Lewis circled around the ring, always with the ropes close, so that a Sonnenberg tackle would carry him into them and not to the mat. At the 30 minute mark, Sonnenberg was raging like a wild man, charging and ramming his way through the heat to get at Lewis. He arm dragged Ed to the mat but the champion wriggled away and put Gus into a headlock. The challenger looked groggy and dazed after he broke free and Lewis jumped on him with another headlock. Gus stumbled away and three times he ducked under Lewis' attempt at another headlock. When Lewis following him to the middle of the ring, Gus slammed into the champion with his hardest flying tackle. Ed head went backward as he was knocked flat. Gus jumped on him with an arm bar and half nelson to get the pin in 37 minutes and 30 seconds.

Newspapers and hats flew through the air as the entire house stood to give tribute to the little man. Lewis laid stunned for a few minutes, with the air completely knocked out of him. He was assisted from the ring. When he returned for the second fall he lifted himself into the ring like a feeble old gentleman, rather than a champion of the world.

Sonnenberg slammed into Lewis at the start of the second fall, driving him into the ropes. Another smashing tackle put a dead look in the champion's eyes. As Gus attempted a third, Lewis woke up and stepped to the side. Sonnenberg missed his target and flew out of the ring, over the heads of startled reporters, to land head-down in a sawdust heap. He land there moaning as the referee counted him out. Sonnenberg couldn't get up and he was carried to the dressing room through the stunned crowd. Lewis' quick move had saved his crown and Sonenberg couldn't continue.

The match was a thrilling affair and everyone left the building wanting a rematch. Ed Lewis had got the football player over and pro wrestling had a new star.[271]

On July 12, Lewis announced he was going to take the summer off to tour England and Europe. He'd then return for a farewell tour of America before retiring at the end of the next year. Lewis left New York City on an ocean liner on July 20. I don't believe he wrestled overseas and it seems to have just been a vacation with his new girlfriend or perhaps he was looking for specialist to treat his Trachoma. He returned home on September 1. He was interviewed in New York, and the reporters commented that Ed looked fat. Lewis claimed the extra pounds came from drinking German beer. He also bought a completely new wardrobe in Paris.

Lewis and Sandow returned to Los Angeles to defeat Joe Malcewicz in two straight falls on October 3, 1928. The match drew a near sellout of 9,300 and a

Toots Mondt as a promoter

gate of over $16,000. The reports were that Lewis had "nice round cheeks" and "appeared to have a lot of excess flesh around his abdomen." One hour and 11 minutes into the first fall, they both were stunned after banging heads together. Lewis luckily landed on top of Malcewicz and got the pin. Malcewicz was still weak following the rest period and Lewis beat him in 2½ minutes with a series of headlocks.[272]

Joe Malcewicz is overlooked by many historians and Halls of Fame, but he was a talented performer and a true wrestler. As a major opponent of Lewis he developed a finishing hold he named the "backward body slam." I believe it was the same hold used by Lou Thesz as a "side suplex" in the 1950's. Malcewicz's hold was used as a counter to Lewis head lock, which couldn't be applied without giving your back to the opposition.

I wonder if it was Lewis, or even Malcewicz, who taught the move to Thesz.

Two weeks later on October 17, he wrestled the "Trust Buster", Marin Plestina, at the Olympic Auditorium. The two had wrestled a couple of other times in Minneapolis during the year, but this was billed as their national showdown—at least in Los Angeles. Lewis won the first fall in 41:26 with a headlock. Plestina surprised everyone by pinning Lewis using a flying mare in 12:45 to win the 2nd fall. This upset Ed and he returned with a vengeance to pin Marin in 2 ½ minutes using Malcewicz's backward slam.[273]

Lewis wasn't touring at the time. He was just headlining in Los Angeles and working a few dates in outlying Phoenix and Salt Lake City. On October 26, he did travel to Philadelphia to draw 7,000 in beating Paul Jones in 48:32.[274]

On the under card was one of the local stars on the East Coast named Dick Shikat, a powerful German wrestler who was being pushed in Philadelphia and the rest of the East Coast. Shikat was a major wrestler, but as a worker he was what was called a "crowbar." He worked some "stuff" and a lot of wrestlers didn't like getting into the ring with him. He was very popular with the type of fan who like their wrestlers to be real wrestlers.

Lewis vs Shikat

The top star in Philadelphia was Jim Londos. The Greek was having a huge year in 1928, with wins over all the major wrestler in Philadelphia, including John Pesek and Ray Steele. On June 25, 1928, Londos established his dominance on the East Coast by beating Dick Shikat on an outdoor card in front of 13,000 fans. Londos was drawing bigger crowds that any non-champion in history. Lewis probably was bought into town because Londos went on a five month tour of Europe. On December 9, 1984, Londos defeated European champion Karol Zbyszko, cousin of Stan & Wladek Zbyszko, in Athens Stadium, Greece, birth place of the Olympic games, in front of 65,000 fans.

Also on the Lewis/Jones under card was Toots Mondt. Toots had left the Sandow company because of a argument with the Baumann brothers. His wrestling career was also slowing down by the end of 1928 due to injuries, so he started working for Ray Fabiani, possibly as the Philadelphia booker. I wonder if it was Toots who got Lewis this booking in Philadelphia, an area he was considered banned in because he only wrestled Bowser contracted performers.

Mondt got a good push in St. Louis by Tom Packs in early 1929. He drew with John Pesek (Jan. 11), defeated Dick Daviscourt (Jan. 29), and jobbed to Jim Londos (Feb. 21). On March 5, Mondt wrestled a 60 minute draw with Dick Shikat. Mondt had known Shikat from Chicago where Dick had worked under cards on Lewis/Sandow cards, without ever being considered for title shots. Mondt knew his wrestling career was about over and Shikat also knew he wasn't going to get promoted over Londos without major promotional help, so Mondt became Dick Shikat's manager soon after the March 5, 1929 match. Mondt put over Londos in a few major matches in 1929, but was never really a major wrestler after 1928. He wrestled off and on for a few years, but only to fill holes and put over talent. You have to give Toots Mondt some credit as a booker/promoter, for he never made the mistake of pushing himself over the other performers—a fault many bookers suffer from.

Mondt was with Ray Fabiani for a short time but alliances with Jack Curley brought Toots into New York City, where he probably booked and bought into Curley's company as a partner. Even if he wasn't a partner with Curley, he became and remained one of pro wrestling's most powerful insiders. Toots Mondt was one of pro wrestling innovators, but it's hard to tell what he did and what he didn't, because he was also a braggart who took credit for everything. One thought on Toots you should kept in mind: Whatever he created, he also destroyed.

On a short vacation in Avalon (November 13, 1928), a small tourist town on the island of Catalina Island, Lewis announced his engagement with Miss Elaine Tomaso, daughter of Mr. and Mrs. Salvatore Tomaso of Glendale, California. It seems that Lewis' marriage with Miss Bessie McNear didn't last long (nothing was ever written about it) and it ended in divorce. The late Salvatore Tomaso was a well-known director and composer, and his daughter Elaine was a pianist and former actress.

Lewis returned to Los Angeles to beat Paul Jones again on November 21 drawing 7,000.[275] The unavoidable rematch with Joe Malcewicz took place on December 19 drawing 8,500 and a gate of $15,000. Billy Sandow missed the match as he was home in his Kansas City sick bed with the 'flu.[276]

Lewis / Sonnenberg, January 4, 1929

On November 14, 1928, President Calvin Coolidge pulled a switch in the White House that turned on the lights in the new Boston Madison Square Garden. The publicity stunt signified the completion of the arena construction. It opened to the public three days later. The Boston Garden was built and designed by Tex Rickard and it was created to be a show house for boxing, but over the years it became known mainly as the home of the Boston Celtics and their many NBA championships. In the 1930's it was second only to New York's Garden as the biggest and most profitable wrestling arena in America. None of this helped Tex Rickard, who died January 6, 1929 at Miami Beach, Florida, from complications following an appendectomy.

In December 1928, Paul Bowser booked the new building to hold the second Lewic / Sonnenberg title match on January 4, 1929. The loss to Lewis had done very little to stem the East Coast enthusiasm for Gus Sonnenberg. Most of the tickets were sold in advance and the event was a sure bet to set the all time indoor gate record. (There was also more betting that night than for any wrestling bout ever staged in Boston.) I wonder how many of those fans realized they were paying admission to see the end of a era in pro wrestling, and the last match in which Strangler Lewis would ever have a claim to the undisputed world title.

As in most major matches, both Lewis and Gus trained in the area for a week leading up to the match. Sonnenberg had the 'flu and there was some thought given to canceling, but it was pro wrestling—so no one thought much of the idea. Both wrestlers agreed that Leon Burbank, the same official that worked the Lewis / Munn match, would be referee.

On January 4, 1929, 20,000 fans crammed into the new Garden, with thousands turned away. Many felt that it would have broken the all-time gate record if only the Garden was bigger. More than 150 police officers were on crowd control, and there were three arrests for selling tickets without a license. Massachusetts Governor Frank Allen, his wife, mother-in-law and his secretary watched the match from a draped box almost directly behind Sonnenberg's corner. The mob was filled with the rich and famous of Boston.

Lewis' experience and skill counted little against Sonnenberg, who was a raving, drooling maniac, determined to

Ed Lewis title loss to Gus Sonnenberg
Boston, January 4, 1929

win the championship. Everyone present felt that Gus gave an exhibition of rough and tumble wrestling that was as exciting as any bout in the city's history The first five minutes was slow as they felt themselves out, but after that it was all action. Lewis attempted to counter Sonnenberg's tackles by turning sideways as he circled the ring, always along the ropes. This took away the "goat's" target and stopped any pinning attempt. Three times Sonnenberg tried ramming into Ed but all he could hit was Lewis' back. Gus's few actual wrestling holds were broken by Lewis without much problem. At one point Lewis kicked Sonnenberg in the head and applied his headlock. Ed shook Gus's head like a cocktail shaker, roughing and mauling him along the ropes while the crowd booed. When Sonnenberg broke the hold, Lewis put on another. Gus broke out again using his legs but the sleeper effects of the headlocks were wearing him down. Lewis beeled Sonnenberg across the ring and, confident of victory, opened his arms in an attempt to put on the finishing headlock. Through the daze, Sonnenberg saw his target, hitting Ed with a flying tackle and then mounted him for the pin. Time was announced as 29:46.

At the end of the first fall, Sonnenberg looked more used up than Lewis, but, when the two returned, Sonnenberg looked fresh and it was Ed that looked like an old man. For the next 8 minutes and 20 seconds Sonnenberg butted Lewis all around the ring. Ed clung to the ropes in an effort to save his title, then Gus's tackles sent the feared Strangler flying out of the ring. Twice he hit the floor and once Ed landed in the ringside press box. After the third time, referee Leon Burbank told Ed he was going to start counting. After seven flying tackles, Lewis laid on the apron, then got to his feet but couldn't make it back into the ring before the count of 10. Burbank then awarded the match to Sonnenberg on a "count out" but the press called the finish a "disqualification."[277]

Billy Sandow jumped into the ring yelling at Burbank saying that Lewis had his foot in the ring and shouldn't have been counted out. Many photos show that Ed had his head and shoulders thought the ropes but both feet were outside the ring.

Sonnenberg jumped out of the ring and headed for the dressing-room but was called back by promoter Paul Bowser. Gus was announced as new world champion and presented the "Ed Lewis belt." In Boston they used a set of rules, since the early 1920's, called AWA rules. Perhaps Bowser had created a fictional commission called the AWA, but whatever, after this match, Sonnenberg's title line would be called the AWA title.

Some reports say that Lewis and Sandow were paid $50,000 for doing the job and dropping the title to Gus (who made $8,000, at least in the newspaper). Why did they do a "screw" count out finish? Lewis never dropped his titles clean but it was also Paul Bowser's style of booking to have a "screw finish" in title changes and to save the clean finish for the rematch. Bowser did it all the time. I think Lewis also realized that regardless of how many clean jobs he did later to the new champions, all that was remembered, and talked about, was the title change. This match was filmed and shown in theaters across America and Europe.

Post Title 1929

There also is a story told in the book *Fall Guys* that says Sandow and Lewis were promised the title back at some point by Bowser. I don't believe it. Lewis would have been 40 years old and no promoter would want a 40 year old fat champion. Lewis had great value as a challenger, but making him champion again is hard for me to believe with Jim Londos and Gus around.

I think the plan in 1928 was for Lewis to go into semi-retirement in Los Angeles and only wrestle major matches, like rematches with Sonnenberg. In time, this would lead to a true retirement in a year or so. Lewis had moved into Glendale, California to be near his new girlfriend and investments. He had plans to co-own a restaurant, but the Depression kicked in during 1929 and everyone was worrying about money. So, from the results, he actually seemed to be more active in 1929 and the following years. Air travel probably made a difference, but he also didn't have to spend 5 days to a week before important title matches, training and doing interviews and other PR duties. Pro wrestling was in a new age with more cities and promoters running more cards, so Lewis was always in demand.

Lou Daro had booked Lewis into a Olympic Auditorium match on January 23,[278] but Lewis cancelled when Paul Bowser wanted Ed for a series of match on the East Coast, including a return to New York City's Madison Square Garden. Daro replace Lewis with none other than Joe Stecher.

In 1929, the Depression's first major "hit" in the country was the farm industry. By the end of the year, farmers were being offered less for grain than they paid for seed. That, and money lost in the stock market, forced Joe and Tony's return to pro wrestling.

During Stecher's return, he was more interested in making money than regaining fame. Joe no longer had ideas of winning titles or controlling wrestling. Stecher joined the Paul Bowser company in late January 1929.

So Joe was brought into Los Angeles to replace Lewis on January 23. He beat Paul Jones at The Olympic drawing 8,000 fans.[279] Bowser then had Stecher return to Boston to resume his 1927 feud with Joe Malcewicz. Joe Stecher then did a clean job to Malcewicz on February 21, 1929, drawing 6,500. This loss set Malcewicz up for a major title match with Sonnenberg and the job by Stecher showed good faith to Bowser and any other promoter who would think about using him. The sign was out to promoters, "Joe Stecher would play ball" and was willing to put people over. On April 17, Lou Daro booked Stecher in a rematch against Malcewicz in Los Angeles. Joe beat him and all the talk was about another match with Strangler Lewis.

Lewis rested for two weeks following the title loss, then beat Jim Clintstock in Philadelphia on January 18. On January 26, 1929 Lewis headlined the new Madison Square Garden (#3) beating Renato Gardini in front of 6,000. That large an attendance would have seemed good in any other arena, but the new Madison Square Garden held room for 20,000 and the rent was high. Still Ed drew a bigger crowd that any other of Bowser men in the arena.

Madison Square Garden, the third New York City arena to be given that name, was opened for boxing on December 11, 1925. Paul Bowser (or a front man using his talent, perhaps Stan Zbyszko), still at war with Jack Curley, began using the building in November 1928. Apparently he was losing money. The November 26, 1928 card drew 1,500.

On January 25, 1929, an Elaine Tomaso of Glendale, California gave an interview announcing she was going to be marrying Ed Lewis very soon. This took place in Chicago where Elaine was visiting relatives with her mother and sister. Her plan was to meet with Ed before his match with Marin Plestina on January 29 and make wedding plans. She was 25 years old, tall and athletic looking with a degree from Northwestern University School of Music.[280]

Lewis arrived in Chicago soon after, beating Plestina in two straight falls.[281] Plestina had become someone that Lewis would beat in just about every town on the wrestling map.

The crowning of the new champion got off to a poor start with other promoters when Tom Packs cancelled a card on January 24 that was to headline a Sonnenberg title defense, because Bowser refused to have Gus wrestle anyone but one of his own contract performers and he also wanted to use his own referee.[282] Packs did book Sonnenberg one semi-final non-title exhibition match (main event was Mondt verse Dick Daviscourt) with an unknown named Frank Jorgenson on January 29. Gus's tackling ability got good reviews but his actual wrestling ability seemed to be weak. He pinned Jorgenson in three minutes and fifty-five seconds and the card drew 4,000.[283] The fans didn't mind Sonnenberg but Packs had another champion he wanted to use, and it would be the last St. Louis would see of Sonnenberg as champion. On February 3, Sonnenberg beat Harold Cantonwine in his

Lewis with his third wife, Elaine Tomaso.

Madison Square Garden début but got a lot of heat from the New York press for only drawing 3,500.

Things pick up with champ Sonnenberg beating Stanley Stasiak in Memphis on February 13 in front of "big crowd."[284] In Chicago Gus drew 8,000 and $16,000 in beating Stasiak on February 25.[285] On April 3, Gus beat Stasiak in what would become his home away from home, Los Angeles, before an almost sold out Olympic Auditorium.[286] Hollywood loved little Gus because they loved stars and that's what Sonnenberg gave them—star power.

Lewis was keeping busy. On February 13 he returned to St. Louis and beat the national favorite Nick Lutze in an hour and four minutes. The card open with a comedy match between two eleven year-olds. "Young Dynamite Sonnenberg" wrestled a draw with "Young Strangler Lewis." Lewis would also beat Jim Clinkstock (March 5) and Nick Lutze in a rematch (March 22) in St. Louis. On February 25, Ed drew 7,000 in New York City beating Kola Kwariani. In Chicago he beat Kola Kwariani (March 11), Joe Malcewicz (March 26), Renato Gardini (April 16) and Matros Kirilenko (April 27).

Lou Daro booked the first ever Lewis/Stecher match in Los Angeles for May 1, 1929 at The Olympic Auditorium. Stecher had challenged Sonnenberg to a title match but was told to beat Lewis first. The Strangler was willing, but he wanted Joe Stecher's famous $10,000 belt to be on the line. After the title change, Lewis had his own belt in St. Louis and the Stecher belt wasn't passed on to the new champion. So the major angle and stipulation for the match was that the winner would get the Stecher belt. It was also billed as a "winner takes all" match.[287]

Stecher was the aggressor in the match. He got rough with the Strangler on numerous occasions but Lewis hung on and was able to out rough and out last him. Stecher got the scissors on and squeezed "Lewis' rather protuberant paunch" for over a minute before turning him over for the pin in 20 minutes and 51 seconds. The finish for the second fall had Lewis on the matt locked once again in the scissors, but this time through sheer strength, Ed stood up with Joe still locked around him. Lewis then slammed Stecher to the canvas and pinned him. It was kind of like a 1929 style "power bomb." Time was 16:02. Stecher was still hurting and dazed at the start of the third fall and Lewis pinned him using a headlock in 4 minutes and 13 seconds. The crowd was 10,395 and the gate, at high prices, was $28,540. A Lewis quote following the match was: "I ruined him at St. Louis when I took the title away from him. He knows I can beat him now." So Lewis showed Joe who was boss.[288]

As for the Stecher belt, the reports say nothing about it. So the stipulation seemed to have been forgotten or never really followed through on. All we know is that Tony Stecher had the belt when he promoted in Minneapolis in the 30's and 40's and all of his champions were photographed wearing it. I would bet Stecher got his cut of the gate too.

Lewis shopping with his third wife, Elaine Tomaso soon after their marriage in Riverside, CA.

On May 8, 1929, Ed Lewis married Elaine Tomaso of Glendale, California at the St. Cecelia chapel in Riverside, California. The Rev. Samuel Hughes did the officiating, Miss Carla Tomaso (Elaine's sister) was the bridesmaid, and Billy Sandow was the best man. Thirty friends of the couple were present. The report had Elaine's age as 25. They claimed Lewis was 34 but he was very close to 39 years old.[289] There were a lot of claims about a honeymoon, but Lewis was back wrestling at The Olympic on May 15, beating Dick Daviscourt.

On May 15, 1929, the Pennsylvania State Athletic Commission suspended champion Gus Sonnenberg for "wrestling unworthy opponents and refusing to met logical contenders."

Lewis, with his new bride, then traveled to Kansas City to beat Matro Kirilenko on May 20. Sandow lived in Kansas City and Lewis had probably stayed in the city for long periods after moving from San Jose. Lewis and Elaine then traveled to Tulsa for another big match up with Joe Stecher for promoter Sam Avey. I think Lewis had ties in Tulsa and probably wanted to show off his new wife. Stecher had set up their next match by beating Joe Malcewicz on May 13 in Tulsa.

The reports before the match claimed Lewis looked fat and every bit of 240. He also didn't train much, claiming he had been in the ring so much in 1929 that he didn't have to work out.

The match was the first wrestling event in the new Magic City Coliseum. Tickets were priced from $2 to $5, with 1,000 $1 seats going on sale when the doors opened. The match drew 6,000 fans.

Lewis was in poor shape for the match, forcing Stecher to do all the work. Joe won the first fall in 30 minutes with the scissor. Lewis won the second using the same "power bomb" finish from Los Angeles in 17 minutes. The third fall only lasted three minutes. Stecher broke his scissor hold because Lewis got to the ropes. In Tulsa, the rules usually were that wrestlers went to the center of the ring after a rope break, but not in this match. As Stecher turn to go to the middle of the ring, Lewis applied a double armlock and rolled backward to pin Stecher. Tony Stecher protested, to the referee, that the move was a foul, but Lewis and Sandow won the argument and the victory. Joe had been cheered through the match and out wrestled the booed Lewis in every way, but he was the loser.[290]

Lewis then took off the first week of June for a trip to Nekoosa to introduce Elaine to his father and mother. On June 4, the two were present at a dinner party at the home of Mrs. J. G. Gutheil. Lewis had owned a summer home or farm in Wisconsin for years. Lewis wrestled two matches in New York City in early June, so the honeymoon may have taken a short venture into the big city.

Paul Bowser had kept Lewis strong and undefeated for six months following the title loss. A lot of fans were used to Lewis and Stecher as champions and figured Sandow was working the same storyline as the Lewis/Munn matches, and that Lewis would get his title back in the rematch. In June Lewis signed to a third match in Boston with Sonnenberg. This time Bowser made sure no fan was turned away, by booking the match into Fenway Park. Both wrestlers trained in the city, and they were ready for a long two out three fall match.

25,000 fans filed into Fenway Park on July 9, 1929. Both the *Boston Globe* and the *New York Times* listed the gate at $90,000 which would have broken the record 1913 gate of Gotch/Hackenschmidt of $87,000 by 3,000.

Once again Sonnenberg was the aggressor, always trying to set up Lewis for one of his tackles. Gus took Lewis down with a sort of arm drag and worked the hold for a few minutes before it was broken. Gus hit his first tackle but it was on Ed's arm and the move only threw the ex-champ to one side. Gus then attempted a running Flying Tackle but Lewis, just like a football lineman, grabbed the incoming wrestler with his powerful arms and tossed him down with a twisting motion. Sonnenberg landed on his back. Lewis jumped onto the dazed champion and with his thirty pound weight advantage, pushed Gus's shoulders to the mat for the first pin fall loss in Sonnenberg's career. Time was 17:41.

In the second fall, Lewis had Sonnenberg dazed and on the verge of collapsing after three headlocks, but as Ed tried for a fourth, he was hit by a tackle in the stomach. Ed fell backward to the mat and as he arose the champion rushed in like a fullback hitting the line and sent Lewis flying. Lewis was helpless and pinned in 18:38.

Lewis had to be lifted from the ring and looked in bad shape on his return. Sonnenberg attacked Lewis with two tackles but on the third attempt Lewis stepped aside and Gus went flying. Sonnenberg should have flown out of the ring, but Gus caught himself in the ropes and saved himself a fall. Lewis attempted a headlock as Gus climbed back into the ring but the champion broke the hold, moved away, and then butted the Strangler over the heart. Lewis was pinned at two minutes and thirdly seconds of the third fall. Ringsiders and reporters claimed the match was thrilling and one of the greatest matches ever staged in Boston.[291]

A 12 minute copy of the Sonnenberg rematch was shown in theaters all over America and Europe.

Except for two Chicago matches with Matros Kirilenko, Lewis was inactive until September. He was back in Los Angeles going through the process of buying a new house in Glendale, so Elaine could stay close to her family. He was also making a deal with an Earl Peyton to go into partnership in a local Glendale restaurant called Earl's Broiler, located at 707-709 South Brand. Once the deal was completed, the name was changed to E. & E. Broiler. The two would later expand to three restaurants, one of which was located at 5th Street and Main, in Alhambra. Much later, Lewis owned part of a restaurant/cocktail bar located at 4300 Long Beach Blvd. in Long Beach. Lewis always claimed that he lost money in the restaurant business but his partnership with Peyton lasted a long time. Lewis' house seemed to have been on East Windsor Street, which was probably within a half mile of the Glendale restaurant.

Ed Lewis playing bartender at
the Glendale E. & E. Broiler

Match book featuring Ed "Strangler" Lewis

E. & E. Broiler match book

Billy Sandow followed Lewis to Los Angeles, buying a home in Brentwood Heights on the southern slopes of the Santa Monica Mountains. Sandow was the neighbor of Tom Gallery who was married to movie star and comedienne Zasu Pitts. Gallery was a minor actor who also became the boxing matchmaker at the Hollywood Legion Stadium during the 1920's and in 1933 at The Olympic Auditorium. He would become a member of the World Boxing Hall of Fame.

Sonnenberg was also in Los Angeles and on July 24 he defeated Joe Malcewicz at the Olympic Auditorium in front of 10, 700 with a LA record gate of $30,392.[292]

On August 7, 1929, the Pennsylvania Boxing Commission stripped Sonnenberg of his world title for not meeting worthy contenders and not agreeing to meet the winner of a Jim Londos/Dick Shikat match. It then sanctioned the August 23 match between Londos and Shikat for the world title.

The August 23 match was the final of a tournament between Londos, Shikat, and Hans Steinke. Londos had defeated Steinke and Shikat, so on July 12 Shikat defeated New York #1 contender Steinke at Philadelphia in 1:04:29 to advance to a final match with Londos.[293] Steinke had some sort of unofficial title recognition in the state of New York, so after his defeat, New York was brought into line with Pennsylvania and also sanctioned the winner of Londos/Shikat for the world title. This storyline was being followed closely in St. Louis newspapers and Tom Packs, who controlled Londos (well maybe it's better said that Londos controlled Packs) seemed more that willing to join Curley and Fabiani in the promotion of a new champion.

On August 23, 1929 a crowd of 25,000 watched Dick Shikat, during a rain shower, defeat the big favorite Jim Londos in one hour and 15 minutes using two crotch holds (I think body slams under a old name) to pin and injure Londos.[294]

Without a title, Londos had become pro wrestling's biggest draw and star. His only rival was the newcomer Sonnenberg, but Londos had been tested and proved to be the real thing. Why then did Curley, Fabiani, and Packs decide to go with Dick Shikat as their new champion? Londos had been working hard for some time all over the country and might have been looking for a major vacation before starting a major push in 1930. With his great conditioning, endurance, and ambition, Londos had been working an unbelievably hard schedule and even he needed time off. Londos, when messed with by promoters, was always willing to walk and leave for another territory, so perhaps his vacation could be seen as a protest to the Shikat crowning, but I've never seen that written anywhere.

Lewis was also being used by Bowser as a policeman for Sonnenberg. When ever challenged by someone they did not control, Bowser would tell whoever that he would first have to prove himself by beating Ed Lewis. Lewis, even at age 39, wasn't someone you wanted to face in a shoot. The Curley group believed that Shikat was a better match up with Lewis. Shikat was a very tough wrestler who was in his prime, unlike Lewis. Managed and trained by Toots Mondt, it's unlikely that Lewis would want to get in the ring with the big German in a shoot situation. So the Curley group wouldn't have to back down from anyone Bowser offered them, which also included Joe Malcewicz.

Londos was also damaged goods with a long history of lost title matches with Lewis and Stecher behind him. Unlike his reputation today, the Londos of pre-1929 was willing to do a lot of jobs to put other people over. He had losses on his record to Lewis, Stecher, Ray Steele, George Calza, Pesek, John Maxos, Dick Daviscourt, Gardini, and Malcewicz. He even had pull over Lou Daro at one point. Londos had also beaten most of those people in rematches and been undefeated for a couple of years, but he had a long history that could be used against him, and Lewis would do just that later.

Also a loss to Shikat didn't hurt Londos much. If Shikat had lost to Londos, it might have killed him. Some time as champion would build Dick into a star that could be used for years. So making Shikat champion probably was good thinking by the Curley group.

In September Lou Daro staged what was called an elimination tournament with the winner to meet Sonnenberg. I don't understand what happened in the tournament or how it was run, but the final had Lewis meeting Joe Stecher again at The Olympic Auditorium on September 4, 1929.

The match drew a near sellout of between 9,000 and 10,000. Lewis won the first fall in 23:34. Stecher used the scissors to win the second in 9:53. In the third fall, Stecher had Lewis locked into an ankle lock for few minutes. Lewis looked in bad shape but he finally escaped by kicking Stecher in the head. Joe fell back but got up dazed. Lewis jumped on him and got the pin in 19:11. The match was described as "workman like" with little emotion and Lewis did most of the work.[295]

So Lewis won the right to meet Sonnenberg for the title on September 18, but his ankle was so damaged from Stecher's ankle lock that he had to refuse to take the match. Stecher replaced Lewis in the title match.

Sonnenberg defeated the ex-champ Stecher on September 18, 1929 in front of 10,400 and a Olympic Auditorium gate of $35,000, which was, if everyone was telling the truth, a Los Angeles record. After the match it was announced that Lewis would get his title match with Sonnenber on October 23.[296]

Jim Londos was vacationing in Long Beach California during September and October of 1929. He was training and running daily on the beach. Londos being Londos, he was also working dates for good friend Pete Sauer (Ray Steele) in Phoenix. It was Steele's home town and it had just opened a new arena called the Phoenix Madison Square Garden. Londos, Steele and Dick Daviscourt were engage in a three man feud and they were drawing well in matches against each other.

On October 4, 1929, Lewis went out of his way to work for a small time rival promoter named Billy Hunefeld in Phoenix. After beating George McLeod, Lewis posted a $500 bond with Phoenix commission for a match with either Jim Londos, Pete Sauer (Ray Steele) or Dick Shikat. He stated he would increase the amount to $2,500 if any of the three accepted the match. Lewis claimed no conditions were attached and would wrestle the match for any promoter, at any time or place—or even wrestle the match in private with only the commission, Phoenix mayor, or city council and newspaper reporters present. This was an obvious grandstand play to make Londos and Steele look bad and take heat away from their feud.[297]

On October 15, Lewis posted a $250 forfeit with the Missouri Athletic Commission as a challenge for a match with Richard Shikat. No action was taken.[298]

On October 22, Gus Sonnenberg left the Los Angeles Athletic Club after a workout and was walking along a busy down town street. He was stopped by a small time wrestler named Pete Ladjimi (Pete Ladjone in the report) on the corner of Broadway and 7th street. Ladjimi pestered Sonnenberg for a match. Gus told him that he wasn't the local promoter, and he should go see Lou Daro. Witnesses claim that Sonnenber started to turn away as he was head butted under the chin by Ladjimi. Gus fell backward to hit his head on the sidewalk. The Police then took Ladjimi into custody, as Sonnenberg charged him with assault. He later was released on $100 bail. Sonnenberg was left with a cut lip and a bruise nose. The report appeared the next day in newspapers across the country. On November 13, 1929 Ladjimi was convicted of assault and battery by a Municipal Court Jury and sentenced to 30 days in jail. His lawyer appeal and Ladjimi was released under a $1,000 bond. In later year Pete Ladjimi would be connected to the Londos group and many people feel this was the Greek's attempt to get back at Lewis, for Phoenix, through his weak champion, Sonnenberg.[299]

The day the report hit the newspapers, October 23, 1929, Sonnenberg and Lewis wrestled for the title at the Los Angeles Olympic Auditorium in front of 10,000 with a gate of $31,000. Sonnenberg took a beating during the first fall but won with a surprise flying-tackle in 23:33. Lewis won the second fall with a series of headlocks in 14:37. Lewis continued applying the headlock in the third and Sonnenberg was being throw around the ring. Suddenly the champion attempted another surprising tackle but Ed stepped aside and Gus sailed through the ropes, landing on his head among the chairs in the front row. Sonnenberg seemed hurt as he slowly crawled toward the ring. At the count of 15, his head appeared above the matt and he started climbing into the ring. All of a sudden, Doc Mullikan, the chiropractic rassler who was seconding Gus, jumped into the ring and started pulling Sonnenberg through the ropes. Referee Don McDonald pushed Mullikan away from the fallen champion, then Jim Charblis, a Lewis second in the corner with Billy Sandow, scrambled into the ring with Sandow pulling at his coat tails. With the timekeeper at the count of 20, Sonnenberg was half in and half out of the ring. With the referee being yelled at by two seconds, a manager and a crazed crowd, Sonnenberg woke up and hit Lewis, who had been standing around watching the events, with another flying tackle. McDonald looked around and saw Gus pinning Lewis, so he gave Ed a three count and raised Sonnenberg's arm. More yelling followed with the referee agreeing that interference should have disqualified both men, but the pin over ruled everything else. Of course, Lewis getting ripped off was grounds for another sold out rematch.[300]

With Strangler Lewis attempting to move into retirement, Billy Sandow went looking for another wrestler. He found one in a former cowboy and amateur wrestler from La Junta, Colorado.[301] It was never stated in a newspaper but I believe that Sandow, living in Los Angeles, had taken the position as booker for Lou Daro at The Olympic Auditorium. It's either that or he bought into Daro's promotion. On the undercard of the October 23 Lewis/Sonnenberg match, Sandow had Marshall defeat Don DeLaun for his first win in town of what would turn into a major push.

The California Commission ruled a rematch would take place on November 13, 1929 with all seconds and managers not allowed ringside during the match. There also was a rule saying that after a wrestler left or fell from the ring and returned, both wrestlers would met in the center of the ring.

The Olympic was once again filled with 10,800 and a gate of $31,000. Sonnenberg won the first fall in 24:45 with the flying tackle. Lewis used his headlock to pin the champion in 13:33. In the third, Lewis dominated Sonnenberg until he missed a headlock and got hit by a tackle. So Ed was pinned in 3:05. Everett Marshall wrestled on the undercard.[302]

On November 16, 1929, Lewis appeared in La Junta, Colorado to help Sandow's new wrestler and lost a handicap match to Everett Marshall in his home town.

Another match with Joe Stecher took place in Kansas City on November 19, 1929. Attendance was more than 4,000. Stecher won the first fall with his scissors in 53:05. Lewis won the second fall in 8:32 and the third in 3:00, both with headlocks. Stecher was the more popular wrestler and Lewis was booed in his own home town.[303]

Lewis then headlined in the upper East Coast and appeared in Toronto on December 9, beating Dan Koloff. He finished his year, on December 16, 1929, in Tulsa. Getting another title shot, Sonnenberg beat him in two straight falls.

Lewis seemed ready to go into semi-retirement in 1930. I believe his Trachoma had become so bad that, at times, he could only see shadows. Ed spent much of his time working in his Glendale restaurant, but he still would wrestle one or two times a week in small territories like Salt Lake City, Phoenix, Portland, and the minor western areas of Canada. Two of his sisters married and moved to Washington, so over the coming years Lewis would spend a lot of time wrestling in the Seattle/Portland area.

Everett Marshall got a major push in Los Angeles headlining the first five cards of 1930. He was given wins over Malcewicz, Stasiak, Dr. Karl Sarpolis, Cantonwine and Nick Lutze. Everett Marshall was a blond youth with good looks and some wrestling ability. Newspapers were comparing him to Earl Caddock. In fact, Marshall had good character, intelligence, and a fine attitude. All Marshall really wanted from wrestling was a good farm. His lack of ego made him easy to work with and he turned out to be a good investment for Billy Sandow. He lived in Glendale near Lewis, so Ed must have been training him. On January 22, Lewis wrestled the semi-main event under Marshall, beating Dick Daviscourt while the two drew 10,000 to the Olympic.

Marshall's string of Olympic main events was broken when Daro booked Lewis to meet Gene LaDoux on March 19, 1930. Lewis won two straight falls and drew 8,500 ($13,000).[304]

Paul Bowser booked Lewis into some matches in late March including a major match in Madison Square Garden, so on March 31 Ed flew to Kansas City to work a draw with Henri Deglane. In New York's Madison Square Garden on April 2, Ed performed in front of a poor crowd of 4,000, beating old Marin Plestina.[305] The next night Lewis beat a feared hooker in Jack Sherry at Boston.

After Everett beat Nick Lutze a second time (drawing 9,000), he had beaten just about every performer in Paul Bowser's stable of contenders but one: Lewis. So Lou Daro made the match on April 16, 1930, with the winner to get a title match with Sonnenberg in Wrigley Field on May 5.

During the 1920's Strangler Lewis' jobs were few. The only loses he had were to Stan Zbyszko, Stecher, Wayne Munn, and Sonnenberg. Before this match, the word was out that he might do another job and the match got national attention in all the newspapers. Marshall went so far as to fly in his family from Colorado to see the match.

Lewis gave Marshall his first lost in the first fall, pinning him after a headlock in 32:16. In the second fall, Lewis began head locking Marshall all over the ring until Everett, in desperation, suddenly picked him up for the backward slam and pin in 10:21. Lewis was groggy at the start of the third fall and Marshall jumped on him to win in 33 seconds. With that, Everett Marshall became a national star and the super match with Sonnenberg was set.[306]

Back on January 11, 1930, The National Boxing Association president Stanley M. Isaacs decided the organization was going take control of pro wrestling and legitimize it, as it had pro boxing. The group had taken control of boxing from a large number of under-funded state commissions (it claimed to rule 31 states) and thought it was powerful enough to extend its domain over wrestling. Its first step was to create a tournament of leading contenders and champions, with the winner being crowned NBA world champion. The men named were Sonnenberg, Shikat, Pesek, Jim Londos, and Pete Sauer (Ray Steele).[307] They were all asked to post a $5,000 forfeit bond. The only two who didn't ignore the NBA was Londos and Pesek. To be fair, Steele lost a match to champion Shikat at Memphis on January 16 to lose his spot on the list.[308] On February 18, Columbus promoter Al Haft won a bidding war for the match and scheduled it for April 9, 1930.

On March 21, John Pesek announced he was withdrawing from the match due to injuries after a fall from horse. The truth was that the injury was a fake. Pesek had learned he was going to be the one losing the match, and he didn't want to job to Londos.

By April 1, the NBA president was fed up with pro wrestling and wanted nothing to do with it. The chairman of the wrestling committee, Col. H. J. Landry, announced it was going to ban all heavyweight wrestlers from NBA territories. A lot of state commission then started to drop out of the NBA and I think Landry changed his mind (and probably took the money he was offered from Londos promoters).

There were other "mark" commissions also making trouble for promoters. In Chicago, Columbus promoter Al Haft appeared before the Illinois Commission asking for Sonnenberg to defend the title against John Pesek. Pesek, claiming the title for himself, posted a $10,000 certified check saying that he could pin Sonnenberg three times in one hour. Then Haft presented world welterweight title holder Jack Reynolds, who post $10,000 for a 2/3 fall match with Sonnenberg. The old student of Farmer Burns (Reynolds) then stated: "This Sonnenberg is only a palooka, who in my opinion, does not know how to wrestle. Honestly, I don't believe he even knows how to put a half nelson on correctly, not to mention the other tricks of the game. This flying tackle stuff, he has been exhibiting, is all hooey-hippodrome blah put on for the benefit of the rag tag and bob ends who love to see roly-poly stuff. My money is up and money usually talks."

The Illinois commission decision was to stage there own tournament. On January 17, 1930 it announced that Londos, Steele and Steinke were to wrestle and the winner was to meet Sonnenberg in a final match. Of course, everyone named refused. Lewis, Plestina, Stasiak and Malcewicz all put up $2,500 forfeits. The commission then suspended all pro wrestling in the state until Londos and Shikat joined the group.

On April 8, 1930, the New York State Athletic Commission got wise and ruled that all wrestling cards had to be billed as wrestling exhibitions and should be classified as theatrical. The commissioner was old time GR wrestling champion, William Muldoom. I think it was the New York Commission that broke the news to the NBA that wrestling was "fake."

You would think a ruling like that would kill pro wrestling in New York City, but it really wasn't anything normal fans didn't know and by the end of 1930 wrestling was drawing bigger than ever in the city. It became the golden period in the sport's—well, exhibition's—history.[309]

After a huge build up, the Gus Sonnenberg/Everett Marshall match in Wrigley Field drew 17,580 and a gate of $69,745.50 on May 5, 1930. With the Depression taking effect and ticket prices dropping soon after this date, it would remain the Los Angeles and California gate record until broken by the Lou Thesz/Baron Leone match in 1953. The numbers are probably very close to the actual (true) numbers of the Fred Blassie/John Tolos card at the L.A. Coliseum on August 27, 1971.

Lewis was ringside and announced before the start of the main event. Marshall was able to avoid the flying tackle during the first fall and won with an airplane spin in 31:13. In the second fall, Marshall broke a Sonnenberg headlock by throwing him to the matt. Gus showed his ring coyness by pretending to be on the verge of collapse. Marshall took the bait and walked in unprotected to be hit in the abdomen by one of

Sonnenberg's tackles. Three more tackles followed and Everett was pinned for the second fall in 11:55. Marshall claimed he had been fouled by a tackle that had landed low in the groin area. The last fall saw Sonnenberg pin Marshall in 1:22 after three flying tackles.[310]

Ed Don George

On the under card was Paul Bowser new super star, Ed Don George, who beat Dan Koloff. George was a well-known Amateur wrestler from at the University of Michigan. He won the AAU wrestling title in 1927 and represented the United States at the 1928 Olympics in Amsterdam. He beat another future pro in Earl McCready to get to the final but lost to another future pro in J. C. Richthoff. His real name was Edward Nye George but he was billed early in his career as Don George. He protested and as a compromise the name was changed to Ed Don George. He actually graduated from the University of Michigan in 1929 with a Mechanical Engineering degree. He worked before and during his career for the Firestone Tire and Rubber Company. Ed didn't wrestle as much as some because of this job outside of wrestling. He was good looking and most reports say he was a fine wrestler. His idol was Ed "Strangler" Lewis. His first pro match took place on November 21, 1929 in Boston. By the time he got to Los Angeles he was well on his way to 50 straight wins. So he was another new star that got a major push by Lou Daro. He beat all the Bowser wrestlers, including Stasiak, Lutze, Lee Wycoff, Malcewicz, Plestina, Bob "Bibber" McCoy and Don DeLaun (later billed as Brother Jonathan, the father of Don Leo Jonathan).[311]

Jim Londos returned to the East Coast where he continued to draw large crowds. Dick Shikat was an adequate draw but he wasn't in Jimmy's league. Shikat was also homesick and planning a trip back to Germany. Talk like that was a sure sign of a "title change."

Shikat and Londos were booked to meet on June 6, 1930 in Philadelphia's Phillies Ball Park.[312] It was to be for Shikat's Pennsylvania and New York world title, plus, because of Pesek dropping out of the Londos match, the NBA world title recognition.

In the rain, it drew a total crowd of close to 15,000 with 13,115 paying $43,622.20. Londos won the three titles in over an hour and 23 minute. After injuring Shikat's leg with a Japanese toe-hold, Londos then grabbed a half-nelson and the uninjured leg and rolled the weaken German into a three count. The crowd loved the idea of Londos being champion, after all the years he had been trying, and a party was held at the Philadelphia Ritz-Carlton until early in the morning. The only person not in a good mood was Shikat.[313]

Jim Londos with the NWA belt.

Ed Lewis must have also hated the idea of the little Greek, he created, being elevated to a champion level at the same time he was being put out to pasture.

After watching the Sonnenberg/Marshall match, Lewis did a another job for champion Sonnenberg in Kansas City on May 20. He then made a short tour of the East Coast before returning to Glendale.

On June 11, 1930, Lewis got a rematch with young Everett Marshall at the Olympic. The winner of that match would get to travel to Seattle for a showdown with Joe Stecher.[314]

The match drew around 9,000 with Lewis' old friend Jack Dempsey ringside. After eating four headlocks, Marshall surprised Ed with a airplane spine that dumped the Strangler on his head. As he tried to get up, Lewis got hit by a Marshall rabbit punch and pinned for the first fall in 31:15. Billy Sandow jumped into the ring to complain about the foul. Sandow was managing both wrestlers but it wasn't known by the public. This is the first time I've found Sandow name mentioned in a report of an Everett Marshall match. So if sides were taken, Billy was still with Lewis.

In the second fall, Marshall was in the process of using the "backward body slam" when Ed reach between his legs and upset Everett who fell back on to the mat. A headlock then finished Marshall in 18:24.

The two went at each other hot and heavy in the third fall with both going for headlocks. Ed got thrown out of the ring but returned just before 20 was counted.[315] He then headlock Marshall three times and pinned him in 8:37. Lewis got his ticket to Seattle and his win back from doing the job to set Marshall up for the Wrigley Field match.

In Seattle, it seemed like a Lewis employee was doing the PR, because the newspaper claimed there had been six matches between Stecher and Lewis, of which Ed had won five. It actually was the 15th match between the two and the record showed, after Joe had been working for Bowser for a year, seven Lewis wins, five Stecher wins, and two draws. Wrestling fans seemed as ignorant of wrestling history in 1930 as their grandchildren were in 1995. The newspaper also wrote that Strangler Lewis was the "most outstanding grappler since the days of Frank Gotch." Lewis was only too happy to write Joe Stecher out of the sport's history.[316]

The match in Seattle was under European rules that had them wrestling under an eight round system.

To win, a wrestler needed to take two falls, and if no one was able to pull that off, the referee would make a decision. Lewis won a fall in the fifth round with his headlock, before Stecher ended the match by pinning Ed with a scissors in the eight. In Europe, a round ends whenever a fall takes place, so the Stecher's pin ended the match. The referee then made his decision and ruled Lewis the winner. Tony Stecher jumped into ring protesting the idea as "a shower of programs, empty cartons, and everything possible except the ringside seats" came flying into the ring showing that the crowd agreed with Tony. The reporter claimed it was a very close match, which could have gone either way.[317]

On June 18, Lewis wrestled Sonnenberg in Milwaukee. I don't know the result, but I have a strong feeling that he lost.

Lewis returned to The Olympic Auditorium on June 25, beating Plestina in the semi-main event on a Marshall / Wycoff card.

Marshall continued to be pushed following the Lewis loss, beating Wycoff, Malcewicz (twice), and on July 9, 1930 he was giving a win over Joe Stecher. This set him up for another match with Gus Sonnenberg for the title. On October 1, 1930, Sonnenberg again defeated Everett Marshall, this time at a sold out Olympic Auditorium (10,400).

Gus Sonnenberg turned out to be a huge draw. In Los Angeles, at the time, no one in history could touch him as a draw in the city. Londos had always been big but with the title he became huge box-office. I think everyone in wrestling, including Bowser and Curley, realized they were presented with a unique situation with two massive drawing cards. A super match between the two, promoted right, outdoors, could shatter all gate records, even if the result was a draw. The thought of the money involved was worth a temporary truce between everyone.[318]

On October 1, 1930, Londos' manager, Ed White, appeared before the Illinois Athletic Commission in an attempt to secure a unification match with Gus Sonnenberg, who was suspended in the state. He offered $10,000 to anyone who could book the match. On October 3, the Commission lifted its ban on heavyweight wrestlers and dropped the suspension of Sonnenberg. Local promoters Doc Krone, Joe Coffey and Ed White were all interested and talking about the unification match. I think the Illinois commission realized the idealistic theory of shoot wrestling wasn't worth losing all the tax money pro wrestling was making for others cities across the nation.

In August 1930, Ed took Elaine with him to Australia for a series of matches with Joe Stecher, booked over two months. The two thought of the trip as a vacation more than a business venture. Lewis arrived in Australia on a Tahiti liner on August 5, 1930. The Stecher family arrived later on the royal mail ship, MV *Aorangi*.

Joe and Tony Stecher resting on deck.

Group photo after training. Unknown person, Joe Stecher, Abe Coleman and Tony Stecher

Lewis had his first match in country on August 9 at Melbourne, beating former Olympian Charley Strack. Reports said that Lewis headlocked Strack unmercifully for four rounds and in the fifth round hit Charley with a headlock and cross body throw so powerful that Strack was knocked out. Lewis couldn't resist clouting the fallen man on the back of the head and got boo'ed by the crowd as a result. Strack was carried out of the ring unable to return.

Victories over Pat McGill, Dr. Karl Sarpolis and Howard Cantonwine followed as they toured such cities as Brisbane and Sydney. In Adelaide he wrestled George Kotsonaros, one of the best "pound for pound" wrestlers of his time. It was said that Lewis amazed the crowd with his size, power, and balance. He broke all of Kotsonaros' holds using his strength and countered the Greek's speed by sidestepping George as he flew out of the ring. Lewis then beat him after five headlocks.

Lewis wrestled Joe Stecher three times on the trip. The first match was in Melbourne on September 6. Stecher won an eight round decision over Lewis, with neither wrestler gaining a fall. Lewis showed a greater varity of hold, but Stecher controlled the match with his scissors.

The second match was also in Melbourne on September 13, with the result an eight round draw. Neither scored a fall.

The third match was held in Sydney on September 20, 1930 in front of 10,500 fans. Stecher won the first fall in the fifth round with a body scissors. Lewis then came back to pin Joe in the seventh and eighth rounds using a headlock and body press in both falls.[319] This is the last match ever recorded between the two rivals.

Stecher would do jobs for rivals John Pesek and Jim Londos, plus a few for major wrestlers like Ray Steele, Jim McMillan, and Jim Browning. But he never wrestled Ed Lewis again.

When Lewis returned to Glendale in October, he had Billy Sandow waiting for him. The two hadn't spent much time together over the last year and a half, and Lewis was once again thinking about training and losing weight for a major comeback. Sandow must have warned Ed that there wasn't much of a market for 40 year old wrestling champions, but Lewis' eyes were better and he was getting the old feelings back. Lewis knew he was old, but with Stecher in line, he didn't feel there was a modern performer who could beat him in a real match. It very well may have been wishful thinking by a washed-up old guy but there were many expert insiders and reporters who agreed with him. Anyway, Lewis was willing to throw his hat into the ring.[320]

Local newspaper articles during Strangler Lewis' 1930 tour of Australia

The News, Adelaide, Friday, 8 August, 1930

FLYING WRESTLER

Strangler Lewis in Melbourne

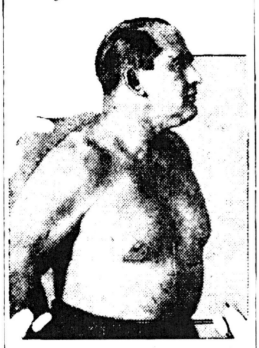

Ed (Strangler) Lewis (formerly heavyweight wrestling champion of the world), who has arrived in Australia, uses the air as a means of travel.

He estimates that in the past six years he has flown a quarter of a million miles. In the last two weeks before leaving for Australia he flew 10,000 miles for nine matches.

This week he travelled by air from Sydney to Melbourne, where he will meet Charlie Strack in his first Australian bout tomorrow night. He will fly back to Sydney on Monday.

Northern Star, Lismore, NSW, Tuesday, 2 September, 1930

WRESTLING

"STRANGLER" LEWIS WINS

SYDNEY. Monday.
At Rushcutters' Bay stadium to-night Ed. "Strangler" Lewis (17-6) defeated "Doctor" Sarpolis (15-4) by one fall to nil in a wrestling match.

The News, Adelaide, Monday, 25 August, 1930

WIFE OF WRESTLER

MRS. "STRANGLER" LEWIS

Takes Advice of Husband

Mrs. "Strangler" Lewis, wife of the famous wrestler, due to arrive in Adelaide tomorrow, said in a recent interview with a Sydney presswoman:—
"We've been married a year and a half. My friends all said, 'Fancy marrying a man like that!' but I discovered that he knew more about things of the mind than I did. And I like his friends; I like the men he knows. They may not know all the right words, but you can stake your life on them, and that is what counts."
Mrs. Lewis is described as an Italian-Belgian-American with a cloud of dark hair shot with red lights, enormous brown eyes and a soft red mouth. Before her marriage she was interested in music, painting, and the pursuit of culture, and thought wrestlers were uncouth.
That is all changed now, and she says she has a tremendous admiration for her husband's mind and always takes his advice.
"Before we were married," she said, "I rang him up at a town 1,000 miles away and asked him what I was to tell the press about our marriage. He told me to be nice to them, because they had to do their jobs. He is always like that. People in all walks of life and in all parts of America go to him for advice, and he helps them.
"He never talks much about the business part of his life. He says that after doing it for 15 years he doesn't want to think about it inside his home as well as out, so I have been to see him wrestle only twice. I was thrilled then, because he is a colorful wrestler. I don't know much about the different holds, but I notice that his feet twinkle. You wouldn't think such a big man could have such small feet."

Ed Don George and Marshall continued to be the major local favorites in Los Angeles but Paul Bowser also sent him another wrestler he wanted pushed. Henri Deglane (born June 22, 1902) was a French wrestler who had won the gold medal in heavyweight Greco-Roman wrestling at the 1924 Olympics in Paris. At age 16, Deglane worked as a truck driver during the war, delivering wine to the soldiers. After the Armistice, he became a member of the Paris Fire Department, which was a semi-military organization with a fine training school in modern athletics. Heni was proficient in wrestling, winning many tournaments, which lead to him being selected to represent France in the 1924 Olympics. After winning the medal, Deglane toured in vaudeville with boxing champion George Carpentier. He later opened a school of physical culture and attempted to promote pro wrestling with little success. Henri also toured Europe and all the leading centers of wrestling on the continent. He was famous in his home country but it wasn't making him rich. Lucien Riopel, Paul Bowser's promoter in Montreal, brought him to Canada and later he moved down to the USA and Boston. Deglane was a good wrestler once he learned catch style wrestling, but he was in his late 20's and lacked the star appeal that Sonnenberg, Marshall, Londos, and George had for

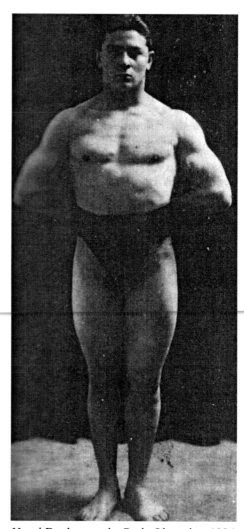

Henri Deglane at the Paris Olympics, 1924

Joe Londos

American audiences. Still, Bowser saw great promise for him in Montreal and he was also planning a move into France.[321]

On October 29, 1930, Gus Sonnenberg defeated Ed Don George in a title match at The Olympic Auditorium. By this time the sport was filled with ex-football players and just regular wrestlers using Gus's Flying Tackle. After splitting two falls, George seemed to have Sonnenberg beat but both attempted flying tackles and they met in the middle of the ring in a head on collision. Both were out but Sonnenberg woke up first and pinned George. Fans and promoter wanted a rematch.[322]

On that card was a Mexican wrestler named Jose Dominguez. Lou Daro knew that if he could ever find a major Mexican wrestler to push, he'd make a ton of money in the city with the largest Mexican population, outside of Mexico City, in the world. He seemed to be working hard on Dominguez, even giving him a win over Joe Malcewicz.

In a semi-final to 2:03:30 draw between Everett Marshall and Henri Deglane at The Olympic on November 12, Strangler Lewis made his come back defeating Jose Dominguez in two straight falls. Los Angeles would have to wait for a Mexican star.

Lewis must have been steaming when he read in the Los Angeles papers that Jim Londos and Jack Curley had returned to New York's Madison Square Garden on November 17, 1930, selling out with over 20,000 fans in attendance (including Mayor Jimmy Walker) as the Greek beat Gino Garibaldi.[323] This was the same building that Lewis had drawn 4,000 on April 2.

Lewis was always willing to tell anyone who'd listen that he had beaten Londos 14 straight times and that got him a lot of press and put pressure on Londos, but at the beginning of Londos title reign he was well known for putting people over. So Curley, Fabiani, Ed White, Packs and Londos himself agreed that, as champion, he wouldn't do jobs of any type. He wouldn't even drop falls to contenders. It wasn't a problem on the East Coast because they booked one fall matches, but in the mid-west, where two out of three fall matches prevailed, it took some creativity to keep people strong and promote rematches. Still 1930 was filled with new stars and Londos was in the process of becoming wrestling biggest drawing star in history. He could and did work every night filling arenas in every city. There seemed to be no limit to how much money Jimmy could make for himself and the promoters.

On November 26, Lewis wrestled another semi-final at the Olympic, wrestling Henri Deglane to an hour draw.

The rematch for the title between Gus Sonnenberg and Ed Don George was booked for December 10, 1930. It drew 10,000 spectators. Sonnenberg won the first fall with the flying tackle in 14 minutes and seven seconds. George won the second with a combination head scissors and double wrist lock. In one of wrestling biggest upsets, George submitted Sonnenberg using a Japanese arm-lock (a standing head scissors with an arm-bar, George's finishing hold in 1930) in 12:52. Gus had been locked in the hold for over five minutes before quitting. The win gave Ed Don George the world title.[324]

The book *Fall Guys* by Marcus Griffin has a story saying that Bowser booked the George/Sonnenberg finish with out telling Sandow or Lewis. The placing of the belt on George supposedly angered both Ed and Billy, because Lewis had been promised in 1929, at some point, to get the title back. The story is only a theory and I have one of my own. Gus Sonnenberg was a huge draw, even without the title. I think Bowser and Daro had plans to run cross promotion matches with Gus and Jim Londos in Los Angeles and a John Pesek/Sonnenberg match in Boston. I think these big money matches were going to be draws or have some screw finish tacked on to them, but he didn't want the title on Gus in case something when wrong. The title on George was good for George's career and with him as champ you didn't have to worry about a double crosses—at least that's what Bowser thought. But George was young and a real wrestler who would be willing to step up if challenged by Londos, Shikat or Steele. Another factor may have been that Sonnenberg had a drinking problem and was becoming an out-of-control drunk.

Lewis returned to the Olympic on December 22, destroying a Joe Stocca in two straight falls in the semi-main event to Deglane beating Nick Lutze.[325]

As the year came to a close, Londos grew more headlines drawing 22,000 (19,715 paying $44,878) on December 29 at Madison Square Garden in beating Ferenc Holuban.[326] This came three days after selling out in Philadelphia against Tiny Roebuck (10,000, $20,213).[327]

Ed Don George and Another Title

On January 1, 1931, the Glendale Chamber of Commerce announce that they were going to stage a $4,000 open golf tournament in the city in December and the sponsors were Glendale residents Lou Daro and Ed "Strangler" Lewis.[328]

The next day, January 2, Lewis was sideswiped by a car in the street in front of his restaurant on the 700 block on South Brand in Glendale. He sustained a severe bruise on his pelvic bone and cuts around his hip. This forced Lewis to cancel some dates in Chicago and the East coast, and he didn't wrestle in January.[329]

He was going to wrestler Frank Judson in Chicago but he was replaced by champion Ed Don George. With the Chicago commission letting up, big time pro wrestling had returned with the two major promotions both running shows. The Bowser promoter was Joe Coffey and a Londos group was being run by Doc Krone.

On January 5, 1931, Lou Daro announced that he had practically ironed out details for a dream match between Gus Sonnenberg and Jim Londos. The Greek had agreed and Daro was going to meet with Sonnenberg in the coming week. Daro had made a lot of money with the Wrigley Field card and he wanted to promote another, even bigger, card in April 1931. Daro was experienced in handling big cards, had a long history with Londos, and was trusted, so he and most everyone else thought he could pull the cross promotion match off. It had the potential to break all attendance records.[330]

The next day, Ed Lewis made an announcement. Lewis said he had a $5,000 bond posted with the state commission for a match with Jim Londos, and demanded that he be given the match with the Greek, not Sonnenberg. Lou Daro stated that Londos refused to have anything to do with a Lewis match. With Sonnenberg in town, building for a rematch with George, the topic of Londos was dropped. Lewis's hatred for Londos and Ed's stunt had cost Daro and Londos their super match.[331] Londos didn't seem to care, on January 26, he drew another 22,200 and gate of $59,496.50 at Madison Square Garden in beating Jim McMillen.[332]

On January 7, 1931, Gus Sonnenberg showed he was still box office without the title by beating Henri Deglane in front of a large crowd on a rainy night at The Olympic. The winner was supposed to get a title match with Ed Don George, but Sonnenberg had commitments on the East Coast so Deglane got the title match on January 21. George then beat Henri at another sold out Olympic.[333]

Sonnenberg went back to Boston to wrestle John Pesek on January 22. Pesek dropped out of the match and had to be replaced by Lee Wyckoff. Sonnenberg still drew a crowd of 14,000.

Lewis returned to the ring on February 4, 1931, beating up Dr. Karl Sarpolis in the semi-final of an Everett Marshall/Ad Santel match.[334] Marshall won and he also beat Deglane in two straight falls on February 18, setting up a title match with George on March 4.

On February 18, promoter Ray Fabiani offered Ed Don George $50,000 to wrestle Jim Londos in Philadelphia or Boston. Later on April 4, Jack Curley offered Ed Don George a match with Londos in New York City. The match would take place outdoors, probably in Yankee Stadium, for the Hearst Milk Fund in April, May, or June. When George didn't respond, Curley booked a rematch between Londos and Ray Steele which drew 21,000 ($63,000) on June 29.

The March 4 title match had George pinning Marshall with The Olympic sold out (10,400). In the semi-final, Lewis wrestled Henri Deglane again in what would be a very interesting match considering the events that would follow in the coming months. Lewis beat Deglane in two straight falls, winning both with headlocks in 30:06 and 4:25. Ed was called "the old war horse" but was said to be looking in good condition after working with Sandow for a few months. It seemed that Lou Daro (or perhaps booker Sandow) was giving Lewis more of a build up than he had had in a few years.[335]

A later match between Everett Marshall and Jim Londos,
Madison Square Garden.

A third match with Everett Marshall took place on March 18, with the winner to meet Ed Don George on an outdoor card in April. Lewis won two straight falls with headlocks in 48:00 and 5:32.[336]

Also on the card was the local debut of Joe Savoldi, the ex-Notre Dame football star. He was the first performer to use the drop kick and he may have been the first wrestler to shave his chest. He would take his place as one of the many stars of the 1930's.

Lou Daro rented Wrigley Field for April 13, 1931, booking the sensational new champion Ed Don George against the legendary Ed "Strangler" Lewis. No one thought Ed was going to win. With so many new stars in the sport, there seemed little reason to put the title back on Lewis, but he still was a force who could draw as a challenger, putting over a young champion. His was a famous name that everyone wanted on their record.

Daro promoted the event by having the two stars give free workouts at The Olympic Auditorium for a week leading up to the match. George would work out first for an hour and then Lewis and Sandow would show Ed doing exhibition type matches with a number of local wrestlers. A PR stunt was pulled on April 9. After working out, George came ringside and sat with Dean Cromwell, Southern California track coach and reporters, while Lewis was working a routine session with Bill Beth. Billy Sandow started yelling at George, saying he couldn't watch Lewis and would stop the workout if George stayed. George told Sandow: "I'm not interested in his training work—we'll settle our argument Monday night. Tell your big fellow to be prepared for a busy night."[337]

The match drew a disappointing 12,000 to the baseball stadium. Most of the fans bought the cheap tickets, and once the first preliminary match started, they rushed down from the grandstands to jam themselves in the higher priced seats. The police spent most of the night moving crashers sitting in a late arriving high roller's seat. A few days after the match, Daro stated he would have made more money running the match at the Olympic, which had a much lower rent.

Lewis with a headlock on Ed Don George
during a match on April 13, 1931.

At some point, Lewis made it known to George that he was going to lose the match and the title. The story is that Ed told him in front of the large crowd: "Ok kid, tonight's the night, and we can do it the easy or the hard way!" The story usually has this happening in the middle of the ring as the referee was giving instructions. About 15 minutes of this match has turned up from newsreels in the last few months, including the introductions. Wrestlers didn't meet in the center of the ring before matches in 1931, so that part of the story needs to be changed.

Anyway, George took this to mean he was dropping the title and they could either do it as a work or a shoot. George did the pro thing and worked the match. Lewis dominated the action and George was never able to try any of the tackles the fans cried for. After 1:10:56 and seven headlocks, Lewis pinned George. The champion looked weak coming out for the second fall. Another headlock had George in major trouble, but Ed Don was able to wriggle out of the pin and crawled dizzily through the ropes for a count of 9. On return, Lewis put him in a body lock that incorporated a hammer lock. Lewis took George to the matt and rolled him over with Lewis on top pushing the champion's shoulders to the mat.[338] The crowd didn't get the significance of the hold, and only when referee Don McDonald dropped to his knees to check George's shoulders did they realize something was about to happen. Lewis held the grip despite George's frantic struggle and Ed's tremendous weight pushed the champ's shoulders down. When the referee patted Lewis' back to end the fall and the match, the crowd was stunned in surprise. Even when Lewis was officially proclaimed the new champion there was but scattering applause for the veteran. Lewis bowed politely and strutted out of the ring, "wrapping a blanket about his ample person with all the dignity and grace of a Roman senator manipulating his toga."[339]

Just about everyone agrees that Lewis stole the title that night. As for the "easy or hard way" quote, I don't know if that happened. It was a story told by Lewis and repeated by Lou Thesz over the years.[340] It's such a good story and line that it has been repeated over and over by Dave Meltzer's *Wrestling Observer Newsletter* throughout the years. I kind of doubt it, but it's such a good line that it will last, regardless of any truth. It can't be seen on the film clips, and it's not mentioned in any newspaper report.

As for Ed Don George, a young Olympic class wrestler, being intimidated into dropping the title by a 40 year old, I really doubt that. I believe that Billy Sandow was either the booker or a partner for Lou Daro in Los Angeles. George was an employee working as a performer for the Bowser group. He had been a pro wrestler for only a year, and had to have been green in the ways things worked. Ed Lewis was his idol and the reason he became a wrestler. He must have seen Sandow, and maybe Lewis, as front office personnel and his boss. So if Billy told him to job, he'd probably do the job. George didn't have a lot of time to think and consult with his manager, being in front of the public. Sure he knew Ed Lewis was a feared old time shooter, but he was a competitive wrestler, too. So I don't see this as some big macho moment in the life of Ed Lewis; I think it was just a young wrestler doing what he was told by a boss.

This was Lewis' fourth time holding this AWA world title but he had also won the Olin world title twice. With Jim Londos holding the New York, Pennsylvania, and NBA world title, it could no longer be called an undisputed title. As soon as Lewis could find a reporter, he was willing to talk about the Greek: "I am ready to meet any grappler in the world, and that includes Jimmy Londos especially. I will smoke him out [as George Bush did with Osama Bin Laden], and if he will venture into the ring with me I'll beat him as decisively as the 14 previous times that I proved my superiority over him."

Lewis/Deglane and The Battle of the Bite

After the match, Lewis and Sandow took their stolen title out on the road. Traveling to Sandow's former home, Kansas City, to defeat Sandow's other wrestling star, Everett Marshall on April 20.

No one can say what went on in the mind of Paul Bowser, but from other situations in wrestling history that resembled this one, the first thought a wrestling promoter has is to accept the situation and negotiate before their title is sold to another competitor. Bowser had been friends and a business partners with Sandow and Lewis for a number of years. I think he realized the need to understand the situation, find out what Sandow and Lewis planned, and if these plans extended beyond just sealing the title, and to find out if Jack Curley was involved. Having the title on Strangler Lewis was one thing, but it being sold to Curley and Jim Londos would ruin him.

Lewis and Sandow had learned, in the years 1926 to 1928, that a title meant nothing without a powerful promoter behind it. To make money they would have to pick between an old friend in Bowser or an old enemy in Jack Curley. If they picked Curley, it would mean doing the job for Jim Londos.

Lewis beat Fred Peterson in Tulsa on April 23 and then traveled to Chicago for a title match with Gene LeDoux on April 28.

Marcus Griffin, in his book *Fall Guys*, claimed that Sandow and Lewis met with Paul Bowser in Chicago before the match. Griffin claimed that Sandow had held $70,000 of Bowser's money as a forfeit. Sandow was given the money as part of the deal made before Lewis dropped the title to Sonnenberg. In Chicago, Sandow returned $50,000 to Bowser and kept $20,000. Bowser then agreed to not try "any funny stuff."

I don't believe that story, as I don't believe Griffin on any of his stories that date before 1933. Most of the facts in *Fall Guys* that take place before Marcus Griffin started working for Toots Mondt's office in 1933—that can be checked through research—have been proven wrong. Errors fill the book.[341] If Bowser had violated the contract with Sandow by giving the title to Ed Don George, why would Billy give $50,000 back to Bowser? (It sounds like too much money anyway.)

I don't believe that the old Lewis was promotable as champion. Bowser knew it—and had other plans of his own. Lewis probably knew it too, but his ego was in the way. I think Lewis wanted a title claim more than the actual title, and a deal was made where he could drop the title and still have the wrestling world think he was the true champion.

Lewis defended the title and beat LaDoux on April 28.

In Montreal on April 28, it was announced that Lewis had agreed to wrestle Henri Deglane for the title in Montreal on May 4, 1931. So why would he agree to go to Montreal, a town run by Paul Bowser, the promoter he double-crossed less than three weeks before? Did Lewis expect everyone to believe he was dumb enough to walk into a trap? (I guess he did.) My guess is that Lewis agreed to lose the title to Deglane for a large sum of money.

A young Henri Deglane

The match took place on May 4 in Montreal in front of 7,000, with prices raised to 75 cents, $1,50 and $3.00. Lewis' attitude leading up to the match was that Henri Deglane, an Olympic champion, was small time and he just wanted to beat him and go home. Deglane presented a problem to Lewis in the first fall by standing erect with his hands high to block any attempt at a headlock, and the younger Frenchman's footwork and speed stopped any attack to his lower extremities. Lewis looked tired, old and on edge. Deglane moved around the ring at a fast pace, making Lewis waste energy following him. After a half hour, Henri stepped on the gas, and hit Lewis with one arm lock after another, until at 33 minutes and 15 seconds he won the first fall with an arm lock followed by a convincing flying mare. The crowd went nuts seeing their French hero win the fall over the old champion.

Lewis and Sandow argued with referee Eugene Tremblay, a former world lightweight champion, so persistent that the police were called into the ring to remove Billy on the grounds he had no license to manage in Canada.[342]

The second fall started with Deglane sailing right in after Lewis' arms again. After 9 minutes and 35 seconds of Henri working over Ed's arms, the challenger managed to get Lewis into a near fall with Deglane on top with one shoulder down and the other on the way. Some reports had Lewis getting a three count.

Deglane then jumped up, yelling that Lewis bit him on the arm. The referee looked at the tooth marks on Deglane's arm (more reliable reports claim it was the wrist that was bitten) and then presented the situation to the Athletic Commissioner, Dr. Gaston Demers, who told the referee to disqualify Lewis, and the fall, the match, and the title were awarded to the challenger.

Sandow ran back into the ring, and it took ten policemen to escort him back to the dressing-room.

As the crowd celebrated, Lewis argued with the referee that Deglane had bit himself. The Montreal commissioner, Demers, backed up referee Tremblay, so Lewis announced that he was going to have a cast made of his teeth to match with the bite marks, but all of that was soon forgotten.[343]

Most wrestling books that have been written over the years have pressed the story that Deglane bit himself and stole the title for Paul Bowser. My view has the match being a "work" from top to bottom. Questions: *1.* How many wrestlers, throughout history, have been disqualified for biting? If there was a plot, what made Bowser think the referee would disqualify Lewis? That would take a ton of guts, taking a title from a legend— for biting, and for the first time in history. The referee and the commissioner would have had to have been in on the plot. *2.* Who would ever defend a title in a town controlled by the very promoter you screwed over three weeks before? For years, Sandow protected Lewis from double-crosses. He wouldn't even let Lewis meet shooters from his own promotion, guys who could make them money like John Pesek, Dick Shikat, and Marin Plestina. In 1928, Sandow wouldn't even let Lewis meet Londos, who was 40 pounds lighter and Lewis was never allowed to ever defend a title verse Joe Stecher. Sandow was suspicious of everything and everybody. So how do you explain Sandow letting Lewis go up to Montreal to wrestle a French Olympic champion? This doesn't make sense. *3.* That being said, why would Lewis give Deglane control of the match by losing the first fall? He also allowed Deglane to be on top for most of the night. Was Lewis that dumb or that bad of a wrestler?

I think the match was a work and just another screw finish that Lewis used whenever he lost. He had to have been in on the finish because he allowed Deglane to be on top with him in a pinning situation, before the bite spot took place. It was too theatrical to be anything but a work. The whole match had to have been agreed upon in Chicago between April 24 and April 27, a day before the match was accepted in Montreal.

Paul Bowser was moving into Montreal and he (and Deglane) were making plans to promote in France. He wanted a French champion, and, after all the jobs Deglane did for Sonnenberg, George, and even Lewis, he was set with a long list of major contenders.

Lewis lost Bowser's Boston AWA title, but the screw finish left him his "heat" and he could still claim the title in his strong cities like Chicago, Los Angeles, Kansas City, and Tulsa. I think Bowser realized that Lewis, with his pride intact, would also be hounding Londos in Chicago and Los Angeles.

Lewis remained in good standing with Bowser and he never expresses the rage like he did with Londos and Curley. If Lewis double-crossed Bowser in Los Angeles, he was forgiven in Montreal. The $20,000 not returned in Chicago was probably just the Lewis cut for dropping the title. It all worked out, and it was probably a lot better to read in Paris that their champion Deglane had beaten the feared Strangler Lewis rather than the rookie Ed Don George.

While Bowser and Lewis played games with their title, Londos continued to break all attendance records as champion. On February 18 he drew 9,000 and $15,000 in beating George Zaharias in Chicago. On February 20, had brought in 10,567 and $19,774 in St. Louis beating Ray Steele. February 23 saw him back in Madison Square Garden, drawing 21,500 and $60,216 in beating Jim McMillen. March 6 he drew 10,000 in Philadelphia beating Karl Pojello. March 13 he drew 12,000 in Boston, defeating Gino Garibaldi. He was back to Madison Square Garden on March 23, drawing 17,000, beating Herb Freeman. On April 22, 1931 in Chicago, he drew 17,250 and $34,419 for a win over Kola Kwariana. Not only was Londos drawing, but the promoters like Packs, Curley and Fabiani had developed a bunch of major performers who the public wanted to watch challenging for the title. Londos' title line couldn't be traced back to Gotch, but the large crowds were strengthening his claim through out the world. The Golden era of pro wrestling had begun.

Four days after the title loss (May 4), Lewis was in Rochester beating Sandow's other wrestler Everett Marshall. Lewis and Sandow were still doing what they always did—claiming the world title. They then left the Baumann home town for a match in Chicago.

Back on April 28, Lewis had posted a $5,000 check with the Illinois Athletic Commission as a challenge to Londos. The commission then gave Londos ten days to sign for a match with Lewis. On May 12, Londos' lawyers notified the commission that he refused to wrestle Ed Lewis. On May 13, the commission announced that the world title was vacant in Illinois and Londos could no longer be billed as champion in the state. Londos claimed he wouldn't wrestle Lewis because Ed was too old and he didn't want to injure an old man. He also said he was returning the same treatment Lewis gave him in 1928, when the Strangler wouldn't defend the title against him.

Londos may have been killing them at the box office but Lewis was winning the PR war in Chicago. On May 10, the *Chicago Tribune* printed a story saying that the Montreal Commission had decided that Henri Deglane bit himself in their recent match and wasn't the champion. The story was a lie, probably planted by Sandow, and the Montreal Commission still considered Deglane the champion—but all that was a long way from Chicago.

On May 13, 1931, Lewis appeared in Chicago defending his world title in beating Frank Judson.

After minor matches in Kansas City and Tulsa, Lewis returned home to Los Angeles to beat Karl Sarpolis at the Olympic Auditorium on June 10, 1931. The California Commission was still recognizing Lewis as world champion and the card drew 9,000.[344]

On September 25, General John V. Clinnin, Chairman of the Illinois State Athletic Commission and president of the National Boxing Association, recognized the title claims of Strangler Lewis and made an invitation to nine wrestlers: Jim Londos, Wladek Zbyszko, John Pesek, George Calza, Kola Kwariani, Gus Sonnenberg, Ed Don George, Henri Deglane and Joe Stecher, to meet Lewis in Chicago, with the winner being named Illinois world champion.[345]

On October 17, the National Boxing Association, through John Clinnin, announced that it was declining to assume responsibility for the conduct of pro wrestling and left the control of the sport to athletic commissions of the various states. Around this time, some of the members branched out to form the NWA (National Wrestling Association). It claimed to have a membership of 16 states (Kentucky, Maryland, Tennessee, Louisiana, Missouri, Michigan, Connecticut, Minnesota, Oklahoma, Georgia, Alabama, Arkansas and Oregon). The NBA officially claimed no affiliation with the NWA, but the NWA felt it was a subsidiary of the NBA. (I don't understand it either.) On September 30, the NWA announced it still recognized Jim Londos as world champion.[346]

A major wrestling star in Chicago was football player Jim McMillen. He had drawn major crowds against Londos in New York and other places while playing for the Chicago Bears. He also owned a part

of the Chicago Bears and would be a vice president of the club under president George Halas. McMillen had been a major wrestler in collage and was a good pro wrestling performer, using all the moves of the football type workers including the flying tackle. He and Londos wrestled in Chicago's Soldier Field on September 7, 1931. Londos won, but the crowd would seem to have been a major disappointment, with only 7,300 showing up. Perhaps the Lewis moment in Chicago hurt the card. (Londos had drawn 17,250 and $34,419 on April 22 in Chicago.) It was also a non-title match because of the commission.

On September 14, the *Chicago Tribune* printed that Londos would be willing to wrestle Lewis but wanted a guarantee of $250,000. In other words, he wasn't going to wrestle Lewis. On September 30, the NWA stated it still recognized Londos as champion.

Lewis wrestling in unidentified backyard.

The only wrestler to answer the commission's challenge was old Wladek Zbyszko. So on November 2, 1931, Lewis and Wladek met one more time; this one was for the Illinois world championship. Lewis won the first fall with the headlock in 23:52. Zbyszko won the second after a flying mare. Lewis used a cross body lock to pin Wladek in the third fall in 7:54. The report claimed it was a good match and Lewis was presented a belt by Gen. John V. Clinnin representing the Illinois title. The spectators responded with "one of the most spontaneous demonstrations Lewis had ever received." The match drew 7,244 and $13,064 but didn't come close to filling the spacious Chicago Stadium.[347] Being the Illinois world champion did Lewis little good and I don't think he ever defended the title in Chicago.

Lewis defended his California world title against another young ex-footballer in Joe Savoldi on November 25, 1931 at The Olympic Auditorium for Lou Daro. Savoldi wasn't much as a wrestler but he was a good-looking guy with a strong looking body, who introduced the drop kick into main stream wrestling. His drop kicks were stupendous, but his overall work wasn't up to the standards of the other young stars of 1931. Savoldi had beaten Marshall twice and Karl Sarpolis to get the title match with Lewis.

Lewis won the first fall with his reverse hammer lock, which he also was using under the name "cross body block." I think it was Lewis' "shoot move" that he used when worried about someone (like Thesz used his STF)—not that Lewis would worry about Savoldi. Joe won the second fall in 7:56 with a head scissors. In the third, Lewis caught Savoldi in the air after a drop kick attempt, and seemed to "power bomb" Savoldi for the pin in 9:15. No attendance was announced, so it may not have been good.[348]

The Ed Lewis Break Up with Billy Sandow

We only have Ed wrestling three more matches after Savoldi in 1931, and those were mainly in the Northwest where he seemed to have family. He seemed to have gone back into semi-retirement, being without a major promoter backing him as champion. Lewis spent his days running his Glendale and Alhambra restaurants, eating, drinking and playing cards until late into the night.[349]

Lou Daro only had two more cards at The Olympic during the year, and he was in the process of dumping the Sandow/Bowser group for the Londos/Pack/Curley team. Los Angeles was always a city willing to change alliances, and go with any promotion or champion that could make them money. Londos had been the top star in town before Lewis had moved in, and Daro wanted him and his title back. Daro knew there was no money in pushing old Lewis or foreigner Deglane as champion.

Billy Sandow either owned a part of Kansas City, MO, or had great influence over it. That continued after leaving Daro, and he also began working with Al Haft of Columbus and John Pesek. Haft was pushing Pesek hard as world champion. Pesek, with an established territory behind him, took great pleasure in beating the old super stars. He started the year on January 1, 1932 by defeating Joe Stecher, and later in the year, on May 11, talked Wladek Zbyszko into jobbing for him in Columbus. Sandow must have been putting pressure on Lewis to do the same and Ed seems to have even signed for such a match. On January 30, 1932, Strangler Lewis was suspended by the Missouri Athletic Commission for failing to follow through on a contract to meet John Pesek in the state. The commission did fail in an attempt to get the NWA to suspend Lewis in all the states affiliated with the organization.

On January 22, 1931, Billy Sandow, visiting his mother in Rochester, announced that his partnership with Ed Lewis was over. The rumor, which was true, was that the Strangler had signed a high paying contract to work for the Jack Curley group on the East Coast.[350] This might explain why Lewis was suspended in Missouri. If the NWA had upheld the ruling it would have upset Lewis' plains on the East Coast and Jack Curley probably had too much influence over the NWA to let that happen.

I've never found anything that made it seem like Sandow or Lewis worked together again. The long relationship between the two friends just ends.

Sandow's break with Lou Daro must have been bitter. In June 1932, Billy started a wrestling war with Lou Daro by promoting at the Hollywood Legion Stadium using Pesek and Marshall as his major stars. On August 25, 1932, Pesek defeated Marshall for a version of the world title in Hollywood.

The New York City War of 1932 and 1933

NWA world champion Jim Londos had continued to draw big crowds in the last part of 1931 and the beginning of 1932. He beat Ray Steele in Madison Square Garden on May 1, 1931, with 12,000 and $33,000. He drew a crowd of 9,000 to the Bronx to see him defeat Renato Gardini on May 8. In the Garden on May 25, he drew 12,000 and $33,000 in beating Sandor Szabo. Londos was rematched with Ray Steele for the big Summer show in Yankee Stadium on June 29, 1931. Some papers gave the attendance at 30,000, but the real figures were 21,000 and $63,000. He wrestled Rudy Dusek in Washington DC on July 17 with a crowd of 12,000. On July 23 he pulled in 11,234 in the Bronx wrestling Herb Freeman. On July 30, 1931 Londos drew a crowd of 11,000 to Coney Island for a match with an ex-Boston Braves pitcher named Al Pierotti. A rematch with Rudy Dusek in Washington DC drew 15,000 on August 12. The next night, August 13, he pulled in 10,000 in beating Kola Kwariani on Coney Island. On September 18, he and Ray Steele worked out doors in the Philadelphia Phillies Ball Park, drawing 15,000. 22,000 St. Louis fans watched Jimmy beat German Hans Kampfer on September 30. His number was 17,000 on November 16 as he beat George Calza in Madison Square Garden. On November 19, 1931 he brought in 15,800, a Toronto indoor sports record, against Gino Garibaldi. A rematch with George Calza drew 15,000 to the Garden on December 7. Another 15,000 spectators returned to the Garden to see another Londos/Steele match on another December 21. 1932 started with another crowd of 17,000 in Toronto for a January 14 match with fellow Greek George Zaharias. Londos drew against every type of opponent, in every city, and he didn't lose a fall all year.

Around early 1932, Londos' contract with the Curley group became void. For three years everyone in Curley's office was getting a percentage of Londos' purses. For being pushed in New York City and being made champion, Londos kicked back a major portion of his pay checks to Jack Curley, Rudy Miller, Jack Pfefer, and "Toots" Mondt.[351] He had the same type of deal that Mondt had in later years with Primo Carnera, Antonino Rocca and Andre The Giant, but Londos was smart about everything and very, very tight with money, so the idea of splitting gates from cities outside of New York City bothered him. So he broke his contract, either through the courts and commission, or it just ran out.

This loss of easy money upset the Curley office and they were worried that Londos would break away to form his own promotion in New York City using their world title. They wanted the title off Londos, so they asked the Greek to drop the belt back to Dick Shikat. He refused.

Toots Mondt had grown powerful in the time spent away from Billy Sandow. He worked for Ray Fabiani for a short period in Philadelphia and then moved on to the Jack Curley promotion. Curley was a major promoter of many different things. I think he used pro wrestling and varies charities, such as the Milk Fund, to make contacts with upper society. It was the way to find moneymen who could invest and finance his different projects. The big money wasn't in pro wrestling, so by 1930 he was mainly a figurehead used in promotion. The real wrestling minds in the office were Toots Mondt, Jack Pfefer, and Rudy Miller. Toots took credit for the creation of Jim Londos and just about everything else that was right with the sport during this period, so it's hard to tell what the truth was.

In late 1931 or early 1932, Toots Mondt visited his old friend Ed Lewis and persuaded him to leave Sandow and accepted a large contract (some say $50,000) to join the Curley's group. Billy was Ed's friend but Lewis knew what he was doing was small time compared with what was happening on the East Coast. Ed also knew that, at age 41, it was his last chance to stay at the top of his profession. He also needed money. With everything adding up, he accepted Toots' offer and dumped Sandow.

Toots had plans, but at the time I don't know if everything was figured out. He felt that Strangler Lewis, even with his age and lack of conditioning, was the ideal opponent to bring into New York to battle Londos, because of his ability to actual wrestle and his many past wins over the little Greek. Lewis hated Jimmy, and Londos respected and feared Ed. Lewis could win a PR battle and drive the little champion out of the city. Shikat couldn't do that. He had already lost twice to Londos and his ego made him as "thick as a brick." If a wrestling war started between Curley and Londos, Strangler Lewis would be someone Mondt wanted on his side.

Lewis began working for Jack Curley in late January 1932. Mondt didn't want to scare Londos, so he kept Lewis out of New York City. He put Lewis on the road, working the schedule of a 1932 pro wrestler, to get him in condition and see if he could handle the work load at his age. Wrestlers didn't perform the long matches, like champions of Lewis' days, but they worked almost every night, with a lot of travel. Ed worked harder in 1932 than at any time in his career. Toots put a lot of pressure on Lewis to lose weight. By the time he got to the big city, he was under 240 pounds. But for five months Lewis worked for Curley in Boston, Toronto, Cleveland, St. Louis, Philadelphia, Baltimore, Newark, and Los Angeles.

Lewis never stopped taking about and challenging Jim Londos. The champion couldn't be interviewed by anyone without being asked about Strangler Lewis. The match would develop into the biggest rivalry since Lewis/Stecher. Fans of 1932 didn't remember all the past matches between the two, and all the great battles Jim had given Ed, all they knew was that the Strangler had won 14 straight times—even if it was another Lewis lie.[352]

One of Curley's new stars was Sammy Stein. Curley told Londos that he planed to use Stein for the big outdoor show they ran every summer. Sammy Stein was a good-looking performer who was capable of drawing a good crowd, but not someone the Greek was worried about, so Londos liked the idea of wrestling him. Curley said he first wanted to build Stein up by having him beat ex-champ Dick Shikat in New York City. He wanted to promote it as a contender's match, with the winner getting a big title showdown with Londos. He asked if he could use a storyline that had Londos agreeing to meet the winner. Londos and his manager Ed White thought the winner was going to be Sammy Stein, so they said yes. Later the New York Athletic Commission had Londos sign legal agreements to meet the winner.

So on March 14, 1932, Sammy Stein wrestled Shikat in New York City. Dick Shikat won and received the contract for a title match with Jim Londos.

Ed White, Londos' manager, went to the commission to try to get out of the match, but they wouldn't budge. White then tried to work on Mondt, but was told that Londos would have to go through with the match and that Shikat was going to get the title back. Londos then quit the promotion, probably around the end of April 1932.

Over the next year and half, a bitter war raged in New York between the Curley group, which consisted of Curley, Mondt, Pfefer, Miller, Shikat and Lewis, and the Londos group, which still had promoters Ed White, Tom Packs, Ray Fabiani, John (Doc) Krone, Jimmy Johnson, and Lou Daro. A lot of Tom Packs' major talent also left Curley. Soon after, Curley's long feud with Paul Bowser ended and the two began working together.

Lewis began touring, outside of New York City, in February 1932. He was pushed very hard and was given wins over many of the stars of the promotion, including Jim McMillen, Jim Clintstock, Taro Myake, George Zaharias, Sandor Szabo, Matros Kirilenko, John Maxos, Rudy Dusek, Hans Kampfer, George Hagen, Renato Gardini, Jack Taylor, Kola Kwariani, Earl McCready, Leo Pinetzki, Tiny Roebuck, and Gino Garibaldi. The only match he didn't win was a 90 minute draw with Londos' policeman Ray Steele on February 24 in Boston, which was billed as a "shoot" match.[353]

Lewis was not billed as world champion, but his title claims were mentioned in interviews. His weight was announced at 238, but he looked to be carrying more poundage. His chest drooped and there seemed to be layers of flesh around his waist. He also looked slow and unsure of himself. In just about every city he was called an old man and given terrible reviews. Like the old gray mare, Lewis wasn't what he used to be.[354]

Lewis was brought into New York City in June and right away was booked into a contenders match with Dick Shikat on June 9, 1932 in Long Island City's (Queens) new Madison Square Garden Bowl. The winner would get a title match with Londos.

Shikat was the favorite and most fans thought he was being groomed for Londos' title. The card was the annual show for the Hearst Free Milk Fund. Curley announced a crowd of 25,000 and a gate of $65,000.

Shikat dominated the early minutes of the match. He put the burly Strangler into hold after hold, only to see Lewis break free. Shikat, in turn, broke a half dozen of Ed's headlocks. Shikat had a wide repertoire of holds while Lewis' offense centered around headlocks. After an hour Shikat slammed Lewis with two body slams, but Ed seemed unhurt and countered with three headlocks that were too much for Shikat to take. Shikat was pinned at the 1:06:07 mark. As a result of the win, the State commission ordered Londos to defend the title against Lewis in September or lose his claim in New York State.[355]

Shikat received $20,000 from Lewis for doing the job. It was to be returned after a rematch and title switch back to Shikat. Lewis didn't have the money, so he borrowed it from his manager, Toots Mondt, who transferred the money to Shikat's manager, Toots Mondt (yes, you read that right). For Lewis, it was better that way, because he had no intention of ever losing to Shikat. After Ed signed off on a new five year contract to be managed by Mondt, the rematch agreement was forgotten by everyone but Dick Shikat.[356]

Jack Curley and Toots seemed to have Jim Londos right where they wanted him. In late June, the New York Commission ordered Londos to sign for a Lewis match by October 31, or be stripped of the title. On July 8, 1932, Londos was ordered by the Pennsylvania Athletic Commission to defend against Lewis with in 60 days or the title would be vacated. Londos continued to refuse, saying he didn't want to injure an old blind man.

The Curley group did everything they could to abuse the Greek's reputation, as Lewis continued to wrestle nightly. The more Ed wrestled, the smaller the crowds became. The New Yorkers wanted Londos back and, until then, they were staying away, uninterested in an old fat man.

Jim Londos

Even with the bad publicity coming out of New York, Londos continued to draw across the nation. Working out of Los Angeles, he broke attendance records in San Francisco and San Diego. On July 18, 1932 a Londos/Steele draw drew 12,000 to Wrigley Field in Los Angeles. Londos even met with President Herbert Hoover on June 2 in Washington DC. He returned to Washington DC on June 23 to defeat Fred Grubmeier in front of a crowd over 10,000. At the September 21 convention of the NWA, the organization put out a statement saying that Londos would continue as their world champion.

In late July, it seemed certain that Lewis would be getting the championship, so Ed was sent to his summer home in Wisconsin to train, much like he always did before winning major title. For six weeks he chopped wood and worked in the forests around his farm.

On August 21, 1932, Toots Mondt was involved in a traffic accident 70 miles north of Toronto near Collingwood, Canada. Driving a Cadillac sports car, a little past midnight, Toots, while speeding around a corner collided head on with a car going in the opposite direction. In Toots' car was his brother Ralph and a woman who claimed to be a dancer. A woman in the other car, Theresa Luccioni, was killed and four others were injured. Toots was arrested and charged on September 2 of manslaughter and criminal negligence. On November 11, Toots was found guilty of criminal negligence by the supreme court of Barrie, Canada and sentenced to a year in jail. Mondt's lawyers appealed and the conviction was overturned in February 1933. Mondt was also sued by the dead girl's mother, the dancer (who lost earrings and suffered), and even his brother Ralph.[357]

Mondt was involved in another auto accident around September 27, 1932. It was a four car collision in New York City, near 116th Street and Riverside Drive. Sandor Szabo was the driver. Toots Mondt suffered a broken right wrist. Dick Shikat was also in the car and he broke his right arm and was forced off the mat for the rest for the year.[358]

So it can be said that Toots Mondt may have started the war with Londos, but for the last part of 1932, he was AWOL.

On September 30, 1932, the New York Commission stripped Jim Londos of the world title, and ordered Ray Steele and Jack Sherry to wrestle on October 10 in Madison Square Garden, with the winner to meet Strangler Lewis for the title. The mark commission didn't seem to understand the problems this created. Both Steele and Sherry were major hookers that were known for working for promotions at odds with Curley. Getting Jack Sherry for the match wasn't really that difficult since Paul Bowser and Curley had ended their long war and were working together. But Ray Steele was Londos' number one contender and policeman. Putting Steele in the same ring with Lewis was trouble and, if it did happen, it would have to be a shoot between the best true wrestlers of two warring promotions. It was a situation very rare in pro wrestling.

Steele refused the match with Sherry, but sent word he'd be willing to wrestle Lewis at a later date. The commission then ruled that Lewis would meet Jack Sherry on October 10, 1932 and the winner would be recognized as world champion in New York.

The match drew 5,000 and a gate of $7,200 to the huge Madison Square Garden. Jack Sherry showed up on orders from Paul Bowser but, at 220 pounds of pure muscle and a true wrestler with a ego to match, wasn't sure if he wanted to do the job. Curley, Lewis or one of the others in the promotion promised him that if he did the job that night, he would later get a rematch with Lewis that would be a true "contest."[359] Sherry agreed, but never got the second match.

For the first hour, the match was all stand up. They tugged, mauled and pushed each other without any form of "show" holds that the fans were used to. Some reports claim that Sherry refused to work and wanted to shoot for the first hour. The few fans in the arena hated all the standing around and started taunting the two giants. Right after the hour mark, Sherry came out of his defensive shell and Lewis started bouncing him around the ring. When they were on the mat, there was little action and one reporter thought Sherry had fallen asleep. After a series of headlocks, Lewis pinned Sherry in 1:23:30.[360]

Everyone but *Ring Magazine* thought the match was terrible. Many of the fans had left before the end. The match was so bad that *The Ring* publish a story defending it, saying the fans were fools and it was a throw-back to the real wrestling of Gotch's era.

Jack Sherry never got his rematch and I don't think he ever had another major match in America. Always looking for a "shoot," he ended up in England claiming the world title. Most of his career, if he had one, is unknown.

So Lewis then had the New York world title to go with his California and Illinois titles. Actually, I think by October 1932, California had been convinced to recognize Londos as champion and Illinois had quit worrying about the title, viewing pro wrestling as type of joke they didn't want to laugh at anymore.

Almost as soon as Ed was crowned, Jack Curley offered Jim Londos $50,000 for a title unification match. Jimmy never called him back.

On November 21, 1932, Lewis headlined a Madison Square Garden card, beating George Calza in front of another small crowd. A lack of Jim Londos was one factor in the drop in attendance, but the under cards were also weakened by a lack of talent. At that point Curley was using the same old Paul Bowser wrestlers to fill out his cards.

Ed Lewis vs George Calza, November 21, 1932.

The commission still required Lewis to wrestle Ray Steele, and the match was made for December 5, 1932 in Madison Square Garden. Steele had had a good year in 1932, and, unlike with Jack Sherry, he was a major national star. At the time he was on a winning streak, with a list including Jim McMillen (September 7), Hans Steinke (September 28), Joe Stecher (September 14), and Bert Assirati (November 9). He was known for doing major jobs for Londos but in his last match with the Greek he worked a draw at an outdoor card in Los Angeles' Wrigley Field (July 18). He also had given Lewis a working over in their 90 minute draw at Boston. Steele, like a few other performers like Billy Robinson and Dick Beyer, had the ability to make true wrestling entertaining, and he was a major draw country wide.[361]

Steele was very good friends with Londos but he was a great guy who made friends everywhere he went. Jack Curley and Lewis both liked and respected him. Unlike with Sherry, he was a hooker who played the game and was willing to put people over. Ray enjoyed life and didn't worry much about being the world's greatest wrestler. Unlike John Pesek, he never was known for hurting people, but when challenged he may have been the equal of any hooker.

Most people considered Steele to be Londos' policeman, but I don't know if he considered himself to be such, and I'm not sure if he liked the idea of doing a shoot in public. I think Curley, Mondt and Lewis took the match with him because they were used to working with him and knew him well. I think they trusted him and figured they could work some type of match that would satisfy everyone. As to the people on Londos' side, insiders, and any type of smart fan — they were sure the bout would be a shoot.

On December 5, the Garden drew a crowd of 8,000 ($11,000) which were divided by the Curley fans and many supporters of the Londos group. Lewis was seconded by his trainer John Evko. Steele used an Indian wrestler called Tom Marvin, who was actually a retired boxer, for his second. The match started slow and stayed slow. Steele stayed away from Lewis and Ed followed him around the ring. It seemed that Steele's plan was to keep the old 240 pound champion moving and to attack his eyes. Steele kept forearming Lewis in the face around the eyes. Everyone knew about Ed's bad eyes and the salty perspiration from both men also clouded his vision. Lewis kept trying to get Steele into a bear hug (probably his pinning body lock), but Ray was able to break every attempt. For 32 minutes the crowd was bored to death, then they came alive as Steele started hitting the old Strangler with more elbows to the head. Three elbows had Lewis groggy, when his second Evko leaped into the ring to protest. Under the rules of 1932, a second entering the ring should result in the wrestler being disqualified. Lewis yelled at Evko: "Get out of here. You have no business in this ring and you have nothing to do with me. Out! Out! Out!" Lewis then pushed Evko through the ropes. The referee Eddie Forbes ordered the wrestlers to resume. Steele immediately started where he had left off by driving his elbow into Lewis chin. The Strangler reeled back into the ropes and Ray let him have it again. Referee Forbes told Steele to stop, ignoring the fact that elbows were legal in a normal wrestling matches, and warned Ray that he would be disqualified if he hit Lewis again. Steele did just that thing and, without hesitating, Forbes stepped between them, waved them to their corners and raised Lewis' arm as the victor. They announced Steele as the loser on a foul.

The end of the Ed Lewis / Ray Steele title match, Madison Square Garden, December 5, 1932.

The crowd was in an uproar, yelling, screaming, stamping and throwing things all over the place. Jack Curley had words with Steele's second Tom Marvin and the boxer threw a punch at the promoter. The blow glanced off the promoter's head, as the police jumped on Marvin, beating him into insensibility with their clubs. They then dragged the boxer to the dressing-room. Fights broke out all over the arena between Lewis and Londos supporters. Riots only stopped with the start of the last match of the night.[362]

After the bout, Steele said he had nothing to say except that what happened in the ring was enough evidence in itself to establish the fact that he was Lewis' master. Steele's people claimed that after a half hour Lewis realized he could do nothing with Steele and gave the signal from his second to jump in the ring and complicate the affair. The reporter also claimed the blows to the head were legal in most states and there were bouts on the under card with wrestlers throwing punches and elbows, and none of them were disqualified.

The story Ed Lewis would tell is that Steele realized that he couldn't beat Lewis, so he started throwing punches to get himself disqualified, bypassing the humiliation of being pinned.

Years later, Ed would claim that Jim Londos had told Steele to wrestle the match in bare feet, and they had become so blistered that Ray didn't want to continue. In the two accounts I've read in newspapers, there is no mention of bloody feet. And Londos wasn't in New York that night.[363]

Of course, it's the Lewis story that has lived on through the years.

On December 6, the New York Athletic Commission announced that Ray Steele was suspended for 60 days and John Evko and Renato Gardini (who jumped into the ring) were suspended indefinitely. The commission was unable to punish Tom Marvin for punching Curley, because he had no license in New York to revoke.[364]

Lewis was still upset over the $20,000 he had given Dick Shikat. A meeting was called with Lewis,

Mondt, and Shikat present. Shikat was told that if he returned the $20,000 and added another $12,000, he would be given a rematch with Ed and the title. Shikat agreed and forked up the money. He was recovering from his broken arm from the car crash, but once he returned he would once again be king of New York wrestling. The title match never happened.

Lewis and Curley attendance continued to bomb. A December 19 handicap match drew 5,000 to Madison Square Garden. On December 15, Lewis traveled to St. Louis to beat Sandor Szabo. The match drew a gross of $326, which didn't pay the expenses for the trip. The fans in New York wanted their Jim Londos back and rejected Lewis completely.

In late 1932, the commission agreed to allow Londos to wrestle in the city if he would not bill himself as world champion. Tom Packs and Ray Fabiani then joined with the Johnson brothers, Charlie and Willee Johnson to bring Londos back to the city. They needed a good wrestling man to book, so Rudy Dusek, who was promoting the South for Curley, also joined the group.

Londos returned on January 11, 1933. In the small St. Nick's Arena, Jimmy beat Abe Coleman in front of a sellout 6,000 with over another 1,000 turned away. The fans, who couldn't get tickets, rioted outside the stadium, breaking windows in an attempt to get in. The riot police had to be called to clear them out. But the economic depression had peaked in the city in 1933 and ticket prices dropped. Some tickets sold as low as 40 cents. The gate was $9,600.[365]

By the beginning of 1933, any hope of promoting Ed Lewis as champion was over. The only problem for Curley, Bowser, Mondt, Pfeffer, and Miller was finding a new champion. Their pick turned out to be a Bowser mid-card wrestler named Jim Browning. Browning had been around for years and had wrestled just about everyone, but had never been pushed as an unbeatable champion. He was long, lean and powerful in the gym and a match for anyone. Why he was pushed to the top in 1933 is hard to say, but he was a very good worker and a major shooter and he probably caught the eye of Mondt and Lewis. In fact he had been around so long that they all were old friends. Browning had also developed a flashy finishing hold called the airplane scissors.

He would put wrestlers in a leg scissors, pick them up just using his legs, spin them around and then crash them into the mat for the pin. As a hooker, he idolized Joe Stecher and was the same type of leg wrestler, working everything around the leg scissors.

On January 23, 1933, Lewis defended the title against Jim Browning in Madison Square Garden, drawing 7,000. Browning out-wrestled Ed during the match and seemed to have the champion beat, but the Strangler turned things around just when it looked the darkest and surprised everyone by pinning Jim. Locked in the scissors, Lewis stood up and power bombed Browning for the win in 34:52.[366]

Lewis headlined the Garden the next month on February 6, drawing less that 5,000 in beating Dr. Fred Meyers.

On February 10, 1933, Henri Deglane returned from France to defend his AWA world title against ex-champ Ed Don George in Boston Garden before a crowd of 12,000. As champion, Deglane had defended the title against George four times in Boston and Buffalo. All four were draws. They may have wrestled in Paris a few times but we have no record of it.

Champion Deglane won the first fall with a side hiplock in 17:24 but had taken a beating in doing so. George pulverized Henri with a series of flying tackles to win the second fall in one minute and 54 seconds. In the third George swarmed all over Deglane hitting

Jim Browning

him with tackle after tackle. After the fifth one, Deglane couldn't get up. Henri had a broken collarbone, so referee Sam Smith awarded the victory and AWA title to George.[367]

The rematch between Lewis and Jim Browning took place on February 20, 1933 in Madison Square Garden, with the New York world title on the line. The attendance was once again a very disappointing 5,000, with a gate of $5,000. Browning was the aggressor throughout the match. He was on top of Lewis most of the time and used a wider, more punishing and effective repertoire of holds. Only once was Lewis able to apply a headlock and it was broken after about a minute. At 57:50 he was pinned after one of Browning's airplane scissors.

Lewis dropping the world title to Jim Browning

Browning was a surprise winner and the crowd gave him an ovation that lasted over five minutes.

This was the first title loss by Strangler Lewis that didn't have some screw finish tied on to it. After a four month reign that ranked as the worst in wrestling history, I think Lewis and all the promoters knew it would be Ed's last major title. He was through as a champion, but fans were still interested in seeing him lose, so he was much more valuable as a challenger, who could lose and give credibility to a champion. The idea of quitting on top wasn't for Ed. He spent his money too easily and would always need a job or go broke.

Dick Shikat was upset when he found out that Browning was the new champion, but Lewis calmed him down by telling him that Browning had double-crossed him. Shikat then wanted to break Browning's neck. The story told in *Fall Guys* is that Lewis and Mondt received $42,000 for dropping the title (considering that the match drew $5,000, I find all these figures hard to believe.). Shikat found out and realized, after four years, that his manager was a rat and started protesting. Curley, Mondt, Pfeffer, and Lewis invited him up to Toots' room at the Hotel Warwick for a conference. Shikat went and got into an argument, calling his partners crooks—which they seemed to be. Lewis punched Shikat and a fight started. Lewis couldn't take care of the German, so Toots jumped in and the two of them beat up Shikat, "giving him the trouncing of his life." Shikat was later treated for his injuries at the Polyclinic Hospital.

I don't know if the *Fall Guy* story is true, but it would explain Shikat motives that resulted in events three years later.

A Lewis / Shikat match did take place as the semi-main event on a March 6, 1933 Browning / Stein card at the Garden. The match was billed as a finish match but was stopped after an hour because of the New York curfew and ruled a draw.

Jack Pfefer's job with Jack Curley was to handle the finances and take care of the books. He also promoted for Curley and brought talent to America from Europe. He had a brilliant wrestling mind but the worms of greed had eaten holes in it and he wanted to run things on his own and be the man who promoted the big Madison Square Garden shows. In early 1933, he jumped from the Curley office to the Londos group. Both companies were doing poorly in New York, but Londos was still the star and drawing as usual outside of the city and it seemed the stronger side. Pfefer dumped Curley and started booking the New York clubs for

Londos with the promise of being the top promoter in New York once the war was over. Pfefer then talked his partner Rudy Miller into jumping over to the Londos side.[368]

On March 20, 1933, Lewis had his third Garden match with New York champion Jim Browning. The title change had brought new interest to the fans of New York and the match drew 15,000 with a gate of $16,500. Lewis could do no better and was pinned after being given a ride in the airplane scissors in 59:58.[369]

Ed Lewis vs Jim Browning

Toots Mondt had been trying to discredit Londos for over a year with no success. Londos was too smart and knew all the tricks. But on April 7, 1933, Londos was booked to defend the title against Joe Savoldi in an outdoor show at Chicago Stadium. The referee was Bob Managoff, the old friend of Lewis who had taken Ed's 'Bob Fredrick' name in 1912 forcing him to take the Strangler identity. Savoldi had been trained by Lewis when the young footballer had worked for Billy Sandow in Los Angeles. Sandow had raised a stink when Savoldi jumped to Lou Daro's promotion, but in hindsight he may have been a plant. Londos had no fear of the non-wrestler Savoldi but he overlooked the damage a paid-off referee could do. After about 26 minutes of wrestling, Londos had Savoldi locked into a Japanese arm bar, with Savoldi standing. They were in the ropes, so when referee Managoff broke the hold Londos thought they were just going to the middle of the ring for a restart. Managoff then pulled one of the most famous double-crosses in ring history by declaring Savoldi the winner and new champion. Managoff claimed that in applying the arm lock, Londos had pinned himself. In 1933, the three count wasn't counted aloud nor were they asked to slap the mat. A pin fall was just the referee's judgment.[370]

Londos went nuts and got his story into the press. He claimed his shoulders were not on the mat and they were raped up in the ropes anyway. Most of the fans present that night couldn't see anything, or they agreed with Londos' story. Outside of New York City, the story was written up like Londos had been double-crossed. The stories in the papers over the next week had Savoldi signing with Joe Corcoran, a money man in the Paul Bowser office and a co-promoter with Toots Mondt in the Queensbury Sports Club of Toronto, Savoldi's wife divorcing him, and referee Bob Managoff signing to officiate Savoldi's matches in Canada. It wasn't hard for the Londos group to prove their point.

The Illinois Commission backed up Managoff's decision and the win by Savoldi but said that the commission didn't recognize anyone as champion in the state, so the match was a non-title match. The NWA also ruled that Londos was still champion. Savoldi was also suspended by the NWA for missing dates in Indiana.

The Illinois commission, aroused by all the talk of "double-crossing," once again banned the sport of pro wrestling in the state. This backfired on Mondt because Chicago promoter John "Doc" Krone had booked a Browning/Lewis rematch for April 11. The commission stated that the show was cancelled but a court order got the show reinstated at the last moment. The fans were left confused so only 800 showed up, producing a tiny gate of $1,100. Browning then beat Lewis using his airplane scissors in 1:03:32.[371]

Jim Browning vs Ed Lewis in Chicago, April 11, 1933

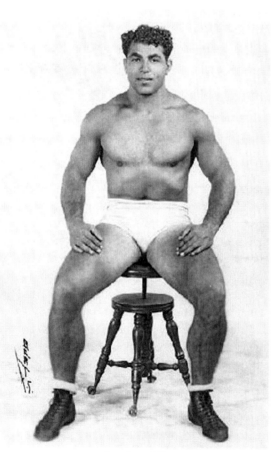

Joe Savoldi

On April 20, 1933, Doctor Benjamin Roller died from pneumonia in New York City.

Before and after Chicago, Lewis had been visiting his home and wife Elaine in Glendale, California. He then worked some dates in Seattle and Vancouver and returned to Los Angeles through San Francisco. In Oakland he beat old Ad Santel on April 28. He defeated Oki Shikina in San Diego on May 9, before flying back to New York for a date in the Garden.

In New York City he met Joe Savoldi, the conqueror of Jim Londos, at the Garden on May 15, 1933. Savoldi was not billed as world champion, but his title claim and win over Londos was being built up in the city. Commissions in Pennsylvania and Illinois had ordered Savoldi to meet Londos in a rematch and Curley, Bowser, and Mondt knew it was going to be hard to keep the non-wrestler away from getting double-crossed by Jim Londos or anyone else. To get the commissions off Savoldi's back, they had Lewis defeat Savoldi by count out (after missing a dropkick, Savoldi fell out of the ring, injured). With Savoldi's title claim resting with Lewis, it ended any noise by Londos or his commissions. A rematch was booked back in Madison Square Garden a week later on May 22, 1933.

But before Lewis could dump his new title claim back to Savoldi, he wrestled Ed Don George for the Paul Bowser AWA world title in Boston on May 17, 1933. This was billed as the rematch of Lewis' title win over George and Ed's first shot at the title he lost to Deglane by foul. The Savoldi title claim in the possession of Lewis also added importance to the match. Smart fans knew he was always a threat. So you could never predict when he would pull a double-cross of his own and steal the title.

The Boston Garden match saw George win the first fall in 22:05 with a crossover toe hold after he had floored Lewis with a couple of flying tackles. The second fall went to Lewis in 7:39 when he broke away from another toe hold and clamped George in a bearish headlock. Another toehold gave Ed Don George the third fall and match in 3:45. The attendance was 10,000. The result complicated any Londos plan to get his title claim back. George was a young fine wrestler and someone Londos would have to talk with before attempting a match.[372]

Curley still had plans for Joe Savoldi in New York City, so on May 22, 1933, he defeated Lewis at Madison Square Garden. After getting thrown around by Lewis headlock, Savoldi made a comeback, pinning the Strangler after two perfect dropkicks. Time was 43:07.[373]

Lewis left New York that night and flew into Chicago where he beat Sammy Stein two out of three falls on May 23. He followed that with a trip to Milwaukee, where he did a job for Gus Sonnenberg (May 24). He then flew home to Glendale to be near Elaine who was feeling sick.

Lou Daro, at The Olympic Auditorium, jumped promotions again, leaving the Londos group for Jack Curley and Paul Bowser. New York world champion Jim Browning had defended his title against Nick Lutze at the Olympic on May 17, billed as New York world champion. On May 28, Daro announced he had signed Browning to wrestle ex-champ Strangler Lewis at the Olympic on June 7, 1933.

In the week leading up to the match, Lewis trained before the public in Idyllwild while Browning training headquarters was at Crystal Pier. I think Browning saw this time as a vacation because Curley and company had been working him hard defending the title nightly all over the west coast. Browning was treated more as an employee than a star with a huge ego. Lewis spent most of his time trying to perfect his headlock which had been losing its effectiveness. The three defeats to Browning had been one fall matches, and Lewis felt he would have a better chance against the champion in a two out of three fall match.

Sammy Stein

That idea worked out. Browning won the first fall in 31:02 with the airplane scissors. Lewis took the second fall after a series of headlocks in 11:11. The third fall saw Lewis forearm Browning into a corner and then put him into a full nelson. Browning then raised up his feet and pushed off the ropes. Both men fell backward with the champion on top, getting the pin. Time was 11 minutes. The match drew 9,000.[374]

Browning then returned to New York City for an out door card with Joe Savoldi at Yankee Stadium on June 12, 1933. The gate was hurt by two factors: it rained, and Savoldi had been shot on by a nobody named Sol Slagel on a Staten Island card. A referee saved Savoldi from defeat after overlooking about 10 pin falls. The Browning/Savodi match went to a 1:58:05 draw and the attendance was 6,000 in the huge stadium.[375]

Gus Sonnenberg had been on the June 7 under card and was upset that Ed had gotten the title match, considering all the wins he had scored over Lewis as champion. This build up led to a contenders match between Gus and

Lewis at The Olympic on June 21, 1933. Sonnenberg won two out of three falls, both falls won with the flying tackle.[376] Sonnenberg then defeated Sammy Stein on June 28. Browning and Sonnenberg were then matched at The Olympic on July 12, 1933, with the California Commission recognizing the winner as champion in the state. Browning won the match and the title.

The semi-final of the July 12 card was a two out of three fall match between Lewis and Sammy Stein. Stein made a fierce comeback to pin Lewis in the third fall using a flying tackle and a cross body block. This win gave Stein an outdoor title match with Jim Browning at Wrigley Field (LA version) on August 28, 1933.[377]

On August 3, Lewis went to Canada to wrestle Jim Browning again, this time in Vancouver. Ed did the job and returned home to Glendale. I believe Lewis had expanded his number of restaurants to three, the new one being located in Pasadena.

On the under card of the Wrigley Field Browning/Stein match, Lewis beat old Marin Plestina in 5:24. The workhorse Browning took two out of three falls from Stein in a good match. The card drew 14,000.

Fred Beell

Fred Beell, who was the dominant wrestler in Wisconsin during Lewis' early years and the last man to defeat Frank Gotch, retired from pro wrestling in 1919. He returned to working his farm in Marshfield, Wisconsin, about 41 miles North-west of Nekoosa. Beel also worked as a relief officer for the Marshfield Police force under Chief of Police William Paape. On August 5, 1933, Beell was shotgunned in the face and killed by a gang of criminals robbing the Marshfield Brewing Company. Beell was 57 years old and had been with the department for twelve years. He is buried at the Hillside Cemetery in Marshfield. He remains today as the only Marshfield police officer to be killed in the line of duty.

On August 29, Lewis and Browning had a match in San Diego. Lewis got a draw with the champion in front of a crowd of 4,000.[378]

Street & Smith's Sport magazine for June, July and August 1933 published Strangler Lewis' life story in three parts. Some of it was true.

The rematch between Browning and Savoldi in Madison Square Garden took place on October 2. Browning defeated Savoldi in 36:51. The attendance was 10,000.

Browning drew a lot better than Lewis in the Garden, and a few of his matches grew as much as 12,000. But he was fair from the draw that Londos was in 1931. The war between Curley and Londos had dragged on too long and both sides were losing money.

Cast photo of 'The Prizefighter and the Lady' (1933), starring Myrna Loy, Walter Huston and Max Baer. Fighters in the photo are Joe Riviera, Bull Montana, James J. Jeffries, Max Baer, Jack Dempsey, Primo Carnera, Ed Lewis, Jess Willard, Billy Papke, and ring announcer Dan Tobey.

Lewis stayed on the West Coast for most of the rest of 1933, working small arenas in San Diego and going north at times for cards in Portland and Salt Lake City. In September he filmed a short bit in the movie 'The Prizefighter and the Lady,' which stared Myrna Loy, and Max Baer as himself. The big scene was a fight between Baer and the actually heavyweight boxing champion, Primo Carnera. The director Howard Hawks wanted Baer to win the fight, but Primo refused, so it ended in a draw. The next year would see Baer defeat Carnera for real and become world boxing champion. Lewis played himself, being introduced before the match, with buddy Jack Dempsey. The film became a big hit when released on November 10, 1933.

In October, Lewis accepted a tour of Texas and New Orleans, but was called back when his wife Elaine Tomaso Friedrich died at her home in Glendale on October 27, 1933. She had been suffering from a pulmonary illness for many months.[379]

At the end of August, Jim Londos left for a six week tour of Europe. On October 22, he defeated Kola Kwariani at Athens, Greece in front of a crowd said to be 110,000. (Film of this match has recently surfaced. The crowd looks huge, but many historians think the real attendance to be around 65,000 due to the size of the stadium. Any uncynically-minded fan who saw the film in 1933 might very well believe 110,000.)

The War Ends (For Some)

While Londos was away, Ed White, Tom Packs, and Ray Fabiani began negotiating with Jack Curley, Paul Bowser, Toots Mondt, Rudy Dusek, and Lou Daro. At one point a meeting was held at the Pennsylvania Hotel. A new wrestling trust was formed consisting of just about every major promoter, except for the Johnson Brothers and the two traitors, Jack Pfefer and Rudy Miller. With the war over, the new Trust would control pro wrestling from one coast to another. It was more of a merger that just an agreement. They were to be partners and all would share in everyone's gates and trade talent.

Jim Londos was not one of the partners. He took the position of world champion and would get his cut from resulting gates. Londos also had a contract that would give him $50,000 if he was beaten by anyone, even in a double-cross.

Londos took many trips to his home country Greece over his career, and it's funny how he always returned to America in a stronger position than when he left. When he came back to America this time, he found himself back on top of the world—everyone's world.

Jim had one other thing written into his new contract: a victory over Strangler Lewis.

When Pfefer found out he had been double-crossed by the new trust, he went nuts. He promised he'd "drink their blood." Pfefer was as smart as anyone and he was willing to destroy the sport to get back at the promoters who had back stabbed him. The one man he hated more that anyone else was Jim Londos.[380]

Pfefer took on the methods of George M. Marsh (Joe Carroll or Ole Marsh), breaking kayfabe and revealing the inner workings of pro wrestling to any newspaper or reporter who would listen. Jack kept complete records on everything and would give newspaper winners and losers before matches took place. He just didn't expose wrestling as the worked sport it was—most knew that. Pfefer brought a cynicism to the sport that told fans and reporters that they were fools for being deceived by low life wrestling promoters. People who weren't wrestling fans began looking down on anyone who enjoyed the sport. For years Pfefer would continue his vendetta against the major promoters, but mostly against Jim Londos. He would even send out a bulletin exposing the "sport" and discrediting wrestling insiders to all the newspaper who would pay attention. No one in the history of pro wrestling did more to hurt the art form than Jack Pfefer.

That being said, Pfefer had a brilliant wrestling mind, and within a year was back in business in New York City promoting light heavyweights. He would be a major part of the business until the 1960's, booking and supplying talent to small territories and outlaw groups.

Lewis putting the squeeze on promoter Jack Pfefer.

After taking care of the affairs of Elaine, Lewis returned to his wrestling career. On November 20, Ed wrestled a 20 minute draw with a young star named Sandor Szabo on the undercard of the Browning / Sonnenberg main event in Madison Square Garden. Lewis, except for a few trips to St. Louis, remained on the East Coast for the rest of 1933.

On November 27, Lewis wrestled in St. Louis against Roland Kirchmeyer for the Jackson Johnson Jr. American Legion post. Lewis won but only drew 1,584 and $658.50, the smallest gate he had ever drawn in the city. This was a promotion working against Tom Packs. Packs was pushing Ray Steele and just four days before the Lewis card (November 23) Steele had defeated John Pesek.

Lewis then moved on to Camden, where he was again defeated by champion Jim Browning on November 30, 1933. Lewis defeated his old rival Wladek Zbyszko in Newark on December 6. Lewis' weight at this time was 264 pounds.

With the new trust in effect, fans were beginning to see "dream matches" in every promotion. The first such match in New York was a title unification match between State world champion Jim Browning and Boston's AWA world title holder Ed Don George. On the December 18 under card, Lewis wrestled a 20 minute draw with Gus Sonnenberg. Later that night, George and Browning wrestled to a 1:40:00 curfew time limit draw. The Madison Square Garden card drew 8,000 and $16,651.

On December 14, 1933, Tom Packs was in court being sued by a former referee Harry Sharpe for $25,000. Sharpe had been injured following a February 17 Jim Londos match, that may or may not have taken place in St. Louis. Ed Lewis was present in the court room; the storyline was that he was a friend of Sharpe and his attorney, Robert Kratky, and was going to be used as a witness. The state Commissioner, Seneca Taylor was also present and was scheduled to testify.

With Packs on the stand, he was questioned by Sharpe's lawyer Kratky. Somehow the topic became the booking policies of the St. Louis promotion. Packs was asked if he refused to use some wrestlers, naming Strangler Lewis as an example. Packs said he would use everyone, including Lewis. He said all Lewis had to do was to step up and sign a contract.

Ray Steele

The spectators were in a uproar as Lewis walked up the center of the aisle toward Packs and Commissioner Taylor to demand that he be signed up then and there. A blank contract was brought into the courtroom. Packs asked Lewis if he'd agree to wrestle Ray Steele or John Pesek. Lewis said he'd wrestle anyone, just so long as he got Londos if he won. Packs said he couldn't guarantee Londos, but he'd give him Steele and cancel his Pesek / Steele rematch if Lewis would agree to the match on December 20. Lewis posted a check for $1,500 as a forfeit with the commissioner and the match was made.[381]

It's hard to believe that a judge would allow a wrestling promoter to use his courtroom to work a wrestling angle, but the newspaper highlighted the story the next day. With the new trust agreements unknown to the public, everyone but insiders knew the match had to be a "shoot" match. The papers were filled with the report of the Garden match and reported that the next match was going to be a true contest "to the finish." In its time, this was the "grand daddy" angle of all time — if it made money.

Steele and Lewis both stated that they would refuse any victory that was disputed in any way. The fans were told there would be no disqualification this time. The commission promised Lewis that all he had to do to get Jim Londos in the ring was beat Ray Steele.

The December 20, 1933 match drew the season's largest crowd of 9,288 and a gate of $9,357.85. The referee was not announced until bell time, and it turned out to be Charley Rentrop, a former wrestler and Memphis promoter. Steele was the crowd favorite and Lewis got his normal boos. The early going was mostly stand up, with the two pushing each other around the ring. Steele attempted two weak side suplexes and Ed missed a few headlocks. At ten minutes, Steele took Lewis to the mat with a double wristlock but Ed freed himself with a headlock. Lewis tried several full body locks, but never succeeded in holding Steele for long. Lewis backed Ray into a corner and landed a terrific elbow under the heart. He then head locked and threw Steele to the mat with Ed's 255 pounds landing on top of him. It looked bad, but Steele managed to get back on to his feet. Lewis kept the headlock on and seemed to be applying great pressure. Steele looked to be out but the referee ruled the hold a strangle and broke it. Rentrop kept Lewis away as Steele recovered by sprinting around the ring until his head cleared. Steele then nailed Lewis with an elbow to the jaw and followed with four front headlock throws. Lewis looked too big to be bothered by the throws and got up unhurt. In fact, Ed became the aggressor, backing Steele into the corner while landing a number of elbows. Forced to break and move back, Lewis broke Steele's attempt at a front face lock. Steele was then stunned by a number of rabbit punches. As Lewis came forward, Steele hit him with a flying tackle. As Lewis got up, he was hit again. As he got back up to his feet again, Steele charged but changed the move into a straight-arm blow to the jaw and the Strangler went down in a heap. Steele then picked Lewis up into the air and slammed him as the crowd stood cheering in anticipation. Steele laid across Lewis and Rentrop ruled Lewis pinned. Time was 36:38. The pin was unnecessary, as Lewis remained out cold for five minutes and had to be carried to the dressing room. Lewis' second, Toots Mondt, protested that Ed had been unfairly slugged prior to the slam, but the commissioner Taylor paid no heed. Steele's second for the night was once again Tommy Marvin.[382]

Neither Steele or Lewis were being built up for a title match with Londos in St. Louis in 1933. Steele had been defeated by Londos in Chicago on December 13. Lewis left St. Louis for Philadelphia and on December 29, 1933 did another job for Jim Browning. Steele's next big match in St. Louis was a 17 minute job for Gus Sonnenberg on January 10, 1934. It drew 7,000 but set up the real super match between Gus Sonnenberg and Jim Londos that drew 15,666 St. Louis fans on February 2, 1934.

Lewis faced a lot of problems at the start of 1934. He had lost his third wife, he had expanded his restaurant business to three sites but none were making him a lot of money, he was 43 years old, overweight (260 pounds), and had lost his ability and willingness to train. He also was addicted to cards and was probably starting to have a drinking problem. He no longer had any major promoters interested in pushing him to a championship. His pluses were his ability as a hooker and his famous name. He had some value as a contender, but if he continued to do frequent well-known jobs, he faced being devalued into a mid-card has-been. Lewis' biggest adventage in 1934 was his feud and known hatred of Jim Londos. The fact that Londos needed a big win over the Strangler gave Lewis something to sell. He also had the ability to talk and promote himself, and the public and most reporters still believed that the wrestling before 1921 was true shoots and that, in a true wrestling contest, Ed Lewis could beat anyone in the sport—if he really wanted to.[383]

By this time Lewis must have been told that a condition given to Londos in the formation of the new trust was one or more wins over Lewis. Another condition may have been a Steele win over Ed too. Londos had many major storylines and feuds in 1934 but he and everyone knew he had to get his win over Lewis. I think Ed convinced the trust that they needed to promote the Londos/Lewis match and give it the spotlight it needed to draw a major gate. Lewis had done major jobs in New York City and Los Angeles, so it would have been a waste to put the match in either of those two cities. They decided to run the match in Ed's home city of Chicago. The trust also understood that Lewis' record needed some big wins before he got in the ring with Londos. Lewis must have explained all of this with promoters, and it was a solid plan that would make money. So in 1934, Strangler Lewis went back to getting a major push.

In January 1934, Lewis worked small towns out of Glendale and then spent a few weeks in the mid-west. He returned to New York City on February 6, dropping a 30 minute decision to Rudy Dusek. He remain in the city and the areas surrounding it for the rest of the month, winning all of his matches.

Londos began what would be the greatest year any pro wrestler would ever have, by drawing 16,000 in defeating Joe Stecher in Detroit on January 12. A rematch and another win over Stecher in Detroit drew

Everett Marshall

16,750 on January 26. The Chicago rematch with Joe Savoldi on January 31 drew 20,200. The Dream match with Gus Sonnenberg in St. Louis drew 15,666 on February 2.[384] A February 10 match in Philadelphia with Everett Marshall drew 15,000. Londos won the match in three hours, four minutes, and forty-five seconds.[385]

Londos had his first match in Madison Square Garden in two years on February 5. Once again working for Jack Curley, Londos beat Ernie Dusek in front of 7,000 for a gate of $10,000. Lewis was ringside to challenge the Greek one more time.[386]

Lewis returned to St. Louis on February 15 to wrestle Joe Malcewicz to a 30 minute draw. The main event was AWA world champion Ed Don George beating Gino Garibaldi. The Bowser champion only drew 5,373 and $4,188.85 for Tom Packs.[387]

Joe Stecher had his last match on February 21, 1934 in Chicago, losing a title match against the man who idolized him, Jim Browning. Joe announced his retirement soon after. He spent his time after that helping his brother Tony promote in Minneapolis. Joe, always quiet and sensitive, developed major health problems. He had an emotional breakdown and suffered from uncontrolled depression. His wife left him, taking his children, and he was institutionalized in a Veterans Hospital for the next 30 years, looked after by his brother Tony.

Lewis returned to the East Coast. Some of the people he beat in the first two months of 1934 were: Rudy Dusek, Matros Kirilenko, Chief Chewacki, Joe Cox, Abe Kashey, Dick Raines, Mike Romano, Hans Kampfer, Eddie Civil, George Calza, and Tiny Roebuck.

Dick Shikat was being pushed in St. Louis to ready himself for a title match with Londos. Packs booked Lewis to a rematch with Shikat on March 1, 1934. Once again the winner was going to be given a match with Jim Londos, so all Ed had to do was win to have all his wishes come true. He lost. Lewis got disqualified for punching Shikat after 34:23 by referee Charley Rentrop. Lewis was upset by Rentrop, so he punched him too. Still upset, Lewis also punched the first arena guard to enter the ring. The police then jumped into the ring to restore order. Lewis was fined $100 and suspended by the Missouri Athletic Commission. Attendance was 6,051.[388]

Shikat wanted a rematch so Lewis' suspension was lifted. On March 15 the two met again in St. Louis but this time Lewis was pinned by Shikat in 34:36. Attendance was 8,219. For the win Shikat was given his match with Jim Londos on April 11. Londos pinned him in 1:10:33 drawing 11,727. Londos would beat Shikat again in St. Louis on May 16, drawing 10,138.[389]

On April 2, 1934, Lewis wrestled AWA world champion Ed Don George in his home town of Buffalo, and lost.

Lewis then returned to Los Angeles and beat Mike Mazurki on the undercard of a Browning title defense against Leo Numa at the Olympic on April 11.

On April 15, 1934, Lewis and Browning traveled to the Mexico City bullring to wrestle for the title. Browning took two out of three falls from Ed, but the strangest oddity of the night was the Mexican fans cheering for Lewis while booing Browning. The card drew 12,000 and $10,000.[390]

Lewis beat a Cowboy Jack Ray on a under card for a Browning win over Dick Daviscourt at the Olympic Auditorium on April 18. It was becoming the fashion to make fun of Lewis' fat, age and ability to sweat.

The Los Angeles Times printed this review: "The old man of the mountain ... with most of the mountain centering around his midsection, Ed (Strangler) Lewis, hardly worked up a sweat in flipping 'Cowboy' Jack Ray on his back in 14 minutes of the third match. Yes, you guessed it, the fall was scored with Lewis's favorite hold, the headlock."[391]

In accepting the job to Londos, Lewis must have made some demands of his own, and from that point forward the push got serious. In the last days of April and the first week of May, Lewis defeated Rudy Dusek, George Hagen, and Sandor Szabo.

On May 14, 1934, Lewis got another match with Ray Steele in New York City, this time at Jack Curley's Seventy-first Regiment Armory. Most of the fans were barely settled in their seats before the finish took place. After some preliminary tussling, Lewis hurled Steele to the mat a dozen times with alternate body slams and forearm punches. After 11 minutes and 7 seconds, Lewis pinned Steele after one of his body slams. The attendance for the card, a rematch of two Hall of Fame wrestlers that had been the talk of the sport the years before, was 2,000.

Sandor Szabo

The small number shows how the war on Londos had killed the sport in the big city.[392] On May 23, Lewis defeated Hans Steinke. Both Steele and Steinke were considered policemen for Londos these wins showed he was serious about beating the Greek.

On May 28, 1934, Lewis was involved in another dream match, this time in Montreal. It was a rematch of the famous "bite match" against Henri Deglane. After negotiations that lasted years, the match was made by the decree of the Montreal Athletic Commission. In front of a crowd of 7,000, Lewis started slow, allowing Deglane to lead the attack and the Frenchman won the first fall in 15:18. After that, Lewis asserted himself and started to rough Deglane up. Little by little, Deglane lost his strength and confidence. At 18:15, he was pinned following a Lewis headlock. Lewis refused to release the hold after the fall was called and seemed determined to embarrass Deglane, if not hurt him. After the rest period, Lewis pounded Deglane with elbows, and punches before finishing him with an armbar in 3:50. Fans booed and threw things at Lewis as he returned to the dressing-room. The reporter felt it wasn't superior wrestling that defeated Deglane, it was Lewis' roughness that Henri couldn't handle. Fans wanted another match, with strict wrestling rules observed. This win seemed to be one of Lewis' demands for

Ed "Strangler" Lewis

wrestling Londos.[393] Lewis was also being build up for an Ed Don George match in Montreal that took place on October 1.

On June 5, Lewis sat ringside to watch Londos defeat Jagot Singh in Chicago. After the match, Lewis again challenged Londos for a title match. Londos didn't refuse.

The title unification match between NWA world champion Jim Londos and New York and California world champion Jim Browning took place out doors in the huge Madison Square Garden Bowl in Long Island on June 25, 1934. The match drew a crowd of 25,000 and a gate of $40,000. Londos spent most on the match on the defense but managed to pin Browning with a series of body slams after 1:10:10.

Jim Londos having his arm raised shortly after pinning Jim Browning, Madison Square Garden, June 25, 1934

On July 6, Londos beat Shikat in Philadelphia drawing 10,000. July 18 in Fenway Park saw Londos and Ed Don George wrestle to a 4 hour and 7 minute draw in front of 28,000 with a gate of $60,110. Victories followed over Everett Marshall (July 20, Washington DC), Gus Sonnenberg (July 21, Trenton), Sandor Szabo (July 24, Baltimore), and Joe Malcewicz (July 26, Rochester). Another draw with Ed Don George took place on August 1, 1934. This one lasted one hour and 30 minute with 14,700 attending. On August 22, Londos repeated his win over Jim Browning in Los Angeles, drawing 9,500.

The 1934 Lewis/Londos Match And A New Gate Record

The super match between Lewis and Londos was signed on July 23 in the office of Arch Ward, sports editor of the *Chicago Tribune*. The match was booked outdoors in Chicago's Wrigley Field with the date being September 20, 1934. It became one of the heaviest promoted matches in history, with the Chicago papers carrying some type of Londos or Lewis story every day. For most of September, Lewis trained in Chicago to help create ballyhoo. The match was billed as a shoot and both wrestlers signed affidavits in front of the commission guaranteeing it was a contest. The match had a 90 minute time limit with two judges, picked by the Illinois Athletic Commission, ready to make a decision if the time limit ran out. This ruling was made to stop the wrestlers from stalling in an attempt to tier out the other wrestler, while boring the crowd. Most felt it gave an advantage to Lewis because Londos was out-weighed by 30 to 35 pounds. Of course, we know today it really didn't matter, because there was no chance it would ever be a true contest. There were only two wrestling matches on the card. The other major match featured Chicago favorite Jim McMillen wrestling Don George. The rest of the card was pro boxing with the best fight being King Levinsky versus Art Sykes.

The match drew 35,625, with a gate of $96,302 breaking the records set by Frank Gotch and Heckenschmidt in 1911 at Comiskey Park. Lewis was the aggressor for most of the match, but his headlocks were broken and he was worn out by 30 minute mark. After both fell out of the ring, Londos body slammed Lewis to the mat and applied a hammer lock and than added a three-quarter nelson to force the Strangler's shoulders down for the three count. The time was announced as 49 minutes and 27 seconds.[394]

In the dressing room, Lewis said that Londos "wrestled a great match, better than I expected." His trainers Toots Mondt and Lou Talaber admitted the same. The long soap opera with Jim Londos was over. Lewis then joined his parents and two sisters, who had been ringside. He spent the next five days in Chicago with his family before returning to Glendale to check on his restaurants.

On August 27 Lewis had added to his win in Montreal over Henri Deglane by beating young Yvon Robert in 1:05:03.[395] This set up an AWA world title match with Ed Don George on October 1, 1934. Lewis lost on a disqualification.

On October 5, 1934, Lewis booked passage on the ocean liner *Ile de France* for a tour of England, France and the rest of Europe. This tour got a big build up in *Ring Magazine*, which claimed Lewis was pro wrestling's greatest ambassador. Lewis was said to have carried letters from several leading American citizens to both Adolph Hitler in Germany and Benito Mussolini in Italy and claims were made that he would visit them. Lewis's headquarters was in London. I think he was sent over by Paul Bowser for another rematch with Henri Deglane. On October 29 he wrestled Kola Kwariani, November 5, 1934, Lewis defeated Charles Rigoulot, and on November 11 he beat Ray St Bernard in Paris, France. The match with Henri Deglane was on November 19, 1934, and Lewis won the match.[396] Some new reports have Lewis losing to Deglane on December 7 (or December 10) at Paris.

Ed Lewis vs Henri Deglane, Paris, 1934.

Danno O'Mahoney

1934 was the greatest year pro wrestling had ever had, but many of the promoters resented the idea of having their businesses and storylines controlled by a performer, namely Jim Londos. Just about every promoter began a quest to find a new champion to replace Jimmy. They needed someone kind of dumb and naïve, who would be willing to work on a cheap salary and not make waves. Boston promoter Paul Bowser figured the best place to find such a man would be over seas, in a poor country like Ireland. Being a Greek immigrant had always been a major part of the Londos' attraction to his fan base and Bowser had been forever trying to create an Irish Londos in Boston. In 1934 Bowser turned his attention to a Dr. Patrick O'Callaghan of Kanturk, Ireland, who had won the hammer event in the 1928 and 1932 Olympics. Bowser sent his friend and front man, Worcester promoter Jack McGrath, to Ireland with an offer for O'Callaghan. It turned out that O'Callaghan was the only man in Ireland with no need for American dollars, but he did know a young Irish soldier named Danno O'Mahoney that might be able to fill the position. After checking O'Mahoney out, McGrath liked want he saw. Danno was a good looking athlete, not too bright, but willing to learn how to perform as a wrestler.

Danno O'Mahoney

In December 1934, Lewis was at the Stadium Club in London, England working out with the feared ripper Bert Assirati. McGrath brought O'Mahoney to England so Lewis could looked the kid over and perhaps teach him a few tricks. Lewis asked a young wrestler named Charles A. Young to go into the ring with O'Mahoney and beat him as fast as he could. Danno lasted two minutes with the unknown wrestler.

On December 6, 1934, O'Mahoney had his first official pro match versus Ed "Strangler" Lewis at London's Stadium Club. Lewis, a many time world champion and one of the most famous true wrestlers in history, was supposed to carry the young athlete to a 60 minute draw, but found the task impossible — so he just pinned Danno after five minute. O'Mahoney did not return for the second fall, so under the English round system it was ruled a draw. This setback made for a bad night, but after considering the boy's inexperience with the pro game and the ability of the man he wrestled, McGrath felt he had stood up well enough in a difficult situation and, in fact, had shown rare poise. McGrath and Bowser agreed to bring their new star to America. Once O'Mahoney was in the Boston, the PR story became that Danno won the London match the over Lewis and was the greatest new talent in pro wrestling since Gotch.[397]

Lewis returned to Glendale by the end of December. On January 2, 1935, he main evented Lou Daro's first card of the year, defeating the giant Hans Steinke at The Olympic in front of 7,000 fans.

Tom Packs had plans for a Londos/Lewis match in St. Louis, so on January 4 Ed drew 7,466 in defeating Ray Steele.

In St. Louis, Lewis heard stories of a sensational young wrestler working out in local gyms. The kid had major wrestling skills, with good looks that rivaled Londos, coupled with a great attitude and dedication to the sport. Tom Packs and the front office felt he was the future of St. Louis wrestling. The boy was 18 years old, and Packs was in the process of booking him to a under card match, but wanted opinions on the boy's potential. Packs asked Lewis to work him out at a local gym and then relay his thoughts back to the office. The boy's name was Lou Thesz. Lewis was always interested in young talent and gladly followed through on the request.

At the St. Louis Business Men's Gym, Lewis was introduced to the young Lou Thesz, only to realize he had met him the year before in Des Moines. Lewis acknowledged Thesz and offered to give the young wrestler a workout. Thesz idolized Ed more that any other wrestler, but he had become cocky after beating many of the local pros. Looking at the fat old Strangler up close, Thesz thought he could beat him, so he was more than willing to get on the mat. The first move Thesz tried was a single-leg take down. Thesz was super quick, but Lewis countered the take down and got behind Thesz, where he stayed. Thesz tried everything to break loose but nothing worked. For 15 minutes, Lewis rubbed Thesz's face into the mat. Lewis then called time, picked Lou up, and slapping him on the back, told him he did "OK." Lewis thanked him for the workout and left.

Thesz was humiliated and so discouraged he packed up his gear and later quit.

Young Lou Thesz

Lewis actually was impressed by the young boys skills and guts, so he told Tom Packs that he was worth the planned investment. When he heard the hard workout had discouraged Thesz, Lewis called Thesz's father, telling him that his son had everything it took to make a lot of money as a pro wrestler. He convinced the father of Lou's future, and Thesz returned to Packs' office the next day. Lou Thesz never forgot Lewis' kind actions, and the two men remained life long friends.[398]

Lewis then flew into New York City to wrestle for the AWA world title against Ed Don George. George won the match with a flying tackle and a double arm lock in 43:48. Lewis then had four wins in the Ohio area before stopping in St. Louis for another victory, this time over George Zaharias before 7,489 (January 16).

During January, Lewis wrestled a few matches around Los Angeles and San Francisco. On the undercard of a Man Mountain Dean / Chief Little Wolf main event at The Olympic (January 23), Lewis beat Jim McMillan on a foul after a third fall tackle landed in Ed groin.[399]

Toots Mondt had become a partner with the brothers Lou and Jack Daro. Mondt was booking talent all over Northern and Southern California and even up into the northwest and down into Texas. Toots' style was to stay in the background and never went out of his way to bill himself as the true promoter, but everyone knew him as a major power in the area. So it's very hard to tell just how many pockets he had his hands in by 1935. He moved west in 1934, after New York City wrestling went into a slump, mainly because of Toots' problems with Londos. Toots' reputation was to destroy everything he created, but it would take him until 1939 to screw up Los Angeles for good.

In 1934, Daro and Toots had promoted Man Mountain Dean into the short term box office king of L.A. He had three huge sellout matches with Jim Londos, all losses, but remained a fan favorite. In 1935, Toots' new project was an Indian wrestler named Chief Little Wolf. On the January 23 card, Little Wolf beat Dean with an Indian death lock and was putting a lot of pressure on Londos for a title match. Also on the card was Bronko Nagurski, who was in town training with the Chicago Bears on Phil Wrigley's Catalina Island. Two other new stars on the card were Mexican Vincent Lopez and Dean Detton.

Man Mountain Dean working out with James Cagney

On January 25, 1934 Lou Daro filed a protest with the California Commission stating that Strangler Lewis had run out on a contract to meet Chief Little Wolf on January 30 at The Olympic.[400] Two days later Lewis replied in the press that he was recovering from an injury suffered from the foul on the January 23. Jim McMillan, also in town with the Chicago Bears, took Lewis' place.[401] That same day, it was announced that

Toots Mondt had taken the position of Little Wolf's manager.[402] This storyline was a complete work. Lewis had been working in San Francisco during the week and he was booked for another super match with Jim Londos in St. Louis on January 31. (In fact, Lewis was in St. Louis when he was reported to be in L.A.) I think Toots and Daro was attempting to put the idea into the head of fans that major wrestlers didn't want to wrestle Little Wolf, because he planned to pull a little trick on champ Londos.

Jim McMillan

On January 31, 1935, Lewis drew 14,921 (and more than $15,000) in St. Louis in another attempt to take the title from Jim Londos. He lost but had a good excuse with Jimmy beating him with a new hold that would later be called a sleeper. Many fans believed Lewis' story, that Londos had been given a "long count" by the referee near the end of the match, and felt the finishing hold was a choke—thus a rematch was ordered for March 6 back in St. Louis.[403]

On February 22, 1935, Lou Daro attacked Jim Londos in the press, noting that Londos was attempting to run out on an agreed match with Chief Little Wolf. Daro then stated that Londos would defend the title against Little Wolf at The Olympic on February 27, 1935, or the Indian would wrestle Gus Sonnenberg with Londos being stripped of the world title in California. An international tournament would then be run in Los Angeles to find a new champion.[404] The pre-match write ups made it known that Londos most likely would "no show" and Wolf would be wrestling Sonnenberg—and that's what happened. Wolf then beat Sonnenberg in front of a sold-out Olympic Auditorium.[405]

Soon after, Londos was suspended by the California commission and this led to Londos being suspended in New York City—again—because some states had agreements to backed up other state commission's decisions. He also was suspended in Illinois.[406] So Toots Mondt was once again putting the screws to the

Greek. Londos called the whole mess a joke and threaten to wrestle in Europe.

Lewis had become a regular in St. Louis and on February 14 he defeated Jim Browning in the city. This had to be viewed as a major win for Ed after all the jobs he had done for Browning over the last year. Browning's stock dropped fast after losing his title and he would spend the rest of his short career putting over others. To show the value of Londos as a draw, this match only drew 5,396.

The March 6, 1935 St. Louis match between Lewis and Londos saw Jimmy on the defense in the early portion of the match, though at one point he did apply the sleeper—but a new referee ruled the hold a choke. Lewis followed with three headlocks but Londos was able to keep his shoulders off the mat and break free. The champion then went into action, hitting Ed with a number of elbows, followed up by a couple rolling front headlocks and then a body block that resulted in the Strangler being pinned. Time was 39:03. It drew 11,438 and a gate of $12,005 on a rainy St. Louis night.[407]

Lewis then headed for home, but first stopped in Atlanta on March 12 for a draw with another young star, Orville Brown. He then traveled through Texas and Arizona, before spending the last few weeks of March working out of Glendale. In San Francisco on March 26 he lost to Joe Savoldi.

Ray Steele was being built up for a Londos match in Minneapolis, and Lewis did a job for him on April 2. After the match, Lewis went nuts and attacked the referee and his own second. Two nights later on April 4 in St Paul, Lewis defeated heel George Koverly in 27:00. Jim Browning defeated Lewis in Chicago on April 11.

Paul Bowser's investment in Danno O'Mahoney was paying off. In Danno's debut match in America, he drew 14,000 to Boston Garden to see him defeat Ernie Dusek.[408] Two weeks later he drew 16,000 in defeating Rudy Dusek at the Garden.[409] On February 18, he defeated Ray Steele in Madison Square Garden[410] and then drew 10,000 winning from Rudy Dusek on February 22 in Toronto. On March 18, Danno returned to New York's Garden, defeating ex-champion Jim Browning in front of 7,500.[411] He also headlined in St. Louis and Chicago. Wherever there were Irish fans, Danno was a major draw. His in ring work was just passable and he actually couldn't wrestle a lick, but he was a good-looking boy who worked hard to improve and did everything asked of him. He also had been given a cool finishing hold called "The Irish Whip."

On April 1, 1935, Jack Curley booked O'Mahoney back into the New York Garden to meet Dick Shikat. Dick Shikat's attitude really hadn't changed much. He was still upset and hostile after all the dirt that had been shoveled on him by Mondt, Lewis, Curley and Jim Londos. He resented doing jobs for Londos, but putting over a young non-wrestler like O'Mahoney must have really burned him up.

6,000 fans watched Shikat dominate O'Mahoney in the early part of the match. Danno looked bewildered and pained. At one point, Shikat threw O'Mahoney into a corner and blocked his escape with elbows, arms, and hands. Danno, who did have boxing experience, lashed out with a punch that caught Shikat squarely on the nose. The Irishman looked apologetic as blood spurted from Dick's nose. Shikat then followed with a series of illegal strangle holds, which had the crowd in an uproar, as referee George Bothner labored frantically to break the holds. Shikit then seemed to calm down as O'Mahoney went on the offense. Headlocks, hammerlocks and a flying mare followed. O'Mahoney then hit Shikat twice with the feared "Irish whip." After the second, Shikat stood up, shook his head, and kicked O'Mahoney twice in the chest. O'Mahoney sank to the canvas, crying that his ribs were broken. With the kid unable to continue, referee Bothner disqualified Shikat and awarded the match to Danno. Standing, O'Mahoney looked unsatisfied, and feebly waved at Shikat to continue, something Shikat seemed more than willing to do. Bothner blocked his path, and Shikat was escorted from the ring by two policemen for safety's sake.[412]

Putting the rookie in the ring with Dick Shikat had to have been considered a terrible mistake, but it was an error they would repeat.

O'Mahoney's next challenge would be Strangler Lewis himself. Lewis flew into Boston on April 20, 1935 and trained for a week in the city before the match on April 26. Part of the match storyline was the London match between the two, with both claiming victory.

The match drew a huge Boston Garden crowd of 20,000. O'Mahoney won the first fall using the Irish whip in 21:27. After the pin, Danno got up and walked to his corner. Lewis then got up and rushed at O'Mahoney swinging. Ed hit Danno and the boy fell through the ropes, but the Irishman scrambled up with blood in his eyes.

By that time, the ring was filled with police, seconds, and a few spectators. A battle royal ensued, with Danno rushing Lewis. Someone clipped Danno from behind and floored him. Standing back up, Danno popped an officer on the jaw, knocking him flat. Throwing people out of his way, he found Lewis in a corner surrounded by would-be peacemakers. Danno and Lewis pushed everyone aside, and exchanged blows, until Lewis was laid out, apparently unconscious in his corner. Danno checked his knuckles and walked coolly to his dressing-room. Lewis was carried by policemen and attendants back stage. When the rest period ended, everyone was in the ring, but Ed—who was unable to continue. The match was awarded to O'Mahoney.[413]

Lou Daro's International Tournament to replace Jim Londos as champion started on April 24, 1935, with a large parade in the morning. With all the wrestlers in cars, they motored down Broadway Blvd. from city hall to the Olympic Auditorium, with hundreds of people lining the street to watch all the goofy wrestlers doing their acts. The actual tournament was the biggest and best since the famed New York City GR tournament of 1915. Over sixty major wrestlers were booked to participate and some were the best in the nation. It was a double elimination tournament, with three cards running each week.[414]

Lewis and O'Mahoney were entered along with such major wrestlers as Chief Little Wolf, Man Mountain Dean, Vincent Lopez, Joe Savoldi, Jim Browning, Nick Lutze, Hans Steinke, Pete Mehringer, Kiman Kudo, Ernie Dusek, Joe Malcewicz, Marin Plestina, Felix Miquet, Mike Romano, Earl McCready, Dean Detton and many more.

Danno flew in to Los Angeles following their Boston match. With them was Paul Bowser, who was part of the rules committee with Jack Curley, Ray Fabiani, Toots Mondt and Tom Packs. Bowser brought with him the famous "Ed Lewis belt," which had been used as the AWA title belt, but was now going to be presented to the winner of the tournament. Ed Don George either had another version of the Lewis belt, or was holding his trousers up by hand. (Perhaps the Rickard Belt was being used.)

Lewis didn't travel directly home, stopping for two jobs for AWA champion Ed Don George (Buffalo on April 29 and Montreal on May 6). On May 22, 1935, Lewis had his first tournament match at the Olympic Auditorium, beating Marin Plestina in 9:55. The newspaper claimed the veterans wrestled for the championship of the old folk's home.[415]

Ed Lewis

Danno O'Mahoney was the early favorite with Chief Little Wolf to win the tournament, and he recorded wins over Howard Cantowine (May 1, 8,500 with 4,885 paid & $5,100) and Man Mountain Dean (10,000 with 7,153 paid & $5,600).

Lewis was scheduled to meet O'Mahoney on May 29, but Danno dropped out of the tournament claiming a injury. Lewis was given a default victory and rebooked with the undefeated Pete Mehringer. Mehringer was an Olympic games champion who was seemingly being developed into a major pro star.[416] Lewis beat Mehringer in 27 minutes using a series of headlocks and a body slam. The joke in the newspaper was Lewis' age and ability to perspire. "Lewis sweat so much the boys in the first row were chanting 'River Stay Away From My Door.'" The loss was Mehringer's first as a pro.[417]

The main event on the May 29 card had a minor upset. Toots Mondt's Chief Little Wolf, after driving Londos out of Los Angeles, and the tournament favorite, was beaten by the town's new star, Vincent Lopez, when the Indian missed a flying tackle and was counted out of the ring in 6:11. The card drew 10,400 with 9,393 paying $9,200. Lou Daro had been looking for a Mexican star for years and with the handsome Lopez he had found his man. Wolf's loss was his first of the double-elimination tournament.

On June 5, Lewis defeated the German wrestler Hans Kampfer at The Olympic in another tournament match.

Lewis then went on the road to Houston to wrestle Jim Londos on June 14 in another NWA title match. The event was held out doors at Buffalo Stadium in front of 9,000 spectators, that paid $12,000, a record for wrestling and boxing in Texas. Londos won the first fall in 21 minutes after KO'ing Ed with a punch during a break. Lewis won the second fall with a headlock in 14:37. Londos took the third fall using his sleeper hold, which the fans thought was a strangle. The crowd was also upset with the fact that Ed's foot was outside the ropes. A rematch was talked about, but the events that followed ended any chance of that happening.[418]

Jim Londos signed for two major matches at the beginning of June 1935. The most publicized was a return to New York City's Yankee Stadium for a match on July 7 with the man who ran him out of Los Angeles, Chief Little Wolf. It was the annual Milk Fund card, which had the backing of the Randolph Hearst newspapers. The other match was the big showdown with the undefeated Danno O'Mahoney on June 27 in Boston's Fenway Park. Londos had continued being wrestling's biggest box office draw, but rumors were flying that he was getting ready to retire and pass on the title. Both of these matches had "title change" written on them. The great Londos was about to fall, and that was something no true fan could miss.

Vincent Lopez

Lewis had his biggest match in the Los Angeles in a co-main event on June 19, 1935 against Vincent Lopez. By 1935, the idea of a long technical match with pacing was over. Fans were coming to arenas to have fun and laugh at the crazy wrestlers brawling and flying out of the ring. It was one big party most nights, and Lopez fit into the style of the time. He had been a amateur wrestler, but in the pros he was just a brawler, whose big finisher was a elbow or punch to the face. So Lewis got punched out by Lopez and lost. After the match, Lewis got up and began slugging Lopez from corner to corner. When the referee and others finally separated them, Lewis was hooted and showered with programs and peanut shells as he left the ring in a huff.[419] The other main event had Little Wolf defeating Sandor Szabo in 15:13 to set up another tournament match with Lopez.

Lewis' last tournament match took place on June 26, 1935, when he lost to Ernie Dusek after a right forearm and a body press in 7:27. The big story was the main event which had Vincent Lopez again beating Chief Little Wolf. The newspapers were filled with stories wondering why Lou Daro would book Lopez over Little Wolf, when the Indian was scheduled 11 days later to be in a New York City Stadium show, supposed to draw $100,000. The newsmen wondered why Daro would kill a Jack Curley event? Was the Curley Trust falling apart? They found out two days later.[420]

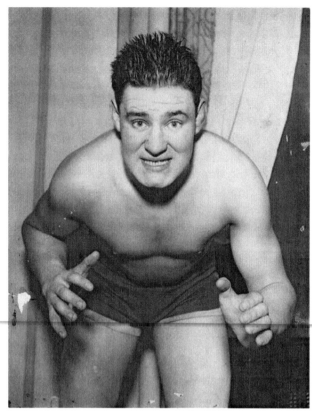

Danno O'Mahoney

On June 27, 1935, Danno O'Mahoney defeated Jim Londos in front of 25,000 fans at Fenway Park, winning the NWA/New York world titles. Londos didn't just lose—he made the young boy look like a champion. For over an hour, Danno threw Londos all over the ring. Whenever Londos applied a hold, O'Mahoney broke it using superior strength. At one hour and ten minutes, as he did in every match, Londos went on the offensive, hitting Danno with a series of super fast moves followed by body slams. But this time the Irishman countered with flying moves of his own. Not using the Irish Whip, Danno threw Londos into the ropes and caught the Greek with three flying mares. Londos was whipped into the ropes a fourth time, followed by O'Mahoney hitting him on the rebound with a flying body scissors. After he fell to the mat under the full weight of Danno, Londos was straddled and pinned. Danno had defeated the great Londos to become champion. It was Londos's first true job in six years and it was also the last one of his career. The time was one hour, 16 minutes and 50 seconds.

In the dressing room following the match, Londos claimed that Danno was the strongest man he had ever faced. His published quote was: "I knew after the first five minutes I would have to be lucky to win. The Kid is green, but with his strength I believe he can beat any man in the world. And when I took the bout the New York people told me I had nothing to fear! I wish I knew as much before I signed … and this bout would have never taken place." Londos, having carried the kid to a good match, and dropped his world title clean in the middle of the ring only to praised the winner as the better man, took his fortune and went home.

Danno's comments were that Londos was "a really great wrestler" but not big enough. He then challenged Ed Don George the AWA World Champion, who was the real champion in Boston.[421]

O'Mahoney then replaced Londos on the Milk Show in Yankee Stadium, beating Chief Little Wolf (July 8, 1935). Without Londos or the threat of a title change, the show bombed, drawing 10,000 to the huge baseball stadium.[422]

On July 10, 1935, back at The Olympic, Lewis defeated Mike Romano on the under card of Ernie Dusek's win over Sandor Szabo. Dusek's win awarded him $5,000 for finishing in third place of the Olympic Tournament.

On that night a Mr. William Focher, an auto mechanic owed money by Lou Daro, attempted to collect on the debt. Daro and Focher had a misunderstanding and Lou directed the police to arrest the other man.

Vincent Lopez and Ed Lewis

Focher ran out of the Olympic Auditorium and soon after was shot to death by the Los Angeles police. When it was revealed that Focher had only been trying to collect money he was justifiably owed, Daro had a major scandal on his hands. On July 24, 1935, out of sympathy to the Focher family, Lou Daro created an account of $5,000 for Mrs. Ivy Focher. From this money, Mrs. Focher could withdraw $25 a week. Daro also gave her $100, so she could take her son on a vacation trip to Catalina Island.[423] This PR move, to counter the damage done to Daro's reputation, didn't really work and Lou's popularity in Los Angeles dropped. Over the next few years, Daro's involvement in pro wrestling at the Olympic, due to this incident and bad health, lessened. With Lou acting as a figurehead for the press, the office was run by Lou's brother Jack Daro and Toots Mondt.

The final of Daro's International Tournament was set for July 24, 1935, with Vincent Lopez taking on Man Mountain Dean. On July 9, Lewis wrestled Lopez in San Francisco, losing two out of three falls. The storyline put out by the Olympic was that Lewis ate lunch with Lopez on July 11. An agreement was made that Lopez would be managed and trained by Strangler Lewis. In the week leading up to the tournament final, Lewis trained Vincent, in front of the public, at the Olympic Auditorium. The storyline was that Lewis bought the contract of Lopez. It's my feeling that this relationship was basically just storyline. Lewis continued to wrestle and promote his own wrestling career outside of Los Angeles. At times the Olympic published Lewis' comments as if he was in Glendale, when Lewis was in other parts of the country. Lewis did manage and second Lopez when in town, and wrestled on Lopez under cards in the north-west.

Vincent Lopez played football and wrestled at the University of Idaho. He was a good-looking guy who came from a well to do family, and gave off the air of a cultured man, much like Enrique Torres in the late 40's and Mil Mascaras in 1969. Lopez was the first true Mexican wrestling star to come out of Los Angeles. Lopez's wrestling style was brawling. I've seen film of him and basically all he could do, or attempt to do, is throw elbows and punches. He was a Mexican version of Danno O'Mahoney, who also was a brawler. Lopez was a good talker, in Spanish and English, so he was over in Los Angeles for a few years. I think Ed Lewis was used by the Daros and Toots Mondt to take the heat off of "babyface" Lopez. Lopez's brawling style might have turned him heel if Lewis wasn't present to direct the heat on to himself.[424]

On July 24, 1935, Ed Lewis seconded Vincent Lopez as he defeated Man Mountain Dean two out of three falls to win the International Tournament, recognition as California world champion, the "Lewis world title belt," and $15,000. The card sold out with 10,400 present, and a gate of $17,000 with another 5,000 people turned away.

A week later on July 31, 1935, NWA world champion Danno O'Mahoney wrestled AWA world champion Ed Don George in a title unification match drawing 40,000 fans to Braves Field in Boston. O'Mahoney won the match after referee and heavyweight boxing champion, James J. Braddock, counted George out of the ring. The win came as a result of the bungling referee Braddock, so a rematch was booked for September 11.[425] O'Mahoney then claimed the undisputed world title. Danno didn't receive George's Lewis (AWA) championship belt because it was being used by California world champion Vincent Lopez.

On July 31, the United Press published a note by Henry McLemore stating that Strangler Lewis had quit active pro wrestling and planed to devote his time to managing and training Vincent Lopez. I don't know if McLemore had some new insight of Lewis' intentions or was just repeating Los Angeles storylines for the rest of the nation. Whatever the case, Lewis did not stop wrestling and, after July 24, 1935, he does act as an in ring second at The Olympic Auditorium for Lopez until March 25, 1936.

Two days after the tournament final (July 26), Lewis wrestled Man Mountain Dean in Seattle, winning via disqualification. On July 31, Lewis lost two out of three falls to Hans Steinke in Portland. On August 13, he main evented in Minneapolis, beating Hal Rumberg. On the under card was young Lou Thesz. On

September 3, Lewis had another rematch with Ray Steele in Minneapolis. After 36:03, referee Mike Nazarian was knocked out of the ring, as Lewis was pinning Steele. When the ref returned, Steele pinned Lewis, who was thinking he had won. This win set Steele up for an O'Mahoney title match two weeks later.

Lewis then wrestled on the under card of the September 11, 1935 Fenway Park rematch of O'Mahoney and Ed Don George, beating Dick Daviscourt. For the main event Lewis seconded for George. This time O'Mahoney proved he was champion by beating George clean in 2:00:05. The card drew 25,000 fans.[426]

After Danno had beaten Lewis on April 26, he admitted that Ed had beaten him in his first bout in London. A rubber match was booked by Paul Bowser for Boston Garden on October 11. O'Mahoney kept his (almost) undisputed world title by beating Lewis in 1:04:57 using the Irish whip. Lewis only drew 8,000, a drop of 12,000 from their first match in Boston.[427]

In 1935, the wrestling noise coming from Texas increased in volume, and the man leading the choir was none other than the hillbilly Hercules, Leo Daniel Boone "Whiskers" Savage. Without ever having an effect on the rest of the nation, Whiskers Savage became a wrestling sensation in Houston during 1935. Like Man Mountain Dean, he was playing the part of an oversized hillbilly and the act went over big—at least in Texas and a few parts of the South. Ed Lewis wrestled him twice for promoter Morris Siegel during the year.

The first took place on October 18. After splitting the first two falls, Whiskers thought he had Lewis pinned but Ed's leg was under the ropes. Savage started to dance around, thinking he had won, but the referee told him different about the same time as he got potatoed by Lewis and pinned. The match drew a good crowd of 6,000. The rematch took place on October 25, and the result had Lewis being disqualified for using the headlock as a strangle. The win over Lewis set Savage up for a title match with O'Mahoney, which he lost.[428]

Lewis had another showdown with the original giant hillbilly as the semi-main event on a November 7 O'Mahoney/Sonnenberg card in St. Louis. This time the hillbilly was Man Mountain Dean himself. Lewis agreed to a handicap match in which he was to pin Dean in 20 minutes. He failed because most of the match was spent trying to revive referee Fred Voepel, after the Man Mountain accidentally fell on him. Anyway everyone had fun, and Danno and Gus drew a crowd of 14,321.[429]

Gus Sonnenberg never gained the respect of Strangler Lewis for his wrestling, but when it came to drinking, bad driving, and badder still marriages, he was Ed's superior.[430] By the end of 1935, Gus needed the use of a babysitter-type driver to get him to his matches sober. In the ring, Sonnenberg could still do his match and draw fans but his push was ending because of his other problems. On November 18, 1935, Lewis beat him at Kansas City.

On November 19, 1935, Denver world champion Everett Marshall, with the support of his manager Billy Sandow and promoter Max Baumann, posted $5,000 with the Missouri State Commission asking for a match with Champion Danno O'Mahoney. Lewis was still close to Paul Bowser and could be considered, at age 45, to be one of Danno's "policemen." Lewis filed a

Pre-match photo of Ed Don George and Danno O'Maohoney with referee and world heavyweight boxing champion, James. J. Braddock

$1,000 check with the commission saying he was willing to meet Everett Marshall at any site he wanted. Jim Browning also posted a challenge to Marshall. The commission then suggested a tournament between Tom Packs' Lewis and Browning against Bauman's Marshall and Lee Wycoff. Nothing came from this, but it should be noted that by 1937 Tom Packs was billing Everett Marshall as champion and Billy Sandow had become a partner in the St. Louis promotion with Packs.

After Man Mountain Dean beat Ernie Dusek in 5 minutes and 30 seconds on Tom Packs' December 5 card, Dean also filed a check with the commission for a match with Marshall. This upset Lewis, who claimed Dean had no business putting up money to bust his way into the tournament. Lewis then offered to drop out of the tournament if Dean could beat him in a straight match.[431] So the two wrestled on December 19, 1935 with Ed winning in front of 4,637. For the win, Lewis was given a St. Louis title match with Danno O'Mahoney on January 29, 1936. Danno won again in front of 9,170.

The O'Mahoney/Shikat Double-Cross of 1936

Being champion wasn't all that much fun for Danno O'Mahoney. Everyone was taking shots at him in the press and, worst still, trying to hook him in the ring. Like with Wayne Munn in 1926, being a non-shooter as champion brought out the worst in opponents.

On February 6 (Ellis Bashara at New Orleans) and on February 7 (Whiskers Savage in Houston), O'Mahoney was set up for double-crosses, but Danno was, on both nights, saved by referee Paul Jones. On February 9 in Galveston, Danno and manager Jack McGrath found out that the locals had a plan for his opponent Juan Humberto to double-cross him. The complete O'Mahoney group then got up and left the arena in front of fans and the state inspector. Lawsuits followed, and a Texas suspension, which led to O'Mahoney being stripped of the NWA portion of his (almost) undisputed world title.[432]

O'Mahoney wasn't any safer back on the East coast when Curley and Bowser booked him into Madison Square Garden against the old malcontent Dick Shikat on March 2, 1936. You would think someone would have learned something after the first Shikat/Mahoney match, but they hadn't. Shikat shot on Danno and made the (almost) undisputed world champion submit in 18:57.[433]

The next edition of every major newspaper in the nation carried the story of Shikat's shoot on the phony champion and the breaking up of the Wrestling Trust. *The Boston Globe* told the story, but its version had Danno and Jack McGrath claiming they had been robbed of the title. Later editions that same day had Bowser saying that O'Mahoney was sick and had simply collapsed in the ring.

On March 4, Bowser announced that the AWA still recognized Danno O'Mahoney as world champion. His first justification was that the match was non-title because the state of New York ruled all matches as exhibitions. That didn't sound right, so the story they settled on was that the AWA title could only change in a two out of three fall match (under Boston rules). So Danno could still be called a world champion, but he was no longer a national champion. He became one of the regional champions that were multiplying by the day. The Boston newspapers took note of the hypocrisy involved and went out of their way to explain who the real champion was—and it wasn't Danno.

It seems the idea of hooking Danno was Dick Shikat's alone and done out of hate for Toots Mondt, Ed Lewis and Jack Curley. Rudy Miller, Florida agent for the trust, Al Haft of Columbus, Adam Weismuller of Detroit, and former mat czar Billy Sandow were told of Shikat's intentions beforehand. Jack Pfeffer wasn't part of the deal but, following the match, he added Shikat in his bookings. But the dirty deed was mainly Shikat's idea.

After the match, Shikat announced that the title was up for sale and just about everyone bid on it. Lou Daro and Toots Mondt offered Shikat $50,000 for two matches versus Vincent Lopez in Los Angeles and Bowser agreed to pay $25,000 for Dick to return the title to Danno or lose to Yvon Robert. The surprise offer was from Jim Londos, who was returning to action and wanted his title back.

Shikat ended up making a deal with the Sandow/Haft group. Then what was left of the Trust started playing tricks with Shikat. Bowser owned a management contract with Shikat's name on it and he began booking Shikat into arenas without his permission. When the star didn't show for the matches he knew nothing about, Shikat was suspended in most states and the whole mess ended up in a Columbus courtroom with every major promoter being call in to testify.[434]

There was another tournament during 1936 in Philadelphia. Credibility for the new star, Dean Detton, was the goal. It took place in February 1936 and the final was Strangler Lewis losing to Detton on February 28, 1936.[435] The win gave Detton the next shot at O'Mahoney title in Philadelphia and that date is said to have been set for March 9, a week after the Shikat double-cross. Some historians think that Toots Mondt was putting a great deal of pressure on Paul Bowser to allow O'Mahoney to drop the title to Detton.[436] Perhaps Toots remembered Wayne Munn, so he knew they had to get the crown on a secure head before someone—like Shikat—cut off Danno's.

The spectacle of the performance sport on trial in Columbus destroyed whatever creditability pro wrestling had left in the eyes of the general public. Wrestling fans always understood that the art form was worked and, like today, they enjoyed it—but the general public couldn't understand the concept as anything but "fake." The court case came to an end when Shikat was allowed to drop the title to a unknown gimmick performer called Ali Baba—which everyone thought was funny. Baba later got double-crossed by a light heavyweight named Dave Levin in an unconvincing way—and before long the wrestling world had at least five champions. Soon every major and minor promoter had their own world champion.

To the public, wrestling was a joke, and when major newspapers stopped covering it attendance dropped. Promoters knew the public thought its product was a joke—so they promoted it like a joke. By 1940 the sport was filled with gimmicks like mud matches or Jell-O matches or dead fish matches. Performing freaks became wrestling's biggest draws.

Before 1936 and the O'Mahoney/Shikat match, wrestling's storylines were national. There may have been more than one champion, but everyone in the country knew who they were and the storylines involving them. After 1936, the whole sport became regionalized, with every territory's storyline walled in from all the others. Promoters no longer wanted intelligent fans that understood the whole picture. They wanted ignorant fans that didn't know they were being lied too. Facts and knowledge was something promoters found hard to deal with. So all the work that Lewis, Stecher, Curley and Sandow did to rebuild the sport after Frank Gotch went to waste as the sport fell into its dark age.

All these changes took place because Dick Shikat shot on Danno O'Mahoney on March 2, 1936.

None of this affected Ed Lewis much. He was no longer in power and the promoters didn't care if he came or went. He was pushing 46 years ago, he was fat, and his work wasn't what it once was. Only Lewis knew how bad his eyes were. If he drew, it wasn't because of his skills—it was his name and his legend.

Following the tournament loss to Dean Detton, Lewis spent most of March working out of Seattle. In April he return to Glendale and the restaurants. It was then that he began seconding Vincent Lopez in his matches. In 1936, he beat George Calza, Sandor Szabo, Bill Longson, Joe Savoldi, Ray Steele, Chief Little Wolf, Orville Brown, and Gus Sonnenberg. He only worked two or three times a week and his losses were being saved for something important—but important matches were becoming hard to find.

Lewis wrestling in an unidentified backyard

Jim Browning retired from wrestling in February 1936. On May 9, 1936 he was admitted to Freeman Hospital in Joplin, Missouri, due to an "ulcerated stomach" and a "liver ailment." Browning seemed to be recovering but he died on the afternoon of June 19, 1936 due to a pulmonary embolism. He was buried at Spring Valley Cemetery at Verona, Missouri.[437]

On or around June 25, 1936, Mike Romano had a heart attack during a Washington DC match with Jack Donovan and died in the ring. Five days later, Lewis turned 46.

On July 26, 1936, Lewis announced that he had sold Vincent Lopez's contract back to the wrestler and was no longer his manager.

In July and the first part of August, Lewis attempt to get back into condition. In workouts he would line up five young wrestlers and wrestle all of them for five minutes one after another. He was feeling so good that he accepted a match with Lee Wykoff in New York City that was an elimination for a match with the new champion, Dave Levin. Lewis accepted Wykoff challenge to make the match a shoot. Wykoff had a reputation as a feared shooter and was trained by Billy Sandow, who had taught Lee all of Lewis' moves.

The match took place at the New York City Hippodrome on August 13, 1936. The match was all stand up for the first hour and 17 minute and they went to the mat only because Wykoff slipped. The rest of the match was tugging and pulling with none of the normal pro wrestling moves and holds being used. It seemed like the match was going to last all night when suddenly the two men fell out of the ring on to the floor. They both made it back into ring, but they were so tired that they had trouble just standing. Finally after a few desperate passes at each other, they fell from the ring again. Referee George Bothner counted both men out and ruled the match a draw. Time was 2:14:45. The crowd for one of the only true shoots in wrestling history was 3,000, but most fans had left the arena by the end of the match.[438]

Lewis was very disappointed in the result and he began to lose interest in his career. He returned to Seattle, but this time he did more jobs. In September 1936, he lost to Sandor Szabo, Pat Fraley, the masked Red Shadow and even one to Tor Johnson.

In mid-September he traveled to Honolulu, Hawaii and beat Ed Don George and Vic Christy. On October 20, he returned to Chicago to job for Jim McMillen. The match only drew 1,500. In November and December he did more refereeing than wrestling. He spent Christmas in Hawaii beating Ed Don George again.

The Last Bride—1937

On January 11, 1937, Lewis married a Miss Bobbie Lee West at Yuma, Arizona. Miss West had formerly lived in Corpus Christi, Texas and Muskogee, Oklahoma. The two had known each other for over twelve years. Bobby Lee was a full blooded Cherokee Indian. Ed seemed to like Indian women and had at least two other Native American girlfriends in his past. Nekoosa and Wisconsin was home to large numbers of Native Americans, so Lewis was comfortable around the Indian people. This was Ed's last marriage, and the two stayed together until Lewis' death.[439]

They purchased a home in the Hollywood Hills near Laurel Canyon for $9,500. The property was located at 8145 Willow Glen Road. It was a seven-room stucco residence with a concrete garage and two cottages on an elaborately landscaped acre of land.[440]

My thought is that Lewis probably sold his interest in what was left of his three restaurants in Glendale, Alhambra and Pasadena, possibly to the Loew's Corporation. His interest in a San Diego hotel also seems to have been sold. Lewis may have continued working as a restaurant greeter for Loew's or did some work for MGM Studios. On March 31, 1937, Robert (Ed "Strangler" Lewis) Friedrich filled for a social security number. (550-16-0364) His employer was listed as Loew's Corporation of Culver City.

Lewis would be associated with a number of jobs over the coming year, none for very long.

Local newspaper articles during Strangler Lewis' 1937 tour of Australia

The Daily News, Perth, Monday, 27 September, 1937

Wrestling Getting Too Rough Says 19-Stone "Strangler" Lewis

Five times wrestling champion of the world, 19-stone "Strangler" Lewis said today that the game is getting too rough.

Lewis, an American wrestler from Hollywood, who is travelling to Colombo to wrestle the Indian champion, Gauma, passed through Fremantle today in the Mooltan.

He said that the new "rough house" methods being employed in wrestling were spoiling the game.

"Personally I used not to wrestle that way myself," he said, "but now I have fallen in with the rest. I don't like it. It is definitely bad wrestling."

"How did you come to get your sobriquet?" he was asked.

"It was an entirely unwarranted title," the "Strangler" declared. "In my bouts I used to specialise in a headlock. It was not a strangle hold at all, but many critics considered it was.

"Actually, I am certain it never interfered with a man's breathing."

Barrier Miner, Broken Hill, NSW, Tuesday, 14 September, 1937

STRANGLER LEWIS BEATS FORSGREN

SYDNEY, Tuesday.—The wrestling bout at Rushcutters Bay Stadium last night was a brief affair, Strangler Lewis (18.6) defeating Jack Forsgren in the third round. Forsgren injured his back when he was thrown from the ring and was unable to continue.

The Referee, Sydney, Thursday, 19 August, 1937

"Strangler" Lewis
Has It All Mapped Out

ED. "STRANGLER" LEWIS, mastodon of the mat and five times heavyweight wrestling champion of the world, is due in Sydney at the end of the month. Lewis is under engagement to Stadiums Ltd.

According to our old friend, Ted Thye, the "Strangler" is engaged in a campaign to uphold the supremacy of the white race in roly poly ring activities.

When he leaves Australia Lewis will invade Mother India, and fling down the gauge to the famous Gama. After defeating Gama (Thye is optimistic), the "Strangler" will journey to England and put the kybosh on "Tiger" Daula, a big Indian, at present busily engaged in breaking the bones of Pukka Sahibs in London.

After that, we presume, the much-travelled Mr. Lewis will return home to settle down on a chicken farm and roam no more.

"Strangler," engaged in the wringing of a rooster's neck, would be a sight for the gods.

The Many Champions of 1937

A light heavyweight wrestler named David Levin beat Ali Baba on a disqualification in New Jersey on June 12, 1936. It was another double-cross, this time the idea of Toots Mondt and Jack Pfefer. He strengthen his claim to the title by beating Vincent Lopez in a Los Angeles unification match on August 19, 1936. Levin, in turn, was beaten by Dean Detton at Philadelphia on September 28, 1936 in a match that lasted 2:05:52.

Very few state commissions supported the Levin win over Ali Baba, so Baba went on to lose his claim to Billy Sandow's wrestler, Everett Marshall, in Columbus, Ohio on June 29, 1936.

Of course, Danno O'Mahoney was still claimed the AWA world title. He even lost his title, but not his claim, to Yvon Robert on July 16, 1936 in Montreal. Later, after Robert actually broke his arm in a match (November 18, 1936), some would think Cliff Olsen was champion—but only outside of Boston.

The NWA title remained vacant until it set up another title tournament, than no one but John Pesek would join. So on September 13, 1937, the NWA recognized Pesek as champion.

Jim Londos returned to America in 1937, having won more than one version of the title in Europe and South Africa.

Lewis was mostly inactive in 1937, but he did accept major jobs to Dean Detton (Sacramento, January 25 and Salt Lake City, March 12), and Sandor Szabo (San Francisco, February 2). None of these matches are remembered for anything other than they had Lewis wrestling.

On May 25, 1937, Lewis did a job for famous football star Bronko Nagurski for Tony Stecher in Minneapolis. This loss by Lewis set Nagurski up for his title win over Dean Detton on June 29, 1937.

Starting on June 25, 1937, Lewis and wife Bobbie Lee sailed on the Matson oceanic liner, S.S. *Mariposa*, on a world tour. Their first stop was in Honolulu, Hawaii, where he won and lost a match over two weeks. In August and the first two weeks of September, Lewis toured New Zealand and Australia. He wrestled at least eight times and only did two jobs for Earl McCready. It's believed he also toured Greece and South Africa. In November, he wrestled and lost to Henri Deglane in Paris, France.

In later life Lewis claimed in stories to Lou Thesz that he wrestled and lost to the Great Gama in India during this world tour, and I've read newspaper reports that said he intended to make that match the center of his tour. It was reported in the January 1938 issue of *Ring Magazine* that Lewis made the trip to India, but the match fell apart when Gama demanded three months to train. Ed then traveled to Paris for the job to Deglane.[441]

Lewis and wife returned to New York City on the United States liner SS *Washington*. He then announced he was retired and planned to spend the rest of his time living in the Hollywood Hills in his new home. He also criticized the state of pro wrestling, saying the current style of "slambang" grappling was "terrible and just awful." He blamed the mess on the public, saying it was just getting the only produce it would pay for and that it hated and booed true scientific wrestling. He didn't mention the part he played over 24 years developing the "slambang" style or how the wrestling promoters would eat their children to make a buck.

Wrestling was well into its "dark age," and he wasn't wanted. The big money days were gone. From his words, it didn't seem like Ed had any plans to wrestle again.

The First Retirement (1938 to 1940)

In late 1937, the book *Fall Guys: The Barnums of Bounce* was written and published by sportswriter Marcus Griffin. It was the first book ever written with an inside view of pro wrestling, and it broke "Kayfabe" in front of the reading public. It was a crudely inaccurate look at pro wrestling history and all the crazy happenings of the 1930's. For years it was the only believable book written on wrestling's history and it was remembered as the facts faded from public's consciousness. Today's researchers finds it to be biased in a hundred ways and inaccurate in many others, whilst promoting a cynical view of the art form.

Marcus Griffin was a newspaper man who was used by Toots Mondt in public relations during the 1932/1933 war with Jim Londos. So most of the views in the book comes from information supplied by Toots Mondt and Jack Pfefer (who talked to anyone who would listen). The overall view in the book is pro Mondt, Lewis, Dean Detton, and Sandow. Others like Londos, Curley, Stecher, Wladek Zbyszko, and Gotch have their reputation dragged through the mud, mainly because they collided with the idea that Ed Lewis was the sport's greatest wrestler. But it has been wrestling history's most influential book, and only after the researchers went to work in the 1990's have we had the information to contest it. That being said, Strangler Lewis came out of the book looking very well in 1938—in a perverse kind of way.

Jack Curley didn't seem to care or defend himself. The man who reformed wrestling into big time entertainment died on July 12, 1937. He left behind a wife named Bessie and two children named Jack and Jean. He was buried at Nassau Knowles Cemetery, Port Washington, Long Island.

Jack Curley in 1912

I can't tell you how long Lewis lived in his luxurious estate. But I can tell you that Ed was easy with money and before long he was looking for more. He continued for some time to manage his old Glendale restaurant, which was, in later reports, called a restaurant and cocktail lounge. But Ed remained famous, and his friends were movie stars and Hollywood types, which would make living on a restaurant manager's salary a tough road to follow. It should be said that everyone in wrestling had stories of The Strangler being an easy touch.

His problems with drinking and his weight worsened as his time became more free. It wasn't long before he weighed more than 300 pounds and from his own stories told during his religious period, he was an alcoholic. It wasn't long before he started missing working out and the life on the road of a pro wrestler.

Lewis didn't just miss pro wrestling—it missed him. The events of 1936 (and after) had killed the sport in the eyes of the public and it no longer got the same treatment from the press. It was considered an off-color joke by most people. The new stars were never able to replace the old ones and business was bad everywhere. The only A-list star left was old Jim Londos. The names of the old stars just got more respect, but there were few of them. If Ed "Strangler" Lewis had anything, it was a great name that people remembered from a better time—a more respected time.

Ed Lewis during bad days

Most old wrestlers aren't allowed to wrestle. If they want to stay around the sport without moving up to management, it was either as a referee or as a manager. Lewis decided he was going to do it all.

On May 18, 1938, Lewis refereed a match in Los Angeles between Jim Londos and Dean Detton. I think Jimmy could thank his Greek gods that Vince McMahon wasn't the booker, because no double-cross took place, and Lewis raised his hand in victory.

Lewis next entered back into the sport as a manager in Southern California in the beginning of 1939. Ed took Arthur White, a mid-card worker and pro football player with the New York Giants, and developed him into a main-eventer. The first sign of something major taking place was a 60 minute draw in San Diego between Arthur "Tarzan" White and Lewis' old rival Jim Londos on March 21, 1939. Londos wrestling draws with major talent and friends like Ray Steele and Ed Don George was one thing, but a draw with a "nobody" must have shook the wrestling world like an earthquake. Why would Londos put an Arthur White over? Maybe he missed his old friend Strangler Lewis and saw some money in continuing the rivalry, with Ed playing the part of a manager.

Lewis then brought White up to Los Angeles and changed his nickname from "Tarzan" to "Strangler."[442] When fans read the name Art "Strangler" White, they knew the manager Lewis was part of the show. Jack Daro's (brother of Lou) business was dying, but the team of Art and Ed drew an Olympic Auditorium crowd of 10,000 to watch White challenge Londos again for the world title. White must have surprised the world by pinning Londos to win the first fall, and the beating continued in the second. Londos looked finished, but he stepped aside at the last second of a flying tackle attempt by White. Without touching the ropes, the pro footballer crashed into the ringside seats, which had luckily been vacated in the nick of time. White was counted out and carried to the local hospital, unable to come back for the third fall.[443]

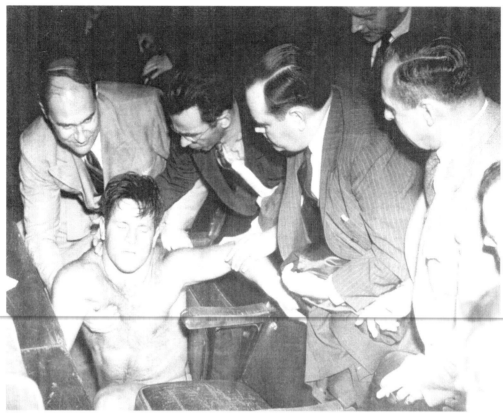

Tarzan White falling out of the ring at the finish of his match with Jim Londos, April 5, 1939

Since it was only bad luck that stopped Londos from dropping the title to White, a rematch was booked by Jack Daro for May 10. Daro did this knowing Londos was booked back East and wouldn't show for the match. Without the star Jimmy, Nick Lutze replaced the Greek and lost to White. Strangler Lewis then claimed the world title for White due to the "default" win. The White/Lutze card drew 8,000, a lot more than they would have drawn with out the false billing.

I think the plan was for a big rematch with Londos, but it never happened. After White beat Sandor Szabo (May 17, 1939), the Masked Marvel (Jim Henry May 24) and The Black Panther (June 21), he and Lewis jumped over to the Olympic's opposition, The Hollywood Legion Stadium. The story in the newspaper had Lewis joining up with his old foe, Joe Marsh (former manager of Marin Plestina, the old time "trust buster" himself) to bring heavyweight wrestling to Hollywood, which normally used the lighter weight wrestlers. I don't believe that story, at the least the part about Lewis, because the true power at the Olympic was Toots Mondt, and I can't believe Lewis would split with his old friend. I think Arthur White jumped from The Olympic because he was getting ripped off on payoffs by Toots and Jack Daro (Lou Daro was sick and in Europe).[444] So White jumped, and got beat the first week in Hollywood by Edward Payson (July 10). A few days later, White was suspended by the California Commission for leaving the Daro promotion. So the Arthur "Strangler" White push and Lewis' involvement was over and Art "Tarzan" White returned to being a mid-level wrestler in the rest of the country.

If the story of Lewis jumping to the Hollywood Legion Stadium is true—with him siding with the wrestlers over the corrupted promoters at the Olympic, which included friend Toots Mondt—I see that as one of the most idealistic moves I've seen Lewis take in my writings.

By the late 30's the money making positions in pro wrestling was the "booking agents." Many of the old promoters had moved on to being agents, booking talent to all the big and small promoters. These men, including Toots Mondt (California, the Northwest, Texas and the Northeast), Jack Pfeffer (East Coast, and outlaw groups all over the country) and Tom Packs (Missouri, Texas, Kansas, and the South) got a cut of every card and didn't take chances like the owners and promoters.

By the end of 1939 and into 1940, the talent (wrestlers) were in revolt at the Olympic Auditorium. They argued that Toots Mondt and the Daro brothers were dishonest and shorting talent payoffs. The new State

Commission investigated and agreed. Toots Mondt, Lou Daro and Jack Daro lost their license to work in California and were banned in the state. Promoting at the Olympic Auditorium was given to George Zaharias and Toots Mondt's booking agency in the state was taken over by Nick Lutze.[445] (Later, on September 2, 1941, the commission approved of Zaharias' selling of the Olympic promotion to Ray Fabiani of Philadelphia.)[446]

On February 1, 1940, Ed's father Jacob Friedrich retired from the Nekoosa Police Department after 28 years of service. He was 81 years old.

On May 17, 1940, Lewis announced his plans to promote boxing in Los Angeles with Jimmy Murray who had just quit as matchmaker at The Olympic Auditorium. Lewis claimed he was backed by sponsors who had $100,000 available for investment. His plan was to stage three outdoor shows during the summer and then begin construction of a $400,000 indoor stadium in Glendale, but nothing came out of this. I know of no cards ever promoted by the two, and he never was able to come up with money, so the arena venture died.

On July 12, 1940, the 290-pound Lewis made the sports page by challenging Jack Dempsey to a mixed march at the Los Angeles Coliseum for the benefit of the Red Cross. Lewis claimed he would train down to 240 pounds for the match. Nothing came from the challenge and the two retired 50 year olds fighting didn't seem like a workable idea.

Lewis was short on money, so he did go into training—which mainly consisted of long walks—but he did lose some weight. He later claimed that at one point, before he started to train, he weighed 365 pounds and had a systolic blood pressure over 200.[447]

Thirteen years after his title win over Joe Stecher (February 20, 1941), Lewis returned to St. Louis to celebrate the anniversary by refereeing a match between NWA world champion Ray Steele and ex-champion Lou Thesz. Steele defeated Thesz in two straight falls after Lou was injured in the first fall. Lewis got good reviews as a referee, moving his 300 pounds around fast enough to keep on top of every move. Between rounds Lewis was the center of attention signing autographs.[448]

Ray Steele as NWA world champion, with Sam Muchnick on his left.

To the South Central Business
associated
A small gang
Ed "Strangler" Lewis
Nov 25 - -41

MVSC, Kansas City Public Library, Kansas City, Missouri

Ed Lewis, 1941

The best part of the night for Lewis was hanging around with old friends like Lou Thesz and Steele. Since Ed's visit with Thesz's father, the young boy had turned into St. Louis' favorite wrestler and a national star after winning two versions of the world title. Thesz still idolized Lewis and the two remained close supporters of each other.

With the world locked into another World War, America was building up its armed forces and the wrestling world was having a hard time finding talent to fill its arenas. Many of the old wrestlers were being recruited to come out of retirement. Lewis would be the most famous star to return.

Following St. Louis, Lewis made some money being a special referee, mainly working in the South. Ed the referee was drawing fans, and he wasn't having any trouble finding work. Lewis continued to work out and he felt he had at least one more comeback left in his career.

The Retirement Ends: WWII

On December 7, 1941 the Japanese attacked American forces at Pearl Harbor, bring the Americans into the war.

Ed Lewis was back wrestling the next week. On December 10, Lewis defeated Joe Marsh in Norfolk. In early January 1942, Lewis announced he was going to make a farewell tour. After taking off 90 pounds by walking, Lewis claimed he was back in good condition.

Lewis with unidentified opponent

He worked his way up the East Coast and on January 27, 1942, he wrestled a draw with Lou Thesz in Montreal. In the same city, he got some type of a win over Montreal world champion Yvon Robert on February 10, 1942.

The War years weren't just good for old wrestlers. Freaks may have been rejected by the armed forces, but they were greeted with open arms by pro wrestling. The greatest of all the freaks was Maurice Tillet, billed as the French Angel, "the ugliest man in the world." With features deformed by the disease Acromegaly, and built at 5'8" and 280 pounds, Tillet became wrestling's greatest attraction in the years 1940 to 1942. During this period, The Angel, under the management of Paul Bowser, won three world titles and beat just about every major star in pro wrestling including Lewis. On February 11, Lewis wrestled and jobbed to Maurice Tillet at Boston. The match was probably was billed for Tillet's AWA world title.[449]

Maurice Tillet versus a Beauty

On February 26 (24) 1942, in a rematch for the Montreal world title, Lewis lost to Yvon Robert. Ed then worked around Philadelphia, beating Rudy Dusek on February 20 before losing to the major East Coast promoter, Ernie Dusek, on March 6. He did another job for Earl McCready in Rochester on March 18. This was followed by Lewis getting beaten again by Maurice Tillet in Toronto on March 19.

Many historians consider Wild Bill Longson to be the major performer of the 1940's. From 1942 to 1948 he dominated St. Louis wrestling, winning the National Wrestling Association world title three times. He was the father of the skilled brawling style later used by Killer Kowalski, Gene Kiniski, Bruiser Brody and Stan Hanson. Some fans claim he was the first heel world title holder, but anyone who has read the history of Ed Lewis in the 1920's knows that isn't true. He was wrestling's biggest draw in the period following the French Angel.

Longson won his first NWA world title on February 19, 1942, beating Sandor Szabo in St. Louis drawing 7,461. His next defense was on March 5, drawing 9,667, beating ex-champ Ray Steele. He won a rematch against Sandor Szabo on March 20 drawing 8,668.

With wrestling's "dark age" in full effect, these attendance marks were considered good, if not great, but on April 8, 1942, Longson tested his title claims versus old fat Strangler Lewis in St. Louis. Longson pinned Lewis in 13:40, but both proved their ability to draw by attracting a crowd of 12,986. This number must have stunned the wrestling world. It was probably the largest American crowd seen since 1937, and this crowd elongated Lewis' career by years.

April 17 saw Lewis wrestling Bill Longson in Houston. He lost by disqualification (attendance 3,000), but that just sent up a rematch on May 17. Ed lost that one clean.

Lewis' father, Jacob Friedrich, died at 7 PM on April 20, 1942, after a lingering illness. The place of death was his home in Nekoosa, and Ed and the rest of the family were present bedside. Surviving Jacob was his wife, Molla Guildenzopf, three daughters, Mrs. John Ambruster and Mrs. George Gladding, both of whom lived in Everett, Washington (which explained why Lewis wrestled in the North West so much) and Mrs.

Jay Buckley, of Wisconsin Rapids and one son, Ed "Strangler" Lewis. Jacob had nine grandchildren and one great-grandchild.

On April 21, 1942, Ed Lewis was the first man to register at the American Legion Hall of Nekoosa in the general registration of all men 45 to 65 years of age. At age 52, nothing came from it.

On May 22 he returned to St. Louis for another match with Ray Steele. Steele won the match but the two drew a healthy 8,405.

Lewis then was signed to appear in a bit part in a classic boxing movie called 'Gentleman Jim,' starring Errol Flynn. Lewis was one of the drinking party that always surrounded Flynn, including the Barrymores and director Raoul Walsh, so he probably got the part because of his old friends. Lewis played the part of a washed-up, bare knuckle pug boxer named Hoghead, who has a fight with Wee Willie Davis, ending up in jail with Flynn and Jack Carson. The placing of the old famous wrestler Strangler Lewis in the cast seemed to be an inside joke, but Ed is very funny in the part. Some reports claim that Ed also worked as a stand-in for Ward Bond, but I don't believe it. In 1942, Bond was very fit and suntanned. Lewis looked very fat and out of shape, resembling George "The Animal" Steele more that Bond. Lewis is very good, reading his lines well, and it's surprising he didn't get more character parts in films.

From May into July, when filming was taking place on 'Gentleman Jim,' Lewis worked in Southern California and San Francisco. He worked three draws with Sandor Szabo and got counted out of the ring in a match with Frank Sexton in San Francisco on July 7.

He also had two matches in San Francisco with Maurice Tillet, August 25 and September 1. Ed lost both matches, but both shows drew well.[450]

At the end of September he moved to the East Coast for a couple of weeks. He then moved on to the mid-west for a bigger push.

Lewis Wins Mid-West Title in 1942

John Pesek was also still wrestling. For over ten years he had been "homesteading" in Nebraska, Iowa, and Ohio. His manager and promoter was Al Haft, who idolized him and protected him from the idea of doing jobs. Pesek wasn't like most wrestlers—he had money and owned a farm and championship stable of racing dogs. Pro wrestling was a part time job for Pesek, and only the opportunity of beating former stars could get him in the ring. Over the years he got revenge over all the wrestlers who had defeated him when he was part of the trust. Late in their careers he got such stars as Joe Stecher, Wladek Zbyszko, Everett Marshall, Hans Steinke and Marin Plestina to come to Columbus or Lincoln to put him over. Pesek himself hadn't done a job since losing to Ray Steele in St. Louis on November 23, 1933. Pesek and Lewis had wrestled at least four times, with Ed always winning. In 1942, Lewis needed money, so he was willing to join Pesek's list.

Whenever in Omaha, Lewis had challenged Pesek to a "shoot" match, but the Ravenna Tiger had been busy racing greyhounds for most of the year. When a break in Pesek's schedule opened up, promoter Max Clayton was able to match the two in Omaha for October 20, 1942. Ticket prices were scaled higher than normal cards, with reserve seats going at $1.65 and $1.10 with general admission tickets listed at 55 cents. The attendance of 4,000, with the mark-up in prices, made the card one of the highest grosses in Omaha in years.

Lewis' age was 52 and he weighed 268 pounds, while Pesek's age was a secret—but I believe he was around 48, and his weight was his normal 190 pounds. The match was billed as two out of three falls with a 90 minute time limit. Everyone claimed the match would be an old style shoot.

Once the match started, Pesek moved around with his old-time agility, as wary and cunning as ever. He usually was in the advantageous position and he had Lewis groaning whenever he applied an arm or leg hold. Most of Lewis's weight was located above his waistline, giving him a "humpty-dumpy" shape. He seemed to have tremendous strength in his arms, and he concentrated solely on applying his headlocks. He had the strategy of a bully, badgering, shoving, letting his weight rest on Pesek, while staying on the offensive. There was a lot of interesting fencing for position, and the two men were on their feet much of the time. After about 25 minutes, Pesek got Lewis down and started to work on Lewis' legs. Breaking away, Lewis started applying major headlocks, but Pesek dropped down and reversed Lewis into a leg lock to win the first fall in 40:05.

The Strangler then battled back to pin Pesek with a headlock in 5:55. During the third fall, Lewis hit Pesek on the jaw and Pesek retaliated. There was some scuffling, and at one point Pesek thought that the

Orville Brown

referee Harry Cadell was holding his arms, so Lewis could get in a few extra licks. Pesek pushed Cadell away and threw the huge Lewis out on the ring. His temper flaring, Pesek then threw the referee out of the ring on top of Lewis. When everyone got back into the ring, Pesek found himself disqualified. Most of the fans in the mid-west had never heard of Pesek losing, and he had everyone believing he was invincible — so the win by Lewis had to be considered a huge victory.[451]

John Pesek's major rivals in the mid-west were Bill Longson and Orville Brown. He wasn't really on the same level as Longson, who held the more nationally know NWA title and worked major territories like St. Louis, Texas, the South and up into Canada. No one drew crowds like Longson, and his only true rival probably was Lou Thesz — but Thesz was locked up with a US Army problem and was out of the wrestling picture. Pesek and Orville Brown were thought of as being on the same level and worked the same area.

Brown was a farmer/cowboy who worked his way threw the minor shoot style of Kansas and Iowa to become a true pro wrestler. During the period of 1933 to 1936 he was considered a major wrestler and a strong contender to Jim Londos' title. After wrestling fell apart as a national sport in 1937, Orville worked on the East Coast and then "homesteaded" in Columbus, Ohio. Brown was good-looking, in a mid-western way, and a fine worker who was powerful and could take care of himself in the ring and out. He got over well in Columbus, but John Pesek was always in the way, refusing to job or drop his MWA world title.[452]

During this time period, which I call the dark ages of pro wrestling, the best way for a star wrestler to make money was to get into promotion and control his own territory. Kind of creating your own world to work out of, and make money for yourself, instead of relying on some cheating promoter. Orville Brown was the prototype for this type of system. In 1940, he took over the Kansas City area of Kansas. From there he worked for other promoters in Des Moines, St. Joseph, Topeka, Louisville, and in small towns all over Kansas, Iowa, and Nebraska. 2,000 fans doesn't sound like much, but at 65 cent to a $1 a head, a good wrestler could make $200 a night, five nights a week, covering the mid-west. There were usually only three matches to a card: the main event, a semi-main usually main up of locals, and an opening match, usually made up of young boys working for a few bucks. Most of the cut went to the main eventers, who earned their payoffs by working long matches. $200 was more money than most people made in a month in 1940. With promoting, and two or three farms, Brown became a wealthy man.

The mid-western fan was much different to the fans in Los Angeles or New York. They didn't pay their money to laugh, watching pure action and performers making fun of the sport. They had a tradition of true wrestling, and that's what they wanted to watch — serious wrestling. It was an area made for Strangler Lewis.

But wrestling was no longer promoted on a national level. These small towns knew very little about the storylines being used in other cities. The local newspapers rarely covered wrestling news from another territories, and the fans were kept in the dark about any storyline other than their own. So the mid-west was filled with different world titles. Champions could lose their title in one town and still be defending a world title in another town against the very guy who beat him and won his title. The promoters had no rules to control them, so they did what they thought could make them the most money.

Orville Brown was a fine booker and he wasn't afraid to do a job or drop a title to keep a storyline going. He was limited in how many stars he could use, so he booked in such a way as to not "blow" anyone off. He wrestled some guys, like Bobby Bruns, a hundred times, but kept it interesting.

On June 13, 1940, Orville Brown defeated Bobby Bruns for a Jack Pfeffer East-coast world title in Kansas City, Kansas, called the Mid-west World Title, which would later be called the Kansas City MWA Title. On June 22, 1940, the Columbus Promoter Al Haft stripped John Pesek of the Columbus MWA world title for being inactive and failing to meet contenders, mainly Orville Brown. (This MWA title had been awarded to Pesek after he had been stripped, for no good reason, by the NWA on August 16, 1938.) Orville Brown then wrestled Dick Shikat on June 27, 1940 for the vacant Columbus MWA world title, with Brown winning. So Brown in 1942 actually held two different MWA titles, but very few fans knew this because each city had different storylines.

Orville hired Ed Lewis in October 1942, and the two worked together throughout 1943.

The first meeting took place, two days after the win over Pesek, on October 22, 1942. 3,600 fans watched Brown defend his MWA title by winning the first fall with an Indian death lock in 19:50. Lewis worked Brown over with headlocks and won the second in 11:20. Between rounds Orville asked for an extra five minutes rest and Lewis agreed. In the third fall, Lewis threw Orville out of the ring and was attempting to block his return but got hit with a tackle and pinned in 5:20.[453]

A young Orville Brown

Omaha wasn't satisfied with the ending of the Pesek/Lewis match so a rematch took place on November 3, 1942. This time the result was different. Pesek attacked Lewis with no mercy, and Lewis resembled a high school football player going against a pro. After 26 minutes and 50 seconds of the first fall, Pesek wriggled out of a headlock to put Lewis into a hold called a "knee-over-toe hold." Pesek had Lewis in the hold for over two minutes when referee Joe Zikmund screamed at Lewis: "You'd better holler 'uncle' or he'll tear the hell out of your leg!" Lewis then lay exhausted, as Pesek was given the first fall. Fans then got up, knowing the result. The rest waited until Pesek returned to the ring before the 10 minute rest was over. Lewis could not continue. In the dressing room, Lewis attempted to raise his leg and groaned: "Cheez, dat guy practically de-legged me. At least der were no fouls, huh?" The match drew 3,700.[454]

Lewis' leg must have recovered fast because on November 5, 1942 in Kansas City, Lewis defeated Orville Brown via a decision. The Kansas City MWA title didn't change hands on a decision, but it did mean there would be another match.

On October 7, 1942 Montreal champion, Yvon Robert, defeated Wild Bill Longson in a title unification match in Montreal, winning the NWA world title. On November 6, Lewis was defeated in St. Louis by the new champion Yvon Robert in 27:58.

On November 18, 1942, Lewis was back in Des Moines for another match with Orville Brown. It wasn't a title match because Brown had lost his claim in Des Moines in a title unification match with Bill Longson back on July 22, 1942. Lewis roughed up Brown in the first fall and pinned him using the headlock. It looked like Ed was going to be a cinch to soon finish his younger adversary, but Brown won both of the next two falls using a reverse toe-lock in 4:05 and 2:55.[455]

On November 25, the movie 'Gentleman Jim' opened nationwide and became one of Errol Flynn's biggest hits. It is still considered a classic even today.

It must have given Lewis some good luck, because the next day, November 26, 1942, Ed defeated Orville Brown in Kansas City for its version of the MWA world title.

On December 1, Lewis got some type of victory over John Pesek in Dayton, Ohio.

Lewis was on a roll, and he defeated Orville Brown in Columbus on December 3, 1942 via count out of the ring in 26 minutes, winning that city's version of the MWA world title.

The MWA champion then wrestled former NWA world champion, Wild Bill Longson, in Louisville on December 8, 1942. The promoter, Heywood Allen, claimed that it was he who changed Robert Friedrich name to Strangler Lewis when Ed performed at the old Buckingham Theater in 1913. That night he allowed any fan, who could prove they had been present in 1913, to watch the show free. Lewis beat Longson on a disqualification.

On December 10, The Strangler defended the title and defeated Lee Wyckoff in Kansas City. This was a rematch of their 1936 Madison Square Garden match, which Lewis claimed was a shoot. Another Kansas City match took place on January 14, 1943 and Wyckoff beat Lewis, taking the Kansas City version of the MWA world title.

The Strangler then lost the Columbus version of the MWA title to John Pesek on January 28, 1943. Time after time Lewis attempted to get the headlock on Pesek, but the speedy Tiger slipped out of the hold. The ending saw Pesek reverse a body slam into a leglock and Lewis submitted in 25 minutes.[456]

At 53 years of age, Strangler Lewis would never be able to claim another world title.

On February 4, Lewis lost to Orville Brown in Kansas City. This set Brown up for a title match with Lee Wyckoff on February 18, a match Orville won, regaining his Kansas City MWA world title.

In March, Lewis' application for a wrestling license in Florida was turned down by boxing commission chairman Frank Markle, saying Ed was too old to wrestle in the state. Lewis countered with a challenge to defeat any five boxers in one night or forfeit a $2,500 bond.

1943 saw Lewis getting pushed in Detroit. He beat Orville Brown twice (March 1 and March 15) and he got two wins over the last (almost) undisputed world champion Danno O'Mahoney (April 5 and April 19).

Lewis' wrestling career was coming to a close, and from that point forward he would be looking for other types of jobs to support his life style. On April 19, 1943, it was announced that Strangler Lewis was the new wrestling promoter at the Detroit Arena Garden. He replaced Louis Markowitz. Lewis' first card drew 1,700. Lewis claimed he wanted a more dignified style of wrestling, but the newspaper pointed out that the only dignified thing at the show was Lewis "dressed to the nines" standing at the front door greeting patrons while a band serenaded them to their seats.[457] The matches were said to be ludicrous. Nothing came from this and

Lewis went back to wrestling in Canada and the North-east.

In Toronto Lewis lost matches to Maurice Tillet (March 18), Leo Numa (June 24) and Earl McCready (July 8). He then return to Kansas to lose MWA title matches to Orville Brown in Kansas City (September 23) and Topeka (September 29).

On August 6, 1943, 'Nazty Nuisance,' a minor film, was released, with Lewis in a small part.

In Chicago, he lost to Kola Kwariani on October 13, 1943. He then spent November touring the East Coast, getting wins over Hans Kampfer, Golden Terror, and Babe Sharkey.

1944 saw Ed getting built up in Minneapolis by Tony Stecher for a big match with Bronko Nagurski. He beat Orville Brown (January 4), Ken Fenelon (January 11) and Ray Steele (January 18), before losing the big match to Nagurski on January 19 in St Paul.

On March 7, 1944, Babe Sharkey won a tournament in Baltimore. This gave him the right to wrestle Strangler Lewis for the Maryland world title on March 14. Sharkey won the match and the world title. Lewis also lost a title rematch to Sharkey in Baltimore on March 28.

Lewis then returned to Minneapolis for a match with his oldest rival Wladek Zbyszko on April 18. Wladek had never stopped wrestling and was a year younger that Lewis. He and his brother Stanislaus lived on a farmer near St. Joseph, Missouri and was active in promoting wrestling in South America. He had wrestled around Kansas for years. At one point he even wore a mask and billed himself as The Great Apollo. Lewis won the match.

The next week in Minneapolis (April 25), Lewis was again beaten by Ray Steele.

Lewis then traveled to Montreal for a series of matches, losing to Frank Sexton on July 5, 1944. Sexton was in the process of becoming one of the top performers of the 1940's. In June 1945, Sexton would defeat Steve Casey for Boston's AWA world title (the title of Lewis, Sonnenberg, and O'Mahoney) and keep it until May 1950. Sexton was the East coast version of Lou Thesz.

Lewis then returned home to the North-West to be near his sister and family. He seemed to be only wrestling part time and his weight got to the 300 pound level. He also owned a home in Tulsa, which he and his wife lived in off and on.

Only August 23, 1944, Lewis had his last match with Wladek Zbyszko in Salt Lake City—and won. A few days later on August 26 at Calgary, Lewis put over Ray Steele.

Gus Sonnenberg had joined the US Navy in 1943, but got sick at the beginning of 1944. On September 9, 1944 Sonnenberg died from Leukemia at Bethesda, MD, Naval Hospital, at age 44. He was buried at Park Cemetery in Marquette.

On September 14, 1944, Bob Managoff, the man who took Bob Friedrich's name thus forcing him to become Strangler Lewis in 1913, died at his home at 2557 Division Street in Chicago.

On September 20, 1944 Lewis gave an interview saying he had just completed a 14 week tour of US Army, Navy, and Marine bases, giving two-hour classes on self defense. He claimed to have visited Japan a number of times and had learned Jiu-Jitsu. His standard interview included stories of having wrestled 6,200 match (not possible), made and spent millions of dollars (don't try to add up the numbers), and having traveled all over the world. At times he claimed to have visited Japan five times. Once is possible, but the Japanese of today have no record of him. Lewis even claim he was a spy for American intelligence, having taken photographs of various buildings and military posts while in Japan.[458]

He traveled to Wichita on December 6 to lose two straight falls to Orville Brown. Reports were being circulated that Lewis was about to retire again. They were denied by Ed.

In 1945, Lewis agreed to manage Cliff Gustafson in the North-West for promoter Tony Stecher. Gustafson was a former University of Minnesota wrestler, who had won the AAU and the intercollegiate title. Stecher had been promoting the wrestler since the end of 1938. Gustafson was a fine amateur, but as a pro he was stiff, colorless and liked to hurt opponents. Stecher needed someone to guild Gustafson during a tour of Seattle, Portland, Winnipeg and other minor cities. Lewis was offered the job of managing Cliff, and Ed accepted. Lewis would help with interviews, second the wrestler in the ring, and sometimes wrestle on the under cards. Ed needed a good job and he performed his duties well.

When not working with Gustafson, Lewis seemed to be visiting Army and Navy bases putting on shows with a group of wrestlers that included Babe Sharkey, Henry Piers, and Milo Steinborn.

Gustafson's tour was cut short on September 17 when he was injured at Seattle in a match with Seelie Samara.[459] The out-of-shape Lewis was forced to take Gustafson's bookings and found himself doing a lot of jobs. Lou Thesz was stationed at Ft. Lewis, in Tacoma, wrestling when off duty. During August and September, Thesz beat Lewis at least four times, mostly in straight falls. Lewis also did jobs for Seelie Samara, Rube Wright (three times), Dick Raines, and Pierre Deglane.

On September 2, 1946, the Japanese surrendered, ending World War II and pro wrestling's labor shortage. Late in 1945, Lewis wrestled on the East Coast, with nothing important happening.

In 1946, Tom Packs was engaged in a major wrestling war with one of his old employees named Sam Muchnick. On January 9, 1946, Lewis wrestled for Muchnick, losing to Ed Virag. The match drew 4,015.

Following the death of Lewis' father, his mother Molly Friedrich continued to live in Nekoosa, but in September 1945 she became ill. She moved to Wisconsin Falls to live with a daughter, Mrs. Jay Buckley. On January 10, 1946, she died at 4 o'clock in the morning. Lewis was present in Nekoosa for the funeral and burial on January 12.[460]

In February, Lewis did jobs for Ali Baba (February 5 and 6 in Baltimore and Philadelphia), and Babe Sharkey (Boston-February 14). He then seemed to stick to refereeing for the rest of the year, in Toronto and then in Northern California.

Late in the year he attempted to market a rubber exerciser called the Strangler Lewis' Health Builder. It resulted in another nothing. Lewis claimed he sold a million of the Health Builders, but also admitted he was broke.[461]

Lewis spent the last part of 1946 and January of 1947 wrestling for promoter George Zaharias in the area around Denver. After putting the young Everett Marshall over nationally in the famous Los Angeles match of April 16, 1930, Lewis had won many rematches and seemed to avoid any loss to Marshall, mainly because of Everett's strong connection with Billy Sandow. The two hadn't met during the years Marshall was recognized as world champion, but with Lewis needing money and Everett making a comeback in 1946, the match seemed to be a natural. The storyline started on December 30, 1946, when referee Lewis screwed up and cost Marshall a Denver match with a Frank Gonzales. Three Denver matches followed. Marshall won the first by disqualification on January 6, 1947. Lewis took the second meeting clean on January 20, and Marshall won the third clean on February 10. During this period, he also did two jobs to Tom Zaharias (January 8 in Colorado Springs) and Ed White (February 12 at Colorado Springs). He then returned to the North-West, both as a wrestler and a referee. He spent May wrestling in the South and lost two matches to Don McIntyre.

Unlike Lewis, Marshall wasn't making a comeback in need of a payday. Since the late 1930's he had owned a large farm, growing mainly onions and cantaloupes. Everett was probably a better farmer than a wrestler. On July 9, 1947, he announced his retirement and, unlike many other stars, he never returned to the ring. In September 1963, Everett, looking to retire from farming, sold three million dollars worth of farm land (110,000 acres) to a group of swindlers and he ended up in bankruptcy court. He still had enough money to help finance the Colorado Boys Ranch, that gave many troubled youths a place to make good in the years that followed. The ranch is still active today. Everett Marshall died on February 10, 1973, at age 67, from complications following surgery. His wife, Harriet Marshall, died at age 92 in 2001. He left many friends and a daughter, Ann Schomburg of Denver, and a son named Bob.[462]

Primo Carnera in his boxing days

Enrique Torres

Lewis moved from Tulsa back to Los Angeles in June, 1947, thinking it would be the easiest place to find work. On June 25, 1947 he wrestled his last title match, meeting California world champion Enrique Torres at The Olympic Auditorium. Lewis lost, but drew a crowd of 9,200.[463]

With the war and the Depression over, pro wrestling started to come out of it's Dark Age, and once television began showing matches it entered a period that rivaled the early 1930's for prosperity. The biggest draw in wrestling during 1947 was ex-boxing champion, Primo Carnera.

On December 7, 1947, promoters matched Lewis with Carnera in Miami. Ed claimed it was the 253rd time he had flown across the country. Primo won the match and Ed took another plane trip back to California.[464]

In later 1947, Jack Sherry was in Hawaii claiming he was the best wrestler in the world and was willing to meet anyone. Sherry had for years been telling people stories about how he was tricked into jobbing to Strangler Lewis in the New York title match in Madison Square Garden (October 10, 1932). After that match, he spent years wrestling in England claiming to be a world champion. He was known as a feared hooker and, after the Lewis match, I have no knowledge of him losing. Honolulu promoters contacted Lewis in Hollywood asking him if he wanted a match with Sherry. Lewis accepted for $2,500 and expenses if he won and nothing if he lost. For a month the 57 year old trained. Word got back to Honolulu that the wrestler getting off the plane was going to be the real Strangler Lewis. On the night of the match (January 28, 1948), Jack Sherry didn't show. With Sherry ducking Lewis, his place was taken by the young star, Butch Levy. Lewis won the match. It was the last match of Lewis' career.[465]

Jack Sherry

In the early part of the year, Lewis took the position of Athletic Instructor and greeter at The Los Angeles Athletic Club.[466] I think Lewis and everyone else believed his future was in public relations of one type or another. Part of Lewis' job entailed talking to boy's clubs, visiting reform schools and giving talks on juvenile delinquency. Ed was fat and looked old in many ways, but he was huge and still had the grace and balance of a champion. He was a good talker who always enjoyed public speaking.

On March 13, Lewis cancelled a match in Fresno with Flash Gordon, claiming an elbow injury.

On March 29, 1948, Lewis' California wrestling license was revoked after he failed the physical examination for journeymen wrestlers. The commission stated he would still be allowed to referee. This, in effect, was the date of Strangler Lewis' retirement as an active pro wrestler.[467]

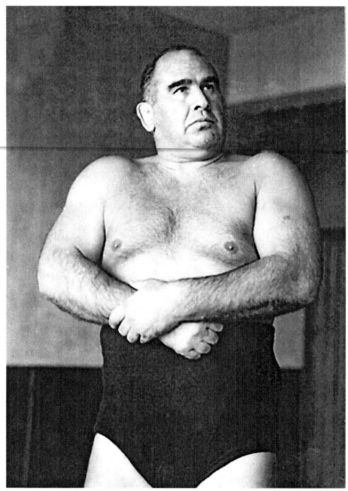

Ed Lewis

Lou Thesz and the Two NWAs

Lewis' friend, Lou Thesz, never had any desire to go over seas to fight Germans. He was a pro wrestler and that was his only obsession. With help from powerful friends he rode out the war working in a medical company stationed at Fort Lewis. In April, 1946 he was transferred to Fort Sam Houston and was discharged from the Army on July 26, 1946.

Thesz was ambitious and it didn't take the two time world champion (MWA and NWA titles) long to win another title. On September 11, 1946, Lou beat his good friend Bobby Managoff for the local world title in Montreal. He then returned to St. Louis to once again became the town's favorite babyface by beating Buddy Rogers in front of 11,085. On January 23, 1947, Thesz had his first match challenging Bill Longson for his St. Louis NWA world title. Lou, while still the Montreal world champion (unknown in St. Louis), lost the match, but the attendance was 15,180.

Whipper Billy Watson

On February 8, 1947, the first television station in St. Louis inaugurated service in St. Louis. The first 6 inch black and white television sets cost $469, but costs were going to drop and most smart people saw it as the future of entertainment.

On February 20, 1947, Lou dropped his Montreal world title to Bobby Managoff, but won it back from Managoff on April 16, 1947. Meanwhile Longson lost his NWA world title to Whipper Billy Watson via a disqualification on February 21.

Thesz then pinned champion Billy Watson in St. Louis on April 25, 1947. At that point Thesz held both the NWA and Montreal world titles. No one could play the champion better than Lou Thesz. He was a classy looking man, who was a super athlete, fine performer, and the best pure wrestler of his generation. He held both titles for most of 1947.

Late in the year, the Montreal promoter Eddie Quinn wanted to put his title back on local star Yvon Robert. Tom Packs didn't want to cheapen the more important NWA title, so they had Thesz first drop his NWA title

back to Bill Longson on November 21, 1947 in St. Louis, and then lose the Montreal title to Robert on November 26. The idea was that Lou would regain his NWA title down.

Around June 5, 1948, Lou Thesz, with money and support from Canadian promoters Frank Tunney, Eddie Quinn and wrestlers Bill Longson and Bobby Managoff, bought the St. Louis promotion from Tom Packs. With the promotion Thesz took complete control of the old National Wrestling Association world title and its belt (called the Thesz belt).

In buying the promotion, Thesz found himself in the middle of the St. Louis wrestling war with his old friend Sam Muchnick. The battle had been going on since 1945, and Thesz's company had always dominated Muchnick's side, but things would change.

On July 18, 1948,[468] a number of the smaller promoters from the mid-west met at the President Hotel of Waterloo, Iowa. The group formed an organization to add in exchanging talent

Lou Thesz

and battling Packs' larger St. Louis promotion. The group consisted of Pinkie George (Des Moines), Tony Stecher (Minneapolis), Sam Muchnick (St. Louis), Orville Brown (Kansas City) and Max Clayton (Omaha). Group president Pinkie George had been using the name National Wrestling Alliance in Des Moines (mainly to confuse fans with Tom Packs National Wrestling Association) and the group agreed to continue using that name and use George's world champion, Orville Brown (who was also the Kansas City MWA world champion). This alliance worked well, and many other promoters liked the idea because it was a way to create a monopoly, control talent and lower costs. Within a few months Al Haft (Columbus) and Harry Light (Detroit) had joined. By 1949, even Paul Bowser was part of the group.

Two days later on July 20 in Indianapolis, Thesz defeated Longson to become the National Wrestling Association world champion.

You could tell Thesz was in charge because, almost immediately, Ed Lewis started finding work. On July 30, Lewis was the special referee for a Thesz/Managoff match in St. Louis. Lewis was also getting referee jobs with Lou's partners in Montreal (Eddie Quinn) and Toronto (Frank Tunney).

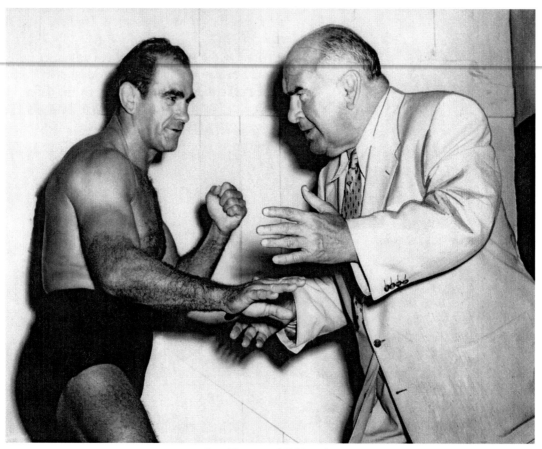

Lou Thesz and Ed Lewis

On November 22, 1948, Ed Lewis was named chairman of a newly organized group called "The Wrestling Promoters' Association of America and Allied Countries." I don't know who these promoters were but my guess it was Thesz's NWAssociation and some New York promoters including Toots Mondt, grouped with Canadian promoters Frank Tunney and Eddie Quinn. I think they were attempting to form an alliance of their own to battle the new NWAlliance. At a press conference held in a New York hotel, Strangler Lewis was promoted to the position of "Mat Czar." The job consisted of public relations, ending the battle over who was the true world champion and bringing back wrestling to New York's Madison Square Garden. Lewis was to be paid $25,000 a year, but claims are that he received very little of that. Three weeks later, Jack Dempsey announced he was working with his friend, Lewis, to bring wrestling back to the Garden. Other than that, nothing really happens while Lewis was this wrestling Czar. In 1949, Lewis continued to referee off and on.

Whatever he was earning wasn't very much, and many people were upset to see the former great champion doing so poorly.

Sam Muchnick's position in the St. Louis war improved with help of the new NWAlliance and its champion Orville Brown. Jack Pefer also helped Muchnick by having his best wrestler, Buddy Rogers, jump from Thesz's group. For years Rogers had been Thesz' only major rival as the best babyface in St. Louis. But Thesz, Longson, and Packs hated Rogers, and did everything they could to keep him down by jobbing him every chance they got. In 1949, Rogers had turned heel, taking on a Nature Boy gimmick in Pfefer's Hollywood promotion. Muchnick started using the heel Rogers and he became a huge draw again in St. Louis.

Buddy Rogers with Pfeffer's belt, after a heel turn in Los Angeles, 1949

By mid-1949, both St. Louis promotions were losing money. Thesz didn't enjoy promoting and wanted to spend all his time wrestling. Muchnick and Thesz had been friends before and talks resulted in both promotions joining as one. Both sides presented their agreement at the July 29, 1949 NWA convention. Members felt that with the nationwide network television stations broadcasting wrestling, promoters could no longer afford multiple champions. So agreements were made for Orville Brown and Thesz to meet in a title unification match in St. Louis on November 29, 1949.

Orville had proved himself a fine champion, but most promoters thought Thesz would be a better national champion. The idea at the time was for Brown to win the unification match and have return matches, with Brown again coming out on top in every major city. When that seemed to be cooling off, Thesz would win the title and start the feud all over again until Brown was of no further use.

On September 11, 1949, Ray Steele—probably the best true wrestler of the 1930's, and good friend to both Lewis and Thesz—died in his sleep from a heart attack at age 49 while hunting in Boise, Idaho. He was buried in Lincoln, Nebraska.

On November 1, Orville Brown was driving from a match in Des Moines to his home in Kansas City when his car skidded underneath a jackknifed trailer-truck. Orville suffered brain damage and was in a coma for five days. When he awoke, he was paralyzed on the left side. These injuries forced his retirement and he relinquished his NWAlliance world title.

Orville Brown's car after his accident in 1949

On November 28, 1949, the National Wrestling Alliance named Lou Thesz as their new champion. The Alliance also agreed that Sam Muchnick would be in charge of the championship bookings. The St. Louis group found themselves in control of the title and the Alliance, so Thesz reigned as NWA world champion for over six years.

Lewis and the Management of the Champion

The convention also named Ed Lewis as its "ambassador of good will." It was seen as a playback position after all of Lewis' years of serves. To help the ailing Lewis financially, each NWA member sent $25 to Lewis each month (other reports claim the amount to be $12,500). Lewis' job had him working as a NWA spokesman, handling controversial issues and wandering from territory to territory ironing out snags between members.[469]

The NWA Convention, 1949.
Ed Lewis is standing at the middle back. Thesz is standing in the right-hand corner.
Every NWA promoter is present, including Bill Longson and Enrique Torres.

In 1950, there are claims that Lewis mentored Timothy Geohagen in Ontario.

On May 3, 1950, a minor film called the 'Bodyhold' opened in theaters. Lewis played a small part as a referee.

Lewis was still working off and on at the Los Angeles Athletic Club, and one of the boys he trained turned out to be Gene LeBell. LeBell, who was to become an AAU National Judo Champion, a pro wrestler, a hall of fame Hollywood stuntman, and a MMA pioneer, was the son of Olympic Auditorium promoter Aileen "LaBell" Eaton. When not in school, Gene would hang around the Olympic getting in trouble. His mother would send him over to the L.A. Athletic Club to keep him out of her hair. LeBell would ride on his bike to the Club and spend his afternoons getting tied into knots by the giant Strangler Lewis. Gene says Lewis weighed over 300 pounds and looked more like a barrel than a man. He learned a lot from Lewis and claimed Ed was impossible to take down.[470]

With Thesz as champion, the NWA grew larger, with just about every major promoter allied or a member. During 1950, Thesz argued that he needed a manager to help him on the road. Thesz pushed for that person to be Ed Lewis. There were some older promoters who felt that the sport owed something to the old champion, while others (like Al Haft) figured Lewis had made his money and spent it, so it wasn't their responsibility to provide the old man with social security checks. But Thesz was a good champion and a very powerful promoter, and everyone knew that to show disrespect toward Lewis was the way to attract Lou's hatred.

So Thesz won the argument and Ed Lewis became Lou's manager in November 1950. Ed would travel ahead of Lou to provide publicity for his major title matches by getting space in local newspapers. Ed was known and liked by sports reporters, and his just walking into a pressroom was news enough to get space on any sports page. Reporters and fans may have not remembered any of his matches, but the name Strangler Lewis was a part of sport's legend that echoed others like Babe Ruth, Jack Dempsey, Bobby Jones, Jim

Thorpe, and Bill Tilden. As Thesz's manager he was billed by promoters and newsmen as pro wrestling's greatest star and a legitimate wrestler. With Gotch dead, Stecher in a nursing home, and Londos running a farm, who was left to say any different? Thesz knew the prestige he'd receive just by having Strangler Lewis in his corner, telling the world that the present champion was as good as any wrestler who ever lived.

Manager Ed Lewis with Lou Thesz, signing a contract with Hawaiin promoter Al Karasik.

Lou Thesz in the ring with manager Ed Lewis, and the belt

Thesz and Lewis were a perfect team. Lou loved Lewis like a father and never got tired of him. Ed told him stories, some of them true, and showed him the best hotels and finest restaurants. Thesz was very good-looking and a dignified champion, but he was reserved around some people and lived a disciplined life style. He was also careful who he made friends with. In fact, Thesz was more like Jim Londos than Strangler Lewis. Lewis was gregarious and attempted to make friends with everyone. In the ring Lewis was always disliked, and boos could be heard during every match; but in life he was liked by just about everyone he came into contact with. Ed was also anything but disciplined. If he wanted food, he ate. If he wanted to party, he stayed up all night. If he had a shot at a woman, he took her. If he had money, he spent it—and worried about it later.

After a match, Lou would eat and then sleep. Lewis after seconding the champion at the arena, would go out drinking, playing cards, and having a good time. In the morning, Lou would get up and find Lewis in the hotel lobby, waiting to eat breakfast. Lewis would then leave for the next city, while Thesz went to the gym.

Lewis didn't stay with Thesz all the time. He seems to have just worked the major cities and major matches. His cut of every card he worked on was 2½ percent of the gate.[471] Many promoters didn't like the deal, but Thesz thought Ed made them money in the long run.[472]

Lewis was enshrined in Wisconsin's Athletic Hall of Fame as a charter member on November 28, 1951.

On October 10, 1954, Anton "Tony" Stecher, brother and former manager of Joe Stecher, who was the long time promoter in Minneapolis, died after a heart attack. His promotion was taken over by his son, Dennis Stecher, and Wally Karbo. Joe Stecher was still alive and in good physical health, living in a nursing home.

Joe & Tony, the Stecher brothers, in Ring 2

The first few years of Thesz's title reign were big money winners, but by the end of 1955 the public grew tired of watching wrestling on television, so business dropped off. In early 1956, the federal government started an investigation of the NWA, claiming the organization was a monopoly—which it was. Most of the smart people in pro wrestling were terrified of the FBI and Thesz was one of them. So in early 1956 (some think December 1955) Thesz sold his share of the St. Louis promotion to Sam Muchnick.

Thesz's body was also suffering from all the years on the road defending the title. In March, Lou injured his ankle (Thesz claimed he broke it) skiing with his wife in California. Needing a vacation, and with the FBI investigation hanging over everyone's head, Thesz made a deal with promoter Frank Tunney to let Billy Watson hold the title threw most of 1956. So on March 15, 1956, Thesz lost the NWA world title to Whipper Billy Watson by "count out of the ring" in front of 15,000 fans in Toronto. The referee was Jack Dempsey.

During these events of early 1956, Lewis lost his managerial job. With Thesz no longer a powerful

Whipper Billy Watson with Thesz's NWA belt

promoter and without the title, there was no longer a use for Lewis. Ed returned to his home in Tulsa to live out what was left of his life with his wife Bobbie Lee West.

If Thesz's ankle was broken, he was a very fast healer. Three weeks after the title loss, Lou was back in the ring with Watson on April 6 at St. Louis. Lou lost that match via a disqualification, a result that got Thesz suspended in town for 60 days. Thesz had moved to the San Fernando Valley near Los Angeles, and had built a strong relationship with Olympic Auditorium promoter Jules Strongbow. After the April 6 match Thesz continued to wrestle, working a least two matches a week for the rest on the year. He had other attempts to take the title away from Watson, wrestling the champion in Houston, Vancouver, Los Angeles, and San Francisco. Thesz's ankle was doing so well that the August 5 match in Los Angeles went to a 90 minute draw.

At the September 1956 conference, the National Wrestling Alliance renewed their pledge to Ed Lewis with a $7,500 annual salary. Thesz wanted Lewis back, but Ed was used to working with other wrestlers like Dory Funk Sr., Bob Ellis, Pepper Gomes and Dick Hutton.[473]

Lewis courted Bob Ellis into pro wrestling during 1956, and stories claim that Ed taught Ellis his "bulldog" headlock.[474]

On October 15, 1956, The National Wrestling Alliance dissolved under a judgment filed in the U.S. district court of Iowa, by Judge William F. Riley. The agreement had the NWA agreeing to cancel all its existing rules, regulations, and by-laws, and then drawing up a new code consistent with the terms of the court order. The agreement was made by the work of Sam Muchnick. This made it safe for a Thesz return.

On November 9, 1956, Lou Thesz defeated Billy Watson in St. Louis by KO to re-win his NWA world title.

Lewis was present at the Floyd Patterson/Archie Moore fight in Chicago on November 30, 1956 and was interviewed by *Ring Magazine*.

Between May 4 and May 12 of 1957, Japanese promoter/wrestler Rikidozan visited Thesz at his San Fernando Valley home. He offered the champion at least $30,000 (real money, unlike some of the other claims in wrestling history) to tour Japan defending the title against Rikidozan. An agreement was made for October 1957. Around this time, plans were also made for Thesz to tour Australia and Singapore.

The NWA and Muchnick didn't like this idea of Thesz visiting Japan. They weren't getting a cut of

Lou Thesz with his NWA belt

the $30,000 and they worried about the title being stolen in a double-cross. Rikidozan changed their point of view by paying them the normal NWA booking fees and giving Muchnick his normal 3%. Sam also may have thought he was going to get a cut of Lou's $30,000, but Lou never let that happen.

To prevent the possibility of a title double-cross overseas, the group got clever and developed a storyline that created two NWA world champions. On June 14, 1957, Lou Thesz seemed to lose the NWA world title to Edouard Carpentier in Chicago. In the third fall, Thesz hurt his back and was defenseless. Lou kept going to the ropes to save himself from being pinned. The referee stopped the match, saying he was disqualifying Thesz for not defending himself. Carpentier was declared the winner and the new NWA world champion.[475] Now, on an "unable to continue" finish, a title can change hands, and that's what seemed to happen. But the referee used the word "disqualify" in announcing the verdict, and NWA rules state that a title cannot change via a "disqualification." It sounded like some type of a mistake, but it was just a way to confuse fans and create controversy. The idea by everyone involved was to create a back-up champion, in case Thesz was double-crossed in Japan and dropped the title to Rikidozan or someone else on the trip. If Lou did lose somehow, the NWA would just claim he wasn't champion, having lost the title to Carpentier.

The plan seemed like there was going to be a title unification rematch in St. Louis on Thesz's return. The promoters would then decide who they wanted as champion, but the plan didn't work out.

After Lou's June 14 loss, the official NWA champion seemed to be Carpentier, but both men defended what they called the NWA world title wherever they appeared. In cities where Thesz was appearing the fans weren't told about Carpentier and they continued like nothing had happened.

On June 27, 1957, Thesz defended his version of the NWA title against Dory Funk (father of Dory Jr. and Terry Funk) in Amarillo. The booker, old Dr. Karl Sarpolis, created a storyline that had Funk paying Ed "Strangler" Lewis to manage and train him for the match. Lewis appeared in Funk's corner, but the match ended up a draw after Lou injured his leg. The angle helped draw a large 8,000 in small Amarillo.[476]

Edouard Carpentier *aka* "Eddy Wiecz"

So it seems that Thesz was still attempting to make his friend Lewis a little money and they may have tried the same storyline in other cities.

A rematch between Carpentier and Thesz took place on July 25 in Montreal. The match, which drew 15,931, ended in a disqualification when Thesz once again injured his back and kept crawling under the ropes to save himself from being pinned by the Frenchman. Carpentier got upset because Montreal referee Yvon Robert refused to disqualify Thesz like the Chicago referee, so he punched him—getting himself disqualified.

On July 27, 1957, Sam Muchnik was quoted in *The Montreal Star* saying that the title couldn't change on a disqualification and that Carpentier was still NWA champion. A 60 minute draw between Carpentier and Thesz followed in Chicago on August 16.

Around that time, Montreal promoter Eddie Quinn realized that he was drawing huge crowds, unlike St. Louis and the rest of the wrestling world, using his own world title, and the prestige of his own top babyface having the NWA world title meant very little in Montreal. The NWA using Carpentier was going to limit his use of his own performer.

Quinn realized that losing dates on his top face wasn't going to make him any extra money. Quinn was also upset that the hated Jack Pfefer was allowed to hang around the NWA convention in St. Louis that started in August. So Quinn pulled Carpentier from the NWA champion storyline, suggesting that the NWA should just rule that Thesz got his title back after the disqualification win in Montreal.

On August 25, 1957, the NWA, at its convention, ruled that the NWA world title belonged to Lou Thesz because the June 14 Thesz/Carpentier match in Chicago was a disqualification, and a title couldn't change on a disqualification. So Edouard Carpentier's name was erased from record books, and as far as the NWA was concerned he was never champion. Basically, the NWA just disowned their past storyline and moved on.

Carpentier was left with a title "claim" which he would use over the next three years, even dropping it in Boston, Omaha, and Los Angeles. This episode in wrestling history pretty much ruined the idea of having only one world champion.

Thesz and Lewis by this time were both fed up with the NWA. Lewis had lost a lot of money because cheap promoters felt his wasn't worth his 3 percent, and Thesz was worn out by his schedule and the days wasted by minor payoffs in small towns. Lewis convinced Thesz that he'd be better off dumping the NWA and going out on his own. Lewis argued that Thesz was a star who played the part of a champion better than anyone. He made Thesz believe that he could draw and that the public would always consider him the champion—even without the NWA name association. This meant no NWA taking its cut of every gate, so Thesz might even make more money without all the work that went with being NWA champion. Lewis also told Thesz about all the money to be made overseas.

During the trip to Australia, Singapore, and Japan, Thesz notified Muchnick by mail that he didn't want the title any longer and that Sam should set up a title change as soon as he returned from Japan.

Muchnick and the NWA members need a new champion and the names worthy of the title were small in number. Most felt that Buddy Rogers would make a good heel champion, but Thesz didn't respect Rogers and had always refused to put him over. Rogers was also under contract to Al Haft of Columbus and they worried about running into the same trouble they had with Eddie Quinn and Carpentier. This also eliminated Verne Gagne, who was owned by Fred Kohler. Another candidate was Pat O'Connor.

Ed Lewis had been a big supporter of Dick Hutton and his comments can be found in an 1956 magazines saying he felt the next champion would be Hutton. Living in Tulsa in 1953, Ed may have even played a part in the training of Hutton before turning pro and managed him for short periods of time when not on the road with Thesz. Hutton was a three time NCAA National Champion on two national championships at Oklahoma A&M, a three times AAU champion, and a 1948 Olympic Games member. Lewis and most amateur officials considered him to be the finest wrestler of his generation. Thesz, who idolized Lewis and was influenced by him, told the NWA that he wanted to drop the title to Hutton. The organization, still wanting Rogers or O'Connor, had to go along with Thesz's wishes because no one in wrestling could intimidate Lou into losing if he didn't want to. And he wanted to lose to the best true wrestler—Hutton.

After terrible trips through Australia and Singapore, Thesz ended his vacation with a very successful tour of Japan. He returned to America in November and wrestled a few matches around Montreal. On November 12, 1957, Thesz wrestled a draw with Buddy Rogers in Minneapolis. One wonders if this had been the promoters planed title change, but Thesz wouldn't "play

Dick Hutton

ball." Thesz was then booked to meet Dick Hutton in Toronto on November 14, 1957.

The storyline for the match resembled the Funk match in Amarillo. Hutton had recruited Strangler Lewis to manage and train him to defeat his former student, Thesz. This time it worked. After 35:15 of a one fall match, Hutton caught Thesz attempting a "Thesz Press" and body-slammed the champion twice. He then applied an abdominal stretch and Lou submitted. Sam Muchnick was present and raised Hutton's hand.

Thesz and Hutton then wrestled a draw in St. Louis on November 22, before Lou left on his European tour, which lasted until late February 1958. When he returned, Thesz was booked out of Los Angeles by promoter Jules Strongbow. He began billing himself as International Champion in Europe and continued as champion in the Los Angeles area for a few years. He also ran a resort hotel in Phoenix.

Pre-match photo of the November 14, 1957 title challenge between Lou Thesz and Dick Hutton,
with Lewis acting as Hutton's manager.

Ed Lewis continued living in Tulsa with his wife. His eyes were worse and his health at age 68 wasn't what it once was. The champion Dick Hutton also lived in Tulsa, and in September 1958 Lewis traveled with Hutton as trainer/manager/publicist in Canada and Minneapolis. On December 26, 1958, he was present in St. Louis to watch Hutton defeat Edouard Carpentier. That major match-up drew only 4,607 spectators.

Hutton was poorly promoted and didn't draw. He lacked color and needed a gimmick. On January 9, 1959, Hutton dropped the NWA title to Pat O'Connor in St. Louis, submitting to an O'Connor toe hold in a one fall match. After losing a number of rematches to O'Connor, he was used in Los Angeles by promoter Jules Strongbow and given a cowboy gimmick. He did very well as Cowboy Dick Hutton in Southern California, but was overshadowed by Lou Thesz, Freddie Blassie and The Destroyer and never won the WWA world title. He retired in April 1964 to marry the daughter of a millionaire and train race horses. After 31 years of marriage, his wife Katherine died from Lou Gehrig's disease. Hutton passed away on November 24, 2003 at the age of 80.

Lou Thesz and Ed Lewis

The Strangler's Last Years

In 1959, Lewis returned to Wisconsin Rapids for the funeral of his sister Hattie Buckley. The only relatives left in Wisconsin Rapids were nephews Patrick Buckley and Ben Buckley. His other two sisters lived in the state of Washington.

In October of 1959 Lewis helped in the pro training of Danny Hodge, three-time national collegiate wrestling champion at Oklahoma University, whose record in school was 46-0 with 36 pins. In early 1960 Lewis seconded Hodge in some of his early pro matches. Lewis was so impressed with Hodge that he gave him one of Billy Sandow's old headlock machines. Lewis still had two such machines in 1960. Today one resides in the National Wrestling Hall of Fame and Museum in Stillwater, Oklahoma, and the other is on display at the Dan Gable International Wrestling Institute and Museum at Waterloo, Iowa.[477]

Paul Bowser promoted a Boston Garden card on July 15, 1960 that saw Lou Thesz and Ed Carpentier draw with Killer Kowalski & Hans Schmidt. Three days earlier, Bowser suffered a heart attack at his home in Lexington and was taken to the Concord Emerson Hospital. After two surgical operations, Paul Bowser died on July 17, 1960. He was buried at Lexington's Westview Cemetery.

By the 1960's, Lewis was legally blind after all the years of suffering from Trachoma. He returned to being fully retired, supported by his wife and helped by donations from acquaintances.[478] He took to religion and preached in many Christian Science churches throughout the mid-west, playing the part of a repentant sinner. He claimed to have been "completely devoted to expounding the message of the Lord." He was once quoted as saying: "They sit out there and listen, because they're afraid, that if they don't, I may get mad and put a headlock on them."[479]

Lewis during his preacher period

Joe Malcewicz, Paul Bowser's best pure wrestler and one of Lewis' top rivals during the 1920's, became the major promoter in San Francisco in 1935. He was a good man known for his honesty and fair payoffs. Lewis always listed him with Stecher and Jim Browning as one of the three top hookers he wrestled in his career. In 1961, Malcewicz was put out of business in San Francisco by Roy Shire, Ray Stevens and local television. He died on April 20, 1962 at the age of 65.[480]

Sam Avey continue to run a strong wrestling promotion in Tulsa, Oklahoma into the 1950's. On September 20, 1952, a lightning strike burned down the Coliseum, leaving him without a major arena. In January 1958 he sold his promotion to Leroy McGuirk. Avey was vice president of Farmers and Merchants State Bank, and served as NWA treasurer until August 1960. Sam Avey died, at age 67, on August 9, 1962.

Lewis' good friend Lou Thesz remained one of wrestling's greatest stars. Pat O'Connor reigned as NWA world champion but was overshadowed by Buddy Rogers, and on June 30, 1961 the two drew 38,000 and a gate of $125,000 in Chicago. Rogers won the title and returned much of its past glory over the next year and half. But Rogers was controlled by Eastern Promoter Vincent J. McMahon and the old school NWA promoters were upset by the few dates they were getting with the Champion. The fact was that the North American territory was simply too big for one champion to cover. Buddy Rogers drew well but his body was shot from years of being a top worker. His work suffered, although fans really couldn't tell, and he missed a lot of action due to injuries. So Sam Muchnick and the other NWA promoters wanted their title back, and on the East Coast Toots Mondt was talking Vincent J. McMahon into forming a new organization with its own champion.

The NWA needed a new champion, and the person they picked was old Lou Thesz. On January 24, 1963, Thesz pinned Rogers in Toronto winning the National Wrestling Alliance world title for the third time. Thesz being asked back as champion has to be considered one of the greatest compliments in pro wrestling history.

Joe Malcewicz

Thesz remain champion for three years, losing it to friend Gene Kiniski (by disqualification) in St. Louis on January 7, 1966.

On November 7, 1965, Thesz had a wrestling date in Tulsa, so he flew into town a day early so he could visit with mentor Lewis. Lewis seemed in good spirits and wanted Lou to take him to Oklahoma City so the two could visit a hotel they used to enjoy during their traveling days. So the two took a day-long trip to the Skillern Hotel. Ed spent the day reminiscing about his career and the people he had know and now were gone. He seemed to enjoy himself, and the two drove back that night so that Lou could defend his title against Sputnik Monroe. Thesz then left the territory, not realizing that the trip was Ed's way of saying goodbye. Several weeks later Thesz got word that Ed was in bad shape after a series of strokes, and had been hospitalized at the Veterans Hospital in Muskogee.

Buddy Rogers with the Ed Lewis Belt, early 1950s

In early 1966, Lewis was honored by his hometown of Nekoosa. A ten-foot-high marker was erected in the city by the South Wood County Historical Corporation. The large plaque memorialized his career and listed the names of many of the great men he had wrestled. A number of his old friends were present, but Lewis was unable to attend because he was confined to a nursing home. The marker still stands today at the intersection of Prospect Avenue (State Highway 73) and 9th Street.

On August 6, 1966, Thesz stopped in Muskogee to see Lewis on the way to some matches in Florida. Lou got to the Veterans Hospital early in the morning and Lewis was sleeping in a wheelchair. The nurses told Thesz that Ed had had a bad night and had been medicated, so Lou left and got on his plane for Tampa. Later that day he got a 'phone call from Jack Pfefer, who had visited Lewis the afternoon following Thesz. Pfefer told Lou that the doctor felt that Lewis was "fading fast." Pfefer told Lou to get back as soon as possible.[481]

Ed "Strangler" Lewis died in his sleep on August 7, 1966 at the age of 76.

Funeral services were held at the Ninde Funeral Home in Tulsa. The private service was officiated over by Willard Russell, a Christian Science reader at Tulsa's Golden Chapel. Lewis was cremated and later buried at Arlington National Cemetery, Arlington, Virginia, in section 53, grave 3546.[482]

The gravestone of Ed Lewis

The two Zbyszko brothers, Wladek and Stan, continued to live together on their pig farm near Savannah, Missouri, north of St. Joseph, Missouri. The two were involved with the development of pro wrestling in South America and it's claimed that Johnny Valentine and Harley Race worked and received some training on their farm. The 88-year-old Stanislaus Zbyszko died on the farm after a heart attack on September 23, 1967. Wladek Zbyszko, one of Lewis' greatest rivals, died on June 10, 1968, and is now resting at the Savannah Cemetery. I believe, if my counting is correct, that he was 75 (born November 20, 1891).

Billy Sandow, Lewis' manager and friend from 1915 to 1932, who should be given full credit for finding Lewis, training him and making him one of sport's greatest stars, was a behind-the-scene promoter of wrestling in Kansas after leaving St. Louis in 1939. The professional break-up seemed to have also ended the friendship, because after 1932 Sandow is written out of Lewis' story. Sandow died on September 15, 1972 at the age of 88.

Aurelio Fabiani, the promoter of Philadelphia and Los Angeles, died at Thomas Jefferson Hospital in Philadelphia on April 26, 1973 at age 82. The man who brought great wrestling to Philadelphia and turned Jim Londos into a superstar has yet to be admitted to any Wrestling Hall of Fame.

Joe Stecher outlived Lewis by almost eight years. Ed's greatest rival, after over 35 years of being institutionalized, died at the Veterans Hospital of St. Cloud, Minnesota on March 29, 1974, at the age of 80. His remains were shipped to San Francisco where his wife lived, and Joe can be found at Cypress Memorial Park, Coma, California (Niche P, Tier 1, in the Garden of Serenity). In public, Lewis always stated that Stecher was the best wrestler he ever met, but that he lacked heart. In private, with friendly insiders like Thesz, he'd say he didn't know who was the better wrestler, and admitted he'd have been beaten in short time if he had gone to the mat with Stecher without stalling.

Jim Londos lived out his life just as he had planned it. Wrestling's greatest box office star had a career that lasted from 1915 to 1959. His last years of life were spent as a rich gentleman farmer in Escondido, California. In the 1960's he sold most of his farm, becoming even richer, and today a large portion of the city of Escondido rests on it. Unlike Lewis, Londos would never have said anything disrespectful about his old bitter rival. When asked about their September 20, 1934 battle in Wrigley Field, Chicago, that broke the all-time gate record, Londos always played down his victory, making a point of saying that Lewis was old and past his prime. Perhaps he knew Lewis' popularity made him invulnerable to critics. Londos suffered a heart attack at Palomar General Hospital and died on August 19, 1975. He was buried at a prime spot, next to his wife, at the Oak Hill Memorial Park, on a green hill overlooking his city of Escondido.

The gravestone of Jim Londos

Toots Mondt remain a power on the East Coast. He played a major part in the promotion of wrestling at Madison Square Garden and formed with Vincent McMahon the Capitol Wrestling Corporation, which later became known as the WWF or WWE. He also played an important part in the careers of Antonino Rocca and Bruno Sammartino. By 1960 Mondt was acting only as a shareholder and was semi-retired, employed only in an advisory capacity. He retired completely in 1969 and moved from Jackson Heights, Long Island, to St. Louis. He died from pneumonia on June 11, 1976. He was 82.

Vince McMahon, Sr., Toots Mondt, Bruno Sammartino, Shelton Weaver and Bill Cardille

On June 2, 1975, the Ed "Strangler" Lewis belt was auctioned off in Boston.[483]

John Pesek never did another job after the Strangler Lewis series of matches in 1942. His last match took place on January 28, 1959. Like Jim Londos, he never dropped his (MWA) world title in the ring. He also ran a productive farm (9 miles south of Ravenna, Nebraska), but Pesek also had one of the most famous kennels of racing dogs in the nation. He was the only man ever enshrined in the Greyhound Racing Hall of Fame and the Pro Wrestling Hall of Fame. It's said that Pesek revolutionized the sport of dog racing, bringing the super dog "Just Andrew" from Australia to America. "Just Andrew" is also in the Greyhound Hall of Fame, with 30 of his offsprings. In 1978, it was claimed that 80% of the greyhounds racing were descended from "Just Andrew." John Pesek died from a heart attack, while eating breakfast in Ravenna with his two older children, Elizabeth and Jack, on March 12, 1978. He was buried at Highland Cemetery, west of Ravenna.[484]

John Pesek and Stanislaus Zbyszko: two farmers, late in life.

In 1979, Bobbie Lee West, Lewis' wife for over 29 years, passed away in Tulsa.

Jack Dempsey remained a sports icon. He continued to make public appearances and ran a famous restaurant in Manhattan. He took a hands-on approach and spent much of his time greeting awe-struck tourists at the door. The press called him sport's greatest gentleman. He died from strokes and heart failure on May 31, 1983, at age 87, and is buried in the Southampton Cemetery in Southampton, New York. Gene Tunney, Dempsey's conqueror, preceded him in death by five years (November 7, 1978). Dempsey's 3,000 word obituary was written by Red Smith and printed on the front page of the *New York Times*. Tunney's death was reported on page 22 with an unbylined obituary of 750 words.[385]

Lou Thesz's career basically ended after a tour of Japan in April 1982. Still in tremendous condition, he remained a legend for his workouts in the gym. In 1984 most insiders felt he was more than a match for WWF world champion Hulk Hogan. At times he still would accept special matches, but that ended in December 1990 in Japan's Tokyo Dome when he injured his hip in a match with Masa Chono. Like Lewis, he stayed in the sport by acting as a special referee and accepted positions with promotions like the UWFI in Japan. With a career that rivaled any in wrestling's history, he was honored by the Cauliflower Ally Club in 1991 and later that year replaced Archie Moore as the Club's President. For the last portion of his life he functioned as pro wrestling's elder statesman, and even was a part of the best pro wrestling history site on the internet, The Lou Thesz Forum at Wrestling Classics.com. He also became a great help to a new generation of wrestling historians, and never showed his annoyance with nobodies who knew historical dates and questioned his memory. Lou could not have a conversation without praising his old friend and mentor, Ed Lewis. Lou Thesz died on April 28, 2002 from complications following open heart surgery. He was 86 years old.

It would be impossible to have a legitimate Pro Wrestling Hall of Fame without the name of Strangler Lewis on its rolls, and Ed is in all of the major ones including: The Wrestling Observer Newsletter Hall of Fame (the initial class of 1996), The Professional Wrestling Hall of Fame (PWHF of Amsterdam, New York) (the initial class of 2002), Wisconsin's Athletic Hall of Fame (initial class of 1951) and The International Wrestling Institute and Museum George Tragos/Lou Thesz Hall of Fame (initial class of 1959).

There is some argument to the idea that Ed "Strangler" Lewis was pro wrestling's greatest shooter, I believe Stecher, Gotch, Caddock, Pesek, Steele, and some of the older and lighter performers have just as much claim to that title as Ed. And I don't believe he surpassed Jim Londos, Gotch, or even Hulk Hogan as a wrestling "star"—but when you follow Ed Lewis' career, you follow the history of the sport.

Left to right: Lewis, Jack Dempsey, Paul Bowser. April 18, 1955

Studio portrait of Ed "Strangler" Lewis in earlier days

Endnotes

1. The story of Ed Lewis, as reported in newspapers, books and articles, is a myth created by Lewis himself, his long-time manager Billy Sandow, wrestling promoters and uninformed sports writers through the years. In the very first sentence we can already find three controversial statements. The first is the spelling of Lewis's true name. The second is the place of birth, and the third is the birth date.

   It is my plan to use newspaper reports of matches to form my base for this paper. I feel that reports of matches, written on the day of the event, have more credibility than stories of events told by the wrestlers themselves years later or stories that have been told and passed on by people who were not present.

   In the late 1940's Lewis attempted to write his biography using a writer/collaborator going by the name Steve McPherson. We don't actually know the identity of this Steve McPherson. During Lewis's life, he was in contact with at least two men using that name. One was a sports editor of a newspaper in Bellingham; the other was a minor promoter of wrestling in Phoenix. McPherson may have been one of these men, but we don't know.

   The godfather of all wrestling historians, J Michael Kenyon, gave me a photocopy of *The Unfinished Lewis Biography* years ago. The paper is basically just of bunch of unfinished notes and stories. Some of it is out of chronological order. In my view, it's a mess—but it is the closest thing we had to Lewis' own words, and it tells stories about parts of his early life we can find in no other place. In forming the early portion of the personal life of Lewis in this paper, I've tried to organize and make sense out of this biography.

   So back to the three controversial statements:

   Ed Lewis true name has been misspelled in number of ways. Fredericks, Friedrick, Fredrich, etc. On legal and family documents it's spelled Robert Friedrich or Robert Herman Julius Friedrich.

   In many reports, most of them from a later date, you'll find Nekoosa, Wisconsin, listed as being the place of birth of Robert Friedrich. In reports from the actual town of Nekoosa, you'll find them saying he was born at Sheboygan Falls. I can't prove anything, but it's my feeling that the family lived in Nekoosa but that the birth took place in Sheboygan Falls, because mother Molly Friedrich's family lived in that city and she might have been looking for support. There also was a medical hospital or clinic located there. Later in Bob's life, his father and brother would both travel to Sheboygan Falls for medical treatment. After the birth, Molly returned to Nekoosa. In 1894 the family lived in Sheboygan Fall for a period before they returned to Nekoosa in 1887, where Friedrich (Lewis) spent most of his childhood. I would consider this statement a theory and not to be taken as fact. It may also be true that the Friedrich family actually lived four and half miles north-east of Nekoosa in Port Edwards. On Lewis' passport application of June 15, 1923, he listed Port Edwards as his place of birth. The best information on this topic can be found in *National Wrestling Alliance: The Untold Story Of The Monopoly That Strangled Pro Wrestling* by Tim Hornbaker (page 62).

   When Molly's father, Carl Guildenzopf, died in 1919, it was written (*Nekoosa Tribune*, April 17, 1919) that he was born on September 9, 1834 in Germany. He moved to America in 1881 and then to Port Edwards in 1886. He was a farmer until he retired a few year before his death, and lived with Molly and family in Sheboygan falls at the time of his death.

   By the time Bob Friedrich got to Chicago in 1913, he was billing himself as being born in 1891. He was being pushed as a young man and I think they dropped a year to fit. For the rest of his career it remained mostly 1891, but legal papers all seem to agree on 1890. Reports from Nekoosa also say 1890.

2. *National Wrestling Alliance: The Untold Story Of The Monopoly That Strangled Pro Wrestling* by Tim Hornbaker states that Jacob Friedrich was born on December 28, 1858 at Deinheim Hessen, Germany, and immigrated to America. Molly (Molla) Gueldenzopf (Guildenzopf) was born in Saxon-Wiemer, Germany on March 23, 1866 and traveled with her family to Sheboygan Falls in 1882. The two were married on September 26, 1887 under the Lutheran faith.

3. Fred Abel is the name used in Lewis' *Unpublished Biography*. Historian Dan Anderson thinks this person is Albert "Babe" Abel, who was born in 1889 in Madison and died in the same city in 1967. He rarely wrestled outside of Madison, and didn't seem to have much success.

4. This match is the first newspaper reference to the man that would become Strangler Lewis. This was a major find by Don Luce, one of wrestling's most respected researchers. The clipping (*Minneapolis Tribune*, February 10 and 12, 1910) has Lewis being pinned. In *The Unpublished Lewis Biography* Lewis claims he lasted out the thirty minutes for the handicap win. I used the clipping's version, except for the Carl Mattson name, which came from Lewis. Sorry if I screwed up a good story, but it is not hard to catch Lewis telling a lie to make himself look good.

5. *The Unpublished Lewis Biography*: Lewis claimed that, in his championship years, he owned 385 silk shirts, 35 to 50 suits, six trunks of clothes, a diamond stud pin, and many canes for every occasion. Because of his 20-inch neck, even neckties had to be made to order. So not all of his money went to ex-wives and old timers down on their luck. It should be noted that Lewis had very good taste in clothes, and this probably helped covered up his lack of education while helping the public accept him as a sophisticated champion.

6. *The Unpublished Lewis Biography.*

7. *The Unpublished Lewis Biography*: Lewis called the famous Gotch/Beel American Title change (December 1, 1906, New Orleans) a "working exhibition." Ed how could you? Don't tell Mark Chapman — please.

8. The times and date came from the *Wood County Times of Nekoosa*, research by Dan Anderson. Details of the match came from *The Unpublished Lewis Biography*. Lewis called the match a "working exhibition." Once again I find it hard to believe that there hadn't been contact between Fred Beell and Bob Friedrich before this date. Beell was one of the most famous wrestlers of his time and owned a big farm in the area in Marchfield. Marchfield is 41 miles north-west of Nekoosa.

9. There is a May 11, 1911 report in the *Wood County Times of Nekoosa* that says Friedrich had wrestled a handicap match with Frank Gotch in or around Grand Rapids sometime after the Beell match, with the result of Bob being pinned in fourteen minutes.

10. The real Bob Friedrich was beating Cyclone Thompson at Galesburg, Illinois on January 10, 1913.

11. The origin of the Ed "Strangler" Lewis name came from *The Lewis Unpublished Biography*, but the story has been backed up in the Louisville newspaper results, and in a Bob Managoff interview that was published in the *Chicago Tribune* of April 9, 1933: 'Referee Defends Action In Awarding Fall To Savoldi' by George Strickler. The only difference in the stories of Managoff and Lewis, is Managoff claiming he created the name (Ed claimed it was Bill Barton) and that he beat Lewis (newspapers list Lewis as the winner).

    Managoff had a long career and is remembered for four things: his part in giving Lewis his name; being in the ring with Frank Gotch on July 18, 1916 when the champion broke his fibula ending any hope of the wrestling world seeing a Gotch/Stecher match; being the referee in the famous Londos/Savoldi double-cross of April 7, 1933; and being the father of a NWA world champion Bobby Managoff in 1942.

12. *Catch Wrestling* by Mark Hewitt, p. 117. Lewis wrestled in bare feet during the September 29, 1913 match. This was something done by wrestlers of the time, mainly Lewis and Londos, when they wanted fans to think a match was a shoot. Without shoes, it is harder for a foe to hook the ankle or use ankle locks. MMA fighters of today know this and go bare foot.

13. *Chicago Tribune*, November 4, 1913

14. From *Catch Wrestling*, a fine book by Mark Hewitt, we find that Lewis returned to Lexington to defeat a Young Olson, billed as the younger brother of feared shooter Charles Olson, but the publicity photos for the match are of Charles Olsen. It's very possible that the wrestler was Charles Olsen, who was always using aliases to rip off gamblers. But I don't buy it, because Charles had wrestled in Lexington earlier in the year.

15. *Chicago Tribune*, November 26, 1913

16. *Chicago Tribune*, November 30, 1913

17. *Chicago Tribune*, December 30, 1913

18. *Chicago Tribune*, February 10, 1914

19. *Lexington Herald*, January 29, 1914

20. *Lexington Herald*, February 5, 1914 and February 6, 1914

21. *Chicago Tribune*, February 11, 1914 and February 29, 1914

22. *Lexington Herald*, March 24, 1914

23. *The Detroit Free Press*, April 6 to April 8, 1914. Most of the storyline about the match being a shoot and Ed's bet with Stan came from *The Lewis Unpublished Biography*. I would believe the idea of it being a shoot if Lewis hadn't used the same storyline in a May 11, 1914 match in Louisville with Charley Cutler.

24. *Buffalo Courier*, April 24, 1914

25. *The Ed Lewis Ring Record*, put together by J Michael Kenyon, Don Luce, Mark Hewett, Steve Yohe, Dan Anderson, Fred Hornby, Richard Haynes, Libnan Ayoub, Vance Nevada, and a number of other wrestling historians. (Reprinted at the end of this volume — see p. 225.) The section on Lewis's stomach illness comes from *The Unpublished Lewis Biography*. Lewis claimed his hatred of Wladek caused the illness and it wasn't until he cleansed himself of the poisons generated by the emotion that he returned to normal. He promised to not get caught up in such emotions again, and from that he gained in strength and confidence. (It should be remembered that the Bio was written during Lewis' Christian period.) The training site used by Lewis, working with a Greek wrestler named Gus Kavaris, was on Mount Osmur on the banks of the Mississippi near Lansing, Iowa.

26. The headlock machine was well known and written about during Lewis's career, but you can read about it in *The Dan Hodge Story* by Mike Chapman, p. 109. Two of the machines exist today, one owned by Danny Hodge and the other is in the Dan Gable International Wrestling Institute and Museum at Waterloo, Iowa. The idea of Alexander being the builder of the machine came from comments to Tim Hornbaker by members of the Sandow family and can be found in *National Wrestling Alliance: The Untold Story Of The Monopoly That Strangled Pro Wrestling* by Tim Hornbaker, p. 65.

27. *Nebraska State Journal*, March 27, 1914

28. *Chicago Tribune*, February 21, 1915. It doesn't seem that promoters had big plans for Charles Cutler. I think they

just needed a champion type wrestler for Stecher to beat. The big money would come later, a Gotch / Stecher super match. I think Cutler was a smart guy who was better suited as a front offices worker. In 1912, Cutler had managed future world heavyweight boxing champion Jess Willard and in 1911 he had played a major part in the promotion of George Hackenschmidt before the super match with Frank Gotch in Chicago. All of this leads me to believe that Cutler was very close to promoter Jack Curley and he seems to have been Curley's booker in New York City. Cutler in ring wrestling career seemed to have peaked with putting Stecher over and he didn't last long.

29. *Louisville Courier-Journal*, May 11, 1915

30. *The Unpublished Lewis Biography.*

31. *Omaha World-Herald*, July 6, 1915

32. *Evansville Press*, October 20 to October 22, 1915. The story goes on to say that pro wrestling was banned in Evansville, at least for a short time. Evansville was later know as a stop-off for Tom Packs' troop of wrestlers between Indianapolis and St. Louis, but it was never considered one of the major wrestling cities. It would seem that they booked the first Lewis / Stecher match in a minor city to set up the rivalry between the two, and I don't think they never planned on a clean finish. The new champion Stecher seemed to be over the shoot period in his career and probably expected a worked match from Lewis. It's impossible to say anything for sure, but it's not beyond imagination that Lewis was uncooperative and refused to job clean. He and Sandow seemed to have formed a pattern of not cooperating in first matches with bigger stars. The loss wasn't important, he just wasn't going to lose his "heat." The finish seemed to have been the worked plan (by Lewis or maybe everyone), coming after all the gambling money on "Lewis over two hours" was assured. Because of the gambling and officials present, these worked matches had to look like true contests, so perhaps the body of this match was the two shooting, but the finish would have to be agreed upon. This match, being a terrible mess, had to be considered Lewis and his boring style's fault. If all of this talk is nonsense and the whole match was a shoot, then Lewis ran from Stecher and was afraid of Joe's skill and scissors. That, to me, makes him look worse than working a bad match. Of course Lewis learned nothing from this match and his lies covered up any embarrassment.

33. The Graeco-Roman or Greco-Roman style of wrestling, wasn't Greek or Roman, but was developed in France — though the rest of Europe resented the French, so they created a name that gave credit to the Romans. For this paper I'm going to refer to Greco-Roman as "GR" and Catch-as-Catch-Can as "Catch wrestling."

34. The tournament style of booking was used mostly in European wrestling. I understand most kinds of sports tournaments, but these tournaments of Germany, France, Russia, Spain, etc. have no form to me. I do not understand them, and no one I've talked to does, either. As far as I know, the only major European wrestling historian known in America was Gerhaed Schaefer, and he died. This created a vacuum that hasn't been filled. These tournaments just seemed like a group of wrestlers converging on a city, and after a month or two months a champion was named. Looking at the results we have, I see no form. So the two 1915 New York City tournaments took this "lack of form" and I can't explain them. One thing you do see is 20-minute draws, followed by a challenge and a finish match (no time limit) to follow the next night or later in the week. Of course, it being New York City, the finish had to end by the curfew time of 1 AM or it would be ruled a draw also.

35. The Manhattan Opera House exists today and was home to the early WWF RAW television shows and at least one ECW PPV. It is a nice building, but kind of small. Used for independent wrestling cards in the city.

36. I'm not sure about Alex Aberg's claim to the GR world title. We know he was defeated by Stanislaus Zbyszko in Boston on February 26, 1914. He lost clean in a 2 / 3 fall match, said to be for the GR world title. Stan, with Gotch retired and Stecher just starting up, was rated by most as the best wrestler in the world, but in 1915 he was out of the country, being held under house arrest during wars in Russia.

37. We have a record of about 80% of the tournaments, but as the days rolled on, the newspapers, probably due to boredom, stopped some of their reports or left out matches. I think there was at least one Lewis victory over Wladek not found. So the results noted are weak, but it is all we have.

38. *Brooklyn Daily Eagle*, December 10, 1915 and *New York Times*, December 10, 1915

39. *Brooklyn Daily Eagle*, December 27, 1915. All the information on the creation of the mask gimmick came from this article.

40. *New York Times* and *Brooklyn Daily Eagle*, December 21, 1915. The part about Lewis crying came from the *Eagle*.

41. *Brooklyn Daily Eagle*, December 30, 1915. Lewis expressed a different opinion in his *The Unpublished Lewis Biography* written in the late 1940's. Ed claimed Aberg was temperamental and jealous of his standing, always demanding top billing. He said that Aberg, with his bald head, paunchy stance, and surly look, didn't endear himself to American fans. Lewis, of course, claimed Aberg didn't beat him, but was strong and tough but very over-rated. He didn't understand why they made him the champion of Europe or the world.

42. *The Jack Curley Bio* by Steve Yohe. Its weak point is having me as the author, but it may be the only place you'll find info on Jack Curley.

43. *New York Times*, January 26, 1916. I believe Rachmann's contract expired with the January 25 match and that

would explain why Wladek was able to meet Stecher in the first place without a Rachmann complaint (January 27) and Wladek's lack of "push" in the last part of the tournament. Wladek seems to have fired his manager at this time and signed with Jack Curley.

44. *Brooklyn Daily Eagle*, January 26, 1916.

45. *Brooklyn Daily Eagle*, January 28, 1916 had the "boost" quote and the *New York Times*, January 28, 1916, had the "Gotch" quote.

46. Alex Aberg's huge New York push goes up in smoke, and I know of no more major matches in America. He returns to Europe and has matches with Stan Zbyszko in 1915 and 1918. The most famous one, in front of the Russian Police, he loses. Aberg died on February 15, 1920, after fighting typhoid and pneumonia, at Armavir in South Russia. He is buried in the same grave as his brother-in-law George Lurich at the Armavir German cemetery.

47. *Chicago Tribune*, July 5, 1916.

48. *Waterloo Evening Courier and Reporter*, December 30, 1916. Lewis admits to the gambling scheme.

49. *National Wrestling Alliance: The Untold Story Of The Monopoly That Strangled Pro Wrestling* by Tim Hornbaker (p. 66) has an example of the story being told in Sandow's words in 1920.

50. *Earl Caddock: The Man Of A Thousand Holds* by Steve Yohe.

51. *The Unpublished Lewis Biography*, page 102. Some of the pages in Ed's *Bio* had numbers, like this one. Lewis claimed the Connolly match was in Butte, Montana.

52. Both Joe and Tony were in the middle of working honeymoons.

53. *Boston Globe*, November 12, 1916. *Reading On The Mat and Off: Memoirs of a Wrestler* by Hjalmar Lundin, I came upon this version of the Stecher/Olin title change. On page 132 Lundin, who managed Olin and got him the match with Stecher, seems to say that, before the match, Olin was willing to do the job and is quoted: "You speak Stecher... he not go so fast... me give good show." So Lundin went to Stecher's dressing room but the manager Tony Stecher wasn't present and he saw no use in talking to Joe. Lundin went back to Olin and told him that: "Stecher says he will beat you in one minute." This upset John who said "Oh... no... not one minute."

During the match, Stecher couldn't hold Olin in the scissors because the Finn could do a very high bridge & break it. Joe was getting upset & Olin was exhausted. John told Lundin he wanted a draw because that would have been a huge thing at that time in Stecher's career. Lundin knew Joe didn't look good and told Olin that there was a Finn in the audience who had bet $1,000 on him, who would shoot him if he quit. So Olin continued. Half an hour later, Stecher quit.

The book says that Olin was told he was the new champion and Olin's words were: "Me...no champion...me country boy...no speaka English...you maka...little money...maybe."

So it's not clear, but it may be that Olin refused the title. More later.

Lundin says he's sure that it would have been a draw if Tony Stecher had been present. Seeing the condition of both wrestlers, he is sure that Tony would have come to him with the offer and Lundin would have taken it because he knew Olin wanted to quit.

All Joe had to say was: "It's all in the game." Stecher was a good loser.

Later in the book (p. 143), while talking about Jack Sherry and different world champion claims, Lundin says: "Years ago a title holder was the champion throughout the country. John Olin defeated the holder of the crown, Joe Stecher, but the former refused the honor, and after that I could not follow up the reign."

So it seems we have the true manager of Olin saying that the title was refused on that night. Perhaps for more money. And that seems to be the reason Stecher could continue his title claim. — Steve Yohe

54. *San Francisco Chronicle*, December 13, 1916.

55. *San Francisco Chronicle*, January 3, 1917.

56. This information on the film 'Reaching For The Moon' was supplied by historian Ken Sandler (Ken Viewer or Ken Writer online), who has been working on finding old wrestling matches through newsreel companies and universities with film libraries. The film seems to exist on DVD, but I've never seen it.

57. *Joe Stecher* by Steve Yohe; *The Des Moines Register*, April 10, 1917; *Chicago Tribune*, April 10, 1917.

58. Statements from the April 11 *Des Moines Register*:

Referee Charley Sherman: "When Caddock came back into the ring for the third fall, Joe Hetmanek, Stecher's manager, came around to Caddock's corner, and in the presence of (Frank) Gotch, Caddock, myself, and I believe Gene Melady, said Stecher had injured his neck and would not come back for another bout. Then I awarded the match to Caddock, which was the only thing to do under the circumstances."

Joe Stecher: "I have but few excuses and no complaint. I was honestly defeated, insofar as the fall I lost was concerned. But as to the final decision of the referee, I must say that when in my room after this fall nobody notified me that the time was up, as either my manager, Mr. Melady, or the referee should, and while I was suffering greatly from a running ear and a surging cold in my head and chest, I was ready to go back, to go on with the match, and intended to, but was not given the opportunity. But I have no harsh words for anyone. I was beaten and that is all there is to it, and in Earl Caddock the game has an honest and deserving successor to myself."

Manager Joe Hetmanek: "I went to Joe's dressing room during the intermission after Caddock's fall, and when the Caddock henchmen were clamoring that the match be awarded to Earl on the grounds that time was up and Joe refused to return, I told Tony to hurry and get Joe out, but he replied that Joe said: "I won't go back and you can't make me go back!" Knowing Joe, I then hurried out and informed the referee that Joe refused to return. But it is all history now and I only want to say that Joe Stecher was not himself. He was ill from several causes, but at that he had Caddock beaten easily, when he did show flashes of his form, and as himself, I think is far and away the better man."

Back to Yohe: You can tell from this that the Stecher did seem to be fed up with Manager Hetmanek, whose only access to Joe was through Tony, and they seemed willing to dump the loss in his lap. I stick to my theory that this was just a worked screw finish designed to give Joe rest away from the title. Everything points to that—and the fact that it was another way to make money off of gamblers to sweeten the idea. Joe was a strange guy and very simple. He just wanted to wrestle and care little about anything else. Tony was the brains and had control. Another theory, not normally stated, is that maybe Joe was told in the dressing room, for the first time, that he was losing—and refused to go back out to job because of ethics or ego. I doubt that, but it's another idea to think about. Some will want me to say it was a shoot and what happens, happens. Everyone is free to think what they want because no one really knows, nor will anyone ever really know. It's just fun.

It should be noted that Stecher proclaimed Caddock the new champion, something that didn't happen after the John Olin match. I think it's a tradition that the old champion has to give the title to the next one. Also Frank Gotch was ringside and in view of everyone. In the official photos, taken before the match, Gotch is standing between Stecher and Caddock. The referee does go out of his way to say that Hetmanek gave up in front of Gotch—as though Gotch's approval of the ruling meant something. This is something to think about in terms of Ed Lewis, who never admits to losing a title until Jim Browning in New York City.

59. *Chicago Tribune*, May 3, 1917. The Olin/Lewis match drew 7,000 fans. The newspaper report said the match was a contest of great strength and endurance but lacked the science and endurance fans were accustomed to in Frank Gotch matches.

60. Bad Yohe joke playing around with the Alfred E. Neuman name. Sorry.

61. An attorney named F. T. Finch showed up at one point to put an attachment on the box office for $1,225, which he claimed was due on a judgment secured against Newman. Charley tried to punch him, but then called it a mix-up and bought off Finch with $300.

62. *San Fransico Chronicle*, June 4 to June 8, 1917, also *Ring Magazine*, 'Memoirs of a Promoter' by Jack Curley (as told to Frank Graham) December issue 1931.

63. *Oakland Tribune*, June 22, 1917.

64. *Oakland Tribune*, April 9, 1919.

65. *Boston Globe*, July 5, 1917.

66. *Earl Caddock: The Man Of A Thousand Holds* by Steve Yohe.

67. *The Houston Chronicle*, November 1 and November 2, 1917.

68. This is an example of just some of the different versions in spelling of Londos's real name. See *The Jim Londos Record Book* (Notes section) by Steve Yohe, Don Luce, J Michael Kenyon and members of the International Historian Club (IHC).

Different spelling of Jim Londos's real name:

Diaspora: Jim Londos The Golden Greek by Steve Frangos—Christos Theophilou
Oakland Tribune (2-24-14) first match—Chris Theopulus
Oakland Tribune (10-23-13)—Theophelus
New York Times Obit by Michael Strauss (8-21-75)—Chris Theophelus
New Times Obit by Red Smith (8-24-75)—Christopher Theophelus
AP Obit (8-20-75—Chris Theophelus
LA Times (1-27-69)—Theophelos
NWA Wrestling Mag—John Contos by Bob Allison—Christopher Theophilus
Fall Guys—Christopher Teophelus
From Milo to Londos by Nat Fleischer—Chris Theophelo
Marriage Certificate—Christ T. Theophelos
San Diego HOF—Chris T. Theophelos
Wikipedia—Christos Theofilou or Christopher Theophelus
Time Magazine—Christopher Theophilus
Boston Globe (7-16-34)—Christopher Theophelou

L A Times, (10-31-34)—Christopher Theophelous
Associated Press (6-28-35)—Christopher Theophilo

Also: Theophalus? Theopolus? Theophilis? Theopholis? Theopolis? Theopelos? Theopphilus? Theopulus?

Historian Steve Johnson: "According to Londos' daughter, he spelled Theopolus about five different ways when he was alive, so it's probably too much to hope for consistency."

69. *The Canton Repository*, November 30, 1917.
70. We have a copy of the cover of the Tournament program. On it we see photos of Stecher, Caddock, Zbyszko and Lewis standing in a row with Frank Gotch (who was on his death-bed and died at the mid-point of the tournament December 15) looking down on them all. It would seem that Curley planed to have all of the big four engaged in the out come, but Stecher never makes an appearance and Caddock leaves.
71. *New York Times*, December 15, 1917.
72. *New York Times*, December 18, 1917.
73. *New York Times*, December 23, 1917.
74. *The Canton Repository*, January 2, 1918.
75. *The Des Moines Register*, January 23, 1918.
76. *The Des Moines Register*, February 10, 1918. Sandy Griswold also talks about the meeting in the *Omaha World-Herald*, February 28, 1918.
77. *The Des Moines Register*, February 9, 1918.
78. To those few people who believe that pro wrestling consisted of "shoots" or "contests," these illusions were forever erased with these agreements and the forming of this version of a Curley trust. The agreement would form the line between the shoot era and the worked period. To the many historians who have read all the reports, the idea of a time line, between real and fake, seems like a joke.
79. Sandy Griswold, one of the best wrestling writers in the history of the sport, wrote this in the *Omaha World-Herald*, February 27, 1918 (*Sandy's Dope*): "Here is a specimen of the stuff some of the New York writers are peddling to the suckers down there. This is from the typewriter of Daniel, a sports writer of much talent, on the *Evening Sun*, and while it proves that Daniel is not what might be called au fait in the ramifications of the mat game, he means well, and must not be wrongly judged. Here's Daniel's comments: B. C. Sandow, manager of the Strangler, charges that a wrestling combination has been formed to the detriment of his grappler... The fact is that in the championship controversy Lewis stands higher than any of the others and with the 'Strangler' asking for a chance to wrestle Zbyszko, Stecher, or Caddock, we fail to see the necessity for an immediate meeting between the Pole and the scissors expert. Stecher has not been in the title hunt for some time, since his defeats by Olin and Caddock, and Zbyszko was eliminated by Caddock recently. The public is entitled to the best bouts available, and if it is convinced that some first-class wrestler is being discriminated against it may decide to give the game the go by." Sandy continued: "Rich, isn't it? This slandering of Ed Lewis, particularly. It is all probably quite true that Lewis is bellyaching for a match with champion Earl Caddock, and runner-up Joe Stecher, and his old stable-mate Wladek Zbyszko, but the opinion is that he'll be allowed to belly-ache for many moons yet. He forever killed his chances for a match with Stecher by his cowardly and unsportsmanlike actions in his match with him two years ago, and so far as Caddock is concerned, he and his manager Gene Melady, are to long-sighted and too business-like to ever give him the slightest consideration—that is, anyway, until after the controversies with all the legitimate adversaries has been settled. No one is anxious to see Lewis perform again, and at that he would be nuts for Caddock, Stecher, or even Zbyszko, that is, of course, providing he gave them a square battle. So far as his headlock is concerned, that's all bosh, and nobody knows it better than he does himself. Oh no, what the public now wants is the return go between Caddock and Stecher."

On March 12, 1918, Sandy writes this about Lewis and his headlock before the March 19 match with Wladek: "Now that is one colossal joke. Lewis' headlock has been one of the commonest holds in wrestling, since that young Babylonian threw the bull in Voltaire's romance—*Zadig*. But Eddie needn't peeve—Zbyszko is his friend. They've only wrestled each other about two dozen times, and Zibby surely isn't going to back on him now."

Yohe: I think the mid-west heat was real, but any problem with Curley at this time was worked. Lewis signed with Curley and becomes one of the gang until 1922. As for the mid-west, he would always be a heel. Some feel that Ed Lewis created the heel character in pro wrestling, but I think his and Sandow personality forced it on him.

80. *The Des Moines Register*, March 10, 1918.
81. *New York Times*, March 20, 1918.
82. The report, *The Canton Repository*, April 6, 1918, claims Dr. Ada Scott Morton was his wife, with the marriage taking place a few months before. We know Scott was following Lewis around the country and continues for some time. It was the only way the two could spend time together. It seems believable that he was passing her off as a wife in 1918. The date of the true marriage was May 8, 1919. It should also be noted that the marriage date set in *The Unpublished Lewis Biography* was March, 1918.

83. *The Kansas City Star*, April 29, 1923.

84. *The Des Moines Register*, May 31, 1919.

85. *Sioux City Tribune*, February 25, 1919.

86. *Chicago Tribune*, March 4, 1919.

87. *Chicago Tribune*, March 4, 1919. Lewis and Stretcher split a purse of $7,200. The promoter in Chicago was actually billed as Jack Herman, who most likely worked for Curley. Quote by reporter Harvey T. Woodruff: "Lewis, by his victory, has placed himself in a position to earn big money in his profession. While not flashy in performance and while his defensive tactics may not always please the crowd, he showed a coolness and strength combined with am improvement since his last appearance here which will make him a most formidable opponent for Champion Earl Caddock when Uncle Sam releases the latter from service."

88. *Chicago Tribune*, March 11, 1919.

89. *New York Times*, March 22, 1919.

90. Lewis wrestled Ben Roller but I see no reason to write about every one of their matches. By April 1919, the record had Lewis winning the last ten matches in straight falls. In *The Unpublished Lewis Biography,* Lewis claimed every one of the Roller matches were shoots. If you want to believe that, go ahead.

91. Beating John Olin was no longer a big deal. He had lost matches to Lewis (4 times), Wladek (3 times) and Caddock (twice). Olin's fluke win over Stecher had added up to many paydays. In 1922, Olin returned to his native country with a bank roll of $50,000. He settled down on a lovely estate with a new wife but in 1926 his luck ran out when he died after a heart attack. *On The Mat and Off: Memoirs of a Wrestler* by Hjalmar Lundin, p. 135.

92. *Lincoln Daily Star*, April 29, 1919.

93. *Lincoln Daily Star, Lincoln Ne*, May 2, 1919.

94. *The Courier-Journal, Louisville*, May 9, 1919.

95. This section cannibalized from my *Earl Caddock: The Man Of A Thousand Holds* by Steve Yohe. The Caddock quotes were from *The Des Moines Register*, May 31, 1919.

96. *Chicago Tribune*, May 19, 1919.

97. *The Des Moines Register*, June 12, 1919.

98. *The Des Moines Register*, June 22, 1919.

99. *The Des Moines Register*, July 5, 1919.

100. *San Francisco Cronical,* August 20, 1919.

101. *Oakland CA Tribune*, September 13, 1919.

102. *Oakland CA Tribune*, October 27, 1919.

103. *New York Times*, November 4, 1919. The play by play of the match was stolen word for word from the *Times*. Lewis' record verses Stecher at that point was one win, four loses, and two draws.

104. *New York Time*, January 31, 1920; *The Beloit Daily News*, January 31, 1919; *Buffalo*, January 31, 1919; *Virginian-Pilot Norfolk*, January 31, 1919.

105. *Fremont Evening Tribune*, February 3, 1920.

106. *Canton Evening Repository*, December 22, 1919.

107. *New York Times*, January 6, 1920.

108. *Virginian-Pilot Norfolk*, February 1, 1920.

109. *Virginian-Pilot Norfolk*, February 5, 1920.

110. *New York Times*, January 21, 1920.

111. The match description comes almost directly from *The New York Times*, March 3, 1920.

112. *New York Times*, March 16, 1920.

113. *Detroit Free Press*, December 23, 1919. Quote from article titled 'Strangler Lewis' Headlock Liked To Knockout Punch': "Lewis with Yankee ingenuity has applied a new twist to old methods, improving by the use of his brain a hold that has been in vogue among grapplers for several years, making it more forceful and feared. Hence the attempt to class it with the now extinct 'strangle' hold… Lewis' headlock is secured from the standing position. Lewis pulls down the opponent's head, reaching over his head with the left hand and getting him into the chancery. With his right hand he reaches under the head of his opponent and grasps his own left hand fitting into the jaw of the defensive wrestler on the right side. The head is drawn in and locked. Then the twist is applied and the opponent is flung to the mat with a cross butlock. Lewis then falls on his victim with all his weight and twists his fist into the jaw. The latter is done so quickly that by the time the referee is on the job, the hold is a chin-lock… Lewis' flying headlock is as good an anesthetic as either or gas. The twisting process which is one of terrific force, acts like a knock out punch, causing the upper part of the jawbone to jar the brain. Wrestlers who have been thrown with Lewis' headlock state that they knew nothing until they began to recover… The headlock is a development of modern wrestling methods."

114. *New York Times*, April 17, 1920. It should be noted that Jack Curley believed in one fall matches and this one and all the other matches of 1920 and before in NYC were one fall to a finish, with no time limit. The WWF or WWE

or WWWF of our time seems to have followed his example.

115. *The Des Moines Register*, June 9, 1920.

116. *San Francisco Chronicle*, December 22, 1920.

117. *New York Times*, December 13, 1920.

118. *New York Times*, December 14, 1920. Most of the description and words used came directly from the *Times* story. I have great respect for the talent of whoever wrote the *Times* reports. I hope this paper makes his work last a little longer. I don't believe anyone of today could match writers such as this from the early 20th century.

    Some who read this may think I'm a mark for giving so much detail in describing these matches, but I really don't care. I don't believe in shoots but I believe they were great pro-wrestling matches. The equal of many of the All Japan matches of the 1990's and I want to give that feeling to the reader if possible.

    Also *The Brooklyn Eagle* December 14, 1920 and *The Arizona Republican* (Phoenix) December 14, 1920. There seems to be some controversy over how many headlocks were used by Lewis in the last great seven minutes. *The Times* said seven, other papers said eight or nine.

119. *The Des Moines Register*, April 1, 1921.

120. *New York Times*, January 25, 1921.

121. *New York Times*, January 31, 1921.

122. *New York Times*, February 4, 1921.

123. *The Des Moines Register*, April 11, 1921.

124. In Armas Laitenen's American debut, he wrestled a one and half hour draw with Stanislaus Zbyszko. The match with Pesek ended with him claiming an arm injury. Pesek tried every hold against him, legal and non-legal, to beat him. Years later Billy Sandow, in an interview, called the shoot "the most impressive" he'd ever seen and went on to relate how Pesek nearly tore the big Finn's arm from his shoulder. Laitenan worked matches as he was told after that. He had a brief career in America and then returned to Finland to become a major law enforcement official. My knowledge of this and most everything else came from my friend and great wrestling historian Mark Hewitt who wrote the book *Catch Wrestling* in 2005. The Pesek/Laitenen match is on page 155. *Catch Wrestling* is one of the few true major wrestling history books and it's not talked about enough.

125. *New York Times*, April 5, 1921. The Lewis/Pesek match was a work, but Pesek himself gave credit to Ed, always saying that Lewis was his master on the mat. Quote: "The Strangler knew how to use his heft expertly." From *Catch Wrestling* by Mark Hewitt, p.155.

126. *Dempsey*, by Jack Dempsey with Barbara Piattelli Dempsey, p. 131.

127. *The Des Moines Register*, April 14, 1921.

128. *New York Times*, May 7, 1921.

129. *New York Times*, December 30, 1921.

130. *The Jack Curley Bio* by Steve Yohe.

131. *Catch Wrestling* by Mark Hewitt, pp.158-160, and *The New York Times*, November 14, 1921. Hewitt offers the theory that Curley was in on the Pesek shoot because he might have been interested in making a mess of rival Tex Rickard's first wrestling card in the Garden. I think Curley saw the mess as another reason to stay away from New York City wrestling. For money reasons, Curley wanted to become part of the city's upper society, and messes like Pesek/Plestina hurt his plans. Pro wrestling had lost its reputation as a place for the upper class, so Curley moved away from it in New York City.

    New York Times, November 29, 1921, and *The Columbus Dispatch*, November 29, 1921. It was the Columbus paper that noted both falls were rolling falls. I've seen reports where Lewis made excuses for this first undisputed title loss by talking about this rematch, with the two rolling falls. Seems to be a mistake or possibly, another lie. He was pinned missing a headlock in the title change.

132. *Oakland Tribune*, December 8, 1921.

133. *Tunney* by Jack Cavanaugh, pp. 238-242. This is a book that set a standard for wrestling history books to follow. *Dempsey* by Jack Dempsey with Barbara Piattelli Dempsey, p.142.

134. *St. Louis Globe*, February 7, 1922.

135. *New York Times*, February 22, 1922.

136. *The History Of Professional Wrestling: Madison Square Garden 1880 To 1999*, published by Scott Teal (P.O. Box 2781, Hendersonville, TN 37077-2781) and researched by Fred Hornby. *New York Times*, 'Tex Rickard Is Denied Wrestling Permit', December 29, 1923

137. *The Wichita Eagle*, March 4 and 5, 1922.

138. *The Wichita Eagle*, March 27, 1922.

139. *St. Louis Daily Globe-Democrat*, March 14 and 30, 1922.

140. *National Wrestling Alliance: The Untold Story Of The Monopoly That Strangled Pro Wrestling* by Tim Hornbaker, pp.280-281.

141. *Boston Globe*, June 8, 1922.

142. Lewis did own a large summer home or ranch in Wisconsin. Most city arenas were very hot or used by the public or out of school children during the summer. The St. Louis Arena was built over a public swimming pool, so the city had very few wrestling shows during the summer unless an outdoor stadium could be found. Most of the ballparks were being used by the different levels of pro baseball, so promoters needed to book their cards around the local baseball teams home games. It wasn't easy. So pro wrestling was seasonal in most places and Lewis took most of the summers off.

143. In a "smart" wrestling book published in 1938, *Fall Guys: The Barnums Of Bounce*, author Marcus Griffin named the group of Billy Sandow / Ed Lewis / Joe "Toots" Mondt the "Gold Dust Trio." I will not be using the name "Gold Dust Trio" in this book because it was a term created by Griffin and used only for his book, and not used by fans or insiders before the book was published. You cannot find the name in print before 1938. Griffin used a writing style that created a number of names in *Fall Guys* for groups and individuals. The book is filled with them: Fall Guys (wrestlers), The Peerless Champion (Frank Gotch) The Big Four (Curley, Tony Stecher, Stan Zbyszko, & Caddock) The Trust (different people at different times in the book), The Brain (Billy Sandow), Trimmer Jim (Jim Londos), Halitosis Kid (Jack Pfefer), The Royal Family of Pugilism (The Johnson Brothers), The Wild Irish Rose (Danno O'Mahoney) and many more—but it is only the "Gold Dust Trio" title that has stuck through time. Today it's constantly used by people who base their knowledge on something other than research. *Fall Guys* was a biased and flawed book with mountains of errors.

Griffin states in the book that Toots Mondt was a partner with Sandow and Lewis. I can't see how that can be true. Lewis, Sandow, and the other Baumann brothers had been together since 1913. They wouldn't let a young wrestler just step into the company as a partner. It's not possible in my mind. Mondt may have had a great mind for wrestling, which he proved later, but in 1922 he was hired as wrestler and coach, and he wouldn't have had as much input as Sandow's brothers Max and Jules.

Fall Guys also says that during Lewis' second reign (1922 to 1925), Mondt created a new style of wrestling and that business prospered. The facts are that 1922 to 1925 was a bad time for pro wrestling in most of the country and most areas hadn't even developed as territories. New York City was dead. The South, Texas, Philadelphia, Montreal, Toronto, Los Angeles, St. Louis were dead or just developing. Most of the network of strong promoters came into the sport around 1925, when new arenas were build all over the country. The Lewis / Sandow group's major areas were Chicago, Kansas City, Wichita, Boston, Tulsa, and cities promoted by the Baumann group. They helped open Los Angeles and St. Louis, and some spots were hit for short periods until the money dried up. For Lewis himself and his contenders, they did great, but you can't see the rest of the country doing much at all.

Fall Guys also claims that there were 500 people in the Sandow company and all the wrestlers were under contract. There wasn't any where near that number of people working with them and I will give the names in this project. Just about all of the major wrestlers jump to the Stecher group after Lewis losses the world title, so if the contracts existed, they weren't written very well.

Fall Guys is about ten years behind on most things talked about in the book, including the five-hour draw between Lewis and Stecher. What Griffin claims happening in 1923, describes 1932 better. The period from 1928 to 1935, is the great period for wrestling in America.

144. *The Kansas City Star*, January 3, 7 and 19, 1923.
145. *New York Times*, December 15, 1922.
146. *Los Angeles Times*, January 11, 1923.
147. *Los Angeles Times*, January 11, 1923.
148. *Catch Wrestling* by Mark S. Hewitt, pp. 164-166. The only other interesting match in Nat Pendleton's career was a rematch with the man who beat him in the controversial final of the 1920 Olympics, Robert Roth of Switzerland. The pro match took place July 26, 1924 in Paris, France. After 30 minutes with no pinfalls, the judges first awarded the decision to Pendleton, then changed it to a draw.
149. *The Kansas City Star*, December 30, 1923.
150. *St. Louis Globe*, Febuary 19, 1923.
151. *St. Louis Globe*, Febuary 21, 1923.
152. *Chicago Tribune*, March 7, 1923.
153. *St. Louis Globe*, March 8, 1923.
154. *San Francisco Chronicle*, April 17, 1923.
155. *St. Louis Globe*, April 13, 1923.
156. *The Kansas City Star*, April 23, 1923. The quote comes from *The Star*.
157. *St. Louis Globe*, May 3, 1923.
158. *The Kansas City Star*, May 3, 1923.
159. *New York Herald*, May 23, 1923.
160. Associated Press, June 21, 1923.
161. *San Francisco*, February 22, 1926.

162. *Wisconsin Rapids Daily Tribune*, October 1 and 3, 1923.

163. *Fresno CA Bee*, October 22, 1923.

164. The *New York Times* reported that Joe Stecher played first base for the Salt Lake Bees against the Oakland baseball team on September 30, 1923. Joe went one for four but drove in two runs with a single in the 5th. He made 9 putouts at first base without an error. I believe Stecher stayed with the team for a week or two replacing an injured star first baseman. Joe Stecher also owned a minor league team in Dodge and would spend money to bring in ringer type pitchers, catchers and hitters to support local players.

165. *St. Louis Daily Globe-Democrat*, December 14, 1923.

166. *The Kansas City Star*, December 16, 1923.

167. *The Kansas City Star*, December 16, 1923.

168. *Associated Press*, December 29, 1923.

169. *The Kansas City Star*, December 19, 1923.

170. *New Yory Herald*, December 31, 1923.

171. *The Kansas City Star*, January 20, 1924.

172. *St. Louis Daily Globe-Democrat*, January 27, 1924.

173. *The Kansas City Star*, February 4, 1924.

174. *The Kansas City Star*, February 11, 1924.

175. *The Kansas City Star*, February 14, 1924.

176. Most of the info on Boston comes from historian and major researcher Mark Hewitt.

177. *Casper Daily Tribune*, February 27, 1924.

178. *Chicago Tribune*, March 26, 1924.

179. *Beloit Daily News*, March 27, 1924, and *Middlesboro KY Daily News*, April 1, 1924.

180. *St. Louis Daily Globe-Democrat*, April 2, 1924.

181. *Philadelphia Inquirer*, April 9, 1924.

182. *Beloit Daily News*, April 30, 1924.

183. *Chicago Tribune*, May 29, 1924.

184. *St. Louis Daily Globe-Democrat*, June 13, 1924.

185. A lot of the Chicago info comes from *Chicago Tribune* results researched by Don Luce, who is the king of wrestling historians.

186. Lou Daro was born in New York City around 1885. His parents were performers. At the age of 7, Daro worked a trapeze act with Barnum and Bailey. Daro, while still a kid, toured Europe with the circus, visiting Austria, Germany, France, and Italy. On his return to America, he was doing a strongman act and wrestling. Around 1905, he appeared at the New York Hippodrome. In 1915, he wrestled in the big tournament at the New York Opera House. He had strong ties with Jack Curley. Curley even visited Los Angeles for over a month around July 1925 to set up the promotion at the new Olympic Auditorium. (This is info from Don Luce research of *Los Angeles Times* 1925.)

187. *San Francisco Chronicle*, July 30, 1924.

188. *Fresno Bee*, August 11, 1924, and *San Francisco Chronicle*, August 11, 1924.

189. *Los Angeles Times*, August 14, 1924.

190. *Los Angeles Times,* August 28, 1924.

191. *San Francisco Chronicle*, September 3, 1924.

192. *Los Angeles Times,* September 5, 1924.

193. *Los Angeles Examiner*, September 26, 1924.

194. *Los Angeles Herald*, October 8, 1924.

195. *Los Angeles Examiner*, October 14, 1924, and *Los Angeles Herald*, October 14, 1924.

196. *Wichita Eagle*, December 12, 1924.

197. *Beloit Daily News*, December 16, 1924.

198. I also believe that the Sandow group, or the Gold Dust Trio, as they are wrongly called by many today, was not as strongly in control as they were put over in the book *Fall Guys*. They had a lot of strong independent promoters to deal with: Paul Bowser (Boston), Ed White (Chicago), Joe Coffey (Chicago), Tom Law (Wichita), Lou Daro (Los Angeles), Tom Packs (St. Louis), Ray Fabiani (Philadelphia) and Gabe Kaufman (Kansas City). Sandow depended on them, and all of them controlled their own cities. Sandow and Lewis also had Jack Curley in hibernation just waiting for them to fail.

199. *From Milo To Londos* by A. D. Phillips, p. 228, published by Nat Fleischer and *The Ring* magazine in 1936.

200. *Philadelphia Inquirer*, April 12, 1925. Monte Munn, a star at the University of Nebraska in football, baseball, and track, like Wayne, graduated in 1922. Became a pro boxer and was better than Wayne. A lawyer, he became a member of the state legislature, and a business man. He moved to Indiana and ran a coal business. In 1932 ran an unsuccessful campaign for the Indiana senate. He suffered a heart attack in 1933, and, after being ill for only a few days, died on March 8, 1933. He was 32. Information came from *Boxrec Boxing Encyclopaedia* on line.

201. A report published in 1929 had John Pesek and Toots Mondt in a argument during the training in Kansas City. The two hookers had a gym match which was won by Pesek. This upset Billy Sandow and he had Max Baumann talk to Pesek. This resulted in Pesek quiting the Sandow company.

202. *Kansas City Times*, January 9, 1915.

203. *Wichita Eagle*, January 11, 1925. There was a big movement to match Joe Stecher with John Pesek in Wichita during this time. It was a storyline that ran over into 1926, and I will cover it later. The newspaper called the *Wichita Eagle* had a smart reporter (just called "Pal") or editor, who was printing "smart" info. On February 1, 1925, he interviewed Max Baumann, brother of Billy Sandow and still manager of John Pesek, and really worked him over with tough questions. In it Baumann claimed there was no wrestling trust. Then Baumann said that Wayne Munn was great and fully entitled to the honor of being world champ, despite his brother's court suit to stop Munn from claiming the title. Baumann said the "suit was mere bunk and just a publicity move." The reporter asked why he was trying to get Pesek a match with Stecher instead of Munn, and Baumann said that Pesek wasn't entitled to a match with Munn, that he had lost to Lewis and Mondt. So he couldn't get the match for Pesek. The reporter then said, "then there must be a wrestling trust?" Baumann again said there wasn't. When asked who should get the match with Munn, Baumann said "Lewis or Stan Zbyszko." The reporter, who knew his results, stated that Stanislaus had lost ten straight matches to Lewis, so why should he get a match? The report then said that the only thing in Zbyszko favor is the fact that he is a "trust" wrestler. Baumann then belittled Stecher, Santel, Plestina, Steinke, and others not in the "trust." He said that the bunch couldn't draw, so shouldn't be champions. The reporter asked whether the championship be decided on wrestling ability or drawing ability? Baumann replied frankly that wrestlers were in the game for the money. So a man who can't draw can't be champion, no matter whether he can wrestle or not. The only reason why Lewis, Zbyszko, Mondt, McGill, Pesek, Munn, Eustace and others wrestle each other continually is because they draw the fans. The fans didn't want a Lewis / Stecher match and they couldn't make any money wrestling Stecher. According to Baumann, the fans were to blame for the condition of the sport of wrestling. The public liked the circus stuff, the throwing of men out of the ring, return matches, etc. Max said that the public didn't care about wrestling wars and didn't care who the champion was, or whether the champion was a real one or not. If the champion was a real showman, that was sufficient. The reporter then wrote at the story's end: "Time and again the writer has been asked why the newspapers do not openly oppose the wrestling trust. If the fans do not care enough about it to protest, if they continue to support the trust wrestlers, if they turn out in thousands for such an event as the Lewis-Munn affair, and go away all enthused, if they demand yards and yards and yards of news of such affairs, then why should the papers kick?"

204. *Chicago Tribune*, January 23, 1925.

205. The Don Luce research on Chicago and the *Beloit Daily News*, February 5, 1925.

206. *Middletown Ohio*, February 19, 1925. Jack Curley had a nationwide news release on February 19, 1925, describing the Shadow / Lewis company in his own words. He laughed at the idea that Munn's win had broken up a wrestling "trust." Curley charged that a bunch of third raters were hogging the wrestling game in the middle west, refusing to let any one outside of their charmed circle get into a big money match with Munn. Quote: "Billy Sandow, manager for Lewis," said Curley today, "is a brother of Max and Jules Baumann. Max manages John Pesek and Jules is going around the country arranging matches for Munn. Munn is playing around with Toots Mondt, Stanislaus Zbyszko, Mike Romano (whom Munn threw twice within ten minutes last night at Chicago), Strangler Lewis, Pat McGill, John Pesek and other third-raters. Munn is not even a good third-rater. I know of ten wrestlers who can beat him. I know of ten wrestlers who will give Munn $10,000 to meet them and they will donate an extra $5,000 to charity if they do not throw him twice in 30 minutes. The ten challengers are Jim Londos, Joe Stecher, Wladek Zbyszko, Hans Steinke, Zaikin, Charles Hanson, Marin Plestina, Jack Sherry, Ad Santel and Nat Pendleton. Not one of these wrestlers can get an engagement with the new champion. His crowd asks that challengers show their right to a match by beating Pesek, their stand-off man."

207. *The Joe Stecher Bio* by Steve Yohe and *The Beloit Daily News*, February 19, 1925.

208. *The Wichita Eagle*, February 9, February 11 and 18, 1925.

209. *The Wichita Eagle*, March 7, 1925.

210. *The Philadelphia Inquirer*, April 16, 1925.

211. United Press, March 18, 1925. On March 17, 1925 Wayne Munn was giving what probably was his vaudeville act at a wrestling match in Nashville, when Wladek Zbyszko climbed into the ring to challenge him. He then took off his coat, while telling Munn he was "ready to go." Munn then left the ring. The promoter / boxer Billy Haack then started throwing punches at Wladek and his friend George Kotsonaros.

212. *The Philadelphia Inquirer*, April 16 and 17, 1925, and *Philadelphia Ledger*, April 16, 1925. Zbyszko's age was listed as 55 or around 50 in post-match reports. I believe he was born April 1, 1878 or 1880. So he was either 47 or 45.

213. *The Philadelphia Inquirer*, April 18, 1925.

214. When Wayne Munn complained of not receiving his championship belt after beating Lewis, it seems the belt in

question was Zbyszko's Rickard belt. While writing this book, I bought a photo of Lewis' Rickard belt from *The Chicago Tribune*. On the back of the photo it states that it was the belt being used on Decoration Day in Michigan City. So it seems the Lewis Belt was staying with The Strangler regardless of who was champion. The two belts looked nothing like each other. After the match, the Rickard Belt disappears from wrestling history and the Lewis Belt is always used by Sandow and later Paul Bowser. Another note: championship belts were always described as being worth $10,000—apparently all of them. The Rickard belt was said to be worth $5,000 the night it was awarded to Zbyszko, so its value had increased 50% in three years. I guess the number $10,000 sounds good.

215. Associated Press, Chicago, May 20, 1925. "Judge Friend heard no witnesses declaring that there was no precedent on which to base the petition for injunction and that it was not the province of the court to decide such a question."
216. *St. Louis Daily Globe-Democrat*, May 31, 1925.
217. *The Wichita Eagle*, June 3, 1925.
218. *Boston Post*, January 10, 1926. For years historians looked for the Caddock/Malcewicz 1919 match but it took the legendary Don Luce to find it in — 1921.
219. I found the story at *Boxing Records* online and the story was also told in *From Milo To Londos* by A. D. Phillips, p. 227.
220. Associated Press, January 9, 1931 and *St. Louis Post-Dispatch*, January 9, 1931.
221. *Los Angeles Times*, August 11, 1925.
222. *St. Louis Daily Globe*, February 11, 1926.
223. *Beloit Daily News*, February 20, 1926.
224. *Boston Post*, March 4, 1926.
225. *Boston Post*, March 12, 1926.
226. Why would Tony Stecher and Jack Curley allow their champion to wrestle for Paul Bowser, a major Lewis promoter, in Boston when the situation looked like a double-cross from the day of the signing? Curley had a bunch of people in the arena that night, and once the cross up started, they all jumped into the ring and led Joe to the dressing room. There also was a ton of pro-Curley press in the locker room for the press conference. It could be that Curley was one step a head of Bowser and anticipated everything that happened that night. His thinking might have been that a messing up match in front of an arena of fans paying to see Joe Stecher wrestle might backfire on Bowser. Screwing up your own card might just alienate your own fan base. 500 fans did ask for their money back once they realized the main event was going to be Malcewicz versus Ned McGuire. The total effect of the stunt was zero. It ended up as just another example of wrestling insiders humiliating themselves in the eye of the public.
227. From Don Luce's research of Chicago. Probably found in the *Chicago Tribune*.
228. The report of the Omaha conference came from *St. Louis Globe-Democrat*, March 27 and 28, 1926. The conference was talked about as part of the build up to the Stecher/Pesek match. What actually happened in the conference is mostly speculation by me, but the topics mention is what promoters normally discussed at these meetings and the result is apparent over the next year.
229. *St. Louis Globe-Democrat*, April 30, 1926. Other research has Lewis wrestling in Boston on the date of the match.
230. *The Philadelphia Inquirer*, June 11, 1926.
231. *Los Angeles Herald*, June 17, 1926.
232. Vernon made the news in the last year (2010). Leonis Malburg, 80, served as mayor and councilman for more than half a century until he was force to resign in 2009. His grandfather, John Basque Leonis, a charismatic Basque immigrant, founded Vernon and the family name came to grace everything from a streets to a power plant. Allegations were made for years that the family didn't even live in the city. In 1978, Mayor Malburg was charged by the grand jury with perjury and fraudulent voting, because he didn't live in Vernon but in a spacious home in Hancock Park. The charges were dropped. But in 2006, he and his son John Malburg were again facing the same charges and on December 5, 2009, they were convicted of voter fraud and conspiracy. Seems they were still living in the same Hancock Park estate that the city's founder, Leonis Malburg's grandfather, once owned. Leonis, at age 80, didn't serve any time, but he wasn't allowed to run for office again. His planned successor son John, went to jail for eight years for sexually abusing children. None of this removed any of the city's other leaders and business continued as usual. In 2011, there is a movement in the California Assembly to disincorporate the City of Vernon, but to do so it will have to battle an army of California's best and most expensive lawyers.
233. *Los Angeles Times*, August 1, 1926. The Vernon promotion was making all kinds of false claims. One of which was that Bill Demetral was the true Greek champion, not Lou Daro's Jim Londos, and that the two wrestlers had never met in the ring. Londos defeated Demetral for the Greek title in a well known match in New York City on January 5, 1920. Londos also beat Demetral in the rematch on March 29, 1920 in New York City.
234. *Los Angeles Times*, August 20, 1926. Stecher: "…I am afraid when the time comes for the match, Mr. Lewis will be conspicuous by his absence."
235. *Los Angeles Times*, August 24, 1926.
236. According to local Dodge historian, Alex Meyer, Tony Stecher was booked to wrestle a John Pevskly in Dodge on

July 4, 1912. Tony took sick and couldn't wrestle, so younger brother Joe took his place and beat Pevskly, "a giant Bohemian" in front of William Vlach's Rialto Theater in Dodge. This result came from a Wilman Vlach, probably a son of William Vlach, who was born on June 16, 1916 and is still alive. Alex questioned Vlach about this match, and stated that he wondered if Pevskly was in fact the great John Pesek. He said this knowing that Pevskly was described as a "giant Bohemian" and Pesek was only six foot and 180 pounds. Mr. Vlach replied immediately: "It was John Pesek! He came to Dodge to wrestle for Dodge's 4th of July celebration that year. They set the wrestling ring up right in front of Dad's theater. You know that building became our Grocery Store and then was Marv's Grocery before he moved across the street." If this was true, it would have been Pesek's first professional match and Stecher's second.

When he was growing up, Vlach lived on the same street with Joe Stecher and by age 12 was training with the champion or at least watching Joe work out. Stecher had a ring set up next to his garage for training in good weather, but at other times would train on the second floor of the Chudomelka's garage. It was in this garage that Mark Chapman found the training equipment on display in his wrestling museum in Iowa. Vlach tells stories of Pesek training with Stecher in the garage.

237. *Los Angeles Times*, and *Los Angeles Herald*, August 26, 1926. The attendance was called a sold out 9,000..

238. *Los Angles Times*, September 1, 1926.

239. *Los Angeles Times*, September 15, 1926.

240. *Los Angles Times*, September 25, 1926.

241. *Los Angeles Times*, October 3, 1926.

242. *Los Angeles Times*, October 7, 1926. You can also read a Pesek family version of the match in *Catch Wrestling* by Mark Hewitt. I consider Hewitt a friend and one of the best historians in pro wrestling, but my feeling is that he spent too much time around the Pesek family and gave a very pro-Pesek view of the match. He seems to think that every Pesek match in 1926 was a shoot, except the match Stecher won. Most of my wrestling knowledge came through Mark Hewitt, so I should just keep my mouth shut. I've also come in contact with Geoff Pesek and think he's a great guy.

243. *Los Angeles Times*, October 9, 1926.

244. *Los Angeles Examiner*, November 22, 1926.

245. www.paladin-press.com

246. *Philadelphia Inquirer*, December 18, 1927.

247. *Philadelphia Inquirer*, January 23, 1927.

248. *Police Gazette*, March 8, 1927. "It was a masterly exhibition that Stecher gave. He even made the Italian grappler look good, though he plainly outclassed him. Like a sleek tiger cat Stecher worked around his man lazily until he had brought about his downfall. Although Gardini is a great poser and strives to make every move a dramatic picture, Stecher has reduced his art to a simplicity that makes of him the true showman and one whose work is well worth watching."

249. *St. Louis Daily Globe-Democrat*, March 27, 1927.

250. Associated Press, January 15, 1917, has the arrest report. The story of the case being thrown out of court was published by the Associated Press on March 3, 1927. Attorneys for both sides agreed that Londos was not in or near Jackson, Tenn. on the date of the crime. Three times Mike Casseras sent lawyers to court, but he never appeared in person before Judge M. R. Patterson. Londos, from day one, claimed he was being set up by wrestling rivals, he may have been right.

251. *St. Louis Daily Globe-Democrat*, January 27, 1927.

252. *St. Louis Daily Globe-Democrat*, April 3 to 7, 1927.

253. *St. Louis Daily Globe-Democrat*, April 8, 1927.

254. *St. Louis Daily Globe-Democrat,* April 9 and 10, 1927.

255. The major source of this story comes from Chapter seven of *Fall Guys* by Marcus Griffin. It claims that Lewis' words were "I'm mat champion of the world. I stand ready to meet any man alive for my title. I have never asked a man to lose to me and I never will. Demetral believes he could have beaten me if he hadn't borrowed money from Sandow. I present herewith a release from Sandow. I also lay before you gentlemen a cash bond of twenty-five thousand dollars and I am willing to pay it to Demetral if he can beat me here before you gentlemen in this room or in any gymnasium you care to name."

256. Read *Tunney* by Jack Cavanaugh—a great book. I also used *Dempsey* by Jack Dempsey and Barbara Piattelli Dempsey.

257. *St. Louis Daily Globe-Democrat*, February 14, 1928.

258. *St. Louis Daily Globe-Democrat*, February 17, 1928.

259. *St. Louis Daily Globe-Democrat* and *St. Louis Times*, February 21, 1928. Most of the backstage information and quotes came from the *St. Louis Times* and reporter Sid C. Keener.

260. *The Chicago Tribune*, February 21, 1928.

261. *St. Louis Daily Globe-Democrat*, February 22, 1928.
262. In *The Unpublished Lewis Biography* Ed claimed that the first fall was a "shoot" and that he and Stecher had agreed to the idea before the match started, even with both knowing Ed would win the match. I don't buy it. Just sounds like Lewis talking. All three pins seem theatrical to me. It was all very dramatic and seemed laid out in advance. It's possible that the first two hours was a shoot, because it was mostly boring stand up like they did in their early matches, but once it reached midnight with no fall, with two more falls after that, and fans needing to go to work in the morning, they went back on script and rushed through the rest of the match. Much of this book is speculation. I think it's easy to pick it apart and figure out what is fact and what is just Yohe giving opinions. I encourage the reader to think for himself and form their own ideas whenever that is possible.

    I don't believe Lewis' headlock was a true shoot move that could be used in a contest. The move that Lewis went to, in what seemed like a shoot situation, was like a bearhug, but Ed would grab his opponent's arm like in a hammerlock and key lock with his other arm. Getting the opponent on the mat, he would shift his upper body weight (most of his weight was in the upper portion of his body, his legs were thin.) over the other wrestler's shoulders. With one arm tied up, the downed wrestler couldn't bridge out or get leverage to kick out. Most of Ed's non-headlock pins came from this move. I think this was the hold that pinned Stecher but Joe legs were hanging over the rope and the side of the ring, making it even harder to escape the pin.
263. *St. Louis Daily Globe-Democrat*, February 24, 1928. Don't believe the numbers being thrown in some of these news reports. It appears that Sandow and Lewis had planned on a European tour before the title change. That makes me think that they knew that Ed wouldn't be champion with a long reign.
264. *Los Angeles Examiner*, May 3, 1928. Lutze was body slammed and then pinned by Lewis using a headlock. Lutze bladed over his eye.
265. *Los Angeles Examiner*, June 14, 1928.
266. *Boston Globe*, June 26, 1928.
267. The first match between Lewis and Plestina, on May 28, 1928, had the two splitting the first two falls. Plestina out wrestling the champion and had Ed on the verge of defeat, when Lewis KO'ed Marin with a punch. The only reason Lewis wasn't DQ'ed was the referee he brought from Chicago, Ted Tonneman. Plestina and everyone in Minneapolis thought he could win with one of their own referees, so a rematch took place on July 9, 1928. Lewis took two out of three falls, winning both falls by tricking Marin.
268. The Plestina story is in Chapter 7 of *Fall Guys*.
269. *The Commercial Appeal, Memphis*, February 10, 1929 and *King of the Ring: Gus Sonnenberg: Lawyer, Football Star, Heavyweight Wrestling Champion of the World* by Joan Oberthaler. To get an idea of what pro football was like in 1928, see the movie 'Leatherheads' starring George Clooney.
270. *Boston Globe*, June 20 to June 30, 1928. I took the description of the match from David F. Egan's report.
271. *Los Angeles Examiner*, October 4, 1928.
272. *Los Angeles Examiner*, October 4, 1928.
273. *Los Angeles Examiner*, October 18, 1928.
274. *Philadelphia Public Ledger*, October 25, 1928.
275. *Los Angeles Examiner*, November 22, 1928.
276. *Los Angeles Examiner*, December 20, 1928.
277. *Boston Globe*, January 3 to January 6, 1929.
278. A hint to how the local fans felt about Lewis work can be found in the *Los Angeles Times* on January 14, 1929, in the build-up to the later cancelled match with Paul Jones: "Without a title to defend, Lewis is expected to take more chances in his wrestling than ever before. His work is expected to be more spectacular and his popularity with the fans is expected to show an upward trend."
279. *Los Angeles Examiner*, January 24, 1929.
280. Associated Press, January 25, 1929.
281. Associated Press, January 29, 1929.
282. *St. Louis Daily Globe-Democrat*, January 20, 1929.
283. *St. Louis Daily Globe-Democrat*, January 30, 1929.
284. *The Commercial Appeal, Memphis*, February 14, 1929.
285. Associated Press, February 25, 1929.
286. *Los Angeles Times*, April 4, 1929.
287. *Los Angeles Times*, May 1, 1929.
288. *Los Angeles Examiner*, May 2, 1929.
289. *Los Angeles Times*, May 10, 1929.
290. *Tulsa Daily World*, May 17 to May 29, 1929.
291. *New York Times*, July 9, 1929, and *Boston Globe*, July 9, 1929. Both newspapers had the gate at $90,000. It was the largest number in Boston History & remained such through the O'Mahoney era when huge cards took place with

more people present but with lower ticket prices. In 1929, it may have been the largest gate in pro wrestling history.

292. *Los Angeles Times,* July 25, 1929.

293. *St. Louis Daily Globe-Democrat,* July 13, 1929.

294. *St. Louis Daily Globe-Democrat* and Associated Press, August 24, 1929.

295. *Los Angeles Times* and *Los Angeles Herald,* September 4, 1929.

296. *Los Angeles Times* and *Los Angeles Herald,* September 19, 1929. During the 1920's many of the Olympic main events lasted past the publish deadline for the *L.A. Times,* so to get a good match report a researcher needs to use a afternoon newspaper like the *Herald* or the *Examiner.*

297. *The Arizona Republican, Phoenix,* October 5, 1929.

298. *St. Louis Globe-Democrat,* October 15, 1929. This was the work of Billy Sandow, who had a home in Kansas City, MO.

299. *Los Angeles Times* and Associated Press, October 23, 1929 and November 14, 1929. The story of the Ladjimi connection to Londos is Associated Press, August 22, 1934. Paul Bowser knew he was in trouble using a non-wrestler as champion and Sonnenberg would wrestle only Bowser wrestlers using Bowser referees.

300. *Los Angeles Times* and *Los Angeles Examiner* story by Jack James, October 24, 1929.

301. Marshall's father owned a ranch in Colorado with a gym and ring. All of the old master grapplers would train there when in the area. So Marshall grew up working out with wrestlers like Londos, Jordan, both Zbyszkos and Toots Mondt. *The Los Angeles Examiner,* May 5, 1930. Marshall also had a pet wrestling bear named Gotch, named after Everett's idol, Frank Gotch. This seems like a good spot to tell my story about wrestling Victor the wrestling bear at a used car lot on Atlantic Boulevard in East LA in 1964, but I'll let the opportunity go… it was a draw.

302. *Los Angeles Times* and *Los Angeles Examiner,* November 14, 1929.

303. *Kansas City Star,* November 17, 1929.

304. *Los Angeles Times,* March 20, 1930.

305. The report of the move that finished the second fall was just called a slam the next day. But in a *Los Angeles Times* interview of May 4, Marshall stated he has used Joe Malcewicz's backward slam to pin Lewis. This move seems to me to be Lou Thesz's side suplex finisher.

306. *Los Angeles Times,* April 17, 1930.

307. Stanislaus Zbyszko retire in April 1930 to promote wrestling shows in the new Madison Square Garden. He seemed to have the backing of Paul Bowser. Jack Curley, by that time, was back on his feet drawing big crowds at the 71st Armory, using Shikat and later Londos.

308. Considering how no one was ever thinking about pushing Ray Steele as a champion, it was a huge compliment to his ability and believability to have been including on the list. Steele was a great draw all over the country and highly respected, but never got the push of a Sonnenberg, Shikat, George, or O'Mahoney. I see him as the Billy Robinson of his time, but a bigger draw and a national star.

309. The best reports I've read on the NBA and wrestling came from *The Commercial Appeal, Memphis.* See April 2, 1930. Memphis was one of the cities upset with the NBA and resigned from the organization over the wrestling issue and from being told who they couldn't book.

310. *Los Angeles Examiner,* May 6, 1930. An article in the *Los Angeles Time,* August 10, 1933 claimed that the attendance was 16,880 and the gate was $68,820.50. This was the outdoor record in California until 1953. The largest attendance for boxing was the George Godfrey / Jaolino Uzcudun fight at 36,605 in 1928. The largest boxing gate was Ace Hudkins / Mickey Walker fight at $150,265.45 (21,370 with a ticket priced at $12. The article claimed it took $10,000 to set up the ring and seats at an outdoor card.)

311. The Ed Don George Bio in *The Historical Wrestling Society # 18: The Ed Don George Record Book* by Richard Haynes, January 1994. George was born June 3, 1905 at North Java NY which is outside of Buffalo, NY.

312. I think this Phillies Ball Park was the old Baker Bowl, also called "The Hump." It had the smallest capacity of any major league park, but no one cared because the Phillies were so bad no one paid to watch them anyway. In 1903, a section of the stands collapsed during a game, killing twelve people. It also had a small field with right field fence only 280 feet away from home. This enabled Phillies right fielder Chuck Klein to win the Triple Crown in 1933 and to set a modern record with 44 outfield assists in 1930. *Ballparks Then And Now* by Eric Enders.

313. *Philadelphia Bulletin* and *Los Angeles Times,* June 7, 1930.

314. *Seattle Times,* June 12, 1930.

315. *Los Angeles Times* and Associated Press, June 12, 1930.

316. *Seattle Times,* June 15, 1930.

317. *Seattle Times,* June 17, 1930.

318. I must say that everything in that paragraph is theory based on data and the way I understand the way promoters think. At least the smart ones interested in making money, like Curley and Bowser. To say that the fact that they were at war and didn't like each other (so they wouldn't work together) isn't enough to overcome the fact that the two end up as partners a couple of years down the road and the two had cross promotion cards, at times, in Boston.

They were rivals but they trusted each others word. They did have the potential of the greatest gate in history looking them in the face. Chicago had been the site of Gotch/Hack with a large available population to draw from, but the city had been dormant for a year because of the mark commission, and they may have felt the promotion was too much for it at the time. Chicago later broke records with Londos/Lewis in 1934 and O'Connor/Rogers in 1961.

319. See *100 Years Of Australian Professional Wrestling* by noted historian Libnan Ayoub. This book ranks with the best books on wrestling history. If you can ever get a copy, it's worth your time. The research of this Australian tour was done by historian Ed Lock.

320. *Los Angeles Times*, March 16, 1931.

321. *Boxing & Wrestling News*, April 1933. *Henri Deglane: The Unknown Champion* by Jim Barrett, p.5.

322. *Los Angeles Times*, December 10, 1930. Details on the finish was used in the pre-match write up for the rematch on December 10.

323. *New York Times*, November 18, 1930; *Madison Square Garden Record Book* by Fred Hornby & Scott Teal.

324. *Los Angeles Times*, December 11, 1930. On page 270 of *From Milo To Londos*. Published by Nat Fleischer in 1936, it claims both Sonnenberg/George matches took place in Boston. It's one of the famous errors in the writing of wrestling history and was carried over into the creation of a title line used by the NWA until the 1990's. The matches took place in Los Angeles.

325. *Los Angeles Times*, December 23, 1930.

326. *New York Times*, December 30, 1930.

327. *The Philadelphia Inquirer*, December 27, 1930.

328. *Glendale News-Press*, January 2, 1931.

329. *Glendale News-Press*, January 3, 1931.

330. *Glendale News-Press*, January 5, 1931.

331. *Glendale News-Press*, January 6, 1931.

332. *New York Times*, January 27, 1931.

333. *Los Angeles Times*, January 8 and January 11, 1931.

334. *Los Angeles Times*, February 5, 1931.

335. *Los Angeles Times*, March 5, 1931.

336. *Los Angeles Times*, March 19, 1931.

337. *Los Angeles Herald*, April 10, 1931.

338. The body lock combined with a hammer lock, was Lewis' major move in a shoot situation and I believe it was the hold Lewis used to win the title in 1929. He would get a hold of his opponent's arm in a hammer lock type position and then he form a body lock by key locking the hand holding the opponent's arm. At that point, it looked like a bearhug, but Lewis would throw the other wrestler or trip him, taking him down to the mat with Ed on top. Lewis would then use his weight and upper body to leverage the opponent's shoulders to the mat for a three count. With one of his arms tied up, the opponent only had one arm to kick out with and a bridge attempt could be warned down by Lewis, who usually carried superior weight and strength. The hold didn't look or sound like much, but it was a killer pinning move.

339. *Los Angeles Times*, *Pasadena Star News* and *Los Angeles Examiner*, April 14, 1931. The *Times* report was very weak, so most of the description of the match came from the *Examiner* story by a Sol Plex. The fact that the coverage in the *Times* was so bad and said so little, adds to the believe that Lewis stole the title.

340. The quote was told by Lewis to Lou Thesz. Ed Don George also seemed to have told a similar story to Thesz and George was quoted by Kit Bauman in his book *Hooker: The Authentic Wrestler's Adventures Inside the Bizarre World of Professional Wrestling*. This is how Bauman wrote the story through Ed Don George: "We were supposed to wrestle a three-fall match, and I was going to win, of course," George said, laughing at the memory. "We came out to the center of the ring for the referee's instructions, and Ed says to me, really casual and friendly, "Well Don, tonight's the night." I knew immediately what he was saying—that he was going to take the title back—and all I could think of was saying was, "Oh no." Ed smiles and says, "Oh yes. Now, how do you want to do it? Do we give the fans a great match or do we wrestle?" We were close friends, and we knew I couldn't beat Ed wrestling on my best day, so I just shrugged and said, "Well, Ed, why don't we just give them a great match, okay? And that's what we did. The only difference was that Ed was the one whose hand was raised at the end."

That seems like a lot of words to be passed around while they were shaking hands. I like the version I printed better. Its seems more poetic, and it's the version that will be remembered.

As I wrote in the biography, I've recently seen 9 minutes of clips of newsreels of this match. The clips have the introduction, and the finish of both falls. There is no meeting in the ring before the match and no words can be seen between the wrestlers. Lewis is big and round with a tire around his waist, but I wouldn't call him overly fat. Standing he looks very quick and clever on his feet. He is not slow and it's not boring. He moves very well on the mat and controls George. He looks very strong, like a hairless gorilla. There seems to be no heat between the two and it doesn't look stiff in any way. I just watched the tape three times and I have to say Lewis impressed me. George—not so much. From what I saw I believe the old man could have beaten Ed Don in a real match. Lewis did get boo'ed through out the match. I liked the style because it felt real, but it wasn't like watching Volk Han, Billy Robinson, or Dick "The Destroyer" Beyer. Only a few people have this match and I'm not at liberty to disclose too much, though at some point everyone will see it.

341. The book *Fall Guys* was written in 1938. It has been consider the first "smart" wrestling book, but is also a very biased book. I will write more about that later.

342. The part of the story that says Sandow was removed came from *From Milo To Londos*. It's not in *The Arena* story.

343. I have always found the Lewis/Deglane title change to be the hardest of all famous matches to research. The major problem is the fact it took place in Canada and I can only get America newspaper from America libraries. The Montreal newspapers were also written in French. A few of the wrestling history books have covered the match but none very well. A lot of semi-unknown facts are important: 1. When did Lewis/Sandow accept the match?; 2. How did they work the finish—was it dramatic, like you would expect in a worked match?; 3. Where was Henri bitten? Was it in a place where someone could bit himself?

Most of the reports are very different. *From Milo To Londos*, printed by *The Ring Magazine* in 1938 (p. 271), had Sandow getting kicked out after Deglane won a fall. I put that in because it sounded right in the storyline. Lewis was pinning Deglane when the bite took place. The bite marks were on his right arm and he claimed Ed bit him more that once. There are a lot of errors in that section of the book. It claims the Lewis double-cross of George took place in Boston and that the National Boxing Commission gave recognition to Lewis following the match (Londos was the NBA champion at the time), among other mistakes. So I have no faith in that report.

Marcus Griffin in *Fall Guys* wrote that the bite took place in the third fall and it was on Deglane's chest. In his story, Dan Koloff did the biting of the "breast" in a washroom during the break between falls. Pretty wild restroom. It also claims that the match led to a break up between Lewis and Sandow, which didn't happen for some time. *Fall Guys* is off on so many things that I don't accept anything it says.

In *Hooker: An Authentic Wrestler's Adventures Inside The Bizarre World Of Professional Wrestling* by Lou Thesz with Kit Bauman, which is basically Ed Lewis' story told through Thesz and then interrupted by Bauman, the bite took place in the third fall, Deglane bit himself on the arm, close to the armpit, and the referee was innocent of any involvement. Backstage, Lewis was met by a gloating Paul Bowser, who had five or six gangsters armed with baseball bats. He also claims the match was three months after the Lewis/George match, instead of three weeks and that Lewis left for a trip to Europe—which didn't happen. Thesz got his information from Lewis himself, so I don't believe too much of it. I loved Lou and like and respect Kit a lot, but the first edition of *Hooker* wasn't a pure history book.

The source I used came from *The Arena* magazine from September 1931 and the story 'Henri Deglane: Conqueror of The "Strangler"' by James Lawton (p. 10). It's an article from a major wrestling and sports magazine printed in 1931. Most of my description of the match came from it—some of it word for word, except the part about Sandow getting kicked out. Until someone comes up with a good newspaper clipping of the match, it's all we have.

I also have a roughly translated (by historian and friend Greg Oliver) report from *Le Devoir De Montreal*, a French Montreal newspaper. The first report of a Lewis/Deglane match is from May 2, 1931, which was the normal argument over referees. Lewis lost that fight and the promoter picked the referee and both wrestlers agree. It was Eugene Tremblay who claimed the "lightweight" title at one time.

The report claims the attendance was 10,000 at "Arena Mont-Royal." In its report Sandow was kicked out after the second fall in the argument over the ruling. Deglane was in the dressing room as the decision was announced, but returned to the ring with his wounded arm in a sling. The crowd wanted to carry Deglane on their shoulders but Henri refused because he was in so much pain.

Another Henri Deglane story I found is in the January 1932 issue of *The Arena* magazine (Volume 4, Number 4, pp. 9-10). It is a cover story called 'Henri Deglane—The World's Champion', also written by James Lawton. The article doesn't hold a great deal of credibility with me, and its main goal seems to be promoting Deglane after his return from France. Seems fans in 1932 were as curious about the bite match as we are, because the closing of the article is a description of the match by Lawton, who claimed to have been present the night of the match:

"There was nothing eventful about the first fall of the match, which came in 33:15, save that Deglane surprised everyone, and especially Lewis, absorbing two devastating headlock just prior to the end and coming back to side-step Lewis' third rush, clamped on a wicked head and arm lock from which there could be no escape, and pinned the big one solidly. The contender then retired to his dressing room for the rest period, while Lewis remained in the ring, listening to his manager 'ragging' the referee in an attempt to get that official excited into doing something like losing his head, but his success was not in evidence."

"In the meantime, Deglane used the time to good advantage, returning to the ring in fine fettle and stepped in the lead by applying two or three headlocks that did the headlock king no good at all. Lewis started weakening, all of which might have had much to do with his following maneuver, and as they milled around on the ropes, action got brisk fast. Deglane, behind the champion, reached for a headlock to pull the big fellow to the center of the ring, only to let go in a hurry and fall to the mat beneath Lewis, nearly pinned. The referee, who had been making for the ropes, called the fall for Lewis, only to note the tooth marks and broken flesh on Deglane's right forearm. Thereupon he quite, properly reversed the decision, giving the fall, the match, and the title to Deglane on a foul."

This version of the match by Lawton is a less detailed account of the match, but makes the finish seem even more theatrical. I just can't see how the match could be anything but a "work" by everyone involved, including Lewis and Sandow.

Two years after I wrote the above, I received another very creditable account of the match from the Montreal newspaer *La Patrie* from one of the major historians in Canada, Patric Laprade. It contained much of the information I was hoping for. His version had the match announced on April 28 in Montreal. Deglane was pinned in the third fall, just as he claimed foul. And the bite mark was on the wrist, which is a better spot that most of the other reports, and there also was no mention of Deglane going to the dressing room between the first and second fall. So in my mind, the "work" theory holds up.

344. *Los Angeles Times*, June 11, 1931.

345. Most of the information comes from Don Luce's study of Chicago wrestling. He researched all of 1931 in Chicago.

346. Associated Press, October 1 and 18, 1931. I can't say that I understand the relationship between the NBA and the NWA. The boxing side of the group gave up on pro wrestling in 1931, but the National Wrestling Association continued into the 1950's usually influenced by Tom Packs in St. Louis until it seemed to unite with the National Wrestling Alliance in 1949.

347. *Chicago Tribune*, November 11, 1931.

348. *Los Angeles Times*, November, 1931.

349. Lewis claimed that he had a "hands on" approach to running his Glendale restaurant, and he seemed to spend time greeting customers. He liked meeting and talking to people and enjoyed the attention it brought. It's also claimed that his restaurant was a good place for any wrestler or boxer to get a free meal. Ed liked playing the big shot by picking up bills. He wasn't the type to save his money.

350. *The Commercial Appeal, Memphis*, January 23, 1932.

351. Most of this information comes from *Fall Guys*, Chapter 15. Marcus Griffin worked in Toots Mondt's office during the war with Londos in 1932, so on this topic he has some credibility. Marcus claimed that Mondt owned 25% of Londos' contract.

352. My records of Lewis and Londos say it stood at: 8 wins for Lewis … 2 handicap wins for Londos … and one draw. We can't be sure if the record is correct because we found two of those matches in the last year and more may show up.

353. *The Boston Globe*, February 24, 1932. Lewis won the first fall in 1:06:15 by painting Steele with a long series of rabbit punches, then he tossed in a few Beels for good measure, butted Ray out of the ring, and gave him one of the old-fashioned headlocks for the pin. Steele got busy with his fist and elbows from the beginning in the second fall and Lewis was always defending himself from that point forward. The ancient Lewis was a gallant figure as he fought off the efforts of the younger man. Still Steele pinned Lewis in 13:33 using a side suplex. Lewis was exhausted but managed to hold on until saved by the 90 minute time limit.

354. Most of that paragraph came from a bad Lewis review in *The Commercal Appeal, Memphis*, April 18, 1932.

355. *New York Times*, June 9, 1932. *The Ring Magazine* covered the match. They claimed the match drew only 15,000. Quote: "…Dick Shikat and Ed Lewis were featured as the headliners. Lewis, far from the 'Strangler' of several years back, came through with an unconvincing victory after an hour, six minutes, and seven seconds of quite ordinary wrestling. It was all Shikat until the finish. Dick toyed with Lewis and had Ed puffing and coughing till the 'Strangler' applied a series of headlocks to pin the clever German. It is our opinion that Shikat could have tossed Lewis had he wrestled as he is capable of doing."

356. *Fall Guys* (Chapter 15) claimed that Shikat received $20,000 as a guarantee that he would get a rematch and a win over Lewis. Lewis had to get the money from Shikat's manager, Toots Mondt. Lewis refused to job for Shikat and Mondt didn't push the issue after Lewis sign a five year contract for Toots to manage him.

357. I used a section from Gary Will's web site *Toronto Wrestling History*: http://garywill.com/toronto/mondt. htm — Toots Mondt was a partner in Jack Corcoran's Toronto office, and was perhaps the majority owner in 1932.

358. *The Commercial Appeal, Memphis*, September 27, 1932.

359. That story about a "later shoot" sounds fishy. I think it was just a story told by Sherry, for the rest of his career, to explain the job to Lewis. He couldn't just tell people he did it because it was the biggest payoff of his career.

360. *Brooklyn Daily Eagle, New York*, and *New York Times*, October 11, 1932. A note: Lewis was bare foot for the match — both Lewis and Londos took the shoes off in matches they wanted fans to believe were shoots. Kind of like in MMA today. You wonder who would understand the reason for doing that in 1932, but it seems there were people with a grappling background who got the point.

361. I would expect that everyone reading this would have gotten the great *Ray Steele Record Book* by Steve Yohe and

members of the IHC.

362. *The Philadelphia Inquirer* and *The New York Times*, December 5, 1932. *The Times* seemed to have attempted to get the Jack Curley version over, while the Philadelphia paper was more detailed and slanted toward Steele and Londos. The Philly paper seemed more creditable to me. The *Ring Magazine* (by "Tex" Austin) also had a version of the match, quote: "The interest of the sport demands that Londos accept the Lewis defy and agree to a match with him to decide the world's championship... The claim has been made by Londos on many occasions that the only reason he refuses to accept a match with the 'Strangler' is because Lewis is blind in one eye, yet Londos did not have any scruples about permitting his chief ally, Ray Steele, a great wrestler, to tackle Lewis. That suggestion of Londos is poppycock. Whether Lewis is old or blind or even both, he certainly demonstrated to the satisfaction of unbiased critics that he is still one of the world's greatest matmen. The manner in which he handled Steele was a revelation. He so far outclassed Ray , that it was truly a surprise to those who figured Ray would have little difficulty in throwing the 'Strangler.' There was not a moment in the entire 32 minutes that the match lasted that Lewis did not prove his superiority to Steele, hence there is no further reason for Londos ducking a match that would mean much to the game in future attendance and revived interest." The bad reaction to the match was credited to the fact that fans of 1932 didn't appreciate true wrestling. *The Ring* then went on, offering the winner of a Lewis/Londos match a $2,000 championship belt.

363. I've read a report that seemed to say that the Lewis/Steele match with bloody feet from blisters took place in Chicago at a later date. It's a match that hasn't been found yet. I've never seen or heard of Ray Steele going bare foot. It was something that Lewis and Londos did in matches billed as shoots.

364. *The Philadelphia Inquirer*, December 7, 1932.

365. *New York Times*, January 12, 1933.

366. *From Milos To Londos*, by A. D. Phillips, p. 276.

367. *Boston Globe*, February 11, 1933, story by David F. Egan.

368. All of that section came from *Fall Guys* by Marcus Griffin, Chapter 16.

369. *North American Newspaper Alliance*, March 21, 1933 and *Los Angeles Times*, March 21, 1933. Also have a report from an unknown New York newspaper that gives the attendance and gate.

370. *Fall Guys* by Marcus Griffin, Chapter 16; also *Chicago Tribune*, April 8 to 14, 1933.

371. *Chicago Tribune*, April 12, 1933.

372. *Boston Globe*, May 18, 1933.

373. *Los Angeles Times*, May 23, 1933.

374. *Los Angeles Times*, June 8, 1933. Newsreel clips of this match can be found on line.

375. *New York Times*, June 13, 1933.

376. *Los Angeles Times*, June 22, 1933.

377. *Los Angeles Time*, July 12, 1933.

378. *San Diego Union*, August 30, 1933.

379. Associated Press, October 27, 1933.

380. Most of the inside information comes from *Fall Guys* (Chapter 18), but it matches up with events and information that came out of later court trials. I don't think Billy Sandow was a major player in the new trust but he may have made money by bringing Everett Marshall to the East Coast for a series of Londos matches. By 1937, Sandow was working with Tom Pack and connected with Paul Bowser.

381. *St. Louis Daily Globe-Democrat*, December 14, 1933.

382. *St. Louis Daily Globe-Democrat*, December 21, 1933. It's interesting that the shoot match (?) in Madison Square Garden is a well-known story that has been covered in *Fall Guys* and *Hooker*, while this St. Louis shoot match is unknown by the public and was never talked about by Lewis. Perhaps Lewis was hit too hard and couldn't remember the event. I've never read anything about Steele bragging about beating Ed in a "shoot'. These two wrestled many times and every match was booked to make the public think the event was a shoot. Lewis and Steele respected each other and were good friends.

383. This reminds me of Wilt Chamberlain's last few years playing basketball with the Los Angeles Lakers. He had aged and bulked up, and the NBA had widen the key so that he couldn't score like he used to. The players had also gotten bigger and more talented, so Wilt concentrated on defense and rebounding. But every announcer, reporter, and fan believed — and said so — that he could still score 50 points in a game, if he just wanted to. And so Wilt was willing to say he didn't feel like playing his best and bragged about it. During their playing careers, most NBA followers thought Bill Russell was a better player than Wilt. Head to head, Russell had made his point over the years by winning. But now in the computer generation, everyone sees Wilt's records and most young fans think Wilt was the man. It's the same problem you have comparing Jack Tunney to Jack Dempsey or Joe Stecher to Strangler Lewis. The public remembers the guy with the most famous name.

384. *St. Louis Daily Globe-Democrat*, February 3, 1934.

385. Associated Press, February 11, 1934.

386. *New York Times*, February 5, 1934.

387. *St. Louis Daily Globe-Democrat*, February 16, 1934.

388. Associated Press, March 2, 1934.

389. *The History Of Professional Wrestling, Vol #6 : St. Louis 1930 To 1959* researched by J Michael Kenyon, Don Luce, James Melby, Scott Teal, and Steve Yohe, published 2002 by Scott Teal and Crowbar Press.

390. *Los Angeles Times*, April 16, 1934.

391. *Los Angeles Times*, April 18, 1934.

392. *The New York Times*, May 15, 1934. I hadn't researched this match until after I had started writing this section and the short match kind of knocked the air out of me after I had made a big deal out of the series of matches between Lewis and Ray Steele. Years ago I put together the *Ray Steele Record Book*, which was a run-through for my later *Jim Londos Record Book*. So I have some ideas about Steele. Unlike with other major wrestlers like Lewis, Stecher, Gotch, and Londos, he was a working-class type wrestling star. He didn't own part of the promotion and he didn't have any major promoters or managers backing him or protecting him. The only thing he had that other normal wrestling performers didn't was talent and a friendship with Jim Londos. Maybe all of that relates to the fact that he had no wrestling ego. Even at his peak, he seemed willing to pull over other wrestlers and do jobs. There is a booking rule in pro wrestling that says the talented wrestlers can afford to do jobs and stay over. The performer types with little talent can't do many jobs without losing what the fans were willing to pay for. So you find guys in the sport like Danno O'Mahoney, Primo Carnera, Hulk Hogan (well I don't know if that is fair, as Hogan was a smart worker and had something, though some fans perceive him as having no talent), French Angel, Antonino Rocca, Undertaker, etc. not doing jobs. As you couldn't really kill the popularity of a Chris Benoit, Hiroshi Hase, or Ray Misterio in the 1990's by making them do jobs, Ray Steele could still keep his fans while putting others over. I see Steele as the Billy Robinson of the 1930's. The thing I do notice is that when Ray does do a job that might be considered below him, he makes it short. All of the great losses to Londos were long matches, some two hours or longer, but for the old fat Ed Lewis of 1934—he went home in 11 minutes. In a huge match with Gus Sonnenberg in St. Louis, he did the job in 17 minutes. I found him doing the same short matches in other minor losses. Maybe it was his way of protesting. It didn't really matter, since in 1940 they made him NWA world champion for a year.

393. This came from a French translation by Greg Oliver from *Le Devoir*, May 29, 1934. This is research by Greg Oliver done just for this project. Everyone please send him a message thanking him. A historical match, not really know about.

394. *Chicago Tribune*, September 21, 1934, *Detroit Free Press*, September 21, 1934, and *Wrestling Life,* 'Londos vs Lewis' by Charles Bartlett, August 1955.

395. This came from a French translation by Greg Oliver from *Le Devoir*, August 28, 1934.

396. *Ring Magazine*, December 1934, and *Wrestling Ambassador* by Ed E. Smith. Lewis "... was sent abroad as a sort of ambassador plenipotentiary, a precursor of good will, a delegate to spread the doctrine among foreign countries and to tell all and sundry just what a fine field there is in this country for wrestling men of merit and intelligence and showmanship and all else that goes to make up the wrestler of this day and age as he is exploited by the able promoters who are doing such an excellent job of mass production." Aaaaaaa... Sometime you wonder if Red Barry ever wrote for *The Ring*. Plenipotentiary is in the dictionary.

397. *Danno Mahoney: Irish World Wrestling Champion* by John W. Pollard with John Levis and Michael P. O'Connell, was a book written in Ireland around 1991 as a tribute to Mahoney. It is idealistic, markish, and very pro Danno O'Mahoney, but it is also seems to be one of the better researched wrestling books and it seems to have had the co-operation of the O'Mahoney family. Also *A Study of Danno O'Mahoney The (Almost) Undisputed World Champion* by Steve Yohe.

398. *Hooker: An Authentic Wrestler's Adventures Inside The Bizarre World Of Professional Wrestling* by Lou Thesz with Kit Bauman, pp. 60-61. (From this point forward I'll refer to the book as *Hooker*.) Kit Bauman places the Lewis workout in January 1936 following Thesz's return form the Minnesota area and before he left for Los Angeles. I'm probably wrong but I think it took place in January 1935, when Thesz was very green having only wrestled in East St. Louis. Thesz might not have known it, and he never comes out and says it, but I think Tom Packs had plans on the young Thesz replacing Jim Londos as the king of St. Louis wrestling from an early age. Thesz's good looks play as big a part in the decision as his pure wrestling ability.

    It should also be noted that during Lou Thesz's actual career the story always had Thesz beating Lewis. This is similar to the story of O'Mahoney beating Lewis in London.

399. *Los Angeles Examiner*, January 24, 1935.

400. *Los Angeles Times*, January 25, 1935.

401. *Los Angeles Herald*, January 28, 1935.

402. *Los Angeles Examiner*, January 26, 1935.

403. *Detroit Free Press*, February 2, 1935.

404. *Los Angeles Times* and *Los Angeles Illustrated Daily News*, February 22, 1935, and *Los Angeles Examiner*, February 24, 1935.
405. *Los Angeles Herald* and *Los Angeles Times*, February 28, 1935.
406. *Los Angeles Illustrated Daily News*, March 2, 1935.
407. *St. Louis Post Dispatch*, March 7, 1935.
408. *The Boston Globe*, January 5, 1935.
409. *The Boston Globe*, January 19, 1935.
410. *New York Times*, February 19, 1935.
411. *New York Times*, March 19, 1935.
412. *New York Times*, April 2, 1935. Story by Arthur J. Daley.
413. *The Boston Globe*, April 27, 1935. Story by James C. O'Leary.
414. *Los Angeles Times*, April 25, 1935.
415. *Los Angeles Times*, May 23, 1935. Quote by Jack Singer.
416. *Los Angeles Examiner*, May 27, 1935.
417. *Los Angeles Times*, May 30, 1935. Quote by Jack Singer
    Also *Los Angeles Times*, June 1, 1935, 'The Sports Parade' by Braven Dyer: "…Ed Lewis, the quondam 'Strangler' should retire…Gray haired and fat, his face wrinkled and shoulders stooped with the weight of years, Lewis is truly a tragic figure as he lumbers about the ring on his short squatty legs…Those of us who remember Lewis as the head-crushing heavyweight champion of the world, hate to see the pathetic Lewis of today…Ed owns a chop house in Glendale."
418. *The Houston Post*, June 15, 1935.
419. *Los Angeles Times*, June 20, 1935. Attendance was 10,400, with paid attendance at 8,748 and $7,900. The paid crowd was later announced by the commission. I think, with three shows a week, Daro gave away a lot of ticket to these cards. Well that, or he lied about attendance.
420. *Los Angeles Times* and *Los Angeles Examiner*, June 27, 1935.
421. *Boston Globe*, June 28, 1935. For dropping the title to O'Mahoney, Londos got $50,000 from the original Trust agreement plus $20,000 from the Fenway Park gate. Some think he got even more money from Bowser. Looking at the newspaper stories at the time, perhaps Londos consented to doing the job because everyone in the Trust was feuding and Jimmy wanted to get his Trust money before the whole organization fell apart. Jim rarely did anything he didn't want to do. On his way home to Escondido, California, he stopped off long enough in St. Louis to tell the world he wasn't retiring. (*St. Louis Globe*, July 9, 1935) His plans were to take time off to build up his Escondido farm and then travel back to Greece to visit family. Then, starting in 1936, the plan had him wrestling in Europe.
422. Probably because of the Hearst newspaper involvement, this is the most disputed attendance figure in wrestling history. The report of "not more than 10,000" came from the *Los Angeles Times* July 9, 1935. Here are the other reports:
    New York Times — 12,000
    Los Angeles Examiner — 15,000
    Los Angeles Illustrated News — not more than 25,000
    Danno Mahoney: Irish World Wrestling Champion — 15,000
    I've learned that the lowest wrestling figure is usually the right number…but you believe what you want to believe.
423. *Los Angeles Times*, July 25, 1935.
424. *Los Angeles Times*, July 7 and 12, 1935. Vincent Lopez was actually Lou Daro's fourth attempt at creating a Mexican star for Los Angeles. The first was Felix Lopez, who was too lazy to develop, followed by Gilberto Martinez, a good looking guy, but a "stiff" and then Frank "Cactus Pete" Aguayo, good worker but too small. Vincent Lopez stayed a star in the area for a number of years. He was followed by such Latin stars as Enrique Torres (1947 to 1963), Pedro Morales (1964 to 1968), Mil Mascaras (1969 to present time) and Chavo Guerrero (1976 to 1982). Lou Daro and the promoters who followed him, found out that Mexico had great workers but few truly good heavyweights. To succeed in Los Angeles, you held on to any of them you could find.
425. *Boston Globe*, July 31, 1935. The finish of the Danno/George match saw O'Mahoney thrown from the ring as the timekeeper or referee James J. Braddock count to 20. The boxing champion didn't know that a 20 count ended the match, and George had to explain the rule to Braddock. By that time, Danno had returned and threw George out of the ring. Ed Don, thinking he had already won, took his time returning, so Braddock counted him out. Braddock, who knew the rules this time, then gave the match to O'Mahoney. The match results appeared the next morning on the front page of the *Boston Globe*.
426. *Boston Globe*, September 12, 1935.
427. *Boston Globe*, October 12, 1935.
428. *Houston Chronicle*, October 13, 20 and 26, 1935.
429. *St. Louis Daily Globe*, November 7, 1935. It seems that 1935 was a good year for "Ref bumps."

430. Associated Press, July 30, 1932. On July 19, 1932, Gus Sonnenberg was driving home drunk from a match when he was involved in a auto accident in the town of North Andover, Massachusetts. In the other car was an off duty police officer named Richard L. Morrissey, who suffered injuries and later died. On July 30, 1932, Gus pleaded "not guilty" in front of District Court of Lawrence, Massachusetts, to charges of manslaughter, driving while drunk, and reckless driving. Sonnenberg was bailed out by Paul Bowser and the trial was set for August 2, 1932. I don't know what happened after that but Gus was back wrestling full time by August 15. Young Lou Thesz would be one of Sonnenberg's drivers in San Francisco in 1936.

431. *St. Louis Daily Globe*, December 8, 1935. Ii is interesting to see Lewis and Sandow pulling their old tricks on each other. Max Baumann was promoting cards in St. Louis, using Sandow's champion Everett Marshall. The split between the two old friends seems real, and I've found nothing in their future reports that makes me think anything ever changed.

432. A more detailed description of the Texas trip can be found in my Danno O'Mahoney biography: "A disastrous tour of the South followed in Feb. 1936. Three times opponents tried to hook O'Mahoney and only Bowser's precautions saved the title. The story told is that Rudy Dusek had once controlled most of the south but had lost territory and control after the creation of the wrestling trust. Using Julius and Morris Siegel the major promoters in Houston and Shreveport, Leon Balkin, his chief lieutenant, and the local booker, Doctor Karl Sarpolis, he made up a plan to outsmart Bowser and steal the title.

  The first two double-crosses took place on Feb. 6 versus Ellis Bashara in New Orleans and on Feb. 7 in Houston versus Daniel Boone Savage (Ed Civil). Danno was saved both times by the Bowser referee Paul Jones. The finish of the Daniel Boone Savage match had Danno throwing the hillbilly over the top rope on to the floor. This was a violation of Texas wrestling rules but the referee Jones didn't call for a DQ. The Texas Commission later ruled that a rematch had to take place within 90 days or Danno would be stripped of the title.

  On Feb. 9 Danno, Manager McGrath, and Paul Jones were present at the Galveston City Auditorium and the wrestler had been examined by commission doctor, when someone told them that his opponent, Juan Humberto, had plans to hook O'Mahoney. The group felt they had enough, so they left the arena during the preliminaries, in front of the local fans and the state inspector of boxing and wrestling. On Feb. 11, 1936, Galveston promoter, Ralph Hammonds, sued O'Mahoney and manager for $15,216.40 due to the run out. Danno was stripped of the title in Texas and the National Wrestling Association soon followed by stripping O'Mahoney of their title. With this, the idea of an (almost) Undisputed World Title was over. When O'Mahoney was unable to return for a title match, a new Texas title line was started on May 8, 1936, with Leo "Whiskers" Savage as world champion. But by that time, there were so many champions, that no one noticed." Also see *Galveston Daily News*, February 9 to 11, 1936 and Associated Press, May 9, 1936. The title line is listed in *Wrestling Title Histories* by Royal Duncan & Gary Will on page 261. This is the greatest of all wrestling history books and should be owned by everyone interested in the topic. Also see *Fall Guys*.

433. *New York Times*, March 2, 1936; *The Boston Globe*, March 2, 1936; *The Ring Magazine*, April 1936. The following is from my O'Mahoney biography: "Two days later (March 2, 1936) history was made in Madison Squire Garden when Danno was matched with his old friend Dick Shikat. Why Jack Curley and Bowser would allow Shikat back into the ring with O'Mahoney, after the April 1, 1935 mess, is hard to explain… My guess is that Danno had run threw every major contender and Shikat was the only fresh name that could draw in New York, so Curley took a chance that Shikat would be happy with a good payday. They were wrong.

  In the Garden ring, Shikat was the aggressor from the moment the bell sounded. In the first minute, he took O'Mahoney to the mat with a wristlock and kept him down for the rest of the match, punishing the Irishman with hold after hold. At no time was Shikat in any danger from Danno and he seemed to enjoy breaking out of any hold attempted by the champion. Hold after hold was applied, with Danno getting freed by crawling to the ropes or by Shikat releasing the lock to go to another. Danno looked to be in agony. The bout saw Danno attempt a wristlock, which Shikat countered with a flying mare followed by a headlock. This was followed by a Japanese arm-lock but Danno broke free, but fell into a hammerlock that the German gave up for a leg lock. Danno went to the ropes for a break only to have Shikat move him to the center of the ring and with a sudden twist take him back to the mat. A body scissors and a grueling toehold followed and were broke only by Danno reaching the ropes. All these moves hurt O'Mahoney and he looked to be in complete agony. Shikat then secured a vicious hammerlock. The more Danno tried to break out of it, the more pressure the German put on. The referee George Bothner a New York commission appointee and one of the most respected men in the sport, twice asked Danno if he wanted to quit. Twice Danno said, 'Yes,' but Bothner did nothing. Shikat then appealed to Bothner that if he didn't stop it, he was breaking O'Mahoney's arm. Bothner got on his knees and asked Danno again in a voice everyone could hear. Danno cried, 'Yes, he's killing me! Stop it, I tell you!' Bothner slapped Shikat on the back and raised the hand of the new champion." (Time: 18:57)

  In the ring and later in the dressing room, O'Mahoney and McGrath gave no indication that there was any doubt in their minds who the champion was. They even praised Shikat but as the night went on they first said that Danno was still tired and sick from the Yvon Robert match two days before. Then Danno claimed, probably after some coaching from Curley or Mondt, he didn't submit, that Bothner had just miss read his Irish brogue, which just made him look bad to the 7,000 fans and reporters who heard him cry out in pain.

434. Most of the story is from *Fall Guys* by Marcus Griffin.

435. *The Philadelphia Inquirer*, February 29, 1936. This match is always called a tournament final, but it was Lewis' only match in the city during that period. Dean Detton had beaten Jim Browning, Hans Steinke, Sergel Kalmikoff, Chief Little Wolf, and Hank Barber. Detton pinned Lewis after a series of flying tackles in 31:51. The newspaper claimed it was Lewis first loss ever in Philadelphia.

436. The only source for this story is *National Wrestling Alliance: The Untold Story of the Monopoly That Strangled Pro Wrestling* by Tim Hornbaker, p. 98. I give the credit to Tim because I think Bowser wanted Danno to drop the title to Yvon Robert and that's the storyline that Bowser follows in the years that followed.

437. See the Tim Hornbaker biography, *The Unknown Champion of the World: The Turnover Scissors King, Jim Browning*.

438. *New York Times*, August 14, 1936. The Lewis/Wycoff card was the first wrestling show to appear at The Hippodrome. It replace all the others arenas to become the best in the city. Story also appears in *Fall Guys* by Marcus Griffin (Chapter 22) and *Hooker* by Kit Bauman & Lou Thesz, p. 56. Lewis told Thesz that he was so confident of beating Wycoff that he wrestled the match with a separated clavicle. He was disappointed with the result but he also thought it was the best contest he ever wrestled.

439. *Los Angeles Times*, January 21, 1937.

440. *Los Angeles Times*, January 24, 1937.

441. *Ring Magazine*, January 1938

"Looking fitter than ever, Ed 'Strangler' Lewis, professional wrestling's ambassador of good will, landed in Paris after a very disappointing trip to India. Here, in the land of turbans, Lewis had made plans to meet Gama, the Ganges giant, who has defied the march of time. The contest was scrapped when the wary Hindu demanded a three month training period. Disgusted that the 'dream-match' of his long career had fallen through, barrel chested Ed sailed for France."

The *Times Of India*, researched by historian Dan Anderson, had these reports:

9-22-1937 *Times Of India*: Strangler Lewis completed his tour of Australia and NZ. He's coming to Bombay to compete in a tournament. A special arena is being built. It will seat 30,000 fans. The winner is to receive 10,000 rupees and a gold cup; second place, 5,000 rupees and a silver cup; third, 2,500 r and a silver cup. Competitors from the Middle East, Central Asia, and Europe are coming.

9-24-1937: Ted Thye, currently in Colombo, Sri Lanka, enroute to Bombay, says he wants to arrange a match between Lewis and Great Gama. "Thye thinks Gama the world's great wrestler."

[…] In Lahore, Hamida, a disciple of Gama has accepted Lewis' challenge. He also accepts Dr. Len Hall's challenge. "I would willingly join issues with Dr. Len Hall and would personally welcome his visit to our country on behalf of professional wrestlers, and like to have a bout with him."

9-25-1937: Ted Thye arrives in Bombay via the *S.S. Strathaird* on Sept 24. Ed Lewis was held up in Australia, and would reach Calcutta the next week. Thye says: "Lewis and I have come out to India at our own expense. Lewis is willing to fight Gama, reputed to be India's best wrestler, on any terms that Gama may offer. We also want to secure matches with other Indian wrestlers, but only with the best of them, provided the terms and condition are acceptable to us." […] "We in the United States think Lewis is the best wrestler. We know Gama's reputation in India. Lewis, in my opinion, is certainly a better wrestler than Zbyszko, whom Gama defeated some years ago."

10-7-1937: Lewis, in Colombo says: "I am disappointed because I cannot meet Gama." He will travel to Europe and may wrestle Tiger Dula, who is in London.

442. United Press, 'Fake Tarzans Are Warned By Author', by Frederick C. Othman, May 19, 1939. White also gave up the Tarzan name because Edgar Rice Burroughs, living nearby in Tarzana, was threatening to sue anyone using the name. I also have to make the point that Arthur White was *not* the wrestler later using the name Ed "Tarzan" White.

443. *Los Angeles Times*, 'White Bows To Londos' by Frank Finch, April 6, 1939.

444. *Los Angeles Times*, 'Stage Seems All Set For Mat Strife In Southland' by Al Wolf, July 3, 1939.

445. *Los Angeles Times*, 'Mondts Give Up Booking Business—Nick Lutze "Adopts" Orphan Wrestlers' by Al Wolf, September 4, 1940.

446. I've stated, earlier in this book, the idea that Toots Mondt destroyed as much as he created. His time in Los Angeles is an example of it. If Mondt wanted to take credit for the good years in the early 1920's with Sandow and Lewis, then he needs to take responsibility for the Wayne Munn blunder. If he want to take credit for building up New York City in 1929, then he need to be responsible for tearing it down by starting a war with Jim Londos in 1932 and 1933. If he wanted to claim he kept an already strong Los Angeles going for four years, fine, but his corrupt ways also

drove it to its knees. The Los Angeles mess wasn't the end of Toots Mondt and he then returned to New York City. He joined with an Alfred "Al" Mayer in a booking agency. He didn't run wrestling in the city, but supplied talent to all the local promotions and continued to have links to promoters all over the country. After seven years with Al Mayer, he broke up the partnership and formed the Manhattan Booking Agency. Mondt then bought a major portion of former boxing champion Primo Carnera's contract and turned him into a pro wrestler. For two years (1947 and 1948) Carnera was wrestling's biggest draw. When Carnera started to decline, Toots stole Antonino "Argentina" Rocca from Kola Kwariani. Rocca was a huge star all over, but really turned into New York City's biggest star since Jim Londos, re-opening Madison Square Garden to large crowds. He was paying a large portion of Toots' gambling debts into 1963. Both Carnera and Rocca ended up broke from working with Toots. Later Toots controlled the early careers of Bruno Sammartino and Andre The Giant. To read more on Toots Mondt see Tim Hornbaker's book, *National Wrestling Alliance: The Untold Story of the Monopoly That Strangled Pro Wrestling*, mainly around page 102.

447. *Detroit Free Press*, March 15, 1943.

448. *St. Louis Daily Globe-Democrat*, February 21, 1941.

449. See *Maurice Tillet: The French Angel* by Steve Yohe.

450. *San Francisco Chronicle*, August 25, 1942. The first match on August 25 saw Lewis drop two out of three falls clean to Tillet. Ed lost the first fall to a leg lock in 9 minutes. Lewis took the second fall via the headlock in 9:06. The French Angel then beat Lewis with his own headlock in 7 minutes. Both men worked very slow.

451. *Omaha World Herald*, 'Pesek's Dynasty Topples' by Robert Phipps, October 21, 1942.

452. See *The Orville Brown Ring Record* by Steve Yohe and the members of the IHC, or *Orville Brown* By Steve Yohe.

453. *The Kansas City Kansan*, October 23, 1942.

454. *Omaha World Herald*, 'Pesek Evens Lewis' Score', November 5, 1942.

455. *The Des Moines Register*, November 18, 1942.

456. International News Service, January 29, 1943. I've heard a rumor, coming from the Pesek family, that there was a gym shoot match, during this time period, between Lewis and Pesek. It's said to have been a draw, but I know very little about this story.

457. United Press, April 22, 1943.

458. *Auckland, New Zealand Star*, September 20, 1944.

459. *Tacoma News Tribune*, September 19, 1945.

460. *Wisconsin Rapids Daily Tribune*, January 10, 1946. The report claimed Mrs. Friedrich's maiden name was Amelia Gueldenzopf. Born in Saxon Wiemer (March 22, 1866), Germany, she came to America at age 16 and settled at Sheboygan Falls. Married Jacob Friedrich in September 1987. She had 9 grandchildren and two great grandchildren.

461. *Oakland Tribune*, December 18, 1946.

462. To read more about Everett Marshall see the biography by Steve Johnson in *The Wrestling Observer Newsletter*, September 28, 2009.

463. *Los Angeles Times*, June 26, 1946.

464. *Miami Herald*, December 2, 1947.

465. *Honolulu Star-Bulletin*, January 19, 1948. Jack Sherry claimed Lewis was old and fat and a match with him would look slow and tame. He thought the match would look fake to the fans, and he didn't want to have a terrible match in front of them. Sherry stayed in Hawaii for a few months working for outlaw promoter, Whitey Grovo, billed as "the uncrowned champion of the world," against the major promoter, Al Karasick. He then returned to the main land, wrestling "off and on" into the 1950's. He died, working as a construction worker, in 1969. No one ever seemed to get rich being a trustbuster. Read Mark Hewitt's book *Catch Wrestling: Round Two*, pp. 247-251, for the complete version of this story.

466. See the section on the Los Angeles Athletic Club under 'Lewis in Los Angeles' section (1924) on page 71.

467. Associated Press and *Oakland Tribune*, March 30, 1948.

468. *National Wrestling Alliance: The Untold Story of the Monopoly That Strangled Pro Wrestling* by Tim Hornbaker, p. 8. The date of the first meeting of the National Wrestling Alliance, July 18, 1948, can be found on page 8. I've also seen the date given as July 14, 1948.

469. *National Wrestling Alliance: The Untold Story of the Monopoly That Strangled Pro Wrestling* by Tim Hornbaker, p. 75. Tim has official NWA papers that he dug up researching the NWA, so I use sections from his book.

470. *The Godfather of Wrestling* by Gene LeBell (The only authorized autobiography), pp. 36-38. I hope I covered this topic well and that LeBell is happy, because I don't want sadistic Gene breaking my arm or nose. I grew up around the Olympic Auditorium and I was always afraid of Gene. Meeting him today at the CAC dinners is wonderful, but I still worry. Read more about Gene at www.GeneLeBell.com.

471. *National Wrestling Alliance: The Untold Story of the Monopoly That Strangled Pro Wrestling* by Tim Hornbaker, p. 75. In 1951, the NWA formed an "Ed Lewis Committee" to preside over all matters related to Lewis. During the 1951convention in Tulsa (Ed's home town), the membership ratified a measure that raised Thesz's per match

income to 15%, giving 2 ½ % to the NWA and 2 ½ % for Lewis' wage. This is information from Tim's research of NWA meetings. Other sources, like Thesz himself and the book *Hooker*, claim Lewis received 3% of the purse.

472. I found a Frankie Cain (The Great Mephisto) story from the sheet *What Ever Happened To...?*, Issue #52 (by Scott Teal, 2002) that showed the Lewis / Thesz relationship in a cool way and I'm going to include it here. Frankie Cain: "Al Haft had a motel and a small restaurant in Reynoldsburg, Ohio. He also had a big farmhouse and a few cabins. There was a ring set up out there where some of the boys worked out. Speedy LaRance used to pick us kids up and take us out there. I never knew what Ed Lewis was doing there, but he would come down, get in the ring, and move around with some of the kids. He was having back problems, so he used to have me walk on his back. He'd say 'Get up on my back,' and he showed me how to place my feet... not on the spine, but on each side of the spine.

One night, Ed and Lou had stayed overnight in one of Al's cabins. Lou, of course, had a busy schedule and was always on the go, so he wouldn't always be in the best of moods. He drove out one day looking for Ed. They had to get a cab to take them to the airport. He walked into the restaurant just after Ed had put in an order for pancakes. Lou got a cup of coffee and sat down at the counter, waiting for Ed to finish. Ed ate the pancakes, a big stack, and he starts looking at the glass case where they displayed the pies. Ed had bad eyes, so he was squinting, trying to see the pies. He asked the waitress, 'What kind of pie is that over there?' She said, 'That's chocolate pie. That's one of our best sellers.' He said, 'Give me a big piece of it. I mean ... a big piece.' Thesz was getting anxious because he wanted to be sure they didn't miss their plane. Lou says, 'Ed, you just ate five pancakes loaded with butter and syrup. Now you're eating a piece of pie. Don't you think you're going to a little extreme?' Ed says, 'Well, I don't worry about it, Lou. I'll just drink a cup of hot coffee. That'll kill all the carbohydrates.' Lou says, 'What did you say?' Ed repeated himself. Lou says, 'Well, by god! You know something that medical science doesn't know.' Ed says, 'That's the trouble, Lou. You think you know every damn thing. That's why you never learned how to wrestle.'"

Thesz goofing with Lewis

473. *National Wrestling Alliance: The Untold Story Of The Monopoly That Strangled Pro Wrestling* by Tim Hornbaker, p. 75.

474. *National Wrestling Alliance: The Untold Story Of The Monopoly That Strangled Pro Wrestling* by Tim Hornbaker, p. 240.

475. *Chicago Tribune*, June 15, 1957 and *Wrestling Life* magazine June 1957. To show how poorly the NWA title was drawling, the attendance was 5,682.

476. *Amarillo Daily News*, June 27, 1957 and June 28, 1957. Funk beat Thesz with a spinning toe hold for the first fall in 30 minutes. Funk put the toe hold on out side the ring in the second fall and was disqualified. Thesz's leg was injured in the process and the match was ruled a draw.

477. *Oklahoma Shooter: The Dan Hodge Story* by Mike Chapman, pp. 107-109.

478. Lewis lived on South Cincinnati Avenue in Tulsa, and the internet report I've found claims he lived with his wife and daughter. If this is true, and the daughter wasn't from some past Bobbie Lee West relationship, it would be a rare appearance of Bobada Friedrich, the child formed from Lewis' marriage with Dr. Ada Scott Morton. Bobada would have been in her 30's.

Frankie Cain served as driver for Lewis during these years and got to know him well. For this project, historian Steve Johnson, who is a editor for *The Washington Post* and a author of many major wrestling books including a forthcoming book on Jim Londos, has gone out of his way to write a short article on Frankie Cain's friendship with Lewis.

A FRIENDLY STRANGLER
by Steve Johnson

Ed Lewis was to wrestling in the Roaring Twenties what Jack Dempsey was to boxing, a larger-than-life figure that was equally at home glad-handing the citizenry as he was mauling opponents. His nickname, "Strangler," lifted from Evan Lewis, no doubt helped; when some newsboy hawking a tabloid shouted "Strangler Lewis Tops Stecher!" the inflection in his voice was probably no different than when he shrieked "Latest on the Manassa Mauler!" or "Sultan of Swat Belts Two!"

Lewis wielded tremendous influence in and out of the ring, but it was not all-encompassing. Growing up around the Columbus, Ohio, wrestling circuit, Frankie Cain followed Lewis' career as a youngster, discussed it with other wrestlers and eventually came to know Lewis to the point that he chauffeured him across the country when the legend's eyes started to fail. "He wasn't a big draw, himself. He had to wait until he got the right opponent. Like everyone else, he was no exception. He wasn't like a Buddy Rogers who could draw without the belt, which he did for years. But Ed, back in those days, he was respected for his wrestling ability. I'd seen him when I was very young and of course, he was over the hill then, but from what the old-timers told me, he was no different than any world champion, as you had to have the right opponent to get those main gates."

What made Lewis stand out from the pack was his hail-fellow-well-met personality, a stark contrast to his in-ring character, whose grinding headlock grip provoked its share of hisses. "If someone told him who was in the rest-room, that he had some fans there, Ed would jump up and go meet him. Actually, he would have made a great politician. Oh yes, oh my, how he could talk!" said Cain, who later became famous as The Great Mephisto. "Ed was probably the only person I've seen who could walk into any newspaper around the country when he was managing wrestlers, and they were thrilled to meet him. He presented himself very well."

His friendly nature probably represented an asset when Lewis aged and remained an active wrestler, since his weight fluctuated between overweight and obese. "I just thought by looking at him in his later years, it must have been a struggle for him to keep in top shape," Cain said. But he came to the ring smiling and he waved at the people. Always had that big smile. That, I think, helped him."

479. *The Wrestler* (magazine), February 1967. 'The Story They Couldn't Tell About Ed (Strangler) Lewis by the Man Who Shared His Secret.' The man, with this untold secret, didn't leave us with his name. I liked his Lewis quotes but don't have a great feel for Lewis' religious pursuits.
480. *National Wrestling Alliance: The Untold Story of the Monopoly That Strangled Pro Wrestling* by Tim Hornbaker, p. 294.
481. *Hooker: The Biography of Lou Thesz* by Lou Thesz with Kit Bauman, pp. 181-182.
482. Over the years, Mark has written a tribute to Strangler Lewis just for this project, and I include it here.

ED "STRANGLER" LEWIS—THE GREATEST
by Mark Hewitt

Ed "Strangler" Lewis boasted that from 1914 through 1940 he was never legitimately defeated in a wrestling match. Was that just bluster, braggadocio, or ballyhoo? There are many opinions on just who was the greatest professional wrestler of all times. Who could have beaten who? Some contend that Frank Gotch ranks as the unbeatable champion heavyweight; other names come up like Joe Stecher and Lou Thesz. How would modern legit grapplers like Kurt Angle and Brock Lesnar or a MMA fighter like Fedor Emelianenko fare against the old-timers? Certainly without a time machine, all this is just conjecture. However, I am in the camp that maintains that Lewis would have ended up on top of the heap in a tournament involving all the greats of all eras.

"Strangler" Lewis was an amazing combination of skill, strength, cunning, and endurance. In fact his stamina was nothing short of phenomenal. He was powerful as a bull. Lewis knew the grappling arts from A to Z. He had an uncanny ability to sense when an opponent was ready to make a move or go after a certain hold, and he was able to block it. "Tigerman" John Pesek, considered by many as one of, if not, the greatest pure catch-as-catch-can wrestlers who ever lived, acknowledged Lewis' mastery on the mat. Pesek remarked stoically, "The Strangler knew how to use his heft expertly."

Lewis' rise to the top really took off on the Lexington/Louisville circuits of Bill Barton and Jerry Walls. When he partnered with the enigmatic Billy Sandow, Lewis exploded onto the national scene, becoming a dominant figure in the pro wrestling heavyweight ranks for the next few decades. Ed Lewis entered into the popular culture of his period. Once his competitive days were past he remained an elder-statesman of the pro wrestling world.

The wild and wooly world of professional wrestling has always been full of smoke and mirrors and circus-like showmanship. But there is also an underlying tradition of tough "shooters" and occasional bona fide contests. Ed "Strangler" Lewis could hold his own on the mat with anybody.

Steve Yohe has done an excellent job of both researching the life and times of Lewis and of penning an interesting and highly-readable biography about this legendary character.

Mark S. Hewitt
2010

483. Over the years, historians have tried to follow the path of the "Lewis Championship Belt." After Joe Stecher dropped the undisputed title to Lewis, he kept his belt (The Stecher Belt). The "Lewis Belt" was awarded to Ed in Kansas City in January 1921 by The Central Athletic Club. When Lewis lost to Stanislaus Zbyszko on May 6, 1921, Stan got the belt along with the title. After defending the title against Lewis on November 28, 1921 in Madison Square Garden, Zbyszko was awarded another belt by promoter Tex Rickard. This belt is called the "Rickard" or Zbyszko belt." In boxing, the tradition is for the new champion to wear the title belt out of the ring, but in the dressing-room, it is given back to the old champion and a new belt is made and later awarded to the new champion. Rickard was a boxing promoter and he gave "Rickard belts" to all the boxing champions, so he gave the same honor to Zbyszko. When Lewis re-won the undisputed title from Stan on March 3, 1922, he got both the "Lewis Belt" and the "Rickard Belt." The "Rickard Belt" is never mention after the May 30, 1925 title title match with Wayne Munn. When Lewis defeated Joe Stecher in St. Louis on February 20, 1928, Stecher again kept his "Stecher Belt" and Lewis just kept using his old belt.

Billy Sandow and Lewis sold the "Lewis Belt," with the title, to Paul Bowser with Gus Sonnenberg victory on January 4, 1929. Sonnenberg gave up the "Lewis" belt after losing in Los Angeles to Ed Don George on December 10, 1930. Lewis did not get the belt back after the double-cross of George on April 13, 1931. Bowser probably gave the belt to Henri Deglane after the bite match in Montreal on May 4, 1931 and passed it back to Ed Don George after losing on February 10, 1933.

George used the belt for a period of time, but by April 23, 1935 Bowser sent the "Lewis Belt" to Lou Daro of Los Angeles. It was awarded to the winner of an International Tournament. Vincent Lopez won the tournament and the "Lewis Belt" on July 24, 1935. Why would Bowser give up his valuable belt? Danno O'Mahoney had been in the tournament and a favorite to win it, but was pulled after Bowser got Jim Londos to agree to job his NWA/NY title to Danno. Lopez used the belt for the rest of 1935 but probably Daro returned it to Bowser in 1936. After that the belt was used over the years as Bowser's AWA championship belt going from Yvon Robert (?), to Steve Casey (February 11-38) to Marv Westenberg (as The Shadow)(March 3, 1939) to Gus Sonnenberg (March 16, 1939) to Steve Casey (March 29, 1939) to Maurice Tillet (May 13, 1940) to Steve Casey (May 13, 1942) to Sandor Szabo (March 29, 1944?) to Yvon Robert (June 14, 1944?) to Steve Casey (May 13, 1942) to Maurice Tillet (August 1, 1944) to Steve Casey (August 15, 1944) to Sandor Szabo (April 25, 1945) to Frank Sexton (May 5, 1945) to Steve Casey (June 6, 1945) to Frank Sexton (June 27, 1945).

From photos the size of the "Lewis Belt" or AWA belt changed, and the feeling of many historians seems to be that there was more than one belt being used. The second belt is not the "Rickard belt," because I have photos, and it looks nothing like the "Lewis Belt."

In 1949, Bowser joined the NWA and he gave the AWA title and use of the belt to Frank Sexton, who was being promoted by Al Haft. It seems Sexton had more than one belt. Frank gave one of them to Don Eagle after dropping the title to Don

Frank Sexton wearing the AWA Lewis Belt, 1946.

Eagle on May 23, 1950. Photos of Eagle from Columbus show him with the belt or a version of the belt. Eagle was kind of a head case and it seems that the title and belt went to Bill Miller (May 1, 1952) and then Buddy Rogers (May 1952). After losing to Eagle, Frank Sexton still claimed the title in Europe and took a very good looking version of the "Lewis Belt" to France, where he dropped both (title and belt) to Felix Miquet in Paris on January 22, 1951. There are photos in the February 1952 issue of *Boxing and Wrestling Magazine* of Felix Miquet presenting the "Lewis Belt" to the man who had defeated him for the European world title, Ivar Martenson.

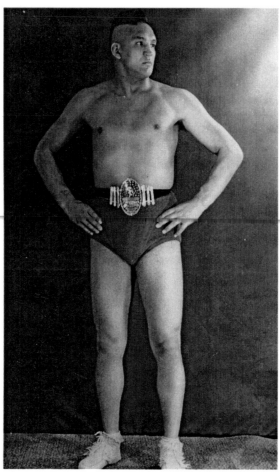

Don Eagle wearing the AWA Lewis Belt, 1951.

I believe the "Lewis Belt" that was used by Buddy Rogers, was returned to its owner Paul Bowser and it remained in his possession until his death in 1960. Attorney George Colbert, executive of the Bowser will, found the belt among Bowser's belongings and put it up for auction in the process of settling the estate. It was purchased by a Boston jeweler, who planned to strip the diamonds and gold. Once he realized the history of the object in his possession, the jeweler changed his mind. A few years later, he sold the belt to George Franklin, head of the Allston Moving Company and a major wrestling fan. He displayed the belt in the window of his office for 18 months, before selling it to local Boston outlaw promoter Tony Santos.

On April 27, 1967, Frank Scarpa won a tournament for the vacant "Big Time Wrestling World Time." After the win, Scarpa was presented with the "Lewis Belt" and there are photos of Scarpa wearing it in Santos' programs next to a Ed Lewis' photo with the belt. Scarpa remained Santos' world champion, until his death in January of 1969. In late 1969 or the early 70's, Santos lent the belt to Cowboy Ron Hill, who used it as a Light Heavyweight title belt. I talked to Hill years ago and he said the belt was dirty and rusted when he got it from Santos, but he cleaned and polished it. Later it was returned to Santos.

On June 2, 1975, the "Lewis belt" was put up for auction, using a sealed bid system, by Santos Promotion (P.O. Box 193 Back Bay, Boston, Mass. 02117). It was billed as the original world's heavyweight title belt, with a picture of Lewis wearing it. It had 34 diamonds 20 pt each and a large center diamond that was 7½ carats. The weight of the gold belt was 2½ pounds. No one knows what happened after that. I think it was stripped and melted down by a jeweler and is in some women's jewelry box today. To me, that Ed "Strangler" Lewis' belt is the Holy Grail of wrestling artifacts.

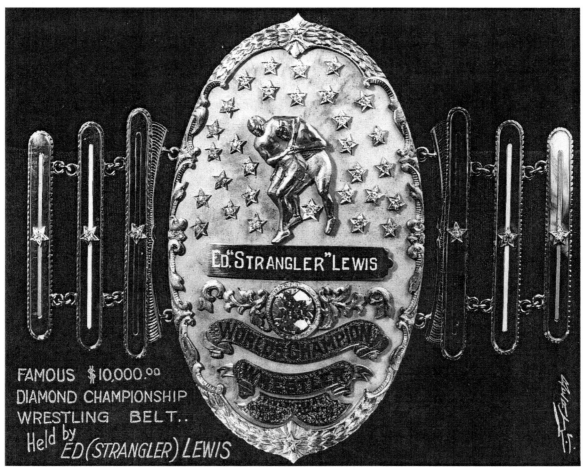

The Ed Lewis Belt

484. *John Pesek: The Wrestler From Ravenna* by Valerie Vierk (granddaughter of John), Mary Lee Pesek (daughter of John) and Geoffrey Pesek (grandson of John).
485. *Tunney* by Jack Cavanaugh, pages 400 to 401.

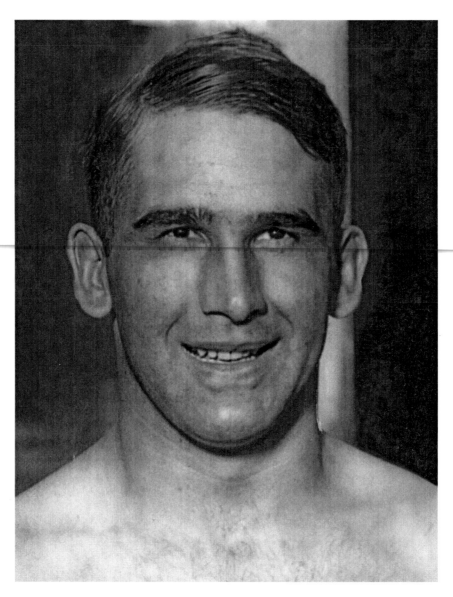

Ed "Strangler" Lewis as a rookie

THE
TITLE HISTORY
&
RING RECORD
OF
ED "STRANGLER" LEWIS

Title History of Ed "Strangler" Lewis

Date Won	Opponent	Date Lost Opponent
AMERICAN TITLE		
1. September 18, 1913	**Dr. Ben F. Roller**	Oct. 22, 1913: William Demetral
2. September 3, 1914	**Dr. Ben F. Roller**	Sept. 29, 1914 Dr. Ben F. Roller
LEWIS PERSONAL WORLD TITLE CLAIM		
1. January 16, 1915	**Dr. Ben F. Roller**	March 21, 1919: Wladek Zbyszko
2. May 19, 1919	**Wladek Zbyszko**	July 4, 1919: Joe Stecher
3. March 3, 1922	**Stanislaus Zbyszko**	Jan. 4, 1929: Gus Sonnenberg
OLIN LINE WORLD TITLE		
1. May 2, 1917	**John Olin**	June 5, 1917: Wladek Zbyszko
2. July 4, 1917	**Wladek Zbyszko**	March 21, 1919: Wladek Zbyszko
UNDISPUTED WORLD TITLE		
1. December 13, 1920	**Joe Stecher**	May 6, 1921: Stanislaus Zbyszko
2. March 3, 1922	**Stanislaus Zbyszko**	January 8, 1925: Wayne Munn
3. February 20, 1928	**Joe Stecher**	January 4, 1929: Gus Sonnenberg
WORLD JIU-JITSU TITLE		
1. December 14	**Taro Miyake**	? (Forgotten)
AMERICAN WRESTLING ASSOCIATION (AWA) WORLD TITLE		
1. April 13, 1931	**Ed Don George**	May 4, 1931: Henri Deglane
ILLINOIS WORLD TITLE		
1. November 2, 1931	**Wladek Zbyszko**	Feb. 20, 1933 ?: Jim Browning
NEW YORK STATE WORLD TITLE		
1. October 10, 1932	**Jack Sherry**	Feb. 20, 1933: Jim Browning
KANSAS CITY MWA WORLD TITLE		
1. November 26, 1942	**Orville Brown**	Jan. 14, 1943: Lee Wykoff
COLUMBUS MWA WORLD TITLE		
1. December 3, 1942	**Orville Brown**	Jan. 28, 1943: John Pesek

The Ed "Strangler" Lewis Ring Record

Researched & Compiled by: J Michael Kenyon, Don Luce, Mark Hewett, Steve Yohe, Dan Anderson, Fred Hornby, Richard Haynes, Libnan Ayoub, Steve Johnson, and Scott Teal.

1890

June 30	Nekoosa, WI	Robert Herman Julius Friedrich born to Jacob and Molla (Molly) Friederich of Nekoosa, Wisconsin. He was the third son in a family with four sons. Two of his brothers' names were Herman and Emil.	

1901

?	Pittsfield, WI	**George Brown**	**Won (UTC)**
?	Nekoosa, WI	Bob apparently moved to Nekoosa	
?	Nekoosa, WI	**Fred Abel**	**Won**
?	Nekoosa, WI	**Ernest Lindsay** (2:00:00)	**Draw**
?	Rhinelander, WI	Bob's Uncle Emil gets him a job lifting 100-pound paper bundles in a paper mill in Rhinelander. Friedrich claimed his great strengh came from this job that he held for two years.	

1903 ?

1908

January 2	Nekoosa, WI	Friedrich left town, after spending holiday with parents, to return to Rhinelander.	
March 26	Rhinelander, WI	Friedrich went to Portage to play for Antigo in a basketball tournament. Marshfield, Wausau, Portage, and Sheboygan in tournament.	
June 18	Nekoosa, WI	Friedrich's parents with sister Emma going to Sheboygan to attend silver wedding anniversary of an uncle Gust Haring.	
July 30	Nekoosa, WI	Friedrich visits his parents in Nekoosa. He came from Camp Douglas were he was camped with the Rhinelander Company of the State Militia.	
October 15	Rhinelander, WI	Friedrich leaves for Wausau after accepting a job at a store there. He also was to play basketball during the winter.	

1909

?	Minneapolis, MN	Left Rhinelander for metropolis of Minneapolis. Worked in the drug store of Oscar Zirker. Lived at an appartment owned by a Mrs. Smith and located at 11th and Hannepin. His roommate was a cook. Rent was $5 a week.	
?	Minneapolis, MN	Worked out with Henry Ordemann.	

1910

?		Played baseball in the Blue Grass League.	
February 10	Minneapolis, MN	**Stanislaus Zbyszko*** Bob Frederick was part of a handicap match Zbyszko had with three men. The other two were Joe Carr and an unknown, possibly Carl Mattson. Managed that night by Billy Potts. Zbyszko praised Ed as the strongest man of his age he had ever seen.	**Lost**
October 21	Nekoosa, WI	In town visiting relatives.	
November 11	Grand Rapids, WI	**Jack Foley***	**Won (2-1)**
November 20 (19)	Rudolph, WI	**Dave Sharkey***	**Won (2-1)**
November 25	Nekoosa, WI	**Dave Sharkey***	**Won (2-0)**
December 19	Arcadia, WI	**Jack Foley**	**?**
December 21	Nekoosa, WI	**Albert Abel***	**Won (2-0)**

1911

January 3	Grand Rapids, WI	**Fred Beell***	**Lost (0-2)**
?	Grand Rapids, WI ?	**Frank Gotch (Handicap Match 14:00)**	**Lost**
February 3	Nekoosa, WI	Bob leaves town for the west. He claims he's booked enough matches to last until June.	
March 10	Glen Ullin, ND	**F. F. Manford** Friedrich defending the Western Championship.	**Won (2-1)**
May 11	Nekoosa, WI	Bob writes home stating he is captain of the Glen Ullin baseball team and plays second base. Says he plans to return home by July 4.	
July 4	Nekoosa, WI	**Abel**	**Won**

July 15	Sheboygan Falls, WI?	**Walter Miller***	**Won (2-0)**
July 24	Sheboygan Falls, WI	**Walter Miller (1:30:00)***	**Won (6-1)**
August 3	Sheboygan Falls, WI	Jacob Friedrich, Marshal of Nekoosa, at Born's Park Sanitarium. Has had a bad back since June. Getting better. He was brought to town by son Bob.	
August 25	Grand Rapids, WI	**Jack (?) Little**	**?**
September 4	Chicago, IL	Friedrich present to see Frank Gotch defeat George Hackenschmidt.	
September 8	Sheboygan Falls, WI	**Fred Beell**	**?**
September 9	Rudolph, WI	**Dave Sharley***	**Won (2-0)**
September 14	Sheboygan Falls, WI	**Jack Downs***	**Won (2-0)**

Bob Friedrich was probably living in McGregor, IA.

October 6	McGregor, IA	**Helmuth Preuss**	**Won**
October 16	Nekoosa, WI	Robert comes to Nekoosa for the funeral of his brother Fred Friedrich.	
November ?	Lansing, IA	?	

1912

January 8	McGregor, IA	**Ed Prior (Boxing)**	**?**
January 27	Sheboygan Falls, WI	**Martin Martenson**	**Won (2-1)**
February 1	Nekoosa, WI	Jacob Friedrich hired as a policeman for the city of Nekoosa. He was 53 years old and stayed on the job for 28 years.	
February 12	La Crosse, WI	Listed as a referee.	
February ?	Lansing, IA	**Jack Little (Handicap)**	**Lost (FTP?)**
March 7	Lansing, IA	**Jack Little** (weight was 210 lbs.)	**Won (2-0)**
March ?	Lansing, IA	**Avery of Madison**	**?**
March 29	La Crosse, WI	**Joe Carr (Handicap Match)** (wrestled as a sub. referee the first match on card)	**FTP**

April 9	Minneapolis, MN	Robert Friedrich applied to work on the police force. Might have been given a position. Dating a Louise Leuhener.	
April 15	Newfoundland, Canada	The ocean liner RMS *Titanic* sinks.	
October 26	Sheboygan Falls, WI	**James Souden** (1:50:00)	**UTC**
November 8	Lansing, IA	Returned from Wisconsin after two week visit.	
November 25	Lansing, IA	Wrestling banned by town mayor.	
December 9	McGregor, IA	**Jud Thompson*** Friederich was billed from Lansing, Iowa & a coach at Kentucky University. From research this would seem to be false.	**FTP**
December 12	Lansing, IA	Newspaper says Robert Friedrich left Tuesday for his home in Wisconsin. He was running a motion picture house in Lansing during this period.	

1913

January 10	Louisville, KY	**William Demetral** Bob Friedrich no show match, and he is replaced by Bobby Managoff, who uses the name Bob Frederick. Later in the month, the real Friedrich shows but his name is being used, so he is given the ring name of Ed "Strangler" Lewis. He uses the name for the rest of his life.	**No Show**
January 10	Galesburg, IL	**Cyclone Thompson**	**Won**
January 24	Louisville, KY	**Bob Frederick (Bobby Managoff)**	**Won**
January 31	Louisville, KY	**William Demetral**	**UTC**
February 6	Lexington, KY	**Bob Fredericks (Bobby Managoff)**	**FTP**
February 7	Louisville, KY	Ringside at Stone / Fredericks match	
Fenruary 19	Lexington, KY	**Jack Stone (Ivan Linow ?)**	**Won**
February 21	Louisville, KY	**Doc Gomer**	**Won**
March 6	Lexington, KY	**Harry Faust**	**Won**
March 12	Lexington, KY	**Gus Chamos**	**Won**

March 14	Louisville, KY	**Young Olsen**	**Draw**
March 28	Lexington, KY	**Young Olsen***	**Won (KO)**
April 8	Lexington, KY	**Ed Schultz**	**?**
April 17	Lexington, KY	**Ed Schultz**	**Won**
April 18	Louisville, KY	**William Demetral**	**Won (2-0)**
April 28	Lexington, KY	**Young Olsen**	**Won**
May 5	Lexington, KY	**Bob Fredericks (Stopped By Police)***	**No Contest**
May 9	Louisville, KY	**William Demetral** (Strangle Hold Barred)	**Lost (0-2)**
May 14	Lexington, KY	**Dr. B. F. Roller*** (Strangle Hold Barred)	**Lost (0-2)**
May 21	Lexington, KY	**Bob Fredericks*** (Lewis vomited during 2nd fall)	**Lost**
June 5	Lexington, KY	**Jack Stone (Ivan Linow)** (3 Hours)	**Draw**
June 17	Lexington, KY	**Dr. B. F. Roller** (Strangle hold barred in 2nd & 3rd falls)	**Lost (1-2)**
June 25	Paris, KY	**Bob Managoff**	**Won**
June 30	Lexington, KY	**Farmer James**	**?**
July ?		Lewis works in Wisconsin and / or Oregon lumber camps as a training regimen during July and August.	
September 12	Lexington, KY	**Gus Costello**	**Won (0-2)**
?	Richmond, VA	**Hjalmar Lundin ?** Lundin claimed to have wrestled lewis in his book.	**Won**
September 18	Lexington, KY	**Dr. B. F. Roller** (American Title Win)	**Won (UTC)**
September 29	Lexington, KY	**William Demetral** (Stopped by police after between fall fight.)	**No Contest**
October 21	Lexington, KY	**William Demetral** (American Title Loss)	**UTC**

November 3	Chicago, IL	**Paul Martinson**	**Won**
November 10	Chicago, IL	Charley Cutler proclaimed himself, as American champion, to be world champion. He claims he was given permission by Frank Gotch.	
November 11	Lexington, KY	**Jack Leroy**	**Won (2-0)**
November 14	Chicago, IL	**Karl Schulz**	**Won**
		Fred Anson	**Won**
November 15	Chicago, IL	**Paul Raas**	**Won**
November 18	Chicago, IL	Lewis got into a fight with Charley Cutler at a downtown restaurant while negotiating a proposed match and purse.	
November 20	Chicago, IL	**The Mysterious Horseshoer (G. Shafford)**	**Won**
November 21	Louisville, KY	**Young Olsen** Paper reports that Lewis was discovered by W. H. Barton while Ed was instructor at University of Kentucky. Now managed by J. M. Wells of Chicago. Young Olsen was billed as the younger brother of Charles Olsen but photos show that it might have been Charles himself.	**Won (2-0)**
November 26	Chicago, IL	**Charles Cutler**	**Lost**
November 29	Chicago, IL	**Jack Sajatoric**	**Won**
December 1	Chicago, IL	**Andre Anderson**	**Won**
December 2	Lexington, KY	**Tom Jenkins**	**Won**
December 5	Lexington, KY	Referee at Billy Jenkins vs Giant Wallace match promoted by Billy Sandow.	
December 15	Lexington, KY	**Billy Jenkins** Jenkins was managed by Billy Sandow.	**Won (2-0)**
December 16	Lexington, KY	**Gus Kervaros?**	**Won**
December 19	Louisville, KY	**Gus Kuvaras**	**Won (2-0)**
December 25	Lexington, KY	**Billy Jenkins**	**Won (2-0)**
December 26	Chicago, IL	Manager is Jerry M. Walls, who promotes in Lexington.	

December 29	Chicago, IL	Gus "Americus" Schoenlein	Lost (0-2)

1914

January 7	Lexington, KY	Referee for Roller vs Mysterious Conductor.	
January 28	Lexington, KY	Dr. B. F. Roller*	Lost
January 29	Lexington, KY	Tommy Devereaux (Exhibition)	Won
January 30	Lexington, KY	Lewis wrestled all comers following performance of Ada Meade Vaudeville Troop.	
February 3	Lexington, KY	Charles "The Mysterious Conductor" Challender*	Won
February 5	Lexington, KY	Billy Sandow* Match followed an Ada Meade Vaudeville Show and Sandow was given $1 for each min. He stayed with Lewis. He made $10. Lewis's manager was still Jerry Walls.	Won
February 9	Chicago, IL	Fred Beel*	Lost
February 10	Lexington, KY	Marvin Plestina* (2:00:00) Billy Sandow managed Plestina.	Draw
February 18	Lexington, KY	Marvin Plestina* (DQ in 1st Fall)	DQ (2-0)
March 23	Lexington, KY	Stanislaus Zbyszko (Handicap)* Zbyszko was to win 2 falls in a hour but only got one. Stanislaus was claiming the world title. Largest crowd in Lexington history.	Won (FTP)
March 27	Louisville, KY	Emil Broggilla	Won (2-0)
March 30	Lexington, KY	Ivan "The Terrible" Mamutoff* Mamutoff's manager was Ed White.	Won (2-0)
April 3	Louisville, KY	Tom Dodge*	Won (2-0)
April 7	Detroit, MI	Wladek Zbyszko	N. C.
April 23	Buffalo	Wladek Zbyszko*	Lost (2-0-UTC)
April 27	Lexington, KY	Charles Cutler*	Lost
?	Springfield, MA	?	?
?	Macon, GA	?	?

May 29	Lexington, KY	**Jack Stone***	**N. C.**
		(Referee stopped match because of torn mat.)	
June 1	Mt. Sterling, KY	**Sebastian Miller**	**?**
December 2	Springfield	**Dr. B. F. Roller**	**Lost**

1915

February 13	Chicago, IL	**Joe Geshtowt***	**Won**
February 20	Chicago, IL	**Paul Martinson***	**Won (2-0)**
February 20	Chicago, IL	In the office of the *Chicago Tribune*, Charles Cutler, the American title holder, claimed Frank Gotch's World Title. He claims to have been undefeated in last two years. His manager was William Rochells.	
April 30	Lexington, KY	**Franz Hockman**	**Won**
May 10	Lexington, KY	**Charley Cutler***	**DQ**
May 28	Lexington, KY	**Yussif Hussane***	**Won (DQ)**
July 5	Chicago, IL	Ringside to see Joe Stecher defeat Charles Cutler for World Title. Lewis claimed he lost $2,500 betting on Cutler.	
October 20	Evensville	**Joe Stecher** (World Title)*	**COR**
October 29	Chicago, IL	**Paul Martinson**	**?**
November 4	Chicago, IL	**Bob Managoff**	**Won**
	New York, NY	Enters international wrestling tournament at Manhattan Opera House.	
November 22	New York, NY	**Loren Z. Christiansen**	**Won**
November 23	New York, NY	**Fritz Mohl***	**Won**
November 25	New York, NY	**Al Maskut***	**Won**
November 26	New York, NY	**Ivan Linow***	**Won (UTC)**
November 27	New York, NY	**Harry Litofsky***	**Won**
November 30	New York, NY	**Wladek Zbyszko** (20 Min)*	**Draw**

December 1	New York, NY	**Pierre Le Colosse***	**Won**
December 2	New York, NY	**Sula Hevonpaa***	**Draw**
December 3	New York, NY	**Wilhelm Ernest***	**Won**
December 4	New York, NY	**Alex Aberg (20:00)***	**Draw**
December 7	New York, NY	**Charles Cutler***	**Draw**
December 9	New York, NY	**Alex Aberg (1:04:00)***	**Draw**
December 10	New York, NY	**Wladek Zbyszko (20:00)***	**Draw**
December 11	New York, NY	**Wladek Zbyszko (20:00)***	**Draw**
December 13	New York, NY	**Wilhelm Ernest***	**Won**
December 14	New York, NY	**Demetrius Tolalos***	**Draw**
December 15	New York, NY	**Hjaimar Johnson***	**Won**
December 16	New York, NY	**Big Hons**	**?**
December 16	New York, NY	**Herman Schilling***	**Won**
December 18	New York, NY	**Demetrius Tolalos***	**Draw**
December 20	New York, NY	**Masked Marvel (Mort Henderson)***	**Won**
December 21	New York, NY	**Sula Hevonpaa***	**Won**
December 22	New York, NY	**Masked Marvel (1:59:00)***	**Draw**
December 23	New York, NY	**Jack McGrath***	**Draw**
December 24	New York, NY	**Albert Vogel**	**Won**
December 25	New York, NY	**Jack McGrath**	**Won**
December 28	New York, NY	**Fritz Muller**	**Won**
December 29	New York, NY	**Alex Aberg (Graeco-Roman Rules)***	**Lost**
December 30	New York, NY	**Carl Vogel**	**Won**

1916

January 3	New York, NY	**Masked Marvel** (2:31:00)	**Draw**
January 6 (7)	New York, NY	**Wladek Zbyszko**	**Draw**
January 8	New York, NY	**Hjalmar Lundin**	**Won**
January 12	New York, NY	**Dr. B. F. Roller**	**Draw**
January 13	New York, NY	**Anton Irsa**	**Won**
January 15	New York, NY	**Dr. B. F. Roller***	**Won**

Manager Billy Sandow claimed World Title as a result of this win.

January 17	New York, NY	**Wladek Zbyszko** (1:21:07)	**Won**
January 18	New York, NY	**Pete Zelesnow***	**Won**
January 19	New York, NY	**Dr. B. F. Roller**	**Draw**
January 21	Boston, MA	Worked out with Renato Gardini	
January 26	Springfield, MA	**Dr. B. F. Roller**	**Won (2-0)**
January 27	New York, NY	**Fritz Mohl***	**Won**
January 29	New York, NY ?	**George Bayley?**	**Won**
February 17	Norfolk	**Masked Marvel (Mort Henderson)**	**Won (2-0)**
February 18	New Haven	**Masked Marvel (Mort Henderson)**	**Won**
February 23	Norfolk	**Dr. Ben Roller**	**Won (2-0)**
March 6	MSG, NYC	**Hans Fuerst**	**Won**
		Albert Miller	**Won**
		Carl Vogel	**Won**
		Carl Nelson	**Won**
		Herman Schilling	**Won**
		Farmer Bailey	**Won**
March 8	Hartford	**Tom Draak**	**Won**

March 16	Norfolk	**Antone Irsa**	**Won (2-0)**
March 22	Hartford	**Soldier Leavitt** Who would become Man Mountain Dean in 1934.	**Won**
April 10	Hartford	**Masked Marvel**	**Won**
April 11	Brattleboro	**Tom Draak**	**Won**
April 26	Norfolk	**Ivan Linow**	**Won (UTC)**
May 2	New York, NY	**Masked Marvel**	**Won (2-0)**
May 17	New York, NY	Alexander Aberg got a temporary injunction from a Judge Mayer to stop Lewis from posing as a champion wrestler, and using posters detailing his defeat of Aberg for world honors. Aberg cited his win over Lewis in a recent bout.	
July 4	Omaha	**Joe Stecher** (World Title)* (Att.: 20,000-Time: 4:51:33)	**Draw**
July 12		Manager Billy Sandow posted $1,000 bond for match with Frank Gotch.	
September 28	Savannah, GA	**Tom Draak** Savannah, GA was promoted by Max Baumann, Sandow's brother.	**Won (2-0)**
October 9	Savannah, GA	**Hjalmar Lundin**	**Won (2-0)**
October 20	Savannah, GA	**Ben F. Roller** Roller was claiming a world title saying he had defeated Charley Cutler.	**Draw**
		Billy Peters	**Won**
November 5	Savannah, GA	**Constant Lemarin** (1:20:00) Lewis injured his shoulder but referee wouldn't render a decision.	**Draw**
November 13	Canton, OH	**Paul Martinson**	**Won (2-0)**
November 20	Canton, OH	**William Demetral** (Handicap)	**FTP**
November 30	Billings, MT	**Pat Connolly**	**Won (2-0-UTC)**
December 3	Savannah, GA	**Constant Lemarin** (1:08:55)	**Won (2-1)**

December 11	Springfield, MA	Joe Stecher is declared a loser when he quits a match with John Olin after 2 hrs and 40 minutes. Stecher still claims the title, but so does Olin and his followers.	
December 12	San Francisco, CA	**Ad Santel** (2:00:00)* (Att.: 7,500)	**WOF**
December 22	Los Angeles, CA	**Nick (Dick) Daviscourt**	**Won (2-0)**
December 25	Savannah, GA	**Constant Lemarin** (1:15:00)	**Won (2-0)**

1917

January 1	Dodge	In a letter to SF promoter Frank Schuler, Stecher's manager refuses to wrestle Lewis in any other city but Omaha due to poor showing by Ed on July 4.	
January 2	San Francisco, CA	**Ad Santel** (2:30:01)* Att: 5,000, $6,275, the largest crowd in West Coast history. Lewis made $1,882.25	**Draw**
January 8	Los Angeles, CA	**Gus Kervaras***	**Won (2-0-DQ)**
January 15	Ogden, UT	**Pete Visser**	**Won (UTC)**
January 15	Excelsior Springs, MO	It is reported that Joe Stecher is recovering from a nervous breakdown. It is rumored this neuritis attack is the reason he was unable to continue versus John Olin.	
January 22	Los Angeles, CA	**Gus Kervaras***	**Won (2-0)**
February 5 (13)	Los Angeles, CA	**Paul Martinson**	**Won (2-0)**
February 19	Canton, OH	**Ivan Linow**	**Won (2-0)**
February 28	Norfolk	**John Freberg** (WC)*	**Won (UTC)**
March 8	Norfolk	**Charley Cutler***	**Won (2-0)**
March 26	Houston	**Charley Cutler**	**Won (2-0)**
April 2	Canton, OH	**Dr. B. F. Roller**	**Won (2-0)**
April 6		United States declared war With Germany and joins WWI.	
April 9	Omaha	Earl Caddock defeats Joe Stecher for World Title.	

April 18	Baltimore, MD	**Americus**	**Won**
May 2	Chicago, IL	**John Olin** (World Title Win-Olin Line)*	**Won (UTC)**
		Time was 2 hrs & 37 mins. Referee was Frank Gotch who praised Lewis.	
May 21	Canton, OH	**Dr. B. F. Roller**	**Won (2-0)**
June 5	San Francisco, CA	**Wladek Zbyszko** (World Title Loss)	**LOF**
June 14	San Francisco, CA	Ed still in town vacationing.	
June 21	San Francisco, CA	Lewis gives a deposition in a court case involving a Dr. Andrew W. Morton suing his ex-wife Dr. Ada Scott Morton in an attempt to recover $70,000 worth of property deeded to her by him in February 1917. Dr. Morton was claiming fraud and misrepresentation.	
July 4	Boston, MA	**Wladek Zbyszko** (World Title win)	**Won (2-1-UTC)**
September 3	Birmingham, AL	**Wladek Zbyszko** (WC)	**Draw**
October 5		World champion Earl Caddock accepted by U.S. Army	
October 8	Canton, OH	Ringside at Londos vs Ed Schultz	
October 29	Canton, OH	**Alan Eustace**	**Cancelled**
November 1	Houston, TX	**Wladex Zbyszko / Charles Cutler***	**No Show**
		Sandow refused to let Lewis wrestle because the promoter hadn't paid $1,000 in advance.	
November 5	Savannah, GA	**Constant Lemarin** (1:20:00)	**Draw**
November 29	Canton, OH	**Jim Londos***	**Won (2-0-UTC)**
December 3	Savannah, GA	**Constant Lemarin** (1:48:00)	**Won**
		Lewis entered internation catch-as-catch-can tournament at Lexington Theater, NYC.	
December 5	New York, NY	**Charles Pospishil**	**Won**
December 6	New York, NY	**Frank Leavitt**	**Won**
December 7	New York, NY	**Fred Pilakoff**	**Won**
December 8	New York, NY	**Sula Hevonpaa**	**Won**

December 11	New York, NY	Ivan Linow	Won
December 14	New York, NY	Pierre Le Belge	Won
December 15	New York, NY	Wladek Zbyszko	Draw
December 17	New York, NY	Wladek Zbyszko* (Att.-3,000)	Won
December 18	New York, NY	Dr. B.F. Roller	Won
December 19	New York, NY	Tom Draak	Won
December 20	New York, NY	George Manich	Won
December 21	New York, NY	Demetrius Tofalos	Won
December 22	New York, NY	Wladek Zbyszko (Tournament Final)* Wladek was given World Title belt for winning the tournament. Headlock was banned in matches and Lewis continued to claim the title via the Olin line.	Lost
December 25	Savannah, GA	Constant Lemarin (1:15:00)	Won

1918

January 1	Canton, OH	Jim Londos (2:30:00)*	Draw
January 4	Savannah, GA	Wladek Zbyszko (1:15:00) (Report had Lewis breaking a rib.)	Draw
January 24	Savannah, GA	Ivan Linow (37:00)	Won
		Constant Lemarin (53:00)	Draw
January 26	Atlanta, GA	Tom Draak	Won (2-0)
February 1	Savannah, GA	Ivan Linow (1:39:45)	Won (1-0)
February 8	Des Moines, IA	Caddock defeats Wladek Zbyszko via decision in a title unification match.	
February 13	Atlanta, GA	B. F. Roller (1:11:07)	Won (2-0)
March 1	Savannah, GA	Ivan Linow	Won
March 13	Atlanta, GA	B. F. Roller (1:04:00)	Won (2-0)
March 15	Savannah, GA	John Olin (1:13:00)	Won

March 19	New York, NY	**Wladek Zbyszko***	**Won (DQ)**
March 21	Canton, OH	**Al Eustace***	**Cancelled**

April 6 — A Canton newspaper reports that Lewis is temporarily retired due to an infectious disease. He was taken to the West coast to see a specialist by his wife, whom he married a few months before.

April 26	MSG, NYC	**Joe Stecher***(2:00:00)	**Draw**
May 10	Louisville, KY	**Wladek Zbyszko***	**Won (Decision)**

May 15 — Des Moines, IA — Manager Billy Sandow is in Des Moines trying to land a match with champion Caddock. He says Lewis is to enter army at Camp Gordon, Augusta, Georgia in a short time, and wants a match before Ed goes to camp.

June 17 (18)	Sioux City, IA	**John Freburg**	**Won (UTC)**
June 21	Des Moines, IA	**Earl Caddock** (WC)*	**Lost (Decision)**

July 18 — Los Angeles, CA — Lewis is in town.

July 27 — Rockford, IL — Ed Lewis was one of the new army recruits stationed at Camp Grant at Rockville, IL. He is on the wrestling team that is scheduled to meet Camp Dodge, home of Caddock, in Chicago on August 9.

August 24 — Great Lakes, IL — Stecher, rookie seaman, wants an Army-Navy championship bout with Lewis, an instructor at Camp Grant.

October 4 — Europe — A ceasefire is called between central powers and allied forces.

November 11 — France — The Armistice is signed and WWI ends.

November 29	Chicago, IL	**Bob Managoff**	**Won (2-0)**
December 7	Chicago, IL	**John Freberg**	**No Show**

December ? — Rockville, IL — A December 30 *Waterloo* report has Lewis discharged from the army.

December ?	Montreal, Canada	**Dr. Ben Roller**	**Won (2-0)**

(The match took place a few days after discharge. He then went home for the holidays.)

1919

January 4   Ringside for Londos vs Joe Turner. He is said to be suffering from injuries incurred in 1918. He is a Sergeant in the U.S. Army.

Date	Location	Opponent	Result
January 18	Chicago, IL	**Paul Martinson**	**Draw**
January 25	Chicago, IL	**Paul Martinson**	**Won**
February 12	Norfolk	**John Olin*** (Biggest crowd of the season, with 200 turned away.)	**Won (2-1)**
February 20	Boston, MA	**Jim Eagan**	**Won (2-0)**
February 20	Chicago, IL	Lewis training with Paul Martinson at the Chicago Athletic Association gym.	
March 1	Chicago, IL	Still in Chicago training for Stecher. He is ringside for the Evans / young Demetral match.	
March 3	Chicago, IL	**Joe Stecher***(2:12:30) (Att.: 7,000, $12,000)	**Won**
March 5	Springfield, MA	**John Freberg**	**Won**
March 6	Richmond, VA	**Ivan Madvas**	**Won (2-0)**
March 7	Norfolk	**Wladek Zbyszko** (2:30:00)(WC)* (Att.: 1,100)	**Draw**
March 14	Utica, NY	**Joe Malcewicz** (WC) (Lewis billed himself as world champion.)	**Won**
March 19	Montreal, Canada	**Dr. Ben Roller**	**Won**
March 20	Boston, MA	**Jim Eagan**	**Won**
March 21	MSG, NYC	**Wladek Zbyszko** (World Title Loss) (Att.: sold out, with 5,000 turned away. 1:34:37)	**Lost**
March 26	Norfolk, VA	**Gus "Americus" Schoenlein***	**Won**
March 27	Richmond, VA	**John Olin**	**Won (UTC)**
April 1	Harrisburg, PA	**Dr. B. F. Roller**	**Won (UTC)**
April 4	Kansas City	**John Olin**	**Won (2-0)**

(Announces engagement to Dr. Ada Scott Morton. She says she operated on Lewis two years previously after he broke his ankle at Butte, Montana.)

April ?	Pontiac, MI	Lewis' grandfather, Carl Guildenzopf, died after a major stroke. He was born on September 9, 1934 in Germany and moved to America in 1881 and Port Edwards in 1886. He was a farmer in the area until a few years before his death. The funeral were held on a Wednesday and internment was in a local cemetery in Nekoosa. The report was dated September 17, 1919.	
April 24	Sheboygan Falls, WI	**?**	**?**
April 28	Chicago, IL	**Wladek Zbyszko*** (Att.: 6,000, $9,924)	**Lost**
May 1	Omaha	Lewis refuses to post $1,500 forfeit with promoter Gene Melady and backs out of the match that was to take place in late May because he would be forced to forfeit money if match didn't go to a two fall finish.	
May 7	Newark	**Anton Swoboda**	**Won (2-0)**
May 8	Chicago, IL	The Associated Press reports that a $2250 belt, emblematic of the World's Championship, will be presented to the winner of the Wladek Zbyszko / Ed Lewis match on May 19, by the Coliseum Athletic Club. Many of the wrestling promoters in the country had contributed to the cost of the trophy. It will become the private property of the holder after he defends it five times.	
May 8	Mercer, PA	Marries Dr. Ada Scott Morton. The two had met in 1917 (?) when the doctor treated Lewis for a broken leg in San Jose, CA.	
May 8	Youngstown	**Ivan Linow**	**Won**
May 14	Excelsior Springs, MO	Lewis has been training with boxer Jack Dempsey who is getting ready for a fight with Jess Willard. Lewis had been in area for a week but leaves soon after for Chicago.	
May 19	Chicago, IL	**Wladek Zbyszko*** (Att.: 6,000, Gate: $11,900, Lewis' purse: $5,287.50, Wladek purse: $1,762.50. Lewis claims World Title.)	**Won (2-1)**
May 23	New York, NY	Sgt. Earl Caddock returns to the USA from the war in France. Says he will try to train at his ranch in Wyoming.	
June 5	Davenport	**John Freberg** (A riot started after Lewis threw Freberg out of ring. Stopped by police.)	**No Contest**
June 9	Grand Rapids	**Tom Draak**	**Won (1-0-UTC)**

Date	Location	Opponent	Result
June 11	Omaha, NE	**Jim Londos***	**Won (2-0)**
July 4	Omaha, NE	**Joe Stecher*** (Referee was Earl Caddock. Att.: 5,000 - the largest in Omaha history. Winner take all match.)	**Lost (0-2)**
July 4	Toledo	Jack Dempsey KO's Jess Willard to win boxing's World Heavyweight title.	
August 5	San Francisco, CA	**Ivan Grandovich**	**Won (2-0)**
August 19	San Francisco, CA	**vs Dante Petroff** (Handicap Match)	**Won**
		vs Jim Londos (Handicap Match)	**FTP**

(Lewis was to pin both in 2 hours. He got Petroff in 1:15:32 and couldn't pin Londos with the remaining time.)

Date	Location	Opponent	Result
September 9 ?	Santa Ana, CA	Visiting his ranch, Lewis spanked a man who was tresspasting on his land after the man pulled a gun.	
October 7	San Francisco, CA	**Tom Draak**	**Won (2-0)**
October 10	Chicago, IL	Cincinnati won the 1919 World Series over the Chicago White Sox.	
October 14	San Francisco, CA	**Tom Draak**	**Won (2-0)**
November 3	Dodgeville, WI	The first Strangler, Evans "Strangler" Lewis, dies.	
November 3	MSG, NYC	**Joe Stecher*** (Att.: Sold Out)	**Lost**
November 6	Boston, MA	**Alex Jarrison**	**?**
November 21	Richmond, VA	**George Stanislaus**	**Won**
November 27	Boston, MA	**Wladek Zbyszko*** (Att.: 6,500. First bout held under new American Wrestling Association championship rules.)	**Lost**
December 1	Chicago, IL	**John Olin**	**Won (2-0)**
December 8	Mason City, IA	**Helmer Myre**	**Won**
December 12	Rockford, IL	**John Freberg**	**?**
December 23	San Francisco, CA	**John Olin**	**Won (2-1)**
December 30	San Francisco, CA	**Gus Kervoras**	**Won (2-0)**

1920

January 9	Kearney	**Tom Draak**	**Won**
January 20	Wichita	**Ivan Linow**	**Won**
January 21	Kansas City, MO	**Ivan Kranloff**	**Won (2-0)**
January 22	Armavir, Russia	George Lurich dies from typhoid.	
January 27	Utica, NY	**John Grandovich** (Handicap)	**Won**
		Joe Malcewicz (Handicap)	**FTP**
January 29	Boston, MA	**Tom Draak**	**Won**
January 30	MSG, NYC	Ringside to see Stecher win title from Caddock.	
January 31	New York, NY	It is announced that Stanisiaus Zbyszko was returning to America.	
February 4	Norfolk, VA	**Jim Londos** (Handicap Match)(2:00:00)	**FTP (0-0)**
		(Ed was to pin Londos three times in 2 hrs. No falls recorded.)	
February 15	Armavir, Russia	Alex Aberg died from typhoid. He and George Lurich were buried in one grave at the Armavir German Cemetery.	
February 16	Kansas City, MO	**Wladek Zbyszko**	**Won**
March 2	MSG, NYC	**Jim Londos** (2:00:04) (Att.: Sold out)	**Won**
March 4	Norfolk	**Salvadore Chevalier**	**Won (2-0)**
March 10	Rochester	**Jack Edwards**	**Won (2-0)**
March 11	Gloversville	**Ivan Madvas**	**Won (2-0)**
March 12	Utica, NY	**Joe Malcewicz** (Handicap)	**FTP**
March 13	Kansas City, MO	**Wladek Zbyszko**	**Won**
March 15	MSG, NYC	**Earl Caddock** (Att.: Sold out, >11,000)	**Won**
March 17	Brooklyn, NY	**Frank Yurko**	**Won**
March 18	Boston, MA	**Stanley Stasiak**	**Won**

| March 25 | Norfolk | **Hassen Managoff** | **Won (2-0)** |

| March 29 | Norfolk | Lewis drops out of match with Jim Londos on March 31. Sandow claimed Lewis was in training for Stecher and didn't want to risk a match with Londos. | |

| April 8 | Boston, MA | **Sampson Orlando**** | **Won** |

| April 16 | New York, NY | **Joe Stecher** (WC)*(3:00:04) | **Lost** |

| April 25 | Norfolk | Promoter Norman Hoffheimer says he's signed Lewis to meet Londos on April 30. | |

| April 29 | Norfolk | Lewis drops out of match with Londos. Sandow says he doesn't want to bring Lewis back East. | |

| May 20 | Boston, MA | **Sampson Jack Orlando** | **?** |

| May 20 | NY State | The James J. Walker Boxing Bill is signed into law by Governor Al Smith. This bill legalized boxing in New York State and has controlled boxing and wrestling in the state to present time. A three man Commission was set up and ruled that virtually everyone connected with ring sports be licensed. | |

| May 21 | The Bronx, NY | **Ivan Linow** (1:29:00) | **Won** |

| May 27 | Boston, MA | **Jack Orlando** | **Won** |

| May 31 | The Bronx, NY | **Ivan Linow** | **Won** |

| June 8 | Des Moines, IA | **Earl Caddock*** | **Lost (1-2)** |

| July ? | San Jose, CA | Lewis's daughter is born. She is given the first name of Bobada. | |

| September 6 | Benton Harbor | Jack Dempsey defends boxing's HWC by KO'ing Billy Miske. | |

| October 27 | Montreal, Canada | **Wladek Zbyszko** | **Won** |

| November 2 | Utica, NY | **Joe Malcewicz** | **Draw** |

| November 18 | Utica, NY | **Joe Malcewicz** | **WOF** |

| November 20 | Kansas City, MO | **Raymond Cazeau** (Att.: 8,000) | **Won** |

| November 22 | New York, NY | **Wladek Zbyszko** (1:25:45)* (Att.: 10,000) | **Won** |

November 25	Boston, MA	**Salvatore Chevalier**	**Won**
November 30	Kansas City, MO	**Raymond Cazeaux**	**Won (2-0)**
December 2	Charlotte	**Jack Rolando** (Largest crowd of the year in Charlotte. Lewis had a $600 guarantee.)	**Won (2-0)**
December 5	New York, NY	Begins training in NYC for Stecher match.	
December 13	New York, NY	**Joe Stecher** (World Title Win)* (Att.: 9,000. $75,000)	**Won**
December 14	MSG, NYC	Jack Dempsey KO's Bill Brennan defending boxing's WHC. Dempsey was boo'ed by crowd for being a WWI slacker. Was Lewis present the day after winning his title?	
December 21	San Francisco, CA	Lewis returns home to San Jose, and is met by wife, Dr. Ada Scott Morton Friedrich and five-month-old daughter Bobada Friedrich. Lewis is wearing sunglasses and says he's been having trouble seeing since before the Stecher bout. During the train trip he was unable to read.	

1921

January 6	Boston, MA	**Renato Gardini** (WC)*(1:38:00) (Att.: 6,000)	**Won**
January 13	Savannah, GA	**Rolando Heracl**	**Won (2-0)**
January 15	Columbia	**Jack Dawson**	**Won**
January 21	Rochester	**Dick Daviscourt** (WC) (Daviscourt was said to have dislocated his vertebrae.)	**Won (2-0-UTC)**
January 24 (23)	New York, NYC	**Earl Caddock** (WC)* (Att.: 8,000. Lewis has to leave ring under guard after Caddock becomes unconscious from the dreaded headlock.)	**Won**
January 27	Kansas City, MO	**Gustav Sulzo** (WC) (Sulzo rendered unconscious from headlock and a riot breaks loose.)	**Won (UTC)**
January ?	Kansas City, MO	Around this time, Lewis is awarded a $10,000 belt, set with 39 diamonds, by the Central Athletic Club. In history it would be called the Lewis Belt.	
January ?	New York, NYC	Jack Curley bans the use of the headlock in a match promoted by him due to injuries. Earl Caddock claims the hold is less dangerous than the toe hold or wristlock. Lewis and Sandow purchase an airplane and were attemping to learn how to fly.	

January 31	Boston, MA	**Renato Gardini** (WC) (Headlock barred. Referee Dr. B. F. Roller.)	**Won**
February 2	Portland, ME	**Bill Martinson**	**Won**
February 11	Savannah, GA	**Tom Draak**	**Won** **(2-0-UTC)**
February 12	Richmond	**Frank Zolar**	**Won**
March 4 (5)	Savannah, GA	**Tom Draak** (1:09:02)	**Won (2-0)**
March 5	Charleston	**Jack Dawson**	**Won (2-0)**
March 15	Wichita	A paper reported that Lewis had ordered a airplane to fly to matches.	
March 31	Appleton, WI	**George Hill** (WC)	**Won (2-0)**
April 3	New York, NY	Lewis says he will retire if defeated by Pesek.	
April 4	New York, NY	**John Pesek** (WC)* (Att.: 4,000)	**Won**
April 7	Springfield, MO	**vs George Hill & ?** (Handicap match)	**FTP**
April 12	Des Moines	**Earl Caddock** (WC)*	**Won (2-0)**
April 13	Chicago, IL	**Jim Londos** (WC)* (Sell out. $7,775)	**Won**
April 20	Boston, MA	**Orlando Jack Sampson**	**Won**
May 6	New York, NY	**Stanislaus Zbyszko** (World Title Loss) (Att.: 10,000) (Referee Dr. Roller)	**Lost**
July 2	Jersey City, NJ	Jack Dempsey KO's George Carpentier in 4th round to defend boxing's WHC.	
October 4	San Francisco, CA	**Joe Stecher**	**Lost** **(Decision)**
November 3	New York, NY	**Joe Polk** (Lewis may injured leg in match and missed a few weeks.)	**Won**
November 8	New York, NY	The New York Athletic Commission lifted the ban on punishing wrestling holds such as the headlock.	
November 23	Philadelphia, PA	**Justiana Silva**	**Won**

November 28	MSG, NYC	**Stanislaus Zbyszko** (WC)*	**Lost**
		(Att.: 7,000. The promoter for the 2/3 fall match was Tex Rickard, and after the win he presented Zbyszko with a diamond-studded belt. Zbyszko won second fall via a rolling or flying fall, while had just been made the rule in NY state.)	
December 6	Kansas City	**Cliff Binckley**	**Won**
December 12	Wichita	**Jatrinda Gobar** * (58:30)	**Won**
		(Undercard for a Joe Stecher vs Wladek Zbyszko match.)	

1922

January 6	Wichita	**Dick Daviscourt**	**Won (2-0)**
January ?	Havana, Cuba	**Alvarez ?**	**?**
January 19		Sandow turns down Zbyszko match in Boston. He thinks the match should take place in a western city like Wichita or Kansas City.	
January 22	New York, NY	Newspapers break story that MSG manager Tex Rickard had been arrested on charges of sexually abusing a number (seven) of young girls, ages from eleven to fifteen. A trial followed.	
February 6	MSG, NYC	**Renato Gardini**	**Won**
February 13		Jack Dempsey is quoted in newspapers saying: "I'll knock out Zbyszko and a half dozen other champion wrestlers in the same ring on the same night." This leads to a series of challenges between Dempsey and Lewis that lasts into the 1940's.	
February 13	Boston, MA	**Dick Daviscourt**	**Won**
February 21	MSG, NYC	**Cliff Binckley**	**Won (2-0)**
February 25	Wichita	Lewis has public workout.	
February 28	Birmingham	**Jack Pauliska**	**Won**
March 3	Wichita	**Stanislaus Zbyszko** (World Title Win)	**Won**
		(Att.: 4,928. $13,000. Lewis was awarded two champion ship belts. This was said to be the first match ever broadcast on radio. Lewis made $5,000 and Stan took home $7,000.)	
March 5	Savannah, GA	**Tom Draak** (WC)	**Won**
March 7	Indianapolis, IN	**John Grandovich** (WC)	**Won (2-0)**

March 9	Nashville, TN	**Joe Petroff** (WC) (1:23:00)	**Won**
March 10	Louisville, KY	**Charles Lebelge** (WC)	**Won (2-0)**
March 11	Lexington, KY	**George "Farmer" Bailey** (WC)	**Won (2-0)**
March 13	St. Louis, MO	**Jack Jurka** (WC)*	**Won (2-0)**
March 14	Fort Wayne, IN	**Jatindra Gobar** (WC)	**Won (2-0)**
March 16	Nashville, TN	Billy Sandow announced that Lewis had posted a $5,000 bond with the sports editor of the *Nashville Banner* as a challenge to boxing champion Jack Dempsey. Says he will beat Dempsey in less than 20 minutes or give him the $5,000. In NYC Jack Kearns said that Demsey was willing to meet Lewis in a mixed match or a wrestling match.	
March 16	Nashville, TN	**Joe Petroff (Joe Zigmund ?)** (WC)	**Won (2-0)**
March 21	Pratt, KS	**John Grandovich**	**Won (2-0)**
March 22	Kirkville, MO	Canceled due to Lewis having carbuncles.	
March 23	Hutchinson, KS	Cancelled due to Lewis having carbuncles on knee.	
March 24	Topeka, KS	**Joe Geshtout** (WC?)	**Won**
March 26	Kansas City, MO	**Yousiff Mahmout** (WC)*	**Won (2-0)**
March 27	New York, NY	Tex Richard's trial for sexually molesting young girls in MSG ends with a not guilty verdict.	
March 28	Des Moines, IA	**Armas Laitenen** (WC)*	**Won (2-0)**
March 29	St. Louis, MO	**Jim Londos** (WC)* (Att.: 5,000. 1st fall Lewis in 1:17:10. 2nd fall Londos in 22:40. 3rd fall Lewis in 14:45.)	**Won (2-1)**
March 31	Appleton, WI	**George Hill** (WC)	**Won (2-0)**
April 6	Tulsa	**Jatrinda Gobar** (WC)	**Won (2-0)**
April 13	Wichita	**Earl Caddock** (WC)	**Won (2-1)**
April 19	Boston, MA	**Dick Daviscourt** (WC)	**Won**
April 25	Kansas City, MO	**Stanislaus Zbyszko** (WC)	**Won (2-1)**
April 27	Tulsa	**Cliff Binckley** (WC)	**WOF**

May 2	Jefferson City, MO	**John Mazzan**	**Won (2-0)**
May 3	Moberly	Promoter F. M. Holtsinger offered Lewis $15,000 for a match with Jim Londos under a circus tent.	
May 4	Minneapolis, MN	**John Freberg** (WC)	**Won (UTC)**
May 6	Oshkosh, WI	**John Grandovich** (WC)	**Won (UTC)**
May 8	Topeka	**Farmer George Bailey** (WC)	**Won (2-0)**
May 11	Arkansas City	**Farmer George Bailey**	**Won**
May 12	Herington, KS	**Jatrinda Gobar** (WC)	**Won (2-0)**
May 31	Muskogee, OK	**John Grandovich** (WC)	**Won (2-0)**
June 2 (22)	Tulsa	**Cliff Binckley** (WC) (Match covered by Tulsa radio station WEH.)	**Won (2-1)**
June 7	Boston, MA	**Earl Caddock** (WC)*	**Won (2-1)**
June 12	Wahpeton, ND	**Jack Sampson** (WC)	**Won (2-0)**
June 14	Minneapolis, MN	**John Freberg** (WC)	**Won (2-1)**
June 17	Chicago, IL ?	John Pesek (WC) ?	Won
June 22 (2)	Tulsa	**Cliff Binckley** (WC) (Match covered by Tulsa radio station WEH.)	**?**
June 29	Oklahoma City	**Dick Daviscourt** (WC)	**Won (2-0)**
July 4	Wichita	**Alan Eustace**	**Won**
July 20	Colorado Springs, CO	Lewis was training at Colorado Springs for a European tour. It is possible that he was working with Toots Mondt, who was coaching at Colorado Agriculture College (later Colorado State University) 133 miles away.	
August 21	Madison, WI	**Scotty McDougall** (WC)*	**Won (2-0)**
September 26	San Francisco, CA	**Renato Gardini** (WC)	**Won (2-1)**
October 10	Eaton, CO	**Goho Gobar**	**Won (2-0)**

(This card was staged by Ralph Mondt, brother of Toots Mondt. Perhaps Lewis and Sandow met Toots at this time and took him east with them? They wrestled November 10 in Boston.)

October 25	St. Joseph, MO	**Jatrinda Gobar** (WC?)	**Won**
November 1	Joplin, MO	**Jatrinda Gobar** (WC?)	**Won**
November 2	St. Louis, MO	**Demetrius Tofalos** (WC)	**Won (2-0)**
November 3	Ottumwa, IA	**Anton Borsa** (WC)	**Won (2-0)**
November 6	Nashville, TN	**Andreas Vassear** (WC)	**Won (DQ 2-0)**
November 8	Columbus	**Cliff Binckley** (WC)	**Won (2-1)**
November 10	Boston, MA	**Toots Mondt** (WC)	**Won**
November 13	Omaha, NE	The *Omaha Bee* reveals that John Pesek's real manager is Maxwell Baumann, brother of Billy Sandow and Jules Baumann, not Larney Lichtenstein.	
November 16	St. Louis, MO	**Bob Managoff** (WC)	**Won (2-0)**
November 17	St. Joseph	**John Grandovich** (WC)	**Won (2-0)**
November 22	Boston, MA	**George Kotsonaros** (WC)	**Won**
November 26	Nashville, TN	Lewis claims he is willing to wager $25,000 that he can defeat Jack Dempsey.	
November 27	Nashville, TN	**?**	**?**
December 8	Kansas City, MO	**Wallace Duguid** (WC)	**Won (2-0-UTC)**
December 10	St. Louis, MO	In town for match with Zbyszko.	
December 14	St. Louis, MO	**Stanislaus Zbyszko** (WC)	**Won (2-1)**
December 18	Wichita, KS	**Dick Daviscourt** (WC)	**Won (2-0)**
December 24	San Jose, CA	Lewis stages Christmas party for the poor and needy children of San Jose.	
December 25	San Jose, CA	Wife Dr. Ada Scott operates on Lewis to relieve blood poisoning in right arm. One report said it was an infected wrist from a match in Kansas City.	
December 27	San Jose, CA	Dr. Morton Lewis operates on Lewis' infected arm at a local hospital.	
December 28	San Francisco, CA	**Tud "Jack" Turner (Joe Zigmund)** (WC)* (Att.: fair)	**Won (2-0)**
December 30	San Francisco, CA	Lewis announced that arrangments had been completed for a mixed match between Jack Dempsey and himself to be held at Wichita. Dempsey, in L.A., claimed nothing had been signed but he was ready for the match. Tom Law, promoter in Wichita, claims to know nothing about the contract for $300,000.	

1923

January 3	Lewis being trained for Dempsey fight by wife Dr. Ada Morton Lewis. Ed says he'll win.		
January 3	Reno, NV	**Frank Yusko** (WC)	**Won (2-0)**
January 7	Kansas City	The rules for the proposed Dempsey / Lewis match were revealed by promoter Tom Law. Includes a three count.	
January 10	Hollywood, CA	**Demetrius Tofalos** (WC)* (Att.: 7,000. l. A. Record)	**Won (2-0)**
January 12	Reno, NV	**Tom Hatchet**	**Won (UTC)**
January 12	Reno, NV	Lewis invited University of Nevada football tackle Bevo Colwell to his Santa Rosa, CA home in the summer to try out as a wrestling sparring partner.	
January 16	St. Louis, MO	**Giovanni Tiverio** (WC)	**Won (2-0)**
January 23	Kansas City	**Toots Mondt** (2:00:00)*(WC) (Att.: 8,000)	**WOF**
February 6	Indianapolis, IN	**?**	**?**
February 15	Kansas City	**Toots Mondt** (WC) (Att.: >10,000)	**Won (2-1)**
February 20	St. Louis, MO	**Jim Londos** (WC)* (Att.: crowded house)	**Won (2-1)**
March 6	Chicago, IL	**Allen Eustace** (WC)* (Att.: 6,500. <$10,000)	**Won (2-0)**
March 7	St. Louis, MO	**Dan Koloff** (WC)	**Won**
April 3	Chicago, IL	**Renato Gardini** (WC) (Att.: 7,000)	**Won**
April 6	Springfield, MO	(Handicap Match)	
		Jack Solar	**Won**
		George Hills (1:15:00)	**FTP**
April 16	Nashville, TN	**Wallace Duguid** (WC)* (Duguid sustained neck injury from headlock.)	**Won**
April 29	Tulsa	**Toots Mondt** (2:00:00)	**Draw**
May 2	Kansas City	**John Pesek** (WC)* (Att.: 15,000)	**Won (2-0)**

Date	Location	Opponent / Notes	Result
May 15	Chicago, IL	**Renato Gardini** (WC)* (Att.: 4,500. Lewis didn't use the headlock)	**Won (2-1)**
May 22	Minneapolis, MN	**Stanislaus Zbyszko** (WC)	**Won**
June 6	Chicago, IL	**Allan Eustace** (WC)	**Won (2-0)**
June 12	Chicago, IL	Ringside for a Stan Zbyszko vs Gardini match.	
June 15	Wisconsin Rapids, WI	Lewis applies for a passport for trip to Europe to start on July 4 on the liner *Layathan*.	
June 21	Stevens Point, WI	Lewis obtains a divorce from Dr. Ada Scott Friedrich of San Jose, CA. The wife claimed to know nothing about it. Lewis charged his wife of cruelty. Ed then said goodbye to his parents, still living at Nekoosa, and headed for the east.	
July 2	Philadelphia, PA	**Renato Gardini** (WC)	**Won (2-1)**
July 4	Shelby, MT	Jack Dempsey defeats Tommy Gibbons to defend boxing's WHC. Dempsey and his manager ripped off the town of Shelby for a purse of $272,000.	
July 21	Kansas City, MO	The K.C. wrestling news reports that Lewis is leaving for a pleasure and recreation tour of Europe. Outside of a few exhibitions in some of the larger cities, he did not wrestle and did not plan on defending the title. On return he will go into training. Toots Mondt was also spending the summer in rest and recreation, having set up camp in the Ozarks near Springfield, MO, for hunting and fishing. His trainer Joe Bruno plans to start a training program around the 1st of September and for him to be in top condition by October.	
July 27	Paris, France	Lewis's trip to Germany was delayed 24 hours when his laundry failed to return to his hotel. He was unable to buy a collar or shirt big enough to fit him in Paris. The biggest he could find was a 17. He proceeded to Berlin the following day.	
August 24	Paris, France	Lewis back in Paris. May wrestle in arenas soon.	
?	Brighton, England	**Goho Gobar**	**Won (2-0)**
?	Brussels, Belgium	**Miller**	**Won (2-0)**
?	Antwerp, Belgium	**La Marn**	**Won (2-0)**
?	Rome, Italy	**George Rode**	**Won (1-0)**
?	Rome, Italy	**La Chevele**	**Won (2-0)**

September 14	New York, NY	Jack Dempsey KO's Luis Firpo in 2nd round to defend boxing's HWC.	
September 29	Rochester	Lewis leaving to marry Princess Marie Traivaska in Chicago. He met her in Europe during the summer, after being divorced from Dr. Ada Morton Friedrich.	
October 2	Nekoosa, WI	Lewis visits home at Woods Farm near Nekoosa. Interviewed by reporter. Talks about mixed match with Jack Dempsey.	
October 26	Kansas City, OK	**John Turner** (WC)	**Won (2-0)**
November 2	Long Beach, CA	**Gus Alex**	**Won (2-0)**
November 16	Sioux City	Wayne Munn was KO'ed by Jack Clifford in round 2 of a boxing match.	
December 4	Ogden	Jim Londos in town attempting to set up a match with Lewis.	
December 7	Kansas City, OK	**Stanislaus Zbyszko** (WC)	**Won**
December 8	Sioux City, IA	Wayne Munn was KO'ed by Charley Paulson in round 4 of a boxing match.	
December 13	St. Louis, MO	**Josef Gurkeweicz** (WC)*	**Won (2-0)**

(Joe Stecher is present and offers Lewis $15,000 for a title match. Sandow refuses by telling Joe to defeat Zbyszko, Mondt, or Pesek first.)

December 14 (15)	Wichita, KS	**Taro Miyake** (WC vs Jiu-Jitsu WC) (Lewis was announced as world Jiu-Jitsu champion after match.)	**Won**
December 18	Chicago	**Joe Zickman (Josef Rogacki ?)** (WC) (Att.: 4,000)	**Won (2-0)**
December 28	Wichita	**Dick Daviscourt** (WC)* (Lewis was arrested following match for hitting a booing fan, William Goodell, after losing the 1st fall. Police released him when the fan didn't press charges. Lewis claimed he punched the wrong fan. It was reported that this was the sixth match between Lewis and Daviscourt in Wichita.)	**Won (2-1)**
December 29	New York, NY	Boxing promoter Tex Rickard is denied permit to promote wrestling in MSG by the license committee of the NY State Athletic Commission who ruled that it would be unfair to the NYC licensed promoters Jack Curley and Matty Zimmerman to have another promoter in the city. Rickard says nothing and cancels a wrestling carnival advertised for January 3, 1924.	

December 29	Kansas City, MO	Signs for Toots Mondt match on January 10.	
December 31	New York, NY	A story in the *New York Herald* reported wrestling the least attented of any professional sport in the city. It said the mat sport was a dead in the city and this condition had its effect throughout the country where there was little activity of major importance. Lewis was the champ but defended the title infrequently because of the dearth of suitable opposition and lukewarm interest.	

1924

January 1 (2)	Chicago, IL	**Taro Myaki** (Att.: 4,000)	**Won**
January 10	Kansas City, MO	**Joe "Toots" Mondt** (WC)*	**Won (2-0)**
January 15	Chicago, IL	**Mike Romano** (WC)	**Won**
January 17	Boston, MA	**Joe Alvarez**	**Won**
January 24	Boston, MA	**Angelo Taramaschi**	**Won**
January 25	Rochester	Ringside for Stecher vs Daviscourt. Rochester promoter was Jules Baumann, brother of Billy Sandow. Another brother Maxwell Baumann was manager of John Pesek in 1925. A fourth brother was Alexander who wasn't involved with wrestling.	
January 28	St. Joseph	**Ali Hassan** (WC)*	**Won (2-0)**
January 31	Kansas City	Promoter Gabe Kaufman announces Stecher vs Mondt match in KC for February 11.	
February 1 (2)	Chicago, IL	**Jack McCarthy**	**Won (2-0)**
February 5	St. Louis, MO	**Renato Gardini** (WC)*	**Won (2-0)**
February 12	New York, NY	**Pat McGill***(WC) (1:15:36) (Att.: 3,000, small)	**Won**
February 14	Boston, MA	**George Kotsonaros**	**Won**
February 17	Kansas City	Joe and Tony meet with KC promoter Gabe Kaufman, in an attempt to sign a match with Lewis. Billy Sandow arrives soon after and talks stop.	
February 26	Chicago, IL	**Stanislaus Zbyszko** (WC)* (Att.: 7,500-$10.000)	**Won**
February 28	Milwaukee, WI	**Jack (Frank) La Mark** (WC) (Att.: Sell-out)	**Won**
February 29	Chicago, IL	**Elmer Saunders** (WC)	**Won**
March 3	Kansas City	**Taro Miyake** (WC)	**?**

March 25	Chicago, IL	**Stanislaus Zbyszko** (WC)* (Att.: 12,000. $23,000)	**Won**
March 26	Chicago, IL	Lewis was married on Wednesday to Miss Bessie McNear of Kansas City, MO. Billy Sandow, Lewis' manager, who had a contract ruling out marriage by Ed while champion, was locked in a hotel room during the ceremony.	
April 1	St. Louis, MO	**Jim Londos** (WC)* (Att.: large)	**Won (KO)**
April 8	Philadelphia, PA	**Renato Gardini** (WC)* (Largest crowd in Philly history. Gardini's partisans rioted.)	**Draw**
April 10	Boston, MA	**Peter Kosloas**	**Won**
April 29	Chicago, IL	**Mike Romano** (WC)* (Att.: 10,000. Fans rioted after Lewis won)	**Won (2-1)**
May 1	Boston, MA	Arrives in town, accompanied by his new wife, to train for match with Stanley Stasiak.	
May 3	Boston, MA	While training at Tyler St. Gym, Lewis got into a brawl with sparring partner Farmer Bailey, who was later fired.	
May 5	Rochester	**Toots Mondt** (WC) (Att.: 3,000)	**WOF**
May 6	Boston, MA	2,000 fans show up to watch Lewis and Stasiak train. The $12,000 purse is the largest ever offered in the North-east.	
May 8	Boston, MA	**Stanley Stasiak** (WC) (Att.: 9,000. Boston record)	**Won (DQ)**
May 21	Philadelphia, PA	**Renato Gardini** (WC) (Att.: 6,500)	**Won (UTC)**
May 24	Winnipeg, Canada	**Dick Daviscourt** (WC) (Att.: 3,000)	**Won**
May 28	Chicago, IL	**Stanislaus Zbyszko** (WC)* (Att.: 5,600-$9,500)	**Won**
June 3	Kansas City	**Jack Yuska** (WC)	**Won (2-0)**
June 12	St. Louis, MO	**Jim Londos** (WC)* (Gate = $14,410)	**Won (2-1)**
June 26	Rochester	Lewis training at Conesus Lake after a minor car accident. Sandow, with Lewis in car, skidded on a wet road and went into a ditch. No one was hurt.	

June 28	Rochester	**Toots Mondt** (WC)	**Won (2-0)**
July 1	Boston, MA	**Stanley Stasiak** (WC)	**Won (2-1)**
July 11	Chicago, IL	**Mike Romano** (WC)	**Won (2-0)**
July 29	San Francisco, CA	**Stanislaus Zbyszko** (WC)* (Att.: sold out. Largest crowd since Stecher/Santel.)	**Won**
August 11	Nester, CA	Four separate charges of battery and one of disturbing the peace were filled in court against Lewis after Ed was involved in a traffic accident, on August 10, with a Mrs. Daisy Haynes on a return trip from Tijuana. Lewis punched out her three sons and pushed Mrs. Haynes around, then left the scene. He later was pulled over for speeding. It took three officers to get Lewis out of his car. Lewis pleaded not gulity and was released on $500 bail.	
August 13	Los Angeles, CA	**Joe "Toots" Mondt** (WC)(1:30:00)* (Sellout of 5,500 with 2,500 turned away.)	**WOF**
August 27	Los Angeles, CA	**Stanislaus Zbyszko** (WC)* (Att.: 5,500—sellout-$16,000)	**Won**
September 2	San Francisco, CA	**Pat McGill*** (McGill sent to hospital. Lewis was also served with a warrant charging speeding in the town of San Juan.)	**Won** **(2-0-UTC)**
September 3	Boston, MA	Arthur Duffey reported the Lewis will soon retire from active wrestling due to suffering from trachoma for over a year.	
September 4	Los Angeles, CA	**Stanislaus Zbyszko** (WC)* (Att.: Sold out, >5,500. 1,000's turned away.)	**Won**
September 23	Urbana, IL	Report has Lewis matched with Jim McMillen on October 17.	
September 25	Los Angeles, CA	**Joe "Toots" Mondt** (WC) (2:00)	**Draw**
October 13	Washington Baseball Park, L.A.	**Toots Mondt** (WC)* (Att.: 10,000-$31,000)	**Won**
October 30	Chicago, IL	**Pat McGill** (WC) (Att.: 4,500)	**Won**
October 31	Chicago, IL	**Hassen Volkoff** (WC)	**Won**
December 1	Chicago, IL	Report has Lewis making a tour of Europe this winter. Will sail in mid-January.	

December 3	Winnipeg, Canada	**Jatrinda Gobar** (WC) (Att.: 2,000)	**Won**
December 11	Kansas City	**Hassain O. Giles (Frank Ogile)** (WC)* (Att.: 10,000. No rules, no referee in ring.)	**Won (2-0)**
December 16	Chicago, IL	**Mike Romano** (WC) (Att.: 11,000)	**won (2-1)**
December 17	Chicago, IL	Lewis worked out at Mullen's gym. Sandow says Lewis will sail for Europe on January 16 for a tour. That night Lewis left for Rochester.	
December 19	Rochester, NY	**Pat McGill** (WC)	**Won (2-0-UTC)**
1925			
January 8	Kansas City, MO	**Wayne Munn** (World Title loss) (Att.: 15,000. Lewis protested the decision and did not give championship belt to Munn. Lewis went to hospital with back injury.)	**lost**
January 9	Kansas City, MO	Lewis keeps two championship belts, one given to him by the central athletic club of Kansas City several years before which is worth $10,000 and has 39 diamonds, and a second belt that was awarded to Zbyszko in NYC by Tex Rickard.	
January 10	Kansas City, MO	Lewis was still in hospital with back injuries and had cancelled all engagements, claiming it would be weeks before he'd be able to walk.	
February 2	Chicago, IL	Lewis training and still claiming World Title.	
February 3	Chicago, IL	**Joe "Toots" Mondt** (WC) (Att.: 9,000. 21,000. On the undercard, Wayne Munn gave an exhibition of the holds he used to beat Lewis. Lewis was still claiming title.)	**Won (2-1)**
February 5	Milwaukee, WI	**Hans Bauer** (1:05:00)	**Draw**
February 6	Chicago, IL	**Joe Zikmund** (WC)	**Won (DQ)**
February 9	Philadelphia, PA	**Mike Romano**	**?**
February 13	Rochester	**Pat McGill** (2:00) (Att.: 2,000)	**Draw**
February 20	Chicago, IL	**Joe Zikmund** (WC)	**Won**
February 25	Milwaukee, WI	**Hans Bauer**	**Won (2-0)**
March 6	Cleveland, OH	**Bill Demetral**	**Draw**

March 17	Chicago, IL	**Tommy Draak**	**Won (2-0)**
March 19	Tulsa	**Pat McGill** (WC)	**Won (2-0)**
March 25	Philadelphia, PA	**Wallace Duguid**	**Won (2-0)**
March 26	Boston, MA	vs **Frank Bruno** (Handicap Match)	**Won**
		vs **Leon Labriola**	**FTP**
April 3	Chicago, IL	**Hans Bauer**	**?**
April 6	Tulsa	**Toots Mondt** (WC)	**Won (2-0)**
April 15	Philadelphia, PA	Stanislaus Zbyszko defeats Wayne Munn for world title. Munn continues to claim title.	
April 16	Boston, MA	**Alex Lunden** (Lewis subbed for Wayne Munn.)	**Won**
May 1	Philadelphia, PA	**Tom Draak**	**Won (2-0)**
May 7	Boston, MA	**Alex Lunden** (Lewis still claiming World Title.)	**Won (1-0)**
May 14	Chicago, IL	Both Lewis and Munn training in Chicago at two different gyms to build interest for May 30 match.	
May 17	Michigan City, IN	Lewis and Munn training. Toots Mondt working for Munn.	
May 23	Chicago, IL	Lewis in town training	
May 29	Michigan City, IN	Both Lewis and Munn training	
May 30	St. Louis, MO	Joe Stecher regains World Title by defeating Stanislaus Zbyszko.	
May 30	Michigan City, IN	**Wayne Munn** (World Title) (Claims title even after Munn lost to Zbyszko. Att.: 14,000-$64,000)	**Won (2-1)**
June 1	Chicago, IL	In Chicago, will return to Wisconsin for a few days.	
June 3	Chicago, IL	Promoter Paddy Harmon offered $50,000 purse for a Lewis / Stecher match.	
June 11	Boston, MA	**Leon Labriola**	**Won**
June 15	Cleveland, OH	**Mike Romano**	**Rained out**
June 18 (19)	Cleveland, OH	**Mike Romano**	**Won (2-0)**
June 29	St. Louis, MO	Joe Stecher turned down a $50,000 purse from Tom Packs to meet Lewis.	
July 9	Tulsa, OK	**Howard Cantonwine** (WC)	**Won (2-0)**

July 24	Tulsa, OK	Film of the Lewis/Munn match shown at local theater.	
August 22	Sand Spring Lake	Lewis training with Jack Roller for Tulsa match with Cantonwine.	
August 28	Tulsa	Returns from Quincy, KS where he was drilling for oil.	
September 2 (3)	Tulsa	**Howard Cantonwine** (WC)	**Won (2-0)**
September 16 (22)	Houston, TX	**Pat McGill** (sub for Mondt)	**Won (2-1)**
September 20	Tulsa, OK	Gabe Kauffman sells Wayne Munn contract to Ed White.	
September 22	Houston, TX	**Pat McGill** (WC)	**Won (2-1)**
September 27	Madison, WI	**Bill Demetral** (WC)	**Won (2-0-UTC)**
October 2	Houston, TX	**Pat McGill**	**Won (UTC)**
October 7	Tulsa	**Wayne Munn** (WC)	**Rain Out**
October 8	Tulsa	**Wayne Munn** (WC)	**Won (2-1)**
October 17	Montreal, Canada	**Scotty McDougall**	**Won**
October 21	Rochester, NY	**Pat McGill** (WC)	**Won**
October 22	Boston, MA	**John "Jack" McPherson**	**Won**
October 29	Boston, MA	**Ned McGuire (Handicap Match)**	**FTP**
November 4	Dallas, TX	**Jack Orlando** (WC)	**Won (2-0)**
November 6	Houston, TX	**Paul Jones** (Handicap Match) (60:00)	**FTP**
November 11	Okmulgee	**Alan Eustace** (WC)	**Won (2-0)**
November 16	Houston, TX	**Wayne Munn** (WC)	**Won (2-1)**
November 23	Cleveland, OH	**Leon Labriola**	**Won (2-0-UTC)**
November 30	Chicago, IL	Ringside for Stecher vs Judson.	
December 2	Chicago, IL	**Mike Romano** (WC) (Att.: 4,000)	**Won (2-1)**
December 2	Sacramento, CA	Marin Plestina gets license to marry.	
December 8 (9)	Denver, CO	**Wayne Munn** (WC)	**Won (2-1)**
December 14	Chicago, IL	**Leon Labriola** (WC) (Att.: 6,000)	**Won (2-0)**
December 16	Tulsa	**Joe O'Dell** (WC)	**Won (2-1)**
December 18	Quincy, IL	**Nick Gotch**	**Won (1-0-UTC)**
December 23	Kansas City, KS	Wayne Munn was KO'ed by Andre Anderson in round 1 of a boxing match.	

1926

January 8	Denver, CO	Ralph Mondt, match-maker for the Denver American Legion Athletic Association, says he will bid $30,000 for a Stecher/Lewis match to be held next summer. Mondt proposes the match be staged in Denver University's new 30,000 seat athletic stadium.	
January 11	Denver, CO	**Wayne Munn** (WC) (Att.: 12,000)	**Won**
January 21	Boston, MA	**Ned McGuire**	**Won**
January 22	Rochester, NY	**Jack Washburn** (WC) (Att.: 3,500)	**Won (2-0-UTC)**
January ?	Milwaukee, WI	**Nick Gotch**	**?**
January 29	Chicago, IL	**Stanley Stasiak** (WC) (Att.: 7,000)	**Won**
February 9	Milwaukee, WI	**Hans Bauer**	**Won (2-1)**
February 11	Tulsa	**Howard Cantonwine** (WC)	**Won (2-0)**
February 18	Cleveland	**Bill Demetral** (WC)(56:00) (Att.: 3,500)	**Won**
February 19	Rochester	**Jack Washburn** (WC) (Att.: 3,400)	**Won**
February 22	San Francisco, CA	Dr. Ada Scott Morton, ex-wife of Ed Lewis, admitted she married Wells Clark, wealthy real estate operator in San Francisco and Washington DC. They met in the east and the wedding followed soon thereafter.	
February 23		Lewis says he has taken Frank Gotch's 12 year old son in tow and will train him to be a champion. Ed says the father taught him many of his wrestling tricks.	
February 25	Denver, CO	**Allan Eustace** (WC)	**Won (UTC 1-0)**
March 1	Chicago, IL	**Stanley Stasiak** (Att.: 9,000, $18,000)	**Won**
March 1	Chicago, IL	Paul Bowser in town trying to sign Stecher or Ed Lewis to face Joe Malcewicz. It's anounced that Stecher had agreed to meet anyone in Boston for $12,500, but Stecher claimed the agreement was to meet Jake Bressler with his own referee on March 11.	
March 8	Tulsa	Newspaper reports that Billy Sandow had paid a handsome sum to Ralph Mondt, brother of Toots, for the Cowboy's contract, good for three years. Lewis wants Mondt to help condition him for his title match vs Wayne Munn.	

March 11	Kansas City	**Wayne Munn** (WC)	**Won (2-0)**
March 11	Boston, MA	Joe Stecher forfits a match with Joe Malcewicz rather that be involved in a trap set-up by promoter Paul Boswer. This results in Stecher being banned in NY State for a short period and Malcewicz claims World Title in Boston.	
April 2	Chicago, IL	Lewis and a 52-year-old broker Charles Wheeler appear before Municipal Judge Padden due to fight that broke out between the two on a snow-drifted street after their automobiles scraped fenders. Charges were dismissed and the two shook hands.	
April 9	Akron, OH	**Nick Gotch (Vanka Zelesniak?)**(WC) (Att.: 1,600)	**Won**
April 10	Canton, OH	**George Hansen** (WC)	**?**
April 13 (12)	Kansas City, MO	**Jim Clinkstock**	**Won (2-1)**
April 15	Boston, MA	**Wayne Munn**	**Won (2-0)**
April 19	Chicago, IL	**Rafaelle Grenna** (WC) (Att.: 8,000)	**Won**
April 29	Boston, MA	**Ncd McGuire** (WC) (Report had Lewis ringside in St. Louis for Stecher/Pesek??)	**Won**
May 11	Chicago, IL	A new boxing and wrestling commission banned all wrestling and amateur boxing shows until they issue licenses to promoters.	
May 6	Kansas City, MO	**Mike Romano** (WC)	**Won (2-0)**
May 14	Boston, MA	**Raffael Grenna**	**Won**
May 17	Tulsa	**Joe O'Dell** (WC)	**Won (2-0)**
May ?	Boston, MA	**?**	**?**
May ?	Boston, MA	**Hans Bauer**	**Won**
May 24	Rochester	**Wayne Munn** (WC) (Att.: 3,000)	**Won (2-0)**
May 26	Milwaukee, WI	**Hans Bauer** (WC)	**?**
June 4	Minneapolis, MN	**Mike Romano**	**Won (2-0)**
June 12	Milwaukee, WI	**Ernst Scharpegge** (WC)	**?**
June ?	Tulsa	**?**	
June 15	Milwaukee, WI	**?**	

June 17	Akron, OH	**William Demetral** (WC)	**?**
June 19	Chicago, IL	The Commission drew up new rules to govern wrestling;	
July 1	Boston (Braves Field)	**Joe Malcewicz** (3:22:30) * (Att.: >10,000. This was a title unification match with Malcewicz reconized as WC in Boston.)	**Draw**
August 2	Tulsa	**Joe Malcewicz** (WC)* (Att.: 8,000)	**Won (DQ)**
August 20	Los Angeles, CA	Lewis and Stecher both post $5,000 with the Calif. State Athletic Commission and seem to agree to meet for the title September 8.	
August 23	Los Angeles, CA	The Lewis and Stecher groups meet before Capt. Seth Strelinger, State Athletic Commissoner, and the match between Lewis and Stecher is set for October 6 at the Olympic Auditorium.	
August 31	Los Angeles, CA	**Mike Romano***	**Won (2-0-UTC)**
September 14	Los Angeles, CA	**Wayne Munn** (WC)*	**Won (2-0)**
September 23	Philadelphia, PA	Jack Dempsey losses every round in dropping boxing's HWC to Gene Tunney. Any hope of a mixed match with Dempsey is gone.	
September 24	Los Angeles, CA	Lewis claims to have broken a bone in his left arm or elbow while working out with Toots Mondt at Garden Grove training camp. Cancels October 6 match with Stecher, and will be out six weeks. Lewis people could not name the bone. Lewis is given 60 days to get ready for the match.	
September 30	Kansas City	Billy Sandow enroute to Rochester. His father-in-law had recently died.	
October 6	Los Angeles, CA	John Pesek subbing for Lewis, shoots on Joe Stecher in match at the Olympic. Stecher is lucky to have match awarded to him via DQ.	
November 5	Chicago, IL	Newspaper rumors are that a chicago businessman offered Stecher and Lewis $100,000 for a World Title showdown.	
November 6	Chicago, IL	Promoter John "Doc" Krone offered a $75,000 purse for a Stecher/Lewis match.	
November 21	Los Angeles, CA	Lewis refuses to wrestle Stecher in L.A. and leaves town for the East coast. His $5,000 forfeit is awarded to Stecher.	
December 6	Tulsa	**Raffael Grenna** (WC)	**Won (2-0)**
December 14	Kansas City	**Ivan Zackowski** (WC)	**Won (2-0)**
December 17	Philadelphia, PA	**Mike Romano***(1:25:00) (Att.: 4,000)	**Won (1-0)**

1927

January 3	Chicago, IL	**Wayne Munn** (WC)	**Won (2-0)**
January 6	Atlanta, GA	**Cliff Binkley** (Att.: 2,000)	**Won (2-0)**
January 13	Boston, MA	**Pat McGill** (2½ hours)	**Draw (0-0)**
January 21	Tulsa	After a match in which Toots Mondt lost to Joe Malcewicz, Mondt had a heated argument with manager Billy Sandow in the dressing-room. It is believed that the two broke off their partnership.	
January 21 (22)	Houston	**Jim Clinkstock** (WC)*	**Won (2-0)**
January 23	New York, NY	Lewis/Sandow and Joe & Tony Stecher meet with promoter Aurelio Fabiani about title match in Philadelphia.	
January 24	Shreveport, LA	**Mike Romano** (WC)	**Won**
February 1	Oklahoma City	**Howard Cantonwine** (WC)	**Won (2-0)**
February 16	Kansas City, MO	**Jack Locker** (WC)	**Won**
February 21	Shreveport, LA	**Jim Mc Clinstock**	**Won (2-0)**
February 24	Boston, MA	**Pat McGill**	**Won**
February 28	Chicago, IL	**Mike Romano** (WC)	**Won (2-1)**
March 9	Shreveport, LA	**Wayne Munn** (WC)	**Won (2-0)**
March 19	Warren, OK	**?**	**?**
March 20 ?	Kansas City	Tom Packs meets with Billy Sandow in Kansas City. Sandow agrees to a match with John Pesek in St. Louis. A future match with Stecher is talked about.	
March 23	Tulsa	**Jack Locker** (WC)	**Won (2-0)**
March 24	St. Louis, MO	Sandow and Lewis stop off to visit with Tom Packs and to set up a training site for April 7 match with John Pesek, then leave for match at Rochester.	
March ?	Rochester	**?**	
March 30	Milwaukee, WI	**Ernest Scharpegge** (WC)	**Won (2-1)**
April 7	St. Louis, MO	**John Pesek** (WC)* (Att.:>9,000. Paid: 8,672. Promoters Paul Bowser, Ray Fabiani, Ed White and Joe Bowman (Rochester) were present with others.)	**Won (2-1)**

April 8	St. Louis, MO	Tom Packs says that Lewis and Sandow responded positively to "feelers" about a match with Stecher in St. Louis. Packs is willing to offer a purse of $75,000. Packs will travel to Hot Springs, AR, to meet with the stechers.	
April 13?	Hot Springs, AR	While on vacation Stecher is visited by Tom Packs, who offers a purse of $75,000 for a match with Ed Lewis.	
April 19	Boston, MA	**Abe Kaplan** (Undercard of a Malcewicz match with Pat McGill that had him billed as world champ.)	**Won (UTC)**
April 28	Kansas City	**Stanley Stasiak** (WC)	**Won (2-0-DQ)**
May 7	Tulsa	Had public work out with Firpo Wilcox.	
May 9	Oklahoma City	**Alexander Garkawienko** (WC)	**Won (UTC)**
June 2	Boston, MA	News report had Toots Mondt breaking off his partnership with Lewis and Sandow.	
June 6	Chicago, IL	Legislature committee's investigation causes the cancellation of June 10's wrestling card.	
June 10	Wrigley Field, Chicago, IL	**Joe Malcewicz**	**Canceled**
June 16	Boston, MA	Lewis was replaced on a card due to a Chicago investigation involving William Demetral's charge that he was forced to post a forfeit guaranteeing he wouldn't defeat Lewis.	
July 1	Chicago, IL	Lewis appeared before a committee investigating the activities of the Illinois Athletic Commission. Claims were made that Billy Sandow headed a trust which controled wrestling, that wrestlers had to make deposits before title matches to insure they were going to job. At one point, Lewis stole the show by offering to wrestle a witness (Bill Demetral) who claimed he could beat the champion.	
July 15	Boston, MA	**Alexander Garkawienko** (WC)	**Won**
July 21	New York, NY	Jack Dempsey defeats Jack Sharkey by a 7[Th] round KO.	
August 3	Madison, WI	**Scotty McDougall**	**Won (2-0)**
September 5	Tulsa	**Stanley Stasiak** (WC)	**Won (UTC)**
September 21	Wichita	**Jim Clinkstock** (WC)	**Won (2-0)**

September 27	Chicago, IL	Gene Tunney defeats Jack Dempsey via 10 round decision to defend boxing's WHC. This was Dempsey's last fight.	
September 28	Tulsa,	**Joe Malcewicz** (WC) (Took place at the McNulty Baseball Park. Gate: $19,000—top seat $10)	**Won (2-0)**
October 27	Tulsa	**Alexander Garkawienko** (WC)	**Won (2-0)**
November 3	Atlanta, GA	**Jack Washburn** (WC)*	**Won (2-0)**
November 8	St. Louis, MO	**Paul Jones**	**Won (2-0)**
November 28	St. Louis, MO	Lewis posts $5,000 bond for a St. Louis match with Joe Stecher. The Stecher brothers arrive in the city to talk with Tom Packs about the match.	
November 29	Atlanta, GA	**Wayne Munn**	**Won (2-0)**
December 12	Tulsa, OK	**Toots Mondt** (WC)	**Won (UTC)**
December 17	Emporia, KS	**Clarence Jenkins** (WC)	**Won**
December 21	St. Louis, MO	Articles signed by Lewis and Joe Stecher for a title unification match in St. Louis new Coliseum, February 20, 1928.	

1928

January 5	Dallas, TX	**Wayne Munn**	**Won (2-0)**
January 9 (11)	Kansas City, MO	**Rudy Dusek**	**Won (2-1)**
January 16	Minneapolis, MN	**Wayne Munn**	**Won (2-1)**
January 23	Tulsa	**Toots Mondt**	**Won (2-0)**
February 20	St. Louis, MO	**Joe Stecher** (World Title Win)* (Att.:>7,500-$65,000)	**Won**
February 29	Kansas City	**Joe Malcewicz** (WC)	**Won (UTC)**
March 6	Atlanta	**Paul Jones** (WC)	**Won (2-0)**
March 12	Chicago, IL	**Alex Garkawienko** (WC)* (Att.: 3,500-$5,000)	**Won (2-0)**
March 14	Boston, MA	**Joe Komar** (WC) (Att.: 5,000)	**Won (2-0)**
March 15	Los Angeles, CA	Lewis signs to defend for Lou Daro.	
March 17	St. Louis, MO	Promoter Tom Packs announces that he and associated promoters in Philadelphia, Chicago, New York and Los Angeles will bar Ed Lewis unless he agrees to meet "legitimate title contenders" including Jim Londos.	

March 30	Houston, TX	**Toots Mondt**	**Won (2-0)**
April 18	Boston, MA	**George Mcleod** (WC) (Att.: 7,000)	**Won**
April 23	Kansas City, MO	**Stanley Stasiak** (WC)	**Won**
April 26	Salt Lake City	**Howard Cantonwine** (Att.: 5,000)	**Won (UTC)**
April 27	Ogden	**Dr. Pete Visser** (WC)	**Won (2-0)**
May 2	Los Angeles, CA	**Nick Lutze** (WC)*(1:29:35) (Att.: <9,000)	**Won**
May 4	Salt Lake City	**Howard Cantonwine**	**Won**
May 5	Logan	**George Nelson**	**?**
May 24	Boston, MA	**George Mcleod** (WC) (Att.:>8,000)	**Won**
May 28	Minneapolis, MN	**Marin Plestina** (WC)*	**Won (2-1)**
May 31	Salt Lake City	**Ira Dern**	**Won (UTC)**
June 1	Price, UT	**Wallace Duguid**	**Won**
June 13	Los Angeles, CA	**Nick Lutze** (WC)* (Att.: 10,000 - Sell Out. $16,000)	**Won**
June 19	Phoenix	**Jack Washburn** (WC?)	**Won**
June 25 (26?)	Houston	**Joe Malcewicz** (WC) (Said to be record crowd. Nation democratic convention in town. Nomination won by Al Smith who later lost to Herbert Hoover.)	**Won (2-1)**
June 25	Philadelphia, PA	Jim Londos defeated Dick Shikat	
June 29	Boston, MA	**Gus Sonnenberg** (WC)* (Att.: 9,500 to 12,000 or 14,000, SRO)	**Won (Utc)**
July 2	Worcester	**Stanley Stasiak** (WC)	**Won**
July 3	Springfield, MA	**Bull Komar** (WC)	**Won**
July 7 ?	Chicago, IL	Lewis was involved in an automobile accident.	
July 9	Minneapolis, MN	**Marin Plestina** (WC)*	**Won**
July 12	Chicago, IL	Lewis states he is going to tour England and Europe for three months and then return for a farewell tour of the USA. Says he will retire by end of next year.	

July 20 (30?)	New York, NY	Lewis sails for England.	
September 1	New York, NY	Lewis returns from a trip to Germany. Looks fat, and says it's from German beer. He says he will train in Canada.	
September 23	Houston, TX	Newspaper reports that Lewis was in Europe during the past summer.	
October 3	Los Angeles, CA	**Joe Malcewicz** (WC)* (Att.: 9,300-$16,000)	**Won (2-0)**
October 5	Salt Lake City	**Ira Dern** (WC?)	**Won**
October 17	Los Angeles, CA	**Marin Plestina** (WC)* (Att.: 10,115)	**Won (2-1)**
October 26	Philadelphia, PA	**Paul Jones** (WC) (Att.: 7,000)	**Won**
November 17	Boston, MA	Boston Garden opens. Designed by Tex Rickard to resemble NYC's Madison Square Garden.	
November 21	Los Angeles, CA	**Paul Jones** (WC)*	**Won (2 St-UTC)**
December 17	Phoenix	**Pat O'Shocker** (WC?)	**Won**
December 19	Los Angeles, CA	**Joe Malcewicz** (WC)* (Att.: 8,500-$15,000)	**Won**

1929

January 4	Boston, MA	**Gus Sonnenberg** (World Title Loss)* (Att.: 20,000. $72,000. Lewis purse=$50,000)	**COR**
January 6	Miami Beach, FL	Tex Rickard dies following an appendectomy in Miami Beach.	
January 18	Philadelphia, PA	**Jim Clinkstock**	**Won**
January 21	MSG, NYC	**Renato Gardini** (Att.: 6,000)	**Won**
January 23	Brooklyn, NY	**George Hagen**	**Won**
January 25	Chicago, IL	Miss Elaine Tomaso of Glendale, CA, announces she will soon be marrying Lewis. She was in Chicago with her mother and sister to see Lewis before the Plestina match. Ed is divorced from Miss Bessie McNear.	
January 29	Chicago, IL	**Marin Plestina***	**Won (2-0)**
February 4	Nashville	**Jim McMillen** (Att.: 3,000)	**Won (2-1)**
February 5	St. Louis, MO	Arrives in town.	

February 7	St. Louis, MO	**Nick Lutze**	**Postponed**
February 11	Tulsa	**Rudy Dusek**	**Won**
February 13	St. Louis, MO	**Nick Lutze***	**Won (UTC)**
February 18	New Orleans, LA	**Mike Romano*** (Att.: 4,000)	**Won (UTC)**
February 20	Portland, ME	**Kola Kwariani**	**Won**
February 22	Ridgewood Grove	**Renato Gardini** (Att.: 4,000)	**Won (1-0)**
February 25	New York, NY	**Kola Kwariani** (1:13:15) (Att.: 7,000)	**Won (UTC)**
February 26	Providence, RI	**Howard Cantonwine**	**Won**
February 28	Boston, MA	**George Mcleod**	**Won**
March 1	Philadelphia, PA	**Gino Garibaldi*** (Att.: 5,000)	**Won**
March 4	New Orleans, LA	**Mike Romero**	**Won (DQ 1-1)**
March 5	St. Louis, MO	**Jim Clinkstock**	**Won**
March 11	Chicago, IL	**Kola Kwariani**	**Won**
March 20	St. Louis, MO	Training with George Tragos at National Gym.	
March 22	St. Louis, MO	**Nick Lutze***	**Won (1-0)**
March 26	Chicago, IL	**Joe Malcewicz**	**Won**
April 1	Kansas City	**Kola Kwariani**	**Won**
April 8	New York, NY	**Matros Kitilenko**	**Won**
April 9	Brooklyn, NY	**Mike Romano**	**Won**
April 12	Philadelphia, PA	**Pat McGill**	**Won**
April 15	Kansas City	**Kola Kwariani**	**Won**
April 16	Chicago, IL	**Renato Gardini** (Gate: $6,000)	**Won (2-0)**
April 19	Minneapolis, MN	**Joe "Toots" Mondt**	**Won (2-1)**
April 19	Chicago, IL	Lewis announced that he had set May 4 as the date for his marriage to Elaine Tomaso of Chicago at Riverside, CA. He claimed it was his third marriage.	
April 22	Shreveport, LA	**Moose Norbeck**	**Won (UTC 1-0)**

April 24	New Orleans, LA	**Milo Steinborn**	**Won (2-0)**
April 25	Baton Rouge, LA	**John Freberg**	**Won (UTC 1-0)**
April 27	Chicago, IL	**Matros Kirilenko**	**Won**
April 28	Chicago, IL	**Gene Le Doux**	**Won**
May 1	Los Angeles, CA	**Joe Stecher***	**Won**

(Att.: 10,395. $28,640. Arena record. Stecher's old championship belt, which he refused to give to Lewis following the 1920 title change, was said to be on the line, but from all we know it remained Stecher's property.)

May 8	Riverside, CA	Lewis married Miss Elaine Tomaso, an art student formerly of Chicago. Billy Sandow was best man. She was 25 and Lewis claimed to be 34 years old. They planned to spend two weeks in Arrowhead, CA.	
May 15	Philadelphia, PA	Champion Gus Sonnenberg was suspended by Pennsyivania State Athletic Commission for not meeting logical contenders.	
May 15	Los Angeles, CA	**Dick Daviscourt***	**Won (2 St-UTC)**
May 20	Kansas City, MO	**Matros Kirilenko**	**Won (COR 2-1)**
May 24	Wichita	**Pat O'Shocker**	**Won**
May 28	Tulsa	**Joe Stecher***	**Won (1-2)**

(Att.: 6,000. Sell-out)

June 3	Nekoosa, WI	Lewis and his new wife, visiting Ed's parents, were guests at the home of Mrs. J. G. Gutheil.	
June 10	New York, NY ?	**Joe De Vito** (30:40)	**Won (1-0)**
June 11	Brooklyn, NY	**Jack Washburn**	**Won**
July 9	Fenway Park, Boston, MA	**Gus Sonnenberg** (AWA WC)*	**Lost (1-2)**

(Att.: 25,000. Jack Curley at ringside. Ed became first person to win fall over Sonnenberg.)

July 31	Chicago, IL	**Matros Kirilenko**	**Won**
August 1	Denver, CO	A 12 minute copy of the Sonnenberg match playing at the America Theater.	
August 7	Philadelphia, PA	Gus Sonnenberg stripped of World Title in state for refusing to meet winner of Shikat/Londos match.	
August 23	Philadelphia, PA	Dick Shikat defeated Jim Londos for WC in Penn.	

August ?	Chicago, IL ??	**Matros Kirilenko ?** (This result from a St. Louis post report on 11-18-29.)	Lost (decision) ?
August 27	Chicago, IL	**Matros Kirilenko**	Won (2-1)
August 31	Greeley, CO	Toots Mondt announces that he is retired from actual wrestling and is manager of Dick Shikat.	
September 4	Los Angeles, CA	**Joe Stecher*** (Att.: 9,000)	Won
September 25 ?	Portland	**Howard Cantonwine**	Won
October 3 (2)	Los Angeles, CA	**Nick Lutze**	Won (2-0-UTC)
October 4	Phoenix, AZ	**George Mcleod** (2/3 falls) (Before match, Lewis posted $500 with Phoenix Boxing Commission for a match with Londos, Sauer or Shikat in that city.)	Won
October 9	Portland	**Howard Cantonwine**	Won
October 14	Seattle, WA	**Andre Adoree**	Won
October 15	Wenatchee, WA	**Bill Reynolds**	Won
October 22	Los Angeles, CA	Gus Sonnenberg was headbutted & KO'ed by small time wrestler Pete Ladjone on the downtown streets of L.A., at 7th (6th?) & Broadway, near L.A. Athletic Club. Ladjone was charged with assault.	
October 23	Los Angeles, CA	**Gus Sonnenberg** (AWA WC)* (Att.: 10,000. $31,000)	Lost
November 12	Los Angeles, CA	Pete Ladjone, the wrestler who attacked Gus Sonnenberg on the streets of downtown Los Angeles, was sentenced to 30 days in jail by municipal judge George L. Bogue. Ladjone was released under $1,000 bond pending hearing on his appeal.	
November 13	Los Angeles, CA	**Gus Sonnenberg** (AWA WC)* (Att.: 10,800--$31,000)	Lost
November 16	La Junta, CO	**Everett Marshall** (Handicap Match)	FTP
November 19	Kansas City, MO	**Joe Stecher***	Won (2-1)
November 20	Des Moines, IA	**Pat O'Shocker**	Won
November 28	Boston, MA	**Joe Devito** (Att.: 2,800)	Won
December 1	Worcester	**Jack Taylor**	Won

December 2	Manchester	**Karl Lemie**	**Won**
December 3	Providence, RI	**Stan Stasiak**	**Won**
December 4	Worcester	**Jack Taylor**	**Won**
December 5	Boston, MA	**Pat McGill**	**Won**
December 6	Holyoke	**Jack Ganson**	**Won**
December 9	Toronto, Canada	**Dan Koloff**	**Won (2-1)**
December 10	Brantford, Canada	**John Katan**	**Won**
December 11	London, ON, Canada	**George Hill**	**Won (2-0)**
December 16	Tulsa	**Gus Sonnenberg** (AWA WC) (Att.: 6,000)	**Lost (0-2)**

1930

January 1	Salt Lake City	**Dr. Karl Sarpolis**	**Won**
January 6	Phoenix	**Dick Daviscourt**	**Won**
January 15	Phoenix	In a attempt to regulare pro wrestling, the National Boxing Commission (NBA) announced a tournament for their World Title. Invited contenders were Sonnenberg, Shikat, Pesek, Londos and Pete Sauer (Steele). Phoenix promoter C. L. McPherson bid $10,000 for one of the bouts.	
January 10	Spokane, WA	**Tom Alley**	**Won (2-0)**
January 13	Seattle, WA	**Howard Cantowine** (Att.: 6,000)	**Won (2-1)**
January 14	Tacoma, WA	**George Mcleod** (Record gate in Tacoma)	**Won (1-0)**
January 17	Chicago, IL	Wrestling was suspended in Illinois until elimination tournament is agreed upon by Londos, Steele, Steinke, with Sonnenberg agreeing to meet survivor. The three refused. Lewis, Plestina, Stasiak and Malcewicz took to put up $2,500 forfeits. This leads to Lewis gaining Illinois title recognition after beating Wladek Zbyszko in November 1931.	
January 22	Los Angeles, CA	**Dick Daviscourt**	**Won (2-1)**
January 24	Salt Lake City, UT	**Ira Dern**	**Won**
January 27	Seattle, WA	**Charlie Hanson** (Largest gate in Seattle history.)	**Won (2-1)**
January 28	Tacoma, WA	**George Mcleod** (Att.: 3,000+)	**Won**
February 3	Phoenix	**Dick Daviscourt**	**Won**

February 7	Salt Lake City	**Dick Daviscourt**	**Won (UTC)**
February 10	Seattle, WA	**Howard Cantonwine**	**Won (2-1)**
February 11	Tacoma, WA	**Dick Daviscourt** (1:10:00) (Att.: Sell out)	**Won (DQ)**
February 13	Vancouver, Canada	**George Mcleod**	**Won**
February 14	Victoria, Canada	**Bob Kruse**	**Won**
February 18	Seattle, WA	**Charlie Hanson** (Hanson was taken to hospital after having convulsions during match.)	**Won (UTC)**
February 28	Salt Lake City, UT	**Ira Dern** (Att.: 6.000)	**Draw**
March 5	New York, NY	**Joe Stocca**	**Won**
March 6	Boston, MA	**Bob "Bibber" McCoy** (45:00)	**Draw**
March 12	Worcester	**Stanley Stasiak**	**Won (2-1)**
March 19	Los Angeles, CA	**Gene La Doux*** (Att.: 8,500-$13,000)	**Won (2-0)**
March 31	Kansas City	**Henri Deglane**	**Draw**
April 2	MSG, NYC	**Marin Plestina** (Att.: 4,000)	**Won**
April 3	Boston, MA	**Jack Sherry***(45:00) (Att.: 5,000)	**Won (2-1)**
April 8	New York, NY	The NY State Athletic Commission ruled that all wrestling cards must be billed as exhibitions. They were classified as theatrical. William Muldoom was on the commission.	
April 9	Milwaukee, WI	**Carl Schultz***	**Won (1-0-UTC)**
April 10	Kansas City	**Dan Koloff**	**Won**
April 16	Los Angeles, CA	**Everett Marshall***	**Lost (1-2)**
May 1	Vancouver, Canada	**Martin Zikov**	**Won**
May 5	Los Angeles, CA	Ringside for the Sonnenberg/Marshall match at Wrigley Field which drew 17,580 and $69,745.	
May 20	Kansas City, MO	**Gus Sonnenberg** (AWA WC)	**Lost**
May 23	Philadelphia, PA	**Jack Smith***	**Won**
May 24	Washington, DC	**Dan Koloff**	**Won**

June 6	Philadelphia, PA	Jim Londos defeated Dick Shikat to win NWA/ NY/Penn. recognition as World champion.	
June 11	Los Angeles, CA	**Everett Marshall***	**Won (2-1)**
June 16	Seattle, WA	**Joe Stecher***(8 rounds)	**Won (Dec)**
June 18	Milwaukee, WI	**Gus Sonnenberg** (AWA WC)	**?**
June 25	Los Angeles, CA	**Marin Plestina**	**Won (2-1)**
July 7	Seattle, WA	**Gus Sonnenberg** (WC)	**?**

Lewis tours Australia with Joe Stecher in September

August 5	Sydney	Lewis arrived in Australia with wife Elaine via the Tahiti liner. Lewis is introduced at a wrestling card that night.	
August 9	Melbourne	**Charley Strack**	**Won**
August 14	Brisbane	**Pat McGill**	**WOF**
August 16	Melbourne	**Dr. Karl Sarpolis**	**Won (1-0)**
August 18	Sydney	**Harold Cantonwine**	**Won (2-1)**
August ?	Sydney	Joe & Tony Stecher arrive in Australia via the liner *Aorangi*.	
August 27	Adelaide	**George Kotsonaros**	**Won (UTC 1-0)**
September 1	Sydney	**Dr. Karl Sarpolis**	**WOF (1-0)**
September 6	Melbourne	**Joe Stecher***	**Lost (Dec 0-0)**
September 13	Melbourne	**Joe Stecher**	**Draw**
September 20	Sydney	**Joe Stecher*** (Att.: 10,500)	**Won (2-1)**
September 28	Sydney	Lewis flies to Brisbane to meet Mrs. Lewis and they take the liner *Nieuw Holland* to tour the far east, before returning to America.	
October 27	Kansas City, MO	**John Turner**	**Won (2-0)**
November 12	Los Angeles, CA	**Jose Dominguez**	**Won (2-0)**
November 21	Fresno, CA	**Moose Norbeck** (Ed claimed to weigh 235 lbs)	**Won (2-0)**
November 26	Los Angeles, CA	**Henri Deglane** (60:00)	**Draw**
November 28	Salt Lake City, UT	**Nick Lutze** (Att.: 3,500)	**Won**
December 4	Vancouver, Canada	**Karl Sarpolis**	**Draw**
December 6	Victoria, Canada	**Charlie Strack**	**Won**
December 10	Los Angeles, CA	Ed Don George defeats Gus Sonnenberg for World Title.	
December 12	Fresno, CA	**Dr. Pete Visser** (Att.: 4,000)	**Won**
December 22	Los Angeles, CA	**Joe Stocca**	**Won (2-0)**

1931

January 2	Glendale, CA	Lewis was hit by a car as he was sideswiped getting out of his auto in front of his restaurant in the 700 block on South Brand. He received a bruised pelvis and a gash on his hip. He said he would cancel all engagements for several weeks. His restaurant was called E. & E. Broiler, formerly Earl's Broiler, located at 707-709 South Brand. Ed co-owned it with an Earl Peyton. Lewis was living at 627 E. Windsor in Glendale. At some point Lewis had part ownership in an E. & E. broiler located in Alhamba at 5th Street and Main. Later Lewis owned part of a cocktail bar named The Virginian at 4300 Long Beach Blvd., Long Beach.	
January 7	Chicago, IL	**Frank Judson**	**Cancelled**
January 9	San Antonio, TX	Wayne Munn died of Bright's disease at Fort Sam Houston Base Hospital. He had been sick for a year after working in the oil business.	
February 4	Los Angeles, CA	**Dr. Karl Sarpolis**	**Won (2-1)**
February 10	Oakland, CA	**Howard Cantonwine**	**Won (2-1)**
March 4	Los Angeles, CA	**Henri Deglane**	**Won (2-0)**
March 18	Los Angeles, CA	**Everett Marshall**	**Won (2-0)**
April 6	Hollywood, CA	Wrestled exhibition with Bill Beth.	
April 13	Wrigley Field, L. A.	**Ed Don George** (AWA World Title win) (Att.: 12,000)	**Won (2-0)**
April 20	Kansas City, MO	**Everett Marshall** (WC)	**Won (2-1)**
April 23	Tulsa, OK	**Fred Peterson** (WC?)	**Won**
April 27 ?	Chicago, IL	The book *Fall Guys* claims that Sandow met Paul Bowser in Chicago and $50,000 of a $70,000 forfeit was returned to the Boston promoter. It's possible that plans were then made to have Lewis drop the title to Deglane.	
April 28	Montreal, Canada	Montreal newspapers announce a Lewis/Deglane in the city match for May 4.	
April 28	Chicago, IL	**Gene Ledoux** (AWA WC) (Att.: 3,107-$6,170)	**Won (2-0)**
April 28	Syracuse, NY	Syracuse promoter Demetrius Tofalos says if Lewis is serious in his challenge to Jim Londos he can have the match at the New York State Fair Coliseum for a guarantee of $10,000. He claims Jim Londos has excepted the match.	
May 1	Montreal, Canada	Promoter Lucien Riopel announced that the Lewis/Deglane match would start before 10:00, so fans from outside town could get home. Prices were raised to 75 cents, $1.50 & $3.00.	

May 3	Montreal, Canada	Reports have both Lewis and Deglane arriving in town.	
May 4	Montreal, Canada	**Henri Deglane** (AWA World Title loss) (Att.: 7,000. Referee Eugene Tremblay)	**DQ (0-2)**
May 8	Rochester	**Everett Marshall**	**Won (2-1)**
May 12	Chicago, IL	Londos's attorney notifies the Illinois Commission that he refuses to meet Ed Lewis. The commission announces that Londos cannot be billed as World Champion in the state.	
May 13	Chicago, IL	The Illinois State Athletic Commission declares the World Title vacant in the state.	
May 13	Chicago, IL	**Frank Judson** (WC)	**Won (UTC)**
May 14	Kansas City, MO	**Babe Luther**	**Won**
May 18	Tulsa	**Nick Velcoff**	**Won (2-0)**
May 21	Topeka	**Ermak Harkovsky**	**Won**
June 5	Salt Lake City	**Ira Dern**	**Won**
June 10	Los Angeles, CA	**Karl Sarpolis** (Calif. WC)	**Won**
June 16	San Diego, CA	**Luther Williams**	**Won**
June 23	San Francisco, CA	**Jack Plummer**	**Won (2-1)**
June 26	Salt Lake City	**Everett Marshall**	**No Show**
July 22	Los Angeles, CA	**Dr. Stanley Lurich**	**Won (1-0)**
July 23	Salt Lake City	**Ira Dern** (WC) (Att.: 5,000)	**Won (DQ)**
September 14	Chicago, IL	The *Chicago Tribune* prints that Londos is willing to meet Ed Lewis in Chicago for a $250,000 guarantee.	
September 17	Kansas City	**Sailor Dick Raines** (WC)	**?**
September 25	Chicago, IL	The Illinois Athletic Commission invites nine of the country's leading wrestlers to meet Ed Lewis in Chicago for world title.	
October 12	Kansas City	**Darna Ostapovich** (WC)	**Won (2-1)**
October 15	Detroit, MI	**Joe Komar** (Att.: 700)	**Won (COR)**
October 22	Chicago, IL	Lewis gives a wrestling exhibition.	
November 2	Chicago, IL	**Wladek Zbyszko** (Illinois World Title win)* (Att.: 7,244)	**Won**

November 21	Los Angeles, CA	Billy Sandow fought off a attempted kidnapping at his home. Although shot in the hand, he wrestled a handgun away from one of the thugs and fired at them as they fled.	
November 6	Albuquerque, NM	**Jack Russell**	**Won (2-0)**
November 25	Los Angeles, CA	**Joe Savoldi** (Calif. WC)	**Won (2-1)**
November 30	Phoenix, AZ	**Count Karl Micheloff**	**Won**
December 7	Seattle, WA	**Marin Plestina**	**Draw**
December 10	Vancouver, Canada	**Howard Cantonwine**	**Won**

1932

January 4	Seattle, WA	**Ira Dern**	**Won**
January 5	Tacoma, WA	**Roland Kirchmeyer**	**Won**
January 6	Portland	**Abe Kaplan**	**Won**
January 7	Vancouver, Canada	**Bob Kruse**	**Won**
January 11	Seattle, WA	**Karl Sarpolis**	**Won**
January 12	Tacoma, WA	**Roland Kirchmeyer**	**Won**
January 13	Portland	**Abe Kaplan**	**Won**
January 14	Seattle, WA	Photos show that Lewis inspected a huge statue of himself by the artist Alonzo Victor Lewis in his studio.	
January 18	Sacramento, CA	**Pete Visser**	**Won**
January 20	Los Angeles, CA	**Michael Gettsonoff**	**Won (2-1)**
January 20	Boston, MA	*Boston Globe* announces that Ray Fabiani has made Toots Mondt match maker and director of his wrestling cards in Boston Garden.	
January 22	Vancouver, Canada	**Tiger Daula** (Att.: 7,300)	**Draw**
January 22	Rochester	Billy Sandow confirms that his 20-year-old partnership with Ed Lewis had ended. It was rumored that Lewis had accepted a $50,000 offer to join the Curley interests in NYC.	
January 23	Seattle, WA	**Karl Sarpolis**	**Won**
January 26	Chicago, IL	Appears on a fight show at Loyola University.	

Lewis starts working for Curley-Mondt group (?) around this time.

Date	Location	Opponent	Result
January 26	Boston, MA	Paul Bowser sought a court injunction stopping Lewis, then aligned with Jack Curley, from appearing on the Fabiani January 27 Boston card, saying that he had an exclusive contract with Ed in the city. Judge Franklin T. Hammond of Suffolk Superior Court refuses to issue an injunction.	
January 27	Boston, MA	**Pat O'Shocker** (Promoter Toots Mondt using Jack Curley talent.)	Won
January 28	Toronto, Canada	**Jim Clinstock**	Won (2-0)
January 30	Missouri	Lewis is suspended by Missouri Athletic Commission for failing to go through with a contract to meet John Pesek. The commission attemps to get the NWA to suspend Lewis in all states affiliated with the organization.	
February 2	Portland, ME	**Taro Myake**	Won
February 5	Ottawa, Canada	**George Vassell**	Won
February 9	Cleveland, OH	**George Zaharias**	Won
February 10	Boston, MA	**Gino Garibaldi** (Att.: 6,000)	Won (2-0)
February 11	Washington, DC	**Tiny Roebuck** (Att.: 7,000. Report has this as Ed's first match with the Curley Group?)	Won
February 12	Philadelphia, PA	**Sandor Szabo**	Won
February 16	New Haven, CT	**Matros Kirlenko**	Won
February 18	St. Louis, MO	**Rudy Dusek** (30:05)	Won
February 23	Baltimore, MD	**Cy Williams**	Won
February 24	Boston, MA	**Ray Steele***(1:30:00)	Draw
February 25	Pittsburgh, PA	**John Maxos** (Lewis breaks Maxos' neck. Arrested, he posts $500 bail.)	Won
February 26	Philadelphia, PA	**Jim McMillen**	Won
March 3(4)	St. Louis, MO	**Hans Kampfer**	Won
March 3	St. Louis, MO	Lewis issued challenge to Jim Londos for a match to decide World Title.	
March 4	Buffalo, NY	**Frank Speer**	Won
March 7	Wilkes-Barre, PA	**Sandor Szabo**	Won

March 8	Jersey City, NJ	**George Hagen**	**Won**
March 9	Newark, NJ	**Renato Gardini**	**Won**
March 11	Detroit, MI	**Frank Brunowicz**	**Won**
March 14	Los Angeles, CA	Promoter Lou Daro offers Londos $100,000 to meet Ed Lewis.	
March 17	St. Louis, MO	**Pat O'Shocker**	**Won**
March 22	Baltimore, MD	**Fred Grubmeier**	**Won**
March 23	Newark, NJ	**Renato Gardini**	**Won**
March 24	Philadelphia, PA	**Jim McMillen**	**Won**
March 29	San Diego, CA	**Vic Christy** (Handicap Match)	**FTP**
March 30	Los Angeles, CA	**Jack Smith**	**Won (2-0)**
April 4	Seattle, WA	**John Freberg**	**Won**
April 5	Tacoma, WA	**Tom Alley**	**Won (2-0)**
April 6	Portland, OR	**Abe Kaplan**	**Won**
April 7	Vancouver, Canada	**Tiger Daula**	**Won**
April 9	Seattle, WA	**Jack Taylor**	**Won (2-1)**
April 12	San Francisco, CA	**Nick Velcoff**	**Won**
April 13	San Jose, CA	**Richard Stahl**	**Won**
April 18	Memphis, TN	**Gino Garibaldi*** (Att.: 4,500)	**Won**
April 19	Atlanta	**Pat O'Shocker**	**Won**
April 25	Birmingham	**Blue Sun Jennings**	**Won**
April 29	Cincinnati, OH	**Milo Steinborn**	**Won**
May 3	Memphis, TN	**Rudy Dusek*** (Att.: 3,500)	**Won**
May 5	Detroit, MI	**Jim Clinstock** (Att.: 2,300)	**Won**
May 10	Boston Garden	**Leo Pinetzki**	**Won (2-0)**
May 11	Montreal, Canada	**Tiny Roebuck**	**Won**
May 13	Philadelphia, PA	**George Zaharias**	**Won**

May 16	Norfolk	**Benny Ginsberg**	**Won**
May 17	Baltimore, MD	**Howard Cantonwine**	**Won**
May 18	Boston, MA	**Kola Kwariani**	**Won (2-0)**
May 19	Toronto, Canada	**Earl McCready**	**Won (2-0)**
May 24	New Haven, CT	**Leo Pinetzki**	**Won**
May 31	Harrisburg	**Herb Freeman**	**Won**
June 1	Montreal, Canada	**Tiny Roebuck**	**Won**

The Curley Group bring lewis to New York City.

June 2	New York, NY	**Leo Pinetzki**	**Won**
June 3	Philadelphia, PA	**Sammy Stein**	**Won**
June 4	New York, NY	**Ralph Wilson**	**Won**
June 5	New York, NY	**Fritz Kley**	**Won**
June 9	Long Island, NY	**Dick Shikat*** (Att.: 25,000. $65,000)	**Won**
June 13	Staten Island, NY	**Sandor Szabo**	**Won**
June 14	Bronx, NY	**Sammy Stein*** (Att.: 7,960)	**Won**
June 15	Brooklyn, NY	**Fritz Kley**	**Won**
June 17	Philadelphia, PA	**Roland Kirchmeyer**	**Won**
June 20	Buffalo	**Leo Pinetzki**	**Won**
June 21	New Haven, CT	**Earl Mc Cready**	**Won**
June 22	Hempstead	**Vanka Zelesniak**	**Won**
June 24	Philadelphia, PA	**Roland Kirchmeyer**	**Won**
June 27	Staten Island, NY	**Sandor Szabo**	**Won**
June 28	Bronx, NY	**Leo Pinetzki**	**Won**

Jim Londos ordered by NY State Athletic Commission to sign Lewis bout by October 31.

June 29	Hempstead	**Vanka Zelesniak**	**Won**
June 30	Freeport, NY	**Cy Williams**	**Won**
July 1	Babylon, NY	**Tiny Roebuck**	**Won**
July 2	Long Beach, NY	**Benny Ginsberg**	**Won**

July 3	Brooklyn, NY	**Fred Donaiff**	**Won**
July 4	Staten Island, NY	**Ralph Wilson**	**Won**
July 5	New York, NY	**Sammy Stein**	**Won**
July 6	Long Beach, NY	**George Manich**	**Won**
July 7	Albany, NY	**George McLeod**	**Won**
July 8	Babylon, NY	**Steve Znosky**	**Won**
July 8	Philadelphia, PA	Jim Londos was ordered by the Pennsylvania Athletic Commission to defend title against Ed Lewis. Londos was given 60 days to defend or vacate title.	
July 11	Staten Island, NY	**Herb Freeman**	**Won**
July 12	New Haven, CT	**Earl McCready**	**Won**
July 14	Long Beach, NY	**Herb Freeman**	**Won**
July 15	Montreal, Canada	**Tiger Daula** (WC)	**Won**
July 16	Toronto, Canada	**Sammy Stein** (WC)	**Won**
July 19	New York, NY	**Sandor Szabo*** (Att.: Small)	**Won**
July 20	New York, NY	**Bill Middlekauff**	**Won**
July 21	Paterson, NJ	**Mike Romano**	**Won**
July 22	Philadelphia, PA	**Tiger Daula**	**Won**
July 23	Long Beach, NY	**Herb Freeman**	**Won**
July 25 (19)	Washington, DC	**George McLeod**	**Won**
July ?	Wisconsin Falls, WI	Lewis trains in the woods of Wisconsin for six weeks.	
July 19	North Andover, MA	Gus Sonnenberg, while driving home drunk around 4:00 AM from a match at Haverhill, is involved in an auto accident which killed patrolman Richard L. Morrissey of the Lawrence Police Department. Sonnenberg suffered lacerations of the lip, right leg, left hand, and a possible fractured rib, but was released from lawrence General Hospital later that day. Morrissey, 42 years old and married, died at the hospital several days later.	
July 30	Belmont, MA	Gus Sonnenberg was arrested at the home of his father-in-law. He was taken to Lawrence, Mass., and charged in District Court with manslaughter, driving while drunk, and reckless driving. Sonnenberg pleaded not guilty and was released after Paul Bowser posted bale of $2,000. The trial was to start on August 2.	

August 21	Collingwood, Canada	An automobile driven by Joseph "Toots" Mondt collided head-on with another car, killing Teresa Luccioni and injuring four others. Mondt was charged with manslaughter and released on $9,000 bail. Toots and brother Ralph suffered cuts and bruises.	
September 3	Wisconsin Rapids, WI	Lewis and wife leave for Chicago after spending several weeks at their cottage in northern Wisconsin.	
September 6	Janesville, WI	**George Mack**	**Won**
September 8	Toronto, Canada	**Howard Cantonwine** (WC)	**Won**
September 9	Philadelphia, PA	**Roland Kirchmeyer**	**Won**
September 12	Staten Island, NY	**Masked Marvel (Joe Cox ?)**	**Won**
September 15	Montreal, Canada	**Sammy Stein** (WC)	**Won**
September 29	Des Moines	**Earl McCready**	**Won**
September 30	New York, NY	Jim Londos stripped of N. Y. World Title for failing to meet Ed Lewis. Keeps N.B.A. Title. The NY State Athletic Commission ordered Ray Steele and Jack Sherry to meet in MSG, October 10, with the winner to wrestle Lewis for the title on October 31. Steele is part of the Londos group and doesn't make the date. This explains why #1 NY contender wrestles a shoot with Lewis on December 5.	
October 3	New York, NY	**Sammy Stein**	**Won**
October 4	New Haven, CT	**Steve Znosky**	**Won**
October 5	Montreal, Canada	**Jack Washburn**	**Won**
October 7	Ottawa, Canada	**Howard Cantonwine**	**Won**
October 10	MSG, NYC	**Jack Sherry** (N. Y. World Title win)* (Att.: 5,000)	**Won**
October 18	Bronx, NY	**Roland Kirchmeyer**	**Won**
October 19	Brooklyn, NY	**Mike Mazurki**	**Won**
October 24	New York, NY	**Bruno Gorrasini**	**Won**
October 25	New Haven, CT	**Pat McClary**	**Won**
October 28	Troy, NY	**Bill Bartush**	**Won**
November 2	Philadelphia, PA	**Earl McCready (WC)***	**Won (1-0)**
November 10	Barrie, ON, Canada	Joe "Toots" Mondt was sentenced to one year in Ontario Reformatory upon his conviction on charges of criminal negligence in connection with the death of a Toronto girl in an automobile accident. He was acquitted of manslaughter. An appeal was made by Toots' counsel.	

November 10	New York NY	George Calza (WC)	Won
November 21	MSG, NYC	George Calza	Won
November 23	Philadelphia, PA	Glenn Munn* (Att.: 6,500)	Won (1-0)
December 5	MSG, NYC	Ray Steele (WC)*(32:55) (Att.: 8,000. $11,000. Riot followed supposed shoot.)	Won (DQ)
December 6	New Haven, CT	Pat McClary	Won
December 7	Buffalo, NY	Frank Speer	Won
December 8	Toronto, Canada	Howard Catonwine (WC)	Won
December 9	Boston, MA	Masked Marvel (Al Getzwich)	Won
December 12	Staten Island, NY	Mike Romano	Won
December 13	Bronx, NY	Sid Westrich	Won
December 14	Detroit, MI	Steve Znosky	Won (2-0-UTC)
December 15	St. Louis, MO	Sandor Szabo	Won
December 19	MSG, NYC	Leo Pinetzki (Handicap Match)	Won
		Sammy Stein (Att.: 5,000)	Won
December 21	Philadelphia, PA	Charlie Strack	Won

1933

January 5	Stockton, CA	Rudy LaDitzi	Won
January 6	Fresno, CA	Jake Patterson	Won
January 9	Seattle, WA	Arrived in town via plane from Los Angeles.	
January10	Tacoma, WA	Bob Kruse	Won
January 11	Portland, ME	Abe Kaplan	Won
January 12	Vancouver, Canada	Tiger Daula (Att.: 6,626)	Won
January 13	Seattle, WA	Ringside	
January 17	San Francisco, CA	Bob Kruse	Won
January 23	MSG, NYC	Jim Browning (NY WC) (Att.: 7,000)	Won

January 25	Boston, MA	**Charlie Strack**	Won
January 27	Holyoke	**Matros Kirilenko**	Won
January 31	Bronx, NY	**Sam Stein** (NY WC) (Att.: 12,000)	Won
February 1	Queens, NY	**Marin Plestina** (NY WC)	Won
February 6	MSG, NYC	**Fred Meyers** (NY WC) (Att.: 5,000)	Won
February 7	Portland, ME	**Pat McGill**	Won
February 9	Lowell, MA	**Gene Le Doux**	Won (2 St)
February 10	Boston, MA	Ed Don George wins AWA WC by beating Henri Deglane.	
February 13	New York, NY	**Nick Lutze** (NY WC) (Att.: 4,000)	Won
February 14	Bronx, NY	**Sam Stein** (NY WC) (Att.: 5,000)	Won
February 15	Philadelphia, PA	**Stan Pinto**	Won
February 16	Camden	**Mike Mazurki**	Won
February 18	Wilmington	**Marin Plestina** (NY WC)	Won
February 20	New York, NY	**Jim Browning** (N. Y. World Title loss)* (Att.: 5,000-$5,000)	Lost
February 21	White Plains,	**Fred Meyers**	Won
February 22	Worcester	**Tiny Roebuck**	Won
February 25	Schenectady	**George Hagen**	Won
March 1	New York, NY	**Matros Kirilenko**	Won
March 2	Camden, NJ	**Sammy Stein** (1:30:00)	Draw
March 3	Buffalo, NY	**Earl Mc Cready**	Lost (Decision)
March 4	New York, NY	**Hans Kampfer**	Won
March 6	MSG, NYC	**Dick Shikat*** (60:00)	Draw
March 7	Bronx, NY	**Sammy Stein**	Won
March 20	MSG, NYC	**Jim Browning** (NY WC)* (Att.: 7,000)	Lost
March 21	Bronx, NY	**Joe Malcewicz** (26:00) (Att.: 3,500)	Draw

March 22	Brooklyn, NY	**Alphonse Geicewicz (Al Getz)**	**Won**
March 24	Buffalo, NY	**Earl Mc Cready**	**Won**
March 27	Chicago, IL	**Leo Pinetzki**	**Won**
April 4	San Francisco, CA	**George Hagen**	**Won**
April 5	Fresno, CA	**Glen Wade**	**Won**
April 6	San Jose, CA	**Richard Stahl**	**Won**
April 7	Chicago, IL	Jim Londos is double-crossed by Joe Savoldi and referee Nanagoff. Savoldi claims World Title.	
April 7	Oakland, CA	**Dan Koloff**	**Won (Utc)**
April 11	Chicago, IL	**Jim Browning*** (Att.: 800-$1,100)	**Lost**
April 15	Clarksdale, MS	President Col. H. J. Landry rules that Jim Londos was still the National Wrestling Association world champion in a press release.	
April 17	Seattle, WA	**Nore Jeristrom**	**Won (UTC)**
April 18	Spokane	**Bob Kruse**	**Won (Dec 1-1)**
April 20	New York City	Dr. Ben Roller died.	
April 20	Portland	**Ira Dern**	**Won (UTC)**
April 21	Vancouver, Canada	**Jack Forsgren**	**Won**
April 25	San Francisco, CA	**George Hagen**	**Won**
April 28	Oakland, CA	**Ad Santel**	**Won**
May 3	Los Angeles, CA	**Tiny Roebuck**	**Won (2-0)**
May 9	San Diego, CA	**Oki Shikina***	**Won**
May 15	MSG, NYC	**Joe Savoldi**	**Won (COR)**
May 17	Boston, MA	**Ed Don George (AWA WC)*** (Att.: 10,000)	**Lost**
May 22	MSG, NYC	**Joe Savoldi*** (Att.: 5,000)	**Lost**
May 23	Chicago. IL	**Sammy Stein** (This match was billed as a contest by the promoter.)	**Won (2-1)**
May 24	Milwaukee, WI	**Gus Sonnenberg**	**Lost**
June 7	Los Angeles, CA	**Jim Browning (NY WC)*** (Att.: 9,000)	**Lost**

June 8	Long Beach, CA	**Glen Wade**	**Won**
June 12	Sacramento, CA	**Dan Koloff**	**Won**
June 15 (14)	San Diego, CA	**Rudy Skarda***	**Won (2-0-UTC)**
June 21	Los Angeles, CA	**Gus Sonnenberg**	**Lost (1-2)**
June 28	Portland	**Bob Kruse**	**Won (2-1)**
June 29	Vancouver, Canada	**Richard Stahl**	**Won**
June 30	Seattle, WA	**Oki Shikina**	**Won (2-1)**
July 4	Alberta, CA	**Jack Taylor**	**Won**
July 6	Portland, OR	**Dan Koloff**	**Won**
July 7	Vancouver, Canada	**Tiny Roebuck**	**Won**
July 12	Los Angeles, CA	**Sammy Stein**	**Lost (1-2)**
July 18	San Diego, CA	**George Hagen***	**Won (2-1)**
July 19	Bakersfield, CA	**Glen Wade**	**Won**
July 20	San Francisco, CA	**Ted Cox**	**Won**
July 26	Los Angeles, CA	**Luigi Bacigalupi**	**Won (1-0)**
July 27	San Francisco, CA	**Marin Plestina**	**Won**
July 28	Fresno, CA	**Jack Ganson**	**Won**
August 3	Vancouver, Canada	**Jim Browning** (WC?)	**Lost**
August 4	Portland	**George Nelson**	**Won (UTC)**
August 5	Marshfield	Fred Beell was shot in the face and killed by gangsters while investigating a robbery as a relief police officer.	
August 8	San Diego, CA	**Louis Bacigalupi***	**Won (2-0)**
August 28	Wrigley Field, L. A.	**Marin Plestina** (5 Min & 24 Sec.)*	**Won (1-0)**
August 29	San Diego, CA	**Jim Browning** (WC)* (Att.: 4,000)	**Draw**
August 31	San Francisco, CA	**Charlie Santen**	**Won**
September 6	Los Angeles, CA	**Ole Anderson**	**Won (UTC)**
September 12	Portland	**Howard Cantonwine** (No show— Gus Sonnenburg)	**Won (DQ)**

September 14	Denver	**Marin Plestina**	**Won**
September 15	Salt Lake City	**Nick Lutze**	**Won (UTC)**
September 19	San Diego, CA	**Sammy Stein*** (Att.: 3,500)	**Draw**
September 20	Los Angeles, CA	**Dale Raines** (handicap)*	**Won**
		Tor Johnson	**Won**
		Louis Bacigalupi	**FTP**
September 21	Stockton, CA	**Tiny Roebuck**	**Won**
September 26	San Diego, CA	**Sammy Stein***	**Won (2-1)**
September 28	Long Beach, CA	**Louis Bacigalupi**	**Won**
September ?	Hollywood, CA	Filmed short appearance as himself in 'The Prizefighter and the Lady.'	
October 2	Pasadena, CA	**Olie Anderson***	**Won**
October 3	San Diego, CA	**Pat O'Hara***	**Won**
October 4	Los Angeles, CA	**Louis Bacigalupi***	**Won**
October 6	Salt Lake City	**Sammy Stein**	**Won**
October 9	Pasadena, CA	**Tor Johnson**	**Won**
October 10	San Diego, CA	**Vic Christy***	**Draw**
October 13	Houston, TX	**Steve Znosky**	**Won**
October 14 ?	Philadelphia, PA	**Paul Boesch** (1:08:49)?	**Won**
October 19	New Orleans, LA	**Mike Romano**	**Won**
October 20	Houston, TX	**Steve Znosky**	**Won**
October 27	Glendale, CA	Mrs. Elaine Tomaso Friedrich died at her home after a pulmonary illness of many months. Lewis is traveling home from the east.	
November 10	Hollywood, CA	Lewis plays himself for a few seconds in the film 'The Prizefighter and the Lady.'	
November 20	MSG, NYC	**Sandor Szabo** (20:00)	**Draw**
November 21	Albany	**Richard Stahl**	**Won**
November 22	Newark	**Bill Middlekauff**	**Won**
November 23	Camden	**Stan Pinto**	**Won**

November 25	New York, NY	**Jim Clinstock**	Won
November 27	St. Louis, MO	**Roland Kirchmeyer**	Won
		(Att.: 1,584. $658.50. A Lewis attendance low in St. Louis)	
November 29	Newark	**Man Mountain Dean**	Won
November 30	Camden	**Jim Browning** (WC)	Lost
December 4	MSG, NYC	**Vic Christy**	Won
December 5	Reading	**Jim Clinstock**	Won
December 6	Newark	**Wladek Zbyszko**	Won
December 7	Staten Island, NY	**Frank Brunowicz**	Won
December 8	Syracuse, NY	**Tiny Roebuck**	Won
December 13	St. Louis, MO	**Mayes McLain***	Won
December 15	Washington, DC	**Jim Clinstock**	Won
December 18	MSG, NYC	**Gus Sonnenberg** (20:00)	Draw
		(Undercard of a George/Browning title unification draw.)	
December 20	St. Louis, MO	**Ray Steele** (No DQ match)*	Lost
December 29	Philadelphia, PA	**Jim Browning** (WC)	Lost

1934

January 9	San Diego, CA	**Mike Mazurki**	Draw
January 10	Los Angeles, CA	**Cy Williams**	Won
January 12	Salt Lake City	**Ira Dern**	Lost
January 16	San Diego, CA	**Sammy Stein**	Won
January 19	Salt Lake City, UT	**Bill Longson**	No Show
January 22	Sioux Falls, SD	**Pat McGill**	Won
January 24	Des Moines	**Sam Leathers**	Won
January 25	Marshalltown, IA	**Mike Markoff**	Won
January 26	Council Bluffs	**Jack O'Dell**	Won
January 29	Kansas City, MO	**Matros Kirilenko**	Won
January 31	Indianapolis, IN	**Chief Chewacki**	Won
February 1	New Orleans, LA	**Joe Cox**	Won

February 2	Knoxville	**Dick Daviscourt**	**Won**
February 3	Wichita	**Abe Kashey**	**Won**
February 5	MSG, NYC	Lewis ringside to challenge as Londos makes first appearance in MSG in two years.	
February 6	New York, NY	**Rudy Dusek (30:00)**	**Lost (Decision)**
February 8	Camden	**Dick Raines**	**Won**
February 13	Wichita	**Abe Kashey**	**Won**
February 14	Kansas City, MO	**Red Devil (Jack Lewis or Joe Cox)**	**Won**
February 15	St. Louis, MO	**Joe Malcewicz***	**Draw**
February 19	New York, NY	**Mike Romano**	**Won**
February 21	Hartford	**Rudy Dusek**	**Won**
February 23	Richmond	**Tiny Roebuck**	**Won**
February 26	Omaha	**Joe De Vito**	**Won**
February 28	Des Moines	**Jake Patterson**	**Won**
March 1	St. Louis, MO	**Dick Shikat**	**DQ**
March 2	Kansas City, MO	**Red Devil**	**Won**
March 5	New York, NY	**Hans Kampfer**	**Lost**
March 7	Brooklyn, NY	**Eddie Civil (Leo Daniel Boone Savage)**	**Won**
March 8	Kansas City	**Joe De Vito**	**Won**
March 15	St. Louis, MO	**Dick Shikat**	**Lost**
March 18	Brooklyn, NY	**Eddie Civil**	**Won**
March 19	Buffalo, NY	**Gene Ledoux**	**Won**
March 20	Youngstown, OH	**John Cope**	**?**
March 21	Rochester	**Ivan Vacturoff**	**Won**
March 22	Erie	**Gene Ledoux**	**Won**
March 23	Boston, MA	**Firpo Wilcox**	**Won**
March 26	New York, NY	**George Calza**	**Won**
March 29	Camden	**Hans Steinke**	**Draw**
April 2	Buffalo	**Ed Don George (AWA WC)**	**Lost**
April 3	New York, NY	**Scotty McDougall**	**Won**

April 6	Houston, TX	**Chief Chewacki**	**Won**
April 11	Los Angeles, CA	**Mike Mazurki**	**Won**
April 15	Mexico City, Mexico	**Jim Browning** (NY WC)* (Att.: 12,000. $10.000. In the Bull Ring)	**Lost**
April 18	Los Angeles, CA	**Jack Ray**	**Won**
April 20	Houston, TX	**Chief Chewacki**	**Won**
April 23	New York, NY	**Rudy Dusek**	**Won**
April 26	Toronto, Canada	**George Hagen**	**Won**
May 2	Newark, NJ	**Sandor Szabo**	**Won**
May 7	Montreal, Canada	**Sandor Szabo**	**Won (2-1)**
May 14	New York, NY	**Ray Steele**	**Won**
May 15	New York, NY	**Harry Fields**	**Won**
May 17	Hempstead	**Sam Cordovano**	**Won**
May 22	Albany	**Rudy Dusek**	**Won**
May 23	Brooklyn, NY	**Hans Steinke**	**Won**
May 28	Montreal, Canada	**Henri Deglane*** (Att.: 7,000)	**Won (2-1)**
June 1	Cedar Rapids	**Ole Olson**	**Won**
June 5	Chicago, IL	Ringside for Londos vs Singh — challanged Jimmy.	
June 12	Marshalltown, IA	**Jack Wagner**	**Won**
June 13	Des Moines	**Roland Kirchmeyer**	**Won**
June 15	Detroit, MI	**Charlie Strack**	**Won**
June 18	Cedar Rapids	**George Mack**	**Won**
June 20	San Antonio, TX	**Jack O'Dell**	**Won**
June 21	Fort Worth, TX	**Sol Slagel**	**Won**
June 22	Houston, TX	**Karl Davis**	**Won**
June 25	New York, NY	NBA WC Jim Londos wins NY WC by beating Jim Browning.	
June 25	Oklahoma City	**Earl Wade**	**Won**
June 28	Fort Worth, TX	**Tiny Roebuck**	**Won**
June 29	Houston, TX	**Joe Cox**	**Won**

July 4	Atlanta, GA	**Karl Davis**	**Won (2-0)**
July 5	New Orleans, LA	**Joe Cox**	**Won**
July 6	Houston, TX	**Sol Slagel**	**Won**
July 10	Chicago, IL	Toots Mondt was called Lewis's manager. In town to set up a match with Jim Londos.	
July 18	Topeka	**Billy Edwards**	**Won**
July 19	Kansas City, MO	**Steve Savage**	**Won**
July 20	Denver, CO	**Joe Savoldi**	**Won**
July 21	Colorado Springs	**Roland Kirchmeyer**	**Won (2 St)**
July 27	Denver, CO	**Karl Sarpolis**	**Won**
July 30	San Antonio, TX	**Billy Edwards**	**Won**
August 3	Lincoln	**Vic Soldat**	**Won**
August 13	Tacoma, WA	**Joe Malcewicz**	**Draw**
August 14	Everett, WA	**Casey Colombo**	**Won**
August 15	Portland, OR	**Masked Marvel (Dick Daviscourt)**	**Won**
August 16	Vancouver, Canada	**Ivan Managoff**	**Won (2-0)**
August 17	Seattle, WA	**Ted Cox**	**Won (DQ 2-0)**
August 22	Portland	**Dick Daviscourt**	**Won**
August 23	Chicago, IL	**George Mack** (Att.: 2,300. Subbed for George Zaharias)	**Won**
August 27	Montreal, Canada	**Yvon Robert** (1:05:03)* (Att.: 6,000)	**Won (1-0)**
August 28	Three Rivers	**George Jenkins**	**Won (2-0)**
September 4	Chicago, IL	Lewis training with Pete Schuh and Zack Malkov. Marin Plestina and Lou Talaber to join later	
September 16	Chicago, IL	Chief Saunooke replaced Pete Schuh in Lewis's camp.	
September 20	Wrigley Field, Chicago, IL	**Jim Londos** (NBA WC) (Att.: 35,265. $96,302)	**Lost**
September 29 (28)	Salt Lake City	**Ira Dern**	**Won**
September 30 ?	St. Louis, MO	**Ray Steele ? or Charles Rigoulot**	**Lost**

October 1	Montreal, Canada	**Ed Don George** (AWA WC) (Att.: 6,000)	**DQ (1-2)**
October 2	Los Angeles, CA	In town on business regarding his restaurants in Glendale and Alhambra.	

Toured France and England

October 5		Booked passage on the ship *Ile de France*. *Ring Magazine* reported he planned on meeting Adolph Hitler of Germany and Benito Mussolini of Italy during his stay in Europe.	
October 19	Paris, France	Lewis arrives in Paris.	
October 29	Paris, France	**Kola Kwariani**	
November 5	Paris, France	**Charles Rigoulot**	**Won**
November 11	Paris, France	**Ray St. Bernard**	**Won**
November 19	Paris, France	**Henri Deglane**	**Won**
December ?	London, England	Worked out with Bert Assirati for 30 minutes at the Stadium Club. Danno O'Mahoney worked out with Charles Smith and was pinned in two minutes.	
December 5	London, England	**Danno O'Mahoney**	**Win or Draw**
December 7 (10)	Paris, France	**Henri Deglane**	**Lost**

1935

January 2	Los Angeles, CA	**Hans Steinke*** (Att.: 7,000)	**Won (2-1)**
January 4	St. Louis, MO	**Ray Steele**	**Won**
January 7	New York, NY	**Ed Don George** (AWA WC)	**Lost (1-0)**
January 8	Albany, NY	**Hans Kampfer**	**Won**
January 9	Cleveland, OH	**Gino Garibaldi**	**Won**
January 14	Cincinnati, OH	**Dick Raines**	**Won**
January 15	Indianapolis, IN	**Charlie Strack**	**Won**
January 16	St. Louis, MO	**George Zaharias** (Att.: 7,486. Man Mountain Dean no showed)	**Won**
January 21	Pasadena, CA	**Mike Mazurki**	**Won**
January 22	San Francisco, CA	**Joe Malcewicz**	**Draw**
January 23	Los Angeles, CA	**Jim McMillen***	**Won (DQ-2-1)**

January 24	Stockton, CA	**Hardy Kruskamp**	**Won**
January 25	Oakland, CA	**Fred Meyers**	**Won**
January 31	St. Louis, MO	**Jim Londos** (NBA WC) (Att.: 14,921)	**Lost**
February 2(1)	Peoria	**Karl Sarpolis**	**Won**
February 7	Camden	**Rudy Dusek**	**Won or Draw**
February 8	Chicago, IL	Chicago promoter Doc Krone dies.	
February 14	St. Louis, MO	**Jim Browning** (Att.: 5,396)	**Won**
February 19 (20)	Evansville	**Dick Raines** (1:02:43) (Att.: Sell-out)	**Won**
February 21	Los Angeles, CA	**Willie Davis**	**Won**
February 25	Phoenix, AZ	**Milo Steinborn**	**Won**
February 26	San Diego, CA	**Frank Speer**	**Won (2-1)**
February 27	Los Angeles, CA	**Willie Davis***	**Draw**
February 28	Long Beach, CA	**Frank Speer**	**Won**
March 6	St. Louis, MO	**Jim Londos** (NBA WC) (Att.: 11,438)	**Lost**
March 7	Chicago, IL	**Danno O'Mahoney**	**Lost**
March 12	Atlanta, GA	**Orville Brown**	**Draw**
March 15	Houston, TX	**Karl Sarpolis**	**Won**
March 18	Phoenix, AZ	**Hans Steinke**	**Won**
March 21	Long Beach, CA	**Paul Boesch**	**Won**
March 22	San Bernardino, CA	**Nick Lutze**	**Won**
March 25	Pasadena, CA	**Frank Speer**	**Won**
March 26	San Francisco, CA	**Joe Savoldi**	**Lost**
March 27	Bakersfield, CA	**Hans Steinke**	**Lost**
March 29	Salt Lake City, UT	**Mike Mazurki**	**Won**
April 2	Minneapolis, MN	**Ray Steele** (22:10) (Att.: 7,000. After natch, Lewis went nuts and attacked the referee and his own second.)	**Lost**
April 3	Duluth, MN	**Ray Richards**	**Won (2-0)**

April 4	St. Paul, MN	**George Koverly** (27:00)	**Won**
April 5	Des Moines, IA	**Lou Plummer**	**Won (2-0)**
April 9	Indianapolis, IN	**Billy Edwards**	**Won**
April 11	Chicago, IL	**Jim Browning**	**Lost**
April 17	Boston, MA	Arrives to train for O'Mahoney match.	
April 20	Boston, MA	Training in Boston, Lewis claims that he'll be 44 years old on June 30 and has earned between $12,000,000 & $14,000,000 in his career. Claims to still own cafes in Glendale, Pasadena and Alhambra, Calif. He lives in Glendale.	
April 24	Los Angeles, CA	Lou Daro's international tournament to crown a new world champion begins. Lewis enters.	
April 26	Boston, MA	**Danno O'Mahoney*** (Att.: 20,000)	**UTC (0-2)**
April 29	Boston, MA	O'Mahoney admits he lost London match to Lewis.	
April 29	Buffalo	**Ed Don George** (AWA WC)	**Lost**
May 1	Trenton	**Joe Dusek**	**Won**
May 2	Brooklyn, NY	**Dick Daviscourt**	**Won**
May 3	Brooklyn, NY	**Fred Grubmeier**	**Won**
May 6	Montreal, Canada	**Ed Don George** (AWA WC)	**Lost (2-1)**
May 10	Houston, TX	**Lou Plummer**	**Won**
May 13	Memphis, TN	**Dick Raines**	**Won**
May 17	Salt Lake City	**Mike Romano**	**Won**
May 20	Pasadena, CA	**Sandor Szabo**	**Draw**
May 22	Los Angeles, CA	**Marin Plestina***	**Won**
May 23	Long Beach, CA	**Pat Fraley**	**Won**
May 29	Los Angeles, CA	**Pete Mehringer*** (This was Mehringer's first pro loss.)	**Won**
June 4	San Francisco, CA	**Milo Steinborn**	**Won**
June 5	Los Angeles, CA	**Hans Kampfer**	**Won**
June 10	Sacramento, CA	**Milo Steinborn**	**Won**
June 11	San Francisco, CA	**Joe Malcewicz**	**Won**

June 14	Houston, TX	Jim Londos (NBA WC)	Lost
June 17	Sacramento, CA	Joe Malcewicz	Won
June 18	San Francisco, CA	Jim Browning	DQ
June 19	Los Angeles, CA	Vincent Lopez* (Att.: 10,400. $7,900)	Lost
June 21	Seattle, WA	Cancelled-Injury	
June 24	Sacramento, CA	Joe Malcewicz	DQ
June 25	San Francisco, CA	Jim Browning	Won
June 26	Los Angeles, CA	Ernie Dusek* (Att.: 10,400. $7,000. Lewis is eliminated from international tournament.)	Lost
June 27	New York, NY	Danno O'Mahoney defeats Jim Londos for NY/ NWA WC.	
June 27	Stockton, CA	Juan Humberto	Won
June 28	Seattle, WA	Lewis is suspended in Washington State for 6-21 no show.	
June 28	Oakland, CA	Willie Davis	Won
June 30	Los Angeles, CA	Lewis turns 45 years old.	
July 3	Los Angeles, CA	Hans Kampfer *	Won (Decision)
July 5	Oakland, CA	Jim Browning	Won
July 9	San Francisco, CA	Vincent Lopez	Lost (1-2)
July 10	Los Angeles, CA	Mike Romano* (This was the night of William Focher's death.)	Won
July 11	Los Angeles, CA	Lewis and Vincent Lopez sign papers making Lewis manager of the future California WC.	
July 11	Stockton, CA	Ted Cox	Won
July 12	Oakland, CA	Joe Malcewicz	Lost
July 23	Los Angeles, CA	Lewis is credited with training Vincent Lopez for tournament final vs Man Mountain Dean.	
July 24	Los Angeles, CA	Vincent Lopez wins tournament final over Man Mountain Dean and is recognized as World Champion in the state of California. Lewis acts as Lopez's manager.	
July 26	Seattle, WA	Man Mountain Dean	Won (UTC 1-1)

July 31	Boston, MA	Danno O'Mahoney becomes undisputed WC by defeating AWA world champion Ed Don George.	
July 31	Portland	**Hans Steinke**	**Lost (1-2)**
July 31	New York, NY	United Press reports that Lewis, after 27 years on the mat, is quitting and will serve as manager trainer to Vincent Lopez.	
August 13	Minneapolis, MN	**Hal Rumberg** (Lou Thesz wrestled on undercard.)	**Won**
August 27	Indianapolis, IN	**Joe Cox**	**Won**
August 28	Detroit, MI	**Carl Hansen**	**Won**
August 29	Merrill, WI	**Howard Blazer**	**?**
September 3	Minneapolis, MN	**Ray Steele** (36:03)	**Lost**
September 4	Waterloo	**Lou Plummer**	**Won**
September 11	Boston, MA	**Dick Daviscourt**	**Won**
September 11	Boston, MA	In corner of Ed Don George during losing match with Dano O'Mahoney, in front of 25,000 at Fenway Park.	
September 13	Jamaica, NY	**Fred Grubmeier**	**Won**
September 16	Montreal, Canada	**Bibber McCoy**	**Won**
September 17	Quebec City, Canada	**Mike Romano**	**Won**
September 23	Buffalo	**Leo Numa**	**Draw**
October 11	Boston, MA	**Danno O'Mahoney** (Undisputed WC)* (Att.: 8,000)	**Lost**
October 16	Evansville, IN	**Joe Cox**	**Won**
October 18	Houston, TX	**Leo Daniel Boone "Whiskers" Savage** (Att.: 6,000)	**Won**
October 19	Fort Worth, TX	**Billy Edward**	**Won**
October 22	Peoria, IL	**Olaf Olsen**	**Won**
October 25	Houston, TX	**Leo "Whiskers" Savage**	**DQ**
October 26	Fort Worth, TX	**Chief Chewacki**	**Won**
November 5	San Diego, CA	**Jack Washburn**	**Won**
November 7	St. Louis , MO	**Man Mountain Dean** (Handicap Match)*	**Ftp**

Date	Location	Opponent	Result
November 12	Indianapolis, IN	?	?
November 18	Kansas City, MO	**Gus Sonnenberg**	**Won (2-1)**
November 19	Indianapolis, IN	**Jim McMillen**	**Draw**
November 19	St. Louis, MO	Everett Marshall, with the support of manager Billy Sandow and promoter Max Baumann, post $5,000 with the State Commission for a match with champion Danno O'Mahoney. Ed Lewis followed that with $1,000 check for the commission for a match with Marshall at any site he wants. Jim Browning also challenges Marshall. The commission then suggested a tournament between Tom Packs, Lewis and Browning vs Baumann's Marshall and Lee Wycoff with the winner meeting O'Mahoney for the title. Chairman Garrett Smalley then gave all four men ten days to post bonds or shut up.	
November 22	Philadelphia, PA	**Tiny Roebuck**	**Won**
November 25	Tampa, FL	**Jack O'Brien** (Att.: 4,000)	**Won**
December 5	Pittsburgh, PA	**Sandor Szabo**	**Won**
December 6	New York, NY	**Harry Fields**	**Won**
December 9	Montreal, Canada	**Danno O'Mahoney** (Undisputed WC)	**Lost (0-2)**
December 10 (12)	Albany	**Vic Christy**	**Won**
December 12	Camden	**Mike Mazurki**	**Won**
December 14	Philadelphia, PA	**Joe Janas**	**Won**
December 16	Kansas City	**Orville Brown**	**Won**
December 17	Indianapolis, IN	**Karl Davis**	**Won**
December 19	St. Louis, MO	**Man Mountain Dean** (7:27) (Att.: 4,637)	**Won**
December 26	St. Louis, MO	**Dick Raines**	**Won**
December 31	Indianapolis, IN	**Henry Piers**	**Won**

1936

Date	Location	Opponent	Result
January 9	St. Louis, MO	vs (Handicap Match)	
		Leo Numa & George Zaharias	**Won**
January 15	Terre Haute, IN	**Ernie Zeller**	**Won**

January 16	Kansas City, MO	**Karl Davis**	**Won**
		Billy Hanson	**Won**
January 27	New York City	**Jack Donovan**	**Won**
January 29	St. Louis, MO	**Danno O'Mahoney** (WC) (Att.: 9,170)	**Lost**
January 31	Kansas City, MO	**Steve Savage**	**Won**
February 5	Los Angeles, CA	**George Calza** (Att.: 7,500)	**DQ**
February 7	Vancouver, Canada	**Tiger Daula**	**Lost**
February 10	Sacramento, CA	**Gino Garibaldi**	**Won**
February 13	Vancouver, Canada	**Tiger Daula**	**Lost**
February 11	San Francisco, CA	**Masked Unknown** (Handicap)* Managed Lopez vs Szabo*	**FTP**
February 14	Seattle, WA	**Mayes McLain**	**Draw**
February 17	Sacramento, CA	**Gino Garibaldi**	**Won**
February 18	San Francisco, CA	**Danny Winters*** Managed Lopez vs Szabo	**Won**
February 20	Stockton, CA	**Chief Little Wolf**	**Draw**
February 21	Oakland, CA	**Billy Bartush**	**Lost**
February 25	San Francisco, CA	**Sandor Szabo***	**Won (2-0)**
February 28	Philadelphia, PA	**Dean Detton**	**Lost**
March 2	New York, NY	**Charles Strack**	**Won**
March 6	Kansas City, OK	**Pat Fraley**	**Won**
March 10	San Francisco, CA	**Billy Bartush**	**Won**
March 12	Vancouver, Canada	**vs (Handicap Match) Mayes Mclain & Willie Davis**	**Draw**
March 13	Seattle, WA	**Rudy Strongberg** Managed Lopez in main event vs Willie Davis	**Draw**
March 16	Tacoma, WA	**Willie Davis** Managed Lopez against Paul Boesch	**Draw**
March 17	Spokane, WA	Managed Lopez vs Mayes McLain	

March 19	Vancouver, Canada	**Jack Forsgren**	Won
March 20	Seattle, WA	**Willie Davis**	Draw
March 21	Longview, WA	**Paul Boesch**	Won (1-0)
March 23	Sacramento, CA	**Joe Malcewicz**	Draw
March 24	San Francisco, CA	**George Calza**	Won
March 25	Los Angeles, CA	Managed Vincent Lopez vs Man Mountain Dean	
March 26	Oakland, CA	**Chief Chewacki**	Won
April 1	Los Angeles, CA	Ringside for Lopez vs Man Mountain Dean	
April 3	Santa Monica, CA	**Wild Bill Longson**	Won
April 9	Long Beach, CA	**Chief Chewacki**	Won
April 11	Santa Monica, CA	**Tony Felice**	Won
April 16	Long Beach, CA	**Joe Savoldi**	Won
April 20	Kansas City, OK	**Pat O'Shocker**	Won
April 21	Indianapolis, IN	**Ray Steele**	Won
April 22	St. Louis, MO	**Gus Sonnenberg** (Att.: 4,968)	Won
April 27	Winnipeg, Canada	**Darna Ostapovich**	Won
April 29	Minneapolis, MN	**Lou Plummer**	Won
April 30	Chicago, IL	**Blue Sun Jennings**	Won
May 1	Detroit, MI	**Jim McMillen**	Draw
May 4	New York, NY	**Hans Steinke**	Won
May 6	Cleveland, OH	**Nick Lutze**	Won ?
May 8	Kansas City, MO	**Gus Sonnenberg**	Won
May 10	Detroit, MI	**Jim McMillen**	Draw
May 13	Memphis, TN	**Dick Raines**	Won
May 15	Knoxville, TN	**Dory Roche**	Won
May 19	Chicago, IL	**Chief Little Wolf** (30:50)	Won
May 20	St. Louis, MO	**Paul Jones** (Att.: 3,195)	Won
May 22	Houston, TX	**Pat O'Shocker**	Won

May 25	Phoenix, AZ	**Vic Hill**	**Won (2-0)**
May 27	Los Angeles, CA	Managed Vincent Lopez vs Joe Savoldi	
May 28	Long Beach, CA	**Tor Johnson**	**Won**
May 29	Houston, TX	**Pat O'Shocker**	**Won**
June 8	Kansas City	**Gus Sonnenberg**	**Won**
June 15	Chattanooga	**Karl Davis**	**Won**
June 17	Atlanta, GA	**Orville Brown**	**Won (UTC)**
June 19	Houston, TX	**Milo Steinborn**	**Won**
June 19	?	Jim Browning dies.	
June 25?	Washington, DC	Mike Romano died in the ring during a match with Jack Donovan.	
June 26	Houston, TX	**Len Macaluso**	**DQ**
July 26	Los Angeles, CA	Lewis announces that he had sold Vincent Lopez contract back to the California World Champion and is no longer his manager. There seems to be heat between the two.	
August 13	New York, NY	**Lee Wykoff** (Shoot-2:14:45)* (Att.: 3,000)	**DCOR**
August 27	Vancouver, Canada	**Stan Pinto**	**Won (COR)**
August 28	Seattle, WA	**Pat Fraley**	**Won**
August 31	Tacoma, WA	**Chief Little Wolf**	**Won**
September 2	Portland	**Sandor Szabo**	**Lost**
September 3	Vancouver, Canada	**Pat Fraley**	**Lost**
September 4	Seattle, WA	**Tor Johnson**	**Lost (Decision)**
September 9	Portland	**Sandor Szabo**	**Won**
September 12	Portland	**Red Shadow**	**Lost**
September 15	Honolulu, HI	**Ed Don George**	**Won**
September 22	Honolulu, HI	**Vic Christy**	**Won**
October 15	Vancouver, Canada	**Pat Fraley**	**Lost**
October 17	Seattle, WA	**Pat Fraley** (Tour)	**Won**
		Harry Kent (Tour)	**Won**
		Dan McIntyre (Tour)	**Lost (Decision)**

October 20	Chicago, IL	**Jim McMillen** (Att.: 1,500)	**Lost (1-0)**
October 29	St. Louis, MO	Ringside for Marshall vs Dory Roch	
		Issues challenge to Marshall and manager Billy Sandow. Says he's beaten Everett 5 straight times.	
November 5	Vancouver, Canada	**Tor Johnson**	**Won**
November 6	Seattle, WA	**Tor Johnson**	**Won**
November 9	Olympia	**Pat Fraley**	**?**
November 12	Vancouver, Canada	Referee Pat Fraley vs Red Shadow	
November 13	Seattle, WA	**Red Shadow**	**UTC**
December 3	Seattle, WA	Referee for Bull Martin vs Red Shadow	
December 4	Vancouver, Canada	**Bull Martin**	**Won**
December 11	Seattle, WA	Referee for Pat Fraley vs Red Shadow	
December 19	Portland	**Red Shadow**	**Lost**
December 27 ?	Honolulu, HI ?	**Ed Don George**	**Won**

1937

January 11	Yuma, AZ	Lewis married Miss Bobbie Lee West, formerly of Corpus Christi, TX and Muskogee, OK. They had know each other for twelve years. Lewis is living in Glendale and still has two restaurants. She claims to be a full-blooded Cherokee Indian. The two remained married for over 29 years, until Lewis's death August 1966. This is Lewis's fourth marriage. His last wife Elaine Tomaso died in 1933.	
January 11	Sacramento, CA	**Brother Jonathan**	**Won (DQ)**
January 24	Los Angeles, CA	Purchases a hillside home at 8145 Willow Glen Road in Laurel Canyon, for $9,500. It is a seven-room stucco residence with two cottages and a garage.	
January 25	Sacramento, CA	**Dean Detton** (CA WC)	**Lost**
January 26	San Francisco, CA	**Jules Strongbow**	**Won**
February 2	San Francisco, CA	**Sandor Szabo*** (Pacific Coast Title)	**Lost (1-2)**
March 10	Los Angeles, CA	**Chief Chewacki**	**Won**
March 12	Salt Lake City, UT	**Dean Detton** (World Title)	**Lost**
March 21	Glendale, CA	Lewis applied for social security card. His SSN was 550-16-0364. His listed age was 47 (June 30, 1980).	

May 20	Kansas City	**Rudy LaDitzi**	**Won**
May 25	Minneapolis, MN	**Bronko Nagurski**	**Lost (0-1)**
June 25	Los Angeles, CA	Lewis and wife sailed on the Matson ocean liner *Mariposa* for a world tour including Greece, India, and South Africa.	
July 6	Honolulu, HI	**Count Francis Fouche**	**Won**
July 12	New York, NY	Promoter Jack Curley dies.	
July 13	Honolulu, HI	**Ray Richards**	**DQ**

Tours New Zealand and Australia

August 2	Auckland, NZ	**Floyd Marshall**	**Won**
August 4	Christchurch NZ	**John Spellman**	**Won**
August 7	Dunedin NZ	**Glen Wade**	**Won**
August 14	Wellington NZ	**Earl McCready**	**Lost**
August 19	Hamilton NZ	**Rusty Westcoatt**	**Won**
August 21	Auckland NZ	**Earl McCready**	**Lost**
September 4	Leichhardt, AUS	**John Spellman**	**Won**
September 13	Sydney, AUS	**Jack Forsgren**	**Won**
September 17	New York, NY	Ray Fabiani reports in the *Hartford Courant* that Lewis was on his way to wrestle the Great Gama in India for $30,000.	
November 29	Paris, France	**Henri Deglane**	**Lost**
November 11	Kansas City	**Cliff Olsen**	**Lost**
December 11	Los Angeles, CA ?	Lewis returned to America on the US liner *Washington*. He announced he would retire from the wrestling ring. In doing so, he criticized the "slambang" style of wrestling. A report has Lewis "half blind from trachoma." He plans on spending the rest of his life living in the Hollywood hills.	

1938

March 30	Los Angeles, CA	Seconded Vincent Lopez vs Broko Nagurski	
May 18	Los Angeles, CA	Referee for Jim Londos vs Dean Detton	
October 19	Los Angeles, CA	Referee for Nagurski vs Szabo	

1939

April 6	Los Angeles, CA	Managed Ed White against Jim Londos
May 3	Los Angeles, CA	Managed Ed White vs Dick Raines
May 10	Los Angeles, CA	Managed Ed White vs Nick Lutze who was subbing for Jim Londos. Because of the no show, Ed claimed WC for White.
May 17	Los Angeles, CA	Managed Ed White vs Sandor Szabo
May 24	Los Angeles, CA	Managed Ed White vs Masked Marvel (Jim Henry)
June 21	Los Angeles, CA	Managed Ed White vs Black Panther
July 10	Hollywood, CA	Managed Ed White vs Edward Payson
November 9	Hollywood, CA	Lewis was appointed matchmaker fo the heavyweights at Hollywood Legion Stadium. Hugh Nichols was in control of the lighter-weights.

1940

February 1	Nekoosa, WI	Jacob Friedrich retires from the Nekoosa Police Department at age 81, after 28 years' service.
May 17	Los Angeles, CA	Lewis announced plans to promote boxing, with ex-Olympic match-maker Jimmy Murray. Claims unidentified backers had supplied him with $100,000 to stage three outdoor cards during the summer. He also claims that he would begin construction the next winter on a $400,000 indoor stadium in Glendale.
July 12	Los Angeles, CA	Lewis challenged Jack Dempsey to a mixed match, promoted by Jimmy Murray, with the purses being donated to the Red Cross. Lewis weighed 280 lbs but claimed he would train down to 240 lbs.
September 4	Los Angeles, CA	Toots Mondt and his brother write a letter to the California Commission requesting a cancellation of his booking office. Commissioner Everett Sanders says it will be accepted. Mondt had been under pressure from wrestlers and the commission over payoffs and money owed. Mondt plans to return to NYC. Art Mondt wants to promote in San Bernardino. The Daro brothers, Lou and Jack, were also out at the Olympic Auditorium.

1941

January 9	Fresno, CA	Referee for James vs Lyons
February 18	Glendale, CA	Lewis is living in Glendale, managing his restaurant and cocktail lounge.

February 20	St. Louis, MO	Referees the Steele vs Thesz NWA Title match	
June 17	Long Beach, CA	Apparently Lewis was operating a restaurant at 4300 Long Beach Boulevard called "The Virginian."	
September 16	Wilmington	Referees Red Berry vs Joe Varga	
October 22	Atlanta	Referees French Angel vs Rudy Strongberg	
November 11	Chicago, IL	**Ole Olson** (Lewis unable to wrestle because of ankle injury. Commission would not let Lewis referee. He may have been ringside.)	**No Show**
November 12	Milwaukee, WI	**Andy Rascher**	**Won**
December 1	Charlotte, NC	Referee for Bobby Bruns vs Swedish Angel	
December 3	Norfolk	Referee for Joe Marsh vs Red Ryan	
December 7	Honolulu, HI	The Japanese attack Americans at Pearl Harbor. The U.S. enters WWII.	
December 10	Norfolk	**Joe Marsh**	**Won**
December 14	Washington, DC	**Jim Henry**	**?**
December 15	Charlotte, NC	**Cowboy Luttrall**	**Won**
December 16	Columbia	**Les Ryan**	**Won**
December 17	Norfolk	**Little Beaver**	**Won**

1942

January		Lewis begins what is billed as a farewell tour at what he claims is 51 years old. He claims to have lost 90 pounds by walking.	
January 8	Washington, DC	**Stan Pinto**	**Won**
January 12	Camden	**Milo Steinborn**	**Won**
January 13	Baltimore, MD	**Hans Kampfer**	**Won**
January 15	Washington, DC	**Ray Steele**	**Lost**
January 16	Philadelphia, PA	**Lou Plummer**	**Won**
January 20	Montreal, Canada	**Jim Henry**	**Won**
January 23	Buffalo	**John Grandovich**	**Won**
January 27	Montreal, Canada	**Lou Thesz**	**Draw**
January 30	Buffalo	**Rudy LaDitzi**	**Won**

February 3	Montreal, Canada	George Koverly	Won
February 4	Hartford	Rudy LaDitzi*	Won (DQ 2-0)
February 10	Montreal, Canada	Yvon Robert (Montreal WC ?)	Won
February 11	Boston, MA	Maurice Tillet	Lost
February 13	Philadelphia, PA	Leo Numa	Won
February 16	Lowell, MA	Lee Henning	Cancelled
February 20	Philadelphia, PA	Rudy Dusek	Won
February 26 (24)	Montreal, Canada	Yvon Robert (Montreal WC ?)	Lost
March 2	Portland, ME	Jim Henry*	Won (DQ)
March 4	Holyoke	Jim Henry	Won
March 6	Philadelphia, PA	Ernie Dusek	Lost
March 11	Boston, MA	Chief Sanooke	Won
March 17	Hamilton	Tommy O'Toole	Won (2-0)
March 18	Rochester, NY	Earl McCready	Lost
March 19	Toronto, Canada	Maurice Tillet	Lost
March 24	Dallas, TX	Fritz Von Schacht	Won
March 27	Houston, TX	Ted "King Kong" Cox	DQ
April 3	Houston, TX	Ted "King Kong" Cox	Won
April 8	St. Louis, MO	Wild Bill Longson (NWA WC) (Att.: 12,986)	Lost
April 17	Houston, TX	Wild Bill Longson (NWA WC)* (Att.: 3,000)	DQ (1-2)
April 20	Nekoosa, WI	Jacob Friedrich died at 7 PM at his home in Nekoosa following a lingering illness. Surviving him were his wife Molla 'Guildenzopf' Griedrich; three daughters, Mrs. John Ambruster, Mrs. George Gladding of Everett, Washington, and Mrs. Jay Buckley of Wisconsin Rapids, and the one son, Ed "Strangler" Lewis. Lewis was present at the time of death.	
April 21	Nekoosa, WI	Lewis was first man to register at the American Legion Hall in the general registration of all men 45 to 65 years of age.	
May 7	Kansas City	Jack Dillon	Won

May 9	North Bergen	**Golden Terror**	**Won**
May 11	Camden	**Joe Cox**	**Won**
May 12	New York, NY	**Max Krauser**	**Won**
May 14	Washington	**Lou Plummer**	**Lost**
May 17	Houston, TX	**Wild Bill Longson** (NWA WC)	**Lost**
May 22	St. Louis, MO	**Ray Steele** (Att.: 8,405)	**Lost**
May 22	Hollywood, CA	Filming for 'Gentleman Jim' begins.	
May 25	Pasadena, CA	**Willie Davis**	**Won (2-0)**
May 27	Los Angeles, CA	**Mayes McLain**	**Won**
May 28	Long Beach, CA	**Dick Raines**	**Won**
June 2	San Diego, CA	**Willie Davis**	**Won**
June 4	Fresno, CA	Referees Savoldi vs Kruskamp	
June 8	Pasadena, CA	**Kolo Stasiak**	**Won (2-1)**
June 9	San Diego, CA	**Sandor Szabo**	**Draw**
June 11	Long Beach, CA	**Rube Wright**	**Draw**
June 15	Pasadena, CA	**Sandor Szabo** (Pacific Coast Title, 60:00)	**Draw (1-1)**
June 16 (17)	San Francisco, CA	**Ivan Rasputin**	**Won**
June 18	Fresno, CA	**Jim Casey**	**Won (2-1)**
June 19	Oakland, CA	**Chief Thunderbird**	**Won**
June 23	San Francisco, CA	**Sandor Szabo**	**Draw**
June 26	Oakland, CA	**Joe Corbett**	**Won**
July 7	San Francisco, CA	**Frank Sexton**	**COR**
July 14	San Francisco, CA	**Tor Johnson**	**Draw**
July 23	Hollywood, CA	Filming for 'Gentleman Jim' ends.	
July 28	San Francisco, CA	**Frank Sexton** (Pacific Coast Title)	**UTC**
August 13	Long Beach, CA	**Kolo Stasiak**	**Won**
August 18	San Francisco, CA	**Cy Williams**	**Won**
August 21	Oakland, CA	**Harry Kent** (60:00)	**Draw**

August 25	San Francisco, CA	Maurice Tillet*	Lost (1-2)
		(Att.: Sell out)	
August 28	Oakland, CA	Jim Clark	Won (UTC)
		(Clark had a "dislocated neck" from Lewis headlock.)	
September 1	San Francisco, CA	Tex Cobb	Won
September 2	San Francisco, CA	Maurice Tillet	Lost
September 3	Fresno, CA	Ted Cox	Lost (1-2)
September 4	Oakland, CA	Maurice Tillet	Lost
September 7	Hollywood, CA	Sandor Szabo	Won
September 8	Wilmington, NC	Dan O'Connor	Won
September 9	Bakersfield, CA	George Zaharias	Won
September 11	Huntington Park, CA	George Zaharias	Won
September 15	San Francisco, CA	Willie Davis	Draw
September 18	Oakland, CA	Harry Kent	Draw
September 30	Des Moines, IA	Emil Dusek*	Won (UTC)
		(Att.: 3,500)	
October 1	Kansas City	Joe Dusek*	Won (UTC)
October 7	Philadelphia, PA	Mike Heller	Won
October 8	Brooklyn, NY	Mike Heller (Haller ?)	Won
October 10	Brooklyn, NY	Ivan Vakturoff	Won
October 14	Philadelphia, PA	vs (Handicap Match)	
		vs Rube Wright & Hercules Tragas	Won
October 15	Brooklyn, NY	Tony Martinelli	Won
October 17	Brooklyn, NY	Fred Brunowicz	Won
October 20	Omaha	John Pesek*	Won (DQ)
		(Att.: 4,000)	
October 21	Des Moines	Joe Dusek*	Won (2-1)
		(Att.: 2,500)	
October 22	Kansas City, MO	Orville Brown (MWA WC)*	Lost (1-2)
		(Att.: 3,600)	
October 24	Brooklyn, NY	Rube Wright	Lost
October 30	Atlanta	Golden Terror	DQ

November 3	Omaha	John Pesek* (Att.: 3,700)	UTC (0-1)
November 5	Kansas City, MO	Orville Brown (MWA WC)	Won (Decision)
November 6	St. Louis, MO	Yvon Robert	Lost (0-1)
November 18	Des Moines	Orville Brown*	Lost (2-1)
November 19	Kansas City	Emil Dusek (Lewis claiming the MWA WC.)	Won
November 25	Los Angeles, CA	'Gentleman Jim' a boxing movie starring Errol Flynn and Ward Bond opens. Lewis has a speaking part as a boxer in a early scene and works as a body double for Ward Bond in the major fight scenes.	
November 26	Kansas City	Orville Brown (MWA World Title Win)* (K.C. Version of MWA Title)	Won
November 30	Charleston, WV	Frank Taylor	?
December 1	Dayton	John Pesek ?	Won
December 3	Columbus	Orville Brown (MWA WC WIN)* (Att.: 4,137. Columbus version of MWA Title)	Won (COR)
December 8	Louisville, KY	Wild Bill Longson (Promoter Heywood Allen, Sr. claims he changed Robert Frederick's name to Strangler Lewis when the wrestler performed at the old Buckingham Theater in Louisville. He alowed any fan who could prove they were present that night in 1913 to see this show free.)	Won (DQ)
December 10	Kansas City	Lee Wyckoff (MWA WC)	Won
December 15	Louisville, KY	Ray Eckert	Lost
December 17	Kansas City, MO	Tom Zaharias (MWA WC?)	Won

1943

January 5	Indianapolis, IN	Roland Kirchmeyer	Won
January 13	Hammond, IN	Fred Carone	Won (2-0)
January 14	Kansas City	Lee Wykoff (MWA World Title Loss) (K.C. Version of MWA Title)	Lost
January 28	Columbus, OH	John Pesek (MWA World Title Loss) (Att.: 6,112. Columbus version of MWA Title)	Lost
February 4	Kansas City	Orville Brown	Lost

February 8	Galveston, TX	Referee for Ray Eckert vs Karl Davis	
February 10	San Antonio, TX	**Juan Humberto**	**Won (COR)**
February 15	Galveston, TX	**Ray Eckert**	**Won (2-1)**
February 19	Houston, TX	**Lou Thesz**	**Lost**
March 1	Detroit, MI	**Orville Brown**	**Won (2-1)**
March	Daytona Beach, FL	Florida Boxing Commission chairman Frank Markle says Ed Lewis is too old to continue wrestling. Lewis counters with a challenge to any five boxers, including Joe Louis. He claims to have posted a $2,500 bond.	
March 12	North Bergen	**Golden Terror**	**Won**
March 13	Toronto, Canada	**Pedro Martinez**	**Won**
March 15	Detroit, MI	**Orville Brown**	**Won (2-1)**
March 18	Toronto, Canada	**Maurice Tillet "The French Angel"**	**Lost**
March 22	Albany, NY	**Chief Chewacki***	**Won (2-0)**
March 25	Washington, DC	**Nanjo Singh**	**Won**
March 26	Harrisburg	**Babe Sharkey**	**Won**
April 5	Detroit, MI	**Danno O'Mahoney**	**Won (1-0)**
April 8	Washington, DC	**George Macricostas**	**Won**
April 9	North Bergen, NJ	**Golden Terror**	**Won**
April 19	Detroit, MI	**Danno O'Mahoney**	**Won**
April 29	Detroit, MI	Lewis was announced as the new promoter of the Detroit Arena Garden shows, replacing Louis Markowitz. His first card drew 1,700. Lewis claimed he would keep wrestling on a more "dignified" level, but the newspaper pointed out that the only dignified thing at the card was Lewis, dressed to the nines, standing at the front door greeting patrons while a band serenaded them to their seats. The matches were said to be ludicrous.	
May 5	Montreal, Canada	**Andre Vadnais**	**Won**
May 13	Toronto, Canada	**Pedro Martinez**	**Won**
May 14	Buffalo	**Lee Henning**	**Won**
June 17	Toronto, Canada	**Lee Henning**	**Won**

June 24	Toronto, Canada	**Leo Numa**	**Lost**
June 25	Buffalo	**George Koverly**	**Won**
July 8	Toronto, Canada	**Earl McCready**	**Lost**
August 6	Toronto, Canada	**John Katan**	**Draw**
August 6	Hollywood, CA	'Nazty Nuisance,' a minor film with Lewis in a small role, was released.	
August 19	Montreal, Canada	**Frank Judson**	**Won**
August 26	Kansas City, MO	**Orville Brown**	**Lost**
September 1	Des Moines, IA	**Emil Dusek***	**Won (2-1)**
September 9	Kansas City, OK	**Orville Brown**	**Lost**
September 16	Kansas City, OK	**John Grandovich**	**Won**
September 23	Kansas City, OK	**Orville Brown** (MWA WC)	**Lost**
September 28	Little Rock, AR	**Tom Zaharias**	**Won**
September 29	Topeka, KS	**Orville Brown** (MWA WC)	**Lost**
October 5	Rockford	**Arthur Van Saxon**	**Won**
October 7	South Bend	**Pete Schuh**	**Won**
October 11	Milwaukee, WI	**Ole Olsen**	**Won**
October 12	Rockford	**Ole Olsen**	**Lost**
October 13	Chicago, IL	**Kola Kwariani**	**Lost**
October 14	Little Rock, AR	**Tom Zaharis**	**Won**
October 21	Kansas City, OK	**John Grandovich**	**Won**
November 4	Trenton, NJ	**Tom Mahoney** (21:22)	**Won**
November 5	Jamaica, NY	**Hans Kampfer**	**Won**
November 9	Baltimore, MD	**The Golden Terror**	**Won**
November 11	Newark, NJ	**Babe Sharkey**	**Won**
November 17	Washington, DC	**Chief Thunderbird**	**Won**
November 18	Trenton	**The Golden Terror**	**?**
November 23	Baltimore, MD	**The Golden Terror**	**Won**
November 25	Boston, MA	**The Golden Terror** (Att.: 6,000)	**Lost (1-2)**

December 13	Chicago, IL	**Kola Kwariani**	**Lost**
December 14	Rockford	**Great Moentezuma**	**Lost**

1944

January 4	Minneapolis, MN	**Orville Brown**	**Won**
January 5	Kansas City, OK	**Orville Brown**	**Lost**
January 5	Topeka, KS	**Tom Zaharias**	**No Show**

(Lee Wyskoff subbed for Lewis. Promoter claimed that Ed was forced off a commercial airline in Omaha.)

January 10	St. Paul, MN	**Jack Ross**	**Won**
January 11	Minneapolis, MN	**Ken Fenelon**	**Won**
January 13	Rochester, NY	**Rass Samara**	**Won**
January 18	Minneapolis, MN	**Ray Steele**	**Won**
January 19	St. Paul, MN	**Bronko Nagurski**	**Lost**
February 3	Brooklyn, NY	**Emil Dusek**	**Won**
February 5	Brooklyn, NY	**Joe Cox**	**Won**
February 6	Camden, NJ	**Lou Plummer**	**?**

(Buddy Rogers on card)

February 10	Brooklyn, NY	**Lou Plummer**	**Won**
March 10	St. Petersburg, FL	**Chief Saunooke**	**Won (DQ 2-1)**
March 14	Baltimore, MD	**Babe Sharkey** (Maryland WC Turn Final)	**Lost**

(Sharkey won a tournament on March 7 to meet Lewis for the Maryland World Title)

March 16	Trenton, NJ	**Leo Wallick** (21:32)	**Won**
March 17	New York, NY	**Hans Kampfer**	**Won**
March 21	Baltimore, MD	**Barto Hill**	**Won**
March 24	New York, NY	**Babe Sharkey** (Maryland WC ?)	**Draw**
March 28	Baltimore, MD	**Babe Sharkey** (Maryland WC ?)	**Lost**
April 7	Buffalo, NY	**Marvin Westernberg**	**Lost**
April 12	Montreal, Canada	**George Lenihan**	**Won**
April 18	Minneapolis, MN	**Wladek Zbyszko**	**Won**
April 25	Minneapolis, MN	**Ray Steele**	**Lost**

April 27	Toronto, Canada	**Bob Wagner**	**Draw**
April 30	Berlin, Gemany	Adolph Hitler comits suicide.	
June 28	Montreal, Canada	**Leo Numa**	**Won**
July 5	Montreal, Canada	**Frank Sexton**	**Lost (1-2)**
July 19	Montreal, Canada	**Bob Wagner**	**Won (DQ)**
August 2	Portland, OR	**Bill Kuusisto**	**Won**
August 3	Vancouver, Canada	**Ray Steele**	**Won**
August 9	Portland, OR	**Jack Ross**	**Won**
		Billy Bartush	**Lost**
August 10	Vancouver, Canada	**Billy Bartush**	**Won**
August 11	Salem	**Cliff Thiede**	**Won**
August 16	Portland	**Billy Bartush**	**Won**
August 17	Vancouver, Canada	**Leo Numa**	**Won**
August 24	Ogden, UT	**Stan Mayslack**	**?**
		(Lewis claims he's headed for the South Pacific to entertain troops.)	
August 26	Calgary, Canada	**Ray Steele**	**Lost**
September 9	Bethesda, MD	Gus Sonnenberg died from leukemia at the Bethesda MD Naval Hospital at the age of 44. He had been there for almost eight months. He served as a navy chief specialist at Great Lakes, IL and Bainbridge, MD. He is buried in Park Cemetery in Marquette.	
September 14	Ogden	**Jack Ganson**	**?**
September 14	Chicago, IL	Bob Managoff died at his Chicago home (2557 Division Street).	
October 2	Phoenix, AZ	**Billy Bartush**	**Won**
November 8	Independence, MO	**Jack Hader**	**Won**
November 16	Kansas City	**Tom Zaharis**	**Won**
November 18	Wichita	**Jerry Meeker**	**Won**
November 20	Cleveland, OH	**Joe Komar**	**Lost**
December 6	Wichita	**Orville Brown**	**Lost (0-2)**

| December 11 | Cleveland, OH | Lewis denies reports that he had retired. His weight is nearly 300 lbs. | |
| December 12 | Cleveland, OH | **Stan Mayslack** | **Lost** |

1945

January 5	Topeka	**Tom Zaharias**	**No Show**
		(Lewis no shows because he is forced off his airplane in Omaha because of a priority passenger. Lee Wykoff subs.)	
February 6	Winnipeg, Canada	Lewis managing Cliff Gustafson visits *Winnipeg Free Press* sports department to promote wrestling card.	
February 24	Winnipeg, Canada	**Robert "Tiny' Lee (Ski Hi Lee)**	**Lost**
		(Claim is that Lewis was the behind-the-scenes promoter with Johnny Petersen. Main event was Gustafson vs Pierre Deglane. Att.: 2,000)	
March 10	Winnipeg, Canada	Lewis is said to be the promoter of a card with Cliff Gustafson in main event. Cliff is said to have a sore throat and Bill Kuusisto subs for him. Attendance is 800.	
April 3	Wisconsin, WI	Appeared on WFHR radio, claiming to have visited Japan five times.	
April 4	Wisconsin, WI	**Don Koch**	**Won**
May 7	San Mateo, CA	Report has Lewis on a tour of 60 army and navy bases with a group of wrestlers that included Babe Sharky, Henry Piers and Milo Steinborn.	
May 7	Cleveland, OH	**& Cliff Gustafson** (Handicap Match) **vs Ernie Dusek**	**Lost**
June 24	Waterloo	**Billy Bartush**	**Rained Out**
July 5	Winnipeg, Canada	**Earl McCready** (11:27)	**Lost**
July 7	Lethbridge, Canada	**Earl McCready** (Match climaxed The Annual Lethbridge Rodeo)	**Lost (0-2)**
July 9	Swift Current, Canada	**Kola Kwariani**	**Lost (1-2)**
July 11	Moose Jaw, Canada	**Cliff Gustafson**	**?**
July 27	Cincinnati, OH	**& Ali Pasha** **vs Frenchy Laranche & Bill Weicher**	**Lost**
July 31	Helena, MT	**Jim Clark**	**Lost**
August 3	Cincinnati, OH	**& Alex Kasaboski** **vs Clete Kaufman & Red Vagnone**	**Won**

August 17	Cincinnati, OH	& Frenchy Laranche vs Frank Marconi & Jack Vansky	Won
August 19	Tacoma, WA	Lou Thesz	Lost
August 20	Seattle, WA	Seelie Samara	Lost
August 21	Tacoma, WA	Lou Thesz	Lost
August 22	Portland	Lou Thesz	Lost
August 25	Victoria	Ted Christy	Won
August 27	Walla Walla	Chief Thunderbird	Won
August 28	Spokane	Ted Christy	Won
September 2	Tokyo, Japan	The Japanese surrender ending WWII.	
September 13	Bremerton	Lou Thesz	Lost (0-2)
September 18	Tacoma, WA	Rube Wright (Sub for protégé Cliff Gustafson)	Lost (0-2)
September 19	Portland	Pierre Deglane	Lost
September 20	Vancouver, Canada	Rube Wright	Lost
September 24	Seattle, WA	Dick Raines	Lost
September 28	Cincinnati, OH	& Frenchy Laranche vs Ali Baba & Alex Kasaboski	Won
October 5	Cincinnati, OH	& Frenchy Laranche vs Red Vagnone & Elmer Estep	Lost
October 13	Canton, OH	Gino Vagnone	Won
October 16	Detroit, MI	Red Vagonne (First appearance in Detroit since Lewis promoted at Arena Gardens in 1942.)	?
October 20	Canton, OH	Elmer Estep	Won
November 6	Detroit, MI	Wild Bill Thornton	Won
November 14	Washington, DC	Jim Coffield	Won
November 15	White Plains, NY	Karol Krauser	?
November 20	New York, NY	Iron Talun	?
November 25	New York, NY	Ed White	Won
November 28	Washington, DC	Gino Garibaldi	Lost

November 29	Brooklyn, NY	**Michele Leone**	**?**
November 30	Philadelphia, PA	**Larry Moquin**	**Lost**
December 3 ?	Detroit, MI ?	**Joe Savoldi ?**	**Won**
December 5	St. Louis, MO	**Jack Conley**	**Won**
1946			
January 9	St. Louis, MO	**Ed Virag** (Att.: 4,015)	**Lost**
January 10	Wisconsin Rapids	Lewis' mother Mrs. Jacob Friedrich dies at 4:00 AM at the home of her daughter Mrs. J. Buckley after a lingering illness. Lewis is living in Tulsa.	
January 11	Chicago, IL	Managed Cliff Gustafson vs Fred Bozik	
January 12	Nekoosa, WI	Lewis' mother's funeral takes place and she rests in Riverside Cemetery.	
February 5	Baltimore, MD	**Ali Baba**	**Lost**
February 6	Philadelphia, PA	**Ali Baba**	**Lost**
February 14	Boston, MA	**Babe Sharley** (Att.: 4,500)	**Lost (0-2)**
March 21	Toronto, Canada	Referee for Billy Watson vs Lee Henning	
March 23 (26)	Buffalo	**Fred Von Schacht**	**Draw**
April 18	Toronto, Canada	Referee for Jonathan vs Von Schacht	
April 19	Buffalo,	**Pat Fraley**	**Lost**
April 23	Hamilton	Referee for Talun vs O'Donnell	
April 25	Toronto, Canada	**Hard Boiled Hannigan**	**Lost**
May 16	Cleveland, OH	Referee for Frank Sexton vs Billy Watson	
September 30	Portland	Referee for tag team match	
October 14	Cleveland, OH	Referee for Joe Savoldi vs Abe Coleman match	
November 4	Emporis, KS	Referee for Villmer vs Hewitt	
November 7	Kansas City, KS	Referee for Lopez vs Graham	
November 16	Wichita, KS	Referee for Orville Brown vs Ede Virag in unification of NWA and MWA titles	
December 3	San Francisco, CA	Refereed Hansen vs Bell	

Date	Location	Event	Result
December 6	Oakland, CA	Refereed Bell vs Hefner	
December 7	Fresno, CA	Refereed Fraley vs Hefner	
December 10	San Francisco, CA	Refereed Lee vs Davis	
December 13	Oakland, CA	**Dutch Hefner**	**Won (DQ 2-0)**
December 14	Fresno, CA	**Pat Fraley**	**DQ (0-2)**
December 18	Oakland, CA	Lewis interviewed by *Oakland Tribune*. Marketing a rubber exerciser called the Strangler Lewis' Health Builder.	
December 20	Oakland, CA	**Billy Hanson**	**?**
December 30	Denver, CO	Refereed Marshall vs Gonzales	

1947

Date	Location	Event	Result
January 1	Colorado Springs	Refereed the whole card	
January 6	Denver, CO	**Everett Marshall** (Att.: 4,600)	**DQ (1-2)**
January 8	Colorado Springs	**Tom Zaharis**	**Lost (1-2)**
January 18	Fresno, CA	Referee Hansen vs Hefner	
January 20	Denver, CO	**Everett Marshall** (Att.: 3,300)	**Won**
January 25	Fresno, CA	**Dutch Hefner**	**Lost**
February 1	Fresno, CA	**Dutch Hefner**	**?**
February 8	Fresno, CA	**Pat Fraley**	**?**
February 10	Denver, CO	**Everett Marshall** (Att.: 3,300)	**Lost (1-2)**
February 12	Colorado Springs	**Ed "Tarzan" White**	**Lost**
February 21	Santa Monica, CA	Referee for Szabo vs Koverly	
February 24	Pasadena, CA	Referee for Levy/Kruskamp vs Babe & Chris Zaharias	
February 27	Long Beach, CA	Referee for Torres vs Szabo	
March 6	Long Beach, CA	**Dutch Hefner**	**?**
March 17	Tacoma, WA	Referee for Fred Atkins vs Chief Little Wolf	
March 26	Portland	**Fred Atkins**	**Lost**
April 7	Pasadena, CA	Referee for Torres vs Russell	

April 10	Long Beach, CA	**Bulldog Clements**	Won
April 12	Fresno, CA	**Len Hall**	Draw
April 17	Long Beach, CA	**& Sam Menacker** (Referee Joe Louis) **vs Swedish Angel & Bob Russell**	Lost
April 19	Fresno, CA	**Len Hall**	?
May 10	Atlanta, GA	Referee for Don Mcintyre vs Jim Coffield	
May 15	Jacksonville, FL	**Jim Coffield**	Won
May 16	Atlanta, GA	**Don Mcintyre**	DQ
May 23	Atlanta, GA	**Don Mcintyre**	Lost
June 10	Wilmington, CA	**Bob Russell**	?
June 12	Long Beach, CA	Referee for Russell vs Kennedy	
June 13	Santa Monica, CA	Referee for McShain vs Becker	
June 16	Pasadena, CA	**Terry McGinnis**	Won
June 18	Los Angeles, CA	**Lee Henning**	Won
June 19	Long Beach, CA	**& Bobby Bruns** **vs Lee Henning & Chris Zaharias**	?.
June 23	Pasadena, CA	Referee for Torres vs Chris Zaharias	
June 25	Los Angeles, CA	**Enrique Torres** (CA World Title) (Att.: 9,200)	DQ (1-2)
June 30	Pasadena, CA	**Chris Zaharias** (12:53)	Won
July 1	Wilmington, CA	**Lee Henning**	?
July 17	Long Beach, CA	Lewis cancels an appearance on Johnny Webb's "Speaking of Sports" redio show on KFOX.	
July 18	Santa Monica, CA	Referee for Ernie Dusek vs Bruns	
July 23	Los Angeles, CA	**Jules Strongbow**	Won
August 5	Wilmington	Referee for Duseks vs Holbrook & Lopez	
August 8	San Diego, CA	**& Danny McShain** **vs Red Berry & Ernie Dusek**	Won
August 11	Pasadena, CA	**Wee Willie Davis**	Won
August 13	Los Angeles, CA	**Jack Kennedy**	Won
August 14	Long Beach, CA	**Ernie Dusek**	Lost

August 25	Hollywood, CA	**& Danny McShain** **vs Ernie Dusek & Red Berry**	**Won**
August 26	San Diego, CA	**& Enrique Torres** **vs Ernie & Emil Dusek**	**Lost**
September 3	Los Angeles, CA	**Vic Holbrook**	**Won**
September 9	South Gate	**Myron Cox**	**Won**
October 9	Long Beach, CA	**Karl Davis**	**Won**

(Interfered with Schnabel vs Moquin main event)

October 14	South Gate	**Willie Davis**	**Lost**
October 16	Long Beach, CA	**Hans Schnabel**	**Won**
October 21	South Gate	**& Larry Moquin** **vs Willie Davis & Frank Jares**	**Lost**
November 4	South Gate	**Willie Davis**	**Lost**

November ?	Los Angeles, CA	Lewis takes job of athletic instructor and public relations man for the Los Angeles Athletic Club.

December 7	Miami, FL	**Primo Carnera**	**Lost**

1948

January 12	Pasadena, CA	Referees Torres vs Szabo

January 25	Honolulu, HI	**Butch Levy**	**Won**

(Lewis came to Honolulu to meet the challenge of Jack Sherry but on arrival Sherry ducked him and refused the match. Levy substituted. Lewis retired from active wrestling after the match.)

February 25	Los Angeles, CA	Referee for Szabo/Garibaldi vs Garza/Mitchell
March 5	Oakland, CA	Referee for Detton vs Eckert
March 6	Fresno, CA	Referee for Flash Gordon vs Pat Fraley
March 12	Oakland, CA	Referee for Holbrook & Gordon vs Jares & Atkins
March 13	Fresno, CA	Referee. Lewis cancelled a match with Flash Gordon because of elbow injury
March 29	Sacramento, CA	Lewis's wrestling license was revoked in California, when he failed the physical examination for journeymen wrestlers.
April 3	Los Angeles, CA	Lewis working as a wrestling instructor at the Los Angeles Athletic Club. He appeared to be living at 1307 North Mansfield, Los Angeles in a small house south of Hollywood High School.
April 7	Los Angeles, CA	Referee for George/Jeffries vs Zaharias brothers

April 15	Long Beach, CA	Referee for Gorgeous George vs Fraley
April 24	Los Angeles, CA	Referee for Gorgeous George vs Tony Martinez
May 27	Long Beach, CA	Referee for Beckers vs Rice & Russell
June 5	St. Louis, MO	Around this time Lou Thesz and a group of promoters bought the St. Louis promotion from Tom Packs. Others in the deal were Eddie Quinn, Frank Tunney, Bobby Managoff and Bill Longson.
June 30	Montreal, Canada	Referee for Yvon Robert vs Henri Deglane
July 14	Waterloo, IA	The National Wrestling Alliance was formed by promoters Pinkie George, Sam Muchnick, Orville Brown and Al Haft.
July 14	Montreal, Canada	Referee for Bobby Managoff vs Ray Eckert
July 15	Toronto, Canada	Referee for Billy Watson vs Bill Longson
July 30	St. Louis, MO	Referee for Lou Thesz vs Bobby Managoff
August 6	Atlanta, GA	Referee for Jim Coffield vs Al Massey
August 25	Los Angeles, CA	Referee for the Dusek brothers vs Carnera / Szabo
November 3	Omaha	Referee for Lou Thesz vs Danny Pleachas
November 22	New York, NY	Lewis was named chairman of the newly organized Wrestling Promoters' Association of America and Allied Countries. Lewis' duties were public relations and ironing out difficulties between promoters.
December 14	Detroit, MI	Jack Dempsey, in town to referee a wrestling main event, said he was working with Ed Lewis, czar of the mat world, to help the sport and bring wrestling back to Madison Square Garden where it will attract the national spotlight. He wants to eliminate all the so-called champions.

1949

January 6	Joplin, MO	Referee for Sonny Myers vs Frank Taylor
February 17	Toronto, Canada	Referee for Billy Watson vs Masked Marvel
February 23	Montreal, Canada	Referee for 6 man tag match
April 14	Toronto, Canada	Referee for Billy Watson vs Fred Atkins
April 21	Kansas City, OK	Referee for Don Eagle vs Dean Detton
June 24	Houston, TX	Referee for Lou Thesz vs Ruffy Silverstein
November 17	Toronto, Canada	Referee for Billy Watson vs Yvon Robert
November ?	St. Louis, MO	Lewis named by the NWA as "Ambassador of Good Will", and he was paid $25 each month by each member.

December 8	Hollywood, CA	A minor wrestling movie called 'Bodyhold' is released. Lewis has a small part as a referee
December 13	Kansas City, MO	Referee for Ali Pasha vs Farmer Jones
December 15	Kansas City, KS	Referee for Bill Longson vs Mike Sharpe
December 16	St. Joseph, MO	As NWA ambassador, Lewis gave a speech at Benton High School.
December 16	St. Joseph, MO	Ringside for Bill Longson vs Mike Sharpe match

1950

January 23	Wichita	Referee for Bill Longson vs Vic Christy
February 4	Racine, WI	Referee for Goeltz vs Gypsy Joe Dorsetti
February 16	Toronto, Canada	Referee for Billy Watson vs Nanjo Singh
March 16	Boston, MA	Referee for Gene Stanlee vs Mike Mazurki
May 3		Movie 'Bodyhold' opens in theaters. Lewis plays a small part as referee.
October 4	Evansville	Referee for Bill Longson vs Ray Eckert
October 10	Atlanta, GA	Referee for Art Nelson vs Jack Kennedy
November 3	Atlanta, GA	Referee for Kennedy vs Art Nelson
November 5	Tampa, FL	Referee for Bob Orton vs Hal Keene
November 8	St. Petersburg, FL	Referee for Jack Wentworth vs Chief Little Fox
November 13	Tampa, FL	Managed Lou Thesz vs Bob Orton. Most likely his first match as manager for NWA World Champion Lou Thesz.
November 15	St. Petersburg, FL	Managed Lou Thesz vs Jack Wentworth
November 23	New Orleans, LA	Managed Lou Thesz vs Hans Herman
December 19	Dallas, TX	Managed Lou Thesz vs Killer Kowalski

1951

July 2	Calgary, Canada	Referee for Bob Langevin vs Mr. X
October 12	St. Louis, MO	Managed Thesz vs Yukon Eric
November 16	St. Louis, MO	Managed Thesz vs Bill longson

1952

February 26	Syracuse, NY	Managed Thesz vs Laverne Baxter
June 12	New Orleans, LA	Managed Thesz vs Gorgeous George.

| June 17 | Dallas, TX | Managed Thesz vs Bill Longson |

1953

January 23	Utica, NY	Managed Thesz vs Hans Schmidt
July ?	Pend Oreille Lake	Lewis on a working fishing vacation with Thesz in Idaho.
July 7	Idaho Falls	Probably managing Thesz vs Warren Bockwinkel
July 9	Salt Lake City	Probably managing Thesz vs Snyder
July 15	Spokane, WA	In town giving interviews.
July 16	Spokane, WA	Manages Thesz vs Red Vagnone
July 20	Seattle, WA	Managing Thesz when not fishing salmon
July 23	Seattle, WA	Probably managing Thesz vs Montana
July 24	Tacoma, WA	Probably managing Thesz vs Lindsey
July 29	Vancouver, Canada	Probably managing Thesz vs Watson
July 31	Tacoma, WA	Probably managing Thesz vs Lindsey
October 19	Memphis, TN	Managed Thesz vs Bill Longson
November 10	El Paso, TX	Managed Thesz vs Lou Plummer

1954

April 8	Spokane, WA	Managed Thesz vs Von Poppenheim
October 10	Minneapolis, MN	Anton (Tony) Stecher, promoter of wrestling and former manager and trainer of brother and world champion Joe Stecher, dies from a heart attack. The Minneapolis promotion is taken over by his son Dennis Stecher and Wally Karbo.
October 19	Baltimore, MD	Managed Thesz vs Buddy Rogers

1955

March 4	St. Louis, MO	Managed Thesz vs Wilbur Snyder. Was punched by Snyder
March 25	St. Louis, MO	Managed Thesz vs Wilbur Snyder. Removed from ringside for coaching.
August 30	Dallas, TX	Managed Thesz vs Gunkel
October 28	Chicago, IL	Managed Thesz vs Don Leo Jonathan
November 27	Atlanta, GA	Managed Thesz vs Jerry Graham

1956

| February 21 | Austin, TX | Managed Thesz vs Manuel Cortez |

1957

| February 8 | Houston, TX | Managed Pepper Gomez as he beat El Medico for the Texas title |

April 26	Atlanta, GA	Managed Thesz vs Red McIntyre
June 27	Amarillo, TX	Managed Dory Funk vs Lou Thesz
October 3	Denver, CO	Managed Bob Elliott (Ellis) vs Charro Azteca
October 10	Kansas City	Ringside for Thor Hagen vs Red Berry
November 14	Toronto, Canada	Managed Dick Hutton as he defeated Lou Thesz for the NWA World Title.

1958

September 7	Winnipeg, Canada	Lewis managing Dick Hutton vs Whipper Watson. Revealed that his life story will be published in November by Harold Rosenthal of the *New York Herald Tribune*.
September 16	Minneapolis, MN	Managed Hutton vs Joe Pazandak
December 26	St. Louis, MO	Managed Hutton vs Ed Carpentier

1959

January 9	St. Louis, MO	Pat O'Connor defeated Dick Hutton for NWA WC.
October ?	Tulsa	Lewis helping in the pro wrestling training of Danny Hodge
October 9	Tulsa	Hodge wins first match over Sasha the Great

1960

March 21	Tulsa	Managed Danny Hodge vs Ali Bey
July 17	Boston, MA	Paul Bowser dies following a heart attack and two heart operations at Massachusetts Hospital at age 74. He was buried at Westview Cemetery.

1963

August 23-25	St. Louis, MO	Attends the NWA convention

1964

October 22	St. Louis, MO ?	Tom Packs dies from a heart attack en route to a hospital.

1965

November 7	Tulsa	Visited by Lou Thesz. The two drive to Oklahoma City's Skillern Hotel for the day.
December 26	Rochester	Jules Baumann dies at age 65.

1966

August 6	Muskogee, OK	Lewis dies at age 76 at the Veterans Hospital in Muskogee, OK.
August 7	Muskogee, OK	Funeral services are held at the Ninde Funeral Home in Tulsa. The private service was officiated over by Willard Russell, a Christian Science reader, at the Golden Chapel. Lewis was cremated and later buried at Arlington National Cemetery, Arlington, VA, in Section 53, Grave 3546.

1967

September 23   St. Joseph, MO   Stanislaus Zbyszko dies on his pig farm after a heart attack at age 88.

1968

June 10   St. Joseph, MO   Wladek Zbyszko dies, and is laid to rest in Savannah Cemetery, Savannah, MO.

1972

September 15   ?   Billy Sandow dies at age 88.

1973

February 10   Fort Collins   Everett Marshall dies at age 67 from complications after surgery.

1974

March 29   St. Cloud, MN   Joe Stecher dies at the Veterans Hospital of St. Cloud, MN. His remains are sent to San Francisco, where his wife lived, for burial. His tombstone can be found at Cypress Memorial Park, Colma California. (Niche p, Tier 1, in the Garden of Serenity).

1975

August 19   Escondido, CA   Jim Londos suffers a heart attack at Palomar General Hospital and dies at age 78.

1976

June 11   St. Louis, MO   Toots Mondt dies after a long illness (pneumonia) at age 82. He had been born on January 18, 1894, in Wayne county, Iowa.

1979

?   Tulsa   Bobbie Lee West dies at age 77.

1999

April 24   Newton, IA   Lewis is inducteed into the George Tragos section of the Wrestling Hall of Fame in the Iowa International Wrestling Institute & Museum with Frank Gotch, Verne Gagne, and Lou Thesz. The pro section of the HOF was controled by Lou Thesz.

INDEX

National Boxing Association, 101, 110, 111, 120, 123, 207 n.309, 209 n.343, 210 n.346, 211 n.383, 271, 289, 290, 292, 294

National Wrestling Hall of Fame and Museum, 186

Nazarian, Mike, 154

'Nazty Nuisance' (*film*), 171, 309

Nebraska State Journal, 194 n.27

Neelsville, 2

Nekoosa, WI, 1, 2, 4, 64, 96, 97, 105, 136, 157, 163, 166, 167, 172, 188, 193 n.1, 194 n.8, 225, 226, 227, 241, 252, 253, 269, 302, 304, 314,

Nekoosa-Edwards Paper Company, 1

Nelson, Art, 319

Nelson, Carl, 234

Nelson, George, 266, 285

Nester, CA, 256

Neuman, Alfred E., 197 n.60

Nevada, Vance, 194 n.25

New Haven, CT, 234, 277, 279, 280, 281, 282

New Orleans, LA, 137, 155, 194 n.7, 214 n.432, 268, 269, 286, 287, 290, 319

New York, NY, 14, 15, 20, 22, 23, 24, 28, 32, 33, 34, 35, 39, 40, 41, 42, 43, 44, 45, 46, 47, 48, 49, 50, 52, 54, 55, 57, 59, 61, 62, 66, 67, 73, 75, 76, 79, 81, 82, 84, 88, 89, 91, 95, 99, 100, 102, 103, 104, 105, 107, 110, 111, 118, 120, 123, 125, 126, 127, 128, 130, 131, 132, 133, 134, 135, 138, 139, 140, 142, 143, 146, 147, 148, 149, 150, 151, 152, 155, 157, 159, 168, 173, 176, 191, 195 n.28, n.34, 196 n.46, 197 n.58, 198 n.79, 200 n.131, 201 n.143, 202 n.186, 204 n.233, 211 n.369, 214 n.433, 215-216 n.446, 224, 232-234, 235, 237, 238, 239, 241, 243, 244, 245, 246, 247, 248, 253, 254, 263, 264, 265, 267, 268, 269, 272, 274, 279, 280, 281, 282, 283, 284, 287, 288, 289, 291, 294, 295, 296, 297, 298, 299, 301, 305, 310, 313, 318

New York Giants, 161

New York Opera House, 20

New York State Athletic Commission, 33, 54, 76, 83, 95, 110, 126, 127, 128, 130, 246, 253, 272, 279, 281

New York Herald, 66, 201 n.159, 254

New York Herald Tribune, 321

New York Times, 105, 191, 195 n.38, n.40, n.43, 196 n.45, 197 n.68, 198 ns.71-73, n.81, 199 n.89, n.103, n.104, n.107, n.110, n.111, n.112, n.114, 200 n.117, n.118, ns.120-122, n.125, n.128, n.129, n.131, n.135, n.136,

201 n.145, 202 n.164, 206 n.291, 208 n.323, n.326, n.332, 210 n.355, n.360, 211 n.362, n.365, n.375, 212 n.386, n.392, 213 ns.410-412, n.422, 214 n.433, 215 n.438,

New Zealand, 159, 215 n.441, 216 n.458, 301

Newark, NJ, 126, 139, 241, 278, 286, 287, 289, 309

Newfoundland, Canada, 6, 228

Newman, Charley, 28, 29, 30, 197 n.61

News, The, Adelaide, 115

Newton, IA, 322

Nieuw Holland (liner), 273

Ninde Funeral Home, Tulsa, 188, 321

Norbeck, Moose, 268, 273

Norfolk, 27, 37, 38, 43,

Norfolk Club, 43, 165, 234, 235, 236, 240, 243, 244, 279, 303

North Andover, MA, 214 n.430, 280

North Bergen, NJ, 305, 308

Northern Star, Lismore (Australia), 115

Northwestern University School of Music, 103

Notre Dame, 74, 119

Numa, Leo, 141, 171, 295, 296, 304, 309, 311

NWA (National Wrestling Association), 80, 112, 123, 124, 125, 127, 133, 143, 151, 152, 153, 155, 159, 163, 166, 168, 169, 170, 174, 175, 176, 177, 178, 179, 181, 182, 183, 184, 185, 186, 187, 194 n.11, 208 n.324, 210 n.346, 212 n.392, 214 n.432, 216 n.469, 216-217 n.471, 217 n.475, 219 n.483, 273, 277, 284, 294, 303, 304, 305, 314, 318, 319, 321

Oakland, CA, 28, 32, 134, 202 n.164, 274, 284, 292, 294, 297, 298, 305, 306, 315, 317

Oakland Tribune, 197 n.63, n.64, n.68, 200 n.132, 216 n.461, n.467, 315

O'Brien, Jack, 296

O'Callaghan, Dr. Patrick, 145

O'Connor, Dan, 306

O'Connor, Pat, 184, 185, 186, 321

O'Dell, Jack, 287, 289

O'Dell, Joe, 259, 261

O'Leary, James C., 213 n.413

Oak Hill Memorial Park, Escondido, 189

Oberthaler, Joan
    King of the Ring, Gus Sonnenberg: Lawyer, Football Star, Heavyweight Wrestling Champion of the World, 206 n.269

Ogden, 236, 253, 266, 311

O'Hara, Pat, 286

Ohio Tigers, 97

Oklahoma City, 187, 149, 163, 164, 289, 321

Oklahoma University, 186

St. Petersburg, FL, 310, 319

Sacramento, CA, 159, 259, 276, 285, 293, 294, 297, 298, 300, 317

Sajatoric, Jack, 230

Salem, 311

Salt Lake City, UT, 99, 109, 137, 159, 171, 266, 267, 271, 272, 273, 275, 286, 287, 290, 292, 293, 300, 320

Salt Lake Bees, 202 n.164

Samara, Rass, 310

Samara, Seelie, 171, 172, 313

Sammartino, Bruno, 189, 190, 216 n.446

Sampson, Orlando Jack, 60, 244, 246, 249, 259

San Antonio, TX, 81, 274, 289, 290, 308

San Bernardino, CA, 292, 302

San Diego, CA, 24, 72, 127, 134, 136, 137, 157, 161, 197 n.68, 275, 278, 284, 285, 286, 287, 292, 295, 305, 316, 317

San Diego Justice Court, 72

San Diego Union, 211 n.378

San Francisco, CA, 24, 25, 26, 28, 29, 30, 32, 35, 39, 40, 47, 52, 57, 60, 61, 65, 66, 71, 72, 82, 127, 134, 147, 148, 149, 153, 159, 167, 182, 186, 189, 214 n.230, 236, 237, 242, 245, 246, 249, 250, 256, 260, 275, 278, 282, 284, 285, 291, 292, 293, 294, 297, 298, 300, 305, 306, 314, 315, 322

San Francisco Chronicle, 196 n.54, n.55, 199 n.100, 200 n.116, 201 n.154, 202 n.187, n.188, n.191, 216 n.450

San Francisco Civic Auditorium, 26

San Jose, CA, 26, 30, 39, 40, 42, 45, 55, 60, 61, 65, 105, 241, 244, 245, 250, 252, 278, 284

San Juan, PR, 72, 256

San Mateo, CA, 312

Sand Spring Lake, PA, 259

Sandow (Baumann), Billy, 10, 11, 12, 13, 14, 15, 16, 18, 19, 20, 22, 23, 24, 25, 26, 29, 30, 31, 32, 33, 34, 35, 36, 38, 39, 41, 43, 44, 45, 46, 47, 49, 50, 52, 53, 54, 55, 56, 57, 58, 59, 60, 61, 62, 64, 65, 66, 67, 68, 69, 70, 71, 73, 74, 75, 76, 77, 79, 80, 81, 82, 84, 85, 86, 87, 88, 89, 90, 91, 92, 93, 94, 95, 96, 97, 99, 100, 101, 102, 105, 107, 108, 109, 112, 114, 117, 118, 119, 120, 121, 122, 123, 124, 125, 133, 154, 155, 156, 157, 159, 172, 188, 193 n.1, 194 n.26, 195 n.32, 198 n.79, 200 n.124, 201 n.143, 202 n.198, 203 n.201, n.203, n.206, 204 n.214, 205 n.255, 206 n.263, 207 n.298, 209 n.342, 209-210 n.343, 211 n.380, 214 n.431, 215 n.446, 218 n.482, 219 n.483, 230, 231, 234, 235, 237, 239, 244, 245, 247, 248, 249, 250, 253, 254, 255, 257, 260, 262, 263, 264, 269, 274, 276, 296, 300, 322

Sandow, Jr., Billy, 73

Sandler, Ken (aka Ken Viewer or Ken Writer), viii, 196 n.56

Sanooke (Saunooke), Chief, 290, 304, 310

Santa Ana, CA, 40, 242

Santa Monica, CA, 107, 298, 315, 316

Santel, Ad (*aka* Otto Carpenter), 17, 24, 26, 27, 28, 52, 71, 76, 118, 134, 205 n.203, n.206, 236, 256, 284

Santen, Charlie, 285

Santos Promotion, 220 n.483

Santos, Tony, 220 n.483

Sarpolis, Dr. Karl, 109, 114, 115, 118, 123, 124, 183, 214 n.432, 271, 273, 274, 275, 276, 290, 292

Sasha the Great, 321

Saunders, Elmer, 254

Savage, Leo Daniel Boone "Whiskers" (Edward Civil), 154, 155, 214 n.432, 288, 295

Savage, Steve, 290, 297

Savannah, GA, 15, 26, 33, 188, 235, 236, 237, 238, 245, 246, 247, 322

Savannah Cemetery, MO, 188, 322

'Saved From The Titanic' (*film*), 6

Savoldi, Joe, 119, 124, 133, 134, 135, 136, 141, 149, 150, 156, 194 n.11, 276, 284, 290, 292, 298, 299, 303, 314

Scarpa, Frank, 220 n.483

Schaefer, Gerhaed, 195 n.34

Scharpegge, Ernest, 261, 263

Schenectady, 283

Schilling, Herman, 233, 234

Schmidt, Hans, 186, 320

Schnabel, Hans, 317

Schoenlein, Gus "Americus", 10, 11, 38, 231, 237, 240

Schomburg, Ann, 172

Schuh, Pete, 290, 309

Schuler, Frank, 26, 28, 30, 52, 236

Schultz, Carl (Karl), 272

Schultz, Ed, 32, 229, 237

Seattle, WA, 28, 41, 109, 112, 134, 153, 156, 157, 171, 270, 271, 272, 273, 276, 278, 282, 284, 285, 290, 294, 297, 298, 299, 300, 313, 320

Seattle Times, 207 n.314, n.316, n.317

Second Army Athletic Team, 38

Sells-Floto Circus, 24, 26

Sexton, Frank, 167, 171, 219-220 n.483, 305, 311, 314

CPSIA information can be obtained at www.ICGtesting.com
Printed in the USA
BVOW05*0651030616

449943BV00013B/15/P